come explore...

different
perspectives
on american
politics

D1254219

popular perspective

Do you know...
that popular television shows, such as *24* and *The West Wing*, may have helped pave the way for the landmark election of an African-American President in 2008?

Turn to page 377

your perspective

Do you know...
that a college sophomore played a significant role in securing passage of the Twenty-seventh Amendment to the U.S. Constitution?

Turn to page 44

AMERICAN GOVERNMENT

HISTORICAL, POPULAR AND GLOBAL PERSPECTIVES
BRIEF VERSION
SECOND EDITION

Kenneth Dautrich
Associate Professor of Public Policy
University of Connecticut

David A. Yalof
Associate Professor of Political Science
University of Connecticut

WADSWORTH
CENGAGE Learning™

Australia • Brazil • Japan • Korea • Mexico • Singapore • Spain • United Kingdom • United States

American Government: Historical, Popular and Global Perspectives, Brief Version, Second Edition

Kenneth Dautrich
David A. Yalof

Publisher: Suzanne Jeans

Executive Editor: Carolyn Merrill

Development Editor: Betty Slack

Associate Development Editor:
  Katherine Hayes

Editorial Assistant: Angela Hodge

Media Editor: Laura Hildebrand

Marketing Manager: Lydia LeStar

Marketing Coordinator: Josh Hendrick

Senior Marketing Communications Manager:
  Heather Baxley

Associate Content Project Manager:
  Sara Abbott

Art Director: Linda Helcher

Print Buyer: Fola Orekoya

Rights Acquisition Specialist, Images:
  Amanda Groszko

Senior Rights Acquisition Specialist, Text:
  Katie Huha

Production Service/Compositor:
  Lachina Publishing Services

Text Designer: Nesbitt Design

Cover Designer: Rokusek Design

For product information and technology assistance, contact us at **Cengage Learning Customer & Sales Support, 1-800-354-9706**.

For permission to use material from this text or product, submit all requests online at **cengage.com/permissions**. Further permissions questions can be emailed to **permissionrequest@cengage.com**.

Library of Congress Control Number: 2010942191

ISBN-13: 978-0-495-90791-6

ISBN-10: 0-495-90791-X

Wadsworth
20 Channel Center Street
Boston, MA 02210
USA

Cengage Learning is a leading provider of customized learning solutions with office locations around the globe, including Singapore, the United Kingdom, Australia, Mexico, Brazil and Japan. Locate your local office at **international.cengage.com/region**.

Cengage Learning products are represented in Canada by Nelson Education, Ltd.

For your course and learning solutions, visit **www.cengage.com**.

Purchase any of our products at your local college store or at our preferred online store **www.cengagebrain.com**.

Printed in the United States of America
1 2 3 4 5 6 7 14 13 12 11 10

This book is dedicated to the next generation of responsible citizens who will inherit the American government; in particular, our students and our own children:

Allison, Benjamin, Jane, Kenny, and Rachel

Brief Contents

BETTMANN/CORBIS   SAUL LOEB/AFP/GETTY IMAGES   AP PHOTO/MATT SAYLES

 FOUNDATIONS

 INSTITUTIONS

 POLITICAL BEHAVIOR

 PUBLIC POLICY

AP PHOTO/MICHAEL CAULFIELD

Contents

AP PHOTO/RICK BOWMER

TAMI CHAPPELL/REUTERS/LANDOV

PART 2

INSTITUTIONS

AP PHOTO/STEPHAN SAVOIA

KEVIN LAMARQUE/REUTERS/LANDOV

CHIP SOMODEVILLA/GETTY IMAGES

MARK WILSON/GETTY IMAGES NEWS/GETTY IMAGES

PART

POLITICAL BEHAVIOR

AP PHOTO/MANUEL BALCE CENETA

JEFF GREENBERG/ALAMY

JUSTIN SULLIVAN/GETTY IMAGES NEWS/GETTY IMAGES

RHONA WISE/AFP/GETTY IMAGES

PART 4

PUBLIC POLICY

YELLOW DOG PRODUCTIONS/GETTY IMAGES

AP PHOTO/MANUEL BALCE CENETA

AP PHOTO

Special Features

American Government In Historical Perspective

American Government In Popular Perspective

American Government In Global Perspective

Your Perspective on Amercian Government

POLITICS InterActive!

Preface

This is a textbook about the American government. It is both concise in its presentation of all the major aspects of the American political system and up-to-date through the outcome of the 2010 midterm elections. The success of American government depends upon a responsible citizenry willing to ask tough questions of its leaders and demand reasonable answers in return. We live in an increasingly interconnected world; more than at any time in American history, the policies and actions of the U.S. government have an impact on the citizens of other nations, just as their governments' policies in turn have an impact on American citizens. Despite all the changes that have occurred over the course of the nation's history, the past is replete with examples from which we can learn. The challenge facing instructors of American government today is how to take adequate account of all these changes while never losing sight of the issues and events from the nation's past and their significance today.

We offer in this second edition of our textbook all the nuts and bolts of the U.S. government and how it works; but as with our first edition, we do not settle for mere surface descriptions and analysis of American government and politics. We also seek to educate students about American politics in ways that go beyond the essentials of government by placing current political issues and debates in perspective. By examining the current state of American politics from different angles, we hope to encourage students to think critically about the significance of certain persons, places, and events in American politics and consider all the different ways in which they might be viewed and interpreted. College students in recent years have been witness to historical shifts in American politics: Barack Obama's presidential campaign and the emergence of a more energetic and younger voting contingent as a force in the 2008 election; the unified resistance of moderate and conservative Republicans to most aspects of the Obama administration's agenda; the rise of the so-called Tea Party movement and its criticism of both parties; the passage of landmark health care legislation and the political fallout of the Obama administration's legislative agenda on the 2010 elections. All of these events offer unprecedented opportunities for testing political theories and concepts against modern-day realities.

As educators, we never want to let students accept at face value these and other essential aspects of American politics—we thus offer alternative perspectives to help students think more critically about American government and politics. For example, we don't want students to assume that all victories in the American political system are equally important; we want them to realize that prevailing political circumstances exert a powerful influence on how different entities may define "victory." Consider that some observers criticized Barack Obama and the Democrats for passing comprehensive health care legislation on the strength of a slim partisan majority; and yet when Lyndon Johnson, at the height of his party's political power in early 1965, was informed by an aide that the White House had just won passage of a desired piece of legislation by a wide margin, the president purportedly remarked: "How much more could we have gotten had we been willing to win by just one vote?" In similar fashion, some defeats may still advance the given cause, such as when losses generate attention or publicity for a previously unrecognized issue. For instance, the newly formed Republican Party's defeat in the 1856 presidential election set the stage for Abraham Lincoln's election as the first Republican president in 1860, and the eloquent dissents written by Supreme Court Justice Oliver Wendell Holmes in the 1920s pointed the way to the more liberal free speech doctrines embraced by a majority of Supreme Court justices in the 1960s.

Throughout the chapters of this textbook, we offer students of American government and politics the means by which to think critically about those topics. Blinded by what is in front of us now, we often ignore lessons from the past. American government has changed dramatically in the more than two centuries of the nation's existence, yet certain issues persist. In this textbook we investigate America's political institutions and processes from a number of different viewpoints in an effort to take the full measure of American politics.

Different Perspectives on American Politics

We offer in these pages no polemic or theoretical argument about what American politics should look like or stand for, either now or in the years ahead. To the degree it is possible, we attempt to avoid normative judgments about American political institutions or individuals based on a particular ideological point of view—whether conservative or liberal, radical or moderate. Instead, we aim to provide a more measured view of government institutions and processes. We complement the text presentation of the essentials of American government with a focus on three perspectives, allowing students to view American government from a variety of angles.

The Historical Perspective

The historical perspective places issues and problems of contemporary American politics within the context of past events and circumstances. Looking back provides important lessons applicable today. In examining the past we find that some of our new and "unprecedented" political controversies are neither new nor unprecedented. The faces may have changed and the policies may have been transformed, but the challenges the nation faces today are often newer versions of past dilemmas and problems.

Viewing American politics through the prism of history allows students to gain a greater appreciation for American government, both its flaws and its successes. Furthermore, placing American government in historical perspective facilitates an understanding of how the modern political system works. For example, the smoke-filled rooms of the nineteenth century in which political party bosses often selected political candidates threatened democracy and undermined accountability to the majority. Those smoke-filled rooms no longer exist today, as progressive reforms introduced in the early part of the twentieth century forced major political parties to use slightly more democratic means to choose candidates. Still, party bosses continue to exert considerable influence by determining where the party will allocate its resources. A thorough examination of past problems, issues, and conflicts does not negate the uniqueness of the current American condition, but it does offer a better understanding of contemporary issues. In some cases, studying the past assures us that the political process does work in a positive way; in other cases, it reminds us that we are not the first to face certain difficulties, and it suggests that we may want to seek more direction from the past about what works and what does not.

The Popular Perspective

The popular perspective offers yet another useful framework for examining political issues. At its core, American government is built upon the bedrock of popular consent. The U.S. Constitution itself and the institutions of government underscore the importance of the role of the people in American government. The biennial election of every member of the House of Representatives and the frequent elections of many state and local officials remind us that securing the popular will has been essential to our system from the beginning. The number and frequency of public opinion polls are further testament to the importance of the popular will. Popular culture also plays a role in influencing the popular perspective. Best-selling books, popular movies, and highly rated television shows all can have a lasting impact on the polity as well through their depiction of American politics . . . the good, the bad, and the ugly.

All these different sources offer a valuable perspective on where hot and not-so-hot political issues stand in the eyes of the public. As popular opinion on the war in Iraq shifted, Bush administration officials responsible for foreign policy were forced to make decisions and advise the president in a more complex (and increasingly hostile) political environment. Students need to take account of shifting political winds to understand why certain events transpired as they did. A popular perspective on American government promotes a deeper appreciation for the nuances of the American political system.

The Global Perspective

The global perspective offers viewpoints and opinions *about* U.S. government institutions and processes from the media, political elites, and the public in other parts of the world. (Though it may help foster some useful comparisons, this global perspective should not be confused with a strictly *comparative* analysis of political institutions and processes in different countries.) Over the years the nations of the world have become increasingly interconnected through communications advances (such as TV, satellite, and the Internet), the improved mobility of people (such as by more routine air travel), economic interdependencies (such as the North American Free Trade Agreement), and political changes (such as the creation of the United Nations after World War II). Now more than ever, American government affects and is affected by events, circumstances, and conflicts all over the world.

Though few would argue that the American government should develop policies based primarily on the views of others, awareness of how "outsiders" view the American government lends a valuable perspective to our understanding of the subject. Franklin Delano Roosevelt's controversial lend-lease agreement with

Britain in 1940 (by which he "traded" war materials to Britain with little hope of repayment) angered many Democrats from his own party who wanted the United States to stay neutral in the conflict in Europe. FDR knew, however, that Western European hopes for victory in the war against the Nazis were fading, and he wanted to assure both the leaders and the citizens of Britain in particular that they were not alone. Almost sixty years later, many were surprised when in 2003 some of the long-time Western European allies of the United States refused to support American military operations in Iraq. American officials' awareness of how their actions are viewed in other parts of the world can only benefit decision makers as they guide the United States through the increasingly interconnected world of global politics.

The three different perspectives described above offer students a broader view to enhance their understanding of American government and politics. Even more importantly, these perspectives provide the means for students to engage in critical thinking about American political issues—in effect, they allow students to challenge more effectively what they read and hear in the media and elsewhere. Does that television news anchor understand that the political rivalry he or she is discussing has roots in the early nineteenth century? Does knowing history affect the significance of an event or change the way political officials should treat the issue? To what extent does that state legislature's controversial policy confront popular approval in its own state and region? Did officials know how the newly occupied nation might react, and did it craft its policies accordingly? These three perspectives are not just helpful—they may be critical to helping students see beyond the here and now.

The Student's Perspective

That said, every student also views American politics through his or her own narrow prism. American military interventions abroad are one thing, but when the U.S. government actually drafts college-age student into the army—as occurred most recently during the Vietnam War—students may come to see the intervention with an entirely different eye. Similarly, the passage of landmark health care legislation means something entirely different for those students who can now remain longer on their family health care policies and thus put off worrying about obtaining their own health care insurance until much farther into the future. The textbook thus offers students **"Your Perspective"** as a window into American politics that looks specifically at students' personal vantage points—with the understanding, of course, that students come from a wide range of backgrounds and experiences.

Organization of the Textbook

Part I ("Foundations," Chapters 1 through 5) of the textbook begins with a discussion of how three different perspectives on American politics can add to and help shape our understanding of American politics and the creation and evolution of its institutions and processes. In Chapter 1, after reviewing the forms and functions of government in general and highlighting fundamental aspects of American political culture, we pose a hypothetical question: Is American democracy on the decline? We then consider evidence that has been offered in recent years to support and contradict that controversial proposition, using an examination of historical perspectives in order to place contentions such as these in their proper contexts. Chapters 2 through 5 begin the textbook's consideration of the American political system with a discussion of the origins of the American government and the Constitution (Chapter 2), the federal system and the rights and liberties that derive from the Constitution (Chapter 3), and the Bill of Rights and subsequent amendments that guarantee equality (Chapters 4 and 5).

Part II ("Institutions," Chapters 6 through 9) considers the major institutions of government formed under the Constitution. Congress (Chapter 6), the executive branch (Chapter 7), and the judiciary (Chapter 9) were all established by the first three articles of the Constitution, though their appearance and functions today might surprise many of founders who designed them. The bureaucracy (Chapter 8) is not specifically mentioned in the Constitution but it is an inevitable product of a government expected to tackle the problems of a nation that is home to a diverse population of over 300 million people.

In Part III ("Political Behavior," Chapters 10 through 15), we consider political behavior and its evolution. Interest groups (Chapter 11) and political parties (Chapter 13) are not modern phenomena; they were outgrowths of the American political system from the beginning. Public opinion (Chapter 10), the media (Chapter 12), voting (Chapter 14), and campaigns and elections (Chapter 15) receive extended attention in this part of the textbook.

In Part IV ("Public Policy," Chapters 16 through 19), we discuss public policy at national, state, and local levels. Following a discussion of the nature of public policy in general, we consider aspects of the nation's economic (Chapter 16), social (Chapter 17), and foreign policies (Chapter 18). In Chapter 19, we examine state and local government, again presenting historical, popular, and global perspectives on the topic.

New to the Brief Second Edition

This revised second brief edition offers new features, updated coverage, and updated features that will assist students as they grapple with the constantly shifting realities of American politics. New features students will find most beneficial are:

- newly created **"Your perspective"** boxes for each chapter, which consider various aspects of American politics from the unique perspective of college students, and which take advantage of the experiences they bring to bear when studying American government;
- succinctly written **learning objectives** provided at the beginning of every chapter, and then repeated throughout each chapter at points in the text that directly address those objectives;
- **critical thinking questions** added at the end of many the thematic boxes, which encourage students to think about the material in new and interesting ways, and which may be used to spark discussion of the material in class;

- a broader scope to the boxes on **popular perspectives**, which now includes discussion of how popular culture (including television shows, movies, best-selling books, etc.) interacts with American politics;
- and newly constituted **chapter summaries** presented in bullet-point format, which now directly parallel each chapter's learning objectives.

Updated Coverage

In recent years we have witnessed a significant transformation of the American political landscape. The collapse of the economy in late 2007 was followed a year later by Barack Obama's historic victory in the 2008 presidential election. The Obama administration's first two years in office proved especially contentious, as the president and his Democratic allies in Congress pushed through their legislative agenda against strong resistance from Republicans and newly formed outside groups such as the Tea Party. The bitterly contested November 2010 midterm elections were a product of this growing unrest. The Second Edition features numerous new chapter-opening vignettes, boxes, tables, and figures that emphasize these recent developments and should help bring students up to speed with new political realities.

Updated Features

- "Now & Then" vignettes at the beginning of Chapters 1 & 13, which consider the role that the Tea Party and other interest groups played in the November 2010 midterm elections; other new vignettes that consider historical parallels for constitutional amendments, incremental policymaking on social issues; the role that states play as "laboratories of democracy" for issues like universal health care; President Obama's methods of prosecuting the war on terror; President Bush's historic rise and fall in the polls; the role of a new medium (the Internet) in shaping policy; how presidents address economic crises; etc.
- New popular perspective boxes on Barack Obama's 2010 State of the Union Address; the role played by White House Web sites and other aspects of the "interactive presidency"; the way that criminal defense attorneys are portrayed heroically in movies; the role of blogs in shaping modern public opinion; television's embracing of women and racial minority presidents long before Barack Obama's historic victory; the use of campaign books by presidential wannabes hoping to get their message across to new audiences; the Oscar-award winning vice president, etc.
- New historical perspective boxes on senators who switch their political parties; the role of sensationalism in driving media coverage; the incorporation of civil liberties (including the Second Amendment Right to Bear Arms) to be applied to state and local governments, etc.;
- New global perspective boxes addressing British perspectives on a new Supreme Court Justice who arose from poverty; Al Jazeera's perspective on Obama's war against terror; the German press's favorable coverage of the Obama campaign in 2008; China's reaction to Obama's fiscal stimulus plan; world perspectives on the Obama administration's new strategy for military intervention in Afghanistan.

Special Instructional Features

We offer a number of recurring special instructional features designed to engage students' interest and provide pedagogical support to help them master chapter material. Several of the recurring features highlight the three perspectives that underlie the book's presentation.

Now & Then

Each chapter (except Chapter 1) begins with an opening vignette entitled **"Now & Then,"** in which some situation relevant to the chapter topic is presented. Many students with at least some exposure to American politics will be able to identify the more recent issue or event (i.e., "Now") to which the situation appears to refer. At the same time, however, the situation also refers to some event or issue in the past (i.e., "Then") that may not be so familiar to students. Those who correctly identified the more recent event may be surprised to learn that the situation presented also describes another event from the nation's past. The "Now & Then" opening vignette thus demonstrates that although people and circumstances may change dramatically, certain issues and problems persist. At the end of the chapter, the section entitled **"Now & Then: Making the Connection"** revisits the two examples from the beginning of the chapter, ties them together, and then connects them to major themes of the chapter as a whole.

Perspectives Features

Nearly every chapter also includes all four features that focus on the different perspectives (historical, popular, global, and your perspective). **"American Government in Historical Perspective"** compares different moments in American history in which the same event or circumstance recurred, albeit with different actors and in somewhat different forms. **"American Government in Popular Perspective"** offers evidence, ranging from public opinion polls to a review of popular culture, about where the American public stands on some issue relevant to the chapter. **"American Government in Global Perspective"** presents material from other countries—perhaps a newspaper editorial, a quote from a foreign politician, or evidence from foreign public opinion polls—that offers outsiders' perspectives on some aspect of American politics. Finally, **"Your Perspective on American Government"** provides material that relates the subject or topic at hand to students' own personal experiences.

Study Aids and Resources

LEARNING OBJECTIVES
★ WHAT YOU WILL LEARN ★

Aids to facilitate study of the material include detailed **learning objectives** at the beginning of each chapter so students can know what will be expected of them at the outset, as well as a **chapter summary** of key points at the end of each chapter that specifically address the learning objectives laid out at the beginning. Additionally, within each chapter **key terms** are highlighted in bold-face type and defined in the margins of the pages. These key terms are also listed at the end of the chapter, and the terms and definitions are repeated in a glossary at the end of the book. Also at the end of each chapter is a list of **resources,** both print and electronic, that students can explore on their own.

Politics InterActive!

The **Politics InterActive!** feature at the end of each chapter presents some contemporary political event or conflict related to the chapter content and instructs students to visit the Wadsworth Web site www.cengage.com/dautrich/americangovernmentbrief/2e accompanying this textbook to explore further Internet resources that offer historical, popular, and global perspectives on that same topic. These Internet resources encourage students' critical thinking and help them realize just how much their views of American politics may be shaped—or reshaped—by their exposure to alternate perspectives. The interactive exercise component of the Politics InterActive! feature then poses a similar issue and asks students to explore Internet resources that offer varying perspectives on that topic.

Many other textbooks subtly (and, in some cases, not so subtly) offer the authors' own "take" on American politics. Although some instructors may appreciate that more polemical approach, we aim to provide something different. Recognizing that students come to the introductory American government course from a variety of different backgrounds and with varying levels of understanding about American politics, we present all the nuts and bolts they need to understand the system in as straightforward and clear a manner as possible. But then we go a step further: To complement that foundation of basic information, we offer materials that present different perspectives on each topic. These different perspectives are intended to encourage students to engage in critical thinking about the political process as a whole.

The historical, popular, and global perspectives—as well as the material that address American politics from students' own perspectives—do not interfere with the description of essential foundations. If anything, they should spark students' interest in revisiting what they learned in high school, from the media, and elsewhere about American politics with a more discerning and critical eye. Perhaps many students will take this critical approach beyond the course and become actual participants in the process. If they do so with a more critical and skeptical eye, our democratic system can only benefit.

Supplements for Instructors and Students

DVDs and CD-ROMs

PowerLecture DVD with JoinIn™ and ExamView® (ISBN-10: 0840035209 | ISBN-13: 9780840035202). This DVD includes two sets of PowerPoint® slides— a book-specific and a media-enhanced set—a Test Bank in both Microsoft® Word and ExamView formats, an Instructor's Manual, JoinIn Clickers, and a Resource Integration Guide.

- Interactive book-specific **PowerPoint lectures,** a one-stop lecture and class preparation tool, makes it easy for you to assemble, edit, publish, and present book-specific lectures for your course. You will have access to a set of PowerPoints with outlines specific to each chapter of *American Government: Historical, Popular and Global Perspectives, Brief Edition* as well as photos, figures, and tables found in the book.

- The **media-enhanced PowerPoints** for each chapter can be used on their own or easily integrated with the book-specific PowerPoint outlines. Audio and video clips depicting both historic and current day events; new animated learning modules illustrating key concepts; tables, statistical charts, and graphs; and photos from the book as well as outside sources are provided at the appropriate places in the chapter. You can also add your own materials—using both types of PowerPoints and your own material—to create a powerful, personalized classroom or online presentation.

- The computerized **Test Bank** in Microsoft Word and ExamView offers a large array of well-crafted multiple-choice and essay questions, along with their answers and page references.

- The **Instructor's Manual** includes learning objectives, chapter outlines, discussion questions, suggestions for stimulating class activities and projects, tips on integrating media into your class (including step-by-step instructions for creating your own podcasts), suggested readings and Web resources, and a section specially designed to help teaching assistants and adjunct instructors.

- **JoinIn** offers book-specific "clicker" questions that test and track student comprehension of key concepts. Political Polling questions simulate voting, engage students, foster dialogue on group behaviors and values, and add personal relevance; the results can be compared to national data, leading to lively discussions. Visual Literacy questions are tied to images from the book and add useful pedagogical tools and high-interest feedback during your lecture. Save the data from students' responses all semester—track their progress and show them how political science works by incorporating this exciting new tool into your classroom. It is available for college and university adopters only.

- The **Resource Integration Guide** outlines the rich collection of resources available to instructors and students within the chapter-by-chapter framework of the book, suggesting how and when each supplement can be used to optimize learning.

Wadsworth News DVD: American Government 2012 (ISBN-10: 0495573094 | ISBN-13: 9780495573098). This collection of three- to six-minute video clips on relevant political issues serves as a great lecture or discussion launcher.

ABC News DVD: Speeches by Barack Obama (ISBN-10: 1439082472 | ISBN-13: 9781439082478). This DVD includes nine famous speeches by President Barack Obama, from 2004 to present day, including his speech at the 2004 Democratic National Convention; his 2008 speech on race, "A More Perfect Union"; and his 2009 inaugural address. Speeches are divided into short video segments for easy, time-efficient viewing. This instructor supplement also features critical thinking questions and answers for each speech, designed to spark class discussion.

Election 2010: An American Government Supplement (ISBN-10: 1111341788 | ISBN-13: 9781111341787). Written by John Clark and Brian Schaffner, this booklet addresses the 2010 congressional and gubernatorial races, with real-time analysis and references.

Political Theatre 2.0 (ISBN-10: 0495793604 | ISBN-13: 9780495793601). Bring politics home to students with Political Theatre 2.0, up-to-date through the 2008 election season. This is the second edition of this three-DVD series and includes video clips of both classic and contemporary political advertisements, speeches, interviews, and more that show American political thought throughout the public sector. Available to adopters of Cengage textbooks.

JoinIn Student Response System (with Installation CD-ROM) (ISBN-10: 0495095508 | ISBN-13: 9780495095507). For even more interaction, combine Political Theatre with the innovative teaching tool of a classroom response system through JoinIn. Poll your students with questions created for you or construct your own questions. Built within Microsoft PowerPoint software, JoinIn is easily integrated into your current lectures in conjunction with the "clicker" hardware of your choice.

The Obama Presidency—Year One Supplement (ISBN-10: 0495908371 | ISBN-13: 9780495908371). Much happens in the first year of a presidency, especially an historic one like that of Barack Obama. This full-color sixteen-page supplement by Kenneth Janda, Jeffrey Berry, and Jerry Goldman analyzes such issues as health care, the economy and the stimulus package, changes in the U.S. Supreme Court, the rescue of the U.S. auto industry, and the effect Obama policy has had on global affairs.

Great Speeches Collection. Throughout the ages, great orators have stepped up to the podium and used their communication skills to persuade, inform, and inspire their audiences. Studying these speeches can provide tremendous insight into historical, political, and cultural events. The Great Speeches Collection includes the full text of over sixty memorable orations for you to incorporate into your course. Speeches can be collated in a printed reader to supplement your existing course materials or bound into a core textbook.

Online Resources

CourseMate (ISBN-10: 0840069731 | ISBN-13: 9780840069733). The CourseMate for *American Government: Historical, Popular and Global Perspectives, Brief Edition* offers a variety of rich online learning resources designed to enhance the student experience. These resources include video activities, audio summaries, critical thinking activities, simulations, animated learning modules, interactive timelines, primary source activities, flashcards, learning objectives, glossaries, and crossword puzzles. Chapter resources are correlated with key chapter learning concepts, and users can browse or search for content in a variety of ways.

NewsNow, a new asset available on CourseMate, is a combination of weekly news stories from the Associated Press, videos, and images that bring current events to life for the student. For instructors, NewsNow includes an additional set of multimedia-rich PowerPoint slides posted each week to the password-protected area of the text's companion Web site. Instructors may use these slides to take a class poll or trigger a lively debate about the events that are shaping the world right now. And because this all-in-one presentation tool includes the text of the original newsfeed, along with videos, photos and discussion questions, no Internet connection is required!

How do you assess your students' engagement in your course? How do you know your students have read the material or viewed the resources you've assigned? How can you tell if your students are struggling with a concept? With

CourseMate, you can use the included Engagement Tracker to assess student preparation and engagement. Use the tracking tools to see progress for the class as a whole or for individual students. Identify students at risk early in the course. Uncover which concepts are most difficult for your class. Monitor time on task. Keep your students engaged.

CourseMate also features an interactive eBook that has highlighting and search capabilities along with links to simulations, animated PowerPoints that illustrate concepts, Interactive Timelines, Videos, Primary Source Activities, Case Studies, Tutorial Quizzes, and Flashcards.

Go to cengagebrain.com/shop/ISBN/ 049590791X to access your Political Science CourseMate resources.

WebTutor™ on WebCT Instant Access Code (ISBN-10: 1111303894 | ISBN-13: 9781111303891).

WebTutor on Blackboard Instant Access Code (ISBN-10: 1111303908 | ISBN-13: 9781111303907). Rich with content for your American government course, this Web-based teaching and learning tool includes course management, study/mastery, and communication tools. Use WebTutor to provide virtual office hours, post your syllabus, and track student progress with WebTutor's quizzing material. For students, WebTutor offers real-time access to interactive online tutorials and simulations, practice quizzes, and Web links—all correlated to *American Government: Historical, Popular and Global Perspectives, Brief Edition.*

American Government CourseReader Printed Access Card (ISBN-10: 111147995X| ISBN-13: 9781111479954)

American Government CourseReader: Politics in Context will enable instructors to create a customized reader. Using a database of hundreds of documents, readings, and videos, instructors can search by various criteria or browse the collection to preview and select a customized collection to assign to their students. The sources will be edited to an appropriate length and include pedagogical support—a headnote describing the document and critical-thinking and multiple-choice questions to verify that the student has read and understood the selection. Students will be able to take notes, highlight, and print content. American Government CourseReader: Politics in Context allows the instructor to select exactly what students will be assigned with an easy-to-use interface and also provides an easily used assessment tool. The sources can be delivered online or in print format.

Aplia (ISBN-10: 1111666156| ISBN-13: 9781111666156). Aplia is dedicated to improving students' learning by increasing their effort and engagement with your American Government course. Founded by an instructor for other instructors, Aplia offers students premium, automatically graded assignments. Aplia saves instructors from spending time on routine grading while giving students an easy way to stay on top of coursework with regularly scheduled assignments organized by specific chapters of their textbook.

Available through a pin-code access, Aplia helps students learn the essential concepts of American Government and apply them to real life through the use of interactive coursework that strengthens their critical thinking and comprehensive reading skills with immediate, detailed explanations for every answer they input. Homework and class assignments help students come to class better prepared. Grades are automatically recorded in the instructor's Aplia gradebook. Aplia provides customer service that's quick, friendly, and knowledgeable.

American Government and Aplia . . . a way to help students engage, prepare, and learn. Aplia will be available with this book for Fall 2011.

Instructor's Companion Web site

The instructor companion site includes the Instructor's Manual; text-specific PowerPoints containing lecture outlines, photos, and figures; and NewsNow PowerPoints, an additional set of multimedia-rich PowerPoint slides posted each week. Instructors may use these slides to take a class poll or trigger a lively debate about the events that are shaping the world right now. And because this all-in-one presentation tool includes the text of the original newsfeed, along with videos, photos, and discussion questions, no Internet connection is required!

Instructors also have access to the Instructor's Guide to YouTube, which shows American Government instructors where on the Internet to find videos that can be used as learning tools in class. Organized by fifteen topics, the guide follows the sequence of an American Government course and includes a preface with tips on how to use Internet videos in class.

About the Authors

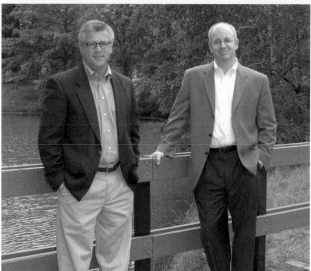

PHOTO COURTESY OF THE AUTHORS

Kenneth J. Dautrich (Ph.D., Rutgers 1995) is an associate professor of public policy at the University of Connecticut. He is also the founder and former director of the Center for Survey Research & Analysis at the University of Connecticut. Previously, Dr. Dautrich was a Research Fellow at the Media Studies Center in New York, and has served as a senior faculty fellow at the Heldrich Center at Rutgers. His first book, *How the News Media Fail American Voters* (Columbia University Press, 1997), received scholarly praise in numerous political science circles. He also co-authored *The First Amendment and the Media in the Court of Public Opinion* (Cambridge University Press, 2002) and *The Future of the First Amendment* (Rowman & Littlefield, 2008). Dr. Dautrich's research and teaching focus on public opinion and American elections. For the past four years he has directed a set of national surveys on civic literacy in the American public and the role of higher education in advancing knowledge about American government. He is currently writing a book on findings from this project.

David A. Yalof (Ph.D., Johns Hopkins University 1997; J.D., University of Virginia 1991) is an associate professor of political science at the University of Connecticut. His first book, *Pursuit of Justices: Presidential Politics and the Selection of Supreme Court Nominees* (University of Chicago Press, 1999), was awarded the American Political Science Association's Richard E. Neustadt Award as the best book published on presidential studies in 1999. He is also the co-author of *The First Amendment and the Media in the Court of Public Opinion* (Cambridge University Press, 2002), *The Future of the First Amendment* (Rowman & Littlefield, 2008), and another textbook, *Constitutional Law: Civil Liberty and Individual Rights* (Foundation Press, 2007). Dr. Yalof has written extensively on issues in constitutional law and Supreme Court appointment politics—his work has been published in *Political Research Quarterly, Judicature, Constitutional Commentary,* and various other journals. He is currently nearing completion of a book-length manuscript about executive branch wrongdoing and the due process of law.

Acknowledgments

This second brief edition of *American Government: Historical, Popular and Global Perspectives* is a product of the hard work of many, many people. First and foremost among them is our executive editor, Carolyn Merrill. At Cengage she has been the prime mover of this project. It is impossible to imagine pulling off a project like this without the management skills, temperament, and good humor that Carolyn provides. Tops among all of the great decisions Carolyn made was the hiring of Betty Slack as our development editor. In our minds, the team of Carolyn and Betty is a hard one to top.

Senior managers at Cengage also played a hands-on role in the development of this second edition, including Sean Wakely, P. J. Boardman, our publisher Suzanne Jeans, and Dan Silverburg. Their guidance and commitment to our book is, as always, greatly appreciated. We also extend our gratitude to the many other members of the Cengage staff we have come to depend upon in writing and producing this book and its supplemental materials: Katie Hayes, Lydia LeStar, Lindsey Richardson, Heather Baxley, Sara Abbott, Jeff Greene, Angela Hodge, Laura Hildebrand, Josh Allen, and Suzanne St. Clair. We would also like to extend a special note of thanks to Lachina Publishing Services for their diligent work in the production process and Carly Bergey for her fine research in selecting pictures.

The many sales representatives at Cengage not only do a great job in getting the word out on our book, but they also have collected feedback from instructors and relayed it back to us. In many instances, our reps have provided their own guidance and feedback as well. Thankfully, all their efforts have helped improve the content of the book, and make it more responsive to the perspective of instructors who use it. Our hats are off to this terrific sales force. Mark, LeDawn, Houston, Sally, Nick, Laura, Davene . . . there are just too many of you to name. We are grateful for your many efforts.

Appreciation also goes to our colleagues at the University of Connecticut, especially those in the Department of Political Science and the Department of Public Policy, of which there are too many to list by name. Their patience, support, and advice in our writing of this second edition have not gone unnoticed; nor has the input we have received from our graduate students and undergraduate users of the text.

The many professionals, colleagues, and students who provide support and advice are not the only ones who influence the writing of a textbook. Our families must live with us through the writing and production cycles. Not only do they tolerate the fact that we often bring our work home, but they also give us strong motivation to get the job done. We cannot thank our better halves, Andrea and Mary Beth, enough. Our children, to whom this book is dedicated, are not shy about offering their ideas either. The book benefits from their youthful perspectives and advice.

Finally, there are many members of our profession and many practitioners in American politics who put in countless hours and intellectual energy aiding in the writing of this manuscript.

We thank the reviewers who commented on drafts of the manuscript:

Reviewers of Second Brief Edition

Amanda Ross Edwards
North Carolina State University

Barbara Headrick
Minnesota State University—Moorhead

Mark Jendrysik
University of North Dakota

Wendy Johnston
Adirondack Community College

William Kelly
Auburn University

Mike Kryzanek
Bridgewater State University

Khalil M. Marrar
DePaul University—Lincoln Park

Sarah Poggione
Florida International University/Ohio University

Daniel Ponder
Drury University

Shane Runyon
Beacon College

Joyce Smith
Hillsborough Community College—Ybor

Julie Stevenson
Minnesota West Community & Technical College

John Vento
Antelope Valley College

Julian Westerhout
Illinois State University

Mohamed Yamba
California University of Pennsylvania

AMERICAN GOVERNMENT

1
Perspectives on American Government

Introduction to Perspectives on American Government

★ Understand that issues and topics in American politics may be viewed from a variety of perspectives, including historical context, popular culture, views from others around the world, and views from college students

Forms and Functions of Government

★ Identify the philosophical underpinnings of the American political system through the exploration of important theories such as the "social contract" theory and the concept of the "natural law"

★ Compare and contrast democracy with other forms of government

American Government and Politics

★ Explain the importance of the value of popular sovereignty, and how that value is realized through "representative democracy" in the United States

American Political Culture

★ Define "political culture" and describe the unique combination of political beliefs and values that form the American political culture, including majority rule, liberty, limited government, diversity, individualism, and equality of economic opportunity

Is American Democracy on the Decline?

★ Assess the health of American democracy and evaluate whether the American system is in decline by reviewing trends in voter turnout, negativity in politics, the influence of money in policy outcomes, etc.

Historical, Popular, and Global Perspectives

★ Appreciate that the American political system is best studied from a variety of perspectives, including historical, popular, and global **CourseMate**

REUTERS/GARY HERSHOM/LANDOV

President-elect Barack Obama and Vice President-elect Joe Biden on the night of their victory in the 2008 presidential election.

AP PHOTO/J. SCOTT APPLEWHITE

Representative Nancy Pelosi and Senator Harry Reid (right) on the November 2006 evening of victories that cemented Pelosi's ascension to Speaker and Reid's becoming Senate majority leader.

Representative John Boehner on election night 2010 gets teary-eyed as he realizes the GOP victory will make him Speaker of the House.

Senator-elect Rand Paul (R-KY) was one of the victorious Tea Party-backed candidates in the 2010 midterm elections.

Placing the 2010 Midterm Elections into Perspective

The Republican Party achieved a major victory in the 2010 congressional elections by picking up more than 60 House seats and thus capturing a majority once again. The GOP also picked up 6 Senate seats, slicing the Democratic margin of control in that chamber from 18 to 6 Senate seats in all. The GOP shift, particularly in the House of Representatives, is significant. Between 1950 and 2008 partisan control of the House of Representatives switched only two times (1995 and 2007). The outcome of the 2010 races was also striking in the way it signaled a dramatic shift in voter preferences over a mere two-year period. When President Barack Obama took the oath of office in January 2009, he had the support of a Democratic-controlled Congress bolstered by successive election cycles that overwhelmingly favored his party. From the 2006 and 2008 election results, many political analysts felt that a permanent shift favoring the Democratic Party was underway. As it turned out, voters in 2010 quickly reversed course, sweeping Republicans into Congress and returning the American political system to a state of "divided government," with a Democrat in the White House and a comfortable majority of Republicans in the House of Representatives. What undercurrents of popular opinion could possibly produce such an abrupt change of course? Did 2010 mark a historically unprecedented midterm election outcome? How schizophrenic does the American electorate appear to the rest of the world, as the decisions made by the U.S. electorate may have significant implications on global policy? Finally, based on the conflicting outcome of the 2008 and 2010 elections, can anybody predict what lies ahead for the 2012 presidential election?

Introduction to Perspectives on American Government

Historical Perspective

At least two things are striking from the 2010 midterm election results. First, the GOP made important and significant gains that should empower the party in the policymaking process, at least through 2012. Second, the electorate abruptly reversed course from the direction it had steered American politics only two years earlier. How unprecedented are these outcomes of the 2010 midterms?

The 2010 GOP gains are by no means historically unprecedented. Since 1914, there have been numerous election cycles that ended with party shifts far greater than those of 2010. In seven elections for the Senate, the partisan gains actually reached into the double digits, and in four of the elections for the House over that same period, at least 75 seats shifted from one party to the other. American voters have never been shy about bringing change to Washington.

Nor has the electorate been reluctant to shift course quickly. Most recently, as the economy began to soften and the Iraqi war lingered in 2006, voters eliminated the GOP's 10-seat Senate margin entirely and transferred partisan control of the House to the Democrats by a 35-seat margin. Two years later, with the economy in a tailspin, voters enhanced Democratic Party control by sending Barack Obama to the White House and increasing Democratic majorities in the Senate to 20 and in the House to 78. This zig to the Democrats clearly zagged back to the GOP in 2010. Before concluding that American voters have developed a schizophrenic voting disorder, however, a glance at history demonstrates that the electorate has zig-zagged over short periods of time in the past as well. In 1946, American voters awarded Republicans 56 new seats in the House and then just two years later sent the Republican Congress packing. Voters similarly zig-zagged in 1992 and 1994 when they first voted into office Democratic President Bill Clinton and a strong Democratic Congress, only to provide the GOP with congressional majorities just two years later. So while the results of 2010 have led some to wonder why the electorate is acting so erratically of late, a view from history shows that such behavior is no anomaly.

Popular Perspective

Understanding the opinions of American voters provides yet another perspective from which to examine the 2010 outcomes. Why would the dynamics of public opinion deliver the White House and strong majorities to the Democrats in 2008, only to punish the Democrats in 2010 with a new GOP House majority?

A review of public opinion from 2006 through 2010 reveals a consistent and salient set of findings: consumer confidence hit new all-time lows, most thought the country was headed in the wrong direction, and voters largely blamed government for the recession. Political scientists have long documented the dynamic nature of public opinion during elections, including the strong inclination of voters to hold the party in power accountable for a problematic economy. Under the theory of "retrospective voting," voters assess their own economic standing and accordingly either blame or reward the party in power. In 2008, most voters held a dim view of their economic prospects and thus were more likely to vote to "throw out the rascals"—in this case that meant jettisoning Republicans from the White House. Two years later, most Americans continued to take a dim view of the economy. While many heard and agreed with the 2008 Democratic theme of change, they did not see much tangible change at all. Finding themselves in the same place as they were in 2008, voters again expressed their frustration with government, this time punishing the Democratic majorities in Congress for failing to deliver. When examining the 2008 and 2010 elections from the popular perspective, it is not so surprising that voters opted in favor of several changes of course.

Global Perspective

It is perhaps a truism today that what happens to America in the 21st century affects what happens in the rest of the world, and vice versa. New communications technologies, the growth in world trade, international travel, multinational corporations, immigration patterns, the common fear of weapons of mass destruction, and numerous environmental problems are just a few of the issues that have heightened the reciprocal impacts of what happens in America and what happens across the globe. Accordingly, understanding how the rest of world views what happens in America has implications for America itself. It is important to understand how other nations reacted to the 2010 midterm elections. This is what led Michael Schulman of *Time* magazine to write the following the day after the 2010 midterm elections:

> With all of this incessant talk about the decline of American global influence, we tend to forget that the U.S. is still by far the world's largest economy, and what happens in the U.S. matters to everyone, everywhere. That's why people from Beijing to Brasilia are watching the midterms with heightened interest. Shifts in U.S. policy, on issues such as trade, China, the budget, banking reform and so on, directly impact the global economy and attempts to reform it. And with the Republicans taking control of the House of Representatives . . . we're definitely in for a shift from the politics and policies of the first two years of the Obama presidency . . .[1]

In this book we examine the major topics and concepts in American government and politics. We attempt to answer sweeping questions about how American government works: How does public policy get made? Who are the major players and institutions that make laws? How do these major players achieve their position? How do disputes get settled? What is the role of the American people in governing? In this discussion, we draw on three perspectives to provide a deeper appreciation for American government and how it works. From a historical perspective, we view contemporary American government as a product of American history. From a popular perspective, we recognize the significant role that the American people play in influencing what government does. And from a global perspective, we examine how the rest of the world views American government and consider how those views might help shape policy. We also encourage you to develop your own perspectives on American government and to use those perspectives to make a difference.

Anarchy
A state of lawlessness and discord in the political system caused by lack of government.

Social contract
From the philosophy of Jean-Jacques Rousseau, an agreement people make with one another to form a government and abide by its rules and laws, and in return, the government promises to protect the people's rights and welfare and promote their best interests.

Authority
The ability of public institutions and the officials within them to make laws, independent of the power to execute them.

Democracy
Form of government in which the people, either directly or through elected representatives, hold power and authority. The word *democracy* is derived from the Greek *demos kratos*, meaning "rule by the people."

Forms and Functions of Government

Government is the collection of public institutions in a nation that establish and enforce the rules by which the members of that nation must live. Even the most primitive of societies have found government to be necessary. Without government, society would be in a state of **anarchy**, a situation characterized by lawlessness and discord in the political system. Thomas Hobbes, a seventeenth-century British political philosopher, wrote that without government life would be "solitary, poor, nasty, brutish and short."[2] Government is necessary to make the rules by which citizens must abide, promoting order, stability, and protection for the society. It exists in part to resolve conflicts that naturally arise when people live in communities. Elaborating on the role of government, Jean-Jacques Rousseau, an eighteenth-century French philosopher, posited that in fact a "social contract" exists.[3] A **social contract** is an agreement people make with one another to form a government and abide by its rules and laws. In return, the government promises to protect people's rights and welfare and to promote their best interests.

A government's **authority** over its citizens refers to the ability of public institutions and the officials within them to make laws independent of the power to execute them. People obey authority out of respect, whereas they obey power out of fear. There are a number of different forms of government with governing authority that can be found among the nations of the world. One such form—the form that will receive extended attention throughout this book—is **democracy**, defined as a government in which the people, either directly or through elected representatives, hold power and authority. The word *democracy* is derived from the Greek *demos kratos*, meaning "rule by the people."

By contrast, an **oligarchy** is a form of government in which a small exclusive class, which may or may not attempt to rule on behalf of the people as a whole, holds supreme power. In a **theocracy**, a particular religion or faith plays a dominant role in the government; Iran is one example of a theocratic nation in the world today. A **monarchy** is a form of government in which one person, usually a member of a royal family or a royal designate, exercises supreme authority. The monarch may be a king, such as King Abdullah of Saudi Arabia, or a queen, like Queen Elizabeth II of Great Britain. In the past, monarchies were quite common; today, they are rarely practiced in the absolute sense. Although the United Kingdom continues to pay homage to its royalty, true political power rests in the Parliament, whose members are elected by the people.

Many of the nations in the world today have an **authoritarian** form of government in which one political party, group, or person maintains such complete control over the nation that it may refuse to recognize, and may even choose to suppress, all other political parties and interests. Most considered the nation of Iraq, before the American military intervention in 2003, to be an authoritarian government under the dictatorial rule of Saddam Hussein. North Korea under Kim Jong-Il is an authoritarian government that still exists today.

An important characteristic of any government, whether democratic or not, is its power to exercise authority over people. **Power** is the capacity to get individuals to do something that they may not do otherwise, such as pay taxes, stop for red lights, or submit to a search before boarding an airplane. Without power, it would be very difficult for a government to enforce rules. The sustained power of any government largely rests on its legitimacy. **Legitimacy** is the extent to which the people (or the "governed") afford the government the authority and right to exercise power. The more that people subscribe to the goals of a government and the greater the degree to which that government guarantees the people's welfare (for example, by supporting a strong economy or providing protection from foreign enemies), the higher will be the government's level of legitimacy. When the governed grant a high level of legitimacy to their government, the government wields its power to make and enforce rules more successfully.

★ LO

Explain the importance of the value of popular sovereignty, and how that value is realized through "representative democracy" in the United States

American Government and Politics

Politics is defined as the way the institutions of government are organized to make laws, rules, and policies and how those institutions are influenced. More than seventy years ago, political scientist Harold Lasswell proposed a brief but very useful definition of politics as "who gets what, when and how."[4] In American politics, the "who" includes actors within and outside the formal government such as citizens, elected officials, interest groups, and state and local governments. The "what" are the decisions the government makes and take the form of what the government funds, the way it raises revenue, and the policies it produces and enforces. The "when" relates to setting priorities about what government does. The concerns and issues that government addresses differ in importance, and issues of greater importance tend to be addressed more quickly. Finally, the "how" refers to the way in which the government goes about its work based on the political institutions that exist and the formal and informal procedures and rules that define the governing process. In describing American politics, this book provides answers to Lasswell's "who gets what, when and how?"

Government in the United States is especially complex. It is organized into multiple layers (national, state, and local), it encompasses a number of political institutions that share power—the executive (the president), the legislature (Congress), and the judiciary (the courts)—and it provides countless methods for individuals and groups to influence the decisions made by those institutions. In this book, we will examine this complex organization of American government, describe the political institutions that exercise power, and explore the varied ways that people and groups exert influence. As we sort through this complexity of American government, we will seek to explain how and why the American political system has been able to endure the conflicts, both internal and external, that it has faced and currently faces. We will attempt to show how the American government is uniquely designed to stand up to its many challenges.

The strength and stability of the U.S. government are grounded in the high level of legitimacy it maintains with the American public. Americans may disagree vehemently with public officials, but rarely do they question their claim to authority. The framers of the U.S. Constitution were keenly aware of the importance of the legitimacy of the system. They knew that if the government was to withstand the test of time, it must serve the people well. These ideas about legitimacy drew largely on the theories of seventeenth-century British political philosopher John Locke (1632–1704).[5] Locke proposed that people are born with certain *natural rights*, which derive from **natural law**, the rules of conduct inherent in the relationship among human beings and thus more fundamental than any law that a governing authority might make.

Oligarchy
A form of government in which a small exclusive class, which may or may not attempt to rule on behalf of the people as a whole, holds supreme power.

Theocracy
A form of government in which a particular religion or faith plays a dominant role in the government.

Monarchy
A form of government in which one person, usually a member of a royal family or a royal designate, exercises supreme authority.

Authoritarianism
A form of government in which one political party, group, or person maintains such complete control over the nation that it may refuse to recognize and may even suppress all other political parties and interests.

Power
The ability to get individuals to do something that they may not otherwise do, such as pay taxes, stop for red lights, or submit to a search before boarding an airplane.

Legitimacy
The extent to which the people afford the government the authority and right to exercise power.

Politics
The way in which the institutions of government are organized to make laws, rules, and policies, and how those institutions are influenced.

Painting of George Washington and the Constitution's drafters at the Constitutional Convention in 1787.

Government cannot violate these natural rights, which include life, liberty, and property. Therefore, government, or human law, must be based on the "consent of the governed"; that is, citizens are responsible for choosing their government and its leaders. This theory loomed large in the mind of Thomas Jefferson as he drafted the Declaration of Independence to justify the American colonies' split with the British government: "All men . . . are endowed by their creator with certain unalienable rights . . . [and] whenever any form of government becomes destructive of these ends, it is the right of the people to alter or abolish it." A government maintains legitimacy as long as the governed are served well and as long as government respects the natural rights of individuals.

Natural law

According to John Locke, the most fundamental type of law, which supersedes any law that is made by government. Citizens are born with certain natural rights (including life, liberty, and property) that derive from this law and that government cannot take away.

Drawing on this philosophy, the framers drafted a Constitution that created a political system able to manage the inevitable conflicts that occur in any society. Mindful of Thomas Hobbes's notion that the essence of government is to manage naturally occurring conflicts, the framers designed a government that encourages conflict and competition rather than attempts to repress it. As we shall see in the chapters that follow, the U.S. Constitution includes a number of mechanisms that allow naturally occurring conflict to play out in as productive a manner as possible. Mechanisms are also in place to resolve conflicts and arrive at consensus on issues. Those who disagree and come up on the short side of political battles are guaranteed rights and liberties nonetheless. Further, the rules by which conflicts are settled are predicated on fairness and proper procedures.

The significance of what the framers of the Constitution accomplished cannot be overstated. They not only addressed the short-term problems challenging the new nation, but they also drafted a blueprint for how government should go about dealing with problems and conflicts into the future. The U.S. Constitution has served as the cornerstone of an American political system that routinely attempts to tackle some of the thorniest problems imaginable. In Chapter 2 of this book, we examine the enduring principles and processes outlined in the Constitution.

The Constitution provides a way for the American government to navigate through the many problems and conflicts that have faced the nation, including severe economic depressions, two world wars, nuclear confrontations with the former Soviet Union, and persisting questions of equality. Through all these difficulties, the American government has endured. The foresight of the framers to create a Constitution that possesses the flexibility to adapt to changing times has served as a basis for the United States' enduring democracy.

World Views on America

The Pew Global Attitudes Project conducted 24,000 interviews with people from around the world in 2008 and asked respondents whether they had a favorable or unfavorable view of America. The following shows the percentage from each country who say they have a favorable view of America.

For Critical Thinking and Discussion

1. What trends do you notice in world opinion about the United States?

2. Can you identify why certain regions of the world, or certain countries in particular, have higher or lower regard for the United States?

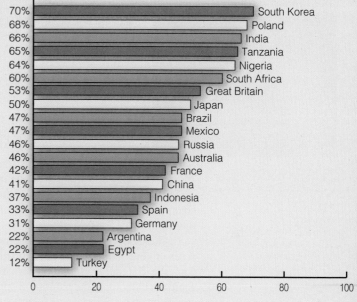

Percentage with a Favorable View of America

Country	%
South Korea	70%
Poland	68%
India	66%
Tanzania	65%
Nigeria	64%
South Africa	60%
Great Britain	53%
Japan	50%
Brazil	47%
Mexico	47%
Russia	46%
Australia	46%
France	42%
China	41%
Indonesia	37%
Spain	33%
Germany	31%
Argentina	22%
Egypt	22%
Turkey	12%

The preamble to the U.S. Constitution perhaps best summarizes the broad goals of American government:

We the People of the United States, in Order to form a more perfect Union, establish Justice, insure domestic Tranquility, provide for the common defense, promote the general Welfare, and secure the Blessings of Liberty to ourselves and our Posterity, do ordain and establish this Constitution for the United States of America.

It is no accident that the first three words of the Constitution are "We the People." With this phrase, the framers acknowledged that the ultimate source of power rests with the people, a concept known as **popular sovereignty**. This "popular perspective" frames our understanding of how the American government works.

The U.S. Constitution provided for a form of **representative democracy**, under which regular elections are held to allow voters to choose those who govern on their behalf. In this sense, individual citizens do not directly make policies, rules, and other governing decisions (a system of government known as a **direct democracy**). Rather, representative democracy, also referred to as *indirect democracy* or a *republican* form of government, rests on the notion that consent of the governed is achieved through free, open, and regular elections of those who are given the responsibility of governing. An important

Popular sovereignty
The idea that the ultimate source of power in the nation is held by the people.

Representative democracy
A form of government designed by the U.S. Constitution whereby free, open, and regular elections are held to allow voters to choose those who govern on their behalf; it is also referred to as indirect democracy or a republican form of government.

Direct democracy
A system of government in which all citizens participate in making policy, rules, and governing decisions.

ARPL/HIP/THE IMAGE WORKS

"I agree to this Constitution, with all of its faults, if they are such: because I think a general government necessary for us, and there is no form of government but what may be a blessing to the people if well administered. I doubt too whether any convention we can obtain may be able to make a better constitution. For when you assemble a number of men to have the advantage of their joint wisdom, you inevitably assemble with those men all their prejudices, their passions, their errors of opinion, their local interests, and their selfish views. From such an assembly can a perfect production be expected? It therefore astonishes me . . . to find this system approaching so near to perfection."

—Benjamin Franklin (1788)

source of the legitimacy of the U.S. government is the nation's commitment to representative democracy, which features the notion of majority rule. Majorities (more than 50 percent of the voters) and pluralities (the leading vote getters, whether or not they constitute absolute majorities) choose the winners of election contests, and so officeholders take their positions on the basis of whom most voters prefer. If officeholders fall from public favor, they may be removed in subsequent elections.

Legitimacy is also enhanced by broad public support for the specific purposes of government stated in the preamble to the Constitution: to "insure domestic Tranquility" (produce laws that maintain a peaceful and organized approach to living in the nation), to "provide for the common defense" (establish and maintain a military force to protect the nation from outside threats), to "promote the general Welfare" (develop domestic policy programs to promote the welfare of the people), and to "secure the Blessings of Liberty" (guarantee basic freedoms, such as the rights of free expression and the ownership of property, even to those in the minority). Although people may have different opinions on how to achieve these broad goals, few in the United States would disagree with the ideals as stated in the abstract or with the broad outlines of our republican form of government. Problems arise when public officials stray so far from these goals that their actions are deemed illegitimate by a near, if not absolute, majority. Yet the political system as a whole has been able to maintain its legitimacy, even under such trying circumstances, because it has been flexible enough to eventually rid itself of those ineffective actors, whether through elections, impeachment, or some other means. The relatively high degree of legitimacy that is maintained in the United States has helped the American government persist under the U.S. Constitution through good times and bad since 1789.

American Political Culture

Political culture refers to the core values about the role of government and its operations and institutions that are widely held among citizens in a society. Political culture defines the essence of how a society thinks politically. It is transmitted from one generation to the next and thus has an enduring influence on the politics of a nation. Every nation has a political culture, and the United States is no exception.

Whereas common ancestry characterizes the core of the political culture of many other nations, the United States has no common ancestry. In many other nations around the world, including France, Britain, China, and Japan,

★ LO Define "political culture" and describe the unique combination of political beliefs and values that form the American political culture, including majority rule, liberty, limited government, diversity, individualism, and equality of economic opportunity.

Political culture
The values and beliefs about government, its purpose, and its operations and institutions that are widely held among citizens in a society; it defines the essence of how a society thinks politically and is transmitted from one generation to the next.

Constitutional Amendments That Have Extended Voting Rights in the United States

In several states, approval of the new U.S. Constitution drafted in 1789 hinged on adding a bill of rights. Supporters of the Constitution agreed, and the first ten amendments, which compose the formal Bill of Rights, were added to the Constitution in 1791. Since then, the Constitution has been amended seventeen times. Six of these seventeen amendments extend Americans' voting rights, and no amendment has ever in any way restricted voting rights. Over the years, changes to the original Constitution have led to greater empowerment of the American people in determining the direction that government takes:

In 1870, the Fifteenth Amendment: provided that the right to vote may not be denied on the basis of race.

In 1913, the Seventeenth Amendment: changed the method of selection of U.S. senators from having state legislatures choose senators to having senators directly elected by the voters of a state.

In 1920, the Nineteenth Amendment: provided voting rights to women by not allowing states to deny women the right to vote.

In 1961, the Twenty-third Amendment: provided residents of the District Columbia with electoral votes in presidential elections.

In 1962, the Twenty-fourth Amendment: prevented states from levying a tax on people before they can vote in federal elections. Some states used a poll tax to discourage poor people and African Americans from voting.

In 1971, the Twenty-sixth Amendment: provided voting rights to those who are eighteen years of age by not allowing states to deny the franchise to those who have reached this age.

a common birth lineage helps define the nation's cultural uniqueness. For example, the Russian people share common political values and beliefs as part of their ancestors' historical experiences with tsars and then later with the communist regime. Britain, despite being a democracy, retains a monarchy as a symbolic gesture toward its historical antecedents. In many nations rich with such common ethnic traditions, these routines often serve to underscore the political culture of the nation.

The United States has no such common ancestry to help define its political culture. Its land was first occupied by many different Native American tribes and then settled by people from many different parts of the world. Most of the immigrants who settled the colonies were seeking a better life from the political or religious persecution they experienced in their native countries, or they were seeking economic opportunities for themselves or their families. As America continued to grow through the centuries, it attracted immigrants from around the world, eager to find a better life. These circumstances had a profound influence on the core values that have become engrained in the American political culture. The ideas generated by democratic political philosophers such as Thomas Hobbes and John Locke also significantly contributed to American political culture. These ideas were used by the founders to justify the Declaration of Independence and the U.S. Constitution, and they continue to underlie American political culture today.

The circumstances surrounding America's first and current immigrants, as well as the ideas generated by seventeenth- and eighteenth-century political

philosophers, form the core set of values that define the American political
culture. One of these core values is **majority rule**. From its earliest times, the
American nation has been committed to the notion that the "will of the people"
ought to guide public policy, thus underscoring the importance of popular
sovereignty in the thinking of the founders. Majority rule is the way popular
sovereignty is actually exercised. Rarely will all of the people agree all of the
time; thus, what the majority of people prefer generally guides decision making. Early local governments, such as town governments in some of the New
England colonies, relied on town meetings, where all citizens were invited to
attend, discuss, and vote to make governmental decisions. Elections for most
local and state offices, and elections for the U.S. Congress, are all based on
the idea that those who make and enforce laws are elected by majorities. A
more recent aspect of U.S. commitment to majority rule is its heavy reliance
on public opinion polling as a gauge to assessing the performance of elected
leaders and to ensure that leaders respect public preferences for certain policy
positions.

While the preferences of the majority rule the day, another core value in
the American political culture is minority rights. Those in the minority enjoy
certain rights and liberties that cannot be taken away by government. The idea
of natural law (for example, that people are "endowed by their creator with
certain unalienable rights" that government cannot deny) is an important cor-
ollary to majority rule. The rights to speak freely, to choose a religion, or to
decide not to practice religion at all are among the many liberties protected by
the U.S. Bill of Rights and are widely endorsed by the American public.

These rights are intended to inspire debate on issues, to guarantee religious
freedoms, and to afford due process rights to those accused of crimes. The
American political culture places a high value on individual liberty. The fact
that many immigrants came to this country for the promise of greater freedom
adds further credence to this proposition. Certainly, there are some terribly
unfavorable marks in American history that belie this claim. Among them are
the perpetuation of slavery in the country up until the Civil War, the internment of Japanese Americans during World War II, and the treatment of early
1960s civil rights protesters in the South. Still, many Americans today view
their nation as the world's "garden" of freedom and liberty, even if it has come
to this status only slowly and sometimes with reluctance during its more than
two centuries of existence.

Another core value in American political culture is the idea of **limited government**. Americans have generally supported the idea expressed by Thomas
Jefferson that "the government that governs least governs best." From the days
of the American Revolution, the colonists believed that the corruptive power
of King George III and the British Parliament led to unfair treatment of the
colonies. Suspicion of the government and those with power is firmly rooted
in the American political culture. The "watchdog" function of the press, the
separation of powers and the system of checks and balances among political
institutions, and the rather negative connotation of the word *politics* all reflect
an appreciation for limits and checks on those with authority. Corresponding
to the value of limited government is the notion that communities and the private sector should take a role in helping fellow citizens. Problems that may be
solved without government should be solved that way. The French journalist
Alexis de Tocqueville observed this tradition when he visited the United States

TABLE 1.1 Daniel Elazar's Typology of American Political Culture

Many observers of American politics have used different approaches and typologies to describe American political culture. The late political scientist Daniel Elazar described three competing political subcultures, which he believed differentiated American political culture from that found in any other country in the world.* Elazar identified the following subcultures:

Subculture	Description
Individualistic subculture	Is skeptical of authority, keeps government's role limited, and celebrates the United States' general reliance on the marketplace
Moralistic subculture	Has faith in the American government's capacity to advance the public interest and encourages citizens to participate in the noble cause of politics
Traditionalistic subculture	Maintains a more ambivalent attitude toward both government and the marketplace, believing that politicians must come from society's elite, whereas ordinary citizens are free to stand on the sidelines

According to Elazar, different subcultures can be found in different geographic areas, and sometimes within a single area itself. For example, he described the political subculture in Texas as part traditionalistic (as manifested in the long history of one-party dominance in state politics) and part individualistic (as seen in the state government's commitment to support for private business and its opposition to big government).

*See Daniel J. Elazar, *American Federalism: A View from the States* (New York: Thomas Y. Crowell, 1966).

in the early 1800s and credited the success of the American political system in part to citizens' strong interest in community and helping one another apart from government.[6]

Since the United States has no common ancestral or cultural bloodline, American political culture recognizes the value and strength derived from the diversity of its population—another important core value. At the base of the Statue of Liberty in New York harbor is inscribed the poem by Emma Lazarus beginning with the phrase: "Give me . . . your huddled masses yearning to be free." Until the U.S. government adopted a restrictive immigration policy in the early 1920s, those huddled masses arrived in waves from different parts of the world, as the United States became the chosen destination for those seeking a better life. Joining freed African American slaves who were originally brought here against their will were legions of Italians, Irish, Germans, and other immigrants from Europe and elsewhere. The United States today is one of the most racially and ethnically diverse nations in the world. Integrating these many peoples into a united nation has not come easy; in fact, resistance to the notion of a "melting pot" has been common. The nation has been wracked at times with racial and ethnic strife to a degree that more homogeneous countries can more easily avoid. Government officials occasionally exacerbate these tensions by promoting policies that discriminate against various groups, including Native Americans, African Americans, Asian Americans, and Hispanic Americans. No stranger to ethnic and racial tensions himself, German dictator Adolph Hitler calculated that the diversity of the United States would

Barack Obama's bid for the presidency in 2008 represented a new chapter in the history of diversity as a value in American political culture.

Individualism

The value that individuals are primarily responsible for their own lot in life and that promotes and rewards individual initiative and responsibility. This value underlies America's reliance on a capitalist economy and free-market system.

eventually hamper its resistance against Germany's totalitarian aggression; in fact, American soldiers of different backgrounds, ethnicities, and religions fought in World War II. Much to Hitler's chagrin, U.S. diversity proved a source of strength rather than weakness. Indeed, many Americans today believe that the heterogeneity of our society enhances the quality of our culture and helps guarantee the fairness of the government.

Americans also generally subscribe to the notion that individuals are primarily responsible for their lot in life—a value referred to as **individualism**. The seeds of this value were sown hundreds of years ago with the Puritans and their commitment to a strong work ethic that stressed "what one sows determines what one reaps." In other words, hard work and intelligence should be rewarded. While the U.S. government has assumed some responsibility to provide a safety net for citizens who suffer economically, the American political culture, through its primary reliance on a capitalist economic system, free markets, and individual effort, is one that promotes individual initiative and responsibility. The value of individualism promotes another core value—equality of opportunity, or the idea that the role of government is to set the stage for individuals to achieve on their own and that everyone should be given the same opportunity to achieve success. Indeed, America has been an attractive place for highly motivated individuals from around the world to immigrate to so that they might have a fair chance of achieving personal success. Many immigrants today, particularly from Asia and Latin America, are attracted to the United States for the opportunities to achieve individual success.

The United States has long set itself apart from nations whose histories include traditions of a rigid class system of privileged aristocracies and oligarchies and peasants with few or no rights or freedoms. In the United States, there is no formal recognition of a class system, nor is there a tradition of royalty, nobility, or monarchy. Indeed, Article I of the Constitution specifically prohibits both the federal government and the state governments from granting any title of nobility to its citizens. Instead, American political culture values the so-called Horatio Alger myth. Alger was a popular writer in the late 1800s whose characters came from impoverished backgrounds but through pluck, determination, and hard work achieved huge success. Although this idealistic rags-to-riches notion often ignores the many harsh economic disparities that exist in the United States, it remains central to the American political culture. The stories of Benjamin Franklin and Abraham Lincoln exemplified this road to success, as do the more recent examples of Presidents Bill Clinton and

Ronald Reagan, both of whom came from less-than-privileged circumstances to win the nation's highest political office and become leaders of the free world. Perhaps it is because of these success stories that so many Americans believe that they have boundless opportunities to better their lot on the basis of diligence and hard work.

These core values provide a window into American political culture. To be sure, there is plenty of room for disagreement as to how these values might be applied to specific situations, which we address in Chapter 10. In addition, these values are often in conflict. At the heart of the debate over affirmative action, for example, lies the value conflict pitting individualism against equality of opportunity. Those who oppose affirmative action in hiring claim that individuals should be evaluated based exclusively on who they are and what they can do rather than on their gender, race, or other demographic characteristic. Those supporting affirmative action claim that historical discrimination has led to a current job market that provides unequal opportunities for certain groups, such as racial minorities and women. While these values do not always solve problems and policy debates, they do lay the groundwork for how American politics goes about settling problems and debating issues.

Is American Democracy on the Decline?

★ LO
Assess the health of American democracy and evaluate whether the American system is in decline by reviewing trends in voter turnout, negativity in politics, the influence of money in policy outcomes, etc.

The old saying that "those who ignore the problems of the past are destined to repeat them" holds as true in American politics as it does in any other context. Certainly, new issues and problems may arise, requiring innovative new thinking to address them. But many other difficulties the United States faces can be effectively addressed by casting an eye on the distant or not-so-distant past. A historical view can help place modern dilemmas in proper perspective.

The Case for Decline

Some recent observers of American politics have suggested that the American political system is in decline. Are we currently witnessing a deterioration of democracy in the United States? Is the American political system in jeopardy? Are the problems that the American system of government faces today beyond repair? To try to answer these questions, let's first look at the factors some cite as contemporary indicators of the decline of American democracy.

- **Voter turnout.** Democratic theorists regard an active, participatory citizenry as a sign of a healthy, vibrant democracy. Thus many point to the half-century trend toward lower voter turnout as a sign of decline. In the 1960s, for example, the percentage of eligible voters who cast a ballot in presidential elections ranged from 62 percent to 65 percent, whereas the range since 1996 has been lower, from 51 percent to just over 60 percent. Ratification of the Twenty-sixth Amendment to the U.S. Constitution in 1971, which guaranteed eighteen-, nineteen-, and twenty-year-olds the constitutional right to vote, expanded the pool of eligible voters, but many of those younger voters have stayed away from the polls in disproportionate numbers, explaining at least in part this downturn in voter turnout. With a smaller percentage of people choosing to participate in elections, many have interpreted the decline as a sign of an ailing democracy.

AP PHOTO/KNOBLOCK

One of the negative ads of the 2008 presidential campaign attacked Democratic candidate Barack Obama for his association with William Ayers, a co-founder of the Weather Underground, a radical 1960s anti-Vietnam War group that carried out bombings at the Capitol and the Pentagon. The Web video ad questioned Obama's judgment for his association with Ayers, seen here in a 1980 photo entering the Criminal Courts Building in Chicago. Ayers, labeled as a terrorist in the ad, is now a college professor, and he and Obama served together on the board of a school reform organization in the mid-1990s.

- **Presidential selection.** For nearly one month after the 2000 presidential election, it remained unclear whether the next president would be Republican George W. Bush or Democrat Al Gore. The closeness of the race in the key state of Florida, along with controversies over how or whether to count certain ballots, left open the question of which candidate actually won the Electoral College vote. In the end, the U.S. Supreme Court indicated that there was insufficient time for a manual recount of Florida's paper ballots, thus effectively awarding Florida's twenty-five electoral votes to Bush, and with them, giving Bush the Electoral College victory. Confounding this outcome was the stark reality that Gore had received approximately half a million more popular votes in total than did Bush. Many regarded this situation as a true constitutional crisis, and called for the abolition of the Electoral College as a means of selecting the president on the basis that a president who takes office without having won the highest number of popular votes lacks the required legitimacy to govern. Four years later a similar electoral crisis was only narrowly averted. A swing of just 60,000 votes in Ohio would have given the Electoral College victory to Democrat John Kerry, even though he garnered several million fewer popular votes nationwide than did the Republican candidate, incumbent President George W. Bush.

- **Money and politics.** In American politics today, most successful election campaigns require large amounts of money. Those who have the financial resources—corporations and wealthy individuals—provide the bulk of the financing. During the 2008 presidential primaries alone, candidates from both major political parties raised more than $1 billion. The winning congressional candidates in the 2006 elections for the House of Representatives and the Senate collectively raised nearly $750 million. Do these huge sums of money, most of which come from corporations and wealthy individuals, influence the behavior of those who win elections? If so, what does that indicate about the state of American democracy?

- **Negative politics.** Negative political advertising, partisan conflicts that degenerate into personal attacks, and exploitation of personal affairs into public spectacles seem to characterize a good deal of modern-day American politics. The inclination of political figures to "go negative," combined with the news media's taste for negative stories, has created a political atmosphere fraught with attacks, counterattacks and much partisan wrangling. From the Republican-driven impeachment of President Bill Clinton in 1998, to claims during the 2004 election that President George W. Bush had avoided serving in the Vietnam War, to the constant barrage of negative political ads throughout the 2006 midterm elections (such as the claim that Tennessee Senate candidate Harold Ford Jr. was a playboy), to the Republican attacks on Barack Obama comparing his celebrity status to that of Britney Spears and Paris Hilton, the measured and orderly democratic process envisioned by the founders seems to have become much less deliberative and civil and much more strident and negative.

Voter Turnout in U.S. Presidential Elections

The popular perspective of the American people finds multiple ways to influence the outcome of policy debates, including reporting poll results, working on campaigns, and donating time and/or money to political candidates and interest groups.

But the most basic way people affect policy is through voting. Prior to 1828, only a limited number of states held popular elections to help determine how a state's electoral votes would be allocated in a presidential election. Since then, most states have held popular elections for electors who in turn select the president. This figure shows the percentage of the eligible electorate that cast a vote in presidential elections since 1900.

Source: From Harold W. Stanley and Richard G. Niemi, *Vital Statistics on American Politics* (CQ Press, 2006). Copyright 2006 CQ Press, a division of Sage Publications.

■ **"Red" state/"blue" state.** The Electoral College maps that the media used to follow the 2008 presidential election returns showed states that Democratic candidate Barack Obama won in blue, and states that Republican candidate John McCain won in red. Whereas the blue states were for the most part clustered in the northeastern United States, the northern Midwest, and the West Coast, the large land block between coasts and throughout the South was predominantly red, with few exceptions. The results of the 2000 and 2004 elections revealed an even sharper divide, with a sea of red extending from Nevada, Arizona, and Idaho in the west all the way to the southeast coast and Florida. (In the 2000 election, New Mexico offered a lone island of blue, while New Hampshire stood by itself as a red state in the Northeast.) It is perhaps no wonder that commentators, referring to this "blue versus red" division of the American public, argue that it represents an electorate widely divided not only along partisan lines, but also along cultural lines. These observers emphasize the divide between the socially moderate-to-liberal values of the Northeast and West Coast and the more conservative values embraced by the Great Plains states and the South.

These dilemmas in contemporary American politics have led some observers to conclude that American democracy is in sharp and deep decline. Yet even with the evidence provided, this may be a rather superficial examination of contemporary American government. If we examine these characteristics of

American politics with the benefit of some historical perspective, it is possible to draw quite different conclusions, which in turn suggest that our system of government is designed to allow conflict and controversy to be managed in a productive way. The system promotes clashes of ideas, sometimes characterized by personal animosity. The system also allows for multiple points of input from a large number of citizens and organized interests.

The Case against Decline

If we reexamine some of the criticisms of contemporary American politics with the benefit of historical perspective, we may reach far different conclusions about whether American democracy is now in a state of decline.

- **Voter turnout.** As shown in the figure on page 17, there has indeed been a general decline in voter turnout, from more than 60 percent in the 1950s to as low as 51 percent in some recent elections. A historical perspective reveals, however, that it has not been uncommon for only half—or even less than half—of voters to cast a ballot in a presidential election. In the elections of 1924 and 1928, turnout dropped below 50 percent. Even in the historically important election of 1932—the election that put Franklin Roosevelt's New Deal coalition into office—voter turnout was less than 60 percent. In the 1948 contest in which Democratic candidate Harry Truman came from far behind to defeat the Republican Thomas Dewey, turnout was a mere 53 percent. Thus by early-to mid-twentieth-century standards, a turnout rate of around 50 percent is not all that unusual. In fact, low voter turnout may even indicate the public's general contentment with the state of the union.

- **Presidential selection.** The confusion surrounding the outcome of the 2000 presidential contest was not unique to that presidential election. In fact, there have been other presidential election contests that either produced no clear winner in the Electoral College or produced an Electoral College winner different from the popular vote winner. The Framers of the Constitution may have even contemplated these possibilities, because they created a compromise that sought to give less populated states disproportionate influence over the outcome. In 1888, for example, Grover Cleveland won the popular vote but lost the Electoral College vote (and thus the presidency) to Benjamin Harrison. In 1876, Samuel Tilden won 51 percent of the popular vote but failed to capture a majority of electoral votes, and Rutherford B. Hayes became president as part of a brokered deal among political party elites. In the 1824 election, Andrew Jackson defeated John Quincy Adams by more than 10 percentage points of the popular votes cast; however, neither candidate won a majority of electoral votes, and the House of Representatives chose Adams as the new president. Even in one of the earliest presidential contests in 1800, the lack of an Electoral College majority was resolved by the House of Representatives awarding the presidency to Thomas Jefferson (it took more than thirty ballots for the House to arrive at this conclusion). What in 2000 seemed like a unique controversy in American politics was only the latest among many in the history of presidential elections.

- **Money and politics.** There is no doubt that the bulk of money for political campaigns comes from corporations and wealthy Americans, and few would question that money greatly influences political campaigns. In addition, some of the most successful interest groups in the United States are funded by the wealthy. But this is by no means a new phenomenon in American politics either. Most of the founders, all of whom were white males, were wealthy landowners. It has been reported that George Washington himself bought one and a half quarts of liquor for each vote he received in his first run for public office in 1758.[7] Just as today's large corporate contributors (such as Microsoft and IBM) and powerful interest groups (such as the American Medical Association and the American Trial Lawyers Association) enjoy disproportionately large influence over politics, so too did the so-called robber barons of the late nineteenth century, such as the financier J. Pierpont Morgan, the industrialist Andrew Carnegie, or the railroad magnate Cornelius Vanderbilt, wield considerable influence over the nation's politics.

- **Negative politics.** The negativity, combativeness, and personal conflict that characterize modern American politics—distasteful though these may be—are nothing new. Negativity and conflict are the product of the vigorous and spirited debate that occurs in a free and open democracy. One of the most negative political campaigns ever waged was the 1800 presidential battle between Thomas Jefferson and John Adams. During that campaign, Jefferson used partisan newspapers to launch a very negative campaign against Adams. The personal attacks that pervaded the impeachment hearings of President Bill Clinton in 1998 were no match for the character assassinations featured during the impeachment of President Andrew Johnson in 1868. And in neither of those cases could the personal attacks match the fatal wounding in 1804 of Alexander Hamilton by Aaron Burr in a duel over political differences that became personal. Nor is the general tone of negativity of the modern-day news media anything new. The intense partisanship of some of the nation's early newspapers, such as Ben Franklin's *Pennsylvania Gazette*, and the sensationalist "yellow journalism" of the late nineteenth century provide a good match for today's focus on negative news.

- **"Red" state/"blue" state.** The Electoral College vote totals of the 2000, 2004, and 2008 presidential elections may appear to depict an unprecedented new geographical divide among the nation's states. Yet nearly half of those states—twenty-three of the fifty—including a handful of states located in

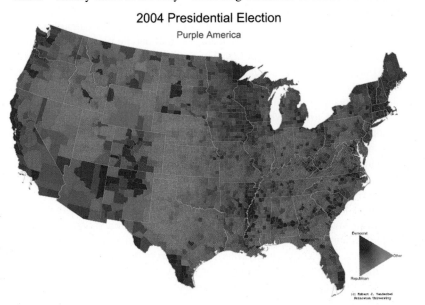

2004 Presidential Election

Purple America

ROBERT J. VANDERBEI, PRINCETON UNIVERSITY

Discussion of the "blue vs. red" political divisions in America ignores the possibility that there may actually be a "purple America," as shown in this map from *Time* magazine. Closely contested districts in 2004 are shown in purple; one-sided Republican districts are shown in red, and one-sided Democratic districts are shown in blue.

every region of in the country, failed to give either presidential candidate as much as 55 percent of the popular vote, a signal that these were in fact not the die-hard "red" or "blue" states that the media often portray them as. In the 2006 congressional elections, Democratic Senate victories in "red" Republican states such as Virginia and Montana helped put Democrats back in the majority not only in the House of Representatives but also in the Senate. Barack Obama moved Virginia, North Carolina, and Indiana into the Democratic presidential column for the first time in decades. Moreover, in some states, such as Ohio, Florida, and Pennsylvania, divisions may be sharper than ever. As political scientist Morris Fiorina argued in his 2005 book, *Culture War? The Myth of a Polarized America*,[8] the percentage of American citizens who went to the polls at the beginning of the twenty-first century with a fairly set idea of how they would cast their votes was actually no greater than it had been a quarter century earlier, or even a full century earlier. Fiorina also discovered that geographic regions differ far less on such issues as abortion, gun control, or the role that religion should play in politics than the stereotypes of red state versus blue state would suggest. Reports of a sharp red–blue divide may be nothing more than a convenient story created by pundits and journalists to generate interest in news stories.

Historical, Popular, and Global Perspectives

History does not literally repeat itself. The specific people, circumstances, and events certainly change. But history can help us identify patterns, recurring problems, and trends in how the American political system functions and resolves conflicts. The preceding discussion of some of the contemporary arguments for why American democracy may be in a state of decline helps us frame current conditions. In doing so, we may gain a greater understanding of the challenges facing the nation today. Many contemporary challenges are no less daunting than problems the nation has encountered over the past two centuries. Throughout this book, a historical perspective on contemporary problems offers a sense of how the past might help us understand politics today.

As past events provide perspective on contemporary American politics, they also make quite clear the significant role that people play in influencing political outcomes and public policy. The "will of the people" is not just a rhetorical phrase used by politicians. Rather, it has guided American politics and government since the country's founding. Throughout this book, we employ a popular perspective to gain a clearer understanding of how our system of government works. Citizens who actively participate in politics through voting, working on campaigns, contributing time and effort to interest group activities, participating in demonstrations, writing to elected officials and the op-ed pages, and running for office have an impact on public policy. In this book, consideration of the popular perspective allows us to see how the will of the people has an impact on American politics.

Finally, a look at American government would not be complete without some perspective on how the rest of the world views the United States. Through advanced technologies such as the Internet, satellites, and air travel, life in the modern world increasingly interconnects people from different nations. The governments of the globe, for better or for worse, are affected by this interconnectedness of the world's peoples. Throughout this book, a global perspective offers insights into how people around the world perceive American government.

POLITICS InterActive!

The Politics of Negativity?

"Isn't it sad that politics have become so negative these days?" Such is a common complaint about contemporary American politics in general, and political campaigns in particular. Poll after poll depicts how much Americans deplore negativity in campaigns, though that doesn't seem to deter its prevalence: In the 2008 presidential campaign, candidates were accused of being celebrities, liars, plagiarists, adulterers, and terrorist supporters. FactCheck.org, a Web site developed and maintained by the Annenberg School at the University of Pennsylvania, is an antidote to some of the negativity and misrepresentation of candidates' records. This Web site examines many of the negative claims that candidates launch against each other in political advertising and seeks to verify the claim or vilify the false accusation.

At www.cengage.com/dautrich/americangovernmentbrief/2e, find the Politics InterActive link for details and examples of negative campaigning in American politics. Consult as well the various links that relate to negativity in American politics in historical, popular, and global perspectives.

© 2012 CENGAGE LEARNING

NORTH WIND PICTURE ARCHIVES

HOOPER Sc.

The duel between Aaron Burr and Alexander Hamilton, which killed Hamilton, is perhaps one of the most famous and extreme instances of negativity in American politics.

Chapter Summary

★ Introduction to Perspectives on American Government

- Issues, topics, and controversies in American politics may be analyzed through a number of different perspectives. This book will encourage analyzing topics through three primary perspectives in particular: a historical perspective, a popular perspective, and a global perspective. Your own perspective will come to bear as well on the state of American politics.

★ Forms and Functions of Government

- The development of the American political system is grounded in the philosophy of John Locke and Jean-Jacques Rousseau, who argued that government is necessary and that it exists for the purpose of protecting the people it serves. The social contract theory states that natural law gives people certain unalienable rights that government cannot take away and that the people give government authority to rule, but the people can withdraw that authority if government does not serve the people's interests.

★ American Government and Politics

- Democracy includes at its core the idea of popular sovereignty. The United States practices a form of democracy known as representative democracy, in which the people indirectly rule by electing leaders who are responsible for making and carrying out policies and laws.

★ American Political Culture

- The political culture in America is reflected in the Constitution and the way in which the political system deals with and decides political debates. Among the core values guiding the American political culture are majority rule, liberty, limited government, diversity, individualism, and equality of economic opportunity.

★ Is American Democracy on the Decline?

- Although the current American government has been in place for more than 200 years, there have been questions raised about whether this political system is in a state of decline. Lower voter turnout, confusing election outcomes, negativity in politics, and the influence of money in policy outcomes have been offered as evidence of a decline. However, a review of historical patterns in American politics suggests that these seemingly contemporary problems are chronic, and the American political system has effectively dealt with these and many other problems.

★ Historical, Popular, and Global Perspectives

- Viewing American government from a historical perspective may enrich our understanding of how the political system works. History can help us identify patterns, recurring problems, and trends in how the American political system functions and resolves conflicts. Many contemporary challenges are no more significant than problems the nation has encountered over the past two centuries.

- Viewing American government from a popular perspective also informs our appreciation of the important role that citizens play in the political system. People play a large role in influencing political outcomes and public policy. The "will of the people" is not just a rhetorical phrase. It has guided American politics and government since the country's founding. Citizens who actively participate in politics through voting, working on campaigns, contributing time and effort to interest group activities, participating in demonstrations, writing to elected officials, authoring letters in op-ed pages, and running for office all have an impact on public policy.

- Viewing American government from a global perspective has become increasingly important in a world that has become interconnected. Through advanced technologies such as the Internet, satellites, and air travel, life in the modern world increasingly interconnects people from different nations. The governments of the globe, for better or for worse, are affected by this interconnectedness of so many different peoples. A global perspective offers insights into how people around the world perceive American government.

CourseMate

Key Terms

Anarchy (p. 6)

Authoritarianism (p. 7)

Authority (p. 6)

Democracy (p. 6)

Direct democracy (p. 9)

Government (p. 6)

Individualism (p. 14)

Legitimacy (p. 7)

Limited government (p. 12)

Majority rule (p. 12)

Monarchy (p. 7)

Natural law (p. 8)

Oligarchy (p. 7)

Political culture (p. 10)

Politics (p. 7)

Popular sovereignty (p. 9)

Power (p. 7)

Representative democracy (p. 9)

Social contract (p. 6)

Theocracy (p. 7)

Resources

Books

Anderson, Terry H. *The Pursuit of Fairness: The History of Affirmative Action.* New York: Oxford University Press, 2004.

Fiorina, Morris. *Culture War? The Myth of a Polarizing America.* New York: Pearson Longman, 2005.

Gilliam, Howard. *Votes That Counted: How the Court Decided the 2000 Presidential Election.* Chicago: University of Chicago Press, 2001.

Greenberg, Stanley B. *The Two Americas: Our Current Political Deadlock and How to Break It.* New York: Thomas Dunne Books, 2004.

Putnam, Robert. *Bowling Alone.* New York: Simon & Schuster, 2000.

Internet Sources

http://www.nara.gov (the Web site for the National Archives; contains a wealth of information on documents relating to American culture).

http://www.whitehouse.gov (the official home page of the White House).

http://www.fjc.gov (the Web site for the Federal Justice Center, which provides detailed information on the federal judiciary).

http://www.house.gov (the Web site for the U.S. House of Representatives).

http://www.senate.gov (the Web site for the U.S. Senate).

The Founding and the Constitution

NOW Man arrested for flag burning on the steps of the U.S. Capitol.

AP PHOTO/CHARLES TASNADI

THEN Preacher speaking at a Methodist camp meeting in Eastham, Massachusetts, during the 1850s.

NORTH WIND / NORTH WIND PICTURE ARCHIVES

NOW & THEN

The Politics of the Amending Process

"Quote the Constitution . . . and if you don't like what it says, demand that it be changed."
The latter political strategy rarely results in actual constitutional amendments, but it does offer considerable benefits for savvy politicians and special interests. Capitalizing on the perception that liberal elites were taking the country in an unwanted direction, several groups formed a movement to propose a constitutional amendment more consistent with their vision of the nation's values. The effort struck a chord, forcing legislators to take it seriously; yet did not earn two-thirds support of both houses of Congress, and so it did not go forward to the states for ratification, Still, the groups' sustained effort found an audience with some of the nation's mainstream politicians, few of whom wished to offend a movement of followers so numerous and passionate. The arduous process of changing the Constitution produces few outright amendments, but nonetheless can provide political victories to those who advocate change.

LEARNING OBJECTIVES
★ WHAT YOU WILL LEARN ★

The Beginnings of a New Nation

* ★ Understand the origins and causes of the American Revolution
* ★ Describe the first national government under the Articles of Confederation, including its weaknesses and struggles

The Constitutional Convention

* ★ Compare and contrast the various plans for the new Constitution and the obstacles to agreement among the different colonies

The New Constitution

* ★ Understand how sovereign powers were divided in the new government

The Ratification Battle

* ★ Evaluate the advantages enjoyed by those seeking to ratify the new Constitution
* ★ Assess the role that *The Federalist* Papers played in ratification
* ★ Explain the origins of the Bill of Rights and its role in securing ratification

Changing the Constitution

* ★ Describe the process of amending the Constitution
* ★ Assess informal types of constitutional change, including different forms of constitutional interpretation

CourseMate

NOW & THEN

Senator Bob Dole (R-KS) speaks in Washington about the recently passed Flag Protection Act of 1989.

The 27th Amendment

"The Congress and the States shall have power to prohibit the physical desecration of the Flag of the United States."

BETTMANN/CORBIS

NOW While efforts to protect the American flag date back to the late nineteenth century, they gained significant and widespread appeal in the 1960s, after Vietnam War protestors discovered the powerful reaction that flag burning could evoke. By the late 1980s, forty-eight of fifty states and the U.S. Congress had passed flag protection laws of some kind, only to see their efforts swept aside when the Supreme Court in 1989 held that all such laws unconstitutionally restricted free expression under the First Amendment. With polls indicating that a majority of Americans favored flag protection laws, specialized interests such as the Citizens Flag Alliance, an umbrella organization of veterans' and other groups, pressed Congress to propose a constitutional amendment that would make an exception to the First Amendment, allowing governments to ban flag desecration. These efforts gained considerable traction, and legislators attempted seven times to pass a flag burning amendment between 1990 and 2006. Though the initiative often garnered House approval, it was never able to generate two-thirds support in the U.S. Senate. To date, more than 3 million citizens have signed petitions asking Congress to pass the amendment, and nearly all state legislatures have passed resolutions urging the same. Legislators of every stripe will continue to oppose this effort only at their own electoral peril.

THEN The First Amendment proved to be a source of frustration in the nineteenth and early twentieth centuries as well, though the battle at that time was waged more on religious rather than patriotic grounds. During the Civil War a coalition of eleven Protestant denominations hailing from seven Northern states directed their anger at the Establishment Clause in the First Amendment to the Constitution, which prohibited Congress from making any law "respecting an establishment of religion." Calling themselves the "Christian Amendment Association," they believed the Civil War was God's punishment for omitting God from the Constitution, and they sought to alter the wording of the Preamble to acknowledge God and profess the idea that civil governments derive their legitimacy from God in general, and from Jesus in particular. As the movement gained momentum, it renamed itself the "National Reform Association" (NRA) and earned the active support of important senators, including John Sherman of Ohio, B. Gratz Brown of Missouri, and the eminent Charles Sumner of Massachusetts. Indeed, the NRA even found an audience with President Abraham Lincoln in February 1864. Despite consideration from Congress in 1864, 1874, 1896, and 1910, the amendment was never able to secure formal passage. Given how quickly the movement had gained popularity, few members of Congress were willing to denounce the cause publicly. That is still a far cry from seeing the amendment proposed and ratified, as the NRA learned repeatedly during the latter part of the nineteenth century.

LIBRARY OF CONGRESS

Senator Charles Sumner (R-MA), a key supporter of efforts to pass the so-called Christian amendment.

Nebraska Senator Ben Nelson once wrote that amending the Constitution "is a delicate endeavor and should be done only on the basis of the most clear and convincing evidence that a proposed amendment is necessary." Certainly the numbers back Nelson up: Of the thousands of constitutional amendments discussed, an average of just one amendment every thirteen years has been ratified since 1791, and that event normally occurs only after years (if not decades) of frustrations and failures. Aware of the odds against them, interest groups often take up the cause of amending the constitution for political reasons: A push to alter the U.S. Constitution can fire up the passions of many Americans; it also enables groups to gauge the support of legislators by holding their feet to the fire. In the case of the "Christian amendment" and the "flag desecration amendment," those efforts went a step further, gaining an audience for their respective supporters before some of Washington, DC's most powerful politicians. Still, no one could have rightfully expected this two-centuries-old document to bend so quickly in either case. To most Americans the document's success is due largely to its capacity to endure and survive in much the same form for over two centuries.

The Beginnings of a New Nation

Throughout the seventeenth and early eighteenth centuries, thousands of people, many of them British subjects, migrated to North America. Many came in search of greater economic opportunities; others fled to escape religious persecution and sought freedom to worship as they pleased. Slowly, a culture dedicated to the protection of social and civil rights began to take shape in the colonies. The political structures that governed the colonies up through the early 1760s roughly paralleled those of England during the same period: (1) royal governors served as substitutes for the king in each individual colony; (2) a governor's council in each colony served as a mini House of Lords, with the most influential men in the colony serving effectively as a high court; and (3) the general assembly in each colony was elected directly by the qualified voters in each colony and served essentially as a House of Commons, passing ordinances and regulations that would govern the colony. Up until the middle of the eighteenth century, the colonies' diverse histories and economies had provided little incentive for them to join together to meet shared goals. In fact, Great Britain feared other European powers attempting to encroach on their American holdings far more than they feared any form of uprising on the part of the colonists.

The French and Indian War that was waged in the colonies from 1754 through 1763 was a significant turning point in British-colonial relations.[1] For nearly a decade, the French, from their base in Canada, fought the British in the colonies for control of the North American empire. Both nations were interested in rights to the territory that extended west of the colonial settlements along the Atlantic seaboard and over the Appalachian Mountains into the Ohio Valley. Britain defeated France, and under the terms of the Treaty of Paris (1763), which settled the war, all territory from the Arctic Ocean to the Gulf of Mexico between the Atlantic Ocean and the Mississippi River (except for New Orleans, which was ceded to Spain, an ally of Britain during the war) was awarded to Britain. But along with the acquisition of all this new territory came a staggering debt of approximately 130 million pounds. Administering its huge new North American empire would be a costly undertaking for Britain.

British Actions

Following the war, Britain imposed upon its colonies a series of regulatory measures intended to make the colonists help pay the war debts and share the costs of governing the empire. To prevent colonists from ruining the prosperous British fur trade, the Proclamation of 1763 restricted them to the eastern side of the Appalachian chain, angering those interested in settling, cultivating, and trading in this new region. The Sugar Act (1764) was the first law passed by Parliament for the specific purpose of raising money in the colonies for the Crown. (Other regulatory acts passed earlier had been enacted for the purpose of controlling trade.) The Sugar Act (1) increased the duties on sugar, (2) placed new import duties on textiles, coffee, indigo, wines, and other goods, and (3) doubled the duties on foreign goods shipped from England to the colonies. The Stamp Act (1765) required the payment of a tax on the purchase of all newspapers, pamphlets, almanacs, and commercial and legal documents in the colonies. Both acts drew outrage from colonists, who argued that Parliament could not tax those who were not formally represented in its chambers. Throughout late 1765 and early 1766, angry colonists protested the Stamp Act by attacking stamp agents who attempted to collect the tax, destroying the stamps, and boycotting British goods. When English merchants complained bitterly about the loss of revenue they were suffering as a result of these colonial protests, Parliament repealed the Stamp Act in March 1766.[2]

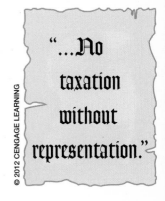

"...No taxation without representation."

Colonial Responses

As a result of the Stamp Act fiasco, positions on the state of British rule were articulated both in the colonies and in Parliament. Following the lead of the Virginia assembly, which sponsored the Virginia Resolves that had declared the principle of "no taxation without representation," an intercolonial Stamp Act Congress met in New York City in 1765. This first congressional body in America issued a Declaration of Rights and Grievances that acknowledged allegiance to the Crown but reiterated the right to not be taxed without consent. Meanwhile, the British Parliament—on the same day that it repealed the Stamp Act—passed into law the Declaratory Act, asserting that the king and Parliament had "full power and authority" to enact laws binding on the colonies "in all cases whatsoever."

> ★ LO
>
> Understand the origins and causes of the American Revolution

Despite the colonists' protests, Parliament continued to pass legislation designed to raise revenue from the colonies. The Townshend Acts, passed in 1767, imposed duties on various items, including tea, imported into the colonies and created a Board of Customs Commissioners to enforce the acts and collect the duties. When the colonists protested by boycotting British goods, in 1770 Parliament repealed all the duties except that on tea. The Tea Act, enacted in 1773, was passed to help the financially troubled British East India Company by relaxing export duties and allowing the company to sell its tea directly in the colonies. These advantages allowed the company to undersell colonial merchants. Angry colonists saw the act as a trick to lure Americans into buying the cheaper tea and thus ruining American tea sellers. On December 16, 1773, colonists disguised as Mohawk Indians boarded ships in Boston Harbor and threw overboard their cargoes of tea. Outraged by this defiant Boston Tea Party, Parliament in 1774 passed the Intolerable Acts (known in the colonies as the Coercive Acts), designed to punish the rebellious colonists. The acts closed the port of Boston, revised the Massachusetts colonial government, and required the colonists to provide food and housing for British troops stationed in the colonies.

The colonists had experienced enough. In September 1774, fifty-six leaders from twelve colonies (there were no delegates from Georgia) met in Philadelphia to plan a united response to Parliament's actions. This First Continental Congress denounced British policy and organized a boycott of British goods. Although the Congress did not advocate outright independence from England, it did encourage the colonial militias to arm themselves and began to collect and store weapons in an arsenal in Concord, Massachusetts. The British governor general of Massachusetts ordered British troops to seize and destroy the weapons. On their way to Concord, the troops met a small force of colonial militiamen at Lexington. Shots were exchanged, but the militiamen were soon routed, and the British troops marched on to Concord. There they encountered a much larger group of colonial militia. Shots again were fired, and this time, the British retreated. The American Revolution had begun.

After the skirmishes at Lexington and Concord in early 1775, a Second Continental Congress met in May of that year, this time with all thirteen colonies represented. This Congress established a continental army and appointed George Washington as its commander in chief, initiating the process that resulted in independence for the colonies and the formation of a new nation, the United States of America.[3]

The Decision for Independence

Despite the events of the early 1770s, many leading colonists continued to hold out hope that some settlement could be reached between the colonies and Britain. The tide turned irrevocably in early 1776, when one of the most influential publications of that period, *Common Sense*, first appeared. In that pamphlet, Thomas Paine attacked King George III as responsible for the provocations against the colonies. Paine's arguments converted many wavering Americans to the cause of independence.[4]

On June 7, 1776, Richard Henry Lee, a delegate to the Second Continental Congress from Virginia, proposed a resolution stating that "these United Colonies are, and of right ought to be, free and independent States." Of course, the Congress needed a formal document both to state their list of grievances and to articulate their intention to seek independence. The Congress thus appointed a committee to draft a document that would meet those objectives.

The committee, consisting of Thomas Jefferson, John Adams, Roger Sherman, Robert Livingston, and Benjamin Franklin, appointed Jefferson to compose the document. At first, Jefferson may have seemed an unlikely choice to produce such a declaration. The thirty-three-year-old lawyer and delegate to the Continental Congresses of 1775 and 1776 had played a relatively minor role in those bodies' deliberations. But according to historian David McCullough, Adams initially believed that the document was really just a symbolic "side show" and quickly justified the choice of Jefferson over himself as follows: "Reason first: you are a Virginian and a Virginian ought to appear at the head of this business. Reason second: I am obnoxious, suspected and unpopular. You are very much otherwise. Reason third: You can write ten times better than I can." Later, Adams fumed for decades over the larger-than-life reputation Jefferson gained on the basis of authoring the nation's first great political document.[5]

The committee submitted its draft to Congress on July 2, 1776; after making some changes, Congress formally adopted the document on July 4. The **Declaration of Independence** restated John Locke's theory of natural rights and the social contract between government and the governed.[6] Locke had argued that although citizens sacrifice certain rights when they consent to be governed as part of a social contract, they retain other inalienable rights. In the Declaration, Jefferson reiterated this argument with the riveting sentence: "We hold these truths to be self-evident, that all men are created equal, that they are endowed by their Creator with certain inalienable rights, that among these are life, liberty and the pursuit of happiness." Jefferson went on to state that whenever government fails in its duty to secure such rights, the people have the right to "alter" or "abolish" it and institute a new one. Through the centuries, America's political leaders have consistently invoked the Declaration of Independence as perhaps the truest written embodiment of the American Revolution. Before independence could become a reality, however, the colonists had to fight and win a war with Great Britain.

The First National Government: The Articles of Confederation

The colonies also needed some sort of government to direct the war effort. The Second Continental Congress drew up the **Articles of Confederation**, a written statement of rules and principles to guide the first continent-wide government in the colonies during the war and beyond. Although the document was initially adopted by Congress in 1777, it was not formally ratified by all thirteen states until 1781. The Articles of Confederation created a "league of friendship" among the states, but the states remained sovereign and independent with the power and authority to rule the colonists' daily lives. The sole body of the new national government was the Congress, in which each state had one vote. The Congress enjoyed only limited authority to govern the colonies: It could wage war and make peace, coin money, make treaties and alliances with other nations, operate a postal service, and manage relations with the Native Americans.[7] But Congress had no power to raise troops, regulate commerce, or levy taxes, which left it dependent on state legislatures to raise and support armies or provide other services. Congress's inability to raise funds significantly hampered the efforts of George Washington and the Continental Army during the war against Britain. Although Congress employed a "requisition system" in the 1780s, which essentially asked that states voluntarily meet contribution quotas to the federal government, the system proved ineffective. New Jersey, for example, consistently refused to pay such requisitions. Reflecting the colonists' distrust of a strong centralized government, the Articles made no provision for a chief executive who could enforce Congress's laws.

The limited powers of the central government posed many problems, but changing the Articles of Confederation to meet the needs of the new nation was no easy task. The Articles could be amended only by the assent of all thirteen state legislatures, a provision that made change of any kind nearly impossible. Wealthy property owners and colonial merchants were frustrated with the Articles for various reasons. Because Congress lacked the power to regulate interstate and foreign commerce, it was exceedingly difficult to obtain commercial concessions from other nations. Quarrels among states disrupted interstate

Declaration of Independence
Formal document listing colonists' grievances and articulating the colonists' intention to seek independence; formally adopted by the Second Continental Congress on July 4, 1776.

★ LO
Describe the first national government under the Articles of Confederation, including its weaknesses and struggles

Articles of Confederation
The document creating a "league of friendship" governing the thirteen states during and immediately after the war for independence; hampered by the limited power they vested in the legislature to collect revenue or regulate commerce, the Articles eventually proved unworkable for the new nation.

commerce and travel. Finally, a few state governments (most notably, Pennsylvania) had come to be dominated by radical movements that further threatened the property rights of many wealthy, landowning colonists.

These difficulties did not disappear when the war ended with the Americans' victory in 1783. Instead, an economic depression, partially caused by the loss of trade with Great Britain and the West Indies, aggravated the problems facing the new nation. In January 1785, an alarmed Congress appointed a committee to consider amendments to the Articles. Although the committee called for expanded congressional powers to enter commercial treaties with other nations, no action was taken. Further proposals to revise the Articles by creating federal courts and strengthening the system of soliciting contributions from states were never even submitted to the states for approval; congressional leaders apparently despaired of ever winning the unanimous approval of the state legislatures needed to create such changes.

Then in September 1786, nine states accepted invitations to attend a convention in Annapolis, Maryland, to discuss interstate commerce. Yet when the Annapolis Convention opened on September 11, delegates from only five states (New York, New Jersey, Delaware, Pennsylvania, and Virginia) attended. A committee led by Alexander Hamilton, a leading force at the Annapolis meeting, issued a report calling upon all thirteen states to attend a convention in Philadelphia the following May to discuss all matters necessary "to render the constitution of the federal government adequate to the exigencies of the Union." At the time, few knew whether this proposal would attract more interest than had previous calls for a new government.

Events in Massachusetts in 1786–1787 proved a turning point in the creation of momentum for a new form of government. A Revolutionary War veteran, Daniel Shays, was one of many debt-ridden farmers in Massachusetts, where creditors controlled the state government. Shays and his men rebelled against the state courts' foreclosing on the farmers' mortgages for failure to pay debts and state taxes.[8] When the state legislature failed to resolve the farmers' grievances, Shays's rebels stormed two courthouses and a federal arsenal.[9] Eventually, the state militia put down the insurrection, known as **Shays's Rebellion**, but the message was clear: A weak and unresponsive government carried with it the danger of disorder and violence. In February 1787, Congress endorsed the call for a convention to serve the purpose of drafting amendments to the Articles of Confederation, and by May, eleven states had acted to name delegates to the convention to be held in Philadelphia.

Shays's Rebellion
Armed uprising by debt-ridden Massachusetts farmers frustrated with the state government.

The Constitutional Convention

Constitutional Convention
Meeting of delegates from twelve states in Philadelphia during the summer of 1787, at which was drafted an entirely new system of government to govern the United States.

The **Constitutional Convention** convened on May 25, 1787, with twenty-nine delegates from nine states in attendance. Over the next four months, fifty-five delegates from twelve states would participate. Fiercely resistant to any centralized power, Rhode Island sent no delegates. Some heroes of the American Revolution like Patrick Henry refused appointments due to their opposition to the feelings of nationalism that had spurred holding the convention in the first place. Meanwhile, the presence of such well-known American figures as George Washington, Alexander Hamilton, and Benjamin Franklin lent authority to the proceedings. Thirty-six-year-old James Madison of Virginia was only beginning to establish a reputation for himself when he arrived in Philadelphia; John Adams and Thomas Jefferson were both on diplomatic assignment in Europe.

TABLE 2.1 The Articles of Confederation and the U.S. Constitution: Key Features

Articles of Confederation Provisions	Problems Generated	1787 Federal Constitution
Unicameral (one-house) Congress with each state having one vote, regardless of population	Gave smaller, less populated states disproportionate power in lawmaking	Bicameral (two-house) legislature with one house (House of Representatives) apportioned by population and second house (Senate) apportioned equally among states (two senators from each state)
Approval by nine of thirteen states required for most legislative matters	Restricted lawmaking by simple majorities, halting the legislative process in most cases	Approval of simple majority (one half plus one) of both houses required for most legislation
No separate executive or judiciary	Legislative abuses went unchecked	Three separate branches of government: legislative, executive, and judicial
Congress did not have the power to regulate foreign or interstate commerce	States negotiated separately among themselves and with foreign powers on commercial matters to the detriment of the overall economy	Congress given power to regulate interstate and foreign commerce
Congress did not have the power to levy or collect taxes	Suffering from the economic depression and saddled with their own war debts, states furnished only a small portion of the money sought by Congress	Congress given power to levy and collect taxes
Congress did not have power to raise an army	Once the war with Britain had ended, states were reluctant to provide any support for an army	Congress given power to raise and support armies
Amendments to articles required unanimous approval of state legislatures	Articles were practically immune from modification and thus inflexible to meet changing demands of a new nation	Amendments to Constitution require two-thirds vote of both houses of Congress, ratification by three-fourths of states

The delegates, who unanimously selected Washington to preside over the convention, were united by at least four common concerns: (1) the United States was being treated with contempt by other nations, and foreign trade had suffered as a consequence; (2) the economic radicalism of Shays's Rebellion might spread in the absence of a stronger central government; (3) the Native Americans had responded to encroachment on their lands by threatening frontiersmen and land speculators, and the national government had been ill-equipped to provide citizens with protection; and (4) the postwar economic depression had worsened, and the national government was powerless to take any action to address it.[10] Of course, on many other matters, the delegates differed. Those from bigger, more heavily populated states such as Virginia and Pennsylvania wanted a central government that reflected their larger

Virginia Plan
A proposal known also as the "large states plan" that empowered three separate branches of government, including a legislature with membership proportional to population.

New Jersey Plan
A proposal known also as the "small states plan" that would have retained the Articles of Confederation principle of a legislature where states enjoyed equal representation.

Great Compromise
A proposal also known as the "Connecticut Compromise" that provided for a bicameral legislature featuring an upper house based on equal representation among the states and a lower house whose membership was based on each state's population; approved by a 5–4 vote of the state delegations.

population bases, whereas those from smaller states like Georgia and Delaware hoped to maintain the one-state, one-vote principle of the Articles.

Plans and Compromises

It quickly became evident that a convention originally called to discuss amendments to the Articles of Confederation would be undertaking a more drastic overhaul of the American system of government. Members of the Virginia delegation got the ball rolling when they introduced the **Virginia Plan**, also known as the "large states plan," which proposed a national government consisting of three branches: a legislature, an executive, and a judiciary. The legislature would consist of two houses, with membership in each house proportional to each state's population. The people would elect members of one house, and the members of that house would then choose members of the second house. The legislature would have the power to choose a chief executive and members of the judiciary and the authority to legislate in "all cases to which the states are incompetent" or when the "harmony of the United States" demands it. Finally, the legislature would have power to veto any state law. Under the plan, the only real check on the legislature would be a Council of Revision, consisting of the executive and several members of the judiciary, which could veto the legislature's acts.

To counter the Virginia Plan, delegates from less populous states proposed the **New Jersey Plan**, which called for a one-house legislature in which each state, regardless of size, would have equal representation. Both the Virginia and New Jersey plans rejected a model of government in which the executive would be given extensive authority. By July 2, 1787, disagreements over the design of the legislature and the issue of representation had brought the convention to a near dead end. The delegates then agreed to submit the matter to a smaller committee in the hope that it might craft some form of compromise.

The product of that committee's deliberations was a set of compromises, termed the **Great Compromise** by historians. (Formally proposed by delegate Roger Sherman of Connecticut, the agreement is also known as the Connecticut Compromise.) Its critical features included (1) a bicameral (two-house) legislature with an upper house or "Senate," in which the states would have equal power with two representatives from each state, and a lower House of Representatives, in which membership would be apportioned on the basis of population; and (2) the guarantee that all revenue bills would originate in the lower house. The convention delegates settled as well on granting Congress the authority to regulate interstate and foreign commerce by a simple majority vote but requiring that treaties be approved by a two-thirds vote of the upper house. The Great Compromise was eventually approved by a narrow 5–4 margin of the state delegations. Connecticut, New Jersey, Delaware, Maryland, and North Carolina approved; Pennsylvania, Virginia, South Carolina, and Georgia opposed; New York and New Hampshire were absent, and the Massachusetts delegation was deadlocked. Thus, a vote margin of just one state paved the way for the creation of a new federal government.

Compromise also resolved disagreement over the nature of the executive. The agreement called for the president (and vice president) to be elected by an electoral college. Because the number of electors equaled the number of representatives and senators from each state, this system gave disproportionately greater influence to smaller states. As chief executive, the president would have

TABLE 2.2 The Virginia Plan, the New Jersey Plan, and the Great Compromise

	The Virginia Plan	The New Jersey Plan	The Great Compromise
	Introduced on May 29, 1787, by Edmund Randolph of Virginia; favored initially by delegates from Virginia, Pennsylvania, Massachusetts	Introduced on June 15, 1787, by William Paterson of New Jersey; favored initially by delegates from New Jersey, New York, Connecticut, Maryland, Delaware	Introduced by Roger Sherman of Connecticut; approved at the convention by a narrow 5–4 vote on July 16, 1787
Branches	Bicameral legislature with one house elected by the people and second house chosen by the first	Unicameral legislature elected by the people	Bicameral legislature with one house elected by the people and second house chosen by state legislatures
Legislature	All representatives and senators apportioned by population	Equal representation among states	Members of one house (representatives) apportioned by population (five slaves counted as three free men); members of second house (senators) apportioned equally among states
	Singular executive chosen by the legislature	Plural executive chosen by the legislature	Singular executive chosen by "Electoral College" (Electors appointed by state legislatures choose President; if no one receives majority, House chooses President).
Other Powers	Congress can legislate wherever "states are incompetent" or to preserve "harmony of the United States"	Congress has power to tax and regulate commerce	Congress has power to tax only in proportion to representation in the lower house; all appropriation bills must originate in lower house

the power to veto acts of Congress, make treaties and appointments with the consent of the Senate, and serve as commander in chief of the nation's armed forces.

The Slavery Issue

The issue of representation collided with another thorny issue looming over the convention proceedings: the issue of slavery. Four southern states (Maryland, Virginia, North Carolina, and South Carolina) had slave populations of more than 100,000 each. Meanwhile, two New England states (Maine and Massachusetts) had already banned slavery, and another four northern states (Vermont, New Hampshire, Rhode Island, and Connecticut) had a combined total of just 4,000 slaves within their borders. The steady march of abolition in the North was matched by a southern slave population that had been doubling every two decades. The convention delegates who advocated a new form of government were wary of the role slavery would play in this new nation, but they were even warier of offending southern sentiments to the point that consensus at the convention would be endangered.

Some delegates from the northern states that had already voted in favor of banning slavery sought a similar emancipation of slaves in all the colonies by constitutional edict. Southerners hoping to protect their plantation economy, which depended on slave labor, wanted to prevent future Congresses from interfering with the institution of slavery and the importation of slaves. Moreover, even among northerners, there was disagreement on how emancipation should proceed. Some favored outright freedom, whereas others argued for some form of colonization of the slaves, which would in effect ship them back to Africa. Many delegates feared that any extended discussion of slavery at the convention would become so divisive that it might bring the entire gathering to a standstill.

Southern delegates also wanted slaves to be counted equally with free people in determining the apportionment of representatives; northerners opposed such a policy for representation because it would give the southern states more power, but they did want slaves counted equally for purposes of apportioning taxes among the states. In an effort to forestall the convention's collapse, the delegates crafted a series of compromises that amounted to misdirection and, in some instances, outright silence on the issue of slavery.[11] By the agreement known as the **Three-Fifths Compromise**, five slaves would be counted as the equivalent of three "free persons" for purposes of taxes and representation. Delegates from southern states also feared that a Congress dominated by representatives from more populous northern states might take action against the slave trade. Most northerners continued to favor gradual emancipation. Once again, neither side got exactly what it wanted. The Constitution said nothing about either preserving or outlawing slavery. Indeed, the only specific provision about slavery was a time limit on legislation banning slave importation: Congress was forbidden from doing so for at least twenty years. In 1807, however, with the slave population steadily outgrowing demand, many southerners allied with opponents of the slave trade to ban the importation of slaves. Not until the Civil War decades later would the conflict over slavery be finally resolved.

On September 17, 1787, after four months of compromises and negotiations, the twelve state delegations present approved the final draft of the Constitution. By the terms of Article VII of the document, the Constitution was to become operative once ratified by nine of the thirteen states.

Three-Fifths Compromise
A compromise proposal in which five slaves would be counted as the equivalent of three free people for purposes of taxes and representation.

★ LO   Understand how sovereign powers were divided in the new government

The New Constitution

As a consequence of the many compromises in the draft Constitution, few of the delegates were pleased with every aspect of the new document. Even James Madison, later heralded as the "Father of the Constitution" for his many contributions as a spokesman at the convention, had furiously opposed the Great Compromise; he hinted at one point that a majority of the states might be willing to form a union outside the convention if the compromise were ever approved, and he convinced the Virginia delegation to vote "no" when it came up for a formal vote.

Nonetheless, the central desire of most of the delegates to craft a new government framework did lead them to consensus on a set of guiding principles that are evident throughout the document. The following principles continue to guide politicians, lawyers, and scholars today as they study the many ambiguous provisions of the Constitution:

- Recognizing that calls for fairer representation of colonists' interests lay at the heart of the Declaration of Independence, popular sovereignty was a guiding principle behind the new Constitution. The document's preamble, beginning with "We the People," signified the coming together of people, not states, for the purposes of creating a new government. Under the Constitution, no law could be passed without the approval of the House of Representatives, a "people's house" composed of members apportioned by population and subject to reelection every two years. Of even greater significance, the delegates agreed that all revenue measures must originate in the House, an explicit affirmation of the principle that there would be "no taxation without representation."

- The delegates recognized the need for a **separation of powers**. The founders drew upon the ideas of the French political philosopher Baron de Montesquieu, who had argued that when legislative, executive, and judicial power are not exercised by the same institution, power cannot be so easily abused. Mindful of the British model in which Parliament combined legislative and executive authority, the drafters of the Constitution assigned specific responsibilities and powers to each branch of the government, giving legislative power to Congress, executive power to the president, and judicial power to the Supreme Court. In the new government, individuals were generally prohibited from serving in more than one branch of government at the same time. The vice president's role as president of the Senate was a notable exception to this rule.

Separation of powers
The principle that each branch of government enjoys separate and independent powers and areas of responsibility.

- While establishing separate institutions, the drafters of the Constitution also created a system of **checks and balances** to require that the branches of government would have to work together to formulate policy. This system of "separate institutions sharing power" helped ensure that no one interest or faction could easily dominate the government. Through the exercise of presidential vetoes, Senate advice and consent, and judicial interpretations and other tools, each institution would have an opportunity to contend for influence.

Checks and balances
A system of limits imposed by the Constitution that gives each branch of government the limited right to change or cancel the acts of other branches.

- Dividing sovereign powers between the states and the federal government—a system later termed *federalism*—is also a defining characteristic of the government framework, established by the Constitution. Rather than entrusting all powers to a centralized government and essentially reducing the states to mere geographic subdivisions of the nation, the convention delegates divided powers between two levels of government: the states and the federal government. The distinction drawn between local concerns—controlled by state governments—and national concerns—controlled by the federal government—was as confusing then as it is today. But the delegates determined that such a division was necessary if they hoped to achieve any consensus. It would be politically impossible to convince the states to become mere geographic subdivisions of a larger political whole.

- Although united by the belief that the national government needed to be strengthened, the framers of the Constitution were products of a revolutionary generation that had seen governmental power abused. Thus, they were committed to a government of limited or **enumerated powers**. The Constitution spelled out the powers of the new federal government in detail, and it was assumed that the government's authority did not extend beyond those powers. By rejecting a government of unlimited discretionary power, James Madison argued, individual rights, including those "inalienable rights" cited

Enumerated powers
Express powers explicitly granted by the Constitution such as the taxing power specifically granted to Congress.

FIGURE 2.1 Checks and Balances in the U.S. Constitution

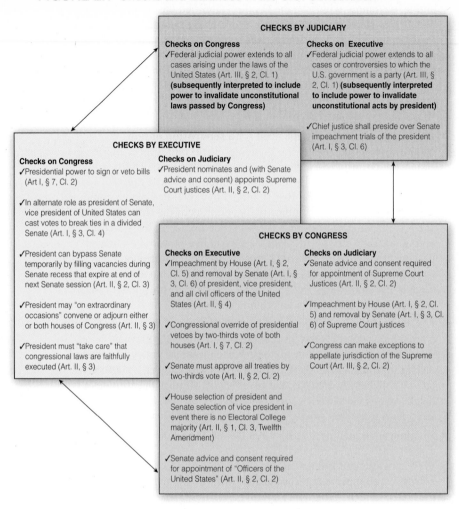

CHECKS BY JUDICIARY

Checks on Congress
✓Federal judicial power extends to all cases arising under the laws of the United States (Art. III, § 2, Cl. 1) **(subsequently interpreted to include power to invalidate unconstitutional laws passed by Congress)**

Checks on Executive
✓Federal judicial power extends to all cases or controversies to which the U.S. government is a party (Art. III, § 2, Cl. 1) **(subsequently interpreted to include power to invalidate unconstitutional acts by president)**

✓Chief justice shall preside over Senate impeachment trials of the president (Art. I, § 3, Cl. 6)

CHECKS BY EXECUTIVE

Checks on Congress
✓Presidential power to sign or veto bills (Art I, § 7, Cl. 2)

✓In alternate role as president of Senate, vice president of United States can cast votes to break ties in a divided Senate (Art. I, § 3, Cl. 4)

✓President can bypass Senate temporarily by filling vacancies during Senate recess that expire at end of next Senate session (Art. II, § 2, Cl. 3)

✓President may "on extraordinary occasions" convene or adjourn either or both houses of Congress (Art. II, § 3)

✓President must "take care" that congressional laws are faithfully executed (Art. II, § 3)

Checks on Judiciary
✓President nominates and (with Senate advice and consent) appoints Supreme Court justices (Art. II, § 2, Cl. 2)

CHECKS BY CONGRESS

Checks on Executive
✓Impeachment by House (Art. I, § 2, Cl. 5) and removal by Senate (Art. I, § 3, Cl. 6) of president, vice president, and all civil officers of the United States (Art. II, § 4)

✓Congressional override of presidential vetoes by two-thirds vote of both houses (Art. I, § 7, Cl. 2)

✓Senate must approve all treaties by two-thirds vote (Art. II, § 2, Cl. 2)

✓House selection of president and Senate selection of vice president in event there is no Electoral College majority (Art. II, § 1, Cl. 3, Twelfth Amendment)

✓Senate advice and consent required for appointment of "Officers of the United States" (Art. II, § 2, Cl. 2)

Checks on Judiciary
✓Senate advice and consent required for appointment of Supreme Court Justices (Art. II, § 2, Cl. 2)

✓Impeachment by House (Art. I, § 2, Cl. 5) and removal by Senate (Art. I, § 3, Cl. 6) of Supreme Court justices

✓Congress can make exceptions to appellate jurisdiction of the Supreme Court (Art. III, § 2, Cl. 2)

in the Declaration of Independence, would be protected from the arbitrary exercise of authority.

- Finally, some delegates believed that the new Constitution should be a "living" document; that is, it should have some measure of flexibility to meet the changing demands placed on it over time. Perhaps the most frustrating aspect of the Articles of Confederation was the near impossibility of any sort of modification. Because any change to the Articles required the unanimous consent of the states, even the most popular reform proposals stood little chance of being implemented. Thus, the framers decided that the new Constitution would go into effect when it had been ratified by nine of thirteen states. Furthermore, once ratified, the Constitution could be amended by a two-thirds vote of each house of Congress (subject to subsequent ratification by three fourths of the state legislatures).

The Ratification Battle
Federalists versus Anti-Federalists

 Evaluate the advantages enjoyed by those seeking to ratify the new Constitution

Once Congress submitted the Constitution to the states for approval, battle lines were formed between the **Federalists**, who supported ratification of the new document, and the **Anti-Federalists**, who opposed it. From the outset, the Federalists enjoyed a number of structural and tactical advantages in this conflict.

- **Nonunanimous consent.** The rules of ratification for the new Constitution, requiring approval of just nine of the thirteen states, were meant to ease the process of adopting the new document.

- **Special "ratifying conventions."** The delegates realized that whatever form the new Constitution might take, state legislatures would have the most to lose from an abandonment of the Articles. Thus, they decided that the Constitution would be sent for ratification not to state legislatures but instead to special state ratifying conventions that would be more likely to approve it.

- **The rule of secrecy.** The Constitutional Convention's agreed-upon rule of secrecy, which forbade publication or discussion of the day-to-day proceedings of the convention, followed the precedent established in colonial assemblies and the First Continental Congress, where it was thought that members might speak more freely and openly if their remarks were not subject to daily scrutiny by the public at large. In the fall of 1787, the rule of secrecy also gave the Federalists on the inside a distinct advantage over outside opponents, who had little knowledge of the new document's provisions until publicized.

- **Conventions held in the winter limited rural participation.** Winter was approaching just as the fight over the new Constitution was being launched. This timing gave the Federalists another advantage, especially in the critical ratification battlegrounds of Massachusetts, New Hampshire, and New York. It would be difficult for rural dwellers—mostly poor farmers resistant to a strong central government and thus opposed to the new Constitution—to attend the ratification conventions if they were held in the dead of winter.

Federalists
Those who supported ratification of the proposed Constitution of the United States between 1787 and 1789.

Anti-Federalists
Those who opposed ratification of the proposed Constitution of the United States.

The Federalist Papers

 Assess the role that *The Federalist* Papers played in ratification

Between the fall of 1787 and the summer of 1788, the Federalists launched an aggressive media campaign that was unusually well organized for its time. James Madison, Alexander Hamilton, and John Jay wrote seventy-seven essays explaining and defending the new Constitution and urging its ratification. Signed under the name "Publius," the essays were printed in New York newspapers and magazines. These essays—along with eight others by the same men—were then collected, printed, and published in book form under the title *The Federalist*.[12] The essays allayed fears and extolled the benefits of the new Constitution by emphasizing the inadequacy of the Articles of Confederation and the need for a strong government. Today, these essays are considered classic works of political philosophy. The following are among the most frequently cited *The Federalist* Papers:

- **Federalist No. 10.** In Madison's first offering in ***The Federalist* Papers**, he analyzes the nature, causes, and effects of factions, by which he meant

The Federalist **Papers**
A series of articles authored by Alexander Hamilton, James Madison, and John Jay, which argued in favor of ratifying the proposed Constitution of the United States; the *Federalist Papers* outlined the philosophy and motivation of the document.

The Continuing Call to *The Federalist* Papers

The Federalist Papers had a significant impact on the birth of the new nation. The essays argued persuasively that the Articles of Confederation were inadequate. Many scholars today attribute the narrow margin in favor of ratification of the Constitution at New York's ratification convention to the sophisticated media campaign waged by the Federalists, especially through *The Federalist* Papers.

In 1905, the Supreme Court's controversial decision in *Lochner v. New York*, which invalidated a New York State health regulation restricting the hours that bakers could be exposed to flour dust, set off a furious political debate about the role government should play in a newly industrialized society. Advocates on both sides of the debate repeatedly cited *The Federalist* Papers to bolster their arguments. Those who supported government regulation argued that it was not the job of courts to disagree with the decisions of legislatures on such public interest issues; even if factions and interest groups had produced such legislation, they cited Federalist No. 10 to justify the proposition that the corrupting spirit of "factions" distinguished democracy from true republics. Opponents of government regulations countered that Madison's preference for more factions was simply his way of reaching toward an ideal politics in which all these factions would cancel themselves out; by contrast,

they argued that factions remained heavily influential in state legislatures. In support of the Court's ruling, they cited Federalist No. 78 in which Hamilton argued that "the independence of the judges may be an essential safeguard against the effects of occasional ill humors in the society." Only a sudden switch by the Supreme Court to stop interfering with industrial regulations in 1937 saved the nation from a constitutional crisis fueled in part by dramatically contrasting readings of *The Federalist* Papers.

In 1996, President Bill Clinton (a Democrat) signed a welfare reform bill that slashed federal welfare spending, reduced welfare benefits, and shifted major responsibilities for welfare programs from the federal government to state governments. To defend the president's actions against incensed Democratic Party leaders like Senator Patrick Moynihan (D-NY), who feared the bill unfairly turned the government's back on the poor, the White House dug into *The Federalist* Papers for its defense. In Federalist No. 51, James Madison defended the Constitution against charges that it unduly transferred excessive powers to the new government: "A double security arises to the rights of people . . . the different governments will control each other, at the same time that each will be controlled by itself." The White House argued that shifting major welfare responsibilities to the states represented a sharing of the duties and responsibilities of government that was consistent with the intentions of the founders.

groups of people motivated by a common economic and/or political interest. Noting that such factions are both the product and price of liberty, Madison argued that by extending the sphere in which they can act, "you make it less probable that a majority of the whole will have a common motive to invade the rights of other citizens."

■ **Federalist No. 46.** In this essay, Madison defended the system of federalism set up by the new Constitution. He contended that the system allowed the states sufficient capacity to resist the "ambitious encroachments of the federal government."

■ **Federalist No. 51.** In perhaps the most influential of the essays, Madison described how the new Constitution would prevent the government from abusing its citizens. His argument is that the "multiplicity of interests" that influence so many different parts of the government would guarantee the security of individual rights. Because the federal system of government divides the government into so many parts (federal versus state, legislative versus executive versus judicial branches, and so on), "the rights of the individual, or of the minority, will be in little danger from interested combinations of the majority."

In late 1787 and early 1788, Anti-Federalists countered *The Federalist* Papers with a media campaign of their own.[13] In letters written under the pseudonyms "Brutus" and "The Federal Farmer" and published by newspapers throughout the colonies, the Anti-Federalists claimed that they were invoking a cause more consistent with that of the revolution—the cause of freedom from government tyranny. For them, the new national government's power to impose internal taxes on the states amounted to a revival of the British system of internal taxation. Perhaps the Anti-Federalists' most effective criticism was that the Constitution lacked a bill of rights that explicitly protected citizens' individual rights. They rejected Madison's contention in Federalist No. 51 that limitations on the central government provided those protections.

Ratification ultimately succeeded but by a somewhat narrow margin. Of the first five states to ratify, four (Delaware, New Jersey, Georgia, and Connecticut) did so with little or no opposition, whereas Pennsylvania did so only after a bitter conflict at its ratifying convention. Massachusetts became the sixth state to ratify when proponents of the Constitution swung the convention narrowly in their favor only by promising to push for a bill of rights after ratification. By June, three more states (Maryland, South Carolina, and New Hampshire) had voted to ratify, providing the critical threshold of nine states required under the Constitution. Still, the Federalists worried that without ratification by the major states of New York and Virginia, the new union would not succeed.

Opposition in Virginia was formidable, with Patrick Henry leading the Anti-Federalist forces against James Madison and the Federalists.[14] Eventually, Madison gained the upper hand with an assist from George Washington, whose eminent stature helped capture numerous votes for the Federalists. Madison also promised to support adding a bill of rights to the new Constitution. Then, Alexander Hamilton and John Jay capitalized on the positive news from Virginia to secure victory at the New York ratifying convention. With more than the required nine states—including the crucial states of New York and Virginia—the Congress did not wait for the votes from North Carolina or Rhode Island; on July 2, 1788, it appointed a committee to prepare for the new government.

ROGER-VIOLLET/THE IMAGE WORKS

Portrait of James Madison, the "Father of the Constitution."

A Bill of Rights

Seven of the state constitutions created during the Revolutionary War featured a statement of individual rights in some form. The Virginia Declaration of Rights of 1776, for example, had borrowed (from John Locke) its grounding of individual rights in a conception of natural law and social contract: "All

Explain the origins of the Bill of Rights and its role in securing ratification

★ LO

men are by nature equally free and independent, and have certain inherent rights, of which, when they enter into a state of society, they cannot, by any compact, deprive or divest their posterity." Later, during the battle over ratification, five state ratifying conventions had stressed the need for amendments to the Constitution in the form of a bill of rights, which would expressly protect fundamental rights against encroachment by the national government.[15]

Still, not all the Federalists saw the need for a federal bill of rights. Madison, for one, believed a bill of rights was unnecessary because the central government held only those powers enumerated in the Constitution. He explained: "The rights in question are reserved by the manner in which the federal powers are granted . . . the limited powers of the federal government and the jealousy of the subordinate governments afford a security which has not existed in the case of the state governments, and exists in no other." Madison was also concerned about the dangers of trying to enumerate all important rights: "There is great reason to fear that a positive declaration of some of the most essential rights could not be obtained," leaving some essential rights omitted for the future. Hamilton underscored this sentiment in Federalist No. 84, arguing that such a list of rights might invite governmental attempts to exercise power over those rights not included in the list.

Among the most ardent supporters of adding a bill of rights to the Constitution was Thomas Jefferson, who warned about the dangers of abuses of power.[16] From his distant vantage point in France, where he continued to serve as an American minister, Jefferson was in the dark about the new Constitution until November 1787. Then, in a December 20, 1787, letter to his friend and political protégé from Virginia, James Madison, Jefferson wrote, "A bill of rights is what the people are entitled to against every government on earth, general or particular, and what no just government should refuse, or rest on inference." Although recognizing Madison's fears of omissions as legitimate, Jefferson continued to argue the point. In a subsequent letter dated March 15, 1789, Jefferson argued that "half a loaf is better than no bread. If we cannot secure all our rights, let us secure what we can."

In the end, Jefferson's arguments prevailed, and Madison (by this time, a congressman from Virginia) became a principal sponsor of a bill of rights in the first Congress. Introducing the bill in the House of Representatives, he declared, "They will be an impenetrable bulwark against every assumption of power in the legislative or executive." On September 9, 1789, the House of Representatives voted to submit a list of twelve **amendments** to the states; ten of these were ratified by the required nine states by December 15, 1791, and compose today's **Bill of Rights**.

Among the rights protected by the Bill of Rights are the rights of free religious exercise, free speech, free press, and assembly (First Amendment); rights against search and seizure without a warrant stating "probable cause" (Fourth Amendment); and rights of due process and no self-incrimination (Fifth Amendment). The two amendments not ratified in 1791 did not relate to individual rights at all. They were (1) a prohibition on salary increases for legislators taking effect prior to the next congressional election (in 1992—more than 200 years later—this became the Twenty-seventh Amendment) and (2) a provision defining the rules for determining the number of members of the House of Representatives.

Amendments
Modifications or additions to the U.S. Constitution passed in accordance with the amendment procedures laid out in Article V.

Bill of Rights
The first ten amendments to the U.S. Constitution, which protect various rights of the people against the new federal government.

Changing the Constitution
The Formal Amendment Process

Describe the process of amending the Constitution ★ LO

Although political circumstances dictated that the Bill of Rights be passed in a relatively speedy fashion, future proposed amendments would not have it so easy. In crafting the rules for amending the new Constitution, the framers sought to balance two competing interests: (1) the need to protect the Constitution from short-lived or temporary passions by making amendments exceedingly difficult to pass and (2) sufficient flexibility to allow for amendments to be added when the needs of the nation demanded change. Their determination to strike such a balance was shaped by their experience in dealing with the Articles of Confederation, whose "unanimous consent of states" rule had left them immune from even the most necessary of reforms.

Article V of the Constitution specifies two ways amendments can be proposed and two methods of ratification. Congress may propose an amendment by a two-thirds vote of both houses; alternatively, two thirds of the state legislatures may apply to Congress to call a special national convention for proposing amendments. Amendments take effect when ratified either by a vote of three fourths of the state legislatures or by special ratifying conventions held in three fourths of the states. To date, all twenty-seven amendments (including the Bill of Rights) have been proposed by Congress, and all but one (the Twenty-first) have been ratified by the state legislatures.

Although twenty-seven amendments have been ratified since 1789, only seventeen of those were ratified after 1791. More than 5,000 amendments have been introduced in Congress since that time, but only thirty-three have been formally proposed by Congress.

FIGURE 2.2 How an Amendment Gets Proposed and Ratified

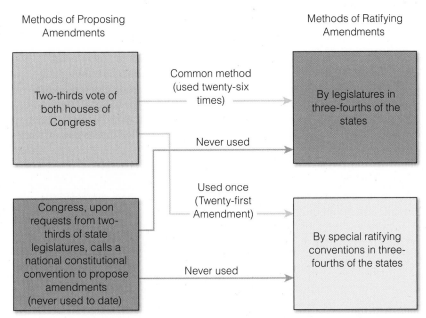

Methods of Proposing Amendments

Methods of Ratifying Amendments

Two-thirds vote of both houses of Congress

Common method (used twenty-six times)

By legislatures in three-fourths of the states

Never used

Used once (Twenty-first Amendment)

Congress, upon requests from two-thirds of state legislatures, calls a national constitutional convention to propose amendments (never used to date)

Never used

By special ratifying conventions in three-fourths of the states

One Student's Term Paper Proves That the Constitution Is Indeed a "Living Document"

College students may be forgiven for assuming that classroom assignments that invite them to propose constitutional amendments are strictly theoretical exercises. Yet in the case of one University of Texas student, such an assignment on constitutional change became much more than theoretical. Gregory Watson chose as the topic for his research a long-forgotten amendment to forbid congressional pay raises from taking effect until an intervening election in the House of Representatives had occurred. Originally proposed in 1789 as part of the Bill of Rights, the amendment was finally ratified 203 years later, thanks largely to Watson. The sophomore had discovered the amendment while doing research for a paper on American government. Watson's final paper—in which he argued that the amendment was still viable for ratification—garnered a mere "C" from his professor. But Watson continued his quest to secure ratification of the amendment. Tapping into the resentment of citizens over various instances in which members of Congress had quietly passed pay raises for themselves without calling attention to their actions, Watson joined forces with several state lawmakers to get the required number of states to ratify the provision. Their efforts succeeded, and the Twenty-seventh Amendment was eventually ratified in May 1992. Although Watson's grade from a decade earlier remained unchanged, he at least had the satisfaction of knowing that he had made history . . . literally.

For Critical Thinking and Discussion

1. What amendments to the Constitution would you like to see implemented?
2. Would you be willing to sacrifice your own time, energy, and resources to organize interest group activities on an amendment's behalf?

The "reasonable time" requirement for ratification of an amendment reached an extreme with the Twenty-seventh Amendment (forbidding congressional pay raises from taking effect until an intervening election in the House of Representatives has occurred). Originally proposed in 1789 as part of the Bill of Rights, it was finally ratified in 1992, just over 202 years later. (See the "Your Perspective" box above for a more detailed discussion of what occurred.)

★ LO Assess informal types of constitutional change, including different forms of constitutional interpretation

Informal Processes of Change

After the Constitution and Bill of Rights were ratified, there remained the difficult task of interpreting those documents for use by the different branches of government. Among the framers, Alexander Hamilton was perhaps most attuned to the danger that Anti-Federalists and other opponents of the new Constitution might attempt to overturn the convention's carefully crafted compromises so many years later by judicial decree. Certainly, most of the Constitution's provisions were vague enough that they allowed discretion for maneuvering by the generation that interprets them. But how much discretion was justified in the process of constitutional interpretation?

TABLE 2.3 Amendments, Date of Ratification, Length of Ratification Process

Amendment	Subject of Amendment	Date Proposed	Date Ratified	Length
Bill of Rights				
First	Free speech, press, religion, assembly	Sept. 25, 1789	Dec. 15, 1791	2+ years
Second	Rights to bear arms			
Third	No quartering of troops in homes			
Fourth	No unreasonable searches/seizures			
Fifth	Right to due process, grand jury; no double jeopardy, self-incrimination			
Sixth	Rights to speedy and public trial, counsel			
Seventh	Right to trial by jury in civil cases			
Eighth	No excessive bail, fines, cruel/unusual punishment			
Ninth	Rights not enumerated retained by people			
Tenth	Powers not delegated to Congress or prohibited to states belong to states or people			
Subsequent Amendments				
Eleventh	No federal cases between state, citizen of other state	Mar. 5, 1794	Jan. 8, 1798	3+ years
Twelfth	Modification of Electoral College rules	Dec. 12, 1803	Sept. 25, 1804	9+ months
Thirteenth	Ban on slavery	Feb. 1, 1865	Dec. 18, 1865	10+ months
Fourteenth	States can't deprive right to due process, equal protection, privileges, and immunities	June 16, 1866	July 28, 1868	2+ years
Fifteenth	Right to vote can't be denied by race	Feb. 27, 1869	Mar. 30, 1870	1+ years
Sixteenth	Congress can levy individual income taxes	July 12, 1909	Feb. 25, 1913	3+ years
Seventeenth	Direct election of senators	May 16, 1912	May 31, 1913	1+ years
Eighteenth	Prohibition of liquors	Dec. 18, 1917	Jan. 29, 1919	1+ years
Nineteenth	Women's right to vote	June 4, 1919	Aug. 26, 1920	1+ years
Twentieth	Dates for inauguration, Congress's session	Mar. 2, 1932	Feb. 6, 1933	11+ months
Twenty-first	Repeal of prohibition	Feb. 20, 1933	Dec. 5, 1933	9+ months
Twenty-second	Presidential term limits	Mar. 24, 1947	Feb. 26, 1951	3+ years
Twenty-third	DC residents' vote for president	June 16, 1960	Mar. 29, 1961	9+ months
Twenty-fourth	Ban on poll taxes	Aug. 27, 1962	Jan. 23, 1964	1+ years
Twenty-fifth	Appointment of new vice president, presidential incompetence	July 6, 1965	Feb. 10, 1967	1+ years
Twenty-sixth	Eighteen-year-olds' right to vote	Mar. 23, 1971	July 1, 1971	3+ months
Twenty-seventh	Congressional pay raises effective only after election	Sept. 25, 1789	May 7, 1992	202+ years

The State of the Union Address

On January 27, 2010, President Barack Obama faced a rocky moment in his young presidency: The economy remained stagnant, his administration's hallmark health care initiative was in peril, and polls showed that his approval rating had dipped below 50 percent for the first time since he took office. Even members of his own Democratic Party were complaining that President Obama had lost sight of the needs of ordinary Americans. And yet for a brief period that evening little of that seemed to matter, as members of Congress of every political stripe, along with the nation's Supreme Court justices, Cabinet members, and others among Washington's political elite, jammed into the Capitol's House chamber to hear Obama speak. What was the occasion? President Obama was giving his first State of the Union address, a yearly right of passage for every modern president. For the ninety or so minutes that Obama spoke, even his most staunch foes in Congress sat quietly and listened, along with millions of television viewers in the United States and around the world.

AP PHOTO/CHARLES DHARAPAK

Loose construction
Constitutional interpretation that gives constitutional provisions broad and open-ended meanings.

As it turned out, the Supreme Court under Chief Justice John Marshall was the first to put its own lasting imprint on the Constitution. Marshall, who hailed from Virginia, served as the chief justice of the United States from 1801 until his death in 1835.[17] Marshall believed in a **loose construction** (or interpretation) of the Constitution, meaning that under his leadership, many of the Constitution's provisions enjoyed broad and quite open-ended meanings. Thus, for example, Article I, Section 8, Clause 18 empowered Congress "to make all laws which shall be necessary and proper for carrying into execution" any of the powers specifically listed in the Constitution. Marshall's loose construction of that provision gave the federal government considerable implied powers (those not explicitly stated) to regulate the economy. For example, in the 1819 case of *McCulloch v. Maryland*,[18] Marshall's court ruled that Congress had the power to create a national bank, even though the Constitution said nothing explicitly about such a power. The Court determined that a national bank was "necessary and proper" to assist in regulating commerce or raising armies. This philosophy of loose constitutional interpretation underlies the concept of a "living Constitution," one that is adaptable to changing times and conditions.

Article III, Section 3 of the U.S. Constitution requires that the president "from time to time give to Congress information of the State of the Union." George Washington personally delivered the first State of the Union address on January 8, 1790, but Thomas Jefferson discontinued the practice, opting instead to send his written address to Congress. Woodrow Wilson reestablished the in-person practice in 1913, and with rare exceptions every president since then has delivered the address personally.

For modern presidents, the State of the Union address offers the chief executive a rare moment when competing politicians defer to him on a mostly unfiltered stage. Though applause for the president is often political in tone (the Republicans in the chamber, for example, refused to applaud when Obama mentioned his administration's controversial stimulus package), most presidents pepper their addresses with patriotic items that will generate applause throughout the chamber. In the case of President Obama's 2010 address, 48 million Americans watched on one of the eleven major TV and cable networks that carried the speech live. Since 1997 the addresses have also been available live on the World Wide Web.

For Critical Thinking and Discussion

1. Should the networks continue to preempt normal programming to cover the president's State of the Union address live? Now that the speech is broadcast on the Internet and elsewhere, is this type of wall-to-wall coverage necessary?

2. Given the increased polarization of the two major political parties in Washington, should the president use his State of the Union address to build bridges to the opposition or to announce new (and potentially controversial) policies? What would you like to see the president emphasize in his State of the Union address?

3. Currently the opposition party is afforded a brief "response to the State of the Union address" delivered by one of its leaders live on all the networks. Would you prefer a more direct give-and-take (i.e., a debate) between party leaders? Or is our current tradition of "dueling addresses" sufficient?

Thomas Jefferson, James Madison, and many others viewed the powers of the central government more narrowly. They favored a **strict construction**, arguing that the government possessed only those powers explicitly stated in the Constitution. Thus, although Article I, Section 8, Clause 3 gave Congress the power to regulate interstate commerce, it could not do so by creating a national bank or utilizing any other means not specifically mentioned in the Constitution. They supported a "fixed" constitution, one that could be changed only by the formal amendment process, not by congressional action or judicial ruling.

The tension between advocates of strict and loose constructions of the Constitution continues to this day. Robert Bork, a former Yale law professor and unsuccessful Supreme Court nominee, argues that overly loose interpretations of the Constitution are outside the court's proper task. In particular, Bork says, the Supreme Court has "simply abandoned" the Constitution by refusing to enforce limits on the subjects that come within congressional reach.[19] In accordance with this philosophy, the conservative Supreme Court of the late 1990s struck down federal statutes regulating guns in the schools and domestic violence on the theory that such regulations were not grounded in any specifically enumerated power of Congress, such as the power to regulate interstate commerce.

Strict construction
Constitutional interpretation that limits the government to only those powers explicitly stated in the Constitution.

This strict-construction approach contrasts markedly with the approach advocated by Professors Lawrence Tribe[20] and John Hart Ely[21] as well as by Supreme Court Justice William Brennan, who argued for a loose or more flexible interpretation of the Constitution. Advocates of a loose construction view the document as evolving with the times. In the 1960s and 1970s, the Supreme Court utilized a loose-construction approach to interpret congressional power more broadly to include the power to create civil rights legislation and federal criminal laws.

With so few amendments proposed and ratified during the nation's history, students of American politics may wonder how a Constitution written in 1787 has developed to meet the needs of a changing nation. In truth, an informal constitutional convention occurs on a frequent basis in the American political system. Congress, the president, and the courts engage in constitutional interpretation every day through their respective activities, both official and unofficial. Thus, the Constitution has not been a straitjacket at all; rather, its elegant vagueness has opened it up to a variety of interpretations.

Making the Connection

When state legislatures in 1791 ratified the Bill of Rights, citizens must have marveled at the flexibility of the new Constitution. After all, it had been amended ten times in just two years! And yet the Constitution has proven remarkably resistant to change since then, incorporating only seventeen additional amendments over the next 220 years. How has the federal Constitution survived so long, and in nearly the same exact form as the original? It is the cornerstone of a political system that encourages discussion, debate, and in some cases outright conflict over the meaning of its provisions, while only occasionally being subject to formal change. In short, the Constitution is forever bending, but it only rarely "breaks." And thanks to the Union's victory over the Confederacy in the Civil War, it has never been permanently broken.

Two amendments pressed by interest groups nearly a century apart—the "Christian Amendment" favored by the National Reform Association beginning in the 1860s, and the "flag desecration amendment" favored by the Citizens' Flag Alliance since the 1990s—made considerable headway in their respective eras. Proposed in Congress on multiple occasions, each gained enough momentum to force even mainstream politicians to take them seriously. Congress never formally submitted either amendment for ratification by the state legislatures, as the threshold requirement of two-thirds support from both houses proved too high to overcome. Still, supporters of each movement were energized by the pursuit, and its leaders were encouraged by the positive support they generated. The constitutional amendment process is supposed to be arduous—how else could the nation's political system ensure that its provisions not be treated like simple statutes? Instead they are treated like scripture—the higher law found in a document that so many deem sacred.

Many provisions in the U.S. Constitution are conveniently vague, affording politicians of different parties and ideologies the chance to interpret the document as they wish. What about constitutional provisions that are extremely specific and less susceptible to interpretation? So long as the two major parties are in agreement, even those provisions may offer few constitutional obstacles. Consider the dilemma facing Senator Hillary Clinton of New York after her appointment as the nation's sixty-seventh secretary of state. By executive order issued in January 2008, the salary of the secretary of state increased from $186,600 to $191,300 per year. What's the problem? Article I, Section 6 of the Constitution reads as follows:

Secretary of State Hillary Clinton greets Indian Foreign Minister S.M. Krishna.

SAUL LOEB/AFP/GETTY IMAGES

> *No Senator or Representative shall, during the Time for which he was elected, be appointed to any civil office under the authority of the United States . . . the Emoluments whereof shall have been increased during such time. . . .*

Did the Constitution bar Hillary Clinton from accepting the post of secretary of state? John F. O'Connor, who has studied the clause in detail, believes that "it is beyond dispute" that Senator Clinton was ineligible under the clause to be appointed as secretary of state.[*] When President Obama selected Senator Ken Salazar of Colorado to be his secretary of the interior, the same issue resurfaced.

Members of Congress, both Republicans and Democrats, quickly resolved the situation by means of the so-called Saxbe fix, named after Senator William Saxbe, who was appointed as attorney general by President Richard Nixon in 1973. In Saxbe's case, Congress reduced the attorney general's salary to pre-1969 levels by legislation and subsequently approved his appointment. In a similar fashion, Congress in December 2008 passed (and President George W. Bush signed) legislation cancelling all salary increases made during Hillary Clinton's Senate term.

Former Attorney General William Saxbe.

AP PHOTO

Several constitutional scholars (including O'Connor) and at least one public interest organization (Judicial Watch) believe the so-called Saxbe fix is unconstitutional. Yet to date no lawsuit has survived. Assuming that both political parties and their leaders in Congress have consented, who is personally aggrieved enough by the "Saxbe fix" to sue? More important, who are the victims of this effort to circumvent plain constitutional language? In an ironic twist, the real victim may be Hillary Clinton herself, who as secretary of state was forced to accept a lower salary than that of her predecessor, Condoleezza Rice.

*See John F. O'Connor, "The Emoluments Clause: An Anti-Federalist Intruder in a Federalist Constitution," *Hofstra Law Review* 24 (1995): 89–178.

Chapter Summary

★ The Beginnings of a New Nation

- Britain's victory in the French and Indian War put the British Empire into significant debt. Following the war Britain imposed numerous regulatory measures on the colonies that were intended to raise money; those measures generated outrage, protests, and eventually outright resistance from the colonists.

- After a series of military skirmishes at Lexington and Concord, the Second Continental Congress in 1776 authorized the drafting of a Declaration of Independence listing the colonists' grievances and justifying the call for independence based on John Locke's theory of natural rights and the social contract.

- The Articles of Confederation created a "league of friendship" among the thirteen states by vesting them with equal authority in the central government during and immediately after America's successful war for independence. Under the Articles, the central government also possessed only limited powers to raise revenue and regulate commerce.

- Congress's inability to raise funds hampered the U.S. government's war effort and its economic relations with foreign nations.

★ The Constitutional Convention

- A constitutional convention consisting of delegates from twelve states convened in the summer of 1787 in an attempt to revise the Articles. The delegates immediately began to consider the "Virginia Plan," which proposed to overhaul the Articles by empowering a new government with three separate branches and the power to raise revenue.

- The Virginia Plan favored large and more populous states by allotting membership in its proposed legislature based on each state's population; delegates from less populous states countered with the New Jersey Plan, based on the principle of equal representation of the states. The Constitutional Convention eventually resolved the conflict by accepting the so-called Great Compromise, which proposed a bicameral legislature with a House of Representatives apportioned by population and a Senate that allots equal power to each of the states.

- With the issue of slavery dividing northern and southern states, the convention sidestepped the issue by settling on the "Three-Fifths Compromise" (counting five slaves as three people for purposes of taxes and representation) and by deferring a ban on slave importation for at least twenty years.

★ The New Constitution

- The new Constitution combined features of popular sovereignty, separation of powers, and checks and balances with a commitment to a system of federalism, which divides sovereignty between state and federal governments.

★ The Ratification Battle

- The battle over ratification was waged between Federalists (who supported the new Constitution) and Anti-Federalists (who opposed it). The Federalists' carefully crafted media campaign, which included publication of the *Federalist Papers* justifying various provisions of the new Constitution, helped ensure its ratification.

- Several state ratifying conventions insisted that the new government add a bill of rights to the Constitution; James Madison, the "father of the Constitution," was initially reluctant to propose such a bill for fear that it might omit important rights, but eventually sponsored a new Bill of Rights in the first Congress.

★ Changing the Constitution

- Article V of the Constitution makes it exceedingly difficult to amend the Constitution. Since the Bill of Rights was ratified in 1791, only seventeen additional amendments have been ratified.

- The Supreme Court under Chief Justice John Marshall favored a loose construction of several constitutional provisions, giving the federal government considerable implied powers; Thomas Jefferson and Jeffersonian Republicans favored a stricter construction of the Constitution's provisions.

CourseMate

Key Terms

Amendments (p. 42)

Anti-Federalists (p. 39)

Articles of Confederation (p. 31)

Bill of Rights (p. 42)

Checks and balances (p. 37)

Constitutional Convention (p. 32)

Declaration of Independence (p. 31)

Enumerated powers (p. 37)

The Federalist Papers (p. 39)

Federalists (p. 39)

Great Compromise (p. 34)

Loose construction (p. 46)

New Jersey Plan (p. 34)

Separation of powers (p. 37)

Shays's Rebellion (p. 32)

Strict construction (p. 47)

Three-Fifths Compromise (p. 36)

Virginia Plan (p. 34)

Resources

Books

Amar, Akhil Reed. *America's Constitution: A Biography.* New York: Random House, 2006.

Bailyn, Bernard. *The Ideological Origins of the American Revolution.* Cambridge, MA: Harvard University Press, 1967.

Beard, Charles S. *An Economic Interpretation of the Constitution.* New York: Macmillan, 1941.

Federalist Papers, various editions, including paperback version, edited by Isaac Kramnick. New York: Penguin Press, 1987.

McDonald, Forrest. *Novus Ordo Seclorum.* Lawrence: University Press of Kansas, 1985.

Maier, Pauline. *American Scripture: Making the Declaration of Independence.* New York: Alfred A. Knopf, 1997.

Rakove, Jack N. *Original Meanings: Politics and Ideas in the Making of the Constitution.* New York: Alfred A. Knopf, 1996.

Wood, Gordon S. *The Creation of the American Republic.* Chapel Hill: University of North Carolina Press, 1998.

Wood, Gordon S. *The Radicalism of the American Revolution.* New York: Alfred A. Knopf, 1991.

Internet Sources

http://lcweb2.loc.gov/ammem/bdsds/bdsdhome.html (Library of Congress exhibit on documents from the Continental Congress and the Constitutional Convention).

http://www.constitution.org/dfc/dfc-0000.htm (the debates of the Constitutional Convention of 1787).

http://www.archives.gov/exhibits/ (exhibit hall of the National Archives and Records Administration on the charters of freedom: Declaration of Independence, U.S. Constitution, Bill of Rights, and so on).

Annotated Constitution
of the United States
# of America

The Constitution of the United States of America

We the people of the United States, in order to form a more perfect union, establish justice, insure domestic tranquility, provide for the common defense, promote the general welfare, and secure the blessings of liberty to ourselves and our posterity, do ordain and establish this Constitution for the United States of America.

As a statement containing the essential reasons for drafting the Constitution and the purposes of the new central government, the Preamble theoretically does not confer any actual power on government. Nevertheless, on numerous occasions the Supreme Court has cited the preamble to illustrate the origin, scope, and purposes of the Constitution, as well as to help discern the meaning of certain constitutional provisions that follow it. Most notably in McCulloch v. Maryland (1819), Chief Justice John Marshall quoted from the Preamble at length to confirm that the Constitution comes directly from the people, and not from the states.

Article I

Section 1. All legislative powers herein granted shall be vested in a Congress of the United States, which shall consist of a Senate and House of Representatives.

The placement of provisions for congressional power in Article I confirms what the Founders undoubtedly assumed to be true: that Congress would be the preeminent branch of the new central government. Section 1 established two important principles. First, by specifying "powers herein granted" it declared that the national government is one of enumerated powers. Despite the broadening of powers implied by the necessary and proper clause of Section 8, this statement of Section 1 still means that Congress theoretically cannot do whatever it wants to do. Rather, it must ground its exercise of power (whether explicitly stated or implied) in a specific provision of Article I. Second, Section 1 established the principle of bicameralism— the presence of two separate but equally powerful legislative bodies as a further safeguard against government tyranny.

Section 2. The House of Representatives shall be composed of members chosen every second year by the people of the several states, and the electors in each state shall have the qualifications requisite for electors of the most numerous branch of the state legislature.

No person shall be a Representative who shall not have attained to the age of twenty five years, and been seven years a citizen of the United States, and who shall not, when elected, be an inhabitant of that state in which he shall be chosen.

Representatives and direct taxes shall be apportioned among the several states which may be included within this union, according to their respective numbers, which shall be determined by adding to the whole number of free persons, including those bound to service for a term of years, and excluding Indians not taxed, three fifths of all other Persons. The actual Enumeration shall be made within three years after the first meeting of the Congress of the United States, and within every subsequent term of ten years, in such manner as they shall by law direct. The number of Representatives shall not exceed one for every thirty thousand, but each state shall have at least one Representative; and until such enumeration shall be made, the state of New Hampshire shall be entitled to chuse three, Massachusetts eight, Rhode Island and Providence Plantations one, Connecticut five, New York six, New Jersey four, Pennsylvania eight, Delaware one, Maryland six, Virginia ten, North Carolina five, South Carolina five, and Georgia three.

When vacancies happen in the Representation from any state, the executive authority thereof shall issue writs of election to fill such vacancies.

The House of Representatives shall choose their speaker and other officers; and shall have the sole power of impeachment.

> *Section 2 of Article I establishes a House of Representatives as the lower House of the Congress. The membership of the U.S. House of Representatives is apportioned according to each state's population; the so-called Three-Fifths Compromise (only three fifths of the population of slaves would be counted for enumeration purposes) helped resolve an impasse at the Convention between Southern states, who wanted slaves to count as more, and Northern states, who wanted them to count as less. Although the number of House members has grown with the population, since 1911 it has been fixed by statute at 435. As constituted, the House is as powerful as the U.S. Senate, and in one respect is even more powerful: the House has the sole power to originate revenue bills. Section 2 also lays out the two-year term rule and qualifications for each House member, as well as providing procedures for apportionment and filling vacancies. Finally, it authorizes the House to choose top officials, including the Speaker.*

Section 3. The Senate of the United States shall be composed of two Senators from each state, chosen by the legislature thereof, for six years; and each Senator shall have one vote.

Immediately after they shall be assembled in consequence of the first election, they shall be divided as equally as may be into three classes. The seats of the Senators of the first class shall be vacated at the expiration of the second year, of the second class at the expiration of the fourth year, and the third class at the expiration of the sixth year, so that one third may be chosen every second year; and if vacancies happen by resignation, or otherwise, during the recess of the legislature of any state, the executive thereof may make temporary appointments until the next meeting of the legislature, which shall then fill such vacancies.

No person shall be a Senator who shall not have attained to the age of thirty years, and been nine years a citizen of the United States and who shall not, when elected, be an inhabitant of that state for which he shall be chosen.

The Vice President of the United States shall be President of the Senate, but shall have no vote, unless they be equally divided.

The Senate shall choose their other officers, and also a President pro tempore, in the absence of the Vice President, or when he shall exercise the office of President of the United States.

The Senate shall have the sole power to try all impeachments. When sitting for that purpose, they shall be on oath or affirmation. When the President of the United States is tried, the Chief Justice shall preside: And no person shall be convicted without the concurrence of two thirds of the members present.

Judgment in cases of impeachment shall not extend further than to removal from office, and disqualification to hold and enjoy any office of honor, trust or profit under the United States: but the party convicted shall nevertheless be liable and subject to indictment, trial, judgment and punishment, according to law.

Just as Section 2 does for the House of Representatives, Section 3 establishes various powers and procedures for the U.S. Senate. Individual senators may be more powerful than their counterparts in the House because of the longer length of their terms (six years) and because there are far fewer members in the body; however, there is no constitutional basis for the claim that the Senate is a superior chamber. Although the vice president theoretically presides over the Senate as its president, and the president pro tempore serves in the vice president's absence, in actual practice the president pro tempore usually deputizes a more junior senator to preside over most Senate business. The provisions of Clause 1 and Clause 2 that state legislatures choose senators have been overturned by the Seventeenth Amendment, which provides that senators are now chosen by popular election.

Section 4. The times, places and manner of holding elections for Senators and Representatives, shall be prescribed in each state by the legislature thereof; but the Congress may at any time by law make or alter such regulations, except as to the places of choosing Senators.

The Congress shall assemble at least once in every year, and such meeting shall be on the first Monday in December, unless they shall by law appoint a different day.

According to Article I, Section 4, states can regulate the time, place, and manner of all federal elections, but Congress can still establish a single uniform date for elections (and it has done so on the first Tuesday following the first Monday in November).

Section 5. Each House shall be the judge of the elections, returns and qualifications of its own members, and a majority of each shall constitute a quorum to do business; but a smaller number may adjourn from day to day, and may be authorized to compel the attendance of absent members, in such manner, and under such penalties as each House may provide.

Each House may determine the rules of its proceedings, punish its members for disorderly behavior, and, with the concurrence of two thirds, expel a member.

Each House shall keep a journal of its proceedings, and from time to time publish the same, excepting such parts as may in their judgment require secrecy; and the yeas and nays of the members of either House on any question shall, at the desire of one fifth of those present, be entered on the journal.

Neither House, during the session of Congress, shall, without the consent of the other, adjourn for more than three days, nor to any other place than that in which the two Houses shall be sitting.

Section 6. The Senators and Representatives shall receive a compensation for their services, to be ascertained by law, and paid out of the treasury of the United States. They shall in all cases, except treason, felony and breach of the peace, be privileged from arrest during their attendance at the session of their respective Houses, and in going to and returning from the same; and for any speech or debate in either House, they shall not be questioned in any other place.

No Senator or Representative shall, during the time for which he was elected, be appointed to any civil office under the authority of the United States, which shall have been created, or the emoluments whereof shall have been increased during such time: and no person holding any office under the United States, shall be a member of either House during his continuance in office.

> *Article I, Section 6 extends to members of Congress various immunities. The speech and debate clause of Section 6 prevents House members or senators from being sued for slander during congressional debates, committee hearings, or most other official congressional business. In deference to the principle of separation of powers, Clause 2 ensures that members of Congress cannot hold another civil office while retaining their legislative seats.*

Section 7. All bills for raising revenue shall originate in the House of Representatives; but the Senate may propose or concur with amendments as on other Bills.

Every bill which shall have passed the House of Representatives and the Senate, shall, before it become a law, be presented to the President of the United States; if he approve he shall sign it, but if not he shall return it, with his objections to that House in which it shall have originated, who shall enter the objections at large on their journal, and proceed to reconsider it. If after such reconsideration two thirds of that House shall agree to pass the bill, it shall be sent, together with the objections, to the other House, by which it shall likewise be reconsidered, and if approved by two thirds of that House, it shall become a law. But in all such cases the votes of both Houses shall be determined by yeas and nays, and the names of the persons voting for and against the bill shall be entered on the journal of each House respectively. If any bill shall not be returned by the President within ten days (Sundays excepted) after it shall have been presented to him, the same shall be a law, in like manner as if he had signed it, unless the Congress by their adjournment prevent its return, in which case it shall not be a law.

Every order, resolution, or vote to which the concurrence of the Senate and House of Representatives may be necessary (except on a question of adjournment) shall be presented to the President of the United States; and before the same shall take effect, shall be approved by him, or being disapproved by him, shall be repassed by two thirds of the Senate and House of Representatives, according to the rules and limitations prescribed in the case of a bill.

Article I, Section 7 is often referred to as the presentment clause. It establishes the procedures by which Congress presents bills to the president for approval; it also lays out the process by which the president may veto legislation, either by refusing to sign it and sending it back, or by keeping the bill for a period of ten days without signing it while Congress has adjourned in the interim (referred to as a pocket veto). In 1996, Congress passed the Line Item Veto Act, which allowed the president to veto specific expenditures at the time of signing; the Supreme Court declared the Line Item Veto Act unconstitutional in Clinton v. City of New York *(1998) because it gave the president the power to repeal parts of duly enacted statutes in a manner different from the "finely wrought and exhaustively considered procedure" described in this section.*

Section 8. The Congress shall have power to lay and collect taxes, duties, imposts and excises, to pay the debts and provide for the common defense and general welfare of the United States; but all duties, imposts and excises shall be uniform throughout the United States;

To borrow money on the credit of the United States;

To regulate commerce with foreign nations, and among the several states, and with the Indian tribes;

To establish a uniform rule of naturalization, and uniform laws on the subject of bankruptcies throughout the United States;

To coin money, regulate the value thereof, and of foreign coin, and fix the standard of weights and measures;

To provide for the punishment of counterfeiting the securities and current coin of the United States;

To establish post offices and post roads;

To promote the progress of science and useful arts, by securing for limited times to authors and inventors the exclusive right to their respective writings and discoveries;

To constitute tribunals inferior to the Supreme Court;

To define and punish piracies and felonies committed on the high seas, and offenses against the law of nations;

To declare war, grant letters of marque and reprisal, and make rules concerning captures on land and water;

To raise and support armies, but no appropriation of money to that use shall be for a longer term than two years;

To provide and maintain a navy;

To make rules for the government and regulation of the land and naval forces;

To provide for calling forth the militia to execute the laws of the union, suppress insurrections and repel invasions;

To provide for organizing, arming, and disciplining, the militia, and for governing such part of them as may be employed in the service of the United States, reserving to the states respectively, the appointment of the officers, and the authority of training the militia according to the discipline prescribed by Congress;

To exercise exclusive legislation in all cases whatsoever, over such District (not exceeding ten miles square) as may, by cession of particular states, and the acceptance of Congress, become the seat of the government of the United States, and to exercise like authority over all places purchased by the consent of the legislature of the state in which the same shall be, for the erection of forts, magazines, arsenals, dockyards, and other needful buildings;—And

To make all laws which shall be necessary and proper for carrying into execution the foregoing powers, and all other powers vested by this Constitution in the government of the United States, or in any department or officer thereof.

Article I, Section 8 may be the most heavily cited clause in the original Constitution, as it lays out all the enumerated powers of Congress. The 18th clause listed, the necessary and proper clause, was the source of significant controversy in the early republic. In McCulloch v. Maryland *(1819), Chief Justice John Marshall interpreted the clause as essentially aiding Congress in carrying out its expressed powers. Combining the powers granted by the 18th clause with other powers allows Congress to exercise implied powers not explicitly listed in the Constitution, so long as those powers offer a theoretical means of achieving the enumerated powers. Thus Congress successfully incorporated a bank of the United States because it was deemed necessary and proper to achieve the power to coin money and regulate its value (Clause 5), as well as other powers. Similarly, Congress chartered a railroad company as a necessary means of promoting commerce (Clause 3) and waging war (Clauses 11–14). No wonder the necessary and proper clause has also been called the elastic clause: it gives Congress the power to enact laws on almost any subject it desires. The power to regulate interstate commerce under Clause 3 has been especially useful in this regard. Citing the commerce clause, Congress since 1937 has regulated minimum wages of state employees, outlawed loan sharking, and passed numerous civil rights laws, among other legislation. The only current limits to that practice were outlined by the Supreme Court in* United States v. Lopez *(1995) and* United States v. Morrison *(2000)—the law in question must regulate activities that are at least directly economic in nature.*

Section 9. The migration or importation of such persons as any of the states now existing shall think proper to admit, shall not be prohibited by the Congress prior to the year one thousand eight hundred and eight, but a tax or duty may be imposed on such importation, not exceeding ten dollars for each person.

The privilege of the writ of habeas corpus shall not be suspended, unless when in cases of rebellion or invasion the public safety may require it.

No bill of attainder or ex post facto Law shall be passed.

No capitation, or other direct, tax shall be laid, unless in proportion to the census or enumeration herein before directed to be taken.

No tax or duty shall be laid on articles exported from any state.

No preference shall be given by any regulation of commerce or revenue to the ports of one state over those of another: nor shall vessels bound to, or from, one state, be obliged to enter, clear or pay duties in another.

No money shall be drawn from the treasury, but in consequence of appropriations made by law; and a regular statement and account of receipts and expenditures of all public money shall be published from time to time.

No title of nobility shall be granted by the United States: and no person holding any office of profit or trust under them, shall, without the consent of the Congress, accept of any present, emolument, office, or title, of any kind whatever, from any king, prince, or foreign state.

Section 9 places some explicit limits on congressional power, including restrictions on the power to ban the import of slaves (at least through 1808), the power to bestow titles of nobility, and the power to lay direct taxes not apportioned to the states' populations. This last restriction was effectively removed by ratification of the Sixteenth Amendment in 1913. It also prohibits Congress from issuing bills of attainder (legislative acts that inflict punishment without a judicial trial) or from passing ex post facto laws (criminal laws that apply retroactively to acts committed in the past).

Section 10. No state shall enter into any treaty, alliance, or confederation; grant letters of marque and reprisal; coin money; emit bills of credit; make anything but gold and silver coin a tender in payment of debts; pass any bill of attainder, ex post facto law, or law impairing the obligation of contracts, or grant any title of nobility.

No state shall, without the consent of the Congress, lay any imposts or duties on imports or exports, except what may be absolutely necessary for executing its inspection laws: and the net produce of all duties and imposts, laid by any state on imports or exports, shall be for the use of the treasury of the United States; and all such laws shall be subject to the revision and control of the Congress.

No state shall, without the consent of Congress, lay any duty of tonnage, keep troops, or ships of war in time of peace, enter into any agreement or compact with another state, or with a foreign power, or engage in war, unless actually invaded, or in such imminent danger as will not admit of delay.

The final section of Article I limits states from exercising powers reserved exclusively to the federal government. Most controversial of these clauses was the contracts clause, which prohibits states from impairing the obligation of contracts. Added to the Constitution largely to prevent state laws that undermined the collection of valid debts, it was later used to protect certain franchises or special privileges that corporations had received from state legislatures. Thus the Supreme Court held in Trustees of Dartmouth College v. Woodward *(1819) that the charter given to Dartmouth by a colonial legislature in 1769 could not be changed without Dartmouth's consent. State legislatures complained that the contracts clause unduly restricted their ability to legislate; thus, the Supreme Court over the course of two centuries has narrowed the meaning of the clause to allow states greater freedom to operate, relying on the theory that such contracts are by implication the laws of the state and thus may be modified by the state. The Court has also upheld state bankruptcy laws when the laws are applied to debts incurred after passage of the law.*

Article II

Section 1. The executive power shall be vested in a President of the United States of America. He shall hold his office during the term of four years, and, together with the Vice President, chosen for the same term, be elected, as follows:

Each state shall appoint, in such manner as the Legislature thereof may direct, a number of electors, equal to the whole number of Senators and Representatives to which the State may be entitled in the Congress: but no Senator or Representative, or person holding an office of trust or profit under the United States, shall be appointed an elector.

The electors shall meet in their respective states, and vote by ballot for two persons, of whom one at least shall not be an inhabitant of the same state with themselves. And they shall make a list of all the persons voted for, and of the number of votes for each; which list they shall sign and certify, and transmit sealed to the seat of the government of the United States, directed to the President of the Senate. The President of the Senate shall, in the presence of the Senate and House of Representatives, open all the certificates, and the votes shall then be counted. The person having the greatest number of votes shall be the President, if such number be a majority of the whole number of electors appointed; and if there be more than one who have such majority, and have an equal number of votes, then the House of Representatives shall immediately choose by ballot one of them for President; and if no person have a majority, then from the five highest on the list the said House shall in like manner choose the President. But in choosing the President, the votes shall be taken by States, the representation from each state having one vote; A quorum for this purpose shall consist of a member or members from two thirds of the states, and a majority of all the states shall be necessary to a choice. In every case, after the choice of the President, the person having the greatest number of votes of the electors shall be the Vice President. But if there should remain two or more who have equal votes, the Senate shall choose from them by ballot the Vice President.

The Congress may determine the time of choosing the electors, and the day on which they shall give their votes; which day shall be the same throughout the United States.

No person except a natural born citizen, or a citizen of the United States, at the time of the adoption of this Constitution, shall be eligible to the office of President; neither shall any person be eligible to that office who shall not have attained to the age of thirty five years, and been fourteen Years a resident within the United States.

In case of the removal of the President from office, or of his death, resignation, or inability to discharge the powers and duties of the said office, the same shall devolve on the Vice President, and the Congress may by law provide for the case of removal, death, resignation or inability, both of the President and Vice President, declaring what officer shall then act as President, and such officer shall act accordingly, until the disability be removed, or a President shall be elected.

The President shall, at stated times, receive for his services, a compensation, which shall neither be increased nor diminished during the period for which he shall have been elected, and he shall not receive within that period any other emolument from the United States, or any of them.

Before he enter on the execution of his office, he shall take the following oath or affirmation:—'I do solemnly swear (or affirm) that I will faithfully execute the office of President of the United States, and will to the best of my ability, preserve, protect and defend the Constitution of the United States.'

Article II, Section 1 lays out the manner by which the president and vice president are selected, the qualifications for those two offices, and the means for removal and succession. (Clause 2 on presidential elections has been replaced by the Twelfth Amendment.) Section 1 begins with the vague declaration that the "executive power shall be vested in a president of the United States of America." Does this clause serve as a source of independent power for the chief executive? Beginning in the twentieth century, the Supreme Court has held that the president possesses broad "inherent powers" to exercise certain powers not specifically enumerated in the Constitution. These vast executive powers included, for example, Franklin Roosevelt's various executive agreements extending the scope of the federal government during the 1930s. On the other hand, the Supreme Court ruled in Youngstown Sheet and Tune Co. v. Sawyer *(1951) that a president's inherent powers did not include President Truman's attempt to seize the steel mills to avert a strike without congressional approval; similarly, in* United States v. Nixon *(1974) the Court held that the chief executive's inherent powers did not encompass President Richard Nixon's refusal to turn over important documents in a criminal matter.*

Section 2. The President shall be commander in chief of the Army and Navy of the United States, and of the militia of the several states, when called into the actual service of the United States; he may require the opinion, in writing, of the principal officer in each of the executive departments, upon any subject relating to the duties of their respective offices, and he shall have power to grant reprieves and pardons for offenses against the United States, except in cases of impeachment.

He shall have power, by and with the advice and consent of the Senate, to make treaties, provided two thirds of the Senators present concur; and he shall nominate, and by and with the advice and consent of the Senate, shall appoint ambassadors, other public ministers and consuls, judges of the Supreme Court, and all other officers of the United States, whose appointments are not herein otherwise provided for, and which shall be established by law: but the Congress may by law vest the appointment of such inferior officers, as they think proper, in the President alone, in the courts of law, or in the heads of departments.

The President shall have power to fill up all vacancies that may happen during the recess of the Senate, by granting commissions which shall expire at the end of their next session.

Article II, Section 2 is striking for how few express powers are granted to the president, as compared to the long list of powers granted to Congress in Article I, Section 8. In the twentieth century the powers granted to the president expanded to create a far more powerful presidency than the Founders envisioned. Thus, invoking their power as commander-in-chief, modern presidents have deployed troops around the world in military battles even without a formal declaration of war by Congress. Recent presidents have occasionally terminated treaties without the consent of the Senate. Presidents have also asserted the power to terminate officers of the United States without cause. The combined Supreme Court precedents of Myers v. United States (1926) and Humphrey's Executor v. United States (1935) authorize them to do so in the case of purely executive officers, but not in the case of independent agency heads.

Section 3. He shall from time to time give to the Congress information of the state of the union, and recommend to their consideration such measures as he shall judge necessary and expedient; he may, on extraordinary occasions, convene both Houses, or either of them, and in case of disagreement between them, with respect to the time of adjournment, he may adjourn them to such time as he shall think proper; he shall receive ambassadors and other public ministers; he shall take care that the laws be faithfully executed, and shall commission all the officers of the United States.

Article II, Section 3 lists numerous presidential responsibilities, including the obligation to give a report on the "state of the union" to Congress (today this occurs in the form of a yearly address), and the duty to "take care that laws be faithfully executed." Citing this latter phrase, presidents have asserted the power to impound money appropriated by Congress, and to suspend the writ of habeas corpus. Though reluctant to afford the chief executive such unbridled authority, the Supreme Court has upheld nearly all efforts by the president to call upon the military to assist in faithfully executing the law. President Eisenhower, for example, exercised this power when he used federal troops to enforce desegregation decrees in Arkansas and Mississippi in the late 1950s.

Section 4. The President, Vice President and all civil officers of the United States, shall be removed from office on impeachment for, and conviction of, treason, bribery, or other high crimes and misdemeanors.

Article II, Section 4 lays out the process of impeachment and conviction of civil officers, but the phrase "high crimes and misdemeanors" is vague and subject to conflicting interpretations. Regardless, the House of Representatives has asserted its authority to decide on its own how to define the term. Only two chief executives have ever been formally impeached under this section: Andrew Johnson in 1868, and Bill Clinton in 1998. However, in both cases, the U.S. Senate failed to provide the required two-thirds vote necessary for conviction.

Article III

Section 1. The judicial power of the United States, shall be vested in one Supreme Court, and in such inferior courts as the Congress may from time to time ordain and establish. The judges, both of the supreme and inferior courts, shall hold their offices during good behaviour, and shall, at stated times, receive for their services, a compensation, which shall not be diminished during their continuance in office.

Section 2. The judicial power shall extend to all cases, in law and equity, arising under this Constitution, the laws of the United States, and treaties made, or which shall be made, under their authority;—to all cases affecting ambassadors, other public ministers and consuls;—to all cases of admiralty and maritime jurisdiction;—to controversies to which the United States shall be a party;—to controversies between two or more states;—between a state and citizens of another state;—between citizens of different states;—between citizens of the same state claiming lands under grants of different states, and between a state, or the citizens thereof, and foreign states, citizens or subjects.

In all cases affecting ambassadors, other public ministers and consuls, and those in which a state shall be party, the Supreme Court shall have original jurisdiction. In all the other cases before mentioned, the Supreme Court shall have appellate jurisdiction, both as to law and fact, with such exceptions, and under such regulations as the Congress shall make.

The trial of all crimes, except in cases of impeachment, shall be by jury; and such trial shall be held in the state where the said crimes shall have been committed; but when not committed within any state, the trial shall be at such place or places as the Congress may by law have directed.

Section 3. Treason against the United States, shall consist only in levying war against them, or in adhering to their enemies, giving them aid and comfort. No person shall be convicted of treason unless on the testimony of two witnesses to the same overt act, or on confession in open court.

The Congress shall have power to declare the punishment of treason, but no attainder of treason shall work corruption of blood, or forfeiture except during the life of the person attainted.

Article III establishes a U.S. Supreme Court, spells out the terms of office of its members, and lists the various cases to which its judicial power extends. Just as important, it provides the basis for a more elaborate judicial system featuring numerous levels of courts, which Congress may establish at its discretion. Note how vague and general this Article is compared to Articles I and II: only one court (the Supreme Court) is specifically mentioned, and there are no provisions that specify the size or composition of the court. Congress subsequently established that federal judges on the courts of appeals and the district courts, like justices of the Supreme Court, are appointed by the president and confirmed by the Senate. They too serve for indefinite terms on good behavior, which provides the equivalent of life tenure to federal judges on those three levels of courts. Article III does not specifically grant the Supreme Court the power of judicial review, that is, the power to review the actions of other branches for their constitutionality. The Supreme Court seized that power for itself in Marbury v. Madison (1803), and it remains a fundamental precept of the federal judicial system today.

Article IV

Section 1. Full faith and credit shall be given in each state to the public acts, records, and judicial proceedings of every other state. And the Congress may by general laws prescribe the manner in which such acts, records, and proceedings shall be proved, and the effect thereof.

Section 2. The citizens of each state shall be entitled to all privileges and immunities of citizens in the several states.

A person charged in any state with treason, felony, or other crime, who shall flee from justice, and be found in another state, shall on demand of the executive authority of the state from which he fled, be delivered up, to be removed to the state having jurisdiction of the crime.

No person held to service or labor in one state, under the laws thereof, escaping into another, shall, in consequence of any law or regulation therein, be discharged from such service or labor, but shall be delivered up on claim of the party to whom such service or labor may be due.

Section 3. New states may be admitted by the Congress into this union; but no new states shall be formed or erected within the jurisdiction of any other state; nor any state be formed by the junction of two or more states, or parts of states, without the consent of the legislatures of the states concerned as well as of the Congress.

The Congress shall have power to dispose of and make all needful rules and regulations respecting the territory or other property belonging to the United States; and nothing in this Constitution shall be so construed as to prejudice any claims of the United States, or of any particular state.

Section 4. The United States shall guarantee to every state in this union a republican form of government, and shall protect each of them against invasion; and on application of the legislature, or of the executive (when the legislature cannot be convened) against domestic violence.

Article IV describes the responsibilities states have to one another under the Constitution, and the obligations of the federal government to the states. It also provides the procedures for admitting new states to the union (no state has been admitted since the entry of Alaska and Hawaii in 1959). In recent years, the most controversial aspect of Article IV has been the full faith and credit clause of Section 1, which theoretically binds states to respect the public acts and proceedings of other states, including the granting of drivers' licenses and child custody rulings. Does the full faith and credit clause apply as well to the institution of same-sex marriage? The federal government and various states have sought to evade the recognition of gay marriages sanctioned elsewhere through legislation, including the Defense of Marriage Act of 1996. (At the time of this writing, five states have sanctioned the practice by a vote of their respective legislatures; three others recognize same-sex marriage under certain conditions, but do not actually grant same-sex marriage licenses.)

The ambiguous privileges and immunities clause of Article IV, Section 2 requires that states not discriminate against citizens of other states in favor of its own citizens, although the Supreme Court has allowed states to establish more favorable terms for in-state residents when distributing certain recreational rights such as amateur fishing licenses or permits to use state parks; taxes on commuters, by contrast, may be unconstitutional if they penalize out-of-state residents who work or do business in the state. The requirement in Section 4 that the United States guarantee to every state a republican form of government was invoked in the 1840s when President John Tyler threatened the use of federal troops after a rebellion occurred in Rhode Island. Today that provision is obscure and little-used.

Article V

The Congress, whenever two thirds of both houses shall deem it necessary, shall propose amendments to this Constitution, or, on the application of the legislatures of two thirds of the several states, shall call a convention for proposing amendments, which, in either case, shall be valid to all intents and purposes, as part of this Constitution, when ratified by the legislatures of three fourths of the several states, or by conventions in three fourths thereof, as the one or the other mode of ratification may be proposed by the Congress; provided that no amendment which may be made prior to the year one thousand eight hundred and eight shall in any manner affect the first and fourth clauses in the ninth section of the first article; and that no state, without its consent, shall be deprived of its equal suffrage in the Senate.

Article V spells out the process for amending the Constitution. By far the most common form of constitutional amendment has been by congressional proposal, with state legislatures ratifying the proposal. Twenty-six of the twenty-seven amendments have been adopted in this way. The sole exception was the Twenty-first Amendment, which was ratified by specially chosen state ratifying conventions to assure that farmer-dominated state legislatures would not undermine the effort to repeal Prohibition. The procedure by which the requisite number of state legislatures (two thirds) apply to Congress to call a convention for proposing amendments has never been used. Article V does not provide a deadline for considering proposed amendments, although Congress has the power to set such deadlines in the language of the proposed amendment. Congress did not do so in the case of the Twenty-seventh Amendment, which received the approval of the required three fourths of states necessary for ratification in 1992— fully 203 years after the amendment was first proposed.

Article VI

All debts contracted and engagements entered into, before the adoption of this Constitution, shall be as valid against the United States under this Constitution, as under the Confederation.

This Constitution, and the laws of the United States which shall be made in pursuance thereof; and all treaties made, or which shall be made, under the authority of the United States, shall be the supreme law of the land; and the judges in every state shall be bound thereby, anything in the Constitution or laws of any State to the contrary notwithstanding.

The Senators and Representatives before mentioned, and the members of the several state legislatures, and all executive and judicial officers, both of the United States and of the several states, shall be bound by oath or affirmation, to support this Constitution; but no religious test shall ever be required as a qualification to any office or public trust under the United States.

Article VI establishes that the Constitution, laws, and treaties are to be the supreme law of the land. In interpreting this supremacy clause, the U.S. Supreme Court has countenanced little resistance. Thus the Supreme Court has consistently struck down attempts by states to control federal institutions, and it has reminded state governments that even state constitutions are subordinate to federal statutes. Even more important, in Cooper v. Aaron (1957) the U.S. Supreme Court stated in no uncertain terms that its own rulings are to be treated as if they are the words of the Constitution itself, heading off attempts by some state governments to resist Supreme Court rulings on desegregation by offering their own interpretations of the federal Constitution as authority.

Article VII

The ratification of the conventions of nine states, shall be sufficient for the establishment of this Constitution between the states so ratifying the same. Done in convention by the unanimous consent of the states present the seventeenth day of September in the year of our Lord one thousand seven hundred and eighty seven and of the independence of the United States of America the twelfth. In witness whereof We have hereunto subscribed our Names,
G. Washington—Presidt. and deputy from Virginia

New Hampshire
John Langdon
Nicholas Gilman

Massachusetts
Nathaniel Gorham
Rufus King

Connecticut
Wm. Saml. Johnson
Roger Sherman

New York
Alexander Hamilton

New Jersey
Wil. Livingston
David Brearly
Wm. Paterson
Jona. Dayton

Pennsylvania
B. Franklin
Thomas Mifflin
Robt. Morris
Geo. Clymer
Thos. FitzSimons
Jared Ingersoll
James Wilson
Gouv Morris

Delaware
Geo. Read
Gunning Bedford jun
John Dickinson
Richard Bassett
Jaco. Broom

Maryland
James McHenry
Dan of St Thos. Jenifer
Danl Carroll

Virginia
John Blair—
James Madison Jr.

North Carolina
Wm. Blount
Richd. Dobbs Spaight
Hu Williamson

South Carolina
J. Rutledge
Charles Cotesworth
  Pinckney
Charles Pinckney
Pierce Butler

Georgia
William Few
Abr Baldwin

Amendments to the Constitution of the United States

The Bill of Rights, ratified in 1791, consists of the first ten amendments to the Constitution. Since that time, seventeen additional amendments have been ratified by the states. Originally the Bill of Rights applied only to the federal government and not to the state governments; however, through a process known as incorporation, the Supreme Court has ruled that the Fourteenth Amendment (adopted in 1868) made most of the provisions found in the Bill of Rights applicable to the states as well. Subsequent amendments have extended the franchise, established (and repealed) Prohibition, and clarified important procedures that the federal government must follow.

Amendment I (1791)

Congress shall make no law respecting an establishment of religion, or prohibiting the free exercise thereof; or abridging the freedom of speech, or of the press; or the right of the people peaceably to assemble, and to petition the government for a redress of grievances.

Although many provisions of the original Bill of Rights are based on aspects of English law, the extensive guarantees found in the First Amendment have no true English equivalent. The First Amendment offered one of the first written guarantees of religious freedom, and it formed the basis for extensive free speech and free press protection as well. Yet its unqualified language notwithstanding, the First Amendment has never conveyed absolute freedom to Americans. Whether it was the Alien and Sedition Acts of 1798, the aggressive application of the Espionage Act during World War I, or the "red scare" of the late 1940s, government has often found ways to evade the First Amendment, especially during times of crisis. The Supreme Court has also specifically exempted obscenity, libel, fighting words, and incitement from free speech protections. Nor has the separate and independent provision for the freedom of the press been interpreted to give members of the press any more protection than is afforded to ordinary citizens. Finally, as noted above, although the first word of the amendment implies that its protections apply only against actions of the federal government, today the First Amendment offers protection against the state governments as well.

Amendment II (1791)

A well regulated militia, being necessary to the security of a free state, the right of the people to keep and bear arms, shall not be infringed.

The Second Amendment originated as a compromise in the debate between those who feared mob rule by the people, and those committed to give the people everything they need to fight governmental tyranny. In 2008, the U.S. Supreme Court ruled for the first time that certain gun control laws may violate an individual's Second Amendment right to "bear arms." Two years later it went a step further, applying those protections against all 50 states governments and their subdivisions. See District of Columbia v. Heller, 554 U.S. ____ (2008); McDonald v. Chicago, 561 U.S. ___ (2010).

Amendment III (1791)

No soldier shall, in time of peace be quartered in any house, without the consent of the owner, nor in time of war, but in a manner to be prescribed by law.

The Third Amendment has been all but lost to history. The Quartering Act, which required the American colonists to provide shelter and supplies for British troops, was one of the grievances that provoked the Declaration of Independence and ultimately the Revolution. Many colonists resented having to house British soldiers in private homes. The Third Amendment aimed to protect private citizens from such intrusions.

Amendment IV (1791)

The right of the people to be secure in their persons, houses, papers, and effects, against unreasonable searches and seizures, shall not be violated, and no warrants shall issue, but upon probable cause, supported by oath or affirmation, and particularly describing the place to be searched, and the persons or things to be seized.

Like the First Amendment, the Fourth Amendment is a uniquely American right. It arose out of colonists' anger over the warrantless searches and so-called General Warrants by which British authorities would conduct raids of colonists' homes virtually at their own discretion. The Fourth Amendment guarantees that with certain carefully specified exceptions (consent of the owner, urgent circumstances, etc.), government authorities can conduct searches only when they possess a reasonably specific warrant demonstrating probable cause. Enforcement of the Fourth Amendment occurs primarily through application of the controversial exclusionary rule, which excludes from trial all evidence seized in violation of a defendant's constitutional rights.

Amendment V (1791)

No person shall be held to answer for a capital, or otherwise infamous crime, unless on a presentment or indictment of a grand jury, except in cases arising in the land or naval forces, or in the militia, when in actual service in time of war or public danger; nor shall any person be subject for the same offense to be twice put in jeopardy of life or limb; nor shall be compelled in any criminal case to be a witness against himself, nor be deprived of life, liberty, or property, without due process of law; nor shall private property be taken for public use, without just compensation.

> *The Fifth Amendment is a collection of various rights, most of which are important primarily to those accused of a crime. Those who "take the Fifth" under oath are normally invoking the privilege against self-incrimination; under current precedents they can invoke that privilege in other contexts as well, such as whenever they are being questioned by police or other authorities. The grand jury requirement has never been incorporated to apply against state governments. The requirement against double jeopardy prevents defendants who have been acquitted from being retried for the same offense by the same government. The due process clause of the Fifth Amendment was later duplicated in the Fourteenth Amendment and applied to states as well. Finally, the takings clause limits the traditional power of eminent domain by requiring that the government must pay compensation whenever it takes private property for public use.*

Amendment VI (1791)

In all criminal prosecutions, the accused shall enjoy the right to a speedy and public trial, by an impartial jury of the state and district wherein the crime shall have been committed, which district shall have been previously ascertained by law, and to be informed of the nature and cause of the accusation; to be confronted with the witnesses against him; to have compulsory process for obtaining witnesses in his favor, and to have the assistance of counsel for his defense.

> *The Sixth Amendment offers the accused numerous constitutional protections. The need for a speedy and public trial dates back to concerns raised by imprisoned enemies of the British crown who were detained indefinitely and without notice. The right to a jury trial—considered a sacred aspect of the American political culture—is not all-encompassing either: it applies only to non-petty offenses (punishable by more than six months of prison).*

Amendment VII (1791)

In suits at common law, where the value in controversy shall exceed twenty dollars, the right of trial by jury shall be preserved, and no fact tried by a jury, shall be otherwise reexamined in any court of the United States, than according to the rules of the common law.

The Seventh Amendment is the only amendment in the Bill of Rights that focuses on elements of civil trials exclusively. It preserves the distinction the English system draws between courts of common law (in which juries grant monetary relief) and courts of equity (in which a judge grants nonmonetary relief, such as an injunction).

Amendment VIII (1791)

Excessive bail shall not be required, nor excessive fines imposed, nor cruel and unusual punishments inflicted.

The Eighth Amendment offers protections that come directly from the English Bill of Rights. The prohibition against excessive bail was established to prevent judges from keeping the accused indefinitely imprisoned while waiting for trials on minor offenses; it has subsequently been interpreted to allow judges to deny bail in instances where the charges are sufficiently serious, or where preventative detention is warranted for the safety of the community. The prohibition against cruel and unusual punishment forbids some punishments entirely (drawing and quartering, burning alive, and other forms of torture), while forbidding other punishments only when they are excessive compared to the crime. Aside from the four-year period from 1972 through 1976, the Supreme Court has consistently held that with proper safeguards, capital punishment is not cruel and unusual punishment. However, consistent with this clause it may not be imposed for rape or crimes lesser than murder, and it may not be imposed against the mentally retarded or against juvenile offenders.

Amendment IX (1791)

The enumeration in the Constitution, of certain rights, shall not be construed to deny or disparage others retained by the people.

The Ninth Amendment has been nicknamed the Madison Amendment in deference to James Madison's general concerns about the Bill of Rights. During debates over ratification of the Constitution, Anti-Federalists called for a bill of rights to protect the people against a potentially abusive new central government. In correspondence with Thomas Jefferson, Madison expressed the fear that by listing exceptions to congressional powers, such a bill of rights would effectively deny the existence of rights that did not happen to appear on the list. Eventually, as a member of the House of Representatives in the First Congress, Madison sponsored passage of the Bill of Rights, but he included this amendment as a way to ensure that the listing of certain rights did not mean that other rights were denied. As interpreted, the Ninth Amendment has not had much impact on the constitutional landscape. Likened by some to an "inkblot," it has been most commonly viewed not as a source of rights, but rather as a loose guideline on how to interpret the Constitution.

Amendment X (1791)

The powers not delegated to the United States by the Constitution, nor prohibited by it to the states, are reserved to the states respectively, or to the people.

The Tenth Amendment lays out in explicit terms that the federal government is limited only to the powers granted to it in the Constitution. For most of the twentieth century, the Supreme Court regarded this amendment largely as a redundant truism, adding little to the Constitution as it was originally ratified. Yet since the early 1990s the Supreme Court has began to put teeth into the amendment, interpreting it as a prohibition on attempts by Congress to force states to participate in federal programs.

Amendment XI (1798)

The judicial power of the United States shall not be construed to extend to any suit in law or equity, commenced or prosecuted against one of the United States by citizens of another state, or by citizens or subjects of any foreign state.

The Eleventh Amendment was ratified to modify the Supreme Court's controversial decision in Chisholm v. Georgia *(1793), which upheld the authority of federal courts to hear lawsuits brought by citizens of one state against another state. The Supreme Court has ruled that the Eleventh Amendment provide states with some form of sovereign immunity, which means that it generally protects states from civil or criminal prosecution. The Supreme Court has also determined that under the Eleventh Amendment, a state cannot be sued by one of its own citizens.*

Amendment XII (1804)

The electors shall meet in their respective states and vote by ballot for President and Vice-President, one of whom, at least, shall not be an inhabitant of the same state with themselves; they shall name in their ballots the person voted for as President, and in distinct ballots the person voted for as Vice-President, and they shall make distinct lists of all persons voted for as President, and of all persons voted for as Vice-President, and of the number of votes for each, which lists they shall sign and certify, and transmit sealed to the seat of the government of the United States, directed to the President of the Senate;—The President of the Senate shall, in the presence of the Senate and House of Representatives, open all the certificates and the votes shall then be counted;—the person having the greatest number of votes for President, shall be the President, if such number be a majority of the whole number of electors appointed; and if no person have such majority, then from the persons having the highest numbers not exceeding three on the list of those voted for as President, the House of Representatives shall choose immediately, by ballot, the President. But in choosing the President, the votes shall be taken by states, the representation from each state having one vote; a quorum for this purpose shall consist of a member or members from two-thirds of the states, and a majority of all the states shall be necessary to a choice. And if the House of Representatives shall not choose a President whenever the right of choice shall devolve upon them, before the fourth day of March next following, then the Vice-President shall act as President, as in the case of the death or other constitutional disability of the President. The person having the greatest number of votes as Vice-President, shall be the Vice-President, if such number be a majority of the whole number of electors appointed, and if no person have a majority, then from the two highest numbers on the list, the Senate shall choose the Vice-President; a quorum for the purpose shall consist of two-thirds of the whole number of Senators, and a majority of the whole number shall be necessary to a choice. But no person constitutionally ineligible to the office of President shall be eligible to that of Vice-President of the United States.

The Twelfth Amendment altered the Constitution's original procedures for holding presidential elections. Under Article II, the winner of a majority of Electoral College votes would become president, and the runner-up would become vice president. The election of 1800 exposed the peculiarity that if every member of the Electoral College voted for both members of a party ticket, each member of the most popular ticket would receive the same number of votes, resulting in a deadlock. The Twelfth Amendment cured that flaw by requiring electors to cast separate votes for president and vice president, and by ensuring that if a deadlock occurred anyway and the House of Representatives failed to choose a president, then the candidate who received the highest number of votes on the vice presidential ballot would act as president (thus all vice presidents must be constitutionally eligible to serve as president).

Amendment XIII (1865)

Section 1. Neither slavery nor involuntary servitude, except as a punishment for crime whereof the party shall have been duly convicted, shall exist within the United States, or any place subject to their jurisdiction.

Section 2. Congress shall have power to enforce this article by appropriate legislation.

The Thirteenth Amendment was the first of the three Civil War Amendments. It officially prohibited slavery in all states, and with certain exceptions (such as in the case of convicts) involuntary servitude. Immediately prior to its ratification in December 1865, slavery remained legal in only two states, Kentucky and Delaware. (Slavery in the former Confederate states had been outlawed by the Emancipation Proclamation of 1863.)

Amendment XIV (1868)

Section 1. All persons born or naturalized in the United States, and subject to the jurisdiction thereof, are citizens of the United States and of the state wherein they reside. No state shall make or enforce any law which shall abridge the privileges or immunities of citizens of the United States; nor shall any state deprive any person of life, liberty, or property, without due process of law; nor deny to any person within its jurisdiction the equal protection of the laws.

Section 2. Representatives shall be apportioned among the several states according to their respective numbers, counting the whole number of persons in each state, excluding Indians not taxed. But when the right to vote at any election for the choice of electors for President and Vice President of the United States, Representatives in Congress, the executive and judicial officers of a state, or the members of the legislature thereof, is denied to any of the male inhabitants of such state, being twenty-one years of age, and citizens of the United States, or in any way abridged, except for participation in rebellion, or other crime, the basis of representation therein shall be reduced in the proportion which the number of such male citizens shall bear to the whole number of male citizens twenty-one years of age in such state.

Section 3. No person shall be a Senator or Representative in Congress, or elector of President and Vice President, or hold any office, civil or military, under the United States, or under any state, who, having previously taken an oath, as a member of Congress, or as an officer of the United States, or as a member of any state legislature, or as an executive or judicial officer of any state, to support the Constitution of the United States, shall have engaged in insurrection or rebellion against the same, or given aid or comfort to the enemies thereof. But Congress may by a vote of two-thirds of each House, remove such disability.

Section 4. The validity of the public debt of the United States, authorized by law, including debts incurred for payment of pensions and bounties for services in suppressing insurrection or rebellion, shall not be questioned. But neither the United States nor any state shall assume or pay any debt or obligation incurred in aid of insurrection or rebellion against the United States, or any claim for the loss or emancipation of any slave; but all such debts, obligations and claims shall be held illegal and void.

Section 5. The Congress shall have power to enforce, by appropriate legislation, the provisions of this article.

The Fourteenth Amendment was ratified in an attempt to secure rights for freed slaves by broadening the definition of national citizenship and offering all persons equal protection of the law as well as due process of law from state governments. In the Slaughterhouse Cases (1873), the Supreme Court held that the privileges and immunities of national citizenship are actually quite limited: they include visiting the seat of government, petitioning Congress, using the nation's navigable waters, and other narrow privileges. By contrast, the equal protection clause provided the basis during the twentieth century for dismantling legally enforced segregation in Brown v. Board of Education (1954) and other cases. It also has been used to extend equal protection to groups other than African Americans, including women and other ethnic minorities. Of equal significance, the Supreme Court has also interpreted the equal protection clause to require states to apportion their congressional districts and state legislative seats on a "one-person, one-vote" basis.

The due process clause has been interpreted to provide procedural safeguards before the government deprives a person of life, liberty, or property. More controversially, in the early part of the twentieth century the Supreme Court in Lochner v. New York (1905) interpreted the clause as providing substantive protection to private contracts and other economic agreements. In later rulings the clause sparked considerable controversy when the Court used it as the basis for protecting substantive privacy rights not explicitly spelled out in the Constitution, such as that of a woman's right to an abortion (in the Court's 1973 Roe v. Wade decision), and of homosexual sodomy (in its 2003 ruling in Lawrence v. Texas).

Amendment XV (1870)

Section 1. The right of citizens of the United States to vote shall not be denied or abridged by the United States or by any state on account of race, color, or previous condition of servitude.

Section 2. The Congress shall have power to enforce this article by appropriate legislation.

The Fifteenth Amendment was ratified in order to enfranchise all the former male slaves. (As was the case with all women, former female slaves would have to wait for passage of the Nineteenth Amendment to gain the franchise.) Unfortunately, the promise of the franchise was subsequently undermined in many states by the proliferation of rigorous voter qualification laws, including literacy tests and poll taxes. Not until passage of the Voting Rights Act of 1965 and the elimination of poll taxes did the franchise become a reality for African American voters in many parts of the South.

Amendment XVI (1913)

The Congress shall have power to lay and collect taxes on incomes, from whatever source derived, without apportionment among the several states, and without regard to any census of enumeration.

The Sixteenth Amendment was ratified in response to the Supreme Court's controversial decision in Pollack v. Farmer's Loan & Trust Co. (1895), which held that a tax on incomes derived from property was a "direct tax." Prior to the Pollack case, income taxes had been considered "indirect" taxes, and thus well within the powers given to Congress by the Constitution. "Direct taxes," by contrast, could be imposed only if they were apportioned among the states according to each state's population (Article I, Section 9). The effect of the Pollack *decision was to make an income tax all but impractical; the Sixteenth Amendment remedied the situation by placing income taxes back in the category of "indirect taxes."*

Amendment XVII (1913)

The Senate of the United States shall be composed of two Senators from each state, elected by the people thereof, for six years; and each Senator shall have one vote. The electors in each state shall have the qualifications requisite for electors of the most numerous branch of the state legislatures.

When vacancies happen in the representation of any state in the Senate, the executive authority of such state shall issue writs of election to fill such vacancies: Provided, that the legislature of any state may empower the executive thereof to make temporary appointments until the people fill the vacancies by election as the legislature may direct.

This amendment shall not be so construed as to affect the election or term of any Senator chosen before it becomes valid as part of the Constitution.

The Seventeenth Amendment changed the method by which U.S. senators were elected, overturning the provisions in Article I, Section 3. The amendment was the culmination of an extended effort of Progressive Era reformers at the beginning of the twentieth century, who frequently targeted institutions marked by economic privilege and corrupt politics. Eventually they demanded that U.S. senators should be more responsive to the public will—the best way to accomplish that goal was to require that senators should be chosen by popular election, rather than by state legislatures. Prior to the amendment's ratification, many states had already amended their primary laws to allow a popular vote for party nominees, and a handful of states had bound their respective legislatures to select the candidate who received the highest number of popular votes in the general election. The Seventeenth Amendment soon followed, receiving the approval of the required number of states (three fourths) less than a year after it was first introduced.

Amendment XVIII (1919)

Section 1. After one year from the ratification of this article the manufacture, sale, or transportation of intoxicating liquors within, the importation thereof into, or the exportation thereof from the United States and all territory subject to the jurisdiction thereof for beverage purposes is hereby prohibited.

Section 2. The Congress and the several states shall have concurrent power to enforce this article by appropriate legislation.

Section 3. This article shall be inoperative unless it shall have been ratified as an amendment to the Constitution by the legislatures of the several states, as provided in the Constitution, within seven years from the date of the submission hereof to the states by the Congress.

The Eighteenth Amendment slipped into the Constitution on the strength of efforts by the Anti-Saloon League and other groups who believed that intoxicating liquors were harmful and sinful. The amendment was proposed immediately after the end of World War I, and the Prohibition era began a year after its formal ratification on January 16, 1919.

Amendment XIX (1920)

The right of citizens of the United States to vote shall not be denied or abridged by the United States or by any state on account of sex.

Congress shall have power to enforce this article by appropriate legislation.

The Nineteenth Amendment was a reform spurred by the Progressive movement. Although women had been fighting for their right to vote since before the Civil War, the drive for woman suffrage started achieving success only with the entry of Western states such as Wyoming, which extended the right to vote to women upon its admission to the Union in 1890. (Five other Western states followed suit in subsequent decades.) By concentrating their efforts on a federal constitutional amendment guaranteeing women the right to vote, woman suffrage activists brought immediate pressure to bear on Congress and the president to support the movement. With momentum clearly on its side, the Nineteenth Amendment was ratified less than fifteen months after it was first proposed.

Amendment XX (1933)

Section 1. The terms of the President and Vice President shall end at noon on the 20th day of January, and the terms of Senators and Representatives at noon on the 3d day of January, of the years in which such terms would have ended if this article had not been ratified; and the terms of their successors shall then begin.

Section 2. The Congress shall assemble at least once in every year, and such meeting shall begin at noon on the 3d day of January, unless they shall by law appoint a different day.

Section 3. If, at the time fixed for the beginning of the term of the President, the President elect shall have died, the Vice President elect shall become President. If a President shall not have been chosen before the time fixed for the beginning of his term, or if the President elect shall have failed to qualify, then the Vice President elect shall act as President until a President shall have qualified; and the Congress may by law provide for the case wherein neither a President elect nor a Vice President elect shall have qualified, declaring who shall then act as President, or the manner in which one who is to act shall be selected, and such person shall act accordingly until a President or Vice President shall have qualified.

Section 4. The Congress may by law provide for the case of the death of any of the persons from whom the House of Representatives may choose a President whenever the right of choice shall have devolved upon them, and for the case of the death of any of the persons from whom the Senate may choose a Vice President whenever the right of choice shall have devolved upon them.

Section 5. Sections 1 and 2 shall take effect on the 15th day of October following the ratification of this article.

Section 6. This article shall be inoperative unless it shall have been ratified as an amendment to the Constitution by the legislatures of three-fourths of the several states within seven years from the date of its submission.

The Twentieth Amendment brought an end to the excessively long period of time between the November election and the March inauguration of a new president. Given advances in transportation and communications systems over the previous century, such a delay in the president taking office—with the outgoing president reluctant to act even during times of crisis—could no longer be justified. The amendment also limited Congress's lame duck sessions that followed the November elections: newly elected members of Congress could now begin their service to constituents in early January, rather than waiting thirteen months until the following December. Finally, the amendment authorized Congress to provide for a line of succession in the event that neither a president-elect nor a vice president–elect qualified to serve by the January 20 date.

Amendment XXI (1933)

Section 1. The eighteenth article of amendment to the Constitution of the United States is hereby repealed.

Section 2. The transportation or importation into any state, territory, or possession of the United States for delivery or use therein of intoxicating liquors, in violation of the laws thereof, is hereby prohibited.

Section 3. This article shall be inoperative unless it shall have been ratified as an amendment to the Constitution by conventions in the several states, as provided in the Constitution, within seven years from the date of the submission hereof to the states by the Congress.

The Twenty-first Amendment repealed Prohibition. The enforcement of the Eighteenth Amendment had proven too difficult and expensive, as thousands of illegal sources arose to meet the continuing public demand for alcohol. Crime gangs involved in the illegal liquor trade spread violence and bloodshed throughout the nation, which pressured politicians to end Prohibition. Finally, when both political parties came out in favor of repeal during the 1932 election, Prohibition's days were clearly numbered. After the Twenty-first Amendment was ratified on December 5, 1933, states would thereafter have the exclusive power to prevent the import and use of liquor in their respective jurisdictions.

Amendment XXII (1951)

Section 1. No person shall be elected to the office of the President more than twice, and no person who has held the office of President, or acted as President, for more than two years of a term to which some other person was elected

President shall be elected to the office of the President more than once. But this article shall not apply to any person holding the office of President when this article was proposed by the Congress, and shall not prevent any person who may be holding the office of President, or acting as President, during the term within which this article becomes operative from holding the office of President or acting as President during the remainder of such term.

Section 2. This article shall be inoperative unless it shall have been ratified as an amendment to the Constitution by the legislatures of three-fourths of the several states within seven years from the date of its submission to the states by the Congress.

Franklin Roosevelt's election to a record fourth term as president in 1944 sent politicians clamoring for a means of restoring the unwritten two-term tradition originally established by George Washington. Within two years of FDR's death, Congress proposed the Twenty-second Amendment, and it was adopted soon thereafter. In addition to setting a limit on the number of terms (two) to which a president may be elected, the amendment also sets a maximum of ten years less one day for a president to serve in the event he or she also succeeds to a part of another president's term. The amendment was worded so as not to apply to the then-sitting president, Harry S. Truman, but it has applied to Dwight Eisenhower and all other presidents since.

Amendment XXIII (1961)

Section 1. The District constituting the seat of government of the United States shall appoint in such manner as the Congress may direct:

A number of electors of President and Vice President equal to the whole number of Senators and Representatives in Congress to which the District would be entitled if it were a state, but in no event more than the least populous state; they shall be in addition to those appointed by the states, but they shall be considered, for the purposes of the election of President and Vice President, to be electors appointed by a state; and they shall meet in the District and perform such duties as provided by the twelfth article of amendment.

Section 2. The Congress shall have power to enforce this article by appropriate legislation.

The Twenty-third Amendment cured the anomaly of U.S. citizens being denied the right to vote for federal officials (including president of the United States) so long as they remained permanent residents of the District of Columbia. Since ratification of the amendment in 1961, DC residents have been entitled to vote for presidential and vice-presidential candidates, but the amendment did not authorize residents of DC to elect members to either branch of Congress. Nor did it provide DC residents with home rule or the power to run their own local government. Since 1973 Congress has authorized the DC government to be run primarily by locally elected officials, subject to the oversight and supervision of Congress.

Amendment XXIV (1964)

Section 1. The right of citizens of the United States to vote in any primary or other election for President or Vice President, for electors for President or Vice President, or for Senator or Representative in Congress, shall not be denied or abridged by the United States or any state by reason of failure to pay any poll tax or other tax.

Section 2. The Congress shall have power to enforce this article by appropriate legislation.

> *The Twenty-fourth Amendment eliminated yet another vestige of legally enforced racism in the South and elsewhere. Many states had already eliminated the requirement that voters pay a tax before voting, a restriction that created an undue hardship on lower economic classes, including disproportionate numbers of racial minorities. Still, as late as 1964, five states (Alabama, Arkansas, Mississippi, Texas, and Virginia) continued to tie a poll tax to the voting privilege. In 1966 the Supreme Court ruled in* Harper v. Board of Education *that poll taxes also violated the equal protection clause of the Fourteenth Amendment.*

Amendment XXV (1967)

Section 1. In case of the removal of the President from office or of his death or resignation, the Vice President shall become President.

Section 2. Whenever there is a vacancy in the office of the Vice President, the President shall nominate a Vice President who shall take office upon confirmation by a majority vote of both Houses of Congress.

Section 3. Whenever the President transmits to the President pro tempore of the Senate and the Speaker of the House of Representatives his written declaration that he is unable to discharge the powers and duties of his office, and until he transmits to them a written declaration to the contrary, such powers and duties shall be discharged by the Vice President as Acting President.

Section 4. Whenever the Vice President and a majority of either the principal officers of the executive departments or of such other body as Congress may by law provide, transmit to the President pro tempore of the Senate and the Speaker of the House of Representatives their written declaration that the President is unable to discharge the powers and duties of his office, the Vice President shall immediately assume the powers and duties of the office as Acting President.

Thereafter, when the President transmits to the President pro tempore of the Senate and the Speaker of the House of Representatives his written declaration that no inability exists, he shall resume the powers and duties of his office unless the Vice President and a majority of either the principal officers of the executive department or of such other body as Congress may by law provide, transmit within four days to the President pro tempore of the Senate and the Speaker of the House of Representatives their written declaration that the President is unable to discharge the powers and duties of his office. Thereupon Congress shall decide the issue, assembling within forty-eight hours for that purpose if not in session. If the Congress, within twenty-one days after receipt of the latter written declaration, or, if Congress is not in session, within twenty-one days after Congress is required to assemble, determines by two-thirds vote of both Houses that the President is unable to discharge the powers and duties of his office, the Vice President shall continue to discharge the same as Acting President; otherwise, the President shall resume the powers and duties of his office.

The Twenty-fifth Amendment clarified several ambiguous aspects of presidential succession. At the outset, it formalized an unwritten precedent first established by John Tyler, who succeeded to the presidency upon the death of William Henry Harrison in 1841: If the office of president becomes vacant because of the president's death or resignation, the vice president becomes president and assumes all powers and duties of the office. If the vice presidency is vacant, the amendment establishes new procedures for filling the position between elections: The president nominates a successor, to be confirmed by a majority vote of both houses of Congress. Since its adoption in 1967, two vice presidents have been selected in this manner: Gerald Ford in 1973, and Nelson Rockefeller in 1974. When Gerald Ford succeeded to the presidency upon the resignation of Richard Nixon in 1974, he became the first—and to date, the only—president in American history to hold that office without being formally elected to either the presidency or the vice presidency.

The amendment also addresses the vexing problem of presidential disabilities. In the early twentieth century, Woodrow Wilson was an invalid for more than a year of his presidency; in the 1950s, Dwight Eisenhower suffered a stroke once during each of his two terms in office. The Twenty-fifth Amendment addresses the problem of presidential disability by providing procedures for the president to temporarily discharge the duties and powers of the office to the officer next in line (normally the vice president), who then becomes "acting president." This has happened only twice: in 1985, when Vice President George H. W. Bush received a transmission of power temporarily while President Ronald Reagan underwent a minor medical procedure; and in 2002, when President George W. Bush temporarily transferred his powers to Vice President Dick Cheney while he underwent a colonoscopy. The amendment further authorizes the vice president and certain members of the executive branch to declare the president disabled or incapacitated, subject (within twenty-seven days) to Congress upholding the finding of incapacity. This final provision has never been invoked.

Amendment XXVI (1971)

Section 1. The right of citizens of the United States, who are 18 years of age or older, to vote, shall not be denied or abridged by the United States or any state on account of age.

Section 2. The Congress shall have the power to enforce this article by appropriate legislation.

The Twenty-sixth Amendment extended suffrage to those age eighteen and older. At the time of its passage, soldiers under the age of twenty-one were fighting in Vietnam, creating intense pressure on Congress and state legislatures to extend the vote to all those who were old enough to fight. The amendment does not apply to the denial of rights other than voting to those who are between eighteen and twenty-one years of age. Thus the National Minimum Drinking Age Act of 1984 obliges states to establish a twenty-one-year-old drinking age or risk the loss of federal highway funds. Additionally, Utah and Alaska have established nineteen as the minimum age for tobacco use.

Amendment XXVII (1992)

No law, varying the compensation for the services of the Senators and Representatives, shall take effect, until an election of Representatives shall have intervened.

The Twenty-seventh Amendment was intended to serve as a restraint on the power of Congress to raise its own pay—it may only do so if the raise takes effect after a subsequent general election. Although the Supreme Court has never ruled on the issue, lower courts have held that this amendment does not prevent Congress from receiving cost of living adjustments immediately.

3 Federalism

 NOW A protester (right) expresses her feelings about the case of Terri Schiavo (below).

THEN Children working in a factory at the turn of the 20th century, before the advent of child labor laws.

NOW &THEN

Dueling Sovereign Powers in the United States

At the time of the nation's founding, worries about an excessively powerful central government threatening the states' sovereignty nearly brought a halt to the American experiment before it had even begun. Now it seemed like some of the Founders' worst fears were being realized, as Congress was attempting to interfere in a matter that until then had been under the strict control of state authorities. State officials were actually divided on the issue in question; some were shocked by the federal intrusion, whereas others welcomed federal assistance in dealing with such a difficult matter. Yet for those who favored federal influence, there was no basis either in tradition or in the words of the Constitution to support such unprecedented infringement in what appeared to be a strictly state matter. Ultimately, the courts stepped in to reassert state control over the issue, and the central government saw its hopes for influence frustrated, at least for the time being. Still, local officials had been put on notice that when Congress disagrees with a state action, that body will not stand by silently and defer without a struggle.

LEARNING OBJECTIVES
★ WHAT YOU WILL LEARN ★

What Is Federalism?

* ★ Define federalism and assess the nature of sovereignty in a federal system

* ★ Compare federalism to other systems of government, including confederations and unitary systems of government

* ★ Understand how the Constitution differentiates between federal government powers, state government powers, and concurrent powers

* ★ Recognize the powers accorded to Congress under Article I, including the necessary and proper clause

* ★ Explain the significance of the supremacy clause, the preemption doctrine, and the full faith and credit clause of Article IV in dividing sovereignty between the federal and state governments

The History of American Federalism

* ★ Define the five eras of American federalism

* ★ Assess the role played by the Supreme Court in articulating the various doctrines and frameworks that determined the relationship between the state and federal governments during the five eras of American federalism

* ★ Distinguish between different forms of federalism (layer cake federalism versus marble cake federalism) in the modern era

Why Federalism? Advantages and Disadvantages

* ★ Recognize the advantages of a system that serves a diverse array of interests

* ★ Understand the disadvantages of federalism in terms of fairness and accountability

CourseMate

NOW & THEN

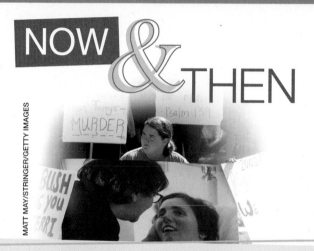

MATT MAY/STRINGER/GETTY IMAGES

NOW   It was a matter of family law, a subject traditionally controlled by state authorities. On March 31, 2005, forty-one-year-old Terri Schiavo died in a Florida hospice. Thirteen days earlier her feeding tube had been removed by court order. Schiavo first went into respiratory and cardiac arrest in 1990; temporarily denied oxygen to her brain, she fell into a short-lived coma. Although she emerged from the coma after two and a half months, Terri Schiavo would live for the next fifteen years in a persistent vegetative state, exhibiting no awareness of her environment. In 1998, Schiavo's husband and legal guardian, Michael Schiavo, petitioned to remove his wife's feeding tube on the grounds that there was no longer any hope for his wife's recovery. His petition thrust him into a protracted legal dispute with his wife's parents. Michael claimed that his wife would never have wanted to be kept alive if she were in a vegetative state; Terri's parents disagreed, and they sought a series of stays against removal of any apparatus necessary to keep their daughter alive.

On September 17, 2003, after five years of hearings, trials, and back-and-forth court orders, a Florida state judge ordered the removal of the feeding tube; less than a month later, the order was executed. Just days after the tube was removed, Florida Governor Jeb Bush ordered the tube to be reinserted in accordance with a new Florida law recently passed to give him that authority. Consistent with their earlier orders, the Florida courts struck down the law as unconstitutional and ordered the tube to be removed; the court's removal order was eventually reinstated on March 18, 2005. Yet at this point the unthinkable happened: federal authorities chose to insert themselves into the state proceedings. On March 21, 2005, President George W. Bush signed newly enacted legislation from Congress that transferred the case over to federal courts for what he hoped would be a different resolution. Unfortunately for Terri Schiavo's parents, this extra layer of federal court review proved no more fruitful, as the U.S. Court of Appeals for the Eleventh Circuit refused to overturn the state court decision. Thus on March 31, 2005, Terri Schiavo died. In the final analysis, the decision over who had the power to determine the medical fate of a patient remained with the state judiciary, Congress's efforts notwithstanding.

THEN The Terri Schiavo case was not the first instance in which the U.S. Congress intervened in a state matter when there was no legal precedent to do so. At the beginning of the twentieth century, many reformers were growing increasingly concerned about the abuses of child labor. By some accounts as many as two million children, often as young as five or six years old, were working long hours in brutal conditions for barely any compensation. In response, state legislatures around the country began passing laws limiting or banning the use of child labor. The result was a patchwork quilt of state regulations, varying in their effectiveness. Reformers in Congress became frustrated with the slow pace of reform at the state level; they wanted uniform standards imposed immediately to prohibit child labor across the nation. But a string of judicial precedents dating back one hundred years cautioned that states alone had the constitutional power to regulate the manufacturing process. Congress then tried a back-door approach to the problem by deploying its power to regulate interstate commerce under the Constitution: in 1916 it passed the Keating-Owen Child Labor Act, which banned the interstate transport of all goods made by children under age fourteen. Some state legislatures were stunned at this aggressive exercise of federal authority. But with its ruling in the case of *Hammer v. Dagenhart* (1918), the U.S. Supreme Court struck down the federal child labor law as unconstitutional. Consistent with its precedents, the Court held that Congress could not ban certain goods from entering interstate commerce, even if its intention in doing so was to regulate manufacturing.

Nineteen years later the Supreme Court—spurred in part by the harshness of the Great Depression and by the appointment of justices more disposed to defer to Congress—gave its approval to federal laws that regulated manufacturing, including new child labor laws. In the end Congress did have its say over the issue. Unfortunately for those who demanded a national solution to the problem of child labor law, conflict between federal and state sovereigns— interpreted by the Supreme Court to prohibit federal intervention in 1918—hamstrung the federal government for the better part of two decades.

LEWIS WICKES HINE/BETTMANN/CORBIS

O nly once in the nation's history have state–federal tensions ignited an all-out military conflict among the parties: the U.S. Civil War of 1861–1865. There have been countless other incidents, however, when the tensions inherent in a system of dual sovereigns have given rise to conflicts between the federal government and state authority. In addition to the Terri Schiavo case in early 2005 and the battle over child labor laws in the early part of the twentieth century, other examples of such conflicts in the not-so-distant past include the protests by many Arizona state officials against a national movement to honor Martin Luther King Jr. with a federal holiday, the movement by Georgians to hoist a state flag with the controversial confederate symbol, and the efforts by Florida state officials to hinder federal attempts to return a young emigrant named Elian Gonzalez to his father's custody in Cuba. In all such instances, tempers eventually cooled and the crisis passed. Passed, but not soon forgotten.

What Is Federalism?

★ LO Define federalism and assess the nature of sovereignty in a federal system

The term *federal* comes from the Latin *foedus*, which means a covenant or an agreement linking different entities. A federal (or federated) system of government is one in which power is divided between a central authority and constituent political subunits. Both types of government are linked to provide for the pursuit of common ends; at the same time, each government maintains its own integrity. **Federalism** is the doctrine underlying such a system. It generally requires the existence of a central government tier and at least one major subnational tier of governments (usually referred to as "states" or "provinces"). Each tier is then assigned its own significant government powers. For a system of federalism to maintain itself, it must sustain this division of powers by whatever means possible, including—but not limited to—a resort to the courts to define the proper bounds of authority.

Federalism
The doctrine underlying a system of government in which power is divided between a central government and constituent political subunits.

Perhaps the greatest challenge facing any federalist system is the task of determining **sovereignty**, defined as the supreme political power of a government to regulate its affairs without outside interference. In a system based on federalism, sovereignty resides not just in the central government but also within each of the subunits or federated states, which in the case of the United States are the individual fifty states. Yet how can there be two separate sovereign governments sharing power over the exact same territory? The distribution of national and local responsibilities to more than one sovereign power depends on how the terms *national* and *local* are defined. These definitions are important, for a government based on federalism must achieve national unity for certain overarching purposes and also preserve local governments' autonomy so they can respond to diverse subsets of citizens.

Sovereignty
The supreme political power of a government to regulate its affairs without outside interference.

Related to these issues are complex questions concerning the nature of national citizenship. American federalism rests on the principle that two separate sovereigns—the state government and the federal government—both exert authority over the individual. But can an individual citizen really be subject to two separate sovereign governments at the same time? U.S. citizens have official status as citizens of the state where they reside and of the nation as a whole. Many take pride in both associations. What remains unclear are the obligations and duties that dual citizenship requires. Is national citizenship every citizen's primary form of identification? To which sovereign government is the citizen obligated when the nation and individual states are in conflict? Although these conceptual difficulties tend to be unique to a federal system, there are other forms of government that involve multiple governments or tiers of government, and these alternative forms have significant problems of their own.

Comparing Federalism to Other Systems of Government

★ LO

Compare federalism to other systems of government, including confederations and unitary systems of government

A federal system of government can be thought of as existing on a continuum of different forms of government. At one end of the continuum is a **confederation** (or "confederacy"), defined as a league of two or more independent states that unite to achieve certain specified common aims. Those aims may be quite limited, as is often the case with offensive or defensive military alliances. For example, the Articles of Confederation, which prescribed the rules of government for the newly independent colonies until 1788, featured thirteen states entering into "a firm league of friendship with each other, for their common defense, the security of their liberties, and their mutual and general welfare.. . ." Recently, the European Union, a collection of European nations united in a commercial alliance, has acquired its own status as a type of confederation.[1] Similarly, the United Nations is a league of countries from around the world that work together to enforce various provisions of international law. Although a confederation may be a useful arrangement to achieve some aims, it can result in political chaos, as when separate member countries bound only by limited rules strike out on their own at critical times, often to the detriment of the larger confederation.

Confederation
A system of government (or "league") in which two or more independent states unite to achieve certain specified common aims.

At the other end of the continuum is a **unitary system of government**, which subordinates the independent aims of constituent states (if any even exist) to the goals of the central whole. Although individual states within such a government may enjoy some form of representation in the central legislature (such as through the election of state senators) and may even assert their own systems of municipal law, sovereignty rests in the central government alone, with states exerting authority over citizens only through the larger government entity. Of the Western industrialized nations, Great Britain and France come closest to this unitary government ideal, with their provinces and subunits having little or no power independent of the national government. Problems with a unitary system of government often arise from the tendency toward hypercentralism—that is, the more or less complete reliance on the central government and the extinguishing of individual state differences. Such a system often hampers local officials from responding to the particular needs of their varying constituencies.

Unitary system of government
A system of government in which the constituent states are strictly subordinated to the goals of the central government as a whole.

A federal system of government is in the middle of this continuum, granting its member states significant power but still subordinating them to the national government in critical instances. James Madison believed this federal system was the preferred "middle ground" of government types. At least twenty countries today, including Canada, Germany, Australia, and Switzerland, may be characterized as federal systems. The United States' brand of federalism, however—first established with the ratification of the Constitution in 1788—represents the most significant breakthrough in the evolution of this government type among modern nation-states.

★ LO Understand how the Constitution differentiates between federal government powers, state government powers, and concurrent powers

Reserved powers
Those powers expressly retained by the state governments under the Constitution.

Concurrent powers
Those powers shared by the federal and state governments under the Constitution.

Government Powers in a Federal System

Under the U.S. Constitution, the national government of the United States was formed to serve a community of thirteen states, and each state delegated to the new central government significant powers while retaining full powers within its own constitutionally designated sphere of authority. The framers of this new government relied on no overarching philosophy or political theory in designing this federalist form of government; federalism was simply a political compromise calculated to build consensus among them. The powers delegated to Congress in Article I, Section 8 of the Constitution are called enumerated powers. The last clause of Section 8 also gives Congress the prerogative to make laws that are "necessary and proper" to carry out its enumerated powers.[2] The powers retained by the states are **reserved powers**. The powers shared by the federal and state governments are generally referred to as **concurrent powers**. Table 3.1 lists the specific powers held by the federal and state governments and the powers they share.

On its face, the Constitution appears to draw clear and explicit lines between the powers afforded the state and national governments. In brief, the national government assumes responsibility for matters of great national

TABLE 3.1 The Powers of the Federal and State Governments under the Constitution

Federal Government Powers (Enumerated Powers)	State Government Powers (Reserved Powers)	Powers Shared by Federal and State Governments (Concurrent Powers)
Borrow money on U.S. credit	Regulate intrastate commerce	Spend money for the general welfare
Regulate foreign commerce	Regulate state militias	Regulate interstate commerce
Regulate commerce with Indian nations	Conduct elections, qualify voters	Establish bankruptcy laws
Conduct foreign affairs	Regulate safety, health, morals	Lay and collect taxes
Coin money, punish counterfeiting	Ratify amendments to the U.S. Constitution	Charter, regulate banks
Establish courts inferior to U.S. Supreme Court		Establish courts
Establish post offices		Establish highways
Establish patent, copyright laws		Take private property for public purposes (with compensation)
Define, punish offenses on the high seas		
Declare war		
Raise and support armies, navies		
Call forth militias		
Govern District of Columbia matters		
Admit new states to Union		
Establish rules of naturalization		

Comparing Views of Federal, State, and Local Government

Surveys conducted by the Pew Research Center for the People and the Press monitor Americans' views of the performance of federal, state, and local governments. As the figure below demonstrates, Americans hold their local and state governments in fairly high esteem. However, positive views of the federal government in 2009 were relatively low by recent standards. Only 42 percent of people said they held a favorable view of the federal government, which is down significantly from 2002, when 64 percent held a favorable opinion. By contrast, 50 percent held favorable views of their state governments and 60 percent held favorable views of their local governments in 2009.

The public's favorable opinion of the federal government in 2002 (favorable opinions outnumbered unfavorable opinions that year by 64 to 27 percent) was a product of the rally-around-the-flag sentiment generated in the months following the terrorist attacks of September 11, 2001. In most years since 2000, state and local governments have fared much better than the federal government in the eyes of the public.

"Now, I'd like your opinion of some organizations and institutions . . . is your overall opinion of (the federal government/your state government/your local government) very favorable, mostly favorable, mostly unfavorable, or very unfavorable?"

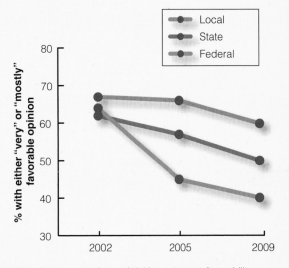

Source: Pew Research Center for the People and the Press, http://people-press.org/report/534/government-favorability.

importance, including the protection of national economic interests, relations with other countries, and the military security of the United States. All local and/or internal matters—including the health, safety, and welfare of citizens—are the province of state governments. Indeed, in a delayed victory for states' rights advocates who had opposed the new Constitution, the Tenth Amendment restates this fundamental division of powers: Any specific power not assigned to the federal government by the Constitution may be exercised by the states, unless the Constitution prohibits the states from exercising that power.

The framers of the Constitution believed that Congress should legislate only within its enumerated powers under Article I; in their view, the **necessary and proper clause** (later referred to as the elastic clause) was *not* to be used as an instrument to expand federal legislative authority unnecessarily. Yet within a few years, competing views of the necessary and proper clause would arise, giving the national government far more discretion in determining how to carry out its enumerated powers.

★ **LO**

Recognize the powers accorded to Congress under Article I, including the necessary and proper clause

Necessary and proper clause
The clause in Article I, Section 8 of the Constitution that affords Congress the power to make laws that serve as a means to achieving its expressly delegated powers.

The Supremacy Clause

Supremacy clause
The provision in Article VI, Clause 2 of the Constitution that provides that the Constitution and federal laws override any conflicting provisions in state constitutions or state laws.

Overlaying this explicit system of enumerated powers for Congress and reserved powers for the states is the **supremacy clause** of Article VI, which provides that the Constitution and the laws passed by Congress shall be "the supreme law of the land," overriding any conflicting provisions in state constitutions or state laws. The supremacy clause gives special weight to the federal Constitution by ensuring that it cannot be interpreted differently from state to state.

The language of the supremacy clause also gives rise to the doctrine of preemption. When Congress exercises power granted to it under Article I, the federal law it creates may supersede state laws, in effect "preempting" state authority. In practice, when a federal law clearly bars state action, the doctrine of **preemption** is relatively uncontroversial. For example, when the federal government acted to regulate the commercial advertising of tobacco products, it essentially "occupied the field," and all state rules governing tobacco advertising immediately gave way to the new federal standard. But when Congress enacts a law that does not clearly articulate its intentions with regard to state laws, a court may have to decide whether the doctrine of preemption applies, subject to later court review. In addition, Congress's lack of action within its enumerated powers opens the door to limited state regulations. For example, a state government can enact transportation regulations affecting truck drivers in the state as long as Congress has not passed any similar laws and the state law does not burden interstate commerce.

Preemption
The constitutional doctrine that holds that when Congress acts affirmatively in the exercise of its own granted power, federal laws supersede all state laws on the matter.

Relations between the States

★ **LO** Explain the significance of the supremacy clause, the preemption doctrine, and the full faith and credit clause of Article IV in dividing sovereignty between the federal and state governments

A federalist system must not only manage relations between the state governments and the federal government, but it must also arbitrate disagreements among member states. A feature of American federalism in this regard is the requirement that individual states must respect the civil laws of all other states, as guaranteed by the **full faith and credit clause** of Article IV, Section 1 of the Constitution. This clause provides that each state abide by the decisions of other state and local governments, including their judicial proceedings. The clause acts to assure stability in commercial and personal relations that extend beyond one state's borders. For example, contracts duly entered into in California under the laws of that state cannot be ignored or invalidated by the courts in Arizona or any other state. Similarly, when an unhappy married couple meets the legal requirements of divorce in one state and ends their marriage, they are not required to meet new divorce requirements in other states, as the divorce decree of one state must be recognized as valid by every other state.

Full faith and credit clause
The provision in Article IV, Section 1 of the Constitution that forces states to abide by the official acts and proceedings of all other states.

In recent years, the proliferation of more controversial family law provisions, such as gay marriage laws, has placed considerable strain on the full faith and credit clause of Article IV. Vermont in 2000 was the first state to sanction so-called civil unions between same-sex partners; a handful of states eventually followed suit in authorizing these types of domestic partnerships. Then, on November 18, 2003, Massachusetts became the first state in the nation to provide for same-sex marriages by decree of its Supreme Judicial Court.[3] Since then at least four other states (New Hampshire, Connecticut, Iowa, and Vermont) and the District of Columbia have legalized marriages for same-sex couples;[4] at the time of this writing, federal courts were busy considering whether a California

The Real-life Benefits of Attending College Close to Home

Many high school seniors dream of attending colleges or universities in distant and exotic locations, far from the watchful eyes of parents or guardians who may be footing the bill. Did you ever dream of attending the University of Hawaii . . . or perhaps the Florida Keys Community College?

While admission standards to such schools may or may not pose an obstacle, the bigger issue may be financial. State legislatures try to attract in-state students by offering lower-cost in-state tuition: They know that those students will often stay in the state after graduation and secure good jobs, contributing to the state's economy. For example, if you live in Wisconsin, and you want to go to the University of Rhode Island, your college tuition in 2008 would have cost you $23,038. But if you were from Rhode Island, it would cost you only

$8,184. UCLA offers perhaps the biggest home-state discount in the country: $26,658 per year for out-of-staters, as compared to just $7,038 in tuition for California residents.

For Critical Thinking and Discussion

1. Did you consider attending (or are you currently attending) a school far from your own home state?

2. As a high school senior, did you know about the significant disparities in tuition charged by some public universities to students from other states?

3. Should states be allowed to discriminate against out-of-state applicants?

Constitutional provision banning same-sex marriage violates the equal protection clause; meanwhile, three other states (New York, Rhode Island, and Maryland) recognize same-sex marriages performed in other states while not actually granting same-sex marriage licenses. Unlike civil unions, full-fledged gay marriage laws allow same-sex couples to gain formal state recognition on an equal plane with everyone else under the traditionally accepted institution of "marriage." Opponents of same-sex marriage contend that equating same-sex and opposite-sex marriage in this way changes the meaning of marriage and its traditions.

Even though the full faith and credit clause has traditionally required states to respect the public proceedings of every other state, many state legislatures have attempted to prevent same-sex couples from asserting their newfound status as married couples. At least thirty states have passed laws denying recognition to same-sex marriages. Legislatures in most other states, including some of those that have sanctioned civil unions, considered but ultimately failed to pass laws of their own that would have denied legal recognition to such out-of-state, same-sex marriages.

Another clause that provides for the equal treatment of out-of-state citizens is the privileges and immunities clause of Article IV. Through this clause,

Gay marriage ceremony in Massachusetts.

AP PHOTO/ELISE AMENDOLA

which guarantees that the citizens of each state are "entitled to all Privileges and Immunities of Citizens in the several States," the Constitution protects the rights of every citizen to travel through other states, to reside in any state, and to participate in trade, agriculture, and professional pursuits in any state.[5] Some states have tried to limit bar memberships to in-state residents or to impose hefty commuter taxes on out-of-staters who cross state lines each day for work. Such legislative efforts potentially conflict with the privileges and immunities clause. Article IV also provides that the criminal laws of individual states must be respected across state lines. When a criminal in one state escapes to another state, he or she is normally *extradited*, or handed over to the original state either to stand trial or to complete a previously imposed sentence.

The History of American Federalism

★ LO Define the five eras of American federalism

In the more than two centuries that have passed since the ratification of the Constitution, different conceptions of federalism have prevailed during different eras. Some of these shifting patterns in state–federal relations were inevitable given the changing state of the nation and the increasingly important role it would play in world politics. The dominance of a global economy in the late twentieth and early twenty-first centuries, changing patterns in population growth, and technological developments in communication and transportation all spurred wholesale reexamination of the nature of federal and state governmental functions. Various government figures—presidents, Supreme Court justices, and members of Congress—have also played a role in shaping the nature of federalism. The flexibility of the federalist system has allowed it to adapt to changing circumstances.

Although a clear delineation of periods may oversimplify history, scholars have identified at least five eras of American federalism: (1) state-centered federalism, 1789–1819; (2) national supremacy period, 1819–1837; (3) dual federalism, 1837–1937; (4) cooperative federalism, 1937–1990; and (5) the "new federalism," 1990–present. Each of these periods is defined by some shift in the power relationship between the national and state governments.

State-Centered Federalism, 1789–1819

The framers' vision of federalism was relatively clear at the time the Constitution was ratified: Other than in those policy areas clearly identified in Article I as subject to the national government's control (the military, foreign affairs, creation of currency, and so on), state governments would have full sovereignty over all other matters. Indeed, it is tough to imagine the Constitution being ratified by the requisite number of states had it called for any further subordination of traditional state authority. With some notable exceptions, the national government's reach was exceedingly limited during the first thirty years of the Constitution's history.[6] For the most part, each state managed its own affairs, often with little interference from the federal government.

President Thomas Jefferson took office in 1801 on the strength of a campaign in which his party, the Democratic-Republicans, offered to curtail the national government's occasional excesses, such as its passage of the Alien and Sedition Acts of 1798, which (among other things) punished individuals who criticized the national government. Jefferson articulated his own "principled distaste" for centralized authority. Notwithstanding his administration's authorization of funds to purchase the Louisiana Territory from France for $15 million, thereby doubling the size of the United States and speeding westward development, federal government functions during Jefferson's administration were usually linked to enumerated national powers. State governments exercised a nearly exclusive role in the administration of education, family and criminal law, civil and property rights, elections, and labor relations during this same period.

National Supremacy Period, 1819–1837

Just before leaving office in 1801, President John Adams installed as chief justice of the United States a fellow nationalist, John Marshall of Virginia. That appointment may have been the most significant act of Adams's presidency; although the Federalists would never again occupy the White House or control Congress, the national government–oriented party would influence American politics through Chief Justice Marshall for the next three decades.

Marshall's **national supremacy doctrine** of federalism is most evident in the Supreme Court decision in ***McCulloch v. Maryland* (1819)**,[7] which concerned the national bank of the United States. As secretary of the treasury during the Washington administration, Alexander Hamilton successfully pushed for Congress to charter the first bank of the United States in 1792, arguing that such an institution would help provide for a sound national currency and a national system of credit. American efforts to obtain needed financial resources throughout the War of 1812 spurred many in the Democratic-Republican Party, including President James Madison, to support the chartering of a second national bank in 1816.

Yet the bank was unpopular in many states where state-chartered banks were forced to compete (often unsuccessfully) with local branches of the national bank for business and influence. The Maryland legislature passed a law that levied taxes on the notes of all banks—including the Baltimore branch of the national bank—that were not chartered by the state. When James W. McCulloch, the cashier for the national bank's Baltimore branch, refused to pay the tax, Maryland sued and won in its own state courts, setting up a monumental showdown on the future of the bank in the U.S. Supreme Court.

Writing for a unanimous 7–0 Supreme Court on March 6, 1819, Chief Justice John Marshall upheld the constitutionality of the bank. According to Marshall, the necessary and proper clause of the Constitution gave Congress the power to do nearly anything it wanted as long as it was a means to exercising its expressly delegated powers, which included the power to borrow money and regulate interstate commerce. The Maryland tax amounted to an unconstitutional interference with national supremacy. "The power to tax involves the power to destroy," the Court declared. Marshall used the occasion of the Court's ruling to articulate a broad vision of the national government's power, asserting that the national government could exercise its powers flexibly to meet the unexpected problems of changing national times. "This . . . is . . . a constitution we are expounding," Marshall noted, "intended to endure for ages to come, and consequently, to be adapted to the various crises of human affairs." According to Marshall, the Constitution altered the position of the states; no longer were they sovereign entities on a par with the federal government. Within the sphere of its own powers, Congress was supreme.

★ LO

Assess the role played by the Supreme Court in articulating the various doctrines and frameworks that determined the relationship between the state and federal governments during the five eras of American federalism

National supremacy doctrine
Chief Justice John Marshall's interpretation of federalism as holding that states have extremely limited sovereign authority, whereas Congress is supreme within its own sphere of constitutional authority.

McCulloch v. Maryland (1819)
The Supreme Court case that established that Congress enjoys broad and extensive authority to make all laws that are "necessary and proper" to carry out its constitutionally delegated powers.

Portrait of John Calhoun, circa 1830.

Gibbons v. Ogden (1824)
The Supreme Court case that held that under the Constitution a federal license to operate steamboats overrides a state-granted monopoly of New York waters.

Marshall's Court also refuted the power of state courts to interpret and apply the Constitution in ways that conflicted with the Supreme Court's own interpretations. Thus, the Constitution assumed its status as the uniform governing law of all the states. To Marshall, the Court's duty was not to preserve state sovereignty but rather "to protect national power against state encroachments." Consistent with this view, the Marshall Court routinely interpreted Congress's legislative authority quite broadly. In ***Gibbons v. Ogden* (1824),**[8] for example, the Court invalidated a monopoly granted by the New York legislature covering the operation of steamboats in New York waters because the New York monopoly was in conflict with a federal license.

The national supremacy doctrine articulated by Marshall was not without its critics. State politicians accused the Court of ignoring the sovereign power of the states. Some national politicians were no less sympathetic. As president, Andrew Jackson opposed the national bank and all internal improvements (such as the building of roads or canals) ordered by Congress as unconstitutional. He even vetoed a rechartering of the bank in 1832. Yet at the same time, he also applied Marshall's national supremacy doctrine in defending the Tariff of 1828. After Congress passed a highly protectionist tariff over the objections of southern free-trade adherents, the South Carolina legislature adopted a series of resolutions negating the tariff on the theory that state sovereignty allowed each state to nullify any law passed by Congress that the state deemed unconstitutional. (New Englanders had used that same argument during the War of 1812 when a convention of the region's states met in Hartford, Connecticut, in early 1815 and endorsed the right of states to interpose themselves against "dangerous infractions" of the Constitution by the federal government.) In response to the action by South Carolina, President Jackson declared that such a nullification was an "impractical absurdity" and rejected the right of individual states to refuse to obey federal laws. A call by South Carolina Senator John Calhoun and others for a "general convention of the states" to reconsider state–federal relations, including possible secession from the Union, elicited enthusiasm from numerous southern states, but eventually, the nullification crisis passed when Congress approved a compromise tariff that progressively lowered rates until they reached their 1816 level.[9]

Dual Federalism, 1837–1937

Marshall's successor as chief justice, Roger B. Taney of Maryland, dedicated much of his twenty-eight-year tenure (1836–1864) on the Court to rearticulating a vision of federalism more consistent with that of the framers. The Taney Court was not a radical champion of state sovereignty. But Taney did abandon the more sweeping aspects of the national supremacy doctrine, which had heralded the federal government as "superior" to state governments. Instead, he maintained that the Constitution was a "compact of sovereign states," with the powers reserved to the states by the Tenth Amendment serving as a limit on congressional power.

Although slavery was a crucial component of the fight between the Union and the Confederacy, the Civil War was at its core a struggle about the relationship between the states and the federal government. The Union's victory undermined dual federalism's "compact of states" premise by rejecting the authority of states to leave the compact. Then, in a series of cases handed down after the Civil War, a newly constituted Supreme Court acknowledged national power and congressional authority to set the terms for readmitting former Confederate states into the Union. This power was considered an outgrowth of Congress's exclusive and unquestioned authority not only to regulate the territories of the United States but also to oversee the admission of new states to the Union. With twenty-four of the fifty states joining the Union between 1836 and 1912, admission to statehood was an important function of the federal government during this period.

Under **dual federalism**, however, the states retained considerable authority to regulate economic affairs that were not directly within the "stream of commerce" between two or more states, including matters concerning the manufacturing of products and the health and safety of factory workers. Ignoring *McCulloch v. Maryland*, the Supreme Court refused to give Congress the discretionary authority it enjoyed during the national supremacy era. Regulatory legislation passed by Congress, such as the child labor laws discussed at the beginning of this chapter, was set aside as unconstitutional. Once again, the Court had greatly diminished the scope of the necessary and proper clause. Despite the onset of the Industrial Revolution, Congress was eventually rendered helpless to regulate the abuses of some businesses. Later, in the 1930s, the Court struck down a series of New Deal laws implementing pension and retirement systems for workers and regulating industrial relations.[10] In this way, dual federalism prevented Congress from addressing the hardships brought on by the Great Depression.

Dual federalism
The doctrine of federalism that holds that state authority acts as a limit on congressional power under the Constitution.

Cooperative Federalism, 1937–1990

Faced with judicial opposition to New Deal policies regulating the workplace, retirement policies, and other subjects traditionally ceded to the states, President Franklin D. Roosevelt (FDR) and his supporters grew increasingly frustrated. To them, the economic hardships of the Great Depression demanded an activist federal government, and a conservative Supreme Court now stood in the way. FDR and his allies in Congress proposed expanding the size of the Supreme Court from nine to fifteen, a move that would allow Roosevelt to "pack" the Supreme Court with advocates of a broader vision of federal legislative power.[11] The proposed "court-packing plan" became unnecessary, however. As public frustration with the Court was mounting, one member of the Court in 1937 (Justice Owen Roberts) suddenly did an about-face, abandoning dual federalist principles in favor of a more expansive view of congressional authority. A shift in just one vote had a significant impact; a shift in two votes on the Supreme Court meant that nearly all federal legislation would now survive high-court scrutiny. Once Roosevelt was able to add his own judicial appointees to the mix, the Court as a whole was ready to support unprecedented exercises of congressional power.

★ **LO**

Distinguish between different forms of federalism (layer cake federalism versus marble cake federalism) in the modern era

Layer cake federalism
Description of federalism as maintaining that the authority of state and federal governments exists in distinct and separate spheres.

Marble cake federalism
Description of federalism as intertwining state and federal authority in an inseparable mixture.

Cooperative federalism
The doctrine of federalism that affords Congress nearly unlimited authority to exercise its powers through means that often coerce states into administering and/or enforcing federal policies.

Social scientists speak of the post–New Deal period as marking a shift from **layer cake federalism**, in which the authority of state and federal governments is distinct and more easily delineated, to a system of **marble cake federalism**, in which state and federal authority are intertwined in an inseparable mixture. This new era, later labeled as the period of **cooperative federalism**, in some ways harkened back to the national supremacy doctrine articulated by John Marshall. Congress once again became the judge of its own powers, including those powers implied under the necessary and proper clause. Congress could, for example, restrict the activities of labor unions, criminalize loan sharking, or enact any policy under the theory that it may be "necessary and proper" to exercise enumerated powers such as the power to regulate interstate commerce. The limits on congressional power under so-called cooperative federalism were thus quite small: As long as some link to commerce could be offered, for example, no matter how tenuous such a link might be, Congress remained free to exert its authority over the states. When Congress passed civil rights laws in 1964 under the premise that racial discrimination in restaurants and hotels "burdened" interstate commerce, the Supreme Court barely batted an eye at what was in fact an extremely broad reading of congressional authority.[12]

Cooperative federalism, however, can be distinguished from Marshall's doctrine of national superiority. Whenever concurrent legislative power is exercised, Congress can act in one of three ways. It can

1. Preempt the states altogether and assert exclusive control over the subject matter;

2. Leave the states to act on their own;

3. Provide that the operation of its own law depends on or is qualified by existing state laws.

This last category provides an opening in state–federal relationships that even Marshall could not have anticipated: the possibility that the federal government might actually enlist state officials and other state actors to implement federal policies.

The positive aspects of cooperative federalism are obvious. The expansion of the central government beginning in the 1930s into the $2.5 trillion per year behemoth that it is today means that federal officials now have huge sums of money at their disposal. Individual states can benefit from this pool of funds whenever the federal government passes on some of its revenues directly to the states to initiate and administer programs. **Grants-in-aid** from the federal government to the states have been used to fund state educational initiatives, build roads, and provide unemployment relief, among other programs that fulfill purposes expressly approved by Congress and/or its federal regulatory agencies. Federal grants also help balance the economic inequities that arise because states have vastly different tax bases. Occasionally, the federal government has transformed grants-in-aid, which are allocated only for specific programs or policies, into **block grants**, which a state or local government may use at its discretion for more generalized programs.

The collaboration between state governments and the federal government in the era of cooperative federalism carried some negative implications for state sovereignty. Federal government officials increasingly insisted that

Grants-in-aid
Grants from the federal government to states that allow state governments to pursue specific federal policies such as highway construction.

Block grants
Grants from the federal government to the states that may be used at the discretion of states to pursue more generalized aims.

federal appropriations to the states be accompanied by various conditions. Often, these consisted of "protective conditions," designed to ensure that the state would administer its program consistent with the objectives of Congress. For example, Congress required that states receiving educational assistance meet federal requirements for educating children with disabilities, including the creation of individualized education programs for students with special needs.

On occasion, however, Congress has imposed coercive burdens on states that increasingly rely on such federal assistance. In 1984, for example, Congress passed the National Minimum Drinking Age Amendment, which withheld 5 percent of federal highway funds from any state "in which the purchase or public possession of any alcoholic beverage by a person who is less than 21 years of age" is lawful. The purpose of the law was to decrease the number of serious automobile accidents among those aged eighteen to twenty; statistics showed that this group was responsible for a high percentage of accidents on the nation's highways. All the states but South Dakota rushed to comply with the directive. South Dakota then sued to keep its highway funds, asserting that the law was "coercive" and exceeded Congress's constitutional powers of taxation and spending. By a 7–2 decision, the Supreme Court rejected South Dakota's claim. With its highway funds threatened, the South Dakota legislature voted to raise the drinking age in the state.

Although the conditions imposed by the National Minimum Drinking Age Amendment essentially coerced state governments to pass laws at the behest of the federal government, the Supreme Court generally approved of such tactics. Yet when Ronald Reagan was elected president in 1980, he openly trumpeted federal initiatives to return policymaking authority to the states. In his first State of the Union Address in early 1981, Reagan proposed to terminate the federal role in welfare and return to the states forty-three other major federal grant programs.

The voluntary transfer of power by the central government to state or local governments is known as "devolution."[13] If Reagan's proposals had been fully implemented, such a large-scale devolution of federal programs would have returned federal–state relations to the version of federalism that existed before the New Deal. As it turned out, however, strong resistance from the Democratic-controlled House led to the defeat of many of Reagan's devolution initiatives. Nonetheless, Reagan administration rhetoric emphasizing federal deregulation and increased state responsibilities set the stage for more sweeping reforms to be implemented in the years ahead.

The "New Federalism," 1990–Present

Scholars assessing the state of federalism since 1990 have failed to reach a consensus on the proper label for characterizing what appears to be a counterthrust favoring states' rights in certain areas. This new era of federal–state

"Sorry, but all my power's been turned back to the states."

1981 *New Yorker* cartoon depicting President Ronald Reagan's plans to return some federal programs to the states.

When Must the Federal Government Put State Governments in Their Place?

Citizens of the United States are also citizens of one of the fifty states. Policies in the states are by no means uniform. Notwithstanding some of the uniform testing requirements imposed by federal "No Child Left Behind" legislation, educational policy differs widely from state to state. So too will an individual accused of a crime find one state's criminal justice system far more onerous and difficult than another. The federal government (which includes federal courts) has occasionally stepped in to smooth out those differences, much to the chagrin of states that prefer to maintain their own unique identity on specific issues. Sometimes uniformity is favored as a matter of good policy; at other times it may be mandated by the Constitution itself. This delicate balancing act between state interests and the need to maintain states' unique political and cultural identities has never been easy to maintain.

In 1850, Congress debated a legislative compromise at a time when Northern and Southern senators were growing increasingly anxious about the future course of slavery in the United States. Though Southern legislators recognized the right of Northern states to forbid slavery, they rejected all efforts to undermine Southern laws that allowed the practice. Especially controversial were "personal liberty laws" passed by Northern states, which mandated a jury trial before fugitive slaves could be moved. (Northern juries often refused to convict those indicted under runaway slave laws). Other states forbade the use of local jails or the assistance of state officials in the arrest or return of such fugitives. Eventually Congress passed the Fugitive Slave Act of 1850 to redress the conflict: Now federal marshals could be held liable for not enforcing runaway slave laws, and former slaves could not request jury trials. In this instance Congress did not mandate uniform laws on slavery; it did, however, bring Northern states into line with the clear expectations of Southern states. A fugitive slave act could shift legal requirements, but it proved to have little effect on

relations has been marked by a resuscitation of state authority, helped by a Supreme Court which, since the early 1990s, has been far more attentive to protecting states' rights.[14] The modern Court's decisions on federalism fit into a number of different categories.

First, although the Supreme Court has continued to allow Congress to place conditions on federal appropriations to the states, it put a stop to coercive conditions that leave the states with no discretion to form their own policies. Faced with the difficult challenge of encouraging states to build radioactive-waste dumps within their own borders, Congress in the mid to late 1980s passed a series of laws that created monetary and other forms of incentives for states to assume that responsibility. Even more extreme, Congress warned that states that shirked their responsibility on the matter might be forced to assume legal ownership of the waste from private companies and thereafter incur all the legal liability that would arise from its hazards. In *New York v. United States* (1992), the Supreme Court ruled that this final provision crossed the line and was unconstitutionally coercive.[15] Recent Supreme Court decisions have also prevented Congress from requiring state officials to implement or carry out federal policies; when the Brady Bill required that local sheriffs conduct background checks of gun purchasers, the Supreme Court in *Printz v. United States* (1997) struck down that provision as unconstitutional.[16]

Northern sentiments. The Northerners' refusal to assist with runaway slaves proved one of many factors that precipitated the outbreak of the Civil War a decade later.

In 1963, uniformity in the treatment of criminal defendants was squarely at issue before the U.S. Supreme Court. By late 1962, close to half of the states were automatically providing indigent defendants a right to counsel whenever jail time was a possibility. In fact, in the landmark Supreme Court case of *Gideon v. Wainwright* (1963), twenty-two of those states urged the Court to adopt this right as a federal standard. By contrast, many states (including Florida) provided such counsel only on a case-by-case basis—if an indigent defendant seemed competent enough to try his or her own case, judges usually insisted that he or she do so. Could such a patchwork of protections stand under the Sixth Amendment? "No," said the Supreme Court, which in 1963 effectively nationalized the requirement that counsel be provided to indigent defendants. Following the landmark *Gideon* decision, the 1960s witnessed the creation of public defenders programs across the country.

In 2010, the U.S. Supreme Court once again inserted itself into a social and cultural debate where individual feelings tend to run high. This time the issue was gun control. In 2007 the Court ruled that the Second Amendment protects an individual's right to possess a firearm for public use. Its ruling was limited, however, to federal restrictions on firearms (in that case it was a DC law); the Supreme Court did not address whether the Second Amendment applied to state laws as well under the process known as *incorporation*. (Incorporation is discussed in detail in Chapter 4). Certainly the possession of firearms has different implications for residents of the South Bronx than it does for residents of rural farmland in Wyoming. Does the Fourteenth Amendment hold all governments accountable to the protections afforded by the Second Amendment? The Supreme Court's answer was "yes." On June 28, 2010, the Court held in *McDonald v. Chicago* (2010) that the Second Amendment right to bear arms applies to all fifty states as well as the District of Columbia.

Second, since the mid-1990s, Congress's virtually unlimited authority to regulate interstate commerce has been scaled back somewhat. In *United States v. Lopez* (1995), the Supreme Court declared that Congress could not ban guns in school zones.[17] Whereas during the cooperative federalism era Congress regulated all manner of criminal and social activities, the present-day Supreme Court has more strenuously insisted that Congress show a clear connection with commerce when exercising its power to regulate interstate commerce. Then, in 1997, Congress ran into more obstacles when it enacted a law entitling sexual assault victims to sue their perpetrators in federal court. Once again, the Supreme Court stood firm for state sovereignty, ruling in *United States v. Morrison* (2000) that the law was unconstitutional on the grounds that domestic abuse had only a slight connection to commerce.[18]

Third, a series of recent Supreme Court decisions has scaled back the doctrine of preemption, at least as applied to Congress's regulation of state government workers and employees. In *Alden v. Maine* (1999), the Supreme Court refused Congress the authority to allow private citizens to sue state governments for damages when the state fails to pay minimum wages required under federal law.[19] A year later, the Supreme Court issued a similar ruling, disallowing private lawsuits against state governments that violated federal age discrimination laws.

Old Rivals Georgia and Florida Do Battle in a Brand New Venue

Free trade between the United States and Latin American countries is theoretically the province of the federal government. Reality tends to be a bit more complicated. In 2003, talks began among thirty-four countries in the Americas to propose an extension of the North American Free Trade Agreement (NAFTA) to countries in Central America and South America as well. The location of this proposed Free Trade Area of America (FTAA) headquarters caused a bit of controversy, however. The city of Miami, Florida, believed it would be a shoo-in for the headquarters, and the Florida state government—with so much to gain from the FTAA—tried mightily to secure Miami as the headquarters. The U.S. government, concerned about the massive anti-corporatization and anti-globalization protests that had taken place at the

FTAA negotiations held in Miami and elsewhere, generally steered clear of these lobbying efforts. The federal government was apparently concerned not just about the possibility of violence; it also wanted to stay neutral in a contest among Florida, Georgia, and other states and cities, all vying to be the FTAA headquarters.

Where does this leave Latin American countries concerned that the U.S. government's "neutrality" about the headquarters site creates a vacuum that may slow down, if not outright derail, the process? Simon Romero, a *New York Times* journalist who currently lives and works in Caracas, Venezuela, tried to capture the Latin American perspective on this competition being waged between the states of Georgia and Florida (his article was reprinted in the *Latin-American Post*):

> If it seems like Mr. [Jorge] Arrizurieta [a Florida-born American working on behalf of his home state] is maintaining a busy traveling schedule, his counterpart in Atlanta, José Ignacio

Why Federalism? Advantages and Disadvantages

Supporters of federalism point to several advantages offered by this form of government, and opponents of federalism counter with arguments of their own concerning the disadvantages of this form of government.

★ LO   Recognize the advantages of a system that serves a diverse array of interests

Advantages of Federalism

Supporters of federalism cite among the specific advantages of this form of government that it is more likely to accommodate the needs of a diverse citizenry, to strengthen liberty by dividing powers between levels of government, to encourage experimentation, and to respond to change.

- **Accommodation of diversity.** If a unitary system of government threatens to treat citizens of different states as interchangeable parts for purposes of quick and easy administration, federalism acts as an important counterbalance to this trend. A citizen of the United States can also take pride in being a citizen of Texas or some other state with a clearly defined culture or character. State and local politicians can perhaps respond to the specific demands or needs of its citizens better than a central government can. The culture of a state may be reflected in that state's handgun control laws, its rules on the

González, is just as frenzied . . . Mr. González and Mr. Arrizurieta crossed paths as they met with the president of Uruguay, Jorge Batlle, and other government representatives on the same day in late August in Montevideo, the Uruguayan capital. Though they did not see each other, they heard of each other's movements from the officials they were meeting with, both men said . . . Mr. Batlle later endorsed Miami's bid, becoming the first government leader in the region to publicly side with any city, even though it is ultimately the Uruguayan trade minister who will put forward his position in a consensus process involving negotiators from throughout the region . . .

Mr. González, the [Georgia] envoy, has taken a different approach from Mr. Arrizurieta's by declining to discuss the negative attributes of his competitors in favor of promoting Atlanta's advantages. "Initially," he said in an interview, "Atlanta might not seem like the most obvious choice but we bring the most to the table

economically, culturally and historically." . . . Atlanta, buoyed by support from local and state political leaders, appears to be doing fairly well in increasing visibility for its bid. Earlier this month, for example, ministers from five Andean countries—Bolivia, Ecuador, Colombia, Peru and Venezuela—met in Atlanta to discuss preparations for next month's talks in Miami. While in Georgia, they dined with former President Jimmy Carter and met with executives from large Atlanta companies . . .

"We're the indisputable gateway to the Americas," Mr. Arrizurieta said, adding that he bristled upon seeing that exact phrase, "Gateway to the Americas," as part of an extensive advertising insert purchased by Atlanta recently in the magazine Latin Trade to win support for its bid. "That really got to me," Mr. Arrizurieta said.

Source: Simon Romero, "Miami Caught in Free Trade Quandary," *New York Times*, October 28, 2003.

distribution of alcohol, or its laws concerning abortion, prostitution, the use of land, and many other issues that tend to receive differing levels of support across America.

- **Strengthening of liberty through the division of powers.** In Federalist No. 51, James Madison argued that "in the compound republic of America" the power surrendered by the people is divided between two distinct governments. This division provides security against a concentration of power in a single, unitary government. Madison also considered the division of such power "essential to the preservation of liberty" because it becomes harder for a corrupt agreement between these two separate governments to last for long—in the unlikely event that one entire government turns corrupt, the other government would still be available to check that government's abuses.

- **Encouragement of laboratories of democracy.** In 1932, Supreme Court Justice Louis Brandeis made famous a metaphor for creative federalism when he wrote that "a single courageous state may, if its citizens choose, serve as a laboratory, and try social and economic experiments without risk to the rest of the country."[20] This notion of states serving as "laboratories of democracy" is encouraged by a federalist system that gives the states authority to craft policies at the outset, while at the same time affording the central government authority to implement policies that prove successful throughout the nation. During the 1930s, FDR borrowed from the

Like this Texan, many citizens take pride in their home states.

experience of various states in crafting many New Deal policies. In 1993, the Brady Bill drafted by Congress drew heavily on successful state gun control provisions that established waiting periods for handgun purchases. The flip side of such successes is also significant: State policies that proved to be failures discourage broad-based applications by the federal government. For example, given that California's deregulation of utilities helped bring about an energy crisis in that state in early 2001, it seems unlikely that other states or the federal government will seek similar forms of deregulation any time soon.

- **Adaptability to changing circumstances.** Some areas of policymaking clearly lie within the purview of the central government: Foreign affairs, the development of a strong military, and the resolution of conflicts between states lead the list. By way of comparison, state and local governments maintain relatively strong control over public education in the state and local communities. Similarly, over the past decade, responsibility for social welfare policies has rested primarily with state governments. In these and other policy areas, state and local control affords considerably more flexibility to officials wrestling with various ways of addressing policy problems. Changing circumstances, such as a sudden influx of students in a state's K–12 educational programs or a migration of welfare recipients to a state, may require a quick and flexible response from government. Federal control over such issues may ensure the benefits of uniformity, but the cost is some loss of flexibility. State control provides the opportunity for legislative reform over a bureaucracy that may be far more manageable in its size.

Disadvantages of Federalism

Chief among the objections claimed by opponents of federalism are the unfairness caused by economic disparities among the states, questions about government accountability for many public programs that are inherent with competing sovereigns, and the system's heavy reliance on the courts to define the nature of federalism.

- **Fiscal disparities among the states.** States differ markedly in the wealth of their citizens and thus in the taxable resources available to them for programs. According to the U.S. Department of Commerce's Bureau of Economic Analysis, Connecticut's citizens in 2007 boasted a per capita personal income of $54,117, nearly twice that of citizens in Mississippi ($28,845).[21] Because of these fiscal differences, the amount of money that states spend on governmental programs varies widely. Furthermore, when the central government defers to state entities in the governing process, such as when it requires states to fund their own welfare programs, wide fiscal inequalities among states (and localities) may mean disparate—and inequitable—programs for citizens in different states.

- **Lack of accountability.** Numerous government programs fall under the exclusive authority of neither the state nor the federal governments; both may act, either may act, or in some cases, neither may act. At least in the abstract, federalism creates the prospect of multiple levels of government

President Barack Obama meets with state and local officials in Grand Isle, Louisiana, to discuss efforts to cap the Gulf of Mexico oil spill.

vying for the opportunity to address economic or social problems. In practice, however, the federal and state governments often play a game of "chicken," each hoping the other will act first and assume greater economic responsibility and perhaps accountability for failures. In an era when public frustration with rising taxes discourages government spending, this "blame game" may go on for years, with both sides accusing the other of shirking its responsibilities to the public. Congress passed legislation in 1996 that transferred welfare responsibilities back to states. Critics charge that this arrangement of shared accountability quickly transforms into a lack of accountability, with neither government accepting responsibility for dealing with problems.

■ **Undue reliance on courts to define the rules of federalism.** Because of the ambiguities inherent within a federalist system, courts play a far greater role in defining this form of government than in defining other forms. Because the federalist system is grounded in a political compromise, the rules are unclear; the limits of governmental power fit into no neat or simple formula. Judicial decision making is a mainstay of most federalist systems because it is necessary; without judicial rulings, it may be difficult if not impossible to balance the competing goals of national and subnational governments. This continued reliance on courts to make these weighty decisions exacts a price, however. Unlike legislators or high-level executives who must win public support to be elected, most judges are appointed and thus never need to directly curry the public's favor. When the courts fail to acknowledge public opinion, as the Supreme Court did when it struck down extremely popular measures to fight the Great Depression in the 1930s, a democratic system such as ours may find the delicate balance of powers tipping too far in favor of the unelected branches of government.

Those who favor expanding states' rights and responsibilities can cite a number of advantages that accrue with a healthy brand of federalism, but those who doubt the capacity of state governments to address complex modern problems are just as passionate when citing its various disadvantages. Debates over the merits of federalism are likely to continue well into the future, as political actors at every level of government stake a claim in difficult public policy problems that have few clear solutions.

Making the Connection

The pride citizens take in their home state connections is inevitable in a republic that celebrates state identities through its formal institutions and structures. The Constitution of the United States guarantees that each state (from California, the most heavily populated, to the least populated states of Delaware, Wyoming, and Alaska) is represented by exactly two members of the U.S. Senate, through which all federal legislation must pass. The presidential election in 2000 came down to the vote count of one state (Florida), whose state-specific and county-specific rules, regulations, and practices figured prominently in the final outcome. Citizens continue to face a dizzying variety of rules and regulations when they move from one state to another. Sometimes, the different rules governing citizens in two different states are more akin to the rules that govern different countries. Indeed, citizens of western New York State crossing by car into Canada often suffer far less culture shock than when they deplane in Texas, Louisiana, or another southern state.

State politicians often push the envelope on the legitimate bounds of state authority, both to win popularity among the state's citizens and to protect what they consider the state's best political interests. In recent years, some states—New York and Pennsylvania, for example—have sought to impose "commuter taxes" on people who live in other states but work in their respective states. In an extreme case of state government action, Massachusetts, to protest human rights violations in the country of Myanmar and to encourage reform in that nation's domestic policies, attempted to apply indirect economic pressure by prohibiting the state of Massachusetts and its agents from purchasing goods or services from anyone doing business with Myanmar.

Are these modern federalism disputes any different from disputes over the reach of federal authority at other times in the nation's history? When Congress attempted to legislate against child labor in the early part of the twentieth century, it ran squarely into a tradition of federalism—enforced by a conservative Supreme Court—that prohibited the federal government from regulating business matters that occurred entirely within the manufacturing stage. When congressional leadership intervened in the Terri Schiavo case nearly a century later, it was once again rebuffed for entering into the kind of political thicket that has divided federal and state lawmakers throughout American history. In all such cases, advocates of state authority must stand strong against federal government's enhanced authority, or they risk being swept aside in the process. The United States of America has not always been the "obedient states" of America, but it is hard to imagine that the founders would have intended the states to act otherwise.

The Medical Use of Marijuana

The federal government's Marijuana Tax Act of 1937 effectively prohibited the use of cannabis as a prescription drug in the United States. Cannabis is the chemical in marijuana plants that provides the mind-altering effects which made it so popular as a recreational drug and thus led to the 1937 law. However, prior to the discovery of aspirin, cannabis was the drug most commonly used to treat headaches and other types of pain in the nineteenth century. The 1937 law was inspired by nonmedical uses of the drug, although it had the effect of banning it for medical purposes as well.

A number of states, including California, have recently passed laws that allow the use of cannabis for medical purposes. In 2002, Angel Raich, a Californian, was using homegrown marijuana prescribed by her physician, who had determined that without it, Raich's high level of pain could endanger her life. Federal agents from the Drug Enforcement Administration seized and destroyed the marijuana plants Raich was using. Raich sued, claiming that her rights were violated and that the federal government could not rely on the commerce clause to trump California law in this instance. In *Gonzales v. Raich* (2005),* the U.S. Supreme Court ruled in favor of the federal government, holding that Congress indeed has the authority under the commerce clause to regulate activities such as marijuana use that have a substantial impact on interstate commerce.

BRUCE ELY/THE OREGONIAN/LANDOV

At www.cengage.com/dautrich/americangovernmentbrief/2e, find the Politics InterActive link for details on why the use of cannabis in medical treatment remains a point of controversy in federal–state relations. Additionally, learn how the National Organization for the Reform of Marijuana Laws (NORML) works with states and policymakers advocating states' rights to allow the use of the drug for medicinal purposes. Consult as well the various links that relate to the "medical marijuana controversy" in historical, popular, and global perspective.

*545 U.S. 1 (2005).

Chapter Summary

★ What Is Federalism?

- The American system of federalism links the central government in Washington, DC, to all fifty state governments. Sovereignty (the power of a government to regulate its affairs) resides concurrently in both the central government and the state governments.

- Federal systems of government can be distinguished from confederations, simple alliances of independent states, and unitary systems of government in which subunits such as states subordinate their aims to those of the central government.

- The framers of the Constitution assigned to the national government matters of great national importance (including foreign and military affairs) and assigned to the states all local and internal matters, including those relating to the health, safety, and welfare of citizens.

- The supremacy clause of Article VI provides that the Constitution and all federal laws override conflicting provisions in state constitutions or state laws.

- The full faith and credit clause of Article IV requires that each state must respect the acts and official proceedings of all other states. Notwithstanding this clause, some states have attempted to prevent same-sex couples married in one state from asserting their status as married couples across state lines.

★ The History of American Federalism

- Beginning in 1819, the Supreme Court under Chief Justice John Marshall substituted the framers' vision of federalism (state-centered federalism) with its own national supremacy doctrine, which held that (1) states possess extremely limited sovereignty and (2) Congress is supreme within the sphere of its own constitutional powers.

- In *McCulloch v. Maryland* (1819), Chief Justice Marshall applied the national supremacy doctrine to uphold the authority of Congress to create a national bank even though the Constitution did not explicitly authorize Congress to do so; congressional authority arose from a broader interpretation of the necessary and proper clause in Article I, Section 8.

- Beginning in 1837, a system of dual federalism, in which state authority under the Constitution served as a limit on congressional power, reigned for nearly a century until the New Deal period of the 1930s.

- The economic hardships of the Great Depression led to an activist federal government; facing these realities, the Supreme Court eventually abandoned its dual federalism principles in favor of a more expansive view of congressional authority.

- The era of cooperative federalism (1937–1990) barely limited Congress in the exercise of its powers. Through grants-in-aid and block grants, the federal government placed huge sums of money at the disposal of states but often attached conditions to those funds.

- Critics of cooperative federalism note that by attaching conditions to the funds it grants, the federal government often coerces states and state officials to administer federal laws. The National Minimum Drinking Age Amendment, for example, required states to increase their drinking age to twenty-one or risk losing national highway funds.

- The rhetoric of the Reagan administration emphasized federal deregulation and increased state responsibilities; Reagan's Supreme Court appointees helped to usher in a period of new federalism (1990–present) in which state sovereignty has once again been resuscitated to prevent certain forms of congressional coercion.

★ Why Federalism? Advantages and Disadvantages

- Federalism carries with it many advantages, including the accommodation of diverse interests in a large republic, the increased protection of individual liberty, and the encouragement of states to serve as "laboratories of democracy" where they might try out new policies. Because of their smaller size, state and local governments are also more flexible in adapting to changing circumstances.

- The disadvantages of a federalist system include the problems caused by significant fiscal disparities among the states, the potential lack of accountability of officials to oversee certain undesirable programs, and the heavy reliance of federalism on unelected courts to define its boundaries and perimeters.

CourseMate

Key Terms

Block grants (p. 66)
Concurrent powers (p. 58)
Confederation (p. 57)
Cooperative federalism (p. 66)
Dual federalism (p. 65)
Federalism (p. 56)
Full faith and credit clause (p. 60)

Gibbons v. Ogden (1824) (p. 64)
Grants-in-aid (p. 66)
Layer cake federalism (p. 66)
Marble cake federalism (p. 66)
McCulloch v. Maryland (1819) (p. 63)
National supremacy doctrine (p. 63)

Necessary and proper clause (p. 59)
Preemption (p. 60)
Reserved powers (p. 58)
Sovereignty (p. 56)
Supremacy clause (p. 60)
Unitary system of government (p. 57)

Resources

Books

Conlan, Timothy. *From New Federalism to Devolution: Twenty-five Years of Intergovernmental Reform.* Washington, DC: Brookings Institution Press, 1998.

Elazar, Daniel J. *Exploring Federalism.* Tuscaloosa: University of Alabama Press, 1987.

Noonan, John T. *Narrowing the Nation's Power: The Supreme Court Sides with the States.* Berkeley: University of California Press, 2002.

Peterson, Paul. *The Price of Federalism.* New York: Twentieth Century Fund, 1995.

Purcell, Edward A. *Originalism, Federalism and the American Constitutional Enterprise: A Historical Inquiry.* New Haven, CT: Yale University Press, 2007.

Walker, David. *The Rebirth of Federalism: Slouching Toward Washington.* New York: Chatham House, 2000.

Internet Sources

http://www.loc.gov/law/help/guide/states.php (Library of Congress Web page that offers an excellent resource for accessing state laws and constitutions, legislative Web sites, state executive branch laws, and state judicial rulings, as well as legal guides and other state sources).

http://www.statenews.org/ (Web site produced by the Council of State Governments with information about state issues and federalism).

http://www.nascio.org (National Association of State Information Resource Executives Web site).

NOW A U.S. soldier walks past a detainee at the Guantanamo Bay Detention Camp, located in Cuba. Between 2001 and 2006, more than 700 people were held at the facility.

BRENNAN LINSLEY, POOL/AP PHOTO

THEN An alien suspected of having "treasonable leanings" is arrested in accordance with the Alien Act of 1798.

MULTIEDUCATOR, INC.

NOW & THEN

Civil Liberties during Wartime

Although Congress had made no formal declaration of war, calls for some form of military intervention remained fierce. Enemies from the other side of the world continued to pose a threat to the United States of America and its security. For years, U.S. officials had thought there was little chance of any real threat emerging from so far away; after all, the nation enjoyed the natural protection of two large oceans and had long tried to steer clear of disputes among warring entities abroad that did not directly threaten U.S. interests. But the United States was now fighting an undeclared war, and the first-term president was determined not to be seen as weak. Congress had already approved far-reaching measures to deal with noncitizens who were perceived as threats. Due process rights for aliens were restricted, if not outright discarded. Though pressured by some to scale back these initiatives, the president and his administration left most of the measures intact. At least for the time being, civil liberties would be forced to take a backseat to national security interests, as they often do when a new president is trying to prove his bona fides as a protector of the nation's security.

LEARNING OBJECTIVES
★ WHAT YOU WILL LEARN ★

The Bill of Rights

★ Compare civil rights to civil liberties; describe the different categories of rights

★ Understand the origin of the Bill of Rights and the process of nationalizing those rights through the process of incorporation

Freedom of Religion and the Establishment Clause

★ Comprehend the free exercise clause and the rules for granting exemptions

★ Identify the rules governing the separation of church and state; recognize the tests for upholding government accommodations of religion

Free Expression Rights

★ Appreciate the theories that justify giving heightened protection to expression rights

★ Understand the scope of free speech rights, free press rights, and symbolic speech; learn the rules for exempting from protection lesser-value speech, including libel and obscenity

The Right to Bear Arms

★ Identify the scope of the right to bear arms and the constitutional limits on gun control laws

The Rights of the Accused

★ Understand the scope of Fourth Amendment rights and the privacy issues raised by advances in technology

★ Understand the rules against double jeopardy and the privilege against self-incrimination

★ Recognize the rights granted under the Sixth and Eighth Amendments

The Modern Right to Privacy

★ Understand the right of abortion and its scope under *Roe v. Wade*, and then later under *Planned Parenthood v. Casey*

★ Become familiar with the privacy rights that apply to government restrictions on sodomy and euthanasia

CourseMate

NOW & THEN

BRENNAN LINSLEY, POOL/AP PHOTO

NOW Certainly many aspects of the scenario just described apply to the "war on terrorism" inherited by President Barack Obama when he took over the White House from President George W. Bush in January 2009. The Bush administration launched wars in Afghanistan and Iraq in the years following the September 11, 2001, terrorist attacks. Congress enacted the USA Patriot Act, authorizing the president to take numerous steps to prosecute the war, including broad new powers to detain suspects without hearings at the Guantanamo Military Base ("Gitmo") in Cuba and elsewhere. The law targeted aliens in particular, allowing authorities to hold noncitizens suspected of terrorism for seven days without charging them and utilized a system of military tribunals with limited due process protections. When Barack Obama campaigned for the presidency in 2008, he promised to scale back many of these Bush-era measures. Yet as president, Obama quickly discovered the dangers of rolling back those measures in the absence of clear guarantees that national security would not be compromised. The new president announced plans to close Gitmo, but was soon thwarted in his efforts to do so by Congress. He halted the use of torture against suspected terrorists, but his administration continued the practice of indefinitely holding prisoners deemed "unlawful combatants," denying them habeas corpus rights. Nearly a decade after 9/11, the state of civil liberties in the United States was still fundamentally different than it had been before the terrorist attacks, even with President Obama in office.

THEN The difficult task of balancing civil liberties and national security interests during wartime is nothing new to American politics. The scenario described above also harkens back to 1798, when the federal government led by first-term President John Adams was gearing up for hostilities against the French dictator Napoleon Bonaparte. Napoleon's forces had already captured Rome and invaded Switzerland and Egypt earlier that year, and now Napoleon's aides intimated to American diplomats that a war against the United States might be next. Congress passed twenty acts to help consolidate the national defense against France and prepare for the possibility of invasion. The most controversial of these were the Alien Act, which authorized the president to deport from the United States all aliens suspected of "treasonable or secret" inclinations; the Alien Enemies Act, which allowed the president during wartime to arrest and imprison aliens subject to an enemy power; and the Sedition Act, which criminalized the publication of materials that brought the U.S. government into "disrepute." According to Adams's biographer, David McCullough, the second president was a reluctant partner in the controversial measures, which he neither asked for nor encouraged.[1] Angered by the treatment of his administration's diplomats and fearful of being viewed as weak on foreign policy, Adams did not oppose their passage, and he eventually signed them into law. And while he did not issue even one deportation order during his presidency, a handful of Republican editors were jailed for violating the Sedition Act. Such was the dilemma faced by an emotional president torn between the need to appear strong to outsiders, and his desire to abide by real constitutional limits.

MULTIEDUCATOR, INC.

n many other nations, restrictions on individual rights—especially during times of tension and upheaval—fail to solicit much intense resistance even from the political opposition. But the founding of the United States rested on a call for protecting the inalienable rights of all people, and the Bill of Rights, added to the U.S. Constitution in 1791, stands as a beacon against the potential tyranny of the majority. That was not always the case: The Bill of Rights has gathered true muscle only during the past seventy-five years. The challenge for so many is how to most effectively recognize the rights that are available to them. That challenge may be especially difficult during times of war, when individual rights come under the greatest threat, although perhaps with all the best intentions.

In this chapter, we take up the subject of **civil liberties**—those specific individual rights that cannot be taken away by government and are guaranteed by the Constitution, such as the freedom of expression and the privilege against self-incrimination. These individual rights, which are subject to formal interpretation by the courts and informal interpretation by those charged with their enforcement, are usually found either in the Bill of Rights or in subsequent amendments to the Constitution. Here, we will focus primarily on the provision of rights guaranteed by the First, Second, and Fourth Amendments and certain provisions within the Fifth, Sixth, Eighth, and Fourteenth Amendments.

Civil liberties are distinguished from *civil rights* (sometimes called *equal rights*), a more modern term that refers specifically to the rights that members of various groups (racial, ethnic, sexual, and so on) have to equal treatment by government under the law and equal access to society's opportunities. This chapter deals with civil liberties, whereas Chapter 5 deals with civil rights.

Civil liberties
Those specific individual rights that are guaranteed by the Constitution and cannot be denied to citizens by government. Most of these rights are in the first ten amendments to the Constitution, known as the Bill of Rights.

★ LO   Compare civil rights to civil liberties; describe the different categories of rights

The Bill of Rights

What are rights? Strictly speaking, they are powers or privileges to which individuals are entitled. The central questions are: Where do rights come from, and are they absolute? *Natural rights*, which are based on the natural laws of human society, exist even in the absence of a formal government. Because natural rights theoretically transcend government entities, no authority can legitimately take them away. As Thomas Jefferson so eloquently stated in the Declaration of Independence, human beings are endowed with certain rights that are "inalienable," which means they cannot be denied by government.

Positive rights, by comparison, are granted by government authority and can usually be shaped and modified by that authority according to certain rules. An indigent person's right to a lawyer paid by the state in felony cases, for example, is a positive right. The term *liberty* refers to a right received from a higher authority, such as a government. As they articulated the basis for a new government, many of the framers grappled with these and other terms in the nation's founding documents.

It is sometimes easy to forget that, as U.S. Supreme Court Justice Antonin Scalia once stated, individual rights are only "the fruits, rather than the roots, of the Constitutional tree."[2] The Constitution of the United States was intended to provide individuals with protection by guaranteeing a framework of limited government based on a theory of enumerated powers; the central government was allowed to exercise only those powers delegated to it by the Constitution. As James Madison wrote in Federalist No. 14, "the general government is not to be charged with the whole power of making and administering laws . . . its jurisdiction is limited to *certain enumerated objects*."[3] Thus, by Madison's logic, separate provisions for the protection of individual rights were unnecessary; protection for those rights was inherent in the nature of limited government with enumerated powers. Because the government possessed no explicit power to infringe on those rights in the first place, they should never be in danger.

★ LO
Understand the origin of the Bill of Rights and the process of nationalizing those rights through the process of incorporation

Yet Madison's logic ran up against an early American tradition that called for the explicit delineation of individual rights. The Declaration of Independence not only formally recognized that certain "unalienable rights" exist, but it also stated that when a government created by "the consent of the governed" fails to protect those rights, the people have the right to "alter or abolish such government." At the time of the founding, individual rights were considered an important element of America's political culture because they embodied the principles that justified the American Revolution. Many of the former colonists wanted those rights clearly spelled out, lest there be any doubt of their significance to the new nation.

When the U.S. Constitution was created in 1787, most state governments already maintained a bill of rights to protect citizens against government encroachment. As the final draft of the Constitution was being debated at ratification conventions in the states, it became evident to the Constitution's supporters that its approval was going to require the inclusion of a more formal bill of rights to protect citizens against the federal government. George Mason and Patrick Henry of Virginia cast votes against ratification, in part because the Constitution lacked a formal statement of rights. Thomas Jefferson was also an early proponent of a bill of rights. To Madison's fears that such a declaration of rights could never be comprehensive, and thus might leave out something important, Jefferson replied: "Half a loaf is better than no bread."[4]

ELIZA SNOW/ISTOCKPHOTO.COM

Eventually, it was Madison who framed the list of rights that the first Congress proposed in 1789—ten amendments to the Constitution were ratified by the required three fourths of state legislatures. These are normally regarded as the Bill of Rights. While the first eight amendments guarantee specific rights, the Ninth and Tenth Amendments offer more general statements describing divisions of power under the Constitution.

The provisions listed in the Bill of Rights enjoyed little influence in late eighteenth- and early nineteenth-century America because they were understood to be restrictions on the federal government only. The Supreme Court confirmed as much in the case of *Barron v. Baltimore* (1833),[5] which pitted a wharf owner against the city of Baltimore. City officials had lowered the water level around the wharves, causing him a significant economic loss. The wharf owner thus sued the city under the Fifth Amendment's "taking clause," which stated that no private property could be taken from an individual for public use without just compensation. But the Supreme Court dismissed the suit because at that time only the federal government could be held up to the standards of the Bill of Rights. In light of the dominant role state governments played in regulating individuals' daily lives during most of this period, the *Barron v. Baltimore* decision essentially reduced the Bill of Rights to paper guarantees that only occasionally provided protection for ordinary citizens.

That all changed in the twentieth century, as the Supreme Court grew increasingly willing to protect individuals against intrusive state actions. Their instrument for doing so was the Fourteenth Amendment (ratified in 1868), which provided that no *state* could "deprive any person of life, liberty or property without due process of law." The Fourteenth Amendment had been passed immediately after the Civil War to protect freed slaves from discriminatory state laws. Yet at the beginning of the twentieth century and increasingly throughout the century, the Supreme Court by a process known as **incorporation** (or "nationalization") demonstrated a new willingness to hold state governments accountable to the Bill of Rights by utilizing the Fourteenth Amendment's vague requirement that states respect "due process." Specifically, the Court carefully considered individual clauses from the Bill of Rights, and if the right was deemed fundamental enough, the Court held that no state could legitimately ignore the right without depriving an individual of the right to "life, liberty and property, without

Incorporation
The process by which the U.S. Supreme Court used the due process clause of the Fourteenth Amendment to make most of the individual rights guaranteed by the Bill of Rights also applicable to the states. Incorporation provided that state and local governments, as well as the federal government, could not deny these rights to citizens.

TABLE 4.1 Incorporating the Bill of Rights to Apply to the States

Provision (Amendment)	Year	Case
Protection from government taking property without just compensation (Fifth)	1897	Chicago, Burl. & Quincy Rwy. v. Chicago
Freedom of speech (First)	1925	Gitlow v. New York
Freedom of the press (First)	1931	Near v. Minnesota
Right to assistance of counsel in capital cases (Sixth)	1932	Powell v. Alabama
Freedom of assembly (First)	1937	Delaware v. Van Arsdall
Free exercise of religion (First)	1940	Cantwell v. Connecticut
Protection from establishment of religion (First)	1947	Everson v. Board of Education
Right to public trial (Sixth)	1948	In re Oliver
Right against unreasonable search and seizure (Fourth)	1949	Wolf v. Colorado
Exclusionary rule (Fourth & Fifth)	1961	Mapp v. Ohio
Protection against cruel and unusual punishment (Eighth)	1962	Robinson v. California
Right to paid counsel for indigents in felony cases (Sixth)	1963	Gideon v. Wainwright
Right against self-incrimination (Fifth)	1964	Malloy v. Hogan
Right to confront witnesses (Sixth)	1965	Pointer v. Texas
Right to an impartial jury (Sixth)	1966	Parker v. Gladden
Right to compulsory process to obtain witnesses (Sixth)	1967	Washington v. Texas
Right to speedy trial (Sixth)	1967	Klopfer v. North Carolina
Right to jury in nonpetty criminal cases (Sixth)	1968	Duncan v. Louisiana
Right against double jeopardy (Fifth)	1969	Benton v. Maryland
Right to keep and bear arms (Second)	2010	McDonald v. Chicago

due process of law." By this incorporation process, states were required to live up to the dictates of the First Amendment free speech clause beginning in 1925, the Fourth Amendment right against unreasonable searches and seizures beginning in 1961, and the Sixth Amendment right to a speedy trial beginning in 1967 (see Table 4.1). Slowly but surely, the provisions of the Bill of Rights were incorporated by the Fourteenth Amendment to apply to state governments as well as to the federal government.

By 1969, nearly every provision of the Bill of Rights had been applied to state governments through the incorporation doctrine. At present, however, there are still several provisions of the Bill of Rights that theoretically provide protection against the federal government only:

- the Third Amendment safeguard against the involuntary quartering of troops;
- the Fifth Amendment requirement that defendants be indicted by a grand jury;
- the Seventh Amendment guarantee of a trial by jury in civil cases;
- the Eighth Amendment prohibition against excessive bail and fines.

All other provisions contained within the first eight amendments of the Constitution are considered applicable to all state governments and to all local governments within the states in exactly the same manner as they are applicable to the federal government.

Freedom of Religion and the Establishment Clause

★ LO
Comprehend the free exercise clause and the rules for granting exemptions

THE FIRST AMENDMENT: Congress shall make no law respecting an establishment of religion, or prohibiting the free exercise thereof; . . .

Although the first words of the Bill of Rights speak to the freedom of religion, the actual rights guaranteeing religious freedom did not become widespread until the latter half of the twentieth century. In early America, Protestantism played a highly influential role in public life, and the First Amendment was intended to provide a limited barrier against its influence. In 1802, Thomas Jefferson described the First Amendment as erecting a "wall of separation" between church and state,[6] but that metaphor captured his hopes more than the reality of the time. Although there existed no official church of the United States, government aid to religion—in particular, to certain Protestant sects—stood little chance of being overturned by a court on constitutional grounds. And for much of American history, minority religious groups such as Mormons, Jehovah's Witnesses, and the Amish were forced to change or abandon some of their religious practices whenever public policy conflicted with them. By the 1940s, however, American public life had grown increasingly secular, and application of the First Amendment's guarantees of freedom of religion was transformed. Even today, the interest in accommodating religion continues to run up against the desire to create a "wall of separation" emphasizing government neutrality.

The Free Exercise of Religion

The **free exercise clause** of the First Amendment bans government laws that prohibit the free exercise of religion. Debate over the clause has largely focused on whether government laws can force adherents of a certain religion

Free exercise clause
The religious freedom clause in the First Amendment that denies government the ability to prohibit the free exercise of religion. Debate over the clause has largely focused on whether government laws can force adherents of a certain religion to engage in activities that are prohibited by their religious beliefs or prevent them from performing acts that are compelled by their religious beliefs.

to engage in activities that are prohibited by their religious beliefs or prevent them from performing acts that are compelled by their religious beliefs. During the heart of World War II, the Supreme Court in *West Virginia v. Barnette* (1943)[7] ordered school officials to reinstate the children of Jehovah's Witnesses who had been suspended for refusing to salute the American flag in their public school classrooms. Yet although those children could claim legitimate religious objections to the law (the Jehovah's Witnesses' creed forbids them from saluting any "graven image"), they also could claim more generally the right of free expression; those who disagreed with the U.S. government were free to withhold displays of public support for the nation's symbol. It remained for the Court in subsequent years to sort out what rights of religious freedom might exist under the free exercise clause.

Seventh-day Adventists and the Refusal to Work. In the landmark case of *Sherbert v. Verner* (1963),[8] the Supreme Court ordered the state of South Carolina to pay unemployment benefits to a Seventh-day Adventist who refused to work on Saturdays. Even though the state's unemployment laws required that she make herself available for work on Saturday, the Court refused to apply the law to her because Saturday was the Sabbath for Seventh-day Adventists. The Supreme Court declared that only a *compelling state interest* could justify denying her such an exception on the basis of religion.

The Mormons and Polygamy Laws. Up until the late nineteenth century, a central tenet of the Mormon Church, also called the Church of Jesus Christ of Latter-day Saints, required some of its adherents to practice polygamy—the act of having multiple spouses "when circumstances would permit." The Supreme Court, in a unanimous decision, rejected the arguments of George Reynolds, secretary of one of the founders of the Mormon Church and the founder of Brigham Young University, that the First Amendment protects plural marriage.[9] The Court ruled that religious practices (such as polygamy) that impair the "public interest" do not enjoy constitutional protection. Since 1890, the Mormon Church has formally renounced the practice of polygamy by its members.

Illegal Drug Use and the Smith Case. In 1990, the Supreme Court adopted a new approach to the free exercise of religion, one that dramatically diminished the likelihood that future religious exemptions might be granted. Two Native Americans were dismissed from their jobs as drug rehabilitation counselors when it was discovered that they had ingested the illegal drug peyote as part of their tribe's religious rituals. Because their drug use violated the Oregon criminal code, the two men were subsequently denied unemployment compensation. The Supreme Court ruled in *Employment Division v. Smith* (1990)[10] that the state's legitimate interest in maintaining its unemployment insurance fund at a high level outweighed the Native Americans' religious rights and thus that it could deny the two men unemployment benefits. State governments may choose to accommodate otherwise illegal acts done in pursuit of religious beliefs, but they are not *required* to do so.[11] Today, *Smith* remains the rule for judicial interpretation of free exercise cases: Instead of being forced to show a *compelling* government interest (which is extremely hard to do), a government interested in applying its neutral laws over religious objections may do so based on any *legitimate state interest* it might claim.

The Establishment Clause

Even more controversial than the debate over religious exemptions from public policies has been the battle over what role religion may play in American public life under the **establishment clause**, which prohibits the government from enacting laws "respecting an establishment of religion." Most Americans take it for granted that during the holiday season they will see Christmas decorations prominently displayed in government buildings, in front of the town hall, and in public squares. But what about nativity scenes? Menorahs? The Ten Commandments? What types of religious activities and symbols are considered acceptable in public places, and which ones run afoul of the First Amendment, whose prohibition of government "respecting an establishment of religion" has been interpreted to mean creating a "wall of separation" between church and state?

Modern debates over the proper role religion may play under the establishment clause generally divide advocates into two camps. Those who advocate a strict dividing line between church and state support a principle of *separation*, which holds that government should have no involvement whatsoever with religious practices, although religion remains free to flourish privately on its own with its own resources.[12] Opponents of strict separation argue instead for the principle of *accommodation*, which holds that government neutrality toward religion requires only that it treat all religions equally. Government should be free to aid and subsidize religious activities as long as it does so fairly across different religions and aids comparable nonreligious activities as well. In recent decades, the Supreme Court has moved from a position of especially strict separation to one that shifts back and forth between principles of separation and accommodation.

Historically Accepted Practices. Certain religious practices have been a part of political and public life for generations, and the Supreme Court has generally allowed such activities to continue. For example, Congress opens each legislative session with a prayer from a clergy member, chaplains serve in religious capacities with the U.S. armed forces, and U.S. currency proclaims "In God We Trust." Even the Supreme Court opens every court session to a marshal's bellowing pronouncement: "God save this honorable court!"

In Kentucky, versions of the Ten Commandments were posted on the walls of several county courthouses. In Texas, a six-foot-high monolith inscribed with the Ten Commandments appears among numerous other monuments and historical markers outside the state capitol building commemorating the "people, ideals, and events that compose Texan identity." In a set of cases handed down in 2005, the Supreme Court ordered the Kentucky courthouses to remove their displays but allowed the Texas display to remain standing. In explaining its different approach to these cases, the Court ruled that even though the Ten Commandments are inherently religious,

Establishment clause
The clause in the First Amendment that prohibits government from enacting any law "respecting an establishment of religion." Separationist interpretations of this clause affirm that government should not support any religious activity. Accommodationists say that support for a religion is legal provided that all religions are equally supported.

A Ten Commandments monument is moved outside the Alabama Judicial Building in Montgomery, 2003.

TAMI CHAPPELL/REUTERS/LANDOV

their placement in a monument outside the state capitol is an essentially "passive" act, whereas their placement within the courthouse had been motivated by a desire on the part of legislators to advance religion.

★ LO   Identify the rules governing the separation of church and state; recognize the tests for upholding government accommodations of religion

Religious Prayers in Public School Classrooms. The public school classroom has always been viewed as a unique context in which to assess claims that the government has violated the establishment clause. Judges and politicians alike assume that students—particularly elementary school students—have not yet formed firm beliefs about religion and thus may be susceptible to even subtle forms of religious coercion. Public officials interested in promoting religion in society as a whole have focused on the school as a place to encourage religious practices; as a consequence, school policies touching on the subject of religion have undergone serious scrutiny in the courts.

In 1962, the Supreme Court in *Engel v. Vitale*[13] invalidated the New York public schools' policy of having each class recite a specified nondenominational religious prayer each day. That prayer, which proclaimed in nondenominational terms, "Almighty God, we acknowledge our dependence upon thee," was held to be a violation of the First Amendment's prohibition against the establishment of religion. In *Abington School District v. Schempp* (1963),[14] the Court refused to allow spiritual Bible readings in public school classrooms, and in *Wallace v. Jaffree* (1985),[15] it outlawed "moments of silence" authorized by government officials to encourage religious prayer during those moments. The Court held that in neither of those instances was the government acting with a "secular purpose"—one not grounded in a desire to "advance religion." Despite these seemingly clear rulings against school prayer, some teachers continue to lead students in prayer in public school classrooms across the country.

Lemon test
The legal test that determines if a government statute aiding public or private schools is an unconstitutional violation of the establishment clause. The statute is unconstitutional if the statute has no secular purpose, if its principal or primary effect advances or inhibits religion, or if it fosters "an excessive government entanglement with religion."

Financial Aid and the *Lemon* Test. Since 1971, issues involving the separation of church and state have often been governed by the **Lemon test** articulated by the Supreme Court in the landmark decision of *Lemon v. Kurtzman* (1971).[16] Under the test, government aid to public or private schools is considered unconstitutional if it fails to meet three separate criteria: "First, the statute must have a secular [that is, not religious] purpose; second, its principal or primary effect must be one that neither advances nor inhibits religion; finally, the statute must not foster 'an excessive government entanglement with religion.'"

Prayers at Graduation Ceremonies and Football Games. In recent years, some school officials have attempted to facilitate student prayers in school contexts outside the classroom. Those efforts have met with little success. In *Lee v. Weisman* (1992),[17] the Supreme Court ordered a Providence, Rhode Island, middle school to stop its practice of reading prayers at the school's graduation ceremony, even though attendance was voluntary. Eight years later, in *Santa Fe v. Doe* (2000),[18] the Court ruled that a student-led prayer before

BOB DAEMMRICH/THE IMAGE WORKS

Group prayer before a high school football game in Austin, Texas.

a football game at a Texas public high school violated the separation of church and state. The Court believed that both practices forced all of those present to participate in an act of religious worship. In addition, these practices could have been interpreted as state endorsements of prayer, which is unconstitutional.

The debate over the role religion should play in American public life remains a highly charged topic. Public schools especially will continue to be a focus of intense interest, as the proponents of a greater role for religion seek ever more creative ways to combine the educational process with efforts at spirituality and religious participation.

Free Expression Rights

THE FIRST AMENDMENT: Congress shall make no law . . . abridging the freedom of speech, or of the press; . . .

Among the many civil liberties guaranteed by the Bill of Rights, the First Amendment rights of free speech and press enjoy especially revered status. That wasn't always the case. The Sedition Act of the late 1790s restricted speech that negatively reflected on the Federalists who were in power; during the Civil War, the Lincoln administration took harsh action against those who sought to undermine the Union's cause. Today, nearly all politicians celebrate rights of free expression, at least in the abstract. For many, these rights of free expression serve as a cornerstone for all other individual rights, facilitating the more effective realization of such freedoms as the right to vote and participate in the democratic process.

What accounts for the lofty status of free expression rights in the American political system? Several theories have been offered to justify this high level of respect.

- **"The marketplace of ideas,"** a phrase coined by Supreme Court Justice Oliver Wendell Holmes in 1919, is a metaphor for the premise that the best test of truth is the free exchange of ideas; only through such free exchange and presentation of all arguments, valid and invalid, can the truth prevail. To ensure a robust marketplace of ideas, government restrictions on speech must be kept to a minimum.

- **Self-governance** is another frequently cited justification for protecting free expression. Speech is considered essential to representative government because it provides the mechanism by which citizens deliberate on important issues of public policy. Free speech also serves as a means for ordinary citizens to check the abuse of power by public officials.

- **Self-fulfillment.** Some philosophers have emphasized the importance of free speech and expression as a means of achieving individual self-fulfillment. The human capacity to create ideas and express oneself is considered central to human existence; government restrictions on free speech threaten that human capacity. Such a justification of free speech rights extends as well to the protection of music, pictures, and other forms of artistic expression.

- **A "safety valve."** Free speech also serves a critical role in encouraging adaptability and flexibility according to the changing circumstances in society. If the suppression of free speech forces citizens to adopt more extreme means of enacting change, such as violence, the promotion of free speech provides an essential mechanism for balancing the need for order with cries for reform.

Free Speech during the Early Twentieth Century: "The Clear and Present Danger Test"

The modern status of free expression rights is a far cry from the low level of protection the First Amendment afforded to free speech nearly a century ago. Many of the early cases pitting dissenting speakers against the government came before the Court when tensions were great—first during wartime, then at the height of the Cold War when fears of communist infiltration in American society gripped many ordinary Americans. In neither instance did free speech fare well.

The Supreme Court gave birth to the clear and present danger test in *Schenck v. United States* (1919).[19] In 1917, when the United States was readying for active participation in World War I, Charles Schenck, a general secretary for the American Socialist Party, was tried and convicted for distributing leaflets arguing that the military draft was immoral. Although the pamphlet posed little danger of interfering with the draft, the Supreme Court refused to release Schenck from jail. Writing the majority opinion for a unanimous court, Justice Oliver Wendell Holmes stated that there was in fact "a clear and present danger" that the pamphlet could bring about the damage being claimed by the government.

In practice, the clear and present danger test soon became a hammer on speakers' rights rather than a shield against government suppression. Under the doctrine, members of the Socialist and Communist Parties were tried and punished for participating in organizational meetings or declaring allegiance to their party's principles. During the late 1940s and early 1950s, when the fear of communism in the United States was reaching a fever pitch, members of the Communist Party were convicted for their advocacy of sedition. In *Dennis v. United States* (1951),[20] the Supreme Court gave a measure of credibility to this red scare when it upheld the convictions of numerous communist defendants for "teaching and advocating the overthrow and destruction of the Government of the United States."

The Warren Court and the Rise of the "Preferred Freedoms" Doctrine

By the late 1950s, fears of subversion and communist infiltration in the United States were beginning to subside. However, it was the ascension of former California Governor Earl Warren to the position of chief justice of the United States in 1953 that eventually changed the Court's free speech doctrine from one that offered little protection to dissenting speakers into one that protected even the most unpopular speakers against suppression by the majority. The Warren Court brought about this change in part by embracing a doctrine first articulated by Justice Harlan Fiske Stone in 1938. In a footnote to the otherwise unnotable case of *United States v. Carolene Products* (1938),[21] Justice Stone declared that various civil liberties guaranteed in the Bill of Rights, including the right of free expression, enjoyed a "preferred position" in constitutional law.

In 1969, the Supreme Court in *Brandenburg v. Ohio* (1969)[22] abandoned the old clear and present danger test and replaced it with a test that was much more protective of free speech. A Ku Klux Klan rally in Cincinnati, Ohio, featured numerous figures in white hoods uttering phrases that demeaned African Americans and Jews. The principal speaker had argued that some form of vengeance be taken against both groups. The group's leader was convicted under a law criminalizing the advocacy of violence. The Supreme Court overturned his conviction.

AMERICAN GOVERNMENT In Global Perspective

The U.S. government has leased the Guantanamo Bay Naval Base, located on the southeastern shore of Cuba, since the Cuban-American Treaty of 1903. Beginning in 2002, the naval base became home to a military prison for "unlawful combatants" in the war on terrorism who do not receive protection under the Geneva conventions. Amnesty International and the United Nations—believing the prison to be the source of fundamental rights abuses—have requested that the facility be shut down. President Obama issued an executive order to that effect on January 22, 2009, but his order was thwarted by the Congress, which forbid the transfer of detainees to other facilities in the United States,

Al Jazeera is an Arabic satellite television network headquartered in Doha, Qatar. It has caused controversy in the Arab world due to its willingness to air competing views. Half a year into Obama's presidency, Al Jazeera provided a voice to the legal charity Reprieve concerning the Gitmo debate:

When Obama became president and said he would close the prison, 34-year-old Ayman al-Shurafa was still being held on the US naval base but should have been one of the first detainees to leave. Although

he had admitted to attending a training camp in Afghanistan, the Pentagon assessed that he posed no threat and should be released. But in the strange world of Guantanamo Bay, degrees of innocence and guilt are only part of the story. Al-Shurafa's case helps to explain why, six months after ordering the closure of Guantanamo Bay, Obama has made so little tangible progress to this end—only 11 of the 242 prisoners he inherited from the Bush administration have been released during his tenure.

In the midst of the political and diplomatic wrangling over Guantanamo's closure, it is easy to forget that at the centre of this story are 229 human beings. Cori Crider, an attorney from the UK-based legal charity Reprieve, says many of the prisoners are losing faith in Obama's promises. "Many of them thought the new administration might finally be the light at the end of their tunnel, but most of them have started to lose hope again," she says. Just last month one of the Yemeni prisoners, Mohammad al-Hanashi, could take no more and committed suicide. It was a stark reminder that every day Guantanamo Bay remains open increases the human cost of a system built on an inherent contradiction—that even if you are found innocent, you are still treated as if you were guilty.

Source: Aljazeera.net, July 22, 2009.

In the process, it declared a new "imminent danger" test for such speech: First, is the speech "directed to inciting or producing imminent lawless action," and second, is the advocacy likely to produce such action? Few of the speakers jailed in the previous half century for seditious speech would have been convicted under this new standard.[23]

Freedom of the Press, Libel Laws, and Prior Restraints

Freedom of the press enjoys a long and storied tradition in the United States. Despite the general recognition of the importance of the press, newspapers traditionally enjoyed few special privileges under the law. That all changed in 1964 with the landmark decision of *New York Times v. Sullivan*.[24] A Montgomery,

Crossing the Bounds of Contemporary Tastes

With regard to obscenity, the First Amendment has often provided a measure of protection against attempts by communities to impose the majority's tastes on the minority. As social mores have evolved—and the bounds of tastelessness have been stretched—the courts have required governmental entities to go beyond oversimplified pleas for decency and good taste in their efforts to regulate sexually explicit material. At the same time, courts remain unwilling to ban any and all forms of regulating obscenity. As a consequence, court rulings attempt to find the fine line between tasteless speech and social mores.

In the late 1950s, a New York State licensing agency denied a movie company a license to show the film *Lady Chatterley's Lover* in the state.

Although the movie's depiction of sexuality would be considered tame even by 1950s standards, the film focused at its core on an adulterous relationship, accompanied by the suggestion that adultery may be "right and desirable" for certain people under certain circumstances. The state banned *Lady Chatterley's Lover* as an "immoral film" that portrayed sexual immorality as "desirable, acceptable or proper." But in 1959, the Supreme Court reversed the licensing decision as a violation of free speech rights. At the same time, the Court distinguished the mere concept or idea of "sexual immorality" from "obscenity" or "pornography," both of which could still be regulated under certain circumstances.

In 1973, during a midafternoon weekday broadcast on contemporary attitudes toward the use of language, a New York City radio station aired satirist comedian George Carlin's twelve-minute monologue titled "Filthy Words." Immediately before the broadcast, the station had advised

---

Alabama, police commissioner sued the *New York Times* in March 1960 for an advertisement the newspaper had published. The ad—charging the existence of "an unprecedented wave of terror" against blacks in Montgomery—had been signed by several black clergymen. In its description of events that had transpired, the ad also contained some minor inaccuracies. Although the police commissioner was unable to prove that he had suffered any actual economic harm, he still sought a $500,000 judgment against the *Times*. But the Supreme Court refused to allow the official to claim damages and in the process articulated a much more stringent test to be met by public officials suing for **libel** (the crime of printing or disseminating false statements that harm someone): They must prove that the newspapers had published false facts with malice (bad intentions) or reckless disregard for the truth (they ignored clear evidence of contrary facts).[25]

In subsequent years, the *New York Times v. Sullivan* decision has applied to public figures as well as public officials; today, a libel lawsuit brought by any famous person—whether it's the president of the United States, Tiger Woods, or Julia Roberts—must prove that the newspaper or magazine in question not only printed false facts but did so either with "malicious intent" or in "reckless disregard" for the truth. Whereas libel laws punish publications after the fact, a **prior restraint** imposes a limit on publication *before* the material has actually been published. Securing a prior restraint is very difficult for government to accomplish. In the *Pentagon Papers Case* (1971),[26] the Supreme Court refused the U.S. government's request to stop the *Washington Post* and the *New York Times* from publishing a classified study of U.S. decision making about the Vietnam War.

Libel
Printing or disseminating false statements that harm someone.

Prior restraint
The government's requirement that material be approved by government before it can be published.

listeners that it would include sensitive language that might be offensive to some. In the monologue, Carlin provided his thoughts about "the words you can't say on the public airwaves, um, the ones you definitely wouldn't say ever," especially the "original seven dirty words." Carlin then repeated the outlawed words in a variety of colloquialisms. When the Federal Communications Commission (FCC) threatened to impose formal sanctions on the radio station, the station sued. In 1978, the Supreme Court narrowly upheld the FCC's authority to impose sanctions. The Court took pains to say that in this particular case, context was all important: "Broadcasting is uniquely accessible to children, even those too young to read." At the same time, the Court hinted that occasional expletives, including even those in Carlin's monologue, might never justify a full criminal prosecution or some more serious sanction.

In 2004, Howard Stern signed his first contract with Sirius Satellite Radio, a medium free from regulations imposed by the FCC. Stern, self-nicknamed "the King of All Media," regularly describes in graphic detail oral, anal, and other forms of sex during his morning radio show, at a time when children may be part of the listening audience. The decision to move to satellite was motivated by business and free speech concerns. Back in 1996, the Infinity network paid over $1.7 million to the FCC to clear more than a hundred indecency claims made against the Howard Stern radio show. Nearly a decade later, Stern accused FCC Chairman Michael Powell of crusading against his radio show by levying huge fines, though never allowing him a day in court to determine if the show was obscene. Since moving to satellite the fines have stopped, though Stern has revealed that he has begun to feel "creatively dead inside." Can Howard Stern survive without the daily rigors of walking on the edge?

Obscenity and Pornography

Despite the exalted status free expression rights enjoy under the Constitution, obscenity has long been recognized as an exception to the rule. Even through the so-called sexual revolution of the 1960s and 1970s, the Supreme Court continued to adhere to the premise that truly obscene speech—words or publications that tend to violate accepted standards of decency by their very lewdness—may under certain circumstances be regulated. When asked how he would define obscene pornography, Justice Potter Stewart in 1964 uttered his now celebrated phrase: "I can't define it, but I know it when I see it." Stewart's statement captures the often confusing state of obscenity law in the United States. The First Amendment does not allow governments simply to ban all sexually explicit materials. But what types of materials can be banned? Should all pornography be considered "obscene"?

In *Miller v. California* (1973),[27] the Supreme Court created the modern legal test for determining what sexually explicit materials may be legitimately subject to regulation under

Poster advertising *Lady Chatterley's Lover*. The film was based on a book that was the target of a New York state ban during the 1950s.

EVERETT COLLECTION

NOW YOU CAN SEE IT!
The most whispered about book in the world becomes the MOST TALKED ABOUT PICTURE OF THE YEAR!

THE FILM WITHOUT FALSE MODESTY!

D. H. LAWRENCE'S CONTROVERSIAL MASTERPIECE

"Lady Chatterley's Lover"

DANIELLE DARRIEUX
LEO GENN
and Introducing ERNO CRISA

A Kingsley International Release

the Constitution. According to the Court, a work is obscene if all of these three conditions are met:

1. The average person applying contemporary community standards would think that the work (taken as a whole) appeals to the "prurient" (that is, lustful) interest.

2. The works depicts sexual conduct in a patently offensive way.

3. The work taken as a whole lacks "serious literary, artistic, political or scientific value."

This third condition has come to be known as the **SLAPS test** (derived from taking the first letter of each word in the quoted phrase). In theory, adherence to the SLAPS test allows a jury to apply its own conception of "contemporary community standards" and thus ban relatively innocent sexual materials. In practice, however, courts have found very few materials able to survive the SLAPS test (after all, who is to say what possesses "artistic value"?). None of the three rules apply to child pornography, which enjoys no First Amendment protection whatsoever under the Constitution.

The rise of the Internet as a medium of communication has caused even more confusion about what types of obscenity and/or pornography can be regulated. In *Reno v. ACLU* (1997),[28] the Supreme Court invalidated a federal law passed to protect minors from "indecent" and "patently offensive" communications on the Internet. The Court feared that in denying minors access to potentially harmful speech, the law had suppressed a large amount of speech that adults have a constitutional right to receive. Still, the question of how to restrict sexually explicit speech on the Internet will remain an issue for years to come.

Symbolic Speech and the Flag-Burning Controversy

When school officials in Des Moines, Iowa, suspended two students for wearing black armbands in protest of the Vietnam War in the 1960s, they claimed they were not restricting free speech rights at all; rather, the students were engaging in conduct that could be regulated by authorities.[29] The Supreme Court in 1969 disagreed, and the students were vindicated,[30] but the line between speech and conduct remains difficult to draw. Protesters often engage in disruptive activities that make powerful statements about important issues of public policy. They may camp out in public parks overnight to bring attention to the plight of the homeless or burn their draft cards as a statement of opposition to a war. Are such forms of **symbolic speech** protected by the First Amendment?

The constitutionality of flag burning has been a source of considerable debate. To many, the American flag is a symbol of nationhood and national unity and thus must be preserved at all costs. For that very reason, protesters seeking to attract publicity for their ideas have burned or desecrated the flag in public places. The Supreme Court ended the legal debate over flag burning with its decision in *Texas v. Johnson* (1989).[31] At a 1984 political demonstration protesting the Reagan administration, Gregory Lee Johnson set an American flag on fire while chanting "America, the red, white and blue, we spit on you." He was then arrested for and convicted of "desecrating a venerated object." The Supreme Court threw out Johnson's conviction because the "government may not prohibit the expression of an idea simply because society finds the idea itself offensive or disagreeable."[32]

Varying Levels of Support for the First Amendment

A recent comprehensive national study of American adults, high school students, teachers, and principals revealed the depth of support that exists for First Amendment free expression rights. The study, analyzed in a 2008 book, found that students are less likely than adults to think that people should be allowed to express unpopular opinions or that newspapers should be allowed to publish freely without government approval of stories. The study also revealed that when it comes to situations more relevant to students' own lives and concerns, students agree at higher rates than adults that certain forms of expression should be allowed (for

example, musicians singing songs with offensive lyrics, or student newspapers reporting controversial issues without administrative approval).

For Critical Thinking and Discussion

1. Why do you think students are less tolerant of civil liberties exercised by professional editors and publishers than they are of their own free press rights? Why aren't the two rights connected?

2. Do you agree that musicians' use of controversial lyrics deserves full constitutional protection? Explain.

3. Print newspapers are on the decline, while Internet newspapers are on the rise. Do you think those different types of publications should be treated the same for First Amendment purposes? Why or why not?

Do you agree or disagree that...
(% who agree with each statement is shown)

Statement	Adults	Principals	Teachers	Students
People should be allowed to express unpopular opinions	83%	97%	99%	95%
Newspapers should be allowed to publish freely without government approval of stories	51%	80%	80%	70%
Musicians should be allowed to sing songs with lyrics others may find offensive	70%	58%	43%	59%
H.S. students should be allowed to report controversial issues in their student newspapers without approval of school authorities	58%	39%	25%	43%

■ Adults ▨ Principals ☐ Teachers ▨ Students

Source: Kenneth Dautrich, David Yalof, and Mark Hugo Lopez, *The Future of the First Amendment* (Lanham, MD: Rowman & Littlefield, 2008).

Hate Speech Codes

Since the 1970s, communities have sought to prevent speakers who preach hatred for certain groups—whether racial, religious, or some other classification—from exercising their rights of free speech in certain specified neighborhoods or other places where the perceived harms may be great. Such efforts have not always passed constitutional muster. In 1977, the courts refused to deny neo-Nazis the right to march in a parade in Skokie, Illinois, home to a large number of Holocaust victims.[33] By contrast, efforts to ban cross burning and other controversial forms of expression have sometimes been upheld. In *Virginia v. Black* (2003),[34] the U.S. Supreme Court ruled that the state of Virginia could prohibit cross burning with the "intent to intimidate any person or group" because the law applied only to intimidation and not to cross burning in general. The law also applied to all groups, not just racial or ethnic groups.

It is a considerable challenge for school officials to restrict hate speech by students at public colleges and universities, even when that speech proves disruptive to the school's mission of providing a constructive environment for learning.[35] In 1988, the University of Michigan passed a regulation subjecting individuals to discipline for "behavior, verbal or physical" that stigmatized or victimized an individual on the basis of race, ethnicity, religion, sex, or a host of other criteria. Stanford University similarly attempted to prohibit "discriminatory harassment," which was defined to include speech intended to stigmatize or insult on the basis of sex, race, and so on. Lower courts invalidated both of these "hate speech codes" on grounds that they violated the First Amendment.

The Right to Bear Arms

> *THE SECOND AMENDMENT: A well regulated militia, being necessary to the security of a free State, the right of the people to keep and bear Arms, shall not be infringed.*

The Second Amendment "right to keep and bear arms" has been something of a puzzle for Americans. On the one hand, the second part of the amendment appears to trumpet the "people's" right to own firearms at their discretion and has taken its place as a central tenet in the platforms of interest groups such as the National Rifle Association (NRA), which opposes nearly all government attempts to restrict gun ownership. On the other hand, the first part of the amendment speaks directly of a "well regulated militia" and implies that some relationship must exist between the private gun owner's rights and more formal state activities. The U.S. Supreme Court finally weighed in on the subject in 2008. In *District of Columbia v. Heller* (2008),[36] the Supreme Court by a 5–4 vote held that the Second Amendment forbids the government from banning all forms of handgun possession in the home for purposes of immediate self-defense. In *McDonald v. Chicago* (2010),[37] the Supreme Court went a step further, ruling that the right to bear arms is incorporated by the due process clause of the Fourteenth Amendment, and thus applies to all fifty states as well. However, this Second Amendment right is not absolute: The Court in *Heller* noted that government can still regulate the commercial sale of handguns; it can also prohibit their possession by felons and the mentally ill, or in sensitive places such as school buildings.

© 2012 CENGAGE LEARNING

Second Amendment considerations aside, Congress has been reluctant to regulate gun ownership; only rarely are the sponsors of gun control able to overcome fierce lobbying efforts by the NRA and others in opposition. Advocates of gun control scored some success following the attempted assassination of President Ronald Reagan in 1981. Reagan was wounded in the attempt, as was James Brady, his press secretary. The subsequent Brady Handgun Violence Prevention Act required a five-day waiting period and a background check on handgun purchases from licensed firearms dealers to ensure that felons, drug users, fugitives, and other specified categories of individuals not be permitted to purchase guns. The NRA avoided any direct court challenges to the law on Second Amendment grounds, hammering instead at more peripheral aspects of the law, such as the requirement that local sheriffs conduct these checks as part of a federal regulatory scheme. In 1997, the Supreme Court struck down this aspect of the Brady Law as a violation of federalism but left the substance of the law in place. Congress has also attempted to restrict the carrying of firearms near schools, even though some of these efforts have been invalidated by the Supreme Court. Recent shooting incidents at Virginia Tech and Northern Illinois Universities have increased criticism of less restrictive gun laws and policies, but political officials in those states and elsewhere remain divided on how to respond.

The Rights of the Accused

A few rights for the accused may be found in the language of the original Constitution. Article I prohibits Congress from passing a **bill of attainder**, which is an act of a legislature declaring a person (or group) guilty of some crime and then carrying out punishment without a trial. It also prohibits **ex post facto laws**, which are new criminal laws retroactively applied to those who engaged in activities when they were not yet illegal. But the vast majority of constitutional rights for those accused of crimes are in the Fourth, Fifth, Sixth, and Eighth Amendments to the Constitution. Despite the seemingly explicit protections found in those four amendments, accused individuals enjoyed only limited substantive protection from arbitrary violations of criminal due process for better than a century and a half of this nation's history, as they protected defendants primarily only against intrusions by the federal government.

Much of that changed in the 1960s with a number of decisions handed down by the Warren Court. During that period, the Supreme Court applied many of the provisions of the Bill of Rights against state governments by incorporating most of the protections given accused persons in the federal judicial system. In addition, the Warren Court gave increased substance to these rights, holding government officials accountable under the Bill of Rights for their actions at highway road stops, during the interrogation of witnesses at the police station, and elsewhere.[38] Even the right to counsel was broadened to extend to far more of those accused of committing crimes. During the late 1980s and 1990s, the Court, under Chief Justice William Rehnquist, scaled back some of these protections. Nevertheless, defendants forced to weave their way through the criminal justice system today still enjoy numerous rights protections that were not guaranteed before the Warren Court era.

Bill of attainder
An act of a legislature declaring a person (or group) guilty of some crime, and then carrying out punishment without a trial. The Constitution denies Congress the ability to issue a bill of attainder.

Ex post facto law
A law that punishes someone for doing something in the past, at a time when the act was not illegal. The Constitution denies government the ability to write laws ex post facto.

Shedding Fourth Amendment Rights at the Schoolhouse Door

Justice Abe Fortas once wrote that "students do not . . . shed their constitutional rights when they enter the schoolhouse door." His comment held true in *Tinker v. Des Moines* (1967), when the Court upheld the rights of students to wear black armbands in protest of the Vietnam War. Yet the Court has not been so kind to students in subsequent civil liberties cases. This has been especially true in the schoolhouse itself, where Fourth Amendment rights may be implicated. When the state's power to search and seize conflicts with student claims of privacy, all the advantages lie with the state.

The leading Supreme Court case addressing students' Fourth Amendment rights is *New Jersey v. TLO* (1985), involving the search of a high school student for contraband after she was caught smoking. The assistant vice principal's subsequent search of her purse without a warrant revealed drug paraphernalia and marijuana. The U.S. Supreme Court held that the search was constitutional so long as it was "deemed reasonable given the circumstances." Since the student was caught and taken directly to the office, it was considered "reasonable" to assume the purse contained some evidence of wrongdoing.

For Critical Thinking and Discussion

1. Do you think the rights of college students on your campus should be equivalent to the rights adults enjoy in the workplace, or should they be equivalent to the more limited rights of high school students?
2. Is the location of the search relevant?
3. Should college students enjoy the same rights against unreasonable searches and seizures in their dorm rooms as they enjoy elsewhere on campus?
4. Should private colleges and universities have greater power to search students than public colleges or universities? Why or why not?

MIKAEL KARLSSON/ALAMY

★ LO Understand the scope of Fourth Amendment rights and the privacy issues raised by advances in technology

Fourth Amendment Rights

THE FOURTH AMENDMENT: The right of the people to be secure in their persons, houses, papers and effects, against unreasonable searches and seizures, shall not be violated, and no Warrants shall issue, but upon probable cause . . .

The right of citizens to be free from unreasonable searches and seizures has a long history in America. Before the American Revolution, colonists loudly protested English abuses of the power to inspect merchants' goods through the use of an unlimited "general warrant." Although the Fourth Amendment had been in place for nearly two centuries, the Warren Court modernized the rules governing police searches with its decision in *Katz v. United States* (1967).[39] The Court's ruling created the ***Katz* test**, which requires that the government attain a warrant demonstrating "probable cause" for any investigative activity that violates a person's reasonable expectation of privacy, whether or not the person is at home. A **warrant** is a document issued by a judge or magistrate that allows law enforcement to search or seize items at a home, business, or anywhere else that might be specified.

Perhaps the most controversial aspect of the Fourth Amendment is the mechanism by which it is enforced. Although no specific provision for enforcing civil liberties is provided in the amendment, since its 1961 decision in *Mapp v. Ohio*,[40] the Supreme Court has demanded that the states adhere to the **exclusionary rule**, by which all evidence obtained by police in violation of the Bill of Rights must be "excluded" from admission in a court of law, where it might have assisted in convicting those who have been accused of committing crimes. Complaints about the exclusionary rule focus on its most likely beneficiaries: those who are guilty of committing some wrongdoing. Since the 1960s, the Court has modified application of the exclusionary rule somewhat, although it has refused to back down from its central requirements. The most significant of these modifications is the **good faith exception** to the rule, which was first instituted in 1984: If a search warrant is invalid through no fault of the police (for example, the judge puts the wrong date on the warrant), evidence obtained under that warrant may still be admitted into court. Police may also under certain circumstances conduct warrantless searches of a defendant's premises. The allowable circumstances for a warrantless search include (1) the search is incidental to a lawful arrest, (2) the defendant has given consent to be searched, (3) the police are in "hot pursuit" of the defendant, and (4) the evidence is in "plain view" of police standing in a place where they have the legal right to be. Police may also briefly stop individuals driving in their cars or conduct a "pat down" of suspicious individuals for weapons; in neither case is a warrant required.

Advances in technology and new innovations in police work have invited new types of Fourth Amendment civil liberties claims and a potential reinterpretation of those rights by the U.S. Supreme Court. Testing defendants for drug or alcohol use through breathalyzer tests and taking blood samples may require the police to jump through a series of procedural hoops imposed on them by the state, but no warrant is generally required in either instance when the defendant is in the legitimate custody of the police. Similarly, the DNA testing of defendants has provided a significant breakthrough in the prosecution of difficult cases that lack eyewitnesses or other "hard" evidence of the crime.

Fifth Amendment Rights

> *THE FIFTH AMENDMENT: No person shall be held to answer for a capital, or otherwise infamous crime, unless on a presentment or indictment of a grand jury . . . nor shall any person be subject for the same offense to be twice put in jeopardy of life or limb; nor shall be compelled in any criminal case to be a witness against himself . . .*

Under the Fifth Amendment, the accused enjoy an assortment of rights that may prove crucial to their defense. The requirement that a grand jury, a jury that meets to decide whether the evidence is sufficient to justify a prosecutor's request that a case go to trial, be convened for serious crimes is theoretically

Katz test
The legal standard that requires the government to attain a warrant demonstrating "probable cause" for any "search" that violates a person's actual and reasonable expectation of privacy.

Warrant
A document issued by a judge or magistrate that allows law enforcement to search or seize items at a home, business, or anywhere else that might be specified.

Exclusionary rule
The legal rule requiring that all evidence illegally obtained by police in violation of the Bill of Rights must be "excluded" from admission in a court of law, where it might have assisted in convicting those accused of committing crimes.

Good faith exception
An exception to the exclusionary rule that states if a search warrant is invalid through no fault of the police, evidence obtained under that warrant may still be admitted into court.

★ LO
Understand the rules against double jeopardy and the privilege against self-incrimination

significant; it forces prosecutors to convince an initial jury that a defendant should rightfully be forced to go to trial. (Grand juries do not decide on a defendant's guilt or innocence.) In practice, however, the grand jury requirement is rarely much of an obstacle to a skilled prosecutor, who can selectively present evidence to the jury members outside the view of the defendant or the defendant's lawyer. Moreover, because the grand jury requirement was never incorporated, it applies only to federal prosecutors in federal court.[41] The **double jeopardy clause** is a source of much greater protection for defendants: It provides that no defendant may be tried twice for the same crime. Prosecutors must weigh carefully their probability of success at trial and bring forth all the relevant resources at their disposal. If the jury acquits the defendant, the prosecutor cannot try the defendant again. Still, the double jeopardy clause does not stop an altogether different government from retrying the defendant for violating that government's own laws.

Double jeopardy clause
The constitutional protection that those accused of a crime cannot be tried twice for the same crime.

DAVID R. FRAZIER/THE IMAGE WORKS

Another provision of the Fifth Amendment is the so-called self-incrimination clause, which prevents individuals from being compelled to testify against themselves. Although originally interpreted to provide protection for defendants only in the courtroom, the self-incrimination clause today offers substantial protection to defendants being questioned by police at the station house or elsewhere. Certainly, the clause protects defendants from being coerced or tortured into confessing to crimes. But the Warren Court truly changed this area of the law in the now famous case of *Miranda v. Arizona* (1966).[42] In that ruling, the Supreme Court announced the requirement that **Miranda warnings** be read to all defendants in custody before they are questioned by police. Chief Justice Warren wrote, "Prior to any questioning, the person must be warned that he has a right to remain silent, that any statement he does make may be used as evidence against him, and that he has a right to the presence of an attorney, either retained or appointed. . . ."

"You have the right to remain silent. Anything you say will be used against you in a court of law. You have the right to an attorney during interrogation; if you cannot afford an attorney, one will be appointed to you."
—Miranda warning, *Miranda v. Arizona*

Miranda warnings
The U.S. Supreme Court's requirement that an individual who is arrested must be read a statement that explains the person's right to remain silent and the right to an attorney.

Thanks to police drama shows and movies, the *Miranda* warnings are better known to citizens today than are any other constitutional protections: Police must routinely tell suspects being questioned that they have the right to remain silent and the right to a court-appointed attorney, and they must confirm that the suspects understand these rights. Perhaps that's why a more conservative Supreme Court conceded in the case of *United States v. Dickerson* (2000) that Miranda has become so "embedded in routine police practice" that the warnings have become "part of our national culture." Thus, a failure to read the list of Miranda rights to witnesses may still result in any subsequent confession to the police being thrown out of court by virtue of the exclusionary rule.[43]

Sixth Amendment Rights

THE SIXTH AMENDMENT: In all criminal prosecutions, the accused shall . . . have the Assistance of Counsel for his defense.

Images of beleaguered and confused defendants trying desperately to defend themselves against experienced and well-seasoned prosecutors are now mostly a thing of the past. In 1963, the Supreme Court in *Gideon v. Wainwright*[44] ordered a new trial for an indigent defendant who had been ordered by the state of Florida to defend himself in a criminal trial, even though he possessed no legal training. Under prevailing Sixth Amendment standards today, no indigent criminal defendant can be sentenced to jail unless the defendant has been provided with a lawyer at no cost. This constitutional right to the assistance of counsel even extends beyond the trial: A court-appointed lawyer must assist the defendant in preparing the case and in all other hearings and meetings before trial. Some critics of the criminal justice system cite the disparity that often exists between the quality of court-appointed counsel and of paid counsel for well-off defendants. Nevertheless, public defenders' offices have been established all over the country in response to the requirement that indigent defendants be provided with lawyers.

Eighth Amendment Rights

THE EIGHTH AMENDMENT: Excessive bail shall not be required, nor excessive fines imposed, nor cruel and unusual punishments inflicted.

The Eighth Amendment deals in a limited way with defendants being held for trial: According to its language, **bail**, which is an amount of money paid to the court as security against a defendant's freedom before trial, may not be excessive. In practice, that provision applies only when bail is proper in the first place; many high-risk defendants are held either to prevent flight or to ensure that they do not cause more harm while on release. In those instances, bail may be denied altogether without any violation of the Constitution.

Bail
An amount of money determined by a judge that the accused must pay to a court as security against his or her freedom before trial.

Far more significant are the concluding words of the Eighth Amendment with respect to "cruel and unusual punishments." No government may impose a cruel and unusual punishment on an individual, but there remains heated debate over what is "cruel and unusual." Traditionally, the clause prohibited only those punishments that even the drafters of the Bill of Rights would have disapproved of—drawing and quartering, beheading, and other forms of extreme torture. By contrast, in April 2008, the Supreme Court upheld Kentucky's protocol for executing prisoners with lethal injections, even though the practice carried with it the risk of "excruciating pain." The Supreme Court has also insisted on "proportionality," which holds that serious punishments may not be imposed for relatively minor offenses. Thus, for example, the Court has struck down imprisonment for the controversial offense of "being addicted to the use of narcotics" on the ground that the state was punishing someone for an illness.

The Supreme Court has never held the death penalty to be inherently cruel and unusual as a general matter. Most modern lawsuits by prisoners on death row focus on the manner by which the death sentence has been imposed. Any judge or jury that imposes capital punishment must have the opportunity to consider mitigating circumstances that might generate some sympathy for the

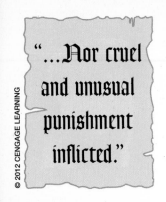

"...Nor cruel and unusual punishment inflicted."

★ LO Understand the right of abortion and its scope under *Roe v. Wade*, and then later under *Planned Parenthood v. Casey*

accused. Nor can a jury impose a death sentence at the same time that it finds the defendant guilty; the defendant's lawyers must be given a chance to argue against imposition of the death penalty without also having to prove the defendant is innocent. Finally, certain defendants may not receive the death penalty. In 2002, the Court in *Atkins v. Virginia* ruled executions impermissible in the case of defendants who are mentally retarded.[45] Then in 2005, the Court also ruled executions impermissible for defendants who committed their crimes while under the age of eighteen.

The Modern Right to Privacy

Perhaps no single constitutional right garnered more controversial attention during the second half of the twentieth century than the right to have an abortion. Unlike all the other rights mentioned so far in this chapter, however, neither the specific right to abortion, nor the more general right to privacy, are explicitly referred to in the Constitution or its amendments. The right to privacy is thus often referred to as an unwritten or "unenumerated" right. The Ninth Amendment counsels against dismissing such rights offhand. It reads: "The enumeration in the Constitution of certain rights, shall not be construed to deny or disparage others retained by the people." In other words, the fact that other rights such as freedom of speech are written down in the Bill of Rights does not mean that the Constitution doesn't also recognize certain unwritten rights.

The recognition of unstated rights in the Constitution raises difficult questions, such as how to justify recognizing certain unenumerated rights but not others. In 1965, the Supreme Court stepped into this controversy with its decision in *Griswold v. Connecticut*,[46] when it invalidated an 1879 Connecticut law prohibiting the dissemination of information about and the sale of contraceptives. Eight years later, the Supreme Court formally recognized the constitutional right to an abortion in *Roe v. Wade*.[47] Lawyers for Norma McCorvey (she used the pseudonym "Jane Roe" for purposes of her lawsuit) argued that the decision to end a pregnancy was a constitutional right that *all fifty states* must adhere to. McCorvey had been unable to secure a legal abortion in Texas and so eventually gave birth and put her baby up for adoption.

In ruling in McCorvey's favor, the Supreme Court affirmed that the Constitution recognizes a right to privacy in general—and thus, a right to abortion more specifically—even though neither of those rights is ever spelled out explicitly. Such a right is not absolute throughout the term of the pregnancy, however. The author of the opinion, Justice Harry Blackmun, divided the pregnancy into three stages as part of a highly controversial *trimester framework*. During the first trimester, a woman's right to end her pregnancy is absolute. During the second trimester, the right is nearly absolute, although the government has the right to restrict abortions that might pose threats to a woman's health. Finally, in the third trimester (when the fetus is potentially viable), the state government is allowed to impose any abortion restrictions on the mother, as long as they do not limit efforts to protect the life or health of the mother.[48]

The number of legal abortions that occurred in the United States rose dramatically in the years immediately following *Roe v. Wade*. The decision also unleashed a fury of controversy from antiabortion interest groups and conservative lawmakers. The election of Ronald Reagan to the presidency in 1980 and his reelection in 1984 set the stage for *Roe v. Wade*'s weakening; as a candidate for high office, Reagan had targeted *Roe v. Wade* as a case of illegitimate judicial activism and had promised to nominate Supreme Court justices who would overturn the controversial decision. Reagan's more conservative Supreme Court appointments began to make their presence known during the late 1980s, when increasingly severe restrictions on abortion were upheld by the Court.

In 1992, the Supreme Court overhauled *Roe v. Wade*'s controversial trimester framework in *Planned Parenthood v. Casey*.[49] Although the Court did not specifically overturn *Roe*, the justices replaced the trimester framework with a less stringent *undue burden test*: Does the restriction at issue—regardless of what trimester it affects—*unduly burden* a woman's right to privacy under the Constitution? One example of this undue burden test is found in the Court's approach to state-mandated twenty-four-hour waiting periods for abortion. In *Casey*, the Court held that such a waiting period does not unduly burden a woman's right to privacy. Other regulations that have been upheld under the *Casey* framework include the requirement that minors seek permission from a parent or a court before having an abortion and the requirement that women seeking abortions be provided with information about the specific medical effects an abortion will have on the fetus.

Not all abortion restrictions are allowed under this new framework. In *Casey*, the Supreme Court invalidated a requirement that women notify their spouses of their intention to have abortions. Yet many more provisions restricting abortion have been upheld since 1992 under the less restrictive *Casey* doctrine. In *Gonzales v. Carhart* (2007),[50] the Supreme Court upheld the Partial Birth Abortion Act of 2003, which effectively banned the use of the "intact dilation and extraction" abortion procedure, most often performed during the second trimester of pregnancy.

Once the unwritten right to privacy became a reality in constitutional law, it seemed inevitable that citizens might try to claim other unwritten rights implicating privacy in the same fashion. Although most efforts to expand the right to privacy beyond abortion and birth control have met with limited success, the Court has not always shut the door on these claims. In 1986, the Court held that a Georgia law that criminalized acts of sodomy by homosexuals was constitutional. Seventeen years later, in the case of *Lawrence v. Texas*,[51] the Court reversed itself, holding that a Texas law making it a crime for two people of the same sex to engage in certain types of intimate sexual conduct did in fact violate the individual's right to due process.

★ LO
Become familiar with the privacy rights that apply to government restrictions on sodomy and euthanasia

Do terminally ill patients have the right to end their life, and if so, can a licensed physician assist them in doing so? Although the Court has been willing to recognize a right of terminally ill patients to end their medical treatment, it has steadfastly refused to extend that privilege to the active termination of one's life. In 1997, the Supreme Court held that no such constitutional right exists, although the justices were significantly divided as to the specific reasons that is so. But the Court also indicated that states are free to legalize physician-assisted suicide. Since then, only one state (Oregon) has enacted an assisted suicide law.

NOW & THEN

Making the Connection

Passionate debates over constitutional rights are hardly a new phenomenon. With a tradition of robust press protections in America dating back to the early eighteenth century, the Sedition Act of 1798 stood little chance of long-term success; America's policy of openness to immigrants from abroad similarly doomed the Alien Act passed that same year. (Both acts were repealed just three years after their passage.) As a candidate, Barack Obama attacked the George W. Bush administration for violating the rights of the accused in prosecuting the war on terror; yet once he became president, he left many of his predecessor's more controversial measures in place, and he failed to effectively modify a handful of others. Where necessary, Obama vigorously defended those initiatives as necessary for national security. Although the actions of the Adams and Obama administrations could have been loosely defined as "wartime measures," not all Americans are equally willing to compromise the Bill of Rights in pursuit of a greater cause. John Adams suffered the public's wrath at the polls in 1800; if President Obama fails to protect the nation from further terrorist attacks, he too may suffer the same fate. Ultimately, a balancing act is required between the interests of national security and the integrity of these constitutional rights. Not all presidents are able to strike that balance with the same degree of political success.

Notwithstanding the enduring conflict between the values of national security and individual liberty, it is quite clear that during the past half century the Bill of Rights has been transformed from a set of mostly paper guarantees with only limited impact on the daily lives of Americans into a truly formidable arsenal of rights that have revolutionized government practices in the public square, at police stations, and in the nation's criminal courts. The Warren Court of the 1960s was responsible for much of this transformation. But the seeds of change were planted much earlier, first through ratification of the Fourteenth Amendment to protect individuals against state intrusion on their rights, and then later, when Justice Harlan Fiske Stone offered a theory of preferred freedoms in 1938 that trumpeted the freedom of speech and other rights that gave citizens their voice in the democratic process. Chief Justice Warren took Justice Stone up on this offer nearly a quarter of a century later, and the rights revolution was born.

In recent decades, the Supreme Court has attempted to return some authority to state governments to manage their own affairs. It has also scaled back some of the more controversial Warren Court decisions. In particular, the Rehnquist Court loosened many of the restrictions on government imposed by the two religious clauses of the First Amendment: the establishment clause and the free exercise clause. It also diluted a woman's right to abortion under *Roe v. Wade* in the 1990s. At the same time, many of the sweeping changes introduced by the Warren Court have been left untouched. And some constitutional protections have even been broadened in the past fifteen years; the right to free speech, for example, now encompasses the right to burn an American flag as a statement of political protest.

POLITICS InterActive!

A Holdout on Capital Punishment

The death penalty is the ultimate punishment for those convicted of crimes—it cannot be reversed once carried out, and it effectively trumps the exercise of all other rights. And yet capital punishment remains a staple of the American criminal justice system, sustained by public opinion polls that have long shown a clear majority of Americans in its favor. An ABC News survey in July 2006 found 65 percent in favor of capital punishment, consistent with many other polls taken in recent years. Moreover, according to a Gallup poll from two months earlier, nearly half the American public thinks the death penalty isn't imposed frequently enough, and fully 60 percent believe it is applied fairly in its current form. Since 1976, the Supreme Court has consistently held that with proper safeguards, the application of the death penalty to competent adults does not violate the Eighth Amendment's prohibition against "cruel and unusual punishments."

AP PHOTO/MICHAEL CONROY

What may seem surprising to many is the degree to which Americans' support for the death penalty defies worldwide trends, which have moved consistently in the opposite direction since World War II. In 1977, sixteen countries were already "abolitionist" regarding the death penalty; by 2010, ninety-five countries worldwide had abolished capital punishment for all offenses. In 2009, just eighteen countries carried out executions, with the United States ranking fifth (fifty-two executions), behind only China, Iran, Iraq, and Saudi Arabia. To a nation that prides itself as a beacon of light for freedom, this seems like unusual company.

At www.cengage.com/dautrich/americangovernmentbrief/2e, find the Politics InterActive link for details on the current state of the death penalty in the United States, the factors that have contributed to its continued support, relevant statistical information, and death penalty studies. Consult as well the various links that help place the current debate over the death penalty into historical, popular, and global perspectives.

Chapter Summary

★ SUMMARIZING WHAT YOU HAVE LEARNED ★

★ The Bill of Rights

- Civil liberties are those specific individual rights guaranteed by the Constitution that government cannot deny to citizens. Most of these rights are found in the Bill of Rights.

- The original Constitution did not include a bill of rights, and the framers guaranteed ratification of the Constitution by promising that the first Congress would propose such a bill.

- Civil liberties are subject to formal interpretation by the courts and informal interpretation by those charged with their enforcement. The courts' interpretation of these rights has evolved greatly over the past two centuries.

- Beginning in the mid-twentieth century, the U.S. Supreme Court, through a process known as incorporation, used the Fourteenth Amendment's due process clause to require state and local governments to uphold most of these protections as well.

★ Freedom of Religion and the Establishment Clause

- The free exercise clause bans government laws that prohibit the free exercise of religion. Debate over the clause has largely focused on whether government laws can force adherents of a certain religion to engage in activities that are prohibited by their religious beliefs.

- The establishment clause prohibits the government from enacting any law "respecting an establishment of religion." In recent decades, the Supreme Court has moved from a position of especially strict separation to one that shifts between separation and accommodation.

★ Free Expression Rights

- The First Amendment rights of free speech and press enjoy especially revered status in the United States because free expression promotes the marketplace of ideas, acts as a watchdog on government, and advances the capacity for individuals to create ideas and improve society.

- The press is afforded a great deal of latitude because the courts have made libel suits very difficult to pursue, and only under very few conditions may government issue a prior restraint on the publication of a story. Speech is not just the spoken word; it also includes such things as flag burning.

★ The Right to Bear Arms

- The Constitution protects the right of individuals to possess a firearm; still, the government retains the power to enact a broad range of firearms laws, including reasonable restrictions on possession by felons, or in sensitive places like schools or government buildings.

★ The Rights of the Accused

- The right of citizens to be free from unreasonable searches and seizures has a long history in America and is the subject of the Fourth Amendment. The basic notion that probable cause is a requirement for a warrant and that a warrant is necessary for a search hold true.

- Modern technologies have given the police and investigators new methods of search and surveillance. Some of these modern police tactics have been successfully challenged on Fourth Amendment grounds.

- Additional rights of the accused are articulated in the Fifth Amendment, including the double jeopardy clause, the grand jury requirement, and the self-incrimination clause. The U.S. Supreme Court has ruled that police must read the "Miranda warnings" to anyone who is arrested.

★ The Modern Right to Privacy

- The Ninth Amendment indicates that just because an individual right is not explicitly spelled out does not mean that the right is not protected. Two such high-profile rights are the subject of much national debate: the right to privacy and the right to die.

- A more recent conservative Supreme Court (since the decision in *Planned Parenthood v. Casey*) has allowed the states to place more restrictions on abortion rights of late.

- Although the Court has been willing to recognize the right of terminally ill patients to end their medical treatment, it has steadfastly refused to extend that privilege to the active termination of one's life. The Supreme Court has also recognized the rights of gays and lesbians to sexual privacy.

CourseMate

Key Terms

Bail (p. 101)

Bill of attainder (p. 97)

Civil liberties (p. 82)

Double jeopardy clause (p. 100)

Establishment clause (p. 87)

Ex post facto law (p. 97)

Exclusionary rule (p. 99)

Free exercise clause (p. 85)

Good faith exception (p. 99)

Incorporation (p. 84)

Katz test (p. 99)

Lemon test (p. 88)

Libel (p. 92)

Miranda warning (p. 100)

Prior restraint (p. 92)

SLAPS test (p. 94)

Symbolic speech (p. 94)

Warrant (p. 99)

Resources

Books

Amar, Akhil Reed. *The Constitution and Criminal Procedure.* New Haven, CT: Yale University Press, 1997.

Brigham, John. *The Constitution of Interests: Beyond the Politics of Rights.* New York: New York University Press, 1996.

Graber, Mark. *Transforming Free Speech.* Berkeley: University of California Press, 1991.

Lewis, Anthony. *Gideon's Trumpet.* New York: Vintage Books, 1989.

Lewis, Anthony. *Make No Law: The* Sullivan *Case and the First Amendment.* New York: Vintage Books, 1991.

O'Connor, Karen. *No Neutral Ground? Abortion Politics in the Age of Absolutes.* Boulder, CO: Westview Press, 1996.

Ravitch, Frank. *School Prayer and Discrimination.* Boston: Northeastern University Press, 1999.

Stone, Geoffrey. *Perilous Times.* New York: W. W. Norton, 2004.

Internet Sources

http://www.aclu.org (the home page of the American Civil Liberties Union; features coverage of a wide range of developments in civil liberties, as well as links to resources and other relevant Web sites).

http://www.fac.org/ (the Web site of the First Amendment Center, which works to preserve and protect First Amendment freedoms in America through information and education).

http://www.eff.org/ (the Web site of the Electronic Frontier Foundation, founded to protect rights and promote freedom on the electronic frontier, including the Internet).

5 Civil Rights, Equality, and Social Movements

NOW Shannon Faulkner at The Citadel in 1995.

AP PHOTO/WADE SPEES, POOL

THEN Autherine Lucy at the University of Alabama in 1956.

BETTMANN/CORBIS

NOW & THEN

Slow Going for a Pioneer in Equal Rights

After fighting a landmark legal battle with the help of civil rights groups, she had finally secured the right to attend this famous southern institution of higher education. The Fourteenth Amendment, the courts had ruled, prohibited the school from excluding her. Bracing for the worst, she expected resentment and hostility from students once she arrived on campus. The torments and continuous taunting were worse than she anticipated. After receiving numerous death threats, she needed an armed escort to accompany her to classes. Soon the isolation proved unbearable, and in less than a week, this landmark experiment in equal rights had reached its premature conclusion. While detractors cheered, the woman packed her bags and left the school she had fought so long and hard to enter. Although equal rights did not prevail at that moment in time, her overall cause was not lost; within a few years, many other students like her would successfully enter that same institution under more favorable conditions, and many of them would go on to graduate. Although her efforts to strike a blow at the backward traditions of the institution had failed for her personally, those efforts had not been in vain.

LEARNING OBJECTIVES
★ WHAT YOU WILL LEARN ★

Types of Equality
* ★ Define the three types of equality: political, social, and economic
* ★ Define civil rights and describe its role as a source of conflict among groups

The Struggle for Equality: Approaches and Tactics
* ★ List the means groups employ to pursue equality

The African American Struggle for Equality and Civil Rights
* ★ Review the history of racial discrimination against African Americans
* ★ Explain the role courts played in initially denying African Americans full equality and then granting that equality in *Brown v. Board of Education*
* ★ Understand the Court-created framework of equality and the challenges it presented
* ★ Trace the civil rights movement's history
* ★ Describe civil rights and voting rights
* ★ Appreciate more recent battles waged over affirmative action and racial profiling

The Women's Movement and Gender Equality
* ★ Understand the history of women's rights from women's suffrage up through the present
* ★ Evaluate the role of the courts in upholding legal challenges to gender discrimination since the 1970s
* ★ Understand Title IX's effect on women's rights

Other Struggles for Equality
* ★ Examine the struggles for equality waged by other racial, religious, and ethnic groups including Native Americans, Asian Americans, Muslims, and Hispanic Americans
* ★ Recognize the struggles of older Americans, Americans with disabilities, and gays and lesbians

CourseMate

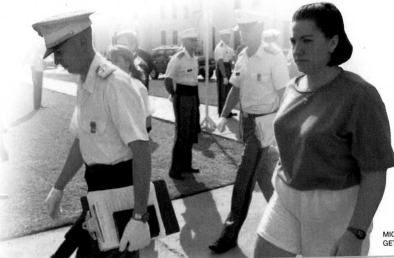

MIC SMITH/AFP/
GETTY IMAGES

NOW In 1995, Shannon Faulkner became a modern-day pioneer in equal rights. The institution Faulkner challenged was The Citadel in Charleston, South Carolina. The Citadel was a 152-year-old male-only military academy that prided itself on producing "citizen-soldiers," men uniquely prepared for leadership in military service and in civilian life. Faulkner had been accepted to The Citadel in 1993 after submitting an application that had failed to reveal her gender. When the school found out Faulkner was a woman, it immediately withdrew her acceptance, sparking a lawsuit filed on her behalf. Eventually, a federal district court ordered The Citadel to admit Faulkner in 1995 on the grounds that no public school could discriminate on the basis of gender. She moved into the barracks on August 12, 1995, accompanied by federal marshals because she had received so many death threats. Although Faulkner began "hell week" with the rest of her classmates, the emotional toll of the death threats and her isolation—combined with the physical toll of intense physical training—eventually proved too much for her. After only a day of training, she was admitted to the infirmary with heat-related symptoms, and on her fifth day at The Citadel, Faulkner dropped out of the school. When the news of her withdrawal got out, the male cadets let out a roar of celebration around campus. But their "victory" was short-lived: Taking advantage of the court order that Faulkner had secured, four more women enrolled at The Citadel the following year. The Citadel finally graduated its first female cadet (Nancy Mace) in 1999; since then over 200 women have successfully navigated The Citadel's grueling program to become full-fledged graduates of the institution.

THEN Faulkner was hardly the first pioneer to face such trying circumstances at an institution of education steeped in tradition. The scenario above also describes the experience of Autherine Lucy, the first African American student to win admission to the University of Alabama. On June 29, 1955, lawyers from the National Association for the Advancement of Colored People (NAACP) secured a court order restraining the university from rejecting Lucy's application on the basis of race; seven months later, on February 3, 1956, the twenty-six-year-old Lucy enrolled as a graduate student in library science at the university's main campus in Tusca-loosa. That's when her personal nightmare began. Immediately upon her arrival, she faced mobs of students yelling "Kill her! Kill her!" wherever she walked on campus. She needed a police escort to get her to class and to protect her in the classroom, where she could hear crowds chanting epithets at her from outside. Just three days after Lucy enrolled, the university's board suspended her, defending its action as necessary "for her safety and that of other students." Although the NAACP's attempts to overturn Lucy's suspension were unsuccessful, within a decade, many more African American students would follow in her footsteps, using a series of court orders to force the integration of the University of Alabama. The battle Autherine Lucy waged against University of Alabama officials was played out over and over again at other educational institutions in the late 1950s and early 1960s as part of a civil rights movement that brought national and international attention to issues of racial discrimination and inequality.

BETTMANN/CORBIS

J ust as Autherine Lucy challenged the white-only traditions of the South, Shannon Faulkner dared to rock the foundations of a well-entrenched male-only institution. Neither of these two women was able to stay in her school long enough to see the institution transformed. Both women, however, made significant contributions to the cause of equal rights. Traditions die hard, and those who battle such institutions in the name of equality must prepare themselves for slow going. Even when court opinions and legislation have transformed the political landscape in favor of equality, social and cultural landscapes often remain products of a stubborn past.

Types of Equality

In the abstract, the word *equality* joins terms such as *liberty*, *freedom*, and *justice* as lofty values that underlie American political culture. Unfortunately, when it comes to settling on a formal definition of equality, no consensus exists. "All men are created equal," Thomas Jefferson wrote in the Declaration of Independence of 1776. But Jefferson never intended that document to extend to African American slaves, at least not in the short run. When Abraham Lincoln warned in 1859 that "those who deny freedom to others, deserve it not for themselves," the future president of the United States did not consider the lot of women in American society, who at that time enjoyed no freedom to vote or own property, among other rights. As with any other abstract ideal, we must fully define equality to understand all that it encompasses.

References to different types of equality tend to appear again and again in discussions of American politics:

- **Political equality** generally refers to a condition in which members of different groups possess substantially the same rights to participate actively in the political system. These rights include voting, running for office, and formally petitioning the government for redress of grievances. In a democracy, the rights to free speech, to free press, and, at least arguably, to a quality education may also be considered necessary elements of political quality, as those who are denied such rights often are less able to exercise influence over the political process in any meaningful way. In the years immediately following the Civil War, some moderates in Congress argued that if freed slaves were simply given formal political equality, other benefits and privileges would inevitably follow. Reality quickly proved otherwise, as even African Americans in the North who were able to exercise their right to vote were generally unable to influence the political process.

- **Social equality** extends beyond the granting of political rights; it refers additionally to equality and fair treatment within the various institutions in society, both public and private, that serve the public at large. Social equality calls for a sameness of treatment in stores, theaters, restaurants, hotels, and public transportation facilities, among many other operations open to the public. Jim Crow laws passed in the South during the late nineteenth century segregated many of these institutions, thus denying social equality to African Americans.

- **Economic equality** remains the most controversial form of equality; indeed, its very mention often touches off heated debate among political officials. To some, society's responsibility to promote economic equality requires only that it provide equality of economic opportunity, by which different groups enjoy

---

★ **LO** Define the three types of equality: political, social, and economic

★ **LO** Define civil rights and describe its role as a source of conflict among groups.

Political equality
A condition in which members of different groups possess substantially the same rights to participate actively in the political system. In the United States, these rights include voting, running for office, petitioning the government for redress of grievances, free speech, free press, and the access to an education.

Social equality
Equality and fair treatment of all groups within the various institutions in society, both public and private, that serve the public at large, including in stores, theaters, restaurants, hotels, and public transportation facilities among many other operations open to the public.

Economic equality
May be defined as providing all groups the equality of opportunity for economic success, or as the equality of results. In the United States, the latter has been the more common understanding of economic opportunity.

substantially the same rights to enter contracts, purchase and sell property, and otherwise compete for resources in society. To others, economic equality extends beyond equality of economic opportunity to something approaching an equality of results. Whichever meaning one gives to the term, economic equality has been exceedingly difficult to achieve. Although the government has introduced a graduated income tax and other resource-leveling measures during the past century to improve economic opportunities for the poor, large variances in the quality of education afforded to different groups continue to render economic equality an elusive ideal.

The term **civil rights** has traditionally referred to those positive rights, whether political, social, or economic, conferred by the government on individuals or groups that had previously been denied them. What type of equality does the guarantee of civil rights promote? Immediately after the Civil War, civil rights legislation that would have provided for extensive social equality (equal accommodations in hotels, restaurants, trains, and other public facilities) was struck down as unconstitutional by the U.S. Supreme Court. As a result, the package of civil rights granted to freed slaves included only limited political rights, including the right to vote. In the late 1950s and 1960s, renewed efforts to guarantee equality in all areas of American life led to the Civil Rights movement.[1]

Many civil rights battles in American history have been waged by African Americans, but other ethnic groups, women, the physically disabled, the aged, and homosexuals have also sought the political, social, and economic equality denied them. The Constitution of the United States and the amendments to it have provided these groups with a framework to win equality. As a result, the meaning of civil rights has been significantly expanded both in the scope of its protection and in the variety of groups who seek its guarantees.

Civil rights
Those positive rights, whether political, social, or economic, conferred by the government on individuals or groups.

The Struggle for Equality: Approaches and Tactics

★ LO
List the means groups employ to pursue equality

The methods and tactics various groups use to achieve equality have evolved since the end of the Civil War. Initially, the battle over what constituted the most effective means of fostering change—at least in the context of challenging racial discrimination against African Americans—pitted two competing philosophies against each other. Booker T. Washington, who founded Tuskegee Normal and Industrial Institute (today Tuskegee University) in Alabama in 1881, advocated a philosophy of *accommodation*, which promoted vocational education for African Americans and opposed confrontation with the mostly white power structure in place in post–Civil War America. Washington urged his fellow African Americans to accept existing conditions, even to the point of tolerating racial segregation and all but surrendering the newly won right to vote.[2] Washington's passive approach contrasted with the philosophy of *agitation*, which challenged racial discrimination and injustice through various forms of political activity. At the beginning of the twentieth century, the most widely recognized proponent of this alternative, W. E. B. Du Bois, proposed a specific platform of legal, political, and social reforms to achieve social, economic, and political equality for African Americans.[3] Agitation eventually replaced accommodation as the dominant mode by which African Americans and other groups sought equality in twentieth-century America. New debates emerged, however, over what would be the most effective means and methods for achieving these reforms. Tactics that various groups have used to seek their civil rights include the following:

- **Working within the political system.** Some groups have used the political process to implement reforms to end discrimination. Various groups have expanded their influence more directly over public policies and programs by lobbying and petitioning government officials; in some cases, members of these groups have been elected to high public office, giving them a place at the table of political power.

- **Litigation.** When the political arena fails to provide adequate remedies to discrimination, a lawsuit brought before a court may afford a better opportunity for success. Founded in 1909 for the purpose of ensuring the political, educational, social, and economic equality of rights of all Americans, the NAACP focused its efforts on legal challenges to discrimination and segregation because the political arena had offered inadequate remedies. These efforts culminated with the U.S. Supreme Court's decision in ***Brown v. Board of Education* (1954)**,[4] which ordered the desegregation of public schools. In subsequent years, women's groups, disabled people, and other victims of discrimination have similarly turned to the courts for remedies to discriminatory practices.

- **Legal boycotts.** The organized refusal to buy, sell, or use certain goods or to perform certain services has long been a tool in economic battles waged between employers and unions. Adopting this tactic for use in the war on racial discrimination, African American citizens of Montgomery, Alabama, refused to ride the city's buses for more than a year in the mid-1950s; their efforts drained the city's public transportation budget and ultimately forced city officials to desegregate the bus system.

Brown v. Board of Education (1954)
The 1954 U.S. Supreme Court decision that declared school segregation to be unconstitutional.

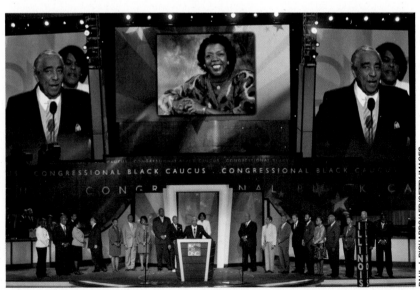

Members of the Congressional Black Caucus at the August 2008 Democratic National Convention in Denver, Colorado.

PAUL J. RICHARDS/AFP/GETTY IMAGES

- **Civil disobedience.** Sometimes, citizens resort to passive resistance to what they see as an unjust government policy or law by openly refusing to obey it. Such a tactic may result in arrests, fines, or even jail time for those who practice it. The Reverend Martin Luther King Jr., who had studied the methods used by Mohandas Gandhi of India and other nonviolent protestors, applied these methods to the civil rights movement in the American South.

The African American Struggle for Equality and Civil Rights

★ LO

Review the history of racial discrimination against African Americans

The period following the American Revolution offered equality primarily to property-owning white men. Nowhere did Jefferson's call for equality, as stated in the Declaration of Independence, seem hollower than in the area of racial discrimination. Throughout the North, African Americans were denied the right to vote and numerous other economic and social privileges enjoyed by white citizens. In the South, the institution of slavery thrived for more than a half century after the Constitution was ratified.

Racial Discrimination: From Slavery to Reconstruction

The organized antislavery movement in the United States began in the late eighteenth century as an effort to eradicate slavery through progressive elimination. Advocates of gradual emancipation believed that by preventing the extension of slavery to new areas and relocating emancipated slaves to areas outside the United States, slavery would eventually die out. Opposed to gradual emancipation were the abolitionists, who sought the immediate emancipation of all slaves. Still, many abolitionists at the time did not believe that emancipation automatically entitled freed slaves to the right to vote or serve on juries. Even among some of the most ardent advocates of equality before the Civil War, a sharp distinction was often drawn between economic rights, which they felt African Americans were entitled to, and basic political rights including suffrage, which were somehow not viewed as natural entitlements.

With the Union victory in the Civil War, the complete emancipation of African Americans after the war was a foregone conclusion. Former slaves were able to legally marry, worship as they wished, and migrate to different parts of the country. But the years following the Civil War—normally referred to as the Reconstruction era (1865–1877) in American history—proved a mixed blessing for the newly freed slaves.[5] The **Civil War Amendments** to the Constitution did grant African Americans the rights of citizenship. The Thirteenth Amendment (ratified in 1865) banished slavery from all states and U.S. territories. The Fourteenth Amendment (ratified in 1868) granted full U.S. and state citizenship to all people born or naturalized in the United States and guaranteed to each person "the equal protection of the laws." Finally, the Fifteenth Amendment (1870) forbade the denial or abridgement of the right to vote by any government on account of race, color, or previous condition of servitude. The Republican-controlled Congress hoped that these three amendments would institutionalize freedom for the former slaves and protect their rights from being undermined by future generations.

During the Reconstruction era, many freed slaves were successful in getting on ballots in the former Confederate states; in all, twenty-two African Americans

Civil War Amendments The Thirteenth Amendment (ratified in 1865) banished slavery from all states and U.S. territories. The Fourteenth Amendment (ratified in 1868) granted full U.S. and state citizenship to all people born or naturalized in the United States and guaranteed to each person "the equal protection of the laws." The Fifteenth Amendment (1870) forbade the denial or abridgement of the right to vote by any government on account of race.

were elected to the House and one (Hiram Revels of Mississippi) was elected to the Senate during the latter part of the nineteenth century. African American participation in Congress tailed off at the beginning of the twentieth century, however, because restrictions on the franchise curtailed the political viability of most black candidates. No African American served in either house of Congress for most of the first three decades of the twentieth century, and just four served in the House up to 1954. After George Henry White (R-NC) left Congress in 1901, no African American was elected from a southern state again until 1973, when Barbara Jordan (D-TX) and Andrew Young (D-GA) were elected to serve in the Ninety-third Congress.

Although African Americans achieved some gains during Reconstruction, the Reconstruction-era generation posed the greatest threat to those civil rights victories. The Civil Rights Act of 1875 attempted to ensure the social and political rights of freed slaves by, among other provisions, prohibiting discrimination in public accommodations. The Supreme Court invalidated the act in *The Civil Rights Cases* (1883),[6] ruling that whereas the Constitution prohibits the states from discriminating by race against certain civil rights, it does not protect the invasion of such civil rights by private individuals unaided by state authority. Therefore, privately owned restaurants and hotels could freely discriminate on the basis of race without violating the Constitution.

This judicial gutting of federal civil rights guarantees opened the way for numerous abuses of freed slaves once the federal government's military occupation of the South ended in 1877. Discrimination against African Americans in all areas of public life soon became the norm. Terrorist groups like the Ku Klux Klan intimidated or threatened African Americans to keep them under control, sometimes backing up their threats with beatings, arson, or murder. White vigilante groups resorted to lynching in an effort to restore white supremacy and deny blacks their rights. Post–Civil War blacks might no longer be slaves, but they could hardly be considered fully equal citizens under the law.

Racial Segregation and Barriers to Equality

In the period immediately following the Civil War, some African Americans were able to use public accommodations as long as they could afford to pay for them. By the turn of the twentieth century, however, growing racial tensions, exacerbated by urbanization and industrialization, led to racial segregation throughout America. The Southern states enacted **Jim Crow laws**, which required segregation of blacks and whites in public schools, railroads, buses, restaurants, hotels, theaters, and other public facilities. In *Plessy v. Ferguson* **(1896),**[7] the Supreme Court upheld a Louisiana law segregating railroad cars on the theory that as long as the accommodations between the racially segregated cars were equal, the equal protection clause of the Fourteenth Amendment was not violated. The Court's ruling established the constitutionality of racial segregation according to the *separate but equal* doctrine.

African American leaders responded to the spread of segregation in different ways. Initially, Booker T. Washington's accommodationist philosophy prevailed. W. E. B. Du Bois, by contrast, advocated direct and militant challenges to segregation. Perhaps the greatest breakthrough against segregation occurred through the legal arm of the organization that Du Bois helped found: the NAACP. Beginning in the late 1930s, NAACP lawyers Charles Houston and Thurgood Marshall began attacking the legal basis for segregation in the courts.[8] The NAACP's

Jim Crow laws
Laws used by some southern states that required segregation of blacks and whites in public schools, railroads, buses, restaurants, hotels, theaters, and other public facilities. The laws excluded blacks from militias and denied them certain education and welfare services.

Plessy v. Ferguson (1896)
The Supreme Court case that upheld a Louisiana segregation law on the theory that as long as the accommodations between the racially segregated facilities were equal, the equal protection clause was not violated. The Court's ruling effectively established the constitutionality of racial segregation and the notion of "separate but equal."

efforts directed at eliminating segregation in education culminated in 1954 with the Supreme Court's landmark decision in *Brown v. Board of Education*. Chief Justice Earl Warren, writing for a unanimous Court, held that racial segregation in any facet of public education constituted a denial of equal protection by the laws. Recognizing the psychological harms of segregation on African American children, the Court declared that segregated schools were "inherently unequal."

The *Brown* decision also confirmed that in all future cases related to racial (and ethnic) discrimination, the Court would apply a standard of **strict scrutiny**, a level of judicial review that requires the government to prove that the racial classification of the law or practice in question is "narrowly tailored" to meet a "compelling state interest." What precisely does this mean? At a minimum, there should be no less restrictive alternative means available for achieving the government's objectives, and those objectives should stand among the most necessary that may be pursued by any government. Many legal scholars and judges say the strict scrutiny standard tends to invalidate nearly all government laws and programs. In the years following *Brown*, the courts would apply the standard of strict scrutiny in decisions on segregated public swimming pools, police forces, and laws banning interracial marriages.

★ LO
Explain the role courts played in initially denying African Americans full equality and then granting that equality in *Brown v. Board of Education*

Strict scrutiny
A legal standard set in *Brown v. Board of Education* for cases related to racial discrimination that tends to invalidate almost all state laws that segregate racial groups.

★ LO
Understand the Court-created framework of equality and the challenges it presented

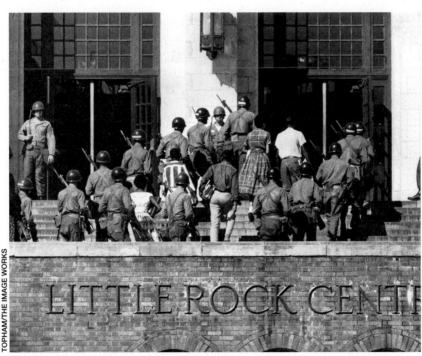

African American students are escorted through the doors of Little Rock's Central High School by the U.S. National Guard on September 25, 1957.

A year after handing down the *Brown* decision, the Supreme Court declared that its implementation should proceed "with all deliberate speed." Despite that decree, many local school boards resisted desegregation. The school board of Little Rock, Arkansas, adopted a plan for "phased integration" over a ten-year period, spurring more lawsuits to speed up the process. Undeterred, Arkansas

Governor Orval Faubus declared that no "*Brown* decisions" enjoyed "the force of law" in his state. Alabama Governor George Wallace blocked a University of Alabama doorway, refusing to allow black students to pass through in 1963. On several occasions, the Supreme Court was even forced to reassert its authority over state governments. In *Cooper v. Aaron* (1957),[9] for example, the Court held that the rights of African American students could "neither be nullified openly and directly by state legislatures or state executive officials . . . by evasive schemes for segregation."

Despite the Supreme Court's increasingly clear edicts against segregation, many school districts in the South and North continued to drag their feet.[10] Significant and widespread change would not occur until after passage of civil rights legislation in the mid-1960s, which gave the executive branch of the government increased power to enforce school desegregation in local districts. Additionally, a sudden influx of federal money into local schools gave extra bite to court desegregation decrees. As scholar Gerald Rosenberg remarked: "Put simply, courts could hold up federal funds." Many school districts in the Deep South, where fewer than half of all blacks were being educated alongside whites as late as 1967, were almost fully integrated by 1971.

In urban areas where whites and blacks lived largely apart, strict adherence to a neighborhood school system meant indefinitely perpetuating a racially unmixed setting; thus, massive court-ordered "busing" in the late 1960s and 1970s became a controversial feature of efforts to integrate these schools. Many such court orders were issued in both northern and southern cities, as the Supreme Court required communities to cease both *de jure discrimination* (segregation sanctioned by the law), which was found mostly in the South, and *de facto discrimination* (segregation in reality, such as that which occurs when different racial groups voluntarily choose to live in different neighborhoods or attend different schools), which was found in both the North and the South. Yet busing was a remedy limited to a single metropolitan area, and comprehensive efforts to integrate schools were further hindered by white flight to suburbia. Today, fully 70 percent of the nation's African American students attend schools that are predominantly black.

The Beginnings of the Civil Rights Movement

Although *Brown* signaled the end of state-sponsored segregation, the Supreme Court took pains to note that its holding applied only to discriminatory acts by the government. The extension of civil rights protections to all public accommodations did not occur until the civil rights movement began to gather momentum in the late 1950s and early 1960s. In December 1955, Rosa Parks, an African American seamstress in Montgomery, Alabama, was arrested for refusing to give up her seat at the front of a city bus. Her arrest sparked a racial boycott of the city's bus system. Leading the boycott was Martin Luther King Jr., pastor of the Dexter Avenue Baptist Church. King's eloquent speeches and his methods of nonviolent civil disobedience brought national attention to the boycott. King had been introduced to these strategies of nonviolent protest when he was a student at Crozer Theological Seminary in Chester, Pennsylvania, and studied the pacifist philosophy of Mohandas Gandhi of India, whose unshakable belief in nonviolent protest and religious tolerance helped secure independence for his country from Great Britain.

In 1957, King and other African American ministers in the South formed the Southern Christian Leadership Conference (SCLC), which encouraged Gandhian practices of nonviolent civil disobedience as a way to gain equal rights for blacks and spur white politicians into action. African American and white college students in numerous cities across the South eventually became the engine for pressing such change. One early tactic the students used was the sit-in. On February 1, 1960, four freshmen from the black North Carolina A&T College in Greensboro sat down at a whites-only lunch counter and refused to move after being denied service. The next day, more students—black and white—joined them. Angry mobs harassed the students verbally and physically. Committed to nonviolence, the students endured the abuse. The episode brought considerable publicity to the civil rights movement. In 1961, interracial groups of students sponsored "Freedom Rides," traveling together from Washington, DC, to the South to test court decisions prohibiting segregation on interstate buses and in bus terminals. Eventually, President John F. Kennedy was forced to nationalize the Alabama police to help assure the freedom riders safe passage.

Birmingham 1963: The Turning Point of the Civil Rights Movement

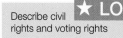

Describe civil rights and voting rights ★ LO

The civil rights movement's strategy of nonviolent civil disobedience reached a climax between 1963 and 1965.[11] The year 1963 will long be remembered as the "Year of Birmingham." Tension was growing between King's SCLC and new civil rights groups that favored more radical and militant action, including the use of violence. Birmingham was a stronghold of segregation; city leaders included the notoriously racist Public Safety Commissioner Eugene "Bull" Connor, who ruthlessly enforced segregation laws throughout the city.

In Birmingham, King led other demonstrators in a nonviolent march downtown, where he was arrested and placed in solitary confinement. While confined, he wrote his famous "Letter from Birmingham City Jail," addressed to the white Alabama clergymen who had criticized King's campaign. In the letter, King explained his philosophy and defended his strategy of nonviolent protest. Despite King's arrest, the demonstration in Birmingham continued. The marchers, including more than a thousand black schoolchildren, were met by attack dogs, cattle prods, and fire hoses. Pictures of children being attacked flashed across the nation's television sets, and newspapers and magazines across the world covered the violence. The nation would be forever aroused by these events; the civil rights movement had finally been transformed into a truly national cause.

President Lyndon Johnson and the U.S. Congress were eventually prodded into action. Johnson signed into law the **Civil Rights Act of 1964**, which banned racial discrimination in all public accommodations, including those that were privately owned. It also prohibited discrimination by employers and created the Equal Employment Opportunity Commission to investigate complaints of discrimination, and it denied public funds to schools that continued to discriminate on the basis of race.[12] The **Voting Rights Act of 1965**, enacted the following year, invalidated literacy tests and property requirements for voting and required that certain states and cities with a history of voting discrimination obtain pre-approval from the Justice Department for all future changes to their voting laws. As a consequence, millions of African Americans were effectively reenfranchised in the South.

Civil Rights Act of 1964
The federal law that banned racial discrimination in all public accommodations, including those that were privately owned; prohibited discrimination by employers and created the Equal Employment Opportunity Commission to investigate complaints of discrimination; and denied public funds to schools that continued to discriminate on the basis of race.

Voting Rights Act of 1965
The federal law that invalidated literacy tests and property requirements and required select states and cities to apply for permission to the Justice Department to change their voting laws. As a consequence, millions of African Americans were effectively reenfranchised in the South.

The focus of the civil rights movement began to shift in the mid to late 1960s with the rise of "black nationalism," which was grounded in the belief that African Americans could not effectively work within the confines of a racist political system to produce effective change. Malcolm X, a leading advocate of black nationalism, sought to turn the characteristic of being black-skinned into a source of strength, and he urged African Americans to shun white culture and the values promoted by white society. Epitomizing a revolutionary vision of society that replaced the strategy of nonviolence with confrontational tactics, the Black Panther Party became a controversial militant presence in some cities.

Black separatist organizations continue to maintain a strong presence. For example, the Nation of Islam (Black Muslims), led by Louis Farrakhan, preaches class consciousness and the concept of black self-rule. In 1995, Farrakhan's Nation of Islam led the Million Man March in Washington, DC, which far outdrew the 1963 March on Washington. This Million Man March garnered international attention for Farrakhan's movement. Four years later, African American women responded with their own million women march.

Barack Obama's historic election as the first African American president in U.S. history may have fundamentally changed how many African Americans perceive their national government. Still, African Americans as a whole face immense challenges in making their voices heard in other institutions on the national political scene. Obama left a Senate chamber in November 2008 in which he had been the only African American then serving, and where he was just the third popularly elected African American senator to serve since Reconstruction. (His replacement as junior senator from Illinois, Roland Burris, also an African American, was appointed to the position.) African Americans enjoyed a bit more success in the other house of Congress, as forty-two African Americans (9.5 percent) served in the House of Representatives during the 111th Congress. Finally, African Americans have been mostly absent from the highest levels of state government: In 2006, Deval Patrick of Massachusetts became only the second popularly elected African American governor in history.

Continuing Struggles over Racial Equality

★ LO Appreciate more recent battles waged over affirmative action and racial profiling

Two contemporary and hotly debated topics related to racial equality are affirmative action and racial profiling.

Affirmative Action. Some observers have called the civil rights movement a "Second Reconstruction" because it eliminated most of the vestiges of racial discrimination and segregation from the books. But would this successful legal revolution translate into real change? Various civil rights leaders in the 1970s and 1980s shifted their focus to affirmative action as a means of promoting African American gains in education and the workplace. **Affirmative action** programs are generally laws or practices designed to remedy past discriminatory hiring practices, government contracting, and school admissions. The women's movement has also benefited from affirmative action programs in the workplace and elsewhere. Although quotas (specifically defined numerical goals for hiring or admitting members of certain groups) have been used in the past, more often such programs involve giving some form of preferential treatment, whether by adding points to a mathematical score due to a person's status as a member of a particular racial group or by creating economic or other

Affirmative action
Programs, laws, or practices designed to remedy past discriminatory hiring practices, government contracting, and school admissions.

incentives for administrative bodies to increase the diversity of their incoming workforce and/or educational institutions.

Proponents of affirmative action argue that past discriminatory practices have deprived certain racial groups and women of opportunities to get the skills or experiences they need to compete for jobs or college admissions on an equal footing with those who have not experienced such discrimination. The issue of affirmative action reached the U.S. Supreme Court in the case of *Regents of the University of California v. Bakke* (1978).[13] Alan Bakke in fact was rejected not once but twice for admission to the University of California, Davis, medical school. In both instances, sixteen applicants with lower grade point averages and MCAT (Medical College Admission Test) scores than Bakke's were admitted to the school under a special minority admissions program. Bakke challenged the program as a violation of the Fourteenth Amendment's equal protection clause. In deciding the case, the Supreme Court ruled that a university could take into account race and ethnicity when making decisions about the admission of students, as long as it did not utilize specifically assigned numerical goals. Opponents of affirmative action thought they had received the victory they were looking for; after all, the Court held that the university could not use fixed racial quotas in this instance. But schools and universities took refuge in the Court's statements favoring the consideration of racial criteria more generally, and in the quarter century that followed, countless schools of higher education utilized race-conscious admissions programs. On June 28, 1978, the Court ordered that Bakke be admitted to the university's medical school. Thus, although Alan Bakke won his personal battle for admission, the war over affirmative action would continue to be waged in the years that followed.

Opponents of affirmative action complain that such programs punish white applicants who played no role at all in the original discriminatory practices. They also claim that a racial divide that currently exists in this country may be exacerbated by affirmative action because members of racial groups who benefit from such programs may be stigmatized by the perception that they are not fully deserving.

A string of Supreme Court decisions in the late 1980s and 1990s has effectively brought an end to explicit affirmative action programs in public employment and contracting.

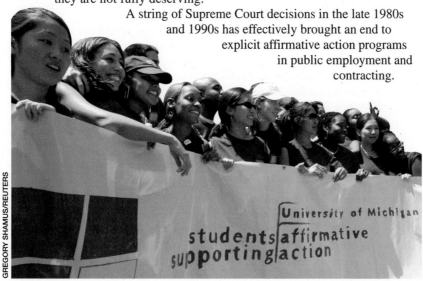

Students at the University of Michigan rally in support of affirmative action. In 2003 the U.S. Supreme Court upheld the use of affirmative action by the University of Michigan's Law School but struck down the affirmative action program utilized in undergraduate admissions.

In *Adarand v. Peña* (1995),[14] the Court held that any racial classification may be considered unconstitutional unless it meets the test of strict scrutiny: It must be "narrowly tailored" to further a "compelling governmental interest," a standard that has proved nearly impossible for the government to meet. In fact, no affirmative action employment plan has been upheld as constitutional since the early 1990s.

By contrast, affirmative action in education remains a source of some controversy. Two University of Michigan cases in 2003 reaffirmed *Bakke*'s finding that diversity constitutes a "compelling state interest" under certain circumstances. In *Grutter v. Bollinger* (2003),[15] the Court upheld the university's law school admission program because it considered race only as a positive factor in a review process where all individual applications were carefully reviewed and analyzed on their own merits. Yet ruling on the same day in *Gratz v. Bollinger* (2003),[16] the Supreme Court struck down the same university's undergraduate admissions program because instead of providing careful, individualized review, it automatically awarded twenty points to all students from underrepresented groups, greatly enhancing their chances of being admitted. The Court declared that such a blanket award of benefits was not "narrowly tailored" enough to promote diversity.

Racial Profiling. Statistics pertaining to the criminal justice system also testify to continuing racial inequality and racial tensions. For instance, although African American youth at the end of the twentieth century represented just 15 percent of the nation's total youth population, they made up 26 percent of the youth arrested, 31 percent of the youth referred to juvenile court, and 44 percent of the youth detained by the police.[17] African American males in particular compose a disproportionate number of those imprisoned. Critics of the system charge that it is racially biased, especially in how it metes out capital punishment. A study conducted by social scientist David Baldus and some associates in the early 1980s concluded that the victim's race was a significant factor in predicting which convicted murderers receive the death penalty. Specifically, killers of whites were 4.3 times more likely to be sentenced to death than killers of African Americans. Still, Baldus's study did not persuade the Supreme Court to abandon capital punishment.

Racial discrimination may also characterize the initial phases of gathering information about a crime. For example, some law enforcement officials admit to using **racial profiling**—the practice of taking race into account when investigating crimes. African Americans may be stopped, questioned, and even held in custody not because there is specific evidence that links them to a particular crime but because they fit a "profile" of the perpetrator that includes the characteristic of race.

Racial profiling became a source of considerable controversy in the 1990s. During the spring of 1999, victims of the New Jersey State Police force's allegedly overaggressive racial profiling testified at hearings held by the black and Latino caucus of the state's legislature. President Bill Clinton publicly condemned racial profiling as a "morally indefensible, deeply corrosive practice." Finally, in March 2003, New Jersey became the first state in the nation to enact an antiprofiling law, which made any profiling by police punishable by five years in prison and a $15,000 fine. Are criticisms of racial profiling exaggerated? Not all racial profiling may be driven by prejudice against African Americans; black civil rights leader Jesse Jackson admitted in 1993 that he was less fearful of white

Racial profiling
The law enforcement practice of taking race into account when identifying possible suspects of crimes.

Securing a Piece of the Franchise

The belief that "all men are created equal" has become part of the American ideology. Yet reality hasn't always kept up with theory. In the early years of the republic, the eligible electorate consisted primarily of white, male property owners. For everyone else, the road to suffrage remained fraught with legal and political struggles.

In 1841, the state of Rhode Island became the last of the United States to liberalize suffrage requirements so that even white males with little or no property enjoyed the right to vote. During the late 1820s and 1830s, the Whig Party had resisted suffrage for all white males, trumpeting the principle of a "hierarchical society" in which voting was treated as a privilege rather than an entitlement. But the rival Democratic Party, worried less about civic virtue and more about government tyranny, called for universal white male suffrage to put electoral pressure on the Whigs. The Democrats converted state after state to their cause. Rhode Island's requirement that a man outright own land worth $134 to be eligible to vote seemed increasingly restrictive once the Rhode Island economy shifted from the emphasis on agriculture to industry. Only after the state held a constitutional convention in 1841, and then a special gubernatorial election that same year, did Rhode Island join the rest of the Union in championing suffrage for all white males.

In 1920, following decades of intense struggles dating back even before the Civil War, the requisite number of states finally ratified the Nineteenth Amendment, granting women the right to vote. Meeting in 1848 in Seneca Falls, New York, some 300 male and female reformers issued a Declaration of Sentiments (modeled on the Declaration of Independence), which included a demand for the right of women to vote. As the movement for women's suffrage grew, it encountered especially well-organized resistance from the liquor industry (which feared female support for prohibition) and the textile industry (which feared female support for restrictions on child labor). The sudden triumph of progressive reforms at the turn of the century, which helped to clean up industrial workplace abuses, made the women's suffrage movement seem less radical by comparison. In 1916, both the Republicans and the Democrats embraced female enfranchisement, and four years later, it became a constitutional reality.

In 1965, the newly passed Voting Rights Act established a foundation for the mass registration of African Americans throughout the South. Their realization of the right to vote should not have had to wait so long; the Fifteenth Amendment, ratified in 1870, had formally guaranteed that the right of U.S. citizens to vote could not be denied or abridged on account of race, color, or previous condition of servitude. But racial intimidation at the polls, the use of poll taxes and literacy requirements, and the manipulation of election laws by local registrars all combined to render the right to vote for African Americans a hollow promise at best. Only when the civil rights movement started making significant headway in the late 1950s did national politicians begin seriously to reconsider the issue of voting rights. The key moment in this struggle came in March 1965, when police in Alabama assaulted marchers making their way from Selma to Montgomery. President Lyndon B. Johnson then demanded passage of an effective voting rights act, and in August 1965, Congress passed and Johnson signed into law the Voting Rights Act. The new act, combined with ratification of the Twenty-fourth Amendment in 1964, which prohibited poll taxes, spelled the effective end to nearly a century of systematic disenfranchisement.

strangers than black strangers on dark streets if only because, statistically speaking, he stands a greater risk of being robbed by a black person than by a white person. At the same time, defenders of racial profiling (as one of many factors in the investigative process) tend to minimize the extent to which the practice adds to the sense of resentment of law enforcement felt by rich and poor blacks alike.

Controversies surrounding affirmative action and racial profiling highlight a vexing challenge in modern society. Even if all vestiges of formal racial classifications under the law are eliminated, calculations of racial differences inevitably enter into the subjective judgments of those in positions of authority. Thus, for all the successful challenges launched against the racist legal and political structures that prevailed in American society during much of the twentieth century, the greater challenge of winning over the hearts and minds of individuals still remains.

The Women's Movement and Gender Equality

The process by which women achieved their own degree of equality during the course of the twentieth century took a circuitous route. In the early part of the century, women's rights leaders linked their calls for equality to other social movements of the same period, including those calling for child labor laws and increased literacy for immigrants. Initially, the women's rights movement pressed for protective laws, arguing that such legislation was necessary because of women's otherwise inferior legal status. For example, in *Muller v. Oregon* (1908),[18] the Supreme Court upheld an Oregon law that prohibited women laundry workers from being required to work more than ten hours a day; similar laws applied to male workers had been invalidated as beyond the government's authority. Yet the reason for the holding could hardly have cheered advocates of women's equality: According to the Court, "a woman's physical structure and the performance of maternal functions place her at a disadvantage in the struggle for subsistence."

Women's Suffrage and the Equal Rights Amendment

After ratification of the Nineteenth Amendment in 1920 guaranteed women the right to vote, women's rights groups began to alter their strategy for pursuing gender equality through the courts. In attempting to expand women's legal rights, these groups now argued that men and women should be treated equally. Their efforts met with only limited success at first. Although the NAACP achieved a string of successful challenges to racial discrimination in the 1940s and 1950s, the Supreme Court refused to view gender discrimination as similarly deserving of suspect scrutiny. In *Hoyt v. Florida* (1961), the Court accepted as legitimate a Florida law that gave only women the right to excuse themselves from jury duty. Thus, the Court continued to accept sex-role stereotypes of women as weak and as dedicated above all else to taking care of the children at home. As the Court pointed out in *Hoyt*, "despite the enlightened emancipation of women from the restrictions and protections of bygone years . . . woman is still regarded as the center of home and family life."[19]

The women's rights movement did not achieve any significant breakthroughs in this regard until the early 1970s. Although the National Women's Party had first proposed an equal rights amendment to the Constitution in 1923 and in nearly every session of Congress since then, the amendment never got very far. In 1966, the newly formed National Organization for Women (NOW) became a forceful advocate for the Equal Rights Amendment and other equal rights in education, employment, and political opportunities for women. NOW and other

International Perceptions of Women as Leaders

A 2007 Pew Global Attitudes survey conducted in forty-six countries around the world queried respondents about gender and the qualities of leadership. Specifically, the surveys asked people whether they thought men or women made better leaders. The table below shows how people from the forty-six nations responded. In the United States, three quarters of those surveyed said that men and women were equally qualified, whereas 16 percent said men were better qualified and 6 percent said women were better qualified. Opinions about gender equality in leadership are similar in Canada, Central and South American nations, and western European countries. As the table shows, however, most eastern European, Middle Eastern, Asian, and African nations strongly favor male leadership.

Which Sex Generally Makes Better Political Leaders?

	Men %	Women %	Both equally %		Men %	Women %	Both equally %
U.S.	16	6	75	Jordan	49	6	42
Canada	10	8	80	Egypt	38	15	43
Chile	26	5	66	Israel	30	14	53
Argentina	17	9	68	Pakistan	54	8	32
Mexico	12	9	76	Indonesia	43	3	52
Brazil	10	15	73	China	28	4	64
France	15	4	81	South Korea	25	5	68
Italy	12	11	74	India	19	17	62
Germany	11	8	80	Japan	16	4	77
Britain	9	6	83	Ethiopia	51	3	45
Russia	40	7	44	Nigeria	48	6	45
Ukraine	34	7	52	Senegal	36	15	48
Poland	23	10	65	South Africa	28	11	61
Czech Rep.	14	11	73	Kenya	27	10	62
Palest. Ter.	64	17	16				

Source: Juliana Manasce Horowitz, *How the World Rates Women as Leaders*, Dec. 5, 2007, Pew Global Attitudes Project (http://pewresearch.org/pubs/650/women-leaders).

women's groups vigorously pressed for passage of the Equal Rights Amendment, which stated simply that "equality of rights under the law shall not be denied or abridged by the United States or any state on account of sex." In 1972, Congress passed the amendment and sent it to the state legislatures for ratification. Even after the deadline for ratification was extended to June 1982, the amendment failed to achieve the approval of the three fourths of state legislatures necessary for passage, falling just three states shy.

Although the Equal Rights Amendment failed, women have recently achieved some noteworthy victories in politics. For example, women made political history in 2003, when Democrat Nancy Pelosi of California was elected minority leader in the House, the first woman ever to hold that high a position in either branch of Congress. When Democrats won control of Congress after the 2006 midterm elections, Pelosi was elected Speaker of the House, again the first woman to hold that exalted position. Pelosi's ascension to such high congressional leadership positions contrasts with the way women in Congress were often relegated to less important committees and noninfluential positions in the past. When the 111th Congress began in 2009, there were seventy-six women serving in the U.S. House of Representatives and seventeen in the U.S. Senate.

Legal Challenges to Gender Discrimination

★ LO Evaluate the role of the courts in upholding challenges to gender discrimination

Ironically, some attributed the failure of the Equal Rights Amendment to other legal developments that may have rendered it unnecessary. The American Civil Liberties Union (ACLU), an organization traditionally dedicated to protecting the First Amendment rights of political dissidents and labor unions, turned its attention to women's rights in the late 1960s. Led in court by board member Ruth Bader Ginsburg (who was later appointed by President Clinton to the U.S. Supreme Court), the ACLU brought suit on behalf of women who charged that they had been victims of gender discrimination. Although the Court refused to accord gender discrimination the strict scrutiny normally reserved for racial discrimination, the ACLU achieved several victories in cases brought before the Supreme Court. For example, in *Frontiero v. Richardson* (1973),[20] the Court struck down a federal law requiring only female members of the armed forces to show proof that they contributed more than 50 percent to the income of their household to receive certain fringe benefits. In the landmark case of *Craig v. Boren* (1976),[21] the Court invalidated an Oklahoma law that prohibited the sale of 3.2 percent beer to males under the age of twenty-one and to women under the age of eighteen.

Since *Craig*, the Supreme Court has applied *intermediate scrutiny* in all gender discrimination cases, a standard requiring the government to show that the gender classification is "substantially related to an important state interest." This level of scrutiny is less than that of strict scrutiny, which tends to invalidate all racial classifications. But under intermediate scrutiny, *nearly* all laws that discriminate against women will be invalidated. That fact alone distinguishes intermediate scrutiny from *rational basis (or "minimum") scrutiny*, which asks only whether the law is "rationally related to a legitimate state interest"—a question to which courts can readily answer "yes" in nearly every instance.

In fact, in the modern era, the Court has upheld only a handful of gender classifications as constitutional. For example, in 1981, the Court upheld a challenge to federal laws that required selective military service registration for males but not for females. That same year, the Court upheld a statutory rape law in California that punished men for having sex with underage females, although not vice versa. In each of those two instances, perceptions of real and relevant differences between men and women persuaded the Court to allow the discrimination to stand.

The highest-profile lawsuits charging gender discrimination targeted two all-male southern military academies: The Citadel in Charleston, South Carolina, and the Virginia Military Institute (VMI) in Lexington, Virginia. Both were classified

Title IX Brings Gender Equality—and Controversy—to a Campus Near You

Every March on college campuses all across the country, many students get caught up in March Madness—the NCAA men's basketball tournament that crowns the sport's annual champion. In April, another event occurs that has become a serious business at many schools as well: the NCAA women's basketball tournament. Women have been crowned as NCAA champions since 1982; before that, between 1972 and 1982, women's college basketball championships were held by the Association for Intercollegiate Athletics for Women. Women who have won the NCAA championship may not realize that they owe some form of debt not just to the parents who supported them and the coaches who coached them, but also to the late Rep. Patsy Mink (D-HI), the first Asian American woman elected to Congress. In 1972 Representative Mink authored the Title IX Amendment to the Higher Education Act, which banned gender discrimination in any "education program or activity" receiving federal assistance. Though Mink's law made no explicit mention of intercollegiate athletics, that is where the law has had its most prominent impact to date.

University of Tennessee women's basketball coach Pat Summit giving instructions to one of her players. Thanks to Title IX, colleges and universities have been forced to provide as many sports teams for women as they do for male athletes.

AP PHOTO/STEPHAN SAVOIA

The implications of Title IX are profound: Courts have interpreted the statute to require gender equality in roster sizes for men's and women's athletic teams in general, as well as to require comparable budgets for recruiting, scholarships, coaches' salaries, and other expenses. The law has not been without controversy. Some schools have eliminated successful men's athletic teams to bring the percentage of women's athletic scholarships up to par; critics complain that men's football and basketball teams are normally the only sports teams that bring in revenue, and so they should be judged independently of all the other sports. Regardless, colleges and universities have fallen into line in the past thirty years; so much so in fact, that in 2006 the Western Kentucky University Board of Regents ordered the upgrading of its football team (from Division 1-AA to 1-A), ostensibly because its share of female scholarship athletes had become disproportionately large.

For Critical Thinking and Discussion

1. Is the intense focus of colleges and universities on gender equality in their collegiate sports programs justified?

2. Would you favor the elimination of a successful men's sports team at your own institution on the basis of an imbalance in male and female scholarship athletes on campus?

3. Do you participate in other aspects of college life such as school-sponsored clubs or the school band where gender inequality exists in some form? Does the intense focus of Title IX enforcement on sports teams in particular tend to obscure gender discrimination where it exists elsewhere on campus?

as state institutions because they accepted significant funds from their respective state budgets; thus, each was hard-pressed to continue excluding women in violation of the Fourteenth Amendment's equal protection clause. Shannon Faulkner's frustrating experience as the first female cadet at The Citadel paved the way for women to apply and be accepted to the institution in subsequent years. In an attempt to fend off gender integration of its own student body, VMI contracted with nearby Mary Baldwin College to create a parallel military program for women called the Virginia Women's Institute for Leadership (VWIL). But in 1996, the Supreme Court ruled that VWIL did not approximate VMI in terms of student body, faculty, course offerings, facilities, or opportunities for its alumni and ordered VMI to accept women. The issue of "separate but equal" that was resolved by the Supreme Court for racial classifications in 1954 was still being litigated for gender classifications well into the 1990s.

As with race discrimination, discrimination against women has been mostly eliminated in the formal sense. **Title IX** of the Federal Educational Amendments of 1972 prohibited the exclusion of women from an educational program or activity receiving financial assistance from the federal government. Courts have interpreted those provisions to force colleges and universities to provide as many athletic teams for women as they do for men, although funding discrepancies continue. Title VII of the Civil Rights Act of 1964 extended to women protection against discrimination in private and public businesses alike. Armed with equal rights to education and to entry in the workforce, women made considerable occupational gains during the twentieth century.

The securing of formal equality under the law and the proliferation of affirmative action programs have not always translated into actual equal opportunities to succeed. Women today continue to earn less than men in comparable positions; calls for "equal pay for equal work" have not always generated substantive changes in the pay structures of private companies or even the government. When women's salaries are compared with those of equally qualified men, the differences remain dramatic. Although Congress passed the Equal Pay Act in 1963 to ensure that women would be paid the same as men for work that is "substantially equal," in the year 2007 a woman on average still earned only 81 cents for every dollar a man received.

Sexual harassment, normally in the form of unwelcome sexual advances by superiors, continues to pose a threat to working women in America. Since the mid-1980s, the Supreme Court has considered such harassment—which includes any and all actions that create a hostile working environment such as putting up provocative posters, making lewd comments, and so forth—to be a form of sexual discrimination actionable under Title VII of the 1964 Civil Rights Act. Still, many such sexual advances in the workplace continue despite the law, either because women remain unclear about the bounds of permissible conduct or because they fear reprisals for reporting the legal violations of superiors. Indeed, more than four in ten women employed in federal agencies say they have experienced some form of harassment.[22]

Other Struggles for Equality

The political and legal systems in the United States directed increased attention during the late nineteenth and twentieth centuries to the plights of African Americans and women. The hardships suffered by these two groups inspired the passage of five constitutional amendments in all (the three Civil War Amendments, the Nineteenth Amendment granting women the right to vote, and the Twenty-fourth Amendment banning poll taxes) as well as many federal and state antidiscrimination laws. But both these groups' continuous quests for

★ LO Understand Title IX's effect on women's rights

Title IX
The section of the Federal Educational Amendments Law of 1972 that prohibits the exclusion of women from an educational program or activity receiving financial assistance from the federal government. Courts have interpreted those provisions to force colleges and universities to provide as many athletic teams for women as they do for men.

★ LO Examine the struggles for equality waged by other racial, religious, and ethnic groups including Native Americans, Asian Americans, Muslims, and Hispanic Americans equal privileges under the law constitute only part of the equal rights land-scape. American history is replete with accounts of discrimination against other underrepresented groups as well. In recent years, these additional groups have begun to see their own claims to fairness and equal treatment recognized and vindicated within the American political system.

Native Americans

One of the nation's most unfortunate tales of mistreatment concerns Native Americans. For much of the eighteenth and nineteenth centuries, vast numbers of white Americans migrated west, pursuing what they viewed as their mani-fest destiny to settle across the continent. Consequently, millions of Native Americans were herded onto reservations according to a removal policy backed by the federal government. By a federal law passed in 1871, the government no longer agreed to recognize Native American tribes or nations as indepen-dent powers capable of entering treaties with the United States; all future tribal affairs were to be managed by the federal government without tribal consent. With passage of the Dawes Severalty Act in 1887, the U.S. government divided tribal lands still in existence among individual Indians who renounced their tribal holdings, further undermining tribal cultures and structures.

Although certain Native Ameri-can tribes received piecemeal U.S. citizenship beginning in the 1850s and the Dawes Act granted citizenship to those who ceded their tribal holdings, the class of Native Americans as a whole was not admitted to full citizenship until 1924, nearly sixty years after freed slaves had been afforded that same privilege. The federal government's attempt to undo the tribal structure did not produce widespread assimilation of Indians into American society as propo-

AP PHOTO

Native Americans protest federal policies by temporarily occupying Alcatraz Island in San Francisco Bay.

nents of the Dawes Act intended; many chose to remain on reservations in an attempt to protect their culture from outside influences. Congress eventually terminated its policy of assimilation and began to recognize the autonomy of Native American tribes to administer federal programs on their own lands. In the past quarter century, the U.S. government has settled millions of dollars in legal claims pressed by Native American tribes and has returned nearly half a million acres of land to the Navajo and Hopi tribes alone.

Asian Americans

Immigrants from East Asia—especially Japan and China—supplied much of the labor that built U.S. railroads in the nineteenth century. Even so, many were excluded from labor unions and denied other civil rights. The government enacted several immigration acts specifically designed to limit or prevent Asian immigration. For example, the Chinese Exclusion Act passed in 1882 prohibited Chinese laborers from immigrating and denied U.S. citizenship to Chinese living in the United States. The 1907 Gentleman's Agreement with Japan prohibited the immigration of Japanese laborers. The National Origins Act of 1924 banned all Asians from further immigration to the United States.

Discrimination was especially rampant on the West Coast, where many Asian American populations were concentrated. Asian children were segregated into separate public schools in San Francisco, and the state of California restricted Japanese immigrants' rights to own farmland. Perhaps the most notorious incident of discrimination against Asian Americans occurred in 1942, when the U.S. government in response to the Japanese bombing of Pearl Harbor forcibly relocated 110,000 Japanese Americans to inland internment camps and seized their property. (The Supreme Court upheld the internment policy in 1944.) In the post–World War II period, Asian Americans enjoyed increased economic prosperity and made significant civil rights gains as well. The ban on Asian immigration was officially lifted in 1952, and provisions of federal law encouraging the immigration of professionals helped attract to the United States large numbers of educated and highly skilled Asian professionals. The Asian American population today stands at less than 5 percent of the American population as a whole.

Muslim Americans

The events of September 11, 2001, had a profound impact on America's foreign policy priorities and its approach to international terrorism. Those events have also taken a toll on citizens' perceptions of Muslim Americans, a group already set apart by its members' distinct religious practices and forms of dress. When plans for an Islamic community center and mosque to be built near the site of "Ground Zero" were revealed in early 2010, anger directed at Muslim-Americans suddenly found a new cause. Polls showed a clear majority of Americans were opposed to the project, even though most also recognized that the Muslim group had a legal right to build there. Many politicians were quick to oppose the proposal, knowing that such opposition would offer them immediate political benefits.

The stereotype that associates the Islamic religion with terrorism is hardly applicable to the vast majority who practice the faith, but post–September 11 initiatives sanctioned by Congress under the USA Patriot Act targeted many Muslim Americans for questioning and in some cases temporary detention. Of course, African Americans have long suffered from racial profiling in criminal law enforcement, but the level and degree to which Muslim Americans have been singled out have created a special source of worry for civil rights groups.

Hispanic Americans

Hispanic Americans are often defined as those of Spanish-speaking descent. A majority descended from Mexicans who were living in the Southwest when it became part of the United States in the 1840s. Even after immigration laws were tightened in the 1890s, hundreds of thousands of Mexicans continued to enter the United States illegally, drawn by opportunities in farming, mining, and other industries. Segregation of Mexican students from white students began in California in 1885 and continued through the 1950s; beginning in the 1960s, many Mexican Americans moved from rural areas to cities. Public schools in California, Texas, and elsewhere were forced to assimilate this growing population, including the children of illegal aliens, into overcrowded school districts.

Of course discrimination against Hispanics also contributes to the overall disproportionate levels of poverty and unemployment in this group. Unlike African Americans, Hispanics were never legally barred from the polls, and in New Mexico and California they have been a large and influential minority for several decades. And yet despite the large number of Hispanic Americans, the group's political power has yet to have its due influence on public policy, perhaps because many Hispanics are not yet citizens, and thus do not have the right to vote. Still, the appointment of Judge Sonia Sotomayor as the first Hispanic to the U.S. Supreme Court in 2009 was a source of pride within the American Hispanic community.

Older Americans

★ LO

Recognize the struggles of older Americans, Americans with disabilities, and gays and lesbians

Today, approximately 12 percent of Americans are over the age of sixty-five, compared with just 4 percent of Americans who were at that age at the beginning of the twentieth century. With their increased numbers has come increased political power; older Americans are among the most politically active of all citizens, and groups such as AARP (formerly the American Association of Retired Persons), with more than 40 million members on its rolls, have become especially influential players on the political scene. This increased influence has been used to counteract incidents of age discrimination in the workplace and elsewhere. The Age Discrimination in Employment Act, passed in 1967 and broadened in 1986, makes it unlawful to hire or fire a person on the basis of age. Older Americans have also been at the forefront of lobbying efforts to protect Social Security trust funds and to ensure the continuation of cost-of-living adjustments to their payments. Ironically, older Americans' success at wielding influence within the political system has given credence to the suggestion that age classifications do not require suspect scrutiny by courts; at least in this instance, the political system appears to protect the civil rights of this particular subset of Americans.

Individuals with Disabilities

As with age classifications, discrimination against Americans with physical and mental disabilities has never received heightened scrutiny from the courts. Misperceptions about the nature of certain disabilities have on occasion led to discriminatory treatment of individuals with disabilities. Today, thanks to significant technological and medical advances, a more enlightened social understanding, and a more sophisticated approach to educating citizens about the nature of these limitations, millions of Americans with disabilities have been mainstreamed into society, attending school, going to work, and living otherwise normal lives. The Americans with Disabilities Act of 1990 established a national commitment to such mainstreaming efforts and extended to those with disabilities protection from discrimination in employment and public accommodations comparable to that afforded women and racial minorities under the 1964 Civil Rights Act.

Gays and Lesbians

Of all the groups that have claimed discrimination in the United States, homosexuals stand among the least successful in having their claims to equal treatment vindicated under the law. Gays and lesbians have traditionally suffered discrimination in society, whether from those whose religions frown on homosexuality in general or from those who are simply uncomfortable with this lifestyle. In the period immediately following World War II, a movement for gay rights emerged with generally integrationist goals, encouraging homosexuals to conform to most existing social standards. Gays and lesbians assumed a more activist quest for equality beginning in the late 1960s, marching for "gay power," urging reluctant gays to "out" themselves by openly admitting their sexual orientation, and interrupting government meetings to draw attention to their cause of equal treatment and nondiscrimination. Some communities reacted by passing laws that prohibited the granting of "any special rights or privileges" to homosexuals. The Supreme Court in *Romer v. Evans* (1996)[23] struck down such a provision of the Colorado Constitution in 1996. Perhaps the biggest court victory of all for gays and lesbians occurred in 2003, when the Supreme Court in *Lawrence v. Texas* struck down a Texas law that forbade same-sex partners from engaging in certain types of intimate relations. Despite these victories, the Supreme Court has still never recognized homosexuals as a protected class on a par with women or African Americans.

Gay-marriage supporters at a Seattle rally in March 2006.

AP PHOTO/SCOTT COHEN

The issue of homosexuals in the military first drew intense national attention when Army Colonel Margarethe Cammermeyer was discharged from the armed forces in June 1992 because, during a routine security clearance interview, she acknowledged that she was a lesbian. In 1993 President Bill Clinton and the Congress agreed on a "don't ask, don't tell" policy that would allow gays still in the closet to stay in the military as long as they never publicized their status. In his 2010 State of the Union address, President Barack Obama indicated that he plans to work with Congress and the military to repeal the "don't ask, don't tell" rule. Still, to many critics this promise should have become reality long ago. Though some European countries have actively recruited gays and lesbians for military service, the U.S. military continues to formally oppose open homosexuality in the armed services.

Recognizing the Legitimacy of Same-Sex Marriage

When New Hampshire in June 2009 became the latest state in the union to formally legalize same-sex marriage, many interpreted the event as just the most recent sign of a trend in favor of increased rights for gays and lesbians. Yet there are contraindications to that trend in the majority of other states that have rejected measures such as civil rights laws that could afford "special rights" or "special status" to homosexuals, as well as the far more controversial institution of same-sex marriage. At the time this book went to press, five states (Massachusetts, Connecticut, Iowa, New Hampshire, and Vermont) and the District of Columbia still perform marriages for same-sex couples (Maine repealed its previous law while California's ban on same-sex marriages was still under review in the courts). Meanwhile, voters in thirty states have approved referenda to ban same-sex marriage.

In 1996, the Defense of Marriage Act—which attempts to ensure that each state retain the option of deciding whether or not to recognize same-sex marriage—was passed overwhelmingly by Congress (85–14 in the House and 342–67 in the Senate) before being signed into law by President Bill Clinton, considered a supporter of gay rights in other contexts. Eight years later, the issue of whether states must recognize same-sex marriages sanctioned in other states was thrown into the spotlight once again when eleven states voted on ballot measures that either defined marriage as between a man and a woman (three states), refused to recognize same-sex civil unions or domestic partnerships from other states (eight states) or banned all such civil unions outright. All these ballot measures were held at the same time as the November 2004 presidential election. And all eleven states passed the measures, with eight of the eleven ballot measures receiving at least two-thirds public support, and four measures topping the 75 percent mark (see the figure below). Then, on Election Day 2008, voters in Arizona and Florida joined Californians in passing measures to ban same-sex marriage in their respective states as well. Gay rights advocates know that so long as these measures retain their overwhelming popularity, an uphill fight for their cause remains.

November 2, 2004: Same-Sex Ballot Measures

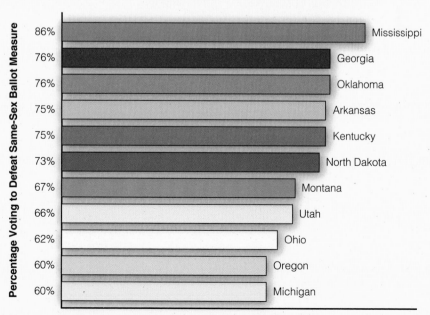

Percentage Voting to Defeat Same-Sex Ballot Measure

State	Percentage
Mississippi	86%
Georgia	76%
Oklahoma	76%
Arkansas	75%
Kentucky	75%
North Dakota	73%
Montana	67%
Utah	66%
Ohio	62%
Oregon	60%
Michigan	60%

Making the Connection

A form of the civil rights movement continues to be waged in modern-day courts and legislatures. Despite all the gains of the past, battles are still being taken up by racial, ethnic, and religious groups, as well as by other traditionally disadvantaged groups, to attain equal rights under the law. Just as Autherine Lucy walked a lonely path to achieve admission for African Americans at the University of Alabama in the 1950s, Shannon Faulkner walked a similar path to achieve admission for female applicants at the all-male Citadel in the 1990s. Both Lucy and Faulkner quickly learned that formal recognition of their rights would not suffice to transform many people's minds and hearts. But their actions provided a foundation for future aspirants to build on their accomplishments and present those stubborn minds with alternative perspectives on equality.

Today, groups such as Native Americans, gays and lesbians, and Muslim Americans walk this path as well, seeking recognition of rights traditionally denied to them by authorities acting on behalf of "the political majority." For every one or two steps they take forward, they are just as likely to take one other step backward. The hearts and minds of the majority are not so easily transformed. Fortunately, the openness of the American political system encourages some form of dialogue between the majority and underrepresented groups, and it shows no sign of stifling that dialogue anytime soon.

Even in Congress, a Muslim Braces for Discrimination

I n 2006, Keith Maurice Ellison, an American lawyer and politician running as a Democrat and member of the Farmer-Labor Party, became the first African American elected to the House from Minnesota when he won the right to represent Minnesota's fifth congressional district. Ellison's race was not as much an issue as his religion: He was also the first Muslim elected to the federal government in American history and became only the fourth elected Muslim official in the United States as of December 2006. Of course, all this occurred when the federal government's war on terrorism has raised questions within the general public about the loyalty of Muslim Americans, the vast majority of whom have done nothing illegal or even suspicious.

Ellison's religion made national news when he was first elected. Yet media coverage of Ellison went through the roof when words of intolerance were directed at him by one of his future colleagues, Congressman Virgil Goode (R-VA). After his victory, Ellison indicated that he planned to use the Koran for his unofficial swearing-in ceremony. This led Goode to send a letter to constituents in which he wrote the following:

ROGER L. WOLLENBERG/UPI/LANDOV

I do not subscribe to using the Koran in any way. The Muslim Representative from Minnesota was elected by the voters of that district and if American citizens don't wake up and adopt the Virgil Goode position on immigration, there will likely be many more Muslims elected to office and demanding the use of the Koran.

Congressman-elect Keith Ellison, being sworn in to the House of Representatives in January 2007.

Ellison criticized Goode about the letter, noting that he was not an immigrant and that Goode does not understand Islam. He has also offered to meet with Goode to discuss the matter. Rather than defusing the issue, Goode went on to state publicly that he was in favor of decreasing legal immigration to the United States and that he hoped to eliminate diversity immigration visas, which might allow people "not from European countries" or from "some terrorist states" to enter America.*

On www.cengage.com/dautrich/americangovernmentbrief/2e, find the "Politics InterActive" link for details about Ellison's political and religious background, as well as statistics about religious diversity in the current and past congresses. Consult these and other links that relate to religious diversity in American government institutions and incidents of current discrimination directed against Muslim Americans, including those who are U.S. citizens.

---

*See http://www.cnn.com/2006/POLITICS/12/21/quran.congress/index.html.

Chapter Summary

★ Types of Equality

- References to equality in discussions of American politics often refer to one of three types: political equality, economic equality, and social equality.

- Civil rights are those political, social, or economic rights conferred by the government to individuals in groups that had previously been denied those rights. The battle for civil rights in American history has focused primarily on African Americans and other ethnic groups (Hispanics, Asian Americans, Native Americans, Muslim Americans), women, older Americans, persons with disabilities, and gays and lesbians.

★ The Struggle for Equality: Approaches and Tactics

- The strategies used by groups seeking to achieve civil rights include working within the existing rules and political process, litigation, boycotts, and civil disobedience.

★ The African American Struggle for Equality and Civil Rights

- The long and hard-fought African American struggle for equality included heated debate as early as the Constitutional Convention. The Civil War and the amendments that passed in its aftermath (Thirteenth, Fourteenth, and Fifteenth) ended slavery, granted citizenship to former slaves, guaranteed all Americans "equal protection under the laws," and denied states the ability to prevent voting rights on the basis of race.

- Despite these amendments, states have used many means to prevent African Americans from obtaining political, social, and economic equality, including black codes, literacy tests, poll taxes, and Jim Crow laws. A number of U.S. Supreme Court decisions, along with congressional legislation and constitutional amendments, have served to bring America closer to the goal of equality for African Americans.

- The *Brown v. Board of Education* decision of 1954 eliminated the "separate but equal" doctrine. The movement toward civil rights to minority groups in all public accommodations began in the later 1950s and emerged as a major force under the leadership of Martin Luther King Jr. and his use of nonviolent civil disobedience.

- King's legacy was memorialized through sweeping civil rights legislation, including the Civil Rights Act of 1964 (which banned racial discrimination in all public places), the Voting Rights Act of 1965 (which effectively reenfranchised millions of African Americans by eliminating the literacy test and property requirements for voting), and the Civil Rights Act of 1968 (which prohibited discrimination in housing and made it a federal crime to deny individuals their civil rights).

- Two contemporary issues relating to civil rights include affirmative action and racial profiling. The courts have struck down many affirmative action programs, but many states continue to try to find ways for government to level the playing field in hiring and college admissions.

★ The Women's Movement and Gender Equality

- The seeds were sown for the movement for gender equality in the early twentieth century with the ratification of the Nineteenth Amendment, guaranteeing women the right to vote.

- But it would not be until after the formation of the National Organization for Women (NOW) and its emergence as a significant political force that the march for women's equality would capture national attention.

- Some of the most heated contemporary debates over equality relate to discrimination against Muslim Americans (and how to protect their civil rights in the post-9/11 era), Hispanic Americans and immigration policy, and the rights of gays and lesbians, particularly as they relate to marriage.

CourseMate

Key Terms

Affirmative action (p. 120)

Brown v. Board of Education (1954) (p. 114)

Civil rights (p. 113)

Civil Rights Act of 1964 (p. 119)

Civil War Amendments (p. 115)

Economic equality (p. 112)

Jim Crow laws (p. 116)

Plessy v. Ferguson (1896) (p. 116)

Political equality (p. 112)

Racial profiling (p. 122)

Social equality (p. 112)

Strict scrutiny (p. 117)

Title IX (p. 128)

Voting Rights Act of 1965 (p. 119)

Resources

Books

Branch, Taylor. *Parting the Waters: America in the King Years, 1954–1963.* New York: Simon & Schuster, 1988.

Gerstmann, Evan. *The Constitutional Underclass: Gays, Lesbians, and the Failure of Class-Based Equal Protection.* Chicago: University of Chicago Press, 1999.

Hochschild, Jennifer. *The New American Dilemma: Liberal Democracy and School Desegregation.* New Haven, CT: Yale University Press, 1984.

Kluger, Richard. *Simple Justice.* New York: Vintage Books, 1975.

Strum, Phillippa. *Women in the Barracks: The VMI Case and Equal Rights.* Lawrence: University Press of Kansas, 2004.

Washington, Booker T. *Up from Slavery.* New York: Airmont Publishing, 1967.

Internet Sources

http://www.civilrights.org (the official Web site of the Leadership Conference on Civil and Human Rights, which is made up of more than 200 civil rights organizations from around the country).

http://www.naacp.org (the National Association for the Advancement of Colored People's home page).

http://www.noi.org (the official Web site for the Nation of Islam).

http://www.hrc.org (the Web site of the Human Rights Campaign, which works on behalf of lesbian, bisexual, gay, and transgender equal rights; features extensive coverage of issues related to gay and lesbian interests, including a comprehensive review of legislation in all fifty states).

http://www.usdoj.gov/crt/ada/adahom1.htm (the U.S. Department of Justice's Americans with Disabilities Act [ADA] home page).

6 Congress

NOW Senator Patrick Leahy (D-VT), Chairman of the Senate Judiciary Committee.

AP PHOTO/TOBY TALBOT

THEN Senator Henry Cabot Lodge (R-MA), Chairman of the Senate Foreign Relations Committee from 1919 to 1924.

HISTORICAL/CORBIS

NOW & THEN

The U.S. Senate Plays the Role of Disloyal Opposition

Once a regal and powerful lawmaking body, the U.S. Senate—like so many other institutions in Washington, DC— had learned to defer to the reality of the modern presidency. An elite group of ambitious politicians advocating their own independent political agendas proved little match for a president determined to make strategic use of the bully pulpit. When the president reached a bit too far in a policy area where the Senate had traditionally exercised significant control, something unexpected happened: The U.S. Senate pushed back. Suddenly the president had to deal with a revitalized institution prepared to stymie the president's objectives by exercising its own considerable tools of political power, including the power wielded by Senate committee chairs to control committee procedures and the ever-present threat of a filibuster. Just when the political system appeared to be under the president's thumb, the upper house of Congress served notice that it remained a vibrant and stubborn obstacle to efforts at presidential steamrolling . . . at least when it wanted to be.

LEARNING OBJECTIVES
★ WHAT YOU WILL LEARN ★

Article I and the Creation of Congress

★ Assess the role of the U.S. Congress as the legislative branch of government, and how that role has evolved over time

The Structure and Organization of Congress

★ Understand the structure and powers of Congress as defined by Article I of the Constitution

★ Explain reapportionment and redistricting

★ Appreciate the role that political parties play in the leadership of Congress

★ Identify key leadership positions and their functions in Congress

The Committee System

★ Compare and contrast the different types of committees found in Congress

How a Bill Becomes a Law

★ Describe the various steps necessary for a bill to become a law

Oversight and Personnel Functions of Congress

★ Explain why Congress often delegates its lawmaking authority to regulatory agencies

★ Learn the role of the Senate in confirming presidential appointments

Constituent Service: Helping People Back Home

★ Assess the "casework" functions of members of Congress in assisting constituents, educating them on policy issues, and performing other services on their behalf

CourseMate

139

NOW & THEN

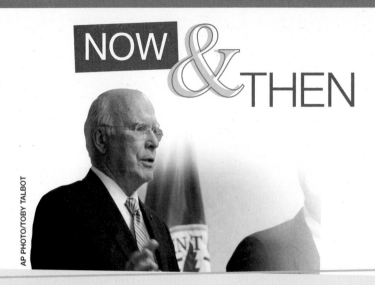

AP PHOTO/TOBY TALBOT

NOW   President George W. Bush arrived in office in January 2001 with both houses of Congress under his own Republican Party's control. That changed on May 24, 2001, when Senator Jim Jeffords (R-VT) announced that he was leaving the party to become an independent, but would caucus with the Democrats. Jeffords's decision swung control of the Senate to the Democrats by a narrow 51–49 margin. Democratic control of the Senate would have negative implications for many aspects of George W. Bush's agenda, but it would have perhaps the most devastating and immediate effect on his plans to pack the federal courts with more ideologically conservative judges—those who, in the words of Senator Charles Schumer (D-NY), lay outside the "judicial mainstream." Notwithstanding the "advice and consent" provisions of the Constitution, with his judicial nominations President Bush paid little heed to senatorial courtesy, the traditional practice of respecting the wishes of both parties' senators. In response, the new chair of the Senate Judiciary Committee, Senator Patrick Leahy (D-VT), announced that some of Bush's judicial nominees would be denied an up-and-down vote in his committee; by exercising this prerogative against the most conservative nominees, the Democrats prevented those nominations from being passed to the full Senate, where a handful of more conservative Democrats might give Bush's nominees the margin for victory. Even after Republicans recaptured the Senate in 2002, ending the committee bottleneck, those controversial nominations that made it to the floor of the full Senate now faced a second obstacle: the threat of a filibuster. That tool of the Senate minority, which stops Senate business based on the vote of just forty-one senators, had rarely been used against judicial nomination in the past. Now, it would serve as a central threat in the Democratic senators' war on judicial nominations: If President Bush did not agree to withdraw his most controversial judicial nominees, Senate Democrats would continue to tie up many of his less controversial choices as well. President Bush was eventually forced to adjust to this new reality, as moderate senators from both parties brokered a deal in the spring of 2005 to allow some, but not all, of the president's controversial nominees through to confirmation.

THEN Nearly a century earlier, another president ran head-first into an emboldened U.S. Senate whose leaders were equally unwilling to defer to the chief executive on issues where its power and authority were constitutionally grounded. Article II, Section 2 of the Constitution affords the Senate a clear role in overseeing treaties—the president can make treaties, but only "by and with the advice and consent of the Senate" and only so long as "two thirds of the Senators present concur." The first sitting president to travel to Europe, Woodrow Wilson participated in the 1919 peace negotiations after World War I, and he worked tirelessly to incorporate a proposed League of Nations (the precursor to the modern United Nations) into the Treaty of Versailles, the treaty that ended the war. But Wilson, a Democrat, was not willing to seek advice from the Senate, especially after control of both houses of Congress went to the Republicans after the 1918 midterm elections. The new Senate Majority Leader, Senator Henry Cabot Lodge (R-MA), was especially irked by Wilson's refusal to afford senators any kind of voice in the treaty negotiations; he and his Republican colleagues already detested Wilson, and they now feared that U.S. membership in the League of Nations would tie the hands of future Congresses over whether to enter international conflicts. Lodge's official "reservations" to the treaty would have allowed passage of the agreement only so long as the U.S. Congress maintained its full autonomy to act at its discretion in the future. As head of the Senate Foreign Relations Committee, Lodge slowed the treaty approval process down to a trickle: He took two weeks to read aloud every page of the 268-page treaty and then solicited testimony from scores of witnesses. The treaty would win approval only if Wilson accepted the "reservations," a path that he refused to take. Wilson was awarded the Nobel Peace Prize in 1919, but the League of Nations itself was formed without U.S. participation, and Wilson left office several months later. He never adjusted to the reality of a Senate willing to stand up to the twentieth-century presidency and reject his peace treaty. Robert Caro put the battle this way: "Woodrow Wilson was defeated by a body he considered both unrepresentative and oligarchical. He was right . . . [b]ut it had the power."

HISTORICAL/CORBIS

W hile lower court judicial nominations and international peace treaties were two very different issues debated at markedly different moments in the nation's history, the characteristics of Senate resistance in opposing the president proved remarkably similar in each instance. Senators with considerable power in their branch of government dug in, used Senate committee and floor procedures to their own benefit, and then let the slow pace of the Senate work its will to frustrate the chief executive. The separation of powers—which affords Congress a significant role in the lawmaking process—was never designed to run quickly, and in both cases described here, that pattern of slow movement was readily apparent. This chapter discusses the complex organization, structure, and processes of both houses of Congress that underlie the often slow and difficult manner in which this important institution does its work. It shows how particular members achieve disproportionate power and influence in the legislative process and offers the rationale for why Congress plays such a central role in dealing with issues of paramount importance to the nation.

Senator Carl Levin (D-MI) grills executives from Goldman-Sachs during an April 2010 committee investigation of the firm's investment practices prior to the collapse of the financial industry. Seated next to Levin is Senator Susan Collins (R-ME).

★ LO   Assess the role of the U.S. Congress as the legislative branch of government, and how that role has evolved over time

Article I and the Creation of Congress

Article I of the U.S. Constitution created Congress, and the fact that it came first was no accident. James Madison, the Father of the Constitution, referred to Congress as the "first branch of government," and as a graduate student, Woodrow Wilson (later the twenty-eighth president of the United States) wrote in his book *Congressional Government* (1885) that "anyone who is unfamiliar with what Congress actually does and how it does it . . . is very far from a knowledge of the constitutional system under which we live."[1] As the legislative branch of the federal government, Congress has ultimate authority for enacting new laws. Because this authority is central to any system of government, the founders took considerable debate and care in building this first branch.

There was little question that a congress of some type would be the central institution in the new political system; a congress had been a central feature in all attempts to organize the states up through and including the Constitutional Convention of 1787. The Albany Congress of 1754 was the first attempt to unite the colonies—at the time for common defense against the French in the pending French and Indian War. The Albany Plan of Union called for the colonies to organize through the vehicle of a "congress." The first official government of the United States, created under the Articles of Confederation, again used a congress as its organizing principle. It is not surprising, then, that Article I, Section 1 of the U.S. Constitution states: "All legislative powers herein granted shall be vested in a Congress of the United States."

The founders engaged in plenty of debate, negotiation, and compromise in defining the powers, functions, and structure of the U.S. Congress. The complexity of this institution continues today. As one observer of Congress put it, "Understanding how Congress works is a little like retelling the story of the blind men who try to say what an elephant is by describing what they can feel. The impression one gets depends on where one is standing." Congress is filled with paradoxes. On the one hand, it is a highly democratic institution in which senators and representatives are selected in free and open elections; on the other hand, Congress often is responsive to an exceedingly narrow set of specialized interests. Citizens and journalists frequently criticize the institution as being too slow to act responsively; yet voters return more than nine in ten of their elected members to office. At times, such as in the weeks following the terrorist attacks of September 11, 2001, Congress can show enthusiasm for tackling large issues expeditiously: Within days of the attacks, it passed the USA Patriot Act, which featured numerous antiterrorism measures. At other times, it seems to avoid taking positions on important issues, such as campaign finance reform and abortion rights.

Most significantly, Congress is the branch of the U.S. government that ensures representation of the people through the direct election of members of the House and, since ratification of the Seventeenth Amendment in 1913, of members of the Senate as well. Through its 535 members, Congress provides representation of many groups throughout the country, such as women, African Americans, Native Americans, and Hispanics.

Joseph Rainey of South Carolina was the first African American elected to Congress. He took office in 1870 and was reelected four times.

The Structure and Organization of Congress

A fundamental characteristic of Congress is its organization into two separate chambers, the Senate and the House of Representatives; thus, it is termed a **bicameral legislature**. At the time the U.S. Constitution was written, ten of the thirteen states featured this type of legislature. Creating a bicameral legislature enabled the founders to reach a compromise between two factions at the Constitutional Convention—those who represented large states and wanted congressional representation according to population and those from small states who favored the model of the Articles of Confederation with each state, regardless of population, equally represented in Congress. The "Great Compromise" reached by the convention delegates allowed for equal state representation in the Senate and representation based on population in the House. These two chambers have shared lawmaking responsibilities since 1789.[2]

Bicameralism has important implications for the legislative process in American politics; passing new laws is difficult because the two chambers, constructed so differently, must come to absolute agreement before a new law

★ LO

Understand the structure and powers of Congress as defined by Article I of the Constitution

Bicameral legislature
A legislature composed of two separate chambers.

is enacted. The slowness that so often characterizes lawmaking in Congress is, in part, a product of this reality. The sharing of power and the "checks" that each chamber has on the other are no mistake. Indeed, the founders intentionally built a Congress that would move slowly and carefully in the adoption of new laws, a process that, although often characterized as gridlock, ensures that change is well contemplated before it is adopted.

The House of Representatives: The "People's House"

★ LO Explain reapportionment and redistricting

The founders intended the House of Representatives to be the "people's house," or the institution through which ordinary people would be represented in government. At the time the Constitution was adopted, the only federal officials directly elected by the people were members of the House of Representatives. (Senators were chosen by state legislatures; the president and vice president were selected by electors in the Electoral College; and judges, ambassadors, and high-ranking officials in the executive branch were nominated by the president and approved by the Senate.) In Federalist No. 51, James Madison admonished, "As it is essential to liberty that the government in general should have a common interest with the people, so it is particularly essential that the branch of it under consideration [the House] should have an immediate dependence on and an intimate sympathy with, the people."[3] The House of Representatives thus directly connects voter sentiment with popular representation.

To ensure that members of the House would be accountable to voters, Article I, Section 2 sets the term of a House member at two years, keeping members constantly attentive to the currents of public opinion. Indeed, because of their relatively brief term of office, members of the House are typically consumed with concerns about winning reelection. This preoccupation has been well documented by scholars such as Thomas Mann, who argues that incumbent House members are in campaign mode most of the time, feeling "unsafe at any margin" of victory.[4]

Article I also ensures that the House of Representatives reflects the popular will by requiring that the number of representatives from each state be proportional to each state's population. States are not equally represented in the House of Representatives; rather, the population of each state is proportionately represented, at least to a large degree. This means that a more populous state has greater representation than a less populous one. The state of California, for example, now has fifty-three seats in the House of Representatives, in contrast to Wyoming, which has only one.

Congressional district
A geographic region (either a state itself or a region located entirely within one state) whose residents select one member to represent it in the House of Representatives.

Reapportionment
The allocation of a fixed number of House seats to the states.

There are 435 **congressional districts**, each represented by one House member. The number of people represented in a congressional district is tied to a number that changes after every census. Since fixing the number of seats at 435, Congress has struggled to find an equitable way to allocate House seats to the states—a process known as **reapportionment**.

Several U.S. Supreme Court decisions in the early 1960s established the basic principle that guides the process of reapportionment after every census—the "one person, one vote" principle.[5] According to this principle, the population size of congressional districts must be as equal as possible. Currently, that amounts to roughly 650,000 people per district. The requirement that each state maintain at least one House district causes some variance among the population sizes of each district. The single congressional district for

Confidence in Congress

Compared with its perceptions of the other institutions in American society, the American public has consistently expressed lower levels of confidence in Congress. The figure below shows the Gallup Poll's 2008 survey on confidence levels in a variety of institutions. As the chart shows, confidence in Congress ranks the lowest.

An important book on the topic of public confidence in Congress is *Congress as Public Enemy* by John Hibbing and Elizabeth Theiss-Morse (New York: Cambridge University Press, 1995). The authors argue that the openness of Congress to public scrutiny is responsible for its lower confidence ratings. Despite the low regard for Congress as an institution, Americans have a much higher opinion of the particular members who represent them in Congress. When national polls ask people to rate their own senator and representative, the average ratings tend to be twenty points higher than those that people give to the rating of the institution as a whole.* Why do people "love their congressperson, but hate Congress?" Individual members' visibility in their home states and districts and the constituent services provided to those they represent tend to promote favorable ratings. In contrast, news about the institution tends to revolve around conflict, debate, and gridlock in the legislative process.

Confidence in institutions

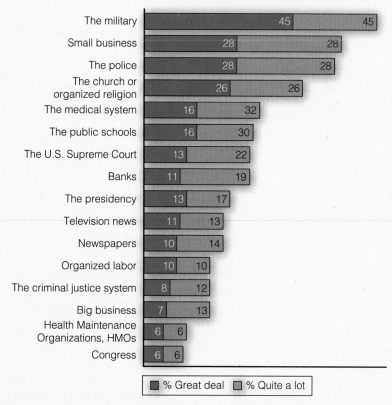

Institution	% Great deal	% Quite a lot
The military	45	45
Small business	28	28
The police	28	28
The church or organized religion	26	26
The medical system	16	32
The public schools	16	30
The U.S. Supreme Court	13	22
Banks	11	19
The presidency	13	17
Television news	11	13
Newspapers	10	14
Organized labor	10	10
The criminal justice system	8	12
Big business	7	13
Health Maintenance Organizations, HMOs	6	6
Congress	6	6

■ % Great deal   ■ % Quite a lot

Source: http://www.gallup.com/poll/108142/confidence-congress-lowest-ever-any-us-institution.aspx.

* *Public Perspective* magazine, 1998.

Wyoming, for example, has a population of about 500,000 because that is the number of people who live in that state. Consequently, Wyoming's population is proportionately "overrepresented" compared with most other congressional districts. Because congressional districts cannot cross state boundaries, the population size of congressional districts across states also varies. Yet once congressional districts are officially allocated to states based on the U.S. census, the size of each district within a state must be as close to equal as possible.

The Constitution requires that a new census of the population be taken every ten years, and the results are used to reapportion seats in the House of Representatives to each state. Each state is then responsible for **redistricting** its congressional boundary lines to achieve equal representation in each of its congressional districts—that is, redrawing congressional district lines to achieve the "one person, one vote" principle within the borders of the state.

The political parties in each state try to optimize the partisan characteristics of each district to their advantage. This drawing of district boundaries to favor one party over the other is referred to as **gerrymandering**, a term named for Elbridge Gerry, who was a signer of the Declaration of Independence, a Massachusetts delegate to the Constitutional Convention, a U.S. congressman, governor of Massachusetts, and vice president under James Madison. While governor, he endorsed legislation that redrew districts in Massachusetts, resulting in huge advantages for his political party, the Democratic-Republicans. The map of one of the new districts took on an odd shape, that of a salamander. Gerry's political opponents, the Federalists, dubbed the plan the "gerrymander plan." The political fallout for Gerry was significant, and he lost his next bid for governor. But the legacy of gerrymandering continues. Every decade or so, parties in states with more than one House member must ultimately negotiate a redistricting plan based on gerrymandered district boundaries that each party hopes will optimize its electoral successes.

Article I requires that all members of the House of Representatives be at least twenty-five years of age, have been a U.S. citizen for a minimum of seven years, and live in the state (though not necessarily the congressional district) from which they are elected. These requirements are somewhat less restrictive than those for the Senate (see below)—another indication of the founders' intention to give the people a greater role in deciding on who members of the House should be.

Redistricting
The act of redrawing congressional boundaries to achieve equal representation in each of the congressional districts.

Gerrymandering
The drawing of House district boundaries to the benefit of one political party over another. The term is named for Elbridge Gerry, a Massachusetts delegate to the Constitutional Convention, who (as governor) redrew districts in this fashion to favor the Democratic-Republicans.

The Senate: A Stabilizing Factor

Whereas the founders wanted to make the House of Representatives highly responsive to the people, their idea for the Senate was quite different. The Senate was to represent the states, with each state having two senators, thus being equally represented. As adopted, the Constitution specified that senators were to be elected not by the people of the state but by the state legislatures, another way to recognize states' importance. Not until passage of the Seventeenth Amendment to the Constitution in 1913 were senators elected directly by the people of the state they represented.

The founders were also concerned that the "people's house" might be too prone to radical changes in membership resulting from swift changes in popular opinion. James Madison in particular regarded the U.S. Senate as "a necessary fence against this danger,"[6] able to resist fast changes in federal legislation because it was less accessible to the people. In fact, during the first five years of our constitutional government, the U.S. Senate met in closed session. By sharing legislative power with the House of Representatives, the Senate, a slower, more deliberative body, would be the mechanism for protecting against the potential tyranny of the masses. Thus, the creation of new laws would be forced to proceed at a more thoughtful pace.

The Constitution sets the term of a U.S. senator at six years, three times the length of that for a House member. The founders staggered the terms of senators. Every two years, only one-third of the seats in the Senate are up for reelection compared with all of the seats in the House. So although in theory all of the seats in the House can change every other year, the Senate may change only by a maximum of thirty-four seats every two years and is thus less prone to drastic changes in membership.

The qualifications for becoming a U.S. senator are also tighter. The minimum age is thirty, five years older than in the House, with the idea being that older people were less likely to endorse radical change. Also, a U.S. senator must have been a citizen for at least nine years (rather than seven for the House) and be a resident of the state that he or she represents.

Article I requires that there be two senators from each state. The total number of senators grew from 26 in 1789 to 100 in 1959, the year Alaska and Hawaii became the forty-ninth and fiftieth states, respectively, to join the Union. Although the size of the Senate has grown, it still remains small, at least relative to the size of the House of Representatives. The smaller size of the Senate is often cited as the primary reason debate in the Senate tends to be more civil and camaraderie between individuals more important.

Political Parties and Leadership in Congress

Unlike the executive branch of American government, which is headed by the president, no one person or office leads Congress as a whole. Leadership is distinct in the Senate and the House of Representatives. Although both chambers must work together to pass new laws, each chamber maintains its own leadership structure to work on bills, pass laws, and conduct its other business. Cooperation between the House and Senate is necessary to accomplish legislation.

The principal factor driving leadership in each chamber is the political party system, which, interestingly, is not mentioned in the U.S. Constitution.[7] The two-party system in America typically generates a majority of members from one of the two major parties in both the Senate and House of Representatives. Since 1851, the majority party in each house has been either the Democratic Party or the Republican Party. Members of the party that has the majority of seats constitute the **majority caucus**, whereas those who are members of the party with a minority of seats constitute the **minority caucus**. The majority caucus in the House and the majority caucus in the Senate use their respective majorities to elect leaders and maintain control of their chamber. The larger the party's majority, and the more discipline and unity among party members, the stronger the power of the majority party's leadership ability.

Leadership in the House. The only guidance the Constitution offers regarding House leadership is contained in Article I, Section 2: "The House of Representatives shall choose their Speaker and other officers." The **Speaker of the House** is the title given to the leader of this chamber. Every two years, when a new Congress takes office, the full House of Representatives votes to determine

★ LO
Appreciate the role that political parties play in the leadership of Congress

★ LO
Identify key leadership positions and their functions in Congress

Majority caucus
The members of the party that has the majority of seats in a particular chamber.

Minority caucus
The members of the party that has a minority of seats in a particular chamber.

Speaker of the House
The leader of the House of Representatives, responsible for assigning new bills to committees, recognizing members to speak in the House chamber, and assigning chairs of committees.

who the Speaker will be from among its 435 members. In practice, the selection of Speaker is made by the political party in the House that holds the majority of seats. Members in the majority caucus meet prior to the vote for Speaker and agree on their leader, who receives virtually all the votes from the majority party members, thus guaranteeing that the majority party will occupy the Speaker of the House post.

The Speaker is a powerful person for a variety of reasons. First, as the person responsible for assigning new bills to committees, the Speaker can delay the assignment of a bill or assign it to a committee that is either friendly or hostile to its contents, a power that gives the Speaker control over much of the House agenda. Second, the Speaker has the ability to recognize members to speak in the House chamber. Because an important part of the legislative process involves members debating bills on the House floor, the Speaker's authority over this process is significant.

Third, the Speaker is the ultimate arbiter and interpreter of House rules. The ability to cast final judgment on a rule of order can make or break a piece of legislation. For example, Republican Speaker Newt Gingrich's decision in 1998 to assign impeachment authority over President Bill Clinton to the House Judiciary Committee rather than to a select committee on impeachment was significant. Gingrich may have surmised that the makeup of the existing Judiciary Committee was inclined toward impeachment. Indeed, the Judiciary Committee ultimately recommended the impeachment of Clinton to the full House. Fourth, the Speaker appoints members to serve on special committees, including conference committees, which iron out differences between similar bills passed in the House and Senate. The Speaker's influence is thus felt in the final changes made to a bill before Congress completes work on it. Fifth, the Speaker plays an influential role in assigning members to particular permanent committees. Some committees, as we will see later in this chapter, are more important than others. Being on the Speaker's "good side" helps in getting a good committee assignment. In addition, the Speaker handpicks the nine members of the all-important Rules Committee. Finally, the Speaker has ultimate authority to schedule votes in the full House on a bill, an authority that allows the Speaker to speed the process or delay it, using timing to either improve or subvert a bill's chances of being passed.

Partisan control of the House is the key factor regarding how that body is organized to do its work. Because the party that holds a majority of seats selects the Speaker, the majority party controls the legislative agenda through members serving in other leadership posts, including chairs of committees. The current Speaker is Nancy Pelosi, a Democrat from California. As of 2007, Pelosi became the first woman in American history to hold a top leadership position in one of the three branches of government. (She shares leadership of the Congress with the Democratic Senate majority leader.) Pelosi was chosen as speaker elect by the House Democratic caucus when it convened in mid-November 2006; she assumed the formal constitutional title of Speaker of the House during the first week of January 2007. Pelosi would relinquish the Speaker's office in 2011, after the GOP won back its majority.

CHIP SOMODEVILLA/GETTY IMAGES

After the Democrats won control of the House of Representatives in the 2006 elections, the new Congress elected Nancy Pelosi as the first woman Speaker of the House. Pictured above, Pelosi takes the gavel from Republican John Boehner in her historic first day on the job as Speaker on January 4, 2007. Four years later in January 2011, Pelosi would relinquish the Speakership to Boehner after the GOP won control of the House.

AMERICAN GOVERNMENT In Historical Perspective

Important Tie-breaking Votes Cast by Vice Presidents in the Senate

The Constitution specifies only two formal functions for the vice president of the United States: to be the presiding officer of the U.S. Senate and to cast a vote in Senate in the event (and only in the event) of a tie. A number of tie-breaking votes by vice presidents have been quite consequential.

In 1790, Vice President John Adams's second tie-breaking vote in the Senate was responsible for moving the capital of the United States from New York City to Washington, DC. The decision to find a permanent capital for the new country was a divisive issue. New York City was the early temporary home of the capital, but southerners feared that the location of the national capital in the North would give that region an unfair advantage on important regional issues, such as slavery and urban development, at the expense of farmers and rural areas. In the House, a deal had already been struck to support moving the capital to a plot of land on the Potomac River bordering Virginia and Maryland. An attempt by several senators to block the move by supporting a bill that would keep the capital in New York resulted in a 13–13 tie. Adams's tie-breaking vote in favor of moving the capital paved the way for passage of a new bill to move the capital to Philadelphia for ten years, while the land that would become Washington, DC, was prepared to be the nation's capital.

In 1881, on March 18, the Senate met to begin its session by selecting a slate of committee leaders and members. For twenty years, the Senate had been controlled by the Republicans, making such votes quite predictable. But in the 1880 elections, Americans sent thirty-six Republicans and thirty-six Democrats to the U.S. Senate, along with two independents. The Senate vote on this day would determine whether the Democrats or the Republicans would control the Senate and thus hold the power to confirm or deny Republican President Garfield's patronage appointments. The initial vote was 37–37, giving Republican Vice President Chester Arthur the all-important deciding vote. Arthur's tie-breaking vote allowed the Senate Republicans to ward off a significant Democratic threat to their power.

In 1993, newly elected President Bill Clinton placed at the cornerstone of his new presidency a budget proposal that included tax increases and new federal spending to stimulate a sluggish economy. Much was riding on this budget proposal, as Clinton had won the election of 1992 over George H. W. Bush based on his criticism of Bush's lack of concern for bringing the nation out of economic recession (made famous by the Clinton campaign slogan "It's the economy, stupid"). Clinton argued that the budget plan was essential not only to economic recovery but ultimately to eliminating the federal budget deficit. Although passed by the House of Representatives, the vote in the Senate ended in a 50–50 tie, setting the stage for Vice President Al Gore to cast the deciding vote to pass the budget. A most remarkable economic development of the 1990s was, in fact, the elimination of federal deficits.

To promote partisan leadership, the majority caucus in the House votes for a House **majority leader**, and the minority caucus votes for a House **minority leader**. These leaders oversee the development of their party platforms and are responsible for achieving party coherence in voting. Other important party leadership positions in the House are the House minority and majority **whips**. Whips report to their respective party leaders in the House and are primarily responsible for counting up the partisan votes on bills; that is, they contact members of their party caucus and try to convince them to vote the way their party leadership wants them to vote. The whips spend much of their time on the floor of the House, on the phone, or in the offices of their party colleagues counting votes and urging their members to vote the party line on bills.

Majority leader
In the Senate, the controlling party's main spokesperson who leads his or her party in proposing new laws and crafting the party's platform. The Senate majority leader also enjoys the power to make committee assignments. In the House, the majority leader is the controlling party's second in command, who helps the Speaker to oversee the development of the party platform.

Leadership in the Senate. The Constitution prescribes that the presiding officer of the Senate is the vice president of the United States. In this capacity, the vice president also holds the title of president of the Senate. Unlike the Speaker of the House, who is necessarily a member of the House of Representatives, the president of the Senate is not a member of the Senate. The president of the Senate cannot engage in debate on the floor of the Senate and has no legislative duties in the Senate, with one notable exception: to cast a vote in the Senate in the event of a tie. John Adams, the first vice president of the United States, was the most frequent tie-breaker in U.S. history, casting a vote twenty-one times in the Senate.

In practice, the vice president rarely shows up on the Senate floor to preside over its session. The presiding officer, in the absence of the vice president, is the **president pro tempore** (*pro tempore* is Latin, meaning "for the time being"). By custom, the official president pro tempore is the senator in the majority caucus who has served the longest number of consecutive years in the Senate. Again, however, in practice, the president pro tempore rarely exercises the authority to preside over the Senate. With fewer rules and a greater culture of respect to fellow members than in the House, the presiding officer of the Senate serves what is largely a ceremonial role.

Leadership in the Senate is principally a function of partisanship, with the majority and minority caucuses organizing through leadership posts similar to those of the House of Representatives. The majority caucus elects a Senate majority leader, and the minority caucus elects a Senate minority leader. These leaders are the main party spokespersons in the Senate, lead their party caucuses in proposing new laws, and are the chief architects of their party's platform. As leader of the majority, the Senate majority leader enjoys special power in making assignments to leadership of committees.

As in the House, the Senate majority and minority leaders are supported by majority and minority whips. The whips in the Senate serve the same function as those in the House; they keep track of how caucus members are planning to vote on upcoming bills, and they communicate the positions of party leaders on upcoming legislative votes.

Leaders in the Senate generally have far less power than their counterparts in the House. The smaller number of senators requires less discipline in membership, and the culture of the Senate includes a greater amount of deference from one senator to another. Because there are fewer rules and formal procedures in the Senate, leaders and rule-making members have less power to control debate in that body.

The GOP House leadership campaigned on "A Pledge to America" to rein in federal spending and reduce the size of government. This campaign helped the GOP cement victories in the 2010 congressional elections.

AP PHOTO/J. SCOTT APPLEWHITE

The Committee System

The work of a member of Congress can be classified into four categories: (1) running for reelection, (2) serving constituents, (3) working on legislation, and (4) providing oversight of federal agencies. Working on legislation involves two activities—working on bills in committees and voting on proposed bills.[8] The bulk of work on legislation consists of what members do in committees, which includes generating ideas for new laws, debating the merits of those ideas, holding hearings, conducting investigations, listening to the testimony of experts, offering modifications and additions to proposed bills, and giving important advice to all House and Senate members regarding how they should vote on a new bill. Committee work also is the means through which members fulfill their role of oversight of federal agencies. Voting, on the other hand, is a rather simple and straightforward process. Members show up to the House or Senate floor and cast a vote of either "aye," "nay," or "present," indicating their support, opposition to, or abstention from voting on a proposed piece of legislation.

Every year, about 10,000 bills are introduced into Congress. A **bill** is a formally proposed piece of legislation, and many bills are long, complex documents with much legal and technical information. It is not practical to assume that each Senate and House member reads and digests every bill that is introduced. As a way to manage the workload, both chambers of Congress rely heavily on a committee system. In both the House and Senate, each member is assigned to a few committees and becomes an expert in the subject area of the committee. Most of members' legislative work revolves around the committees to which they are assigned.

Congressional committees also include subcommittees, providing for even more specialization and division of labor. Currently, there are more than 100 subcommittees in the House alone. Each of the subcommittees is also assigned a chair, so many members in the majority party of the House are chairs of either a committee or subcommittee. In the Senate, with fewer members, all members of the majority are usually the chair of at least one committee or subcommittee. A House member sits on an average of five different committees, whereas a senator sits on an average of seven committees.

What makes the committee system so powerful a force in legislation? It is the deference that most members give to the work of their colleagues in committees. Recognizing specialized knowledge, respecting the need for division of labor, and protecting one's own authority in the committees on which one serves all lead senators and House members to vote on the basis of a committee's recommendation on a bill.

Types of Committees in Congress

There are four general types of congressional committees: standing committees, select committees, conference committees, and joint committees.

Standing committees are permanent committees that exist in both the House and Senate. Most standing committees focus on a particular substantive area of public policy, such as transportation, labor, foreign affairs, or the federal budget. A few focus on procedural matters of the House and Senate, such as the House Rules Committee and the Senate Rules and Administration Committee. The most significant power of the standing committee is that of **reporting legislation**, which means that the full House or Senate cannot vote on a bill unless the committee votes to approve it first. No other type of congressional committee has the power to report legislation. Standing committees have been the heart and soul of congressional organization since the very early 1800s. Just like today, standing committees then were divided into substantive policy areas and had plenty of authority to determine the future of a bill within its jurisdiction. For example, in

Bill
A proposed law presented for consideration to a legislative body.

Standing committee
A permanent committee that exists in both the House and Senate; most standing committees focus on a particular substantive area of public policy, such as transportation, labor, foreign affairs, and the federal budget.

Reporting legislation
The exclusive power of standing committees to forward legislation to the full House or Senate. Neither chamber can vote on a bill unless the committee votes to approve it first.

1802, the House of Representatives established the Ways and Means Committee to set policies for America's federal tax system. Any bill dealing with changes in the tax system had to pass through this committee, as it does still today. The House Ways and Means Committee remains the primary author of tax bills, including the tax cuts approved by Congress and signed into law by President Bush in 2001 and 2003.

Although most standing committees focus on a substantive area of public policy, such areas of focus are often broad and complex. To further divide labor and provide for even greater levels of specialization, most standing committees include subcommittees. For example, the House Transportation and Infrastructure Committee includes the following subcommittees: Aviation; Coast Guard and Marine Transportation; Economic Development, Public Buildings, Hazardous Materials, and Pipeline Transportation; Ground Transportation; Oversight, Investigations, and Emergency Management; and Water Resources and Environment.

Before the House of Representatives or the Senate can vote on any bill, it must first be approved by a majority of members on the committee. A number of factors can affect a committee's consideration of a bill, which can seriously slow down the process of a bill becoming law and create a sense of "legislative gridlock." When a committee gets a new bill, the chair usually directs the bill to a subcommittee. The subcommittee discusses the bill, holds hearings, and makes changes, additions, or deletions to the bill. Usually, after a successful subcommittee vote, the bill moves back to the full committee, where additional debate and hearings might occur. Only after a successful committee vote is the bill ready for consideration by the full House and/or Senate. This process occurs in both the House and the Senate. There are, therefore, many opportunities for standing committees to slow the policymaking process or bring it to a grinding halt.

Select committee
A committee established by a resolution in either the House or the Senate for a specific purpose and, usually, for a limited time.

A second general type of committee in Congress is the **select committee**, a special committee established to examine a particular issue of concern. Select committees do not have the power to report legislation, and they are not permanent. Once their work on a particular issue is complete, the select committee is dissolved. Select committees are often formed to deal with a particularly serious national problem—a problem for which legislation may not be considered but rather a recommendation might be made. Recently, for example, select committees have been established to investigate the problem of illegal immigration and the national drug problem. House or Senate leaders may choose a select committee to deal with an issue for political reasons as well. If leaders suspect that a standing committee might have trouble reporting a bill to the full chamber, they might appoint a select committee, which does not have reporting power.

Conference committee
A joint committee of Congress appointed by the House of Representatives and the Senate to resolve differences on a particular bill.

A third type of committee found in Congress is the **conference committee**. As described earlier in this chapter, the House and Senate are equal players in the legislative process. This means that both chambers debate, hold hearings on, comment on, and vote on individual pieces of legislation. A bill, then, is considered, modified, and voted on by both the House and the Senate. Assuming that a bill survives both chambers and passes, it is likely that the changes made to the bill during the standing committee process will differ between the House and Senate. Conference committees consist of both House members and senators, who work together to iron out differences in the House and Senate versions of a bill.

A fourth type of committee is the **joint committee**, which consists of members from both chambers. Joint committees do not propose legislation and have no reporting power but rather are investigative in nature, focusing on issues of general concern, such as oversight of programs that are administered by the executive branch of the federal government. Unlike select committees, which are temporary and focus on a narrower topic, joint committees are typically permanent and focus on broader policy areas. An example is Congress's Joint Economic Committee. This committee keeps tabs on the performance of the nation's economy and provides oversight to the Federal Reserve Board, the unit that, among other things, has authority to adjust the federal prime interest rate.

Joint committee
A committee comprising members of both the House and the Senate that is investigative in nature.

Leadership of Congressional Committees

Although there are a handful of broad leadership positions such as "presiding officers" and "party leaders" in the House and Senate, the vast majority of leaders are the chairs of the many committees and subcommittees in the two chambers. The power of the majority caucus is fully felt in the committee and subcommittee chairs, as all chairs are members of the majority caucus. Committees are where Congress gets most of its work done, and the chairs of committees have a great deal of power in determining what gets done and when it gets done.[9]

For example, the chairs decide how much time, if any, to spend on a new bill; they choose the people who will testify before the committee; and they allot the time to be spent on testimony and committee discussion. House and Senate leaders choose committee chairs from members of the majority caucus, a selection generally based on seniority and party allegiance. For each committee, the majority party's ranking, or senior, member is typically the person who becomes the committee chair, although the Speaker of the House ultimately determines the chairs for House committees, and the Senate majority leader does the same for Senate committees.[10] Although seniority remains important, congressional reforms in 1974 and 1994 have somewhat reduced the power of seniority in the determination of committee chairs. More recently, the selection of chairs and the chairs' adherence to party leadership have provided a strong basis for party influence in congressional leadership.

Partisan Nature of the Committee System

The large number of standing committees and subcommittees, along with the significant power of the committee given its expertise in the policy area, disperses legislative power. It is in the interest of the majority party, however, to control what bills are given priority, how bills are written, and what bills get passed. Thus, the primary organizational characteristic of most committees in Congress is partisanship. To control the committee agenda and the committee votes, the majority caucus ensures that all committees have a majority of members of their party.[11] Furthermore, the chair of each committee is from the majority caucus. In addition, the majority caucus typically reserves a "supermajority" of seats on the most powerful committees, such as the Rules and Appropriations Committees.

Congressional Staffing

The 435 House members and 100 senators are supported by a large professional staff, many of whom are young, recent college graduates. Staffers

AP PHOTO/RUSTY KENNEDY

Congressman Patrick Murphy (D-PA) is congratulated by his wife (immediate left) and staff after his reelection victory in 2006. Murphy lost his reelection bid in the GOP landslide of 2010.

perform a variety of support functions related to the roles of members of Congress. They conduct background research on bills, help generate new ideas for bills, provide services to constituents, and aid in the oversight of executive agencies. There are three categories of congressional staff.

First is the member's **personal staff**. Members of Congress are given a budget to support a group of staffers to assist them. They typically have a staff in their Washington, DC, office and one in their home district office. The personal staffers serve a number of legislative support functions, including tracking bills that the member has introduced and conducting research on ideas for new bills. They also work with the local media in the member's home district, answering journalists' questions and providing information on the member's legislative activities. Perhaps the personal staffers' most important responsibility is responding to constituents in the district. House and Senate members receive many kinds of communications from constituents, ranging from requests for information about bills and explanations of why they voted a particular way to letters expressing opinions on various issues and requests for speaking engagements. The personal staffers are responsible for dealing with these myriad constituent inquiries.

Congressional personal staff
A group of workers who assist an individual member of Congress in performing his or her responsibilities.

Congressional agencies
Government bodies formed by and relied on by Congress to support members of Congress in performing their functions.

Another form of support for members of Congress comes in the form of **congressional agencies**. The volume of legislative work has grown substantially over the years, as has the complexity of the federal budget and the policy issues that Congress deals with. One way that Congress has dealt with problems of growth and complexity has been to delegate authority to executive agencies of government, a consequence of which was that Congress began to lose control of the ability to keep tabs on what those agencies were doing. The explosion of budget deficits in the 1970s and suspicions about the administration that were inspired by the Watergate scandal also left Congress feeling that it lacked necessary information for effective monitoring of executive agencies under presidential control. Through the 1970s, Congress relied on budget data from the Office of Management and Budget (OMB), which reports to the president. Congress suspected that the budget figures produced by OMB were compiled with an eye toward supporting the president's point of view. In response, in 1974, Congress created a new congressional agency, the Congressional Budget Office (CBO), to monitor the nation's economic situation and provide objective projections of the national budget. It reports directly to Congress. With the CBO, Congress no longer needs to depend exclusively on the executive branch to gather economic data and produce information to help Congress oversee the budget process.

At the same time, Congress also substantially expanded the size and funding of the Government Accountability Office (GAO; formerly called the General Accounting Office) and the Congressional Research Service (CRS). Congress uses the GAO to monitor executive agency expenditures. Essentially, the GAO audits the spending of federal organizations to find and remove any abuses. The CRS is Congress's information and statistical data archive. It provides members with information they might need in preparation for writing a bill, conducting a hearing or investigation, or making a speech. Other important agencies of Congress include the Library of Congress, which acts both as the de facto national library of the United States as well as a research arm for congressional members. The Government Printing Office prints and provides access to documents produced by and for all three branches of the federal government.

A third type of staffing resource at Congress's disposal is the congressional committee staff. Each standing committee of Congress employs a professional staff, many of whom are policy or legal experts in the policy area of the committee.

How a Bill Becomes a Law

Describe the various steps necessary for a bill to become a law ★ LO

It is not easy for a bill to become a law. Although most work on bills occurs in committees, there are numerous other points at which a bill might be "killed." The Speaker of the House, the Senate majority leader, and the president all have means at their disposal to kill a bill. There are other points, as well, when bills might be stopped dead in their tracks. Not surprisingly, of the 10,000 or so bills introduced annually in Congress, only about 500 to 1,000 end up becoming law. And rarely does a bill, as originally introduced, become law without significant revision in the process. An important book on the process of a bill becoming law is *The Dance of Legislation* by Eric Redman.[12] As the title suggests, the lawmaking process involves many people and much politicking; the process is difficult and often follows no regular or consistent path. The steps to a bill becoming law are also highly influenced by partisan politics, lobbyists and special interests, public opinion, and powerful voices in and out of government. Even though the actual dance of legislation typically follows no neat pattern or order, we describe here the general way a bill becomes a law.

Step 1: A Bill Is Introduced

With the exception of tax or revenue proposals, which must originate in the House of Representatives, a bill can be first introduced into either the Senate or the House. The revenue exception, as stipulated in the Constitution, is a product of the American colonial experience with England and the famous cry, "no taxation without representation." Because the House provides popular representation, and representation is the philosophical basis undergirding taxation, the founders gave the House sole authority to originate tax and revenue bills.

Whereas the Constitution requires that only a House member or a senator can introduce a bill, the ideas for new bills come from a variety of sources. Many come from the president of the United States or someone in the president's office or executive branch of government. Others come from lobbyists. Because House members and senators depend on lobbyists for information and lobbyists represent groups who support candidates for congressional office, those with access to members are an important source of ideas for new legislation. Business leaders, educators, journalists, and regular constituents may also generate ideas for new bills. The next step for those with a suggestion for a new law is to find a sponsor in the House or Senate to introduce the idea in the form of a bill.

FIGURE 6.1 The Steps in a Bill Becoming a Law

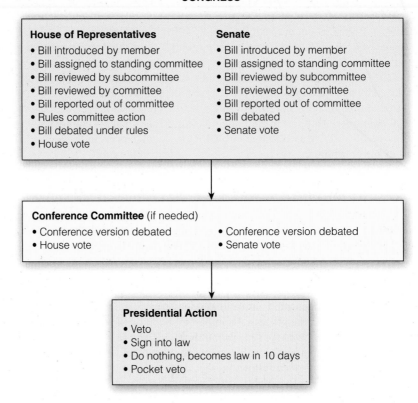

CONGRESS

House of Representatives
- Bill introduced by member
- Bill assigned to standing committee
- Bill reviewed by subcommittee
- Bill reviewed by committee
- Bill reported out of committee
- Rules committee action
- Bill debated under rules
- House vote

Senate
- Bill introduced by member
- Bill assigned to standing committee
- Bill reviewed by subcommittee
- Bill reviewed by committee
- Bill reported out of committee
- Bill debated
- Senate vote

Conference Committee (if needed)
- Conference version debated
- House vote

- Conference version debated
- Senate vote

Presidential Action
- Veto
- Sign into law
- Do nothing, becomes law in 10 days
- Pocket veto

Whether the idea for a law comes directly from a member of Congress or from some other source, the first official step in the process is for the sponsoring member to submit the bill to the House or Senate clerk, who issues a unique number to the bill. The clerk in the House sends the bill to the Speaker of the House; the Senate clerk forwards the bill to the Senate majority leader.

Step 2: The Bill Is Sent to a Standing Committee for Action

The next step in the process requires the bill to be assigned to the standing committee that has policy jurisdiction over the topic the bill addresses. A bill introduced in the Senate to raise the minimum wage, for example, would likely be sent to the Senate Labor and Human Resources Committee; a bill proposing increased criminal penalties for mail fraud introduced into the House might be assigned to the House Judiciary Committee.

Most bills die during their initial consideration by the committee. In some cases, the committee chair simply sits on the bill and ignores it. In other cases, the full committee, without deliberation, votes to kill the bill. If the committee decides to give the bill serious consideration, the committee chair usually assigns it to a subcommittee. The subcommittee may hold hearings, conduct investigations, and deliberate on the merits of the bill. Often, the

FDIC Chair Sheila Blair, Assistant Treasury Secretary Neel Kashlari, and Assistant HUD Secretary Brian Montgomery attend an October 2008 hearing of the Senate Banking Committee, which was meeting to address the U.S. financial crisis.

subcommittee will make amendments to the bill before sending it back to the full committee.

When a bill is back in full committee, the recommendations of the subcommittee may be accepted, rejected, or further revised. The full committee may conduct additional hearings, call more witnesses and experts to testify, and debate the bill. At the end of this process, a *markup*, or final version of the bill, is prepared. The markup is the proposed legislation on which the full committee will vote. If a majority of committee members vote against the bill, the bill goes no further, so here is another point in the process when a bill might be stopped. If a majority of committee members vote in favor of the bill, it moves forward in the process.

Step 3: The Bill Goes to the Full House and Senate for Consideration

At this next stage, the full House or Senate debates the bill and proposes amendments. The start of this process differs between the House and Senate. In the House, a bill that makes it through the committee is immediately assigned to the House **Rules Committee**. The Rules Committee decides when the bill will be debated, the amount of time that will be allotted for debate, and the extent to which amendments may be added from the floor of the House. The ability to control the timing and amount of time for debate is significant, thus making this committee one of the most important ones in the House. The ability to control the amendment process is even more powerful. If the Rules Committee issues a **closed rule**, House members are severely limited in their ability to amend the bill. An **open rule** order, on the other hand, permits amendments to the bill.

In the Senate, there are no rules set up ahead of time for debate. The Senate majority leader decides when to bring a bill to the floor. But in theory, there are no limits on the amount of time the bill will be debated, and all senators are given the courtesy of speaking on any bill if they so wish. The fact that the Senate includes far fewer members than the House allows for less structured debate. With no rules about how long a senator might speak, there is a possibility that a minority of senators—or even one senator—might try to block a bill from passage by refusing to end discussion, a process known as a **filibuster**.[13]

Rules Committee
A committee in the House of Representatives that determines the rules by which bills will come to the floor, be debated, and so on.

Closed rule
A rule of procedure adopted by the House Rules Committee that severely limits the ability of members of Congress to amend a bill.

Open rule
A rule of procedure adopted by the House Rules Committee that permits amendments to a bill.

Filibuster
The action by a single senator or a minority of senators to block a bill from passage by refusing to end discussion.

In 1917, a group of senators successfully filibustered to thwart a bill that would have armed American ships in anticipation of the nation's entry into World War I. In response to this event, the Senate adopted a **cloture** rule, which permitted the Senate to end debate and force a vote on a bill by approval of a two-thirds vote. The Senate left a loophole in place, however: If any senator, once properly recognized, refuses to concede the floor, he or she can exercise the equivalent of a one-person filibuster for as long as his or her voice will hold out. In 1957, South Carolina Senator Strom Thurmond spoke for more than twenty-four hours in an attempt to block the Senate from passing civil rights legislation. For many years, Senate filibusters successfully blocked legislation supported by a majority of senators. Then in 1975, the Senate modified the cloture requirement so that currently a less stringent three-fifths vote of the Senate (60 of 100 senators) is required to end debate.

At the end of the debate and amendment process, the House and Senate take a vote on the proposed bill. Passage of a bill must achieve a majority of votes (half of all present for voting, plus one) from members on the floor. A majority of votes must be achieved in both the Senate and House for the bill to survive to the next step in the legislative process.

How any one member of the House or Senate makes the decision to vote "aye" or "nay" on a given proposed bill differs from one bill to another and from one member to another. But there are six common explanations, which vary in importance, depending on the situation.

1. **Personal opinion and judgment.** Many members of Congress have strong personal opinions and convictions on issues and cast their votes on bills on the basis of those opinions. Rep. Henry Waxman (D-CA), for example, is an ardent environmentalist and consistently votes this position on environmental bills. Similarly, Rep. Chris Smith's (R-NJ) pro-life stance on abortion leads him to vote that position on bills.

2. **Constituent opinion.** Members of Congress want to be liked by their constituents, and most want to be reelected. In voting on particular bills, members often use results of polls, editorial commentary in local media, and letters written to them by their constituents to help them make up their minds in voting on a particular bill.

3. **Interest groups and lobbying.** As a way of achieving their goals, interest groups exert influence on congressional voting in a number of ways, including making contributions to congressional campaigns and hiring lobbyists to provide arguments to members regarding why they should vote a particular way on a bill. So members use both information provided by lobbyists to aid in their voting and the campaign support from interest groups to prompt how they will vote.

4. **Political parties.** Party affiliation often conveys quite a bit about a member's political positions and ideology, with Democrats tending to be more liberal on social and economic issues and Republicans tending to be more conservative on these issues. So party membership is an important cue. In addition, the leadership of each party is organized to influence party members to vote the "party line" on bills. Members voting with their party tend to be rewarded with better committee assignments and greater campaign funding, thus making party a very important factor in voting on legislation.

5. **The president.** Presidents are the focus of national attention and have, as President Teddy Roosevelt once said, a "bully pulpit" to make their case and influence others, including members of Congress. Presidents are quite influential in directing congressional members of their own party how to vote but often exert influence on members of the opposition party as well. Particularly in times of international crisis, presidents can effectively make appeals to put partisanship aside and convince members to vote in the interests of the country.

6. **Logrolling.** Members often enter into an agreement with other members to vote a certain way on one bill in exchange for a favorable vote on another bill. This process is known as logrolling. Members vote on thousands of bills every term. Giving up a vote on less important bills in exchange for favorable votes on more important bills is a common practice that often guides congressional voting behavior.

Logrolling
The trading of influence or votes among legislators to achieve passage of projects that are of interest to one another.

Step 4: Conference Committee Action

As discussed earlier in this chapter, often the version of a bill that passes the Senate differs from that passed by the House. To iron out any differences between Senate and House bills, Congress appoints a conference committee to work out the kinks. The conference committee consists of House and Senate members— usually those who are on the standing committees that worked on the bills.

Step 5: Presidential Action

The president plays both an informal and a formal role in the passage of new laws. The president's informal role is to develop new ideas for laws and urge members of Congress to introduce them. The president also lobbies Congress, attempting to persuade members to support or oppose certain bills. The president's strong presence in the American political system, along with attention from the national media, offers the president a unique platform to lobby on behalf of or against certain legislation.

OLIVIER DOULIERY/PHOTOSHOT

President Obama signs the health care reform bill into law at the White House in March 2010.

★ LO   Explain why Congress often delegates its lawmaking authority to regulatory agencies

The formal constitutional role that the president plays in legislation is the fifth step in the process by which a bill becomes law. Once both chambers of Congress have agreed to a bill, the bill is sent to the president for action. The president has three options for dealing with the congressionally approved bill. First, the president can sign the bill, which officially makes it new law. Second, the president can **veto** (or refuse assent to) the bill, which stops the bill from becoming law. If the bill is vetoed, Congress has one more opportunity to pass the bill by **overriding** the presidential veto. An override requires a two-thirds vote in favor of passage in both the Senate and the House, a margin substantially more difficult to achieve than the simple majority vote required prior to a presidential veto. Third, the president can decide not to act on a bill (that is, neither sign it nor veto it), in which case the bill automatically becomes law after it has been on the president's desk for ten days. If Congress passes a bill and sends it to the president within ten days of the end of a congressional session and the president does not act on the bill, then the bill does not become law, a process known as a **pocket veto**.

Oversight and Personnel Functions of Congress

In addition to creating new laws, Congress performs four other important constitutional functions: oversight of federal agencies, confirmation of top federal executives and judges, approval of treaties, and impeachment of top federal executives and federal judges.

Congressional Oversight

Congress's principal responsibility is to enact new laws to deal with national problems and concerns. But given the complexity of many issues (nuclear and toxic waste disposal, creating new sources of energy, promoting the role of high technology, and enhancing the performance of a multitrillion-dollar economy that has become highly integrated in the global economy, to name just a few), Congress often lacks the scientific and technological expertise needed to enact laws. In addition, for political reasons, sometimes Congress prefers not to deal with issues on its own but rather to "pass the buck" to a bureaucratic agency. Defining the limits of genetic cloning is one such political hot potato. Whether the reason is technical capability or politics, Congress often delegates more specific legislative authority to the executive branch, which has the resources and expertise to make more highly technical policy decisions. The delegation of congressional power to the executive branch has become more frequent as our society has become more complex.

This delegation of authority, however, is not carried out blindly or without accountability. When Congress delegates its authority, it generally monitors the activities of agencies and administrators who are given this power through congressional oversight. One agency to which Congress has delegated considerable authority is the Federal Reserve Board (known as "the Fed"). Established by the Federal Reserve Act of 1913, the Fed has authority over credit rates and lending activities of the nation's banks. Congress created the agency because it recognized that maintaining a viable economy required specialized monitoring of the economy and the technical expertise

World Views of the United States

In March 2010, the House and Senate both held hearings to investigate the image of the United States around the world. The Foreign Relations committees in both houses called upon international relations and public opinions experts to provide their perspectives on what people from around the world thought of the United States, and how these views are changing. Andrew Kohut, the president of the Pew Research Center, presented findings to the House Foreign Relations Committee from the Pew Global Attitudes Project. The project features surveys in 57 countries conducted since 2002. A "U.S. Favorability Rating" is a standard question used in these surveys. The table below shows the U.S. Favorability Rating around the world, as reported to the Foreign Relations Committee. (Data from 1999/2000 are from a survey conducted by the U.S. State Department.)

U.S. Favorability Rating

	1999/ 2000 %	2002 %	2003 %	2005 %	2006 %	2007 %	2008 %	2009 %
U.S.	--	--	--	83	76	80	84	88
Canada	71	72	63	59	--	55	--	68
Britain	83	75	70	55	56	51	53	69
France	62	62	42	43	39	39	42	75
Germany	78	60	45	42	37	30	31	64
Spain	50	--	38	41	23	34	33	58
Poland	86	79	--	62	--	61	68	67
Russia	37	61	37	52	43	41	46	44
Turkey	52	30	15	23	12	9	12	14
Egypt	--	--	--	--	30	21	22	27
Jordan	--	25	1	21	15	20	19	25
Lebanon	--	36	27	42	--	47	51	55
Palest. ter.	--	--	*	--	--	13	--	15
Israel	--	--	78	--	--	78	--	71
China	--	--	--	42	47	34	41	47
India	--	66	--	71	56	59	66	76
Indonesia	75	61	15	38	30	29	37	63
Japan	77	72	--	--	63	61	50	59
Pakistan	23	10	13	23	27	15	19	16
S. Korea	58	52	46	--	--	58	70	78
Argentina	50	34	--	--	--	16	22	38
Brazil	56	51	35	--	--	44	47	61
Mexico	68	64	--	--	--	56	47	69
Kenya	94	80	--	--	--	87	--	90
Nigeria	46	76	61	--	62	70	64	79

Source: The Pew Research Center for the People and the Press, Pew Global Attitudes Project, http://pewglobal.org/2009/07/23/confidence-in-obama-lifts-us-image-around-the-world. 1999/2000 survey trends provided by the Office of Research, U.S. Department of State.

of economists to make decisions about credit rates and lending activities. The act gave the Fed the authority to adjust the supply of money to banks and to shift money from where there is too much to where there is too little. The Fed also has the power to take means to ensure that banks do not overextend themselves in lending so that a sudden economic scare will not cause a sudden run on banks for money. For nearly 100 years, Congress has given this agency the power to set important monetary policy for the nation. But Congress retains its authority to exercise oversight of the Fed. The Joint Economic Committee in Congress carefully monitors the Fed's performance and regularly holds hearings to inquire about its policies and decisions. In addition, newly appointed members of the Federal Reserve Board must be approved by Congress.

In his book on Congress titled *Congress: The Keystone of the Washington Establishment*,[14] political scientist Morris Fiorina notes other important reasons for congressional delegation of power to executive agencies, including garnering political rewards while shifting blame to the executive branch, enabling Congress to blame federal agencies for failing to fulfill legislative intent, and taking credit for problem solving by holding oversight and investigative hearings.

★ LO Learn the role of the Senate in confirming presidential appointments

Confirmation of Presidential Nominations and Approval of Treaties

The U.S. Senate plays a pivotal role in the selection of cabinet officers, other agency and executive branch heads, federal judges, and foreign ambassadors. The president nominates individuals for these posts, but the Senate must consent to the nomination with a majority vote in favor of the candidate. This function is one performed solely by the U.S. Senate and not the House of Representatives.

At the beginning of a new presidential administration, the U.S. Senate is typically quite busy reviewing the president's nominations for high executive office positions.[15] Although the Senate usually endorses most nominees, there have been a number of high-profile instances when the Senate has been unwilling to confirm the nominee, typically occurring during eras of divided government when the political party of the president is different from the majority party in the Senate.

When there is a vacancy on the U.S. Supreme Court, an event that often draws considerable interest from both the press and the public, the president nominates a new justice, whom the Senate also must confirm with a majority vote. Under certain circumstances, Congress may also become involved in the selection of president and vice president of the United States. When no candidate receives a majority of electoral votes, the House of Representatives chooses the president and the Senate chooses the vice president. This has happened three times in the history of the nation—in 1801, when the House chose Thomas Jefferson as president; in 1825, when the House chose John Quincy Adams; and in 1877, when the House appointed a commission to resolve the controversial 1876 election (it chose Rutherford B. Hayes).

In the event of a vacancy in the vice presidency, the Twenty-fifth Amendment to the Constitution stipulates that the president's nomination of an individual to fill that position is subject to the approval of both the House and Senate by

An Internship as a Steppingstone

Many college students interested in politics and public policy seek internships with Congress during the summer. Such an experience allows them to see firsthand how Congress works, gain valuable experience, and prepare for a possible job with the federal government. In early 2010, the job search website Monster.com estimated that job opportunities in the federal government would grow from 2.1 million to 2.5 million by end of 2012. Building one's resume with an internship in Congress can help to jump-start a successful career in public service.

The dozens of committees in Congress all have spots for college interns, as do large congressional agencies such as the General Accounting Office, the Congressional Budget Office, and the Library of Congress. In addition, all 535 members of Congress maintain offices in Washington, DC, as well as in their home state/district. Interns are commonly found helping with casework in many of these offices. Moreover, the partisan leadership offices, such as the majority and minority leaders

A recent group of interns who work with the Congressional Hispanic Caucus.

CONGRESSIONAL HISPANIC CAUCUS INSTITUTE

and whips, frequently staff college interns to help them do their work, as do the Democratic and GOP House and Senate campaign committees. Many senators and representatives first got introduced to Congress through an internship that they themselves had. At a minimum, an internship with Congress provides a great resume item when applying for a full-time position in some part of the federal government.

If you are interested in a congressional internship, there are a number of ways to get one. You can contact the office of a member of the House and/or Senate directly and inquire about future openings. You can visit the internship coordinator at your college or in your university's political science department and ask what might be available and how to apply. Or you can click on the following websites for information about ongoing internship opportunities:

- http://dc.about.com/od/jobs/a/Internships.htm
- http://www.twc.edu
- http://www.cbo.gov/employment/intern.cfm

majority vote. This has happened twice since adoption of that amendment: in 1973, when Vice President Spiro Agnew resigned and Nixon's nomination of Gerald Ford was quickly approved, and in 1974, when Ford became president due to Nixon's resignation and Congress approved Ford's nomination of Nelson Rockefeller as vice president.

Finally, the Senate has the power to approve treaties that the president negotiates with foreign countries. The Constitution stipulates that approval of a treaty requires the consent of two thirds of the Senate. Even though the standard for treaty approval is much higher than a simple majority, most treaties do obtain the necessary two-thirds approval. Perhaps the most important rejection concerned the Versailles Treaty following World War I. The relatively low number of rejected treaties may be due to presidents' reluctance to negotiate treaties that they are not reasonably certain will pass. President Woodrow Wilson's failure to consult with the Senate and consider their objections to the Versailles Treaty led to the treaty's twice being rejected by the Senate, once in 1919 and again in 1920. More recently, the House has also played an important role in approving treaties because most of them involve financial issues that require the approval of that chamber.

Constituent Service: Helping People Back Home

★ LO Assess the "casework" functions of members of Congress in assisting constituents, educating them on policy issues, and performing other services on their behalf

Much of what has been discussed thus far in this chapter pertains to what members of Congress do in Washington. As the people's representatives, members are sent to Washington to develop new laws and deliberate on important issues. They are expected to safeguard the nation's security, act as watchdogs against fraud, and ensure that judges and high-ranking executive officers are qualified for office. An integral part of the way members serve their constituents is by reflecting the opinions and input of those whom they represent while carrying out these legislative functions.

However, the service of members of Congress does not stop with the work they do in Washington. Often, constituents will call upon a House member or senator to provide information about federal programs, to render assistance in getting benefits from federal programs, or to prepare a talk or visit with a community group to educate them about the political system or on a specific legislative or policy topic. Members are often asked by officials in state or

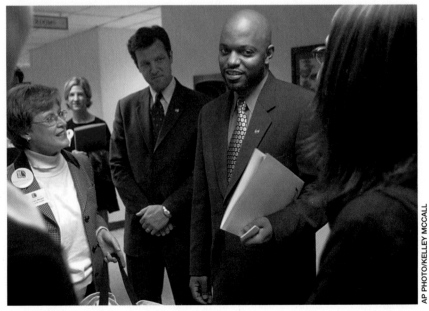

Missouri Congressmen Russ Carnahan (left) and Rodney Hubbard (right), both Democrats, visit with some constituents back home.

AP PHOTO/KELLEY MCCALL

local government to facilitate federal help for a local or state issue. The direct assistance that a member provides to a constituent, community group, or a local or state official is referred to as **casework**. A now classic book by Richard F. Fenno, titled *Home Style: House Members in Their Districts*, provides a rich description of this role played by members of Congress.[16]

Casework is important for a number of reasons. First is its electoral importance to members of Congress. Casework raises the visibility of members in their home state or district, which reflects positively on how well the member is regarded and gives members an advantage over their opponents in elections. More than nine in ten House and Senate members who run for reelection are returned to office, and effectively managing casework is an important reason for this high return rate.

It has also become an implicit responsibility of members to help their constituents navigate the complex federal bureaucracy. Federal programs are varied and complex, and constituents are often overwhelmed in their efforts to obtain the benefits for which they are eligible. For example, under the Workforce Development Act, the federal government has programs that provide assistance to "displaced workers," defined as those who have lost their jobs due to technological or broad trends in the workplace. Many workers in the U.S. manufacturing industry have lost their jobs over the past decade as the national economy has shifted away from manufacturing and toward technology and information services. A variety of programs are available for these displaced workers to help them obtain training in new skills necessary to adapt to the new workforce. Finding these programs is often difficult, and members of Congress provide information to connect constituents with available programs.

Third, casework provides a direct connection between members and their constituents. Casework requires members to keep in touch with the people they represent. Giving a speech to a local Rotary club or League of Women Voters meeting, showing up to "cut the ribbon" at an opening of a new local school building or park, and coming to speak to a group of students or employees all provide face time between the members and their constituents. The experiences that members have and the type of work they do in Washington can shelter them from the real-life concerns of their constituents back home. Casework provides a constant reminder of the needs and interests of those whom members represent.

Another aspect of constituent service involves what is known as "pork-barrel" politics. The federal budget includes a great deal of money for local projects, such as parks, dams, or road improvements. Members secure federal funds to support these projects in their states and districts through what is often referred to as **pork-barrel legislation**. The pork-barrel reference is based on the idea that members are "bringing home the bacon." Members use their influence on congressional committees and leadership positions to add amendments to bills that authorize pork-barrel spending on projects back home. Although many observers of the political system decry the unfairness of pork-barrel legislation, it has been an important aspect of constituent service since the beginning of our political system and promises to remain so in the future.

Casework
The direct assistance that a member of Congress provides to a constituent, community group, or a local or state official.

Pork-barrel legislation
A government project or appropriation that yields jobs or other benefits to a specific locale and patronage opportunities to its political representative.

NOW & THEN

Making the Connection

This chapter began with examples of Senate resistance in two issue areas at two very different points in American history—the approval of the League of Nations provisions of the Treaty of Versailles following World War I, and lower court judicial nominations in the first decade of the twenty-first century. In both instances, the Senate moved at a glacier pace, frustrating an impatient president at every turn. When Senate leaders offered the president compromises that might speed up the process, he was reluctant to give up any of what he viewed as "executive prerogative," and so the stalemates continued. Putting these two instances of Senate resistance in the context of the information presented in this chapter, what conclusions can we draw about the way the Congress as a whole, and the Senate in particular, tend to work?

First, and most apparent, when Congress is dealing with major problems or issues of the day, the process of creating new laws, approving new treaties, and approving presidential appointments can be very slow indeed—many observers use the word "gridlock" to describe congressional inaction. Congress's actions are slow and deliberate; there are many points at which the process may be halted, and many actors with the capacity to hinder progress. Second, the compromises necessary to achieve success in Congress rarely prove entirely satisfactory to everyone involved. In the case of the Treaty of Versailles, Senator Henry Cabot Lodge's reservations to the treaty, which rejected any advance U.S. obligation to enter international conflicts to defend the autonomy of another country, were considered unacceptable to President Wilson, and so the Senate rejected the treaty and U.S. membership in the League of Nations. In the case of George W. Bush's judicial nominations, Senate Democratic leaders proposed to speed up the nomination process for some nominees, only if his more controversial nominees were withdrawn.

Both these conflicts also highlight the power and significance of individual actors in the legislative process. Strong individuals such as Senator Henry Cabot Lodge and Senator Patrick Leahy dominated the debate over these issues. Congress is not simply two houses of 535 individuals who vote, with a majority obtaining victory. Those in leadership positions can exert a disproportionate influence on the process. Those with special communication skills enjoy more power, as do those who are highly informed on a particular issue. The better part of a century separated Senate debate and action on the Treaty of Versailles and President Bush's judicial nominations. However, in both instances the same principles guided Senate activity and worked to produce similar approaches to resisting the chief executive.

POLITICS InterActive!

Replacing Members of the U.S. Senate: Special Elections or Gubernatorial Appointment?

On August 25, 2009, Democratic Senator Ted Kennedy of Massachusetts passed away. His death created a vacancy in the U.S. Senate and reduced the Democratic majority from 60 to 59, thus allowing Senate Republicans to filibuster the Obama administration's health care reform legislation. The temporary replacement of a Senate seat is a matter determined by state law. In Massachusetts, the law in 2009 required a special election to be held between 145 and 160 days of the vacancy arising. In 2004 the Democratic majority in the Massachusetts State legislature withdrew the authority of then-governor Republican Mitt Romney to fill a Senate seat vacancy, anticipating that presidential candidate John Kerry, a Democratic senator from Massachusetts, might win the 2004 election. (As it turned out, he lost.) Senator Kennedy strongly encouraged the Democrats in the state's legislature to override Governor Romney's veto of that change, and they did. Ironically, in 2009 the vacancy created by Kennedy's death now threatened to hold up or even kill the federal health care reform legislation that Kennedy himself had championed.

Newly elected U.S. Senator Scott Brown (R-MA) celebrates his victory in the January 19, 2010, special election.

Seven days before his death, Senator Kennedy was again lobbying the Democrats in the Massachusetts legislature. Now with Democrat Deval Patrick as governor and the fate of health care reform in question, Kennedy urged yet another change in the law: allowing the governor to make a temporary appointment prior to the special election for Senate seat vacancies. On September 22, 2009, the Massachusetts legislature posthumously approved Kennedy's request, paving the way for Patrick to appoint long-time Kennedy aide Paul Kirk as interim senator, thus temporarily protecting the Democrats' veto-proof majority until the January 19, 2010, special election. Republican Scott Brown eventually won that special election, and his election eliminated the veto-proof majority once again.

The political circumstances surrounding the actions of the Massachusetts legislature in 2004 and 2009 raise questions about how vacated Senate seats get filled. Changes in the Massachusetts laws are not the only examples of political gamesmanship in state legislatures. What is the best process for filling vacated seats in the Senate—special elections or gubernatorial appointments, or a hybrid approach such as the one adopted by Massachusetts in 2009? As a result of the 2004 and 2009 actions by the Massachusetts legislature, some have called for an amendment to the U.S. Constitution standardizing the manner in which interim vacancies get filled, thus removing political considerations from the process. Do you think that the Constitution should or should not be amended for this purpose?

On www.cengage.com/dautrich/americangovernmentbrief/2e, find the Politics InterActive link for details on filling vacated Senate seats. Consult the various links that relate to the process of filling vacated Senate seats across the fifty states, as well as historical, popular, and global perspectives on the topic.

Chapter Summary

★ Article I and the Creation of Congress

- Congress was the central institution in America's new political system at the beginning of the republic. At that time, it was the only one of the three branches to ensure representation of the people.

- Like most of the early state governments, the federal government featured a bicameral legislature. The federal version included a "people's house" apportioned by population and a Senate in which the states have equal representation.

- To ensure the principle of "one person, one vote" in the House, the population of congressional districts must be made as equal as possible based on the results of a federal census conducted every ten years. Parties try to maximize their advantage in the House of Representatives by "gerrymandering," which means that they draw district boundaries that favor their party on Election Day.

★ The Structure and Organization of Congress

- The relative strength of political party membership determines leadership in each legislative chamber. The Constitution designates that the leader of the House carry the title Speaker of the House. The Speaker is responsible for assigning new bills to committees and recognizing members to speak in the House chamber. The Constitution also prescribes that the vice president is to be the presiding officer of the Senate. Unlike the Speaker, the president of the Senate can vote only to break ties. When the vice president is absent from the Senate chamber (as is quite often the case), the presiding officer is the president pro tempore ("for the time being").

★ The Committee System

- There are four types of congressional committees: standing committees (permanent), select committees (established to look at a particular issue for a limited time), conference committees (reconcile differences between House and Senate versions of a bill), and joint committees (include members from both houses, investigative in nature). Most members defer to committee recommendations on a bill.

★ How a Bill Becomes a Law

- The lawmaking process is often slow, and bills that survive frequently receive significant revisions along the way. After a bill is introduced by a member of Congress, it is usually sent to a committee for consideration (often in the form of hearings) and possible action. If the bill is endorsed by a majority of the committee, it then goes to the full House and Senate for consideration. Finally, if it is endorsed by a majority of each chamber, a conference committee reconciles differences in versions between the chambers, and then after a vote on the bill's final version, it goes to the president for signature.

- If the president vetoes the final bill, Congress can override the presidential veto by a two-thirds vote of both houses of Congress.

★ Oversight and Personnel Functions of Congress

- Congress delegates considerable legislative authority to the executive branch, whether because it lacks the expertise of bureaucrats or because it wishes to shift blame for policies to the executive branch. Still, Congress may exercise oversight to ensure that the implementation of laws and regulations is consistent with national problems and concerns.

- The U.S. Senate plays an important role in consenting to the president's selection of cabinet officers, other executive branch officials, and judges.

Key Terms

Bicameral legislature (p. 143)

Bill (p. 151)

Casework (p. 165)

Closed rule (p. 157)

Cloture (p. 158)

Conference committee (p. 152)

Congressional agencies (p. 154)

Congressional district (p. 144)

Congressional personal staff (p. 154)

Filibuster (p. 157)

Gerrymandering (p. 146)

Joint committee (p. 153)

Logrolling (p. 159)

Majority caucus (p. 147)

Majority leader (p. 149)

Minority caucus (p. 147)

Minority leader (p. 150)

Open rule (p. 157)

Overriding a veto (p. 160)

Pocket veto (p. 160)

Pork-barrel legislation (p. 165)

President pro tempore (p. 150)

Reapportionment (p. 144)

Redistricting (p. 146)

Reporting legislation (p. 151)

Rules Committee (p. 157)

Select committee (p. 152)

Speaker of the House (p. 147)

Standing committee (p. 151)

Veto (p. 160)

Whip (majority and minority) (p. 150)

Resources

Reference Works

Barone, Michael, and Richard E. Cohen, eds. *The Almanac of American Politics.* Washington, DC: National Journal, 2010. This almanac is published biannually with each new Congress and contains in-depth profiles of the 535 members of Congress along with the states and congressional districts they represent.

The *Congressional Record* is the official proceedings of Congress. It contains a record of all the proceedings of the House and Senate.

Books

Dodd, Lawrence C., and Bruce Oppenheimer, eds. *Congress Reconsidered.* 9th ed. Washington, DC: CQ Press, 2008.

Fenno, Richard F. *Congressmen in Committees.* Boston: Little, Brown, 1973.

Fenno, Richard F. *Homestyle: House Members in Their Districts.* Boston: Little, Brown, 1978.

Fiorina, Morris. *Congress: Keystone of the Washington Establishment.* New Haven, CT: Yale University Press, 1979.

Hibbing, John R., and Elizabeth Theiss-Morse. *Congress as Public Enemy: Public Attitudes Toward American Political Institutions.* New York: Cambridge University Press, 1995.

Smith, Stephen S., Jason M. Roberts, and Ryan V. Vander Wielen. *The American Congress.* New York: Cambridge University Press, 2007.

Internet Sources

http://www.thomas.gov (offers links to the *Congressional Record*, which provides the text of bills, floor debate, committee hearings, and reports).

http://www.congress.org (offers links to information and statistics about Congress, including demographic characteristics of members, current leaders in both houses, and e-mail addresses of members).

7 The Presidency

NOW Economic Recovery Advisory Board Chairman Paul Volcker meeting with President Obama in March 2009.

THEN President Franklin Delano Roosevelt (left), and British Economist John Maynard Keynes (right).

NOW &THEN

A Leader's Determination to Stick to His Principles during a Severe Economic Crisis

The president of the United States was no economist, so he kept economists close by to help him make sense of detailed economic data. He understood that economic forces could make or break his administration. He also knew that the United States was facing a financial crisis of epic proportions, and achieving a recovery would require forceful action. Keynesian economic theory—named after its founder, the British economist John Maynard Keynes—justified what the president had in mind: using massive financial government investments to stimulate the economy and increase private economic activity. The president hoped that active public sector spending would provide the spark for economic recovery. His administration sponsored comprehensive legislation in line with this philosophy, and Congress followed the president's lead. Not everyone in Washington agreed with the president's approach: His policy choice would explode the deficit, and some economists believed to do so was dangerous given the difficult economic times. But the president had been elected to deal with the crisis, and as the nation's chief legislator and crisis manager, he alone would take the lead in choosing the road to recovery.

Where Do Presidents Come From? Presidential Comings and Goings

* ★ Assess the requirements for serving as president

* ★ Understand the process by which presidents may be impeached and removed from office; know the order of presidential succession

The Evolution of the American Presidency

* ★ Trace the evolution of the presidency from "chief clerk" in the late 18th and 19th centuries to eventual political dominance

* ★ Understand how the modern presidency has persevered in the recent era of divisiveness

Express Powers and Responsibilities of the President

* ★ Recognize the formal powers vested in the president under Article II of the Constitution

* ★ Explain how presidents use the veto, appointment and removal, and the pardon

* ★ Define the powers and limits of the president as commander in chief

Implied Powers and Responsibilities of the President

* ★ Recognize the implied powers of the presidency not spelled out in the Constitution, including those exercised as the nation's crisis manager and political party leader

* ★ Explain how presidents exercise power through executive orders and agreements

Presidential Resources

* ★ Describe the other individuals and offices in the executive branch that contribute to the modern presidency

Important Presidential Relationships

* ★ Recognize how the power of the presidency is enhanced by communications with the public, the Congress, and the media

CourseMate

NOW & THEN

CHARLES OMMANNEY/CONTOUR BY GETTY IMAGES

NOW Though John Maynard Keynes had been dead for over sixty years, his economic theories were alive and well in the Obama administration during the early months of 2009. Since the 1980s, many economists had argued that the United States was in a "post-Keynesian world" where manipulating interest rates (instead of massive government spending) offered the best chance of staving off serious economic recessions. Then came December 16, 2008, the day the Federal Reserve tried to stabilize an economy in crisis by lowering the interest rate to 0 percent; the economy only continued to worsen in the weeks that followed.

After huddling with his top economic advisors, newly elected President Obama in February 2009 threw his administration's weight behind a quintessentially Keynesian solution: a $787 billion fiscal stimulus plan. The American people looked to Obama as the nation's chief legislator and crisis manager for a recovery plan, and Obama in turn pressed successfully for the American Recovery and Reinvestment Act (ARRA) of 2009. The new act expanded unemployment benefits, increased government spending in education, health care, and energy, and invested over $100 billion in transportation and other infrastructure. A year later, several independent macroeconomic firms, including Moody's and IHS Global Insight, estimated that the stimulus had saved or created 1.6 to 1.8 million jobs. On the other hand, the Congressional Budget Office conceded that the ARRA had increased the deficit by $200 billion for 2009 alone. By favoring the Keynesian route to recovery, Barack Obama cast his nation's lot with a British economist who had spearheaded a revolution in economic thinking more than seventy-five years earlier.

THEN   John Maynard Keynes was nearly fifty years old and at the height of his prestige as an economic theorist when Franklin D. Roosevelt took office as president of the United States in March 1933. FDR had remained open-minded about how his administration should tackle the Great Depression: During his first year in office he offered many different legislative solutions, and all offered hope, but little in the way of tangible improvements to the underlying economy. On a visit to the White House in 1934, Keynes urged the president to forget about the steep deficit that arose when tax revenues dried up during the Great Depression and instead engage in massive government spending to create jobs, build the nation's infrastructure, and assist struggling industries. These suggestions squared with FDR's deeply held belief that the government needed to be active and aggressive, rather than passive, about the economy. The Roosevelt administration eventually relied on these tools of fiscal policy to pass laws aimed at increasing productivity: The Public Works Administration increased its outlays in 1934, eventually spending over $3 billion to fund more than 35,000 public works projects. In the spring of 1938, FDR launched a $5 billion spending program in an effort to increase mass purchasing power in his second term. As chief legislator and crisis manager, FDR enjoyed considerable deference in taking this road. In doing so he ignored the protests of his own Treasury Department officials, who had advocated greater fiscal responsibility by tightening the government's belt. Of course they were right in one respect: The deficit quickly mushroomed, and only the onset of World War II curbed the out-of-control budget shortfalls that resulted. But no one questioned FDR's duty to point the direction to recovery.

TIME LIFE PICTURES/GETTY IMAGES

BETTMANN/CORBIS

P residents Roosevelt and Obama arrived at the White House more than seventy-five years apart, but they both faced serious economic crises, and the nation looked to both men for solutions. The Constitution vests in Congress the power to pass laws, and it says nothing about special rules that govern during a crisis, whether military, economic, or otherwise. Yet in the modern era, it is practically impossible for a Congress of 535 members to provide decisive leadership, and when the nation's economy has run out of gas, a "wait and see" approach is not likely to gain much approval. In this environment, the president must step to the forefront and use the formidable powers as chief legislator and crisis manager to command the nation's attention, direct its spirits, and act decisively. Competing economic theories may point down different paths, and so the president must sort through the evidence and choose a solution. Of course he may end up on the wrong side of history as a result of his difficult choices: The roads to recovery chosen by Herbert Hoover and Jimmy Carter, for example, failed to achieve much, and both men lost their bids for reelection. FDR and Barack Obama knew the stakes. But both recognized that a refusal to lead might be the greatest failing of all.

★ LO   Assess the requirements for serving as president

Where Do Presidents Come From? Presidential Comings and Goings

As a formal matter, the adage that "anyone can grow up to be president" is not literally true. Article II of the Constitution imposes three prerequisites on those who aspire to the Oval Office. Every president must be (1) a "natural born" citizen, (2) thirty-five years of age or older, and (3) a resident within the United States for at least fourteen years. Although the Constitution poses no other formal obstacles to the presidency, as a practical matter the first forty-three holders of the office have tended to fall into several clearly identifiable categories. All chief executives but one have been white males (Barack Obama is the lone African American president) between the ages of forty-two and seventy-seven. All were born Christians, and nearly all identified themselves as Protestants at one point or another in their lifetimes. (John Kennedy was Catholic; Lyndon Johnson was mostly nonobservant in his adulthood.) When George Washington, after serving two terms as the nation's first president,

★ LO   Understand the process by which presidents may be impeached and removed from office; know the order of presidential succession

Changing images of FDR, seen here in 1932, 1936, 1940, and 1944.

AMERICAN GOVERNMENT In Historical Perspective

Presidential Sex Scandals

The American political system has seen its share of corruption, including scandals that have directly implicated some of the men who have occupied the Oval Office. Like it or not, presidential personal lives have become a matter of public interest, and the chief executives have occasionally seen their administrations swept up in sex scandals that captured the public's attention for weeks, if not months, at a time.

In 1802, rumors that President Thomas Jefferson had secretly fathered children by his slave Sally Hemings were published by one of Jefferson's political rivals, James Callender. Hemings herself was the daughter of Jefferson's father-in-law and another female slave. Such personal attacks were not unusual in the early politics of the republic, and historians dismissed the rumors as scurrilous for the better part of two centuries. Finally, in 1998, the British journal *Nature* published the results of DNA tests that suggested Jefferson was the "probable father" of at least one descendant of Hemings. Recent

reunion celebrations that included both descendants of Jefferson and descendants of Hemings may have put this issue to rest once and for all.

In 1922, President Warren Harding entertained a mistress, Nan Britton, in the White House. Three years earlier, while Harding was still a U.S. senator, Britton had given birth to a child fathered by Harding. The Republican Party effectively buried evidence of the relationship during the 1920 presidential campaign, but once elected, Harding resumed his liaison with Britton. Four years after Harding's death in 1923, Britton wrote a tell-all bestseller disclosing her relationship with the president, including details of intimate acts performed in an anteroom near the White House.

Between 1995 and 1997, President Bill Clinton had a series of sexual encounters with White House intern Monica Lewinsky. The affair became public when an independent counsel investigating Clinton's activities with respect to another alleged affair came across evidence of his affair with Lewinsky. Clinton was ultimately impeached for lying to a grand jury and obstructing justice with respect to the Monica Lewinsky affair. The Senate eventually acquitted him of both charges, but the scandal would occupy the Clinton presidency for more than a year.

---

declined to run again, he established an unwritten two-term precedent. No president challenged that precedent until Franklin Roosevelt sought a third term in 1940. FDR's successful election to four consecutive terms (he won in 1932, 1936, 1940, and then again in 1944) led to passage of the **Twenty-second Amendment** in 1951, which restricts any one person from being elected to the presidency "more than twice" or from acting as president for longer than two and a half terms. Four chief executives were assassinated while in office, and four others died of natural causes while serving as president, including Franklin Roosevelt, who died in 1945, only a few months into his unprecedented fourth term.

The constitutional means of removing a president from office is by **impeachment** and subsequent conviction. Article II, Section 4 of the U.S. Constitution provides that the president may be removed from office upon impeachment by a majority vote of the House and conviction by two thirds of the Senate of "Treason, Bribery, or other high Crimes and Misdemeanors." Just what type of offense qualifies as a "high crime and misdemeanor" is difficult to say. Only two presidents, Andrew Johnson and Bill Clinton, have ever been impeached under these provisions, and both were impeached for primarily political reasons: Johnson was charged with illegally firing a cabinet member, pardoning traitors, and impeding ratification of the Fourteenth Amendment; Clinton was accused

Twenty-second Amendment
Passed in 1951, this constitutional amendment restricts any one person from being elected to the presidency "more than twice," or from acting as president for longer than two and a half terms.

Impeachment
The first step in a two-step process outlined in Article II, Section 4 of the U.S. Constitution to remove a president or other high official from office. The House of Representatives, by majority vote, may impeach if the official has committed "treason, bribery, or other high crimes or misdemeanors." The second step requires a conviction in the Senate by a two-thirds vote.

of lying to a grand jury about his sexual relationship with an intern and for obstructing justice. Both men were acquitted on all charges by the U.S. Senate and served out their respective terms. The only president to resign was Richard Nixon, who was accused of obstructing justice in the now infamous Watergate burglary and political scandal.

When President John Adams was defeated for reelection in 1800 and turned over the White House to arch-rival Thomas Jefferson, he helped establish a precedent of peaceful transition between chief executives that has held firm to this day, despite the hostile feelings that sometimes exist between successive presidents. In the case of the president's removal by death, resignation, or inability to serve, the Constitution requires that the powers and duties of the president "devolve" on the vice president. When William Henry Harrison died barely a month after becoming president in 1841, Vice President John Tyler took over all the powers, duties, and responsibilities of the presidency, rejecting any notion that he was simply there to serve as a more limited "acting president" until the next election. Since Tyler, seven vice presidents have become chief executive in this manner, including most recently Lyndon Johnson, who assumed office after John Kennedy was assassinated in November 1963. Of the last six vice presidents thrust unexpectedly into office, four—Theodore Roosevelt, Calvin Coolidge, Harry Truman, and Lyndon Johnson—eventually secured election as presidents in their own right.

© 2012 CENGAGE LEARNING

★ LO Trace the evolution of the presidency from "chief clerk" in the late 18th and 19th centuries to its eventual political dominance

The Evolution of the American Presidency

The U.S. Constitution appears to place as many limitations on the office of the presidency as it grants the president specific powers and duties. As a review of the history of the presidency reveals, the institution has evolved over the past two centuries not so much because of any constitutional expansion of the chief executive's powers but rather through practice, tradition, and the personal energy of some presidents. The changing dynamics of policymaking in the United States from a mostly local concern to a national phenomenon have given presidents the opportunity to exert unprecedented influence over the process, and many have done exactly that. In many ways, the growth of power of the presidency has paralleled the growth of the United States.

The President as "Chief Clerk" of the United States: 1789–1836

The earliest presidents established the office as a forceful power in the national government. Still, even the most popular presidents of the period were careful to avoid interfering with the clear legislative prerogatives of Congress. Several played a major role in helping steer America away from or toward war, despite the inclinations of Congress. But the truly dominant chief executive would not emerge until many years later.

When George Washington, the immensely popular former general of the Continental Army, agreed to be nominated as the nation's first president, he rejected entrapments of royalty such as being referred to as "Your Majesty," preferring instead to be called "Mr. President." Washington also established the executive's influential role in crafting public policy, siding with his Secretary of Treasury

Alexander Hamilton's plans for industrialization and the creation of a national bank and striving to maintain an isolationist foreign policy.

During the four decades after Washington's retirement, most presidents of the United States served more as chief "clerks" than chief "executives," doing Congress's bidding and performing mostly administrative duties on behalf of the federal government. Upon winning the presidency in 1800, Thomas Jefferson (1801–1809)* put into practice his theory that "government is best which governs least." Accordingly, the Jefferson administration abolished many judgeships, trimmed government economic planning efforts, and scaled back the armed forces. The one crucial exception to such downsizing occurred in the area of land acquisition: Jefferson personally arranged for the purchase of the vast Louisiana territory from France, more than doubling the physical size of the country.

A presidency characterized by limited executive powers soon confronted unexpected challenges. When tensions between Great Britain and the United States erupted into the War of 1812, President James Madison (1809–1817) found himself hampered both by the small size of the federal army and by the lack of a powerful national bank capable of funding

MARY EVANS PICTURE LIBRARY/THE IMAGE WORKS

Portrait of General Andrew Jackson, later the seventh president of the United States.

the government's prosecution of the war. This war with Britain revealed the limited powers of the president to influence national matters without strong institutional resources at his disposal. Madison's successor, James Monroe (1817–1825), exercised most of his influence in foreign affairs. Monroe's Secretary of State John Quincy Adams, who himself was president from 1825 to 1829, helped craft the Monroe Doctrine, which declared that the United States would thereafter regard as an "unfriendly act" any attempt by a European nation to increase its possession or otherwise intervene on the American continent. Meanwhile, Congress led the way in domestic matters, crafting key compromises over slavery and paying off much of the public debt incurred during the War of 1812.

Andrew Jackson, who served as president from 1829 to 1837, remade the presidency into an office of tremendous political power. The military hero of the Battle of New Orleans in 1815, Jackson came to the White House as a political outsider but with overwhelming popular support. Capitalizing on this resource, Jackson wielded presidential power in a way that few of his predecessors had, dismissing hundreds of officeholders, forcing out cabinet members who angered him, using his constitutionally authorized power to veto Congress's bill to recharter the Second National Bank of the United States, and introducing the so-called spoils system of doling out federal offices to individuals as rewards for political service.[1]

---

* Dates provided after a president's name refer to year(s) of service as President of the United States.

The Weakened Presidency in the Wilderness Years, 1837–1900

After Jackson's stormy eight years in office, subsequent presidents played a far less active role in the American political system, at least up until the Civil War.

The presidency of Abraham Lincoln (1861–1865) proved to be an exception to the rule of weak chief executives during this period. He thrived due to a rare combination of factors. Frequently underestimated as a great political mind, Lincoln was confronted with the single greatest threat in the history of the republic—the secession of eleven southern states and the great battle between North and South to restore the Union. Although Lincoln proceeded carefully in his prosecution of the war against the South for fear of alienating crucial border states, those acts he did undertake were bold and unprecedented. At the outset of the war in April 1861, with Congress not even in session, Lincoln proclaimed a blockade of southern ports and called on the northern states to provide 75,000 soldiers for battle. He (at least in one court's opinion[2]) unconstitutionally suspended the writ of habeas corpus, by which anyone arrested is to be brought before a judge or court to determine if there is sufficient reason to hold the person for trial. Suspending the writ allowed Lincoln to hold some criminal defendants indefinitely.

Following Lincoln's assassination in April 1865, Congress, dominated at that time by radical Republicans determined to punish the former Confederate states, quickly reasserted its control over the nation's agenda. For the remainder of the century, Congress would determine domestic policy. Indeed, after the former Civil War hero Ulysses Grant left office in 1877, no sitting president won election to a second term until William McKinley accomplished the feat in 1900.

President Abraham Lincoln delivering the Gettysburg Address in 1863.

The Birth of the Modern Presidency and Its Rise to Dominance, 1901–1945

The beginning of the twentieth century marked the onset of a new era for the American presidency. In an increasingly global and interconnected world, the power of the presidency grew disproportionately. By the time two world wars had concluded, the presidency had emerged as the premier institution in American politics.

In the fall of 1901, William McKinley was assassinated during the first year of his second term, thrusting into office his young and ebullient vice president, forty-two-year-old Theodore Roosevelt. Roosevelt's presidency (1901–1909) ushered in a new era of presidential authority. He injected a forceful energy and enthusiasm into the office, using his position as "a bully pulpit" (Roosevelt's own words). As one observer noted, "He wanted to be the bride at every wedding; the corpse at every funeral." Unlike many of his predecessors, Roosevelt was willing to gamble political capital on bold assertions of presidential power: His efforts to break up corporate monopolies were narrowly upheld by the Supreme Court and forced Congress to enact new antitrust legislation. Roosevelt, through the creative use of executive orders, increased the acreage of national parks fivefold.

TABLE 7.1 The Ten Greatest Presidents of All Time

More than half a century ago, historian Arthur M. Schlesinger Jr. began the process of polling historians to rank the presidents of the United States. Recent surveys continue to borrow heavily from Schlesinger's original methodology. In 2009, the C-SPAN Survey of Presidential Leadership ranked the opinions of presidential historians and "professional observers of the presidency." Another poll of presidential scholars was conducted by *The Wall Street Journal* in 2005, with support from the Federalist Society. Interestingly, the results vary. Among the most significant differences: Ronald Reagan was ranked at No. 6 in the *Wall Street Journal* poll but barely broke the top ten in the C-SPAN poll; Woodrow Wilson and John Kennedy landed in the top ten of the C-SPAN poll but were ranked eleventh and fifteenth, respectively, in the *Wall Street Journal* poll. While Washington, Lincoln, and Franklin D. Roosevelt usually top most lists, presidential scholars substantially disagree on how to complete the list of greatest presidents.

C-SPAN Survey—2009 Top 10	*Wall Street Journal* Poll—2005 Top 10
1. Lincoln	1. Washington
2. Washington	2. Lincoln
3. Roosevelt, F.	3. Roosevelt, F.
4. Roosevelt, T.	4. Jefferson
5. Truman	5. Roosevelt, T.
6. Kennedy	6. Reagan
7. Jefferson	7. Truman
8. Eisenhower	8. Eisenhower
9. Wilson	9. Polk
10. Reagan	10. Jackson

A Nominee with African Roots, as Viewed by a Writer in Kenya

In securing the Democratic nomination for the presidency in 2008, Barack Obama became the first major party nominee with direct roots to Africa, as his father was from Kenya. One foreign journalist asked: How might that connection affect Obama's policy on U.S.-African relations as president of the United States? John Harbeson wrote as follows in the August 16, 2008, edition of the *Daily Nation,* an English-language newspaper serving the East African countries of Kenya and Nairobi:

Obama needs to align himself as both a "black" politician and an exemplar of post-black politics, keeping alive the civil rights agenda while crowning the success of the civil rights generation by merging it with the agendas of mainstream liberal American politics. But what has all this to do with

AP PHOTO

Senator Barack Obama of Illinois in the attire of a Somali Elder during a visit to Kenya, the homeland of his father.

African politics? The connection is between building on the achievements of the civil rights generation in America and those of the generation that has spearheaded African political liberation from colonial rule.

Neither agenda has been completed. America has made real civil rights progress over the past half-century, and African nationalism has largely expelled colonial political oppression over the same period. But affirmative action in the US is still needed, and Nepad (New Partnership for Africa's Development) has in many ways only just begun. So here's the question, common to both the American and African contexts.

How possible, indeed how legitimate and politically viable, will it be for Obama to continue the civil rights agenda while crowning its success by moving beyond it, and for post-independence generations of African leaders to maintain continuity with the political liberation agenda while building on its successes to embrace new and wider issues? There are many parallels between Obama's challenge and analogous challenges for Africa's political leaders. . . .

Source: John Harbeson, "Obama's Dreams and the African Agenda," *Daily Nation,* August 16, 2008 (http://www.nation .co.ke/News/world/-/1068/457288/-/rx0emi/-/index.html; accessed on August 19, 2008).

As president from 1913 to 1921, Woodrow Wilson achieved some significant successes and suffered some great failures: His aggressive industrial reform agenda marked a mostly well-received first term in office; during his second term, he eventually led the United States into World War I and received accolades at the Paris Peace Conference following the war. But Wilson's hopes for a stable international order based on a system of collective security ultimately confronted political reality, as Senate leaders whom Wilson had excluded from the peace talks rejected U.S. membership in the League of Nations.

The onset of the Great Depression during Herbert Hoover's presidency (1929–1933) and the looming threat of a second world war in the late 1930s called for a new and innovative approach to the office. Franklin Delano Roosevelt placed his own indelible stamp on the nation by transforming the presidency into an institution marked by permanent bureaucracies and well-established repositories of power. FDR tackled the Great Depression with **New Deal** policies that tied the economic fate of millions of Americans to the fate of the American government: A social security program of old-age insurance and unemployment insurance would provide income for workers who retired or lost their jobs; the government would guarantee deposit accounts in commercial banks through the Federal Deposit Insurance Corporation (FDIC); and the government would provide federal jobs to the unemployed to perform various public works. Roosevelt communicated extensively with the American people through the media, and millions listened to his fireside chats on the radio. By restoring public confidence with his energetic support for New Deal programs, FDR redefined the presidency as a source of national leadership. Future presidents would enjoy significant resources of power simply by taking the helms of the formidable institution FDR established.

Like Theodore Roosevelt and Woodrow Wilson, FDR felt especially at home in foreign affairs. When America entered World War II in 1941 after being attacked at Pearl Harbor, presidential power in this international context was put on full display. FDR met personally with British and Soviet leaders to craft military plans; then, near the end of the war, the Allied leaders carved Europe and the Middle East into "spheres of influence" that would establish an American presence in those parts of the world for the remainder of the century. With the president playing a dominant role in both national and world affairs, the imperial presidency that took root at the beginning of the twentieth century came to fruition by the close of World War II.

The Imperial Presidency Comes Under Attack, 1945–1980

By the end of World War II, the presidency had emerged as a very powerful office. FDR's fireside chats on the radio linked average Americans to the occupier of the White House in a way that the founders never imagined. In the late 1940s, television became a central influence in American life, and presidents honed their skills with this new medium to further nurture their relationship with the public.

Now recognized as powerful chief executives, those who followed in FDR's footsteps confronted a new and unprecedented threat to American national security: the presence of a second world military superpower—the Soviet Union. With presidential authority greatest in the area of national security, waging the Cold War that began in the late 1940s consumed much of these presidents' energies. Harry Truman, FDR's immediate successor, proclaimed the Truman Doctrine in foreign policy, by which the United States pledged military and economic aid to any nation threatened by communism or the Soviet Union. Like Truman, Presidents Eisenhower and Kennedy also focused their administrations' energies on containing the Soviet communist threat. As long as the Soviet Union challenged American interests, the presidency would remain the center of power in the American political system.

Not until the presidency of Lyndon Johnson (1963–1969) was a president able to enact a sweeping domestic agenda similar to FDR's

New Deal
A set of aggressive federal domestic policies proposed by President Franklin Roosevelt in the 1930s and passed by Congress as a response to the Great Depression; it ultimately transformed the presidency into an institution marked by permanent bureaucracies and well-established repositories of power.

President Lyndon Baines Johnson.

New Deal. Johnson's **Great Society** program featured more than sixty reform measures, including increases in federal aid to education, the enactment of Medicare and Medicaid, and legislation that guaranteed civil rights and extended voting rights. But Johnson's domestic policy success was offset by his failures in foreign policy. Exercising his authority as commander in chief, Johnson sent more than half a million troops to Vietnam to fight an increasingly unpopular war. The failure to stop the communists from taking over South Vietnam was laid squarely at the feet of Johnson, just as earlier foreign policy successes had been credited to his predecessors.

The presidents who followed Johnson came under increasing attack in the 1970s. Richard Nixon achieved foreign policy success by improving America's relationship with the Soviet Union and China, but in 1974, he became the first president in history to resign from office before the end of his term when the Watergate scandal enveloped his presidency. Jimmy Carter's presidency (1977–1981) was beset with hardships, as the nation's economy faltered in the 1970s.

Redefining the Presidency in an Era of Divisiveness, 1981 to the Present

The election of Republican Ronald Reagan to the White House in 1980 marked the return of the chief executive as an unmatched force over American politics. No president in the twentieth century (save perhaps FDR) could match Reagan's prowess as a "great communicator"; by speaking directly to the American people in terms they could understand, Reagan bypassed Congress and enjoyed early victories with passage of an economic program marked by tax cuts, decreased social spending, and a marked increase in defense spending. Reagan's legislative success was all the more remarkable given that he was working with a divided-party government. The Democrats controlled the House of Representatives in every year of Reagan's presidency; his legislative success thus contrasted favorably with that of previous presidents who had struggled to get legislation passed by a Congress controlled by the opposite party. In foreign policy, Reagan's aggressive program of military buildup combined with his own hard-line position against the Soviet Union is credited with helping bring about the fall of communist regimes in Eastern Europe, the breakup of the USSR, and the end of the Cold War. In addition, Reagan's immense popularity allowed him to weather numerous crises and scandals in a way that few of his predecessors had.

Reagan's successors also faced the reality of divided-party government at different points in their respective presidencies. George H. W. Bush took the lead in foreign policy, overseeing the dismantling of the Soviet Union and forging international alliances prior to mounting a successful war against Iraqi aggression in Kuwait. However, by compromising with the opposition Democrats on tax legislation, he frustrated some of his more conservative constituencies and undermined his efforts at reelection. Bill Clinton became the first Democratic president in a half century to serve two full terms. Clinton appealed to moderates largely by in effect borrowing central elements of the opposition party's domestic program. His three main legislative successes (free-trade agreements, budget cutting, and welfare reform) were all programs that had been more closely associated with Republicans than Democrats at the time Clinton took office in the early 1990s.

Another "Tweet" from the Commander in Chief: The Interactive Presidency of Barack Obama

THE U.S. NATIONAL ARCHIVES AND RECORDS ADMINISTRATION

Web page from the George W. Bush White House Web site.

In the age of the Internet, most private companies and government agencies maintain a Web site. The White House is no different. The George W. Bush administration's White House Web site featured extensive videos and links to speeches and addresses by the forty-third president. (See the photo of the Bush White House home page at right.) What the Bush White House Web site lacked, however, was more cutting-edge interactive features: There was a simple tool that allowed visitors to "ask the White House" a question, and a "White House interactive" feature with officials answering basic questions from students, but little more.

Enter the Obama administration and its brand new state-of-the-art Web site at http://www.whitehouse.gov. The site hosts no less than eleven substantive blogs, all archived and indexed by category; a tool that allows the visitor to receive e-mail updates on the latest White House news and events; live streams of the president and his top aides speaking from around the world; and archived podcasts available on nearly any subject imaginable. This site also offers visitors the chance to stay connected to presidential events by Twitter, Facebook, mySpace, Flickr, and a number of other social networking sites. President Obama also

maintains his own personal Web site at http://www.barackobama.com—as of August 1, 2010, the president's daily (and sometimes hourly) "tweets" were followed by nearly 5 million people around the world. In fact, that same day twittaholic.com's statistical algorithm ranked President Obama as the fifth most popular Twitter user in the United States, trailing behind only Ashton Kutcher, Britney Spears, Ellen DeGeneres, and Lady Gaga.

For Critical Thinking and Discussion

1. What types of information would you expect to find on http://www.whitehouse.gov that is not available on other media Web sites or other Internet sites that follow the presidency?

2. What advantages does a modern president have in the ability to communicate with a younger generation of citizens?

3. Do the political views of a Web surfer affect his or willingness to visit the White House Web site? Why or why not?

MLADEN ANTONOV/AFP/GETTY IMAGES

Web page from the Barack Obama White House Web site.

In the aftermath of the terrorist attacks of September 11, 2001, President George W. Bush moved quickly to position his administration as the eminent world leader in an emerging war on terrorism. His early efforts to fight terrorism at home and abroad enjoyed congressional support from both parties: His aggressive military intervention against the Taliban-controlled government in Afghanistan in late 2001 proved extremely popular and helped cement his administration's image of toughness and resolve. Yet when the Bush administration expanded the war on terrorism to include military intervention in Iraq, justified on the basis of inaccurate reports that Iraq possessed weapons of mass destruction, these same policies became much more divisive. Barack Obama's presidency began—as most presidential terms do—buoyed by feelings of good will coming from both sides of the political aisle. A clear majority of the public hoped he would successfully tackle the economic crisis that befell the nation in 2008. They also hoped the young president was serious about his promises to bring "change" to Washington.

Obama's "honeymoon period" ended quickly, however, as the details of his administration's proposals for reform were laid bare for debate. President Obama benefitted from strong Democratic majorities in Congress; he muscled through his legislative agenda almost entirely on the strength of those majorities, and with little support from Republicans. The $787 billion fiscal stimulus bill (the American Recovery and Reinvestment Act of 2009) passed with the help of just three Republican senators and no Republican House members; the landmark health care reform bill of 2010 was even more partisan, garnering not a single Republican vote from either branch of Congress. Obama thus learned an important political lesson: The rhetoric of bipartisanship does not easily translate into bipartisan votes. Regardless, Obama had just enough Democratic support to rack up some significant legislative successes during his first two years as president; few expected similar successes after the congressional elections of 2010.

★ LO   Recognize the formal powers vested in the president under Article II of the Constitution

Express Powers and Responsibilities of the President

Article II of the Constitution provides that the president of the United States holds executive power, but it is not very detailed about what constitutes executive power. In fact, the Constitution lists only four specific powers of the president: (1) commander in chief of the armed forces, (2) power to grant reprieves or pardons, (3) power to "make" treaties (subject to Senate approval), and (4) power to make certain appointments, including those of ambassadors and justices of the Supreme Court (again subject to Senate approval). Despite this limited number of constitutionally expressed powers, presidents today serve many important functions in the American political system. Noting these varied roles, political scientist Clinton Rossiter referred to the many different "hats" that the president must wear during the course of a week or even during just one day.[3] Some of these are specified in the Constitution and laws of the United States, which conceive of a limited executive but one who possesses the authority to react quickly and energetically to unexpected crises.

Head of State

The office of the presidency combines the political and symbolic functions that are often divided in other countries. As the nation's head of state, the president fulfills numerous formal duties and obligations on behalf of the country. Most visiting foreign heads of state meet directly with the president; sometimes, those visits include an official state dinner at the White House hosted by the president and attended by key political leaders from throughout Washington. Article II of the Constitution also carves out a more formal role for the president in foreign affairs; the president's role in receiving ambassadors and other public ministers has often been interpreted as granting the president the discretion to give or deny official recognition to foreign governments. Although such a power may seem mostly honorary, it can have a real political impact in some circumstances. President Woodrow Wilson's refusal to recognize the new government of Mexico in 1913 caused considerable consternation among American supporters of the Mexican revolution and led to growing tensions between the two neighbors. More recently, American presidents during the 1970s and 1980s refused to recognize the Palestine Liberation Organization as the legitimate representative of the Palestinian people, buttressing Israel's own hard-line stance against that organization.

President Obama at the 2009 G-8 Summit in L'Aquila, Italy, surrounded by (from left to right) Prime Minister Silvio Berlusconi of Italy, French President Nicolas Sarkozy, Russian President Dmitri Medvedev, U.N. Secretary General Ban ki Moon, and Libyan Leader Muammar Gaddafi.

Chief Executive and Head of Government

The framers of the Constitution vested all executive power in the president alone. Unfortunately, they failed to define that power with any specificity. At a minimum, the Constitution grants presidents alone the responsibility to execute laws of the United States, which encompasses the implementation and enforcement of measures passed by Congress—in other words, to see that Americans abide by those laws in practice. A president's failure to "take care that the laws be faithfully executed," whether intentionally or due to negligent administration of his subordinates, can have obvious implications for the effectiveness of such laws. Actual levels of execution sometimes lie squarely within the discretion of the chief executive. Republican President George W. Bush and the Democrats in Congress sparred not just over the written terms of the USA Patriot Act but also over the Bush administration's aggressive enforcement of those provisions against some individuals, which gave the laws far more teeth than some had originally anticipated.

★ LO

Explain how presidents use the veto, appointment and removal, and the pardon

The president's power to see that laws are faithfully executed also implies some power to hire and fire those charged with administrative authority to help execute federal laws. The **power of appointment** thus stands among the president's most important executive powers.[4] The Constitution specifically authorizes the president to appoint ambassadors and other public ministers, judges of the Supreme Court, and all other federal officers under his charge. Additionally, the president appoints all federal judges. Most of these appointments require the consent of the Senate. In recent years, senators have subjected the president's nominees to intense scrutiny, occasionally even rejecting the president's choices. President George W. Bush's second choice for the Supreme Court, White House Counsel Harriet Miers, was withdrawn from consideration before even receiving a formal Senate vote in October 2005.

The president's removal power has proven a source of controversy as well. The Supreme Court's decision in *Myers v. United States* (1926) established that chief executives have the power to remove "purely executive officers" without congressional consent. Although federal judges and independent agency heads can be removed only by congressional action, cabinet heads and military officials can be terminated by the president alone. In one famous instance during the Korean War, President Truman decided in 1951 to fire the extremely popular General Douglas MacArthur, commander of the UN forces in Korea.

Not only is the president responsible for the enforcement of all federal laws, but the Constitution also authorizes the president to grant reprieves and pardons to individuals who violate those laws. The founders vested this power in the chief executive because they believed that the prerogative of mercy, on which the pardon power is based, is most efficiently and equitably exercised by a single individual, as opposed to a body of legislators or judges. A **reprieve** reduces the severity of a punishment without removing the guilt; a full **pardon** relieves an individual of both the punishment and the guilt. A president's decision to exercise the pardon power can invite considerable negative comment and political backlash. Not surprisingly then, most presidents wait until the end of their presidential terms to grant reprieves or pardons. President Clinton issued 140 pardons on his last day in office in 2001, including one to Marc Rich, who had previously fled the country for tax evasion and whose wife was a major contributor to Clinton's political campaigns. No president received more criticism for granting a pardon than Gerald Ford, who as vice president succeeded to the presidency when Richard Nixon resigned in 1974. Ford's pardon of his former boss for involvement in the Watergate scandal helped undermine his prospects for election to the White House in 1976.

Chief Diplomat

As chief diplomat of the United States, the president has the power to negotiate treaties and appoint diplomatic representatives to other countries, including ambassadors, ministers, and consuls. The president's power over treaties is limited to negotiation and execution; enactment of any treaties requires approval by two thirds of the Senate. Still, the power to negotiate and execute the terms of treaties affords the president immense authority in the field of foreign affairs. John F. Kennedy used this power to negotiate an end to the Cuban missile crisis in 1962;[5] Jimmy Carter personally presided over the negotiation of the Panama Canal Treaty of 1977–1978, which relinquished U.S. control over the canal by the year 2000. Every president during the latter stages of the Cold

War conducted arms control negotiations with the Soviet Union, working to check the spread of nuclear weapons to other nations.

Chief Legislator

Although Congress is the branch of government authorized to make laws, modern presidents are involved in nearly every stage of federal lawmaking.[6] The Constitution's express provision that the president recommend for the consideration of Congress "such measures as he shall judge necessary and expedient" barely hints at the president's real role in this context: Major legislation is often the product of a give-and-take process between the president and congressional leaders. In the **State of the Union address**, an annual speech made to Congress laying out the status of the nation, the president typically proposes suggestions for legislation. The president then plays a critically important role in helping to set the lawmaking agenda for Congress, especially when the president's party is also in control of the legislative branch of government. Congress's reorganization of various executive branch agencies into a unified Department of Homeland Security in 2002 was based on a plan drafted by officials within the Bush administration. House and Senate leaders made few significant modifications to their respective health care bills in 2009 without first huddling with President Obama and his top White House aides; and it was the president's willingness to meet frequently with moderate Democratic members of Congress that kept many in the fold for the final passage of health care reform in 2010.

The **White House Office of Legislative Affairs** serves as a liaison between the president and Congress and helps develop the strategy used to promote passage of the president's legislative agenda. Administration officials often testify before congressional subcommittees on behalf of legislation, and presidents meet with congressional leaders frequently throughout the lawmaking process to negotiate details and discuss strategy. The president's legislative authority also includes the constitutional power to veto, or reject, legislation that he opposes. While Congress can technically override a veto by a two-thirds vote of both houses, barely 4 percent of presidential vetoes have been overridden in history.

During the twentieth century, vetoes became a routine form of political exercise for presidents, especially those confronting Congresses controlled by the opposite political party. For Richard Nixon, Gerald Ford, and George H. W. Bush, the only three presidents during this span who never enjoyed unified party rule, the veto became something of an art form. Nixon and Bush vetoed forty-three and forty-four bills, respectively. (Only eight of those vetoes were overridden.) Gerald Ford vetoed sixty-six bills in just two and a half years, but more than one in five were overridden, a clear sign of the limited power Ford held during his brief term as president.

Commander in Chief

One of the defining features of the American political system is its firm commitment to civil control of the military, embodied in the president's status as head of the nation's armed forces. As commander in chief, the president is the nation's principal military leader, responsible for formulating and directing all military strategy and policy. Although the Constitution grants Congress the formal power to "declare war," the balance of war-making power has shifted

State of the Union address
An annual speech that the president delivers to Congress laying out the status of the nation and offering suggestions for new legislation.

White House Office of Legislative Affairs
A presidential office that serves as a liaison between the president and Congress. This office helps the president develop the strategy used to promote passage of the president's legislative agenda.

★ LO
Define the powers and limits of the president as commander in chief

TABLE 7.2 Vetoes Issued by Modern Presidents (through October 15, 2010)

President	Congresses	Regular Vetoes	Pocket Vetoes	Total Vetoes	Vetoes Overridden
Theodore Roosevelt	57th–60th	42	40	82	1
William Taft	61st–62nd	30	9	39	1
Woodrow Wilson	63rd–66th	33	11	44	6
Warren Harding	67th	5	1	6	0
Calvin Coolidge	68th–70th	20	30	50	4
Herbert Hoover	71st–72nd	21	16	37	3
Franklin D. Roosevelt	73rd–79th	372	263	635	9
Harry Truman	79th–82nd	180	70	250	12
Dwight Eisenhower	83rd–86th	73	108	181	2
John F. Kennedy	87th–88th	12	9	21	0
Lyndon B. Johnson	88th–90th	16	14	30	0
Richard M. Nixon	91st–93rd	26	17	43	7
Gerald Ford	93rd–94th	48	18	66	12
Jimmy Carter	95th–96th	13	18	31	2
Ronald Reagan	97th–100th	39	39	78	9
George H. W. Bush	101st–102nd	29	15	44	1
William Clinton	103rd–106th	37	1	38	2
George W. Bush	107th–110th	11	1	12	4
Barack Obama	111th	2	0	2	0

overwhelmingly from Congress to the president during the past century, as modern executives have assumed nearly unlimited power to send troops into combat.[7] Terming it a "police action," President Truman sent troops to Korea in June 1950 without even asking Congress for a formal declaration of war. In 1973, over President Nixon's veto, Congress passed the War Power Resolution, which theoretically limits the power of the president to unilaterally commit troops to battle. Ignoring the resolution's provisions, Presidents Reagan, George H. W. Bush, and Clinton deployed U.S. troops to invade Grenada (1983), Panama (1989), and Haiti (1994), respectively. Similarly, in February 2009 President Obama simply announced his plans to bolster the U.S. military presence in Afghanistan by over 17,000 new troops. Of course, presidents are not entirely immune from public pressures in this context. In the two most recent Gulf War conflicts, the weight of popular opinion led both President Bushes to seek congressional authorization for the invasions of Iraq in 1991 and 2003.

Implied Powers and Responsibilities of the President

Recognize the implied powers of the presidency not spelled out in the Constitution, including those exercised as the nation's crisis manager and political party leader

★ LO

Article II of the Constitution does not specifically spell out all the powers that a president may exercise; during the past two centuries, presidents have assumed the right to exercise some "implied" or "inherent" powers not listed in the Constitution, and the Supreme Court has for the most part acceded in their right to do so. These implied powers allow the president to act quickly in crisis situations, to serve as leader of his political party, and to issue executive orders and make executive agreements that do not require congressional approval.

Crisis Manager

More than any other official in government, the president is in a unique position to respond quickly and effectively to unexpected crises. Consequently, Americans look immediately to the president under such circumstances to provide assurances, comfort, and where appropriate, a plan to address the difficulties. When a natural disaster strikes, the president will often visit the scene, meet with family members, and in many cases, provide aid from the Federal Emergency Management Agency (FEMA). Domestic and international terrorism has posed special challenges for presidents in this regard. Even President Clinton's bitterest critics praised his efforts in 1995 when he led the nation in mourning the loss of 168 lives from a truck bombing at a federal building in Oklahoma City. In the days following the September 11 attacks, George W. Bush redefined his presidency as a fight against terrorism. His visits to Ground Zero, the site of the attacks on the World Trade Center, and his address to a joint session of Congress created indelible images in the media and won him widespread public support. President Obama continually expressed his personal resolve to tackle the nation's economic crisis up to and after his inauguration as president in 2009: Within weeks he pressed forward with a proactive economic stimulus plan in hopes that it might reassure the public that his administration was not taking a passive approach to the problem.

LUKE SHARRETT/THE NEW YORK TIMES/REDUX PICTURES

President Obama campaigning with New Jersey Governor (and fellow Democrat) John Corzine in 2009.

Party Leader

Once elected, the president of the United States assumes the position of de facto leader of his own political party. Not surprisingly, presidents are normally well attuned to how their political decisions will reflect on the party as a whole. A popular president is often expected to campaign for the party's congressional candidates and, if possible, help secure control of Congress for the party. Any assistance the president provides to congressional candidates seeking election may have an important side effect: The president may now have the leverage to demand support from those members of Congress for his own legislative programs. Similarly, the "coattail effect," by which voters who cast their ballots for the president automatically vote for congressional candidates and state and local officials of the president's party, may strengthen the president's position with party members during the upcoming term.

Executive Orders and Agreements

Executive orders
Rules or regulations issued by the chief executive that have the force of law and do not require the consent of Congress.

On their own, presidents can issue **executive orders**, which are rules or regulations issued by the chief executive that have the force of law. Once thought to be an unconstitutional exercise of Congress's lawmaking power, executive orders have now become a routine feature of American government.[8] Since the beginning of the twentieth century, presidents have issued more than 13,000 executive orders regulating all manner of topics, including affirmative action, civil service, federal holidays, the classification of government documents, public land designations, and federal disaster relief. Many executive orders dealt with the nation's armed services: Truman used an executive order to end segregation in the armed forces in 1948; Clinton's "don't ask, don't tell" policy, which allowed homosexuals to serve in the military as long as they did not reveal their sexual orientation, was similarly established by an executive order (albeit one that Clinton modified in response to congressional and public uproar). President George W. Bush issued more than 150 executive orders during his first term in office alone. On his first full day in office, Obama issued an executive order mandating that the interrogation of terrorism suspects not include torture.

Executive agreement
A pact reached between the president and a foreign government that does not require the consent of Congress.

An **executive agreement** is a pact, written or oral, reached between the president and a foreign government. As with executive orders, these agreements do not require the consent of Congress, although Congress does have the power to revoke them. Executive agreements have become important tools by which presidents conduct foreign affairs. In recent years, the U.S. government's military alliances with Great Britain and other countries in response to Iraqi aggression came in the form of executive agreements between President Bush and the British government.

Presidential Resources

Nearly a half century ago, Professor Richard Neustadt defined the central problem that all presidents face from the moment they are sworn into office: How do presidents mobilize the powers of the office to work for them? The federal bureaucracy has grown so vast that presidents cannot simply command the bureaucracy to do their will. So what exactly can presidents do to make their will felt within the executive branch and to carry out their choices through that "maze of personalities and institutions called the government of the United States"?

In his landmark book, *Presidential Power: The Politics of Leadership,* Neustadt argued that the president's most fundamental power is the "power to persuade."[9] Presidents use this power most effectively by keeping themselves informed, employing a system of information that allows them to be at the center of the decision-making apparatus, and carefully cultivating the image of a powerful president. Modern presidents have tended to emphasize certain individuals and offices under their control that play critical roles in the success of their administrations.

The Vice President

Next in line for succession and thus "only a heartbeat away" from the presidency, vice presidents have often been relegated to the very fringes of presidential power.[10] FDR barely communicated with John Nance Garner, who was vice president during FDR's first two terms in office. Of course, Garner did not have a very high opinion of the vice presidency either, referring to the position (in a sanitized version of his remarks) as not worth "a bucket of warm spit." Up through the 1950s, vice presidents maintained their principal offices on Capitol Hill near the Senate chamber, where they occasionally performed their one clearly defined constitutional responsibility: to preside over the Senate and to cast a vote in the event of a tie.

The vice presidency, however, has undergone a transformation in recent decades. Modern-day vice presidents have assumed roles as key advisers and executive branch officials working on behalf of the president. Walter Mondale developed U.S. policy on South Africa and was one of President Jimmy Carter's most trusted advisers. Al Gore headed the National Performance Review for the Clinton administration, leading to reforms to increase the federal government's efficiency and reduce its costs. Perhaps no federal official was more influential with President George W. Bush than Vice President Dick Cheney. According to journalist Bob Woodward, Cheney was the driving force behind President Bush's controversial decision to invade Iraq in March 2003.[11] The current vice president, Joe Biden, has become famous for his salty language and verbal gaffes; but Biden is a trusted counselor to President Obama and the former senator is credited with helping to press the administration's legislative agenda forward with his former colleagues.

Constitutionally, the vice president is also the first in line to succeed the president in the event of the death or incapacitation of the chief executive. By statute, if the vice president is not available to serve, succession falls in turn to the Speaker of the House, the president pro tempore of the Senate, and then to cabinet-level officials.

The Cabinet

The Constitution specifically affords presidents the power to solicit the advice of the principal officers in each of the executive departments. Thus, in addition to running their own executive departments within the large federal bureaucracy, principal officers also serve as key advisers. Together, they form the president's **cabinet**. Today's cabinet consists of fifteen heads of departments and six other important officials considered of cabinet rank. In reality, such a large body of individuals with different areas of expertise can serve only limited functions for a president, and recent chief executives have convened their full cabinets to serve more as a sounding board and a communications device than as a significant instrument of policymaking. Nevertheless, in individual meetings, cabinet-level officials may still provide critical input to the president on issues related to their own departments.

Cabinet
The collection of the principal officers in each of the executive departments of the federal government who serve as key advisers to the president.

The White House Interns Program

College basketball star Joy Cheek found a pretty good job after graduating with a public policy degree from Duke University in 2010: She got to play professional basketball during the summer with the Indiana Fever of the WNBA. Joy maintains a back-up plan, however, in case her athletic dreams don't work out in the long run: She wants to work in politics. And in the summer of 2009 she got quite a head start toward that dream when she held a fourteen-week internship working in the office of the vice president on economic policy. While friends were working in fast-food restaurants or as lifeguards, Joy was attending weekly lectures with top White House officials, assisting at White House social events, and even hobnobbing with Vice President Biden.

The White House Internship program is one of the most prestigious of its kind, placing interns from across the country in one of twelve different White House offices, including the office of the Vice Presidency, where Cheek landed. Competition for a spot in the program is normally quite stiff: Applicants go through a rigorous screening process that includes filling out a questionnaire, writing a pair of 300-word essays, and undergoing in-depth interviews. Yet the rewards of service are unarguable: Past White House interns of note include NBC news anchor Brian Williams, Fox news journalist Neil Cavuto, and the Academy Award–nominated screenwriter Nora Ephron.

If you are interested in getting first-hand experience working at the White House, you can apply online through the White House web page (www.whitehouse.gov/about/internships/apply). But don't count on it being a particularly lucrative experience: Summer White House interns are unpaid.

AP PHOTO/MARK DUNCAN

ARISTIDE ECONOMOPOULOS/STAR LEDGER/CORBIS

Former White House interns Brian Williams, nightly news anchor for NBC News (left), and Neil Cavuto of Fox News (right).

The Executive Office of the President and the White House Staff

Created in 1939 to bring executive branch activities under tighter control, the Executive Office of the President (EOP), with nearly 2,000 federal employees, consists of numerous agencies that assist with the management and administration of executive branch departments. Some of these agencies, such as the Office of Management and Budget, the President's Council of Economic Advisors, the National Security Council, and the Office of the U.S. Trade Representatives, have near permanent status. Other EOP agencies come and go depending on the policy priorities of the current administration. Thus, during the height of the Cold War, the EOP included agencies that focused on preparedness and civil defense in the event of a nuclear attack.

The EOP also includes an expanded White House staff. Until 1939, this staff consisted mostly of assistant secretaries and clerks who helped the president with correspondence; the White House staff today consists of nearly 600 employees and runs on an annual budget of almost $730 million. In charge of this bureaucracy is the **White House chief of staff**, who manages and organizes the staff to serve the president. Some modern presidents, including Ronald Reagan and George H. W. Bush, have adopted management styles that rely heavily on the chief of staff to control access to the president. Others, such as President Clinton, have utilized a "spokes-of-a-wheel" arrangement in which five or six different advisers have direct access to the president.[12] Regardless of the arrangement chosen, the White House chief of staff has a significant hand in the operation of the modern presidency. The principal duties of the White House staff include, but are not limited to, speechwriting, advance work for presidential appearances, scheduling, congressional relations, public relations, and communications.

White House chief of staff
The manager of the White House staff, which serves the president's organizational needs, including speechwriting, advance work for presidential appearances, scheduling, congressional relations, public relations, and communications.

The First Lady

All but one president (James Buchanan) have been married at some point in their lifetimes, and the spouses of sitting presidents, now referred to as first ladies, have come to assume an important role in the affairs of the nation. Until recently, presidents mainly relied on their spouses to help them perform social obligations, such as hosting state dinners. Woodrow Wilson's two wives broke somewhat with this mold: His first wife, Ellen, took public positions on bills being considered for Congress, and his second wife, Edith, served as an intermediary between the president and other government leaders while Wilson was recovering from a massive stroke in the fall of 1919. Eleanor Roosevelt, wife to Franklin Delano Roosevelt, launched one of the earliest civil rights organizations, the Southern Conference on Human Welfare; actively supported the building of model communities; and lobbied for refugees fleeing Nazi persecution. Occasionally, she even disagreed publicly with some of FDR's policies in foreign affairs.

Although none of the first ladies after Eleanor Roosevelt so boldly challenged their

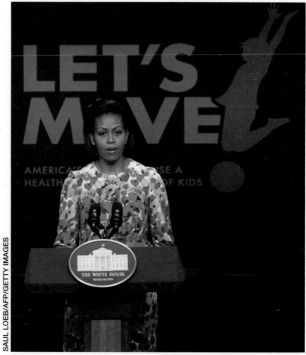

SAUL LOEB/AFP/GETTY IMAGES

First Lady Michelle Obama speaking at an event related to her "Let's Move" campaign against childhood obesity.

husbands' policies in the media, many did stake out policy areas where they could contribute, and some have become active members of their husband's administrations.[13] They have been assisted in this regard by a formal Office of the First Lady, now staffed by more than twenty aides.

★ LO   Recognize
how the power of the
presidency is enhanced by
communications with the
public, the Congress, and
the media

Important Presidential Relationships

The power of the president is influenced by the relations that a president develops and cultivates with three important constituencies: the public, Congress, and the news media.

The President and the Public

Catering to the needs and demands of the public mattered little to presidents prior to 1824, when presidential nominees were chosen by congressional leaders in secret caucuses. By contrast, the presidency today is a truly public institution that depends heavily on public popularity for political effectiveness. Modern presidential nominations and elections are won on an arduous campaign trail in which aspiring chief executives must reach out, communicate with, and ultimately gain acceptance from large segments of the public. Once in office, presidents must remain constantly attentive to the sentiments of the public at large. FDR was the first president to rely on public opinion polls, and his administration utilized them to monitor support for his New Deal policies. Through his fireside chats, he reached into the living rooms of millions of Americans, winning their support for and confidence in his domestic and foreign policies.

Top: President Ronald Reagan giving a "set speech" from the Oval Office in 1986. Right: President Bill Clinton interacting with the public at a "town meeting" in 1993. Bottom: President Obama takes his campaign for health care to large, arena-sized audiences across America.

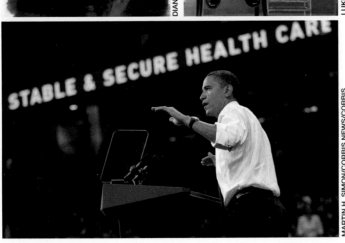

Most modern presidents continuously engage the public to support administration policies, whether through the annual State of the Union address to Congress and other special televised messages, staged events, or interviews and press conferences with the media where they attempt to promote the benefits of their programs. Presidents Richard Nixon and Ronald Reagan preferred the "set piece" speech presented from the Oval Office during prime time; Presidents Jimmy Carter and Bill Clinton occasionally held "town meetings" to discuss issues in open forums with concerned citizens. In bypassing legislators and appealing directly to their constituents, modern presidents have perfected the art of what social scientist Samuel Kernell calls "going public."[14]

The President and Congress

The history of the American political system is marked by the ebb and flow of power between the president and Congress. For much of the nineteenth century, a form of "congressional government" prevailed, with most presidents acting as dutiful administrators of the laws passed by Congress. Buoyed by advances in communications technology that placed modern presidents at the center of American politics, presidents today play far more influential roles in the legislative process, at times even prodding Congress forward to meet their administrations' goals. Because credit for a program's success is rarely spread evenly between the two branches, tensions are inevitable and compromises are often difficult to come by. President Clinton's willingness to sign a welfare reform bill in 1996 aided him in that year's election, when he claimed to have lived up to his earlier promise to "end welfare as we know it." The Republican Congress that actually drafted and passed the welfare bill received far less credit for its accomplishments. In foreign policy, presidents continue to act nearly independent of Congress.

Presidents have many tools at their disposal to influence Congress. As party leader, the president can campaign for congressional candidates and then leverage that assistance into support. Personal contacts by the president with members of Congress can be effective as well. The White House Office of Congressional Relations (OCR) serves as a liaison to Congress, rounding up support and monitoring events on Capitol Hill. Still, the most effective lobbying for a president's policies comes from members of Congress friendly to the administration, who persuade other members of Congress to vote in favor of the policies. The rewards for such service often come in the form of future appointments, pork-barrel projects for home districts or states, or financial support from the political party for future election bids.

The President and the Media

Effective media management has been a hallmark of the most successful modern presidents. Much of the responsibility rests with the **White House press secretary**, who plays an especially important role in briefing the press, organizing news conferences, and briefing the president on questions he may be forced to address. The administration that ignores media management does so at its own peril. Social scientists Kathleen Hall Jamieson and Paul Waldman revealed how the mainstream media today do not so much report the news about presidents as create it, transforming "the raw stuff of experience into presumed fact" and "arranging facts into coherent stories" that can prove crucial to presidential success.[15] The media's focus on President George W. Bush talking with recovery workers at Ground Zero and issuing warnings to terrorists through a megaphone emphasized his toughness and compassion in dealing with the terrorist attacks of September 11, 2001. Yet nearly four years later, that same press corps emphasized perceptions of President George W. Bush's aloofness aboard Air Force One after Hurricane Katrina killed thousands in and around New Orleans, Louisiana.

Today, the president also relies on the White House director of communications to articulate a consistent and effective message to the public.[16] But even before that office came into being, chief executives felt the need to craft a message and hone their public images. Franklin Roosevelt worked hard to cultivate good relations with the media, allowing his administration to set the news agenda and influence the content of the news. Many of his press conferences included off-the-record commentary that fed the media's appetite for information yet allowed the president to change his position as circumstances changed. John F. Kennedy perfected the modern press conference in the East Room of the White

White House press secretary
The person on the White House staff who plays an especially important role in briefing the press, organizing news conferences, and even briefing the president on questions that may be asked.

House; his colorful banter with reporters played well as sound bites on the evening television news. Ronald Reagan's reputation as the "great communicator" was enhanced by the use of "staged" or "pseudo" events, which presented the president in a positive light—perhaps visiting flag factories or reading Shakespeare to children at elementary schools—all packaged in time for the evening newscasts.

Borrowing from Reagan's playbook, Presidents George W. Bush and Barack Obama have avoided live press conferences whenever possible, preferring controlled situations that could be molded to fit their respective messages.

Making the Connection

When unexpected crises confront the nation—military, economic, or otherwise—leadership must come from the president of the United States. As the nation's chief legislator and executive, he can propose legislation to address the crisis and can implement that legislation in the best interests of the nation. As the nation's chief crisis manager, he must act boldly and decisively to reassure the nation that he has a plan to address whatever difficulties it may be facing. In the cases of FDR and Barack Obama, John Maynard Keynes's economic theories offered a basis for their administration's similar approaches to dealing with financial crises facing the nation. Other presidents have chosen markedly different approaches to leading the nation through economic difficulties. Both Presidents Ronald Reagan and George W. Bush relied on the theory of supply-side economics to cure the nation's fiscal woes. Regardless of the approach adopted, modern presidents are expected to act decisively in times of crisis.

Unfortunately, the Constitution does not spell out all of the roles and responsibilities that have become central to the modern presidency. The office has evolved over the course of the nation's history, and much of that evolution has occurred in response to crisis situations, economic or otherwise. Unlike the Congress, the president is just one person and so can act quickly and decisively. Additionally, the president and the vice president are the only two officials elected by the entire nation; thus, the president alone can claim a mandate to act on behalf of the American people as a whole rather than on behalf of a state, a district, or one political party. In times of crisis, citizens look to presidents for strength because they alone are in a position to provide it. For that reason more than any other, presidents only rarely need to demonstrate their continued relevance in the modern political system.

POLITICS InterActive!

A Honeymoon for the President?

I mmediately following his inauguration as president on January 20, 2009, President Obama could look forward to a "honeymoon period" with the press and the public during his first few months in the White House. The question was not whether that honeymoon would occur, but how, if at all, the newly elected president would seek to take advantage of it. In the case of Obama, this period was marked by numerous legislative achievements: the $787 billion fiscal stimulus bill, a budget reconciliation bill, and massive intervention in the housing and credit markets.

Still, Obama's honeymoon period proved disappointing in at least one respect. Past U.S. presidents have found that during this honeymoon period, even congressional opposition is likely to support some of the new president's more controversial initiatives. Ronald Reagan, for example, was able in 1981 to win support from the Democratic-controlled House of Representatives for some of the largest tax cuts in American history. FDR in 1933 was able to pass a record number of bills during his administration's first 100 days with the support of many Republicans. Barack Obama's legislative victories, by contrast, were achieved almost entirely on the strength of Democratic congressional majorities.

AP PHOTO

Realistically, Barack Obama's honeymoon period began to wind down during May 2009, as his approval ratings plummeted into the 50 percent range on a regular basis. By then the nation was already growing frustrated with its continued economic woes, and many were willing to transfer at least some of the blame to the new administration (concerns about the growing deficit also hurt Obama's standing). Other presidential honeymoons have been cut short by pronounced presidential missteps. Gerald Ford enjoyed high approval ratings in 1974 when he took over the presidency following Richard Nixon's resignation; but when he pardoned the ex-president just a month into his own presidency, Ford suffered an immediate 30-point drop in his approval ratings. Bill Clinton rode a wave of high hopes into the White House in 1993. Yet when during his first week in office he announced his plans to allow gays in the military, support for his administration began to diminish.

DENNIS BRACK/LANDOV

Even the most careful presidents know that these honeymoons don't last forever. By the summer of a president's second year in office, the nation begins to turn its attention to the midterm elections; the following year, the president is usually gearing up to run for reelection.

On www.cengage.com/dautrich/americangovernmentbrief/2e, find the Politics InterActive link for details on presidential agenda-setting and the short "honeymoon period" presidents work with during their first term in office. Consult as well the various links that relate to how different presidents began their administrations with ambitious policymaking agendas. Historical, popular, and global perspectives on the issue are also presented.

Top: President Gerald Ford announced on September 8, 1974, that he granted Nixon a "full, free and absolute pardon" for "all crimes committed against the United States" during Nixon's presidency.

Bottom: President Obama, flanked by Vice President Joseph Biden, listening intently during a meeting with the National Governors' Association early in his presidency. The new president faced immediate resistance to his proposals for economic recovery from Republican governors, among others.

Chapter Summary

★ SUMMARIZING WHAT YOU HAVE LEARNED ★

★ Where Do Presidents Come From? Presidential Comings and Goings

- Although, theoretically, any American who is at least thirty-five years old, a "natural born" citizen, and has lived in the United States for fourteen years is eligible to be president, in fact, the forty-three individuals who have been elected to the presidency have been mostly older, well-educated, Caucasian Protestant men with prior political experience.

- Only two presidents in history have ever been impeached by the House, and none were removed by the Senate. When a president does leave office, succession falls to the vice president.

★ The Evolution of the American Presidency

- The office of the president has evolved over the nation's history and over time has accumulated more power. For the century after George Washington's term, Congress dominated the federal government, with only a few exceptions—namely, during the presidencies of Andrew Jackson and Abraham Lincoln.

- The birth of the modern presidency occurred with the ascension of Theodore Roosevelt to office in 1901. His strong personality forced itself on the office. Taking strong pro-American positions in foreign policy and aggressive antimonopoly positions during the industrialization period, Roosevelt promoted power in the executive office.

- FDR's New Deal policies, in response to the Great Depression of the 1930s, cemented a large role for the president in the American constitutional system. The growth of the federal bureaucracy under FDR significantly changed the power of the presidency and the role that the president would play and the power that office would yield.

- The emergence of the United States as a superpower after World War II cemented the role of the U.S. president as a dominant player in world and national politics. Contemporary presidents find themselves as the focal points of American politics, setting the political and legislative agenda and leading American foreign and domestic policy.

★ Express Powers and Responsibilities of the President

- The powers of the president, as expressly stated in the Constitution, are (1) to be commander in chief of the armed forces, (2) to grant reprieves or pardons, (3) to "make" treaties (subject to Senate approval), and (4) to make certain appointments, including those of ambassadors and justices of the Supreme Court (again subject to Senate approval).

★ Implied Powers and Responsibilities of the President

- Beyond the express powers granted to the president in the Constitution, presidents today also play a key role in setting the legislative agenda, managing national and international crises, and serving as leader of their political party.

- The singularity of leadership in the executive branch affords the president a unique position in the American political system, giving the president the power to command the attention of the nation's people, Congress, and the media—thus enhancing the president's ability to persuade others what to do.

★ Presidential Resources

- The cabinet, the Executive Office of the President, and the White House staff provide large organizational support for the president to administer federal programs and agencies and lead the national government.

★ Important Presidential Relationships

- The president enhances his power by continually communicating with the public, maintaining a strong working relationship with congressional leaders from both parties, and cultivating a good relationship with the media through strategic management of the White House's activities.

CourseMate

Key Terms

Cabinet (p. 191)

Executive agreement (p. 190)

Executive orders (p. 190)

Great Society (p. 182)

Impeachment (p. 175)

New Deal (p. 181)

Pardon (p. 186)

Power of appointment (p. 186)

Reprieve (p. 186)

State of the Union address (p. 187)

Twenty-second Amendment (p. 175)

White House chief of staff (p. 193)

White House Office of Legislative Affairs (p. 187)

White House press secretary (p. 195)

Resources

Books

Beschloss, Michael. *Presidential Courage: Brave Leaders and How They Changed America.* New York: Simon & Schuster, 2007.

Dallek, Robert. *Hail to the Chief: The Making and Unmaking of American Presidents.* New York: Oxford University Press, 2001.

Greenstein, Fred. *The Hidden-Hand Presidency: Eisenhower as Leader.* New York: HarperCollins, 1982.

Greenstein, Fred. *The Presidential Difference: Leadership Style from Roosevelt to Clinton.* New York: Free Press, 2000.

Kernell, Samuel. *Going Public: New Strategies of Presidential Leadership.* Washington, DC: CQ Press, 1993.

Neustadt, Richard. *Presidential Power.* New York: John Wiley & Sons, 1980.

Peterson, Mark. *Legislating Together: The White House and Capitol Hill from Eisenhower to Reagan.* Cambridge, MA: Harvard University Press, 1993.

Internet Sources

http://www.whitehouse.gov/ (the home page of the White House, including information on broader aspects of the presidency, a virtual library, and so on).

http://www.americanpresidents.org C-SPAN-sponsored site on the presidency, including life portraits and a video archive of all American presidents).

http://www.archives.gov/presidential-libraries/index.html (the official National Archives site on presidential libraries, featuring links to all the individual libraries, a digital classroom, a research room with a searchable index, and so on).

8 The Federal Bureaucracy

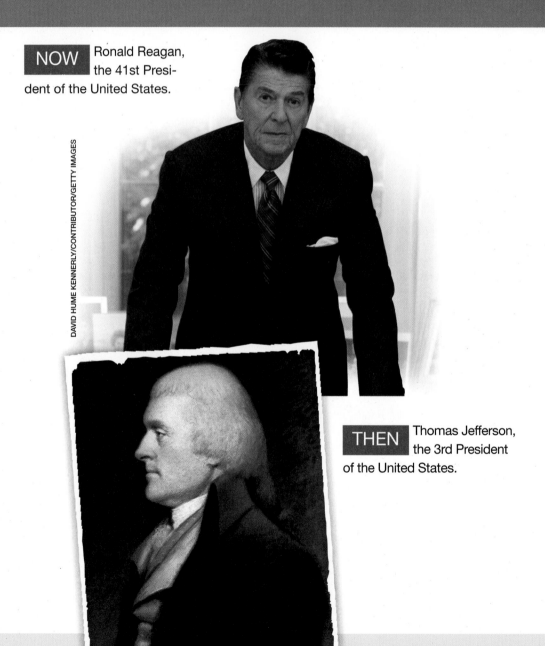

NOW Ronald Reagan, the 41st President of the United States.

DAVID HUME KENNERLY/CONTRIBUTOR/GETTY IMAGES

THEN Thomas Jefferson, the 3rd President of the United States.

AP PHOTO

NOW & THEN

The Elusive Goal of Reducing the "Bloated" Bureaucracy

The new president took office armed with a mandate to reduce the size of the federal government. His successful campaign for the Oval Office featured an often-repeated pledge to reduce government excesses—the bureaucracy had grown rapidly in the years that preceded his leadership, and in his opinion the federal government needed to become more frugal and tighten its belt. Soon after winning election, the new chief executive set out to make good on his pledge. Commentators described this initiative by the new president as a "revolution" of sorts—one that would streamline government and reduce the burden of the federal bureaucracy on the American people. Hefty federal spending in previous years also encouraged him to make reducing the national debt a top priority. But the president soon realized that to accomplish other objectives he would need even greater resources and an even larger bureaucracy. Though he accomplished other policy objectives, he ultimately failed to make good on his pledge to reduce the size of government. Ironically, by the time he had left office, the federal government had grown bigger than it had been when he first arrived.

CourseMate

NOW & THEN

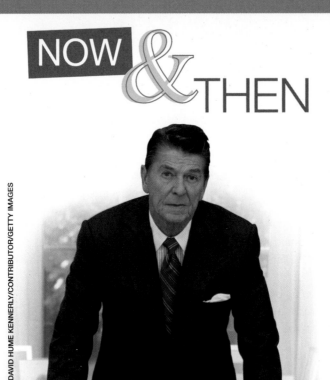

DAVID HUME KENNERLY/CONTRIBUTOR/GETTY IMAGES

NOW Consider Ronald Reagan's presidency, which lasted from 1981 through 1989. The "Reagan Revolution" aimed to reduce the burden of government. In his presidential campaign of 1980, Reagan criticized the federal government for growing beyond the means of the American people to support it. Getting rid of waste, reducing cumbersome red tape, eliminating expensive and inappropriate federal programs, and paying off the national debt were cornerstone themes of Reagan's campaign.[1] Accordingly, early in the Reagan administration a significant tax cut package was passed to reduce the size of the federal government. During his eight years in office, however, Reagan found that he often needed to increase the size of government to accomplish other objectives, such as defeating the Soviet Union in the Cold War, a feat that many historians now call the single greatest success of the Reagan administration. But such success came only after a substantial increase in the size of the federal bureaucracy and the budget to support that bureaucracy. Defense Department programs and budgets grew substantially during the Reagan years. Indeed, defense spending during this period amounted to the largest peacetime buildup in the nation's history. Ultimately, the Soviet Union proved no economic match for the United States, and Reagan's significant expansion of resources for the federal bureaucracy played a part in winning the Cold War. But in the process of winning it, Reagan reneged on his pledge to reduce the size of the federal government, thus leaving office in 1989 with a much larger bureaucracy than the one he inherited in 1981.

THEN Ronald Reagan was certainly not the first president to fall prey to this contradiction. Nearly two centuries earlier, Thomas Jefferson talked the talk of cutting the bureaucracy, but similarly failed to walk the walk of containing its growth. As with Reagan, political commentators of the time described Jefferson's triumph over John Adams as a "revolution" of sorts.[2] In his campaign, Jefferson stressed the need for "frugality" when it came to federal spending, and in his first inaugural address in 1801, he talked about the need to cut the waste. As president, Jefferson eliminated several federal agencies. In an effort to reduce the national debt, he closed down American embassies and cut the budgets of the Army and Navy.

Yet just like Reagan would do almost two centuries later, Jefferson pursued a policy agenda that ultimately required more government, more federal resources, and a larger bureaucracy. His agenda featured the expansion of the nation's borders, including the purchase of the Louisiana Territory from France, which more than doubled the geographic size of the United States. At a cost of $11,250,000 for the land and the assumption of $3,750,000 in French debts, the price tag was fairly steep for its time. Even more expensive, however, were the increases to the federal bureaucracy necessary to settle the region, fight the Indians who lived in the area, and fund a new agency called the General Land Office.[3] Many historians today view the Louisiana Purchase as President Jefferson's greatest accomplishment. To achieve it, however, Jefferson, like Reagan, had to forgo his commitment to reduce the size of the federal bureaucracy. When Jefferson left office in 1809, the federal bureaucracy was much larger than the one he had inherited in 1801.

AP PHOTO

T hose aspiring to high office sometimes trumpet as one of their primary goals the downsizing of the bureaucracy. Reducing costs, rooting out inefficiencies in spending, improving program effectiveness, reducing unnecessary red tape, and eliminating waste are promises that strike a positive chord with many voters. Presidential candidates in particular often run campaigns focused heavily on just such a pledge. Once elected to office, however, they quickly learn that to accomplish their policy goals, the bureaucracy sometimes must grow rather than contract. By the end of their terms in office, they frequently discover that their work as chief executive has contributed more to increasing the size of government than to reducing it.

What Is Bureaucracy?

Bureaucracy is a term that usually conjures up negative images. It often refers to overgrown government, excessive rules and paperwork, or a burdensome process for getting something done. Political candidates cite the vices of "the unresponsive, fat bureaucracy" to strike a sympathetic chord with voters.[4]

Despite the negative connotations of the term, bureaucracy is necessary for any government. Laws must be enforced, programs must be administered, and regulations must be implemented. Without a federal bureaucracy, the government could not function. To be sure, there are many problems with bureaucracy. It is often hard to get things done in an efficient manner, to fire workers who do not perform well, or to reward deserving workers. The buck often passes from one desk to another, and silly or irrelevant rules often dictate the actions of the bureaucrats. Despite its problems and the "bad rep" that the term sometimes conjures up, bureaucracy is absolutely essential for any government to implement and carry out its laws and public policies.[5]

Bureaucracy
An organization set up in a logical and rational manner for the purpose of accomplishing specific functions.

A **bureaucracy** is an organization set up in a logical and rational manner for the purpose of accomplishing specific functions. Sociologist Max Weber (pronounced VAY-ber), an early student of bureaucratic organizations, identified six characteristics of effective bureaucracies:[6]

1. **Bureaucracies are organized on the basis of specialization, expertise, and division of labor.** The organization is divided into subunits based on function, and subunits are staffed by employees who are qualified to administer those tasks.

2. **They are organized in a hierarchical manner with an identifiable "chain of command" from top to bottom.**

3. **A common set of rules for carrying out functions characterize the operation.** These rules are often referred to as standard operating procedures (SOPs). Employees are trained to know and use these SOPs so that functions are performed smoothly and consistently.

4. **Bureaucracies maintain good records, or a "paper trail," of actions taken and decisions made.** Good record maintenance enables periodic review, efficiency of operation, and proof of action.

5. **Bureaucracies are characterized by an air of professionalism on the part of employees.**

You, Your Parents, and the Dreaded FAFSA Form

You have probably seen it. Your parents or legal guardians have seen it. Most of your college friends have seen it too. It is the dreaded "FAFSA" (Free Application for Student Aid) form. The joy and satisfaction of getting accepted into college is often met with the red tape and complexity of applying for student financial aid. The FAFSA form must be filled out by all students applying for federal support to offset the increasingly high costs of college tuition. Most states and colleges also require the FAFSA to help make their own decisions about a student's financial need and thus the aid that may be required. The U.S. Department of Education begins accepting FAFSA applications on January 1 for eligibility during the school year that begins the following fall. FAFSA requires documentation for a myriad of financial information about college students and their legal guardians. If you have never seen the form, either because your parents have done the leg work for you or because you haven't applied for financial aid, take a look at it at on the Web at http://www.fafsa.ed.gov.

Financial planners and other consultants have built an industry out of aiding college students and their families in their efforts to navigate the cumbersome FAFSA form. The detailed financial information that FAFSA requires is not always handy— gathering that information can be an especially time-consuming and aggravating task. However, the goal of FAFSA remains a laudable one: to fairly and equitably distribute aid to college students based on documented financial need. Still, the challenge of filling out FAFSA and meeting all its requirements can offer a rude awakening indeed to prospective and returning students who have never before confronted the federal bureaucracy in all its glory.

U.S. DEPARTMENT OF EDUCATION

For Critical Thinking and Discussion

1. What do you think about FAFSA? Is it too cumbersome or tedious?

2. Is the federal government transforming a simple process into one that is too complex to be effective? Or do you believe this form of red tape is necessary to ensure that colleges and universities can make fair decisions about financial aid for the nation's college students?

6. **The hiring and promotion process within effective bureaucracies is characterized by merit-based criteria and insulated from "politics."**

Bureaucracies are created within many types of organizations. Organizations typically exist to carry out a function or set of functions. Bureaucracies are what actually carry out these functions. Large private companies typically have bureaucracies that divide labor functions into categories or departments such as sales, accounting, human resources, MIS (management information systems), and other divisions. Colleges and universities have bureaucracies that usually include an admissions department, a registrar's office, an academic counseling center, an athletics department, and so on. Even small organizations such as physicians' offices feature a bureaucracy that includes medical support staff (such as nurses), a front-office staff (receptionist and secretary), and business offices (accountant and medical insurance specialist).

Mixed Views on Bureaucracy

Public opinion surveys about the federal bureaucracy tend to provide mixed reviews. People generally support the idea of government addressing important problems, but many are of the opinion that when government does act, it tends to waste money and act inefficiently. As the figure at right shows, Americans exhibited mixed feelings about the expansion of the federal government in response to the economic problems during the recessionary period of 2007–2010. While a slim majority—53 percent—approved of government's expanded role to help improve the economy, they only supported that expansion for the short term. More than eight in ten Americans either disapproved of government's expanded role or wanted government's role to retract once the recession was over.

Americans were asked by the *USA Today/*Gallup Poll: "Thinking about the way the federal government has responded to the financial crisis in recent months, generally speaking, do you approve or disapprove of the expansion of the government's role in the economy?" Those who approved were then asked if they thought the role of government should be reduced once the crisis is over. Here is how they responded:

*Source: USA Today/*Gallup Poll, conducted March 27–29, 2009.

Most governments maintain bureaucracies to carry out specific governmental functions, and the federal government is no exception. As with political parties, there is no reference to the bureaucracy in the U.S. Constitution. But like parties, the federal bureaucracy is arguably one of the most important features of the American political system. Americans have come to depend on it for many important things such as the defense of U.S. interests around the world, protection against terrorist attacks, cleaning up the destruction caused by natural disasters, a financial safety net for those who are unemployed or retired, the maintenance and expansion of the nation's roads and airways, and research for cures to such health problems as heart disease, cancer, and AIDS. In American government, the federal bureaucracy has traditionally come under the authority and jurisdiction of the president and the executive branch. As we will see, however, the modern federal bureaucracy is a complex set of agencies and organizations, parts of which are accountable to the legislative and judicial branches as well.

Citizens are more likely to come into direct contact with the bureaucracy than any other part of government, and so for many Americans, the bureaucracy comes to symbolize what government is. A visit to an unemployment office to register for unemployment benefits, a check in the mail from the Social Security Administration, a trip to the Department of Motor Vehicles to renew a driver's license, or a visit to the Web site of the Consumer Protection Agency to inquire about the safety of a child's car seat—these are just a few of the many ways citizens interact with the bureaucracy.

The federal bureaucracy, in fact, is a huge set of organizations that is expected to serve many different functions. It includes hundreds of departments, offices, agencies, bureaus, councils, foundations, commissions, boards, services, and authorities. Each of these units, as Weber's analysis of bureaucracies suggests, specializes in an area of public policy, is hierarchically organized to carry out its particular duties, conducts its operation on the basis of a set of standard operating procedures, maintains records of its actions and decisions, is trained to carry out functions in a professional manner, and engages in hiring practices that are based on merit. The vast size and level of responsibility of these units make the federal bureaucracy a complex and often confusing system to study.

What Does the Federal Bureaucracy Do?

★ LO

Understand the critical role that the bureaucracy plays in the implementation of federal policy

Most of the federal bureaucracy is within the executive branch of government and ultimately reports to the president of the United States.[7] Article II of the Constitution states that "the executive power shall be vested in a President of the United States of America." The executive power, or the power to carry out, administer, and enforce specific laws, then, falls mainly under the purview of presidential responsibility. The president uses the federal bureaucracy to exercise executive authority.

Policy Implementation

The full range of activities in which the federal bureaucracy engages is known as **policy implementation**. Policy implementation is the process of carrying out a law. Laws that are passed by Congress often include the development of new or modification of existing federal programs or services. To carry out the specific programs or services outlined in a law, the federal bureaucracy is assigned the task of implementation. For example, in 1935, Congress passed the Social Security Act to provide older Americans with a stable source of income during their retirement years and to offer support for the children of deceased workers. The act created the Social Security Administration as the agency in the federal government that had the authority to carry out the provisions of the act. Today, the Social Security Administration remains the unit in the federal bureaucracy responsible for maintaining records and authorizing benefits to those eligible for Social Security payments.

Policy implementation
The process of carrying out laws, and the specific programs or services outlined in those laws.

Implementation of a law requires translating the congressional legislation into action. Bureaucratic units begin the process of implementation by developing **regulations**, or a set of rules that guide employees of the agency in carrying out the program or service. These rules are supported by the force of law. The Social Security Administration, for example, has a detailed set of regulations defining who is and who is not eligible for Social Security retirement benefits. The rules include a schedule for the amount of monthly payment benefit based on a person's age, the number of years he or she contributed to the Social Security system while working, and other criteria. Regulations are useful not only because they translate laws into actions but also because they are written down and are usually very specific. In addition, they provide a basis for employees in the bureaucracy to apply them consistently from one case to the next.

Regulations
Rules or other directives issued by government agencies.

Federal Register
The journal that publishes draft regulations that implement a federal program.

Once an agency drafts a set of regulations to implement a program, the regulations are published in the ***Federal Register***. This federal government publication is widely accessible to elected leaders, interest groups, corporations, the media, and regular citizens. The agencies authoring the regulations have an open period during which they accept comments on the proposed rules and decide whether to redraft based on the commentary they receive. If the agency refuses to redraft based on an objection, the objector can ask Congress to require the agency to modify the regulations, or the objector might take the matter to court based on the agency's acting outside Congress's intentions in the law.

Bureaucratic Legislation

★ LO   Explain "delegated authority" and describe the conditions under which such authority is granted

The types of laws passed by Congress are many and varied, and thus, policy implementation encompasses many different bureaucratic activities. Some laws are very vague and offer agencies very little guidance about implementation. Other laws can be very specific in directing the agency how they are to be implemented. When laws are vague, agencies are said to have **administrative discretion**, which gives them considerable freedom in deciding how to implement the law. Vague laws require an agency to spend more time and effort in developing regulations.

Administrative discretion
The freedom of agencies to decide how to implement a vague or ambiguous law passed by Congress.

Two policy areas in which congressional legislation tends to be vague and agencies have much latitude in making rules and regulations are environmental quality and workplace safety. Important pieces of legislation, such as the Clean Air Act and the Occupational Safety and Health Act, have given agencies such as the Environmental Protection Agency (EPA) and Occupational Safety and Health Administration (OSHA) much discretion in setting specific standards for car emissions, pollution, and workplace safety standards. This discretion usually is the product of at least one of two conditions. First, Congress often does not have the technical expertise to define how to achieve clean air or workplace safety, and so it gives agencies that have such technical capabilities the discretion to set standards. Second, Congress sometimes chooses not to deal with politically difficult issues such as how to clean up toxic-waste dumps, and so it shifts the responsibility to the bureaucracy, forcing an agency to resolve the problem. When an agency makes an unpopular decision as a result of Congress's "passing the buck," the agency's action contributes further to the negative image of bureaucracies.

Delegation of congressional power
Congress's transferring of its lawmaking authority to the executive branch of government.

When Congress writes vague legislation and thus transfers legislative authority to an agency, it gives that agency the effective power to make laws, a constitutional power that is supposed to rest with the Congress alone. When Congress does this, it is said to have **delegated congressional power**. Laws that relate to the authority of administrative agencies and the rules promulgated by those agencies are referred to as **administrative law**. Congress has delegated considerable legislative authority to the EPA and OSHA to craft both environmental and workplace safety laws. Similarly, Congress has delegated a substantial amount of authority to the Federal Reserve to manage the nation's economy. The Fed has the power to adjust the prime interest rate in response to economic conditions to encourage investments and ward off inflation.

Administrative law
A law that relates to the authority of administrative agencies and the rules promulgated by those agencies.

Congressional oversight
Congress's exercise of its authority to monitor the activities of agencies and administrators.

Delegation of power from Congress to bureaucratic agencies is not, however, typically open-ended. Congress may cede lawmaking authority to the bureaucracy, but it does not relinquish all power. **Congressional oversight** is the term that describes Congress's regular monitoring of bureaucratic agency performance.

★ LO   Describe the oversight function of Congress over the bureaucracy

Although the vast bulk of bureaucratic agencies ultimately report to the president as chief executive, Congress through its oversight function commands a significant amount of accountability from executive agencies.[8]

If Congress is not satisfied with an agency's performance, it has a variety of means to coerce change: It can reduce or eliminate an agency's budget; it can refuse to confirm presidential appointments to that agency; it can eliminate the agency; it can conduct investigations into the activities and performance of the agency; or it can establish a new agency and shift resources and powers to it. This strong system of checks often renders the federal bureaucracy just as (if not more) responsive to Congress as to the president.

Bureaucratic Adjudication

Just as policy implementation sometimes includes the writing of legislation, it also may involve **bureaucratic adjudicating**, or determining the rights and duties of particular parties within the scope of an agency's rules or regulations. Such adjudication might include ruling on whether an individual is eligible to receive Social Security payments or whether a company has violated an air pollution rule. Most adjudication takes place in the court system. However, Congress, which has the authority to create federal adjudicating agencies, has placed judicial power in some bureaucratic agencies as well. For example, the Equal Employment Opportunity Commission (EEOC) has the authority to adjudicate cases in which an individual or a group of individuals charges that a company has violated federal laws preventing discrimination in hiring or promotion practices in the workplace. The EEOC can try a case against a company, and if it finds that the company violated federal law, the EEOC is authorized to prescribe a punishment or corrective action.

The EEOC and other agencies such as the EPA, the National Labor Relations Board, and the Federal Communications Commission (FCC) employ the personnel, procedures, and case law more typically seen in the judicial branch. Bureaucratic judicial personnel and powers include "administrative judges," appellate courts within the agency, and administrative hearings that resemble a trial. Ultimately, any administrative court decision may be appealed to the federal court system because the power of adjudication ultimately rests with the judicial branch. In reality, however, federal courts routinely uphold cases appealed from administrative courts.

The Development of the Federal Bureaucracy

The executive branch of government during the first four years of George Washington's presidency was extremely small. Congress created just three departments to aid the first president in executing the law: the Department of State to oversee foreign affairs, the Department of Treasury to oversee fiscal affairs, and the Department of War to oversee military affairs. Washington selected and the Senate confirmed Thomas Jefferson, Alexander Hamilton, and Henry Knox to lead these departments, respectively. Shortly after these departments were created, the president was authorized to hire an attorney general and a postmaster general. During the first year of the Washington administration, the federal bureaucracy employed only about fifty individuals.

Bureaucratic adjudicating
Determining the rights and duties of particular parties within the scope of an agency's rules or regulations.

As the role of government expanded and as the United States added new territories, there was a need to expand the size of the federal bureaucracy. Military operations, such as those conducted during the War of 1812, required increased support services and agencies to assist military operations. Westward expansion brought with it the need for federal services to settle the new areas. A centralized national bank required federal agencies to centralize the economic and monetary system. By the mid-1800s, Congress saw the need to create a new cabinet department, the Department of the Interior, to manage federally owned lands and to aid in the westward expansion of the nation. The important role of farming in the nation's growth and development led to the establishment of the Department of Agriculture in 1862 to support and promote farming and farm product commercialization. The Department of Justice was established in 1870 to aid the attorney general in the post–Civil War era in prosecuting violators of federal law and representing the federal government in the courts.

In 1884, a Bureau of Labor was created to address the concerns of the labor force that arose with the growth of the industrial economy. Large-scale industrialization and economic development led to the development of a Commerce Agency in 1888 to help regulate interstate and foreign trade. These agencies were elevated to cabinet status in the early 1900s to reflect the growing role they played in the federal government. The Great Depression set the stage for the election of Franklin Delano Roosevelt in 1932. The FDR administration advocated an activist role for the federal government in responding to the economic crisis. Consequently, FDR's New Deal created a myriad of new federal agencies to deal with the nation's fiscal woes, including the Social Security Administration, the Securities and Exchange Commission, the Civilian Conservation Corps, and a host of public works programs to provide jobs for the large number of unemployed. In 1936 Roosevelt established the Brownlow Committee to investigate how to make the growing bureaucracy more efficient and more responsive to the president.[9] The committee unanimously agreed that the president's power should be enhanced to give the president greater authority as manager of the bureaucracy. The Brownlow Committee's recommendations led to the consolidation of presidential authority over the bureaucracy.

By 1940, the federal government accounted for 10 percent of the nation's gross domestic product (GDP), with $9.5 billion spent on federal programs, including the employment of about 700,000 Americans in the federal bureaucracy. The increased role of government led to greater demands for federal services, which in turn necessitated growth in the federal bureaucracy. Between 1940 and 1975, the federal bureaucracy experienced an unprecedented growth spurt. During this period, the number of federal employees more than tripled to 2.2 million, the federal budget increased to $332 billion, and the federal budget as a percentage of the gross domestic product reached 22 percent.[10]

Two factors accounted for this massive growth in the bureaucracy. First was President Lyndon B. Johnson's Great Society program of the 1960s. The Great Society encompassed numerous new laws aimed at social and economic improvements to American society through a highly activist role of the federal government. The post–World War II prosperity of the American economy allowed Johnson to convince a Democratic Congress that programs promoting social justice, a safety net for the impoverished, improvements to urban life, health care for the elderly, and greater access to educational opportunities should

One Italian Writer Experiences American Bureaucracy

Americans tend to think that our bureaucracy is far too large, complex, and difficult for most average citizens to navigate. Of course, the Italian bureaucracy can more than hold its own in a battle with the American version; it is renowned for its size, power, and grip on Italian government, as well as for its overall complexity for Italian citizens. In his book *Ciao, America!: An Italian Discovers the U.S.*, Italian journalist Beppe Severgnini of Italy offers a dose of perspective to Americans by chronicling the relatively pleasant experience he had with the bureaucracy in Washington, DC.

For Italians coming to live in the United States, the greatest satisfaction . . . is grappling with American bureaucracy. Why is that? It's because, having trained on the Italian version, we feel like a matador faced with a milk cow. It's a pushover. . . . After sorting everything out, an Italian has a craving for a few more phone calls to make, some last-minute problem to unravel, or another clerk to convince. What now follows is the story of one short but exciting morning in action against the bureaucratic legions of Washington:

The "battle station" was a phone booth at Sugar's, a Korean coffee shop on the corner of P and Thirty-fifth streets. Weapons and ammunition—five quarters, paper, pen, passport, map of the city, a good command of English, and a moderate degree of optimism. The first thing, in a country where everything is done over the phone, was to get a telephone. All this took was a call to C&P (the local—private and therefore efficient—equivalent of the Italian Telecom) to ask for a number. The clerk asked a few questions of the kind that any student on

a beginner's English language course could answer—name, surname, age, address. At the end of the conversation, the same clerk told me, "Get your pen and write. This is your number. You'll be connected in twenty-four hours." Total time required for the transaction—ten minutes. Cost—twenty-five cents.

At this point, it is necessary to connect your new phone to a long-distance carrier. Competition among AT&T, MCI, and Sprint is ruthless. Each provider offers special conditions, such as discounts on numbers you call frequently, on calls to a foreign country of your choice, at particular times of day or on certain days of the week. Time required to decide—fifteen minutes. Cost—nothing. Each company has its own free phone number (which in the USA begin with 1-800).

But to apply for a Social Security number, which is the de facto equivalent in the United States of an identity card, the phone is not enough. You need to go to the appropriate office, where a clerk asks you questions and types your answers straight into a computer. Queue (sorry, line)—none. Forms—ditto. Interview time—five minutes.

Then we made a visit to the police for a temporary parking permit. (Time—fifteen minutes. Cost—nothing.) After which to open a bank account, all you need to do is turn up with the money (essential), and proof of domicile. The address on a letter is okay. A photocopy of your rent contract is even better. A temporary checkbook is issued on the spot and you can choose the definitive version from a catalog. There's the classic model, the old-fashioned type, and one with Sylvester the cartoon cat on every check. My wife, of course, insisted on Sylvester. That was perhaps the most trying moment of the entire morning.

Source: Beppe Severgnini, *Ciao, America!: An Italian Discovers the U.S.* (New York: Broadway Press, reprint edition 2003), 13–14.

be guaranteed to all Americans and funded by the great wealth of the American economy. These programs had a large influence on the growth of the bureaucracy through the 1970s.

A second factor contributing to the massive growth in the bureaucracy was the Cold War. World War II resulted in two superpowers, the United States and the Soviet Union, vying against each other for global influence. From 1945 to 1991, these superpowers developed expensive nuclear and other war technologies in search of military superiority. The federal budget for defense programs grew dramatically, as did the programs to support intelligence operations and aid to foreign nations for diplomatic purposes.

Getting Control of the Growing Bureaucracy

★ LO Explain methods for attempting to control or reduce the size and scope of the federal bureaucracy through privatization, devolution, deregulation, and accountability

During the mid to late 1970s, the American economy began to slump. Whereas the prosperity of the 1960s facilitated the creation of a larger government to accomplish a number of policy goals, the sluggish economy of the late 1970s was unable to support the by now very large federal bureaucracy. Federal budget deficits began to accumulate, and the United States could no longer afford the huge federal bureaucracy it had created. Ronald Reagan was elected president in 1980 with an agenda to scale back the federal bureaucracy. The Reagan administration targeted domestic programs to achieve the reduction in government. Since the 1980s, various administrations have attempted to reduce the size of the federal bureaucracy. The methods they have used include the following:

Privatization
The process of replacing government-provided services with services provided by the private sector.

- **Privatization. Privatization** means replacing government-provided services with services provided by the private sector. The theory of privatization is that if private companies compete to provide services, the cost of those services will be less than if government provides those services directly. Additionally, some contend that private corporations can more flexibly adapt to changing circumstances because they are not weighed down by civil service restrictions and government red tape. Accordingly, a number of federal programs were privatized during the 1980s. For example, the U.S. Department of Labor frequently provided job training services to the unemployed during the 1960s and 1970s. Federal laws passed in the 1980s eliminated much of the federal management of job training and contracted out these services to private companies. More recently, the federal government has used a number of private contractors, including Halliburton (the company once run by former Vice President Dick Cheney) to help rebuild Iraq after the second Persian Gulf War, under the idea that the costs would be even greater if the federal government played a more direct role.

Deregulation
The elimination of government oversight and government regulation of certain activities.

- **Deregulation.** The development of rules and regulations to achieve a policy goal requires units in the bureaucracy to ensure that such rules and regulations are followed. **Deregulation**, that is, eliminating government oversight and regulation of certain activities, results in less government to do the regulating. Prior to the mid-1970s, the trucking and railroad industries, long-distance telephone service, prices for air flights, and the activities of savings and loan institutions were regulated by the federal government. Deregulation of these and other activities resulted in the abolition of a number of federal agencies, including the Civil Aeronautics Board and eventually the Interstate Commerce Commission.

- **Devolution.** A central question in our federal system of government is which level of government—national or state—should have the authority to provide programs and services to citizens. The New Deal and Great Society programs gave the national government increased responsibility and authority for such services. In response to extensive growth of the national government, the 1980s witnessed a **devolution** of power and responsibility back to the states, mainly to shrink the size of the national government. For example, welfare reform in the mid-1990s shifted much responsibility for welfare from the federal to the state governments.

- **Reinventing government.** When Bill Clinton was elected president in 1992, he promised to "reinvent government." This promise translated into an eight-year effort to promote bureaucratic accountability. The Clinton administration instituted mechanisms such as customer satisfaction research with those who received federal services and freedom of information policies that gave the public and the news media access to government documents to help promote accountability. In addition, the Government Performance and Results Act, passed in 1997, required that agencies establish goals and set out a plan for achieving those goals. In the book *Reinventing Government*, David Osborne and Ted Gaebler describe how bureaucracy and other aspects of the public sector in the United States have undergone a transformation.[11] They contend that the "entrepreneurial spirit" brought to bear on government performance, which includes market-driven and business-oriented planning, has improved the effectiveness and efficiency of bureaucracy at all levels of government.

Devolution
The transfer of power and responsibilities for certain regulatory programs from the federal government back to the states.

In addition to implementing these strategies for reducing the size of the federal bureaucracy, the Cold War, which concluded in 1991 with the collapse of the Soviet Union, put an end to escalating defense budgets to support the arms race with the Soviets.

The end of the Cold War and the implementation of strategies that contain, if not reduce, the size of the federal bureaucracy do appear to have reversed the decades-long trend toward increasing the size of government. Between 1990 and 2000, the number of civilian employees in the federal government declined by about 500,000,[12] and the percentage of the GDP accounted for by federal spending dropped from 21.9 percent to 18.2 percent. Despite these efforts, however, federal spending on the bureaucracy continues to increase annually at a pace that exceeds inflation. In particular, defense spending to fight the war on terrorism and the war in Iraq in recent years has increased federal spending. Also, the Department of Homeland Security, created in response to the terrorist attacks of September 11, 2001, required increased federal dollars to protect the nation within its own borders.

© 2012 CENGAGE LEARNING

More recently, the election of President Barack Obama and increased majorities of Democrats to Congress in 2008 during an economic recession ushered in a new growth spurt for the federal bureaucracy. A $787 billion federal spending plan to provide an economic stimulus along with a health care reform package and increased regulations of the financial services industry all significantly increased the scope and size of the bureaucracy. Most notably, the Obama administration championed the creation of a powerful new Consumer Financial Protection Bureau designed to provide stricter regulations on the mortgage financing industry in particular.

★ LO   Define the
different types of agencies
in the federal bureaucracy
including cabinet depart-
ments, independent agen-
cies, regulatory agencies,
government corporations,
and the Executive Office
of the President

The Organization of the Federal Bureaucracy

The federal bureaucracy is made up of a variety of different types of agencies that are empowered to carry out laws and federal programs. Some of these organizations have broad authority over a public policy area, whereas others have a narrow focus; some are empowered to implement laws and programs established by Congress, whereas others have the added responsibility of creating rules and policies and adjudicating. Some report directly to the president, whereas others answer to both the president and Congress. Also, although most organizations in the federal bureaucracy are part of the executive branch, some are part of the legislative and judicial branches. Units of the federal bureaucracy include cabinet departments, independent agencies, regulatory agencies, government corporations, and the Executive Office of the President.

Cabinet Departments

Cabinet departments
Those federal agencies that
qualify as the major administrative organizations of the
executive branch.

Amid the complex web of bureaucratic units is a select set of fifteen organizations called **cabinet departments**, which are the major administrative organizations of the executive branch. These departments vary in terms of both size and importance. The Department of Defense, for example, employs nearly 1 million civilian workers and another 1.5 million military personnel. By contrast, the Department of Education has only about 5,000 employees.

At the head of each cabinet department is a secretary (with the exception of the Department of Justice, which is headed by the attorney general) who reports directly to the president. Along with a few other high-level presidential advisers and the vice president, these secretaries compose the president's cabinet, a set of high-level administrators who report directly to the president. Cabinet heads and their deputies are

President Obama meets with his cabinet in the Cabinet Room at the White House.

nominated by the president and must be confirmed by the Senate. Typically, a secretary shares the same views as the president on policy matters and often is a loyal political supporter (if not close friend) of the chief executive. The "inner cabinet" is a term used to describe the secretaries of the most important departments in the cabinet: State, Defense, Treasury, and Justice. Whereas the cabinet once served as the president's primary advisory panel, the growth in the Executive Office of the President, discussed later in this chapter, has shifted primary advisory responsibilities to that office.

Cabinet departments (sometimes referred to as executive departments) generally have a broad scope of authority over a particular policy area, such as the nation's military (the Department of Defense), federal law enforcement (the Department of Justice), the federal road and highway system (the Department of Transportation), and protecting the nation from terrorism and responding to emergency situations (Department of Homeland Security). The scope of activities in any one department tends to be so broad that most departments are best viewed as a collection of many different agencies and subagencies, each with a narrower policy focus.

The U.S. Department of Labor, for example, is charged with promoting the American labor force and the interests of labor. It is organized into a large array of agencies and offices, each of which focuses on a particular aspect of labor issues. The Occupational Safety and Health Administration develops standards to promote safe workplace environments and implements regulations to ensure that employers live up to those standards. The Bureau of Labor Statistics is responsible for compiling data on the labor force on a regular basis. The Office of Labor-Management Standards sets policies for the conduct of negotiations between employers and employees. Likewise, the U.S. Department of Defense manages the armed forces and is organized into a number of subunits, including the Army, Navy, Air Force, and National Guard. The hierarchical organization of departments facilitates the bureaucratic goals of area specialization, division of labor, and chain of command.

Although the head of a cabinet department advises and reports directly to the president, only Congress has the authority to create a new department or eliminate an existing one. The power to define the scope, authority, and indeed the very existence of a specific major department in the federal bureaucracy is an important "check" that Congress exercises over the president.

Special situations, particularly crises, have led the U.S. government to create cabinet-level departments to deal with large-scale national problems. The creation of the Department of Defense in 1947, for example, was in response to large and costly inefficiencies in military operations during World War II. The Department of Energy was established in 1977 in response to the severe energy crisis and gasoline shortage that plagued the country during the 1970s. President Reagan successfully pressed for the creation of a Department of Veterans Affairs in 1988 to promote his administration's appreciation of those who served in the U.S. military. The newest cabinet department is the Department of Homeland Security (DHS), established in 2002.

In addition to maintaining the authority to carry out many of the nation's laws, the cabinet also plays a symbolic role in the political system. Many interest groups provide input to the president through leaders in the cabinet, and the voices of community and business leaders are often heard first by cabinet department officials. As the highest level units in the bureaucracy, cabinet departments theoretically represent the most important policy areas. Increasingly, presidents have used their cabinet secretary appointments to demonstrate diversity in government. For nearly two centuries, cabinet secretaries were almost exclusively white men, but over the last twenty years, presidents have used race and gender as factors influencing their appointments. President Clinton made history by naming women to the inner cabinet for the first time: Janet Reno as attorney general in 1993 and Madeleine Albright as secretary of state in 1997. President George W. Bush similarly made history by appointing the first African American to the inner cabinet: Colin Powell as secretary of state in 2001. In 2005, Bush appointed an African American woman, Condoleezza Rice, as Powell's replacement; he also appointed the first Hispanic to the inner cabinet when he named Alberto Gonzales as the nation's attorney general during his second term in office. President Obama's cabinet is also diverse, featuring in

Conflicts within the President's Cabinet

Presidents choose the leaders of their cabinets, and those chosen are most often high-level political supporters and friends of the president, as well as those who agree with the chief executive on key issues of public policy. Even though the president makes all these high-level appointments, conflicts between department heads are not uncommon. Discord among high-ranking officials may sometimes play out in the media and become a source of embarrassment to presidents. Most recently, a 2010 book by Bob Woodward entitled *Obama's Wars* depicts top White House officials in conflict over how to resolve the war in Afghanistan. Yet cabinet leaders' differences of opinion on key policy matters may not always be a bad thing because they give the president a variety of perspectives from which to make a choice.

From 1789 through 1793, President George Washington's cabinet included Secretary of State Thomas Jefferson and Secretary of the Treasury Alexander Hamilton. Washington's desire for his cabinet officers to work closely with each other and provide coordinated advice to him was soon dashed as severe conflicts broke out between these two men. Their primary disagreement was over Hamilton's proposal to create a central national bank. Hamilton believed that the federal government had the authority to establish such a bank, which he saw as necessary to solve the nation's economic problems. For Jefferson, the creation of a central bank exceeded the authority of the central government. The conflict between these top two cabinet officials reflected a battle between Jefferson's "state's rights" beliefs and Hamilton's "strong central government" views. In the end, Washington sided with Hamilton, and a central bank was created.

From 1977 through 1979, President Jimmy Carter's foreign policy team included Secretary of State Cyrus Vance and National Security Adviser Zbigniew Brzezinski. Brzezinski was a close adviser to the president and over time came to take on more and more of the responsibilities normally under the purview of the secretary of state. For example, Carter in 1978 sent Brzezinski to Beijing to help normalize China–U.S. relations. As an emissary for Carter, Brzezinski assumed state functions beyond those of a policy adviser. The role Brzezinski played caused mounting friction between himself and Vance. This friction came to a head in 1979 over the U.S. response to the Iranian hostage crisis. Vance favored a policy of recognizing the Ayatollah Khomeini and negotiating with him, whereas Brzezinski favored U.S. military action to remove Khomeini. When Brzezinski convinced Carter to approve a plan to rescue the hostages by force (which failed), Secretary of State Vance resigned.

In 2003, George W. Bush found two of his inner circle cabinet secretaries locked in a profound battle over the question of whether the United States should militarily intervene in Iraq. Iraqi leader Saddam Hussein had continuously defied UN resolutions regarding inspections to locate sites used for the development of weapons of mass destruction. Secretary of State Colin Powell advocated a diplomatic solution, threatening the use of the U.S. military only if the UN would endorse such action. Secretary of Defense Donald Rumsfeld argued for U.S. military action even without UN approval (France, Germany, and Russia, and members of the UN Security Council had refused to support military intervention). In the end, President Bush sided with Rumsfeld, and the United States went to war with Iraq without the UN's full support. These conflicting positions between the president's top two foreign policy advisers reflect Rumsfeld's "hawkish" military perspective and Powell's more "realist" perspective. Powell resigned after President Bush's reelection in 2004; Rumsfeld remained secretary of defense until December 2006, resigning soon after the 2006 midterm elections.

prominent positions four women (Secretary of State Hillary Clinton, Secretary of Health and Human Services Kathleen Sebelius, Secretary of Homeland Security Janet Napolitano, and Secretary of Labor Hilda Solis) and two African Americans (Attorney General Eric Holder and U.S. Trade Representative Ron Kirk).

Independent Agencies

A number of units in the federal bureaucracy do not have the high status of a cabinet department but do report directly to the president. Whereas cabinet departments tend to concentrate on broad areas, such as labor, energy, defense, or education, these **independent agencies**, which are not part of any executive cabinet department, tend to focus on a narrower scope of issues. NASA, for example, focuses on the U.S. space program, whereas the Small Business Administration concentrates on low-cost loans and support to encourage the development of small businesses. Independent agencies tend to be smaller than cabinet departments. The heads of these agencies are appointed by and report to the president.

Independent agency
A department that focuses on a narrower set of issues than do higher-status cabinet departments.

Regulatory Agencies

Regulatory agencies are responsible for implementing rules and regulations governing individual or corporate conduct related to some aspect of the economy. Such agencies are supposed to be staffed by nonpartisan individuals who are entrusted to make sound decisions that promote fairness and weed out corrupt practices on fiscal matters. To accomplish this, regulatory agencies (unlike cabinet departments and independent agencies) are not under the control of the president. They are created by Congress and are run by independent boards or commissions that are not supposed to exert partisan influence.

Regulatory agency
A government body responsible for the control and supervision of a specified activity or area of public interest.

The first regulatory agency was the Interstate Commerce Commission (ICC), created by Congress in 1887.[13] As with the creation of most regulatory agencies, the ICC was the federal government's response to widespread corruption. In the case of the ICC, the target was corruption in the railroad industry, which led to the high cost of railroad transportation. The ICC's scope of responsibility extended to regulation of commerce via not only railroad but also pipeline, barge, automobile, and aircraft. The ICC established a complex set of rates for both passenger and freight transportation via the various modes of transport. ICC rules were intended to guarantee that transportation companies pay a fair fee on the value of property they used in carrying out their services. Congress abolished the ICC in 1995 because it determined that the agency was overregulating and thus hindering growth in certain business sectors.

Today's federal bureaucracy includes a number of important regulatory agencies:

- **The Federal Trade Commission (FTC).** Established in 1914, the FTC has the authority to develop and implement rules and regulations to encourage competition in industry. Over the years, the FTC has played an instrumental role in preventing "price fixing" policies of corporations.

- **The Federal Communications Commission (FCC).** The FCC was established in 1934 with the authority to regulate radio, television, and interstate telephone companies. Unlike newspapers, which are not regulated, radio and TV stations use public airwaves, making them subject to regulations developed and administered by the FCC.

- **The Securities and Exchange Commission (SEC).** Created in 1934 in response to the stock market crash of 1929, the SEC is responsible for making rules with respect to the stock market and corporate bookkeeping practices.

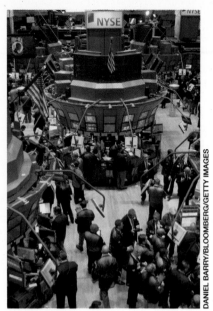

The SEC, a regulatory agency, regulates the activities of traders on the busy floor of the New York Stock Exchange, pictured above in May 2007.

Government corporations
Units in the federal bureaucracy set up to run like private companies that depend on revenue from citizens to provide their services.

- **The Equal Employment Opportunity Commission (EEOC).** Created by Congress to help administer the Civil Rights Acts of 1964, the EEOC is charged with investigating violations of the act.

- **The Environmental Protection Agency (EPA).** The EPA was created in response to the environmental protection movement of the 1960s and 1970s. Concerns about air and water quality, as well as hazardous waste materials, led Congress to pass a number of important laws that addressed antipollution measures and empowered the EPA (in 1970) to implement environmental regulations. The EPA is the largest of the regulatory agencies.

- **The Consumer Product Safety Commission (CPSC).** Consumer advocacy was also a movement that gained steam in the 1960s and 1970s. Efforts to make manufacturers produce products that were safer for consumers were an important feature of that movement. The CPSC was created in 1972 to protect the public against risks associated with consumer products.

Government Corporations

A small number of units in the federal bureaucracy are set up to run like private companies even though they serve an important public purpose. These are called **government corporations**. The idea behind a government corporation is that there is a market of customers who are willing to pay individually for the services provided by the corporation. The revenue on which the government corporation relies comes primarily from citizens paying for the service provided by the corporation. Unlike private corporations, government has a special interest in the solvency of government corporations because they serve an important public purpose. Consequently, when the revenue of a government corporation falls short of meeting expenses, government often will intervene to keep the unit in business.

The most widely known and used government corporation is the U.S. Postal Service (USPS), which employs nearly 1 million workers. The primary source of funds for the USPS comes from the sale of U.S. postage stamps. Similar to a private business, the USPS has a product to offer (mail delivery) and charges a fee (the cost of postage) for use of that service.

Another government corporation is the Tennessee Valley Authority (TVA), which serves the power needs of seven states in the Tennessee Valley and operates the system for navigation and flood control of the Tennessee River. Users of TVA's generated power pay for service, as do those who navigate on the Tennessee River. Another well-known government corporation is Amtrak, a railroad service operated by the National Railroad Passenger Corporation. Amtrak maintains more than 20,000 miles of track and operates 500 stations across the nation. Its revenue is largely derived from the sale of passenger tickets; however, in recent years low ridership has forced Congress to subsidize Amtrak from the general revenue fund.

The Executive Office of the President

The president of the United States has an office staff that reports directly to the president, provides advice and counsel, and helps the president manage the rest of the federal bureaucracy. The **Executive Office of the President** is managed by the White House Chief of Staff and includes a Communications Office, a press secretary, a Council of Economic Advisers (to provide advice and management of the bureaucratic agencies responsible to the economy), a National Security Council (to provide advice on foreign and military affairs), an Office of Management and Budget (to coordinate and provide data on the national budget), a White House Counsel (to provide legal advice to the president), an Office of Science and Technology, an Office of the U.S. Trade Representative, and an Office of National Drug Control Policy, among others.

Executive Office of the President
The staffers who help the president of the United States manage the rest of the federal bureaucracy.

The Federal Workforce

The federal bureaucracy encompasses an immense workforce. Currently, it employs approximately 2 million civilian personnel, 85 percent of whom work outside of Washington, DC.[14] In addition, there are about 1 million U.S. postal workers and another 1.7 million U.S. military personnel.

★ **LO**
Appreciate the large scope of the federal workforce and the civil service rules governing federal employment

Political Appointees and Career Professionals

About 8,000 members of the federal workforce are presidential appointees, some of whom must be confirmed by the Senate. Those requiring Senate confirmation include cabinet secretaries and the attorney general, heads of independent agencies, ambassadors, U.S. attorneys, and other high-level officers who have administrative responsibility. When a president's term of office expires, the new president generally fills these positions with new appointees. Presidential appointees are frequently referred to as "political" appointees because the job often represents a political reward for past service to the president or the president's political party.

Another 7,500 civilian federal employees are part of what is called the **Senior Executive Service (SES)**. These are senior officers in the federal bureaucracy who are career professionals. Those in the SES do not leave their positions when a new president takes office but work closely with presidential appointees and provide continuity in the operations of the federal bureaucracy from one presidential administration to the next. Congress established the SES in the late 1970s as a means of providing this continuity in leadership. Congress also spelled out a nonpartisan process for hiring SES officers based on educational background, work experience, and other qualifications.

Senior Executive Service (SES)
Since the late 1970s, a defined group of approximately 7,500 career professionals in the federal bureaucracy who provide continuity in the operations of the bureaucracy from one presidential administration to the next.

Presidential appointees are largely selected to reflect the political orientation of the president, and senior executives are selected primarily to find highly qualified career professionals who will maintain stability in the operations of the bureaucracy. Together, these groups of employees provide leadership and senior management of the units in the federal bureaucracy.

The Civil Service

The vast majority of the federal bureaucracy workforce is known as the **civil service**. Similar to the SES, civil service workers in the federal bureaucracy are theoretically hired based on their qualifications and remain employees beyond the term of a particular president. Thus, they are supposed to be immune from partisan political maneuvering. Civil service jobs were not always insulated from partisan politics, as they are today.

Civil service
The system whereby workers in the federal bureaucracy are supposed to be immune from partisan political maneuvering.

During the early years of the American republic, continuous recruitment of well-educated, upper-middle-class men characterized the development of the federal bureaucracy. Presidents Washington, Adams, and Jefferson hired political, business, and social elites to carry out the activities of the federal bureaucracy. With the exception of top posts in government such as cabinet secretaries, those in federal jobs usually remained from one presidential administration to the next. This tradition ensured an able and effective federal workforce, albeit not a diverse one.

President Andrew Jackson, elected to office in 1828, undertook a massive restructuring of the federal workforce. Jackson ran for the presidency as a populist advocating for the interests of the "common man." Upon taking office, he removed from the bureaucracy individuals who were not at all "common," and who found themselves politically at odds with the new president. Resistance among many in the bureaucracy to follow Jackson's orders, along with the president's own desire to see that the bureaucracy more closely reflected the demographics of American society, led Jackson to undertake a major overhaul of the bureaucratic workforce.

Spoils system
The postelection practice of rewarding loyal supporters of the winning candidates and party with appointive public offices.

Patronage
The act of appointing people to government positions.

Jackson replaced the long-term, upper-middle-class bureaucrats with political supporters and friends who came from many walks of life. This **spoils system** of hiring federal workers quickly became a steadfast American tradition. To the victors of presidential elections went the spoils of jobs in the federal government. Under this system of **patronage**, campaigning, political party activities, and governing became intertwined. Political parties enticed people to work on political campaigns by promising the payoff of a good federal job with an electoral victory. Often, those who were given a job were expected to return a percentage of their salary to the political party—a very clever fund-raising strategy. Strength of partisan support became the key criterion for landing and maintaining a good job.

Needless to say, this system of hiring workers produced a number of problems. Because qualifications to do the job were not important in the hiring decision, the bureaucracy became inefficient. Bureaucrats were more concerned about campaigning and supporting the political party than they were about doing their job. Further, the bureaucracy lacked any sort of continuity, for when the partisan control of the presidency changed hands, federal workers were fired en masse and replaced by a new set of underqualified political appointees.

Pendleton Civil Service Reform Act
The 1883 law that created a merit system for hiring many federal workers, protected them from being fired for partisan reasons, and set up a Civil Service Commission to oversee the hiring and firing process.

Merit system
A system of appointing and promoting civil service personnel based on merit rather than political affiliation or loyalty.

By the time of the Civil War, the spoils system was entrenched, and the bureaucracy was thoroughly corrupt. A civil service reform movement arose in the post–Civil War era, advocating an end to the spoils system and the development of a "professionalized" bureaucracy. Strong resistance from the political party bosses stalled the reform movement's agenda. But the 1881 assassination of President James Garfield by a disgruntled party worker who did not receive the federal job he thought he deserved gave strength to the movement. In 1883, Congress passed the **Pendleton Civil Service Reform Act**, which did the following:[15]

- It created a **merit system** for hiring many federal workers based on qualifications for the job, including educational background, related job experience, and performance on civil service tests.

- It prevented employees from losing their federal jobs when the presidency changed hands.

- It set up a Civil Service Commission to oversee federal hiring and firing practices.

Initially, the Pendleton Act applied only to a limited portion of the federal workforce, but it provided the basis for Progressive Era reformers of the early 1900s to develop a more professional bureaucracy through additional reform legislation. Today, job qualifications in federal hiring and federal worker immunity from patronage are firmly rooted in the federal bureaucracy's employment practices. These principles now apply to more than 90 percent of federal workers.

The **Hatch Act of 1939** further insulated the civil service from partisan politics by (1) prohibiting the dismissal of an employee for partisan reasons (with the exception of certain high-level political appointments) and (2) prohibiting federal workers from running for office or actively campaigning for a political candidate. In the early 1990s, revisions to the Hatch Act relaxed some of the more stringent requirements of the law and allowed federal workers more flexibility in engaging in political activities. Those in the civil service can now participate in campaigns outside their work hours, contribute money to a candidate or party, express partisan opinions, and wear campaign buttons, among other activities. However, under the current law, federal workers still cannot be candidates in a partisan election or use their official position to raise money or influence votes.

The **Civil Service Reform Act of 1978** replaced the Civil Service Commission with the Office of Personnel Management (OPM) and the Merit Systems Protection Board (MSPB). OPM and MSPB, bureaucratic agencies themselves, manage the civil service system today. Their functions include administering the system of federal hiring, protecting the rights of federal employees, conducting hearings and deciding cases where there are charges of wrongdoing in hiring and firing of employees, evaluating the effectiveness of federal hiring and retention practices, and regulating the ways federal workers can participate in politics.

Hatch Act of 1939
The 1939 law that insulated the civil service from partisan politics by prohibiting employee dismissals for partisan reasons and by prohibiting federal workers from participating in political campaigns.

Civil Service Reform Act of 1978
The federal act that replaced the Civil Service Commission (the agency that oversaw federal hiring and firing practices) with the Office of Personnel Management (OPM) and the Merit Systems Protection Board (MSPB).

Getting a Job in the Federal Government

Applying for a job in the federal government is much different from applying for a job at a company. For one thing, most federal jobs require that the applicant take and pass a civil service examination. And those who land a federal job often find that the job is much different from a job in the private sector. In his book *Insider's Guide to Finding a Job in Washington*, Bruce Maxwell lists four primary advantages of having a job in the federal bureaucracy:[16]

- "The federal government is the nation's largest employer, and has lots of jobs. In January 1999, in the Washington area the executive branch employed 293,584 people—and that's just civilians. Between January 1998 and January 1999, federal agencies and departments together hired an average of 3,272 new employees each month in the Washington area."

- "Federal jobs provide excellent job security. It's true that the federal government has been on a downsizing kick in recent years, but the vast majority of the job cuts have occurred through attrition and buyouts, not layoffs. The downsizing trend has now largely tapered off. In fact, between January 1998 and January 1999, the number of executive branch employees in the Washington area grew by 4,254."

- "In general, federal wages and benefits are good, and are comparable to those in the private sector. Federal workers in the Washington area got a 3.68 percent pay hike in January 1999, raising the salary of the average white-collar employee to $59,307."

- "Workers who retire from the federal government receive excellent pension benefits."

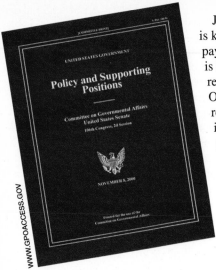

Job openings in the federal bureaucracy are advertised in what is known as a "vacancy announcement," which includes job title, pay grade level, application submission deadlines, where the job is located, a description of the job duties, a description of the job requirements, and procedures for applying for the position. The Office of Personnel Management (OPM) is the federal agency responsible for coordinating and distributing information on hiring and vacancy announcements in the federal government. OPM provides updated information on jobs at the following Web site: http://www.usajobs.opm.gov.

Pictured above is the "plum book," which provides a listing of all job openings in the federal bureaucracy.

NOW & THEN

Making the Connection

The federal bureaucracy has grown dramatically since the George Washington administration. As new presidents seek to advance new policy goals, federal departments and agencies have been created and expanded. These agencies have aided presidents in accomplishing new feats and bringing the United States to world "superpower" status. Jefferson's expansion of the bureaucracy was necessary to accomplish the tremendous growth of the nation through the Louisiana Purchase. Reagan's expansion of the bureaucracy helped expand the defenses of the nation to the point that it helped win the Cold War. Many other presidents have found a bureaucracy necessary to help implement federal initiatives. These include Lincoln's efforts to withstand the secession of the Southern states and preserve the Union; Theodore Roosevelt's drive to tame the corporate monopolies, Franklin Roosevelt's priming of the federal workforce to tackle the Great Depression, and Barack Obama's attempt to jump start the economy by helping to pass a nearly $1 trillion stimulus spending plan in 2009.

Over the centuries, presidents, with the support of the American people, have used the bureaucracy to accomplish important policy goals. The bureaucracy has also served as the "whipping boy" in rhetorical campaigns for political office. In many instances the bureaucracy has earned its reputation as wasteful, inefficient, and bloated. But without the federal bureaucracy, the most important national initiatives could not have been realized. Even those presidents who campaigned on a platform to cut the bureaucracy ended up using it to advance important initiatives. The federal bureaucracy is an easy target of criticism, yet there is no denying the fact that it has contributed as much to the development of the American political system as any other part of the political system.

The official title of "czar" was once used by Russia to signify that nation's monarchial head. In previous centuries Russian czars, like other European monarchs such as kings and queens, were quite often dictators, reaching high office through undemocratic means while exercising broad legislative and executive authority. Today in the United States a number of positions in the executive branch of government are referred to unofficially as "czars." The title seems to have caught on for one of two reasons: Either (1) the person selected for the job was expected to lead an effort to solve a particularly difficult problem (e.g., the "drug czar" coordinates the federal effort to mitigate the illegal drug trade in the United States), or (2) the person was selected by the president with the clear expectation that congressional approval was unnecessary. Often both reasons apply to the appointment of these special bureaucratic leaders. As coordinators of a very wide array of agencies, they usually enjoy close working relationships with the president. No wonder the modern czar is considered such a powerful force in American politics.

Presidents since Franklin D. Roosevelt have been making these special czarist appointments. During the administrations of FDR and most of his successors, the number of bureaucratic czars appointed per president was in the single digits. President Kennedy appointed none, Nixon just three, Reagan just one, and George H. W. Bush a mere two czars in all. A new trend began with George W. Bush, who created more than thirty of these positions, and continued with Barack Obama, who in his first fifteen months in office set a record number of czarist appointments at thirty-eight. While a handful of Obama's appointments have been confirmed by the Senate, the vast majority of them were never approved, making them the target of critics who believe the president has usurped congressional authority. The criticism may have reached its peak in August 2009 when Van Jones, President Obama's "Special Advisor" for "Green Jobs, Enterprise and Innovation," resigned when it was discovered that he supported a number of socialist policies. The Senate approval process might have turned up this concern much earlier.

Some of the high-profile Obama-appointed czars include the following:

- John Brennen, Assistant to the President for Homeland Security and Counterterrorism
- George Mitchell, Special Envoy to the Middle East
- Cameron Davis, Special Advisor to the EPA Administrator
- Paul Volcker, Chairman of the Economic Recovery Advisory Board
- Kenneth Feinberg, Special Master for TARP (Troubled Asset Relief Program) Executive Compensation
- Carol Browner, Assistant to the President for Energy and Climate Change
- Ed Montgomery, Director of Recovery for Auto Workers and Communities

Do you think that all high-level appointments made by the president should require congressional confirmation? Should czars be formally confirmed by the Senate just as all cabinet-level and many subcabinet-level appointments are? What accounts for the increased use of czars by Presidents George W. Bush and Barack Obama? Has the growth and increased complexity of the federal bureaucracy created an atmosphere wherein presidents need a special advisor to coordinate agencies in a specific problem area?

At www.cengage.com/dautrich/americangovernmentbrief/2e, find the Politics InterActive link for details on czars in the federal government.

Chapter Summary

★ What Is Bureaucracy?

- Although the term *bureaucracy* often conjures up negative images, the government could not function effectively without bureaucratic organizations.

- Most units in the vast federal bureaucracy are part of the executive branch of government, and most engage primarily in policy implementation. Such implementation begins with the development of regulations that guide employees of the agency in carrying out particular programs or services.

★ What Does the Federal Bureaucracy Do?

- Because Congress lacks technical expertise, it often gives agencies wide administrative discretion to decide how to implement laws. Sometimes, Congress also delegates important programs to agencies because it wants to avoid thorny political issues.

- Congressional oversight of executive agencies may occur through legislative hearings or through the use of congressional agencies such as the CBO and GAO. Congress may threaten poorly performing agencies with reduced funding, a refusal to confirm appointments to the agency, or, in some extreme cases, the elimination of the agency.

- Congress has given some bureaucratic agencies judicial power to help them determine the rights and duties of parties within the scope of the agency's authority.

★ The Development of the Federal Bureaucracy

- The size of the federal bureaucracy exploded as the federal government played an increasingly active role in regulating the U.S. economy, overseeing new territories, and conducting overseas military operations. After FDR's New Deal was enacted during the 1930s, the federal government accounted for a sizable portion of the nation's economy as a whole. The bureaucracy continued to expand in the 1960s and beyond to meet the needs of President Lyndon Johnson's Great Society program and to compete with the Soviet Union in the Cold War.

★ Getting Control of the Growing Bureaucracy

- Beginning in the 1980s, some administrations attempted to reduce the size of the federal bureaucracy through (1) the privatization of certain government-provided services, (2) the deregulation of some federal activities, (3) the devolution of various powers and responsibilities back to the states, and (4) efforts to promote greater bureaucratic accountability through initiatives such as the Government Performance and Results Act.

★ The Organization of the Federal Bureaucracy

- The federal bureaucracy is organized into fifteen cabinet departments, including the recently created Department of Homeland Security, numerous independent agencies that focus on a narrower scope of issues, regulatory agencies that implement rules and regulations of private conduct, government corporations, and the Executive Office of the President.

★ The Federal Workforce

- The federal workforce includes 8,000 presidential employees who received their positions through political patronage, a Senior Executive Service consisting of approximately 7,500 senior career professionals, and a vast number of civil service workers whose jobs are immune from partisan politics. Today, most lower level federal workers are hired through a merit system rather than through the spoils systems that prevailed throughout much of the nineteenth and early twentieth centuries.

CourseMate

Key Terms

Administrative discretion (p. 208)

Administrative law (p. 208)

Bureaucracy (p. 204)

Bureaucratic adjudicating (p. 209)

Cabinet departments (p. 214)

Civil service (p. 219)

Civil Service Reform Act of 1978 (p. 221)

Congressional oversight (p. 208)

Delegation of congressional power (p. 208)

Deregulation (p. 212)

Devolution (p. 213)

Executive Office of the President (p. 219)

Federal Register (p. 208)

Government corporations (p. 218)

Hatch Act of 1939 (p. 221)

Independent agency (p. 217)

Merit system (p. 220)

Patronage (p. 220)

Pendleton Civil Service Reform Act (p. 220)

Policy implementation (p. 207)

Privatization (p. 212)

Regulations (p. 207)

Regulatory agency (p. 217)

Senior Executive Service (SES) (p. 219)

Spoils system (p. 220)

Resources

Books

Cook, Brian J. *Bureaucracy and Self-Government.* Baltimore: Johns Hopkins University Press, 1997.

Johnson, Ronald N., and Gary D. Libecap. *The Federal Civil Service System and the Problem of Bureaucracy.* Chicago: University of Chicago Press, 1994.

Neiman, Max. *Defending Government: Why Big Government Works.* Upper Saddle River, NJ: Prentice Hall, 2000.

Osborne, David, and Peter Plastrik. *Banishing Bureaucracy.* New York: Plume Books, 1997.

Stivers, Camilla, ed. *Democracy, Bureaucracy, and the Study of Administration.* Boulder, CO: Westview Press, 2001.

Wildavsky, Aaron. *The New Politics of the Budget Process.* 2nd ed. New York: HarperCollins, 1992.

Wilson, James Q. *Bureaucracy: What Government Agencies Do and Why They Do It.* New York: Basic Books, 1989.

Internet Sources

http://www.usa.gov/ (the U.S. government's official Web portal, this site provides links to all units and subunits of the Executive Office of the President, the fifteen cabinet departments, and most of the independent agencies, regulatory agencies, and corporations of the federal government).

9 The Judiciary

NOW Judge Sonia Sotomayor, nominated to the U.S. Supreme Court, testifying at her Senate confirmation hearings in July 2009.

CHRISTY BOWE/CORBIS

THEN Solicitor General Thurgood Marshall, preparing to testify at his Supreme Court confirmation hearings in 1967.

AP PHOTO/JOHN ROUS

NOW & THEN

A Pathbreaking Appointment Offers a New Look—and Possibly a New Perspective—to High Court Deliberations

? *Demographically speaking, the U.S. Supreme Court has never been a truly representative judicial body. Eventually, presidents in the twentieth century made small inroads into promoting a more diverse Court, naming justices from different religions, for example. A racially and ethnically diverse Court, by contrast, took more time. Eventually a president recognized for his dedication to racial diversity in other facets of American politics took that cause to the high Court, nominating an individual who would become the first justice hailing from this significant racial minority. Though the president's opponents in the Senate would find other grounds for opposing the nominee, there would not be enough opposition to defeat the history-making appointment. And when the new justice was finally seated on the Court, the president would rightfully take credit for having moved the Court yet another step away from its more traditional all-white moorings.*

CourseMate

227

NOW & THEN

MARK WILSON/GETTY IMAGES
NEWS/GETTY IMAGES

NOW President Barack Obama's election as the nation's forty-fourth president broke perhaps the most visible racial barrier in American politics. Building on themes from his election campaign, Obama did not downplay the potential significance his own victory offered for race relations in America. And yet other racial barriers remained. Every session of the U.S. Supreme Court between 1967 and 2008 featured a bench made up of eight Caucasians and just one African American. While the Court included two Italian Americans (Antonin Scalia and Samuel Alito), Hispanics and Latinos, who together constitute the largest nonwhite ethnic group in the nation, remained unrepresented on the Court when Obama first took office.

President Obama dramatically altered that landscape when he nominated Judge Sonia Sotomayor, a woman of Puerto Rican descent, to the Supreme Court on May 26, 2009. Once confirmed, her appointment promised to diversify the high Court and gave Obama instant credibility with a large and powerful ethnic group. The road to Sotomayor's confirmation was rocky at times: Senate Republicans complained of comments she made about how the experiences of a "wise Latina woman" might help her reach better conclusions than a "white male who hasn't lived that life." But Sotomayor's strong academic pedigree, her extensive prosecutorial experience, and her seventeen years of judicial experience combined to secure the votes of every Senate Democrat and over twenty Senate Republicans, allowing her to coast to confirmation. Would Sotomayor's unique ethnic background give her a different perspective on the hardest cases? Debates over that question would be waged in the years to come.

THEN The thirty-sixth president of the United States, Lyndon Baines Johnson, was a product of the Texas hill country; as a young politician in the 1930s and 1940s, he cut his teeth on the rough-and-tumble, sometimes racist world of Texas politics. Few would have predicted that a politician hailing from that background would one day secure a legacy right next to Abraham Lincoln as the chief executive most responsible for advancing the cause of racial equality in America. Yet Johnson rightfully earned credit for shepherding civil rights and voting rights legislation through a Congress that had once seemed impregnable to such initiatives. With that legacy secure, President Johnson went a step further in 1967, appointing the African American solicitor general, Thurgood Marshall, to the all-white U.S. Supreme Court.

Marshall's credentials to become the first African American justice seemed impeccable: the former federal appeal judge made his name as a leading Supreme Court advocate on behalf of the NAACP, having successfully argued the landmark case of *Brown v. Board of Education*, among other cases. Eleven southern senators opposed Marshall's appointment by publicly emphasizing nonracial considerations: they claimed his addition to the Court would create a "built-in activist majority" that would favor criminal defendants at the expense of the public good. But Marshall's detractors were far outnumbered, and he coasted to confirmation by a 69–11 vote. Was Marshall's voting record as a Supreme Court justice for the next twenty-four years influenced by his race and background? On this one point, Marshall's enemies and supporters would both answer in the affirmative.

AP PHOTO

Because justices serve for life, they are not normally accountable for judicial decisions rendered while on the bench. Their decisions are influenced by a number of factors: ideology, past experience as a jurist or in other government positions, and in all likelihood, the justice's personal characteristics and traits that help frame how he or she views a given set of facts or laws. Since the outset of the republic, presidents have pursued diversity for the high Court. During the nineteenth century the diversity they looked for was mostly geographical, as they sought representation for different regions; in the early part of the twentieth century, presidents sought to have different religions represented on the high Court. In recent decades presidents have occasionally emphasized ethnic and racial diversity as well. It may be impossible to prove that demographic traits and characteristics systematically affect the way a justice approaches a Supreme Court case, but presidents and senators clearly assume they will have some effect; otherwise, the emphasis on diversity would be for symbolic purposes only. No doubt Presidents Lyndon Johnson and Barack Obama thought their pathbreaking nominations of the first African American and Latina justices, respectively, would carry symbolic importance. But to cement their legacies in terms of actual judicial decision making, the two presidents and their supporters were no doubt hoping for more than just a symbolic effect.

Article III of the U.S. Constitution vests in the Supreme Court the power to decide legal cases or controversies that come before it. As one of the three primary branches of the federal government, the judiciary enjoys a special status in our constitutional system. Many scholars have suggested that courts enjoy heightened prestige over other actors in government as a result of their own conscious efforts to foster the perception that they somehow stand "above the political fray." The solemn formalities that pervade so many judicial proceedings conducted by "high priests of the law"—the black robes, the prohibition of cameras in the U.S. Supreme Court, and the general reluctance of judges to seek publicity—contribute to a mythology about courts in general and a "cult of the robe" that carries credence with many Americans.[1]

In this chapter, we explore the nature of the federal judiciary and the specific role it plays in the U.S. political system by examining types of law and the manner in which the legal system in the United States is organized. We also explore the role state courts play in the political system and how individuals come to occupy all types of judgeships. We then focus on the U.S. Supreme Court more closely, with an eye toward learning how cases come to and are resolved by the nation's highest tribunal and how that court is confronting some of the great issues of the day.

★ LO   Compare different categories of law

Types of Law

The concept of law defies simple understanding. Although law is normally defined simply as "authoritative rules made by government," the philosopher John Locke argued that certain laws precede society and government. These natural laws are God given, exist within human beings from the time they are born, and are intrinsic to the nature of individuals. Locke's notions of natural law (as distinguished from human-made or government-issued law) have influenced the legal systems of many nations, including the United States. Prior to the Civil War, opponents of slavery challenged its legitimacy with the claim that it ran counter to natural law. During the 1960s, civil rights advocates seeking to overhaul discriminatory practices presented similar arguments.

Still, even the foremost advocates of natural law concede that the rules imposed by sovereign governments enjoy some measure of legitimacy in most instances. Those rules and laws may be created and passed down in different ways. **Civil law** (also called *statutory law*) refers to legislative codes, laws, or sets of rules that are enacted by authorized lawmaking bodies such as Congress, state and local legislatures, or any executive authority entrusted with the power to make laws.[2] **Common law** refers to judge-made law handed down through judicial opinions, which establish slowly evolving precedents over time. Many European legal systems, such as those of France, Germany, and Italy, are characterized as primarily civil law systems due to their extensive reliance on detailed legislative codes. The legal system in Britain, by contrast, is recognized as mainly a common law system. The modern U.S. legal system features a combination of these two approaches. Other categories of law include the following.

- **Criminal law** is the body of rules and regulations that declare what types of conduct constitute an "offense against society" and that prescribe the punishment to be imposed for those offenses. Criminal laws against murder, rape, and burglary can be found in almost any legal system. The body of noncriminal law—which includes the law of property, contracts, and other issues dealing with the private rights of citizens—is sometimes referred to as "civil law."

- **Constitutional law** is the body of rules and judicial interpretations of rules found in the fundamental law of the nation or state, such as the Constitution of the United States. Normally, constitutional law is considered "supreme" and overrides any statutes or executive decisions with which it comes into conflict.

- **Administrative law** is the body of rules, regulations, orders, and decisions issued by administrative agencies of a government, such as the Federal Trade Commission, the Environmental Protection Agency, or a state department of health.

- **Public law**, a term used more by academics than practitioners, refers to the laws and rules that govern disputes and issues involving the government directly acting in its official capacity. Constitutional, administrative, and criminal laws are all subcategories of the general rubric of public law.

- **Private law** refers to all parts of the law concerned with the definition, regulation, and enforcement of rights in cases where either (1) all the parties directly implicated are private individuals (such as a divorce settlement) or (2) the government is acting like any other private citizen when it sues or is sued. For example, when a private person crashes his car into a government mail truck, the government's lawsuit against that person is usually a matter of private law rather than public law.

Significant overlap exists among all these categories of law. Knowing something about the different types of law is useful in helping to understand courts and the functions they serve in the American political system.

The Structure of the U.S. Legal System

Every court occupies a unique position within the larger hierarchy of state and federal courts. As a result, each court performs a variety of specific roles dictated by where it happens to be situated within the larger court structure.

Civil law
This term has two meanings: (1) legislative codes, laws, or sets of rules enacted by duly authorized lawmaking bodies such as Congress, state and local legislatures, or any executive authority entrusted with the power to make laws; (2) the body of noncriminal laws of a nation or state that deal with the rights of private citizens.

Common law
Judge-made law handed down through judicial opinions, which over time establish precedents.

State Legal Systems and State Courts

Most criminal and civil law matters in the United States first find their way into one of the fifty states' legal systems. Together, the state governments process nearly 35 million cases each year, more than 95 percent of the nation's litigation. About a third of the cases in state legal systems involve criminal matters. Each state system features its own unique characteristics and different nuances, an outgrowth of the states' different historical origins and significant population differences. Still, some common elements exist across all states.

Every state maintains trial courts, which do the bulk of work processing cases at the lower levels of the state legal system. These trial courts (often called *district courts* or *circuit courts* depending on the state or locality) may hear appeals from subordinate courts such as traffic courts; they also serve as sites for trials of more significant crimes. Thirty-nine of the fifty states have intermediate appellate courts, to which all appeals from trial courts must first be directed. All fifty states maintain at least one high supreme court. (Texas and Oklahoma have separate supreme courts for criminal and civil cases.) State supreme courts (or their equivalent of a different name) generally provide the final source of appeal for each state legal system.[3] To appeal beyond the state supreme court directly to the U.S. Supreme Court, a losing party must first exhaust all the remedies available at the state level, including the loss of his or her case at the state system's court of final appeal. He or she must also demonstrate there is a federal question at issue, whether based on the interpretation of a federal statute or of the U.S. Constitution.

In theory, state courts must comply with pronouncements from the U.S. Supreme Court over the meaning of the federal Constitution. The reality is much more complicated. During various periods of American history, rebellious state courts tried to evade certain Supreme Court pronouncements by distinguishing or limiting the Supreme Court ruling and, on occasion, even by denying the Supreme Court's jurisdiction over the matter. The Virginia Supreme Court resisted various pronouncements of the U.S. Supreme Court in the early part of the nineteenth century; more than a century later, state courts sometimes ignored U.S. Supreme Court decisions protecting the accused. Although the Supreme Court can usually exert its will over defiant state courts, it must be willing to expend key institutional resources and prestige to do so.

Development of the Federal Court System

Article III of the Constitution establishes a Supreme Court and any "inferior courts" that Congress may wish to create. Accordingly, Congress provided at the nation's outset for the creation of district and circuit courts, the latter of which bear little resemblance to modern circuit courts. Specifically, these early federal circuit courts were staffed by Supreme Court justices and district court judges, and they performed both trial and appellate functions. Thus, in addition to their formal duties on the high Court, Supreme Court justices in the early days of the republic were also required to "ride circuit," traveling to their assigned circuits on a regular basis. (This practice formally ended when Congress reestablished the U.S. Courts of Appeals in 1891.)

During the nation's early history, the Supreme Court was seen as a weak third branch of government with limited enforcement powers. With his ruling in *Marbury v. Madison* (1803),[4] Chief Justice John Marshall established the Court's power to review all acts of Congress for their constitutionality; even so, during

FIGURE 9.1 The Federal Court System*

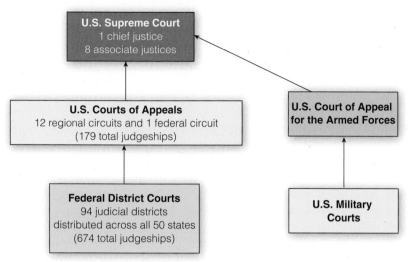

*Chart does not include specialized courts including courts of international trade, tax courts, claims courts, etc.

Marshall's thirty-four-year reign as chief justice the Court struck down just one act of Congress as unconstitutional.

Cases today begin in the federal court system, rather than the state court system, only when they fit into one of three categories: (1) the lawsuit requires interpretation of the U.S. Constitution, a federal law, or a treaty of the United States; (2) the federal government is suing or prosecuting someone or is itself being sued; or (3) the lawsuit is between two citizens of different states suing for an amount of more than $75,000. Many of the highest-profile legal cases in recent years became federal cases because they featured defendants accused of committing federal crimes.

The federal judicial system today also features a number of specialized courts, including tax courts, bankruptcy courts, and military courts. Most parties to a federal case start out in one of the ninety-four federal district courts located throughout the country. Federal district court judges have original jurisdiction (the power to rule in the first instance) over criminal and civil trials, and along with federal magistrates, they provide the initial sources of potential legal relief available in the federal judicial system.

After the federal district court has rendered its judgment, appeal is available to one of thirteen federal appeals courts (also referred to as circuit courts of appeals) across the country. With some exceptions, federal appeals are normally decided by a panel of three judges selected at random from the pool of ten or more judges authorized to serve on that court. In some cases, litigants can appeal from the three-judge panel to the full circuit court—this type of hearing is called *en banc*.

Litigants who receive an adverse judgment in the federal appeals court and wish to be heard in the U.S. Supreme Court may petition for a *writ of certiorari*, which is the pleading a losing party files with the Supreme Court asking it to review the decision of a lower court. Currently, the Supreme Court enjoys near absolute discretion over its docket, and so it remains a long shot (less than 3 percent) that it will even grant the writ of certiorari in the first place.

Petitioning the U.S. Supreme Court for review is the final option available to state court litigants who suffer adverse decisions in the highest state court and to federal court litigants who suffer adverse decisions after exhausting all forms of appeal in the federal court system. In a normal year, approximately half of the cases heard by the Supreme Court come from federal appellate courts, and the other half are from the fifty state court systems.

The Adversarial System of Justice

Some European legal systems are based on an *inquisitorial system of justice*, in which judges, working on behalf of the government, are responsible for gathering information relevant to the disposition of a particular case. For example, in France, which adheres to the inquisitorial model, judges may initiate a criminal investigation against an individual, commission experts to investigate and report on special aspects of the crime, and even call witnesses and question them intensely. By contrast, the American legal system is primarily an *adversarial system of justice*, in which opposing parties contend against each other for a result favorable to themselves. In jury trials, judges act merely as independent referees overseeing the contest; in so-called bench trials where no jury is present, judges must still remain objective arbiters as they prepare to make final decisions on the merits.[5] In an adversarial system, the judge is entrusted only with ensuring that the litigants achieve procedural fairness and plays no active role in evidence gathering or in the advocacy of one side over the other. Supporters of this system contend that adversarial proceedings pitting zealous representatives of parties against one another offer the best prospect of allowing the judge or jury to determine the truth. Critics counter that inquisitorial systems tend to be free of the many strategic "maneuvers" parties so frequently practice in U.S. courtrooms, such as withholding crucial evidence or presenting evidence that bears only a minimal relationship to the actual facts at issue.

Elements of Civil Litigation

Litigation
Any judicial contest, including all the events that lead up to a possible court event.

Plaintiff
The party that chooses to initiate formal legal proceedings in a civil case.

Complaint
A document written by the plaintiff arguing why the court is empowered to hear the case and explaining why the plaintiff is entitled to some form of relief under the current law.

Defendant
The target of a plaintiff's complaint.

Countless disputes among individuals or entities are resolved quietly, long before the threat to litigate is even invoked. Still, whenever one private party contests another over the definition or enforcement of certain legal rights or the legal relationship that may exist between them, the disagreement may wind up in the form of a lawsuit brought before a judge in a court of law. Any such judicial contest, including all the events that lead up to a possible court event, is referred to as **litigation**. Although the procedural rules governing such private disputes vary widely from state to state and system to system, some elements of civil litigation are common among all systems. Normally, the complaining party who chooses to initiate formal legal proceedings (usually called the **plaintiff**) does so by filing a **complaint**, which is a written document justifying why the court is empowered to hear the case and explaining why the plaintiff is entitled to some form of relief (usually an amount of money) under the current law. The target of the complaint, the **defendant**, normally must respond to the complaint with a formal written defense, in which he or she either admits to or denies what the plaintiff has said.

If the defendant convinces the judge either that the court has no power to hear the case (perhaps it was filed in the wrong court) or that there is no law that provides a remedy to the plaintiff, the case may be dismissed. If the defendant's argument is unsuccessful, the case then moves forward to the stage of pretrial litigation normally referred to as **discovery**. During discovery, each side has the right to find out what information the other side has about the case by requesting documents or materials, access to property, and/or examinations or by offering answers to questions about the litigation either in written form or verbally at a deposition.

The vast majority of civil disputes never make it to trial. In some cases, one party may succeed in convincing the judge that no trial is necessary and that the judge should rule in that party's favor immediately. Far more often, the sides agree to a legally binding settlement of claims made against each other, in which one side pays money to the other side or agrees to cease and desist a certain practice to avoid the costs and uncertainties of trial. In civil litigation, judges often play an active role in encouraging the two parties to settle their differences out of court, saving resources for them and the judicial branch that would have been wasted in a long, drawn-out trial.

In some instances, the parties are not able to reach an out-of-court settlement, and a formal trial becomes necessary. In a bench trial, the parties present evidence to a judge rather than to a jury of citizens. A jury trial usually takes far longer than a bench trial because of the many procedures required to prevent undue prejudice of the jury. Even if a jury trial is necessary, the judge still plays a role in the courtroom by ensuring that the jury is properly selected and that fair procedures are adhered to during the trial. One of the most crucial roles played by a judge in either type of trial is to rule on the admissibility of evidence that may be used to reach a decision. Only relevant evidence, which logically tends to prove or disprove a disputed fact, may be admitted into the trial proceedings. In civil cases, the complaining party is obligated to prove its allegations by a preponderance of the evidence, which is generally thought to be anything greater than 50 percent. Although there is widespread disagreement on what this standard exactly means, it is clearly well below the high standard imposed on prosecutors in criminal cases to prove guilt beyond a reasonable doubt.

Once the judge or jury has reached a final decision on the case, normally called the *verdict* in the case of a jury trial or the *judgment* in a bench trial, and the judge or jury has settled on a monetary amount to be awarded, the trial stage of the process comes to an end. Some posttrial motions may be available, and a dissatisfied party is also free to appeal the decision to a higher court.

The Criminal Justice System at Work

Most criminal prosecutions begin with the arrest of a suspect by some law enforcement official at the federal, state, or local level. Once the suspect is formally accused, he or she is also referred to as the defendant. Because some criminal charges may be later revealed as groundless or unsubstantiated, the government must quickly demonstrate in one of two ways that the charges against the defendant are valid. Some prosecutors elect to present initial evidence at a preliminary hearing held before a magistrate or trial judge, where they must demonstrate that there is probable cause to proceed to trial against the suspect. Far more often, the prosecutor convenes a **grand jury**, whose duty is to receive complaints, hear the evidence offered by the prosecutor, and

Discovery
A stage of pretrial litigation in which the plaintiff and defendant have the right to learn what information the other side has about the case by requesting documents or materials, access to property, and/or examinations, or by offering answers to questions about the litigation either in written form or verbally at a deposition.

★ LO
Understand the criminal justice system

Grand jury
A jury whose duty it is to hear the evidence offered by a prosecutor and determine whether a trial is justified.

Indictment
A decision by a grand jury authorizing the government to proceed to trial against the defendant.

Plea bargain
A pretrial negotiated resolution in a criminal case in which the defendants seek to reduce their jail sentences by pleading guilty and in return prosecutors are willing to trade down the severity of the punishment.

determine whether a trial is justified. In the overwhelming majority of cases, the grand jury does indeed return a bill of **indictment** authorizing the government to proceed to trial against the defendant.

Most criminal prosecutions in the United States are resolved through a negotiated **plea bargain** between the defendant and the prosecutor.[6] Indeed, over 90 percent of all convictions are the direct product of negotiated plea bargains. Many defendants seek to reduce their jail sentences by entering plea agreements that lead to smaller punishments. Much of the negotiation that occurs between prosecutors and defense attorneys is over the appropriate charges that will be formally filed, as most courts have adopted the equivalent of "going rates" for particular crimes.[7] Prosecutors willingly trade down penalties for crimes either because they are seeking that defendant's cooperation at another trial or because they wish to avoid the uncertainty and huge expenditure of resources that come with a trial.

In criminal cases that do go to trial, the burden rests squarely on the prosecutor to prove that the defendant committed the crime "beyond a reasonable doubt." Defendants, by contrast, do not have to prove their innocence. Unless a defendant waives the right to a jury trial, she or he must be tried by a jury of peers. State courts require anywhere between six and twelve jurors, whereas the federal court system require twelve jurors in all cases where a jury is present. The Sixth Amendment has been interpreted to guarantee each indigent defendant the right to a government-provided lawyer in any instance where they face the possibility of jail time. Unfortunately, many public defenders' offices are overworked and underfunded, placing defendants at a relative disadvantage. By comparison, wealthy or well-connected defendants who do enjoy access to top legal talent and other resources at trial often fare much better. Clearly, the American legal system does not always offer the same types of outcomes to those who are not similarly situated or well connected.

Former football star O. J. Simpson (left) confers with his "dream team" of high-priced legal talent at his murder trial in 1995.

POOL/GETTY IMAGES

★ LO Define the power of judicial review

Judicial Review and Its Implications

Courts in general, and judges in particular, serve in a variety of capacities: supervising the disposition of legal controversies between private parties, overseeing preliminary hearings or trials of criminal defendants, and ruling on important issues concerning the procedures to be followed or the evidence to be introduced at trial. Indeed, the role many judges play as independent magistrates is fundamental to the effective functioning of the American legal system. But courts and judges also play a significant and far-reaching role in overseeing the operations of the other branches of government, both by supervising conflicts between those branches and by protecting citizens against government action that may violate the Constitution.

Criminal Defense Attorneys as Heroes of the American Cinema

Few real-life criminal defense attorneys are likely to win popularity contests any time soon: After all, within the criminal justice system, they are the ones normally responsible for helping criminal defendants escape jail on technicalities. Yet when the public goes to the movies, the heroic image of the criminal defense attorney tends to predominate. In numerous Oscar-winning performances, the criminal defense attorney is the one who fights for a heroic cause (his or her factually innocent defendant) against the evil government, prosecutors, and lying witnesses who are seeking victory at all costs. The most famous of these cinematic attorneys was the character of Atticus Finch (played by Gregory Peck), who defended an innocent African American defendant in a racist Southern town in *To Kill a Mockingbird* (1962). Other defense attorneys followed in Atticus Finch's footsteps on the big screen, including Jake Brigance (played by Matthew McConaughey) in *A Time to Kill* (1996) and the irrepressible Vinny Gambini (played by Joe Pesci) in *My Cousin Vinny* (1992).

UNIVERSAL STUDIOS/GETTY IMAGES

Actor Gregory Peck as Atticus Finch in *To Kill a Mockingbird*.

For Critical Thinking and Discussion

1. Are criminal defense attorneys unfairly celebrated on the big screen?

2. Can you think of any examples in which a criminal defense attorney was *not* afforded heroic status in a full-length movie feature?

3. Why do you think popular culture tends to boil the criminal justice system down to a simple battle between good (defense attorneys) and evil? Are there any dangers to this pattern?

This judicial authority has been magnified by the general recognition that American courts enjoy the added power of **judicial review**, by which they may declare acts of the other branches of the federal or state governments unconstitutional and thus invalid. This dimension of judicial authority is not mentioned anywhere in the U.S. Constitution.

The power of the Supreme Court to exercise judicial review was first established by the fourth chief justice of the United States, John Marshall, in the highly controversial case of *Marbury v. Madison* (1803).[8] In his final hours as president, John Adams, a Federalist, appointed sixteen circuit court judges and forty-two new justices of the peace for the District of Columbia (all loyal Federalists). Immediately after Thomas Jefferson and his Secretary of State James Madison formally took office in March 1801, they learned that several of the commissions for the new justices of the peace appointed by Adams had never been delivered—including one for William Marbury. Preferring that fellow Jeffersonian Republicans get the judicial posts, Jefferson ordered Madison to withhold the commissions. Marbury then asked the Supreme Court to issue a *writ of mandamus*, a judicial order commanding an official (in this case,

Judicial review
The power of a court to declare acts of the other branches of government or of a subordinate government to be unconstitutional and thus invalid.

Madison) to perform a ministerial duty over which his discretion is limited (namely, the formal delivery of a duly signed and sealed commission). As authority for the Supreme Court's power to issue such a writ, Marbury cited the Judiciary Act of 1789, which appeared to give the U.S. Supreme Court exactly that authority.

Marbury assumed the Court, composed of fellow Federalists including Chief Justice John Marshall, would be sympathetic to his plight. In truth, it was Marshall who was really at fault in the case; as Adams's secretary of state, he had failed to properly mail the commission. (Marshall should have recused himself from the case, refusing to participate as a judge in the first place.) Yet the Supreme Court rejected Marbury's request. Recognizing the tense political situation that surrounded the case—and all too aware that Jefferson might not abide by court order—Marshall lambasted the Jefferson administration for its refusal to perform their statutorily mandated duty but denied that the Supreme Court possessed the power to issue the writ as requested.

Why the refusal to help his fellow Federalist? Marshall acknowledged that the 1789 law did in fact authorize the Court to issue such a writ in "original jurisdiction." But, Marshall ruled, that law was in explicit violation of Article III, Section 2, Clause 2, which did not specifically list "writs of mandamus" among the types of cases over which the Supreme Court had original jurisdiction. Nor could Congress extend the Court's original jurisdiction by mere statute. Thus, Marshall decided, the 1789 law was repugnant to the Constitution and was therefore null and void. With this decision, Marshall seized for the Court a power of judicial review over congressional laws that is unmentioned in the Constitution. The Supreme Court exercised this power only once more before the Civil War, although it has struck down well over 150 acts of Congress since then.

Two rulings more than a decade later further established the Supreme Court's authority in interpreting the Constitution. In *McCulloch v. Maryland* (1819),[9] the Court upheld the constitutionality of the Bank of the United States, thereby establishing the precedent that congressional power extends beyond those powers specifically listed in Article I of the Constitution. In *Martin v. Hunter's Lessee* (1816),[10] the Supreme Court ruled that the power of federal courts to review government actions for their constitutionality was not just applicable to other federal institutions; the supremacy clause ("The Constitution . . . shall be the Supreme Law of the Land") meant that the Supreme Court could also invalidate any actions of state governments that it believed were in conflict with the U.S. Constitution. In the two centuries since Marshall served as chief justice, the Supreme Court has invalidated more than 1,200 state laws. In 1958, it once again reaffirmed the principle of judicial supremacy in *Cooper v. Aaron*[11] in response to official defiance of a lower court's desegregation rulings: Governors and state legislatures were bound to uphold decisions of the Supreme Court just as they were bound by oath to uphold the Constitution.

★ LO Recognize the structural limitations on courts

Limitations on Courts

In Federalist No. 78, Alexander Hamilton deemed the judiciary "the least dangerous" branch because it had "no influence over either the sword or the purse . . . and can take no active resolution whatsoever." Despite Hamilton's opinion, courts have played a critically influential role in the American political system. When the Supreme Court aggressively interposes itself between aggrieved citizens and the government, as it did when it ordered desegregation of public schools in *Brown v. Board of Education* (1954),[12] or when it helps resolve some great political crisis, as it did when it ordered President Richard Nixon to hand over controversial tapes of White House conversations in *United States v. Nixon* (1974),[13] the judiciary appears more like an all-powerful branch than one that is weak and inconsequential.

© 2012 CENGAGE LEARNING

The power of American courts is great, but the method by which courts participate in the political system is far more circumscribed than that of the other two branches. The limitations that courts must adhere to include the following:

1. **Courts cannot initiate or maintain lawsuits.** Unlike legislatures, which can propose and pass bills on their own initiative, judges in the United States cannot decide issues that are not currently before them in a legitimately filed lawsuit. If none of the actors in a controversy elect to involve the courts directly, the court has no role whatsoever in resolving the conflict.

2. **Courts can hear only those lawsuits that constitute true "cases" or "controversies."** Article III imposes on the Supreme Court and all federal courts the same type of limitation that applies to nearly all other courts: Judges may hear and resolve only those lawsuits that amount to legitimate "cases" or "controversies" and must ignore mere "hypothetical" or "theoretical" conflicts. In practice, courts tend to refuse to decide lawsuits that are moot (that is, it is too late to provide any effective remedy) or to decide cases that are not yet ripe (that is, the actual conflict is still sometime in the future). Accordingly, courts normally refuse to provide executives with what amounts to "legal advice" about future controversies that have not yet occurred.

   The courts have also maintained a long-standing tradition of refusing to decide cases where the Constitution has explicitly entrusted the issue to be decided by one of the other branches of government; such issues are generally referred to as "political questions.".Related to the "case or controversy" rule is a requirement that courts impose on the parties themselves: Courts will hear lawsuits only from parties that have proper **standing**, meaning that they are "uniquely" and "singularly affected" by the controversy. For example, courts usually reject lawsuits brought by individuals who are frustrated with the allotment of their tax dollars because those individuals are not "singularly affected." Congress and many state legislatures have loosened these harsh standing requirements by authorizing lawsuits brought by large numbers of people with clearly defined common interests. Such **class action lawsuits** can proceed through the legal system even when not every member of the class has formally signed on. High-visibility class action lawsuits in recent years include those brought by tobacco users across the country and those by people who have suffered from the effects of asbestos.

3. **Courts must rely on other branches for enforcement.** Unlike the other branches of government, courts rely on other political institutions to put their opinions or orders into direct effect; police officers, marshals, and executive branch officers, among others, must carry out the courts' mandates. In some rare cases, a court's decisions may be met with outright disobedience.

   Controversial Supreme Court decisions in the 1950s and 1960s occasionally led to significant resistance on the part of ordinary citizens as

Standing
The requirement that a party must be uniquely or singularly affected by a controversy in order to be eligible to file a lawsuit.

Class action lawsuit
A lawsuit filed by a large group of people with clearly defined common interests.

well.[14] The landmark decisions in *Brown v. Board of Education*, which first held that segregated public schools violated the equal protection clause and then commanded that public schools be desegregated "with all deliberate speed," met with violent reaction in the South. Ultimately, President Dwight Eisenhower sent U.S. marshals to the South to enforce the desegregation decrees; otherwise, there might have been even greater resistance to the Court's controversial decisions. The Supreme Court's 1962 decision invalidating school-sponsored religious prayer in public schools (*Engel v. Vitale*)[15] is ignored in many parts of this country even today. In one instance, a federal district court in Alabama was forced to prohibit prayer in public schools throughout the state in response to reports of widespread defiance.

Appellate jurisdiction
The authority of a court to review decisions handed down by another court.

Original jurisdiction
The authority of a court to be the initial court in which a legal decision is rendered.

In addition to these limitations, courts must also adhere to limitations that arise from the constitutional or statutory law. For example, Congress can by statute alter the Supreme Court's **appellate jurisdiction**, which is the power to review prior decisions handed down by state and lower federal courts. Thus Congress could in theory declare that federal courts as a whole are not empowered to hear abortion cases. In fact, foes of the Supreme Court's abortion decisions proposed just such a bill in the 1980s, but it was never passed. However, Congress cannot alter the Court's **original jurisdiction**, which is the power to hear a lawsuit at the outset. Article III authorizes the Court's original jurisdiction in cases involving ambassadors and cases in which states are the only parties.

★ LO Learn how state judges are selected

Electing and Appointing Judges

The state and federal court systems differ dramatically in the way judges are selected. State court judges tend to be selected in one of five ways. Some states hold partisan elections, with prospective and sitting justices required to campaign for their party's nomination and then to run in a general election. Many other states hold nonpartisan elections, in which party designations are eliminated from the election process. The "Missouri Plan," or merit plan selection process, features a three-step process in which a judicial nominating commission initially screens candidates and then submits a list of three potential nominees to the governor, who then selects the judge from the list. Shortly thereafter, the new judge must secure voter approval in a nonpartisan retention election.[16] Several other states authorize gubernatorial appointment of judges, in which the governor appoints judges, subject to approval of the state senate. Finally, a handful of states require that the state legislature appoint judges.

The selection of federal judges follows a more universal formula: All federal district court judges, federal appeals court judges, and Supreme Court justices are appointed by the president, subject to confirmation by a majority vote in the U.S. Senate. Whereas the Constitution dictates this formula for appointment of Supreme Court justices, Congress in its discretion authorized the appointment of lower federal court judges to require the Senate's advice and consent as well. Because all federal judges and Supreme Court justices hold their offices during "good behavior"—the functional equivalent of life tenure—they are thought of as more independent than those state judges who must run for reelection. In fact, the retention rate for state judges is often so high (due to low voter turnout and other factors) that even elected state judges tend to enjoy a large degree of independence in rendering decisions.

The Nomination Process

Learn how federal judges and Supreme Court justices are selected

★ LO

During a single term in office, a president can expect to make hundreds of federal judicial appointments. In practice, a tradition of deference to home-state senators (often called "senatorial courtesy") provides legislators in the upper chamber—especially those hailing from the president's party—with considerable influence over the selection of district court judges in their own states. (Senatorial courtesy also has a more limited impact on the selection of appeals court judges, as circuits cross individual state boundaries.) In recent decades, presidents have not only relied on senators' recommendations to generate nominees for judgeships, but they also consider ideological factors and the personal characteristics of potential nominees.

Some modern presidents have sought to place their own ideological stamp on the lower courts (whether liberal or conservative) by utilizing a committee of White House and Department of Justice attorneys to screen and suggest candidates.[17] The Reagan and George W. Bush administrations were especially active in seeking to use the appointment of lower court judges as a means of moving the constitutional landscape in a conservative ideological direction. When the presidency and the Senate are held by different parties, battles over judicial nominees may become especially fierce. In 2002 and 2007–2008, the Democrat-controlled Senate Judiciary Committee gave heightened scrutiny to President George W. Bush's more conservative nominees. Though in the minority, Senate Republicans sought to return the favor to President Obama, delaying many of his lower court nominees in 2009 and 2010.

Given its place atop the U.S. legal system, vacancies on the U.S. Supreme Court tend to draw far more political attention than do other judicial vacancies. Because the president, the U.S. Senate, and the media follow personnel changes on the Supreme Court far more closely, the process by which justices are nominated and confirmed is a major news event.

CHIP SOMODEVILLA/GETTY IMAGES NEWS/GETTY IMAGES

President Barack Obama introduces his second nominee to the U.S. Supreme Court, Elena Kagan, in 2010.

STEVE PETTEWAY, COLLECTION OF THE SUPREME COURT OF THE UNITED STATES

The U.S. Supreme Court Justices, as pictured at the start of the Court's Fall 2010 term. Standing, from left to right: Sonia Sotomayor, Stephen Breyer, Samuel Alito, and Elena Kagan. Seated, from left to right: Clarence Thomas, Antonin Scalia, John Roberts (Chief Justice), Anthony Kennedy, and Ruth Bader Ginsburg.

TABLE 9.1 Current Membership of the U.S. Supreme Court

Member	Gender	Position	Date Born	Year Appointed (President)	Law School	Party	Religion
John Roberts	M	Chief Justice	1/27/55	2005 (Bush II)	Harvard	Republican	Roman Catholic
Antonin Scalia	M	Associate Justice	3/11/36	1986 (Reagan)	Harvard	Republican	Roman Catholic
Anthony Kennedy	M	Associate Justice	7/23/36	1988 (Reagan)	Harvard	Republican	Roman Catholic
Clarence Thomas	M	Associate Justice	6/23/48	1991 (Bush I)	Yale	Republican	Roman Catholic*
Ruth Bader Ginsburg	F	Associate Justice	3/15/33	1993 (Clinton)	Harvard/Columbia	Democrat	Jewish
Stephen Breyer	M	Associate Justice	8/15/38	1994 (Clinton)	Harvard	Democrat	Jewish
Samuel Alito	M	Associate Justice	4/1/50	2006 (Bush II)	Yale	Republican	Roman Catholic
Sonia Sotomayor	F	Associate Justice	6/25/54	2009 (Obama)	Yale	Democrat	Roman Catholic
Elena Kagan	F	Associate Justice	4/28/60	2010 (Obama)	Harvard	Democrat	Jewish

* At the time of his 1991 appointment, Clarence Thomas regularly attended an Episcopal church but later returned to Roman Catholicism, the faith in which he had been raised.

In choosing nominees to the high Court, presidents in recent decades have considered several factors:

- **The nominee's ideological and policy preferences.** This factor has enjoyed a place of special importance in presidential calculations. A nominee's views on abortion, school prayer, and other hot-button issues may well tip the balance of the Court in favor of the president's stated views.

- **Judicial competence.** Most presidents have an interest in appointing especially qualified candidates for the high Court, if only because it assists in speeding along the confirmation process. The American Bar Association (ABA), an interest group of lawyers, rates candidates for every federal judicial vacancy on a scale from "highly qualified" to "not qualified" on the basis of their legal background and accomplishments. Ethical considerations may also be considered because the ABA may be reluctant to approve candidates who have previously been convicted of crimes, for example. Although a negative rating from the ABA does not always eliminate a candidate, it may present significant obstacles in the Senate confirmation process. Early in his first term, President George W. Bush announced that he would no longer vet judicial candidates through the ABA prior to their formal nomination.

- **Political loyalty.** Although loyalty has diminished somewhat as a priority in recent years, presidents still occasionally practice old-fashioned politics in the selection of Supreme Court nominees, choosing a justice based on a background of service to the president's party or to the president. During the twentieth century, well over 90 percent of all Supreme Court nominees were members of the president's political party.

- **Demographic factors.** A president may choose a candidate for the diversity the nominee adds to the demographics of the current Supreme Court.[18] As was noted at the outset of this chapter, Lyndon Johnson appointed Thurgood Marshall as the first African American to the Court in 1967; Ronald Reagan appointed Sandra Day O'Connor as the first female justice in 1981; and President Obama appointed Sonia Sotomayor as the first Latina justice in 2009. Obama also appointed a second female, Elena Kagan, to the Court the following year, bringing the number of women on the Court up to three for the time being. The selection of nominees who can diversify the Court may pay political dividends for the White House as well: The president may be counting on such nominations to build support among certain groups.

- **The current political environment.** Supreme Court vacancies do not occur in a vacuum; presidents are well aware of the political conditions that surround a particular Court vacancy, and more often than not, they respond to it through their nomination choices. Such factors as low presidential approval ratings, a Senate controlled by the political opposition, or the need to achieve other legislative proposals may convince the president to select a more moderate or less controversial nominee.

The Confirmation Process

Until the late 1960s, most confirmation processes tended to be little noticed events, drawing little public attention or press coverage. Beginning at that time, however, with the growth of federal regulatory schemes placing more and more cases in the federal courts, presidents began to routinely utilize judicial appointments as a means of shaping public policy. The confirmation process for those nominees was simultaneously opened up to unprecedented high levels of public scrutiny. All hearings for Supreme Court nominees have been televised live on C-SPAN since 1981. Interest groups have become increasingly active in confirmation proceedings, lobbying senators directly and testifying in favor of or against particular nominees. With the ideological stakes raised, presidents and their aides have become increasingly active in lobbying for their nominees.[19]

The Senate confirms the vast majority of Supreme Court nominees; between 1900 and 2010, fifty-nine of the sixty-three Supreme Court candidates who came up for a formal Senate vote on their respective nominations were confirmed. Nevertheless, controversial nominees in recent decades have experienced their share of public scrutiny—and in some cases, humiliation—when subjected to the glare of the confirmation process. Ronald Reagan's nomination of Judge Robert Bork to the Supreme Court in 1987 was defeated in the Senate amid a cloud of interest group cries that Bork would reverse liberal precedents on free speech

PABLO MARTINEZ MONSIVAIS/ASSOCIATED PRESS

John Roberts, nominee for chief justice of the United States, testifying before the Senate Judiciary Committee in September 2005.

Still a Nation Where Anyone Can Grow Up to Be a Supreme Court Justice . . .

Sonia Sotomayor, age 7.

Justice Sonia Sotomayor.

When Supreme Court nominee Sonia Sotomayor went before the Senate Judiciary Committee during the summer of 2009, the symbolism of her nomination was obscured somewhat by the storm of political rhetoric flying in every direction. From the right came accusations that she would allow her gender and ethnicity to affect her decision making, and from the left came countercharges that critics were judging Sotomayor by a double standard as she was forced to appear bland and "mainstream" even while Latin Americans were celebrating the meaning of her pathbreaking nomination.

Foreigners—especially those who hail from countries with a rich heritage of aristocracy and royalty—were perhaps less likely to ignore the symbolism of Sotomayor's "rags to riches" story. Just consider this commentary from BBC News Editor Justin Webb, who returned to the United Kingdom in 2009 after spending eight years as BBC's Washington-based editor.

Out on route 17 in South Carolina, you can do very well or very badly. You can crash and burn, or you can fill up with cheap petrol and ride off into the sunset. If you do not like yourself in South Carolina, you can hire a self-drive hire truck and take it to Seattle. If you do not like your life and you have drive and luck, you can change it because—being American—you believe you can change it. Sitting in a dingy apartment in New York

watching Perry Mason on the TV, you can decide to make it big in law as eight-year-old Sonia Sotomayor once did. This summer, now in her fifties, she becomes a Supreme Court justice and the latest American story to send shivers down the spines of dreamers of the American dream.

But if Sonia Sotomayor is to make it big, there must be something creating the drive, and part of that something is the poverty of the alternative, the discomfort of the ordinary lives that most Americans endure and the freedom that Americans have to go to hell if that is the decision they take.

Source: Justin Webb, "Checking out of 'Hotel America,'" BBC website, August 1, 2009, accessed at http://news.bbc.co.uk/2/hi/programmes/from_our_own_correspondent/8176448.stm.

---

and abortion.[20] Bork, a former Yale law professor, sported a record of opposition to many Supreme Court doctrines supported by political liberals, including the doctrine of constitutionally protected abortion rights that the Court articulated in *Roe v. Wade* (1973).

The Senate eventually defeated Bork's nomination by a 58–42 vote. Presidents since then have come to understand the new politics of judicial confirmations, working closely with interest groups to mount their own campaigns in favor of judicial nominees. The Bork nomination gave rise to a new term in Washington's political lexicon—"to Bork"—which defines the act of challenging a president's nominee through well-financed and organized interest group opposition. The Bork confirmation fiasco also encouraged subsequent presidents to favor nominees who either possess no paper trail at all or who would be far more circumspect than Bork in their willingness to engage the Senate on constitutional issues.

In recent years, the confirmation process for lower court nominees has been politicized as well, with battles waged with extra ferocity over appointments to the U.S. courts of appeals. Before the Democrats regained control of Congress in the 2006 midterm elections, Senate Democrats opposed to some of George W. Bush's nominees on ideological grounds began to take advantage of Senate rules to stop votes on contested nominees. Specifically, they utilized the filibuster to block ten of President Bush's appellate court nominees during his first term in office. Bush renominated nine of those blocked nominees at the start of his second term, and a frustrated Republican Senate leadership began to consider rule changes to foreclose the use of filibusters against future nominees. Senate Democrats referred to any such rule change as the "nuclear option" because they were prepared to respond by shutting down Senate business through use of the filibuster rule in all other instances. On May 24, 2005, this growing crisis was averted, as a group of fourteen moderate senators (seven Republicans and seven Democrats) settled on a plan to allow several of Bush's most controversial nominees to be confirmed in return for the promise that the filibuster would be reserved for use against judicial appointments when there are "extraordinary circumstances."

How a Case Proceeds within the U.S. Supreme Court

★ LO

Follow a Supreme Court case as it proceeds from writ of certiorari to final opinion

The vast majority of cases that come before the U.S. Supreme Court arrive by a **writ of certiorari**, the formal term for an order by which the Court acts in its discretion to hear a case on appeal. Losing parties in the highest state court, a federal circuit court, or, in extremely rare cases, a federal district court can properly file a "cert petition" with the Supreme Court, asking the Court to hear its case. Decisions to grant a writ of certiorari generally follow the *Rule of Four*: If four of the nine justices vote to hear the case, it is placed on the Court's official docket of cases that it will hear during the coming year. Of the many thousands of cert petitions that arrive at the Court during a given year, barely more than 1 percent (fewer than ninety overall) are normally granted.

In theory, the justices decide to hear only those cases considered so important that they justify intervention at such a high level. Two other factors may also increase the likelihood that the Supreme Court will grant a writ of certiorari: (1) when the federal government intervenes in the case or (2) when there is a split among two or more of the U.S. circuit courts of appeals on a similar issue. Denial of a cert petition theoretically casts no aspersions whatsoever on whether a case has been wrongly or rightly decided, although it does allow the lower court decision to stand as the controlling legal decision for the parties in that case. For example, the Supreme Court's 1997 denial of a cert petition in a case concerning affirmative action at the University of Texas did not necessarily imply high Court

Writ of certiorari
The formal term for an order by which the Supreme Court acts in its discretion to review a case from a lower court.

Briefs
Written documents filed by parties in an appealed case arguing why constitutional or statutory law weighs in favor of their respective positions.

Amicus curiae briefs
Written documents filed by outside parties in the case with an interest in the outcome of the litigation expressing their own views on how the Court should decide a particular case.

Solicitor general
The lawyer representing the U.S. government before the U.S. Supreme Court.

dissatisfaction with affirmative action; rather, it simply left intact a U.S. Court of Appeals decision that applied only to the three states in that circuit: Texas, Mississippi, and Louisiana. The U.S. Supreme Court waited until six years later to articulate new rules for affirmative action that would become applicable in all fifty states.

If the Court elects to issue a writ of certiorari and hear a case, both the losing and winning parties in the lower court file written documents called **briefs** arguing why constitutional or federal statutory law weighs in favor of their respective positions. Outside parties with an interest in the litigation may also elect to file briefs, known formally as **amicus curiae briefs** (*amicus curiae* is Latin for "friend of the court"), expressing their own views on how the Court should decide a particular case.

The **solicitor general** argues on behalf of the U.S. government in most cases when the federal government is a party. That office also stands among the most

FIGURE 9.2 From Cert Petition to Final Judgment in the U.S. Supreme Court

In some exceptionally rare cases, a final judgment from a federal district court may receive expedited review from the U.S. Supreme Court and thus bypass the U.S. Court of Appeals.

influential "friends of the court," filing amicus briefs on behalf of the federal government in approximately a quarter of all cases heard by the Supreme Court each year. Acting through the solicitor general, the U.S. government has enjoyed a disproportionate share of success in affecting Supreme Court case discretionary grants of review and case outcomes.[21]

After all party and amicus briefs have been filed, the Supreme Court justices normally hear oral arguments from opposing counsel in the Supreme Court's chamber. Attorneys licensed to practice before the Supreme Court present their client's view of the law and facts within an allotted period of time (normally thirty minutes); most of that time is spent answering questions and inquiries from the justices. If a justice is truly undecided, he or she may be affected in the margins by the positions of advocates at oral arguments; the give-and-take with the lawyers may also suggest ways to more effectively draft the final opinion. Still, there remains little evidence that the oral arguments actually shift the votes of most justices.

Shortly after the oral arguments are completed and the case has been formally submitted, the justices meet in conference to discuss the case, offer initial votes, and assign opinions. The chief justice presides over all conferences, which culminate in the assignment of opinions to be researched and written by individual justices in accordance with the conference discussions. Each justice employs four clerks—selected from a pool of the top law school graduates from across the country—who work behind the scenes researching the law and creating initial drafts of written opinions according to the justice's specific wishes. In some cases, clerks enjoy even more influence over the justices they work for, assisting them as they sort through competing legal arguments.

A **majority opinion** requires agreement of at least five of the Court's nine members; only a majority opinion carries the force of law. The chief justice has just one vote like the associate justices, but a chief justice in agreement with the majority also has the crucial power to choose who will write the Court's main opinion. (If the chief justice is not in the majority, the senior-most associate justice in the majority retains that power of assignment.) Individual justices may choose to write other opinions either on their own or on behalf of a minority of justices. A **concurring opinion** agrees with the end result reached by the majority but disagrees with the reasons offered for the decision. A **dissenting opinion**, on the other hand, disagrees with the result reached by the majority. Justices write concurring and dissenting opinions both to register their differences with the majority and to lay the groundwork for the future, when those alternative grounds may one day secure the support of a Court majority.

Why the Justices Vote the Way They Do

Although it is difficult to determine what causes Supreme Court justices to vote as they do on certain issues, social scientists and legal scholars have identified a number of factors that may play a role in a judge's decision making.

- **Legal rules and precedents.** The law itself—including constitutional law, statutes, rules and regulations, and past court decisions interpreting those sources—may be unambiguous enough to counsel one particular application to the case at hand. Previous court decisions are especially hard to avoid; when judges follow the decisions of past judges ruling in similar cases, they

Majority opinion
The opinion of a majority of members of the U.S. Supreme Court, which carries the force of law.

Concurring opinion
The opinion of one or more justices that agrees with the end result reached by the majority but disagrees with the reasons offered for the decision.

Dissenting opinion
The opinion of one or more justices who disagree with the result reached by the majority.

★ LO

Examine the factors that influence judges

Cases That Kept a Nation on Edge

Decisions of the U.S. Supreme Court are often highly watched and frequently have a profound impact on the political system. Sometimes, a decision of the Court is characterized by both high visibility and huge consequences. Following are three points in the nation's history when all eyes were on the Supreme Court's decision.

In 1819, the nation was suffering from a financial panic brought on by intense inflation, overextended investments in manufacturing, the collapse of foreign markets, and the contraction of credit nationwide. Exacerbating these ills was the mismanagement of the Second Bank of the United States, which had been chartered by Congress in part to provide stability during just such a crisis. In fact, the national bank had also increased the hardship on state banks by offering competition for scarce resources. When several states passed laws that either taxed the national bank or restricted its operations, the very constitutionality of a national bank came under question in a case (*McCulloch v. Maryland*) that weaved its way up to the U.S. Supreme Court. The economic solvency of various state banks rested on the Court's decision, and many eagerly awaited the Court's verdict. The suspense ended in 1819, when John Marshall, speaking for a unanimous Court, upheld the national bank of the United States as constitutional and rendered it immune from inferior entities.

In 1951, Americans were gripped by a "red scare" brought on by rising tensions in the Cold War with the Soviet Union. Back at home, Senator Joseph McCarthy (R-WI) was charging that communists had infiltrated the Department of State and the U.S. Army. Two years earlier, eleven top leaders of the U.S. Communist Party had been convicted in a high-profile trial for violating the Smith Act of 1940, which made it a crime to "knowingly and willfully advocate" the necessity or propriety of overthrowing the government. All eleven appealed their convictions to the U.S. Supreme Court, claiming that the Smith Act violated the First Amendment guarantee of freedom of speech. McCarthy's forces triumphed: The Court ruled on June 4, 1951, that the First Amendment did not bar the government from making the advocacy of violent overthrow of the government a criminal act. McCarthy's personal comeuppance would have to wait three and a half more years until December 1954, when the Senate voted to censure McCarthy for his abusive conduct by a 67–22 vote.

In 2000, more than a month after Election Day, Florida's twenty-five electoral votes remained up for grabs between presidential contenders George W. Bush and Al Gore. Although an electronic recount of the state's ballots indicated that Bush held a slim lead, Gore claimed that voter confusion had led the machine recount to inaccurately record the "intent of the voter," and his lawyers demanded a manual recount of the ballots in four counties. The Florida supreme court agreed with Gore's position, but the U.S. Supreme Court stopped the recount and agreed to hear the case on expedited review. With a nation of citizens left wondering if the outcome of the election would be resolved in time for the January inauguration, a narrowly divided Supreme Court issued its 5–4 decision on the evening of December 12, 2000. The Court's five more conservative justices ruled that a manual recount of the ballots in the disputed counties would violate the Constitution's equal protection clause and was thus invalid. With no time left to conduct a complete manual recount of the ballots in the entire state under a more uniform standard, Gore conceded the election the following evening to Bush. Five weeks later, Bush was sworn in as the forty-third president of the United States.

are adhering to the long-standing doctrine of *stare decisis*, which is Latin for "stand by the decision" that has already been settled. For example, although Justice Byron White dissented from the original decision in *Miranda v. Arizona* (1966)[22] providing unprecedented rights to the accused, in later decisions he actively applied the *Miranda* holding to other cases, deferring to a high Court precedent that he personally opposed.

- **Changes in circumstances.** Sometimes, changes in real-life conditions and circumstances may influence how laws are interpreted. In the school desegregation cases of the 1950s, the Supreme Court openly considered the newly discovered harmful effects of segregation on African American children. Similarly, in 1973, the Supreme Court took into account changes in modern medicine when it formulated the definition of constitutionally protected abortion rights in *Roe v. Wade*. Some jurists and scholars believe such changes in circumstances are irrelevant; rather, they view the Constitution as fixed in time and thus limited in scope to what the framers envisioned. The search for the framers' original intent about the Constitution is often referred to as *originalism*. By contrast, other judges and scholars advocate the more flexible view of the Constitution as a "living, breathing document," which must adapt to changing circumstances and conditions.

- **Ideological "attitudes."** Many political scientists argue that Supreme Court justices' personal attitudes (liberal or conservative on law enforcement issues, free speech, and so forth) influence their judicial decision making. This model of understanding how justices decide cases has been labeled "the attitudinal model." Defenders of the model cite numerous statistics that support their understanding of the way judges decide cases. For example, William O. Douglas was a New Deal liberal who voted in the liberal direction in criminal procedure cases nearly 90 percent of the time and in civil rights cases 93 percent of the time.[23]

- **Personal traits and characteristics.** Males and females may approach political events differently; accordingly, the gender of a Supreme Court justice affects his or her reaction to legal issues and cases to some degree. Just as some demographic groups tend to be more conservative, justices who fit into those groups may be expected to vote accordingly. A justice's personal experiences may also play a role in how he or she judges. Biographers of Justice Oliver Wendell Holmes, for example, contend that Holmes's near-death experiences as a soldier in the Civil War colored his approach to judging.[24]

- **Intracourt politics.** A justice's interest in maintaining good relations with fellow justices may push him or her to vote in a certain way; behind-the-scenes bargaining and negotiating have also been features of Supreme Court politics throughout its history. In the late 1950s and early 1960s, Chief Justice Earl Warren and Justice William Brennan were famed for their ability to sway undecided justices in their favor; by contrast, Justice Felix Frankfurter's condescending attitude toward his fellow justices persuaded few and alienated many.

- **External political pressures.** Although Supreme Court justices enjoy life tenure and are thus theoretically immune to outside political pressures, the reality is much more complicated. *Roe v. Wade* survived its widely predicted demise in 1992 because at least two conservative justices feared its reversal would deal a blow to the Supreme Court's prestige. Public opinion may also play a role in determining the language of opinions and even the outcome of some cases.

Making the Connection

Alexander Hamilton's assumption that the judiciary would be "the least dangerous branch" has not been realized—at key periods in our nation's history, Supreme Court justices have used the power at their disposal to exert important influence on the American political system. Even when the Court has been forced to retreat somewhat from its activism, it leaves an imprint on the political terrain by legitimating the decisions of the other branches. U.S. judges are more than just innocent "umpires" calling balls and strikes within the political system; by opening up their courtrooms to certain cases, presiding over trials, and interpreting the laws and rules that govern individuals, they play a significant role in this nation's political and legal systems.

In the modern era, some presidents have placed added emphasis on the need to diversify the Court, moving it beyond the all-white tribunal that presided up through the 1960s. President Lyndon Johnson named the first African American (Thurgood Marshall); President Barack Obama named the first Latina (Sonia Sotomayor). Both nominations generated some controversy, but both were eventually confirmed by comfortable margins. As result, the Court would look different and—in the eyes of many—the Court's decision making would be influenced by the addition of new and unique perspectives. Does the racial and ethnic identity of a Supreme Court justice affect his or her judicial decision making, or does the law mean the same thing to those of every race, ethnicity, gender, etc.? Such a connection may be difficult to prove, though many of those who supported the two nominations were no doubt hoping for exactly that result.

POLITICS InterActive!

Overturning *Roe v. Wade*

Since 1973, the Supreme Court's controversial decision in *Roe v. Wade* has galvanized the nation like few other Supreme Court decisions in history. By a 7–2 vote, the Court in *Roe* struck down abortion laws in forty-six states and the District of Columbia. Opposition to *Roe* exploded from the outset, with a pro-life camp forming in heated resistance to the decision. Self-labeled "right to life" groups gained even more legitimacy when President Ronald Reagan made opposition to *Roe v. Wade* part of his litmus test for all judicial appointments. In response to *Roe v. Wade*, several states passed laws limiting abortion in various ways, such as requiring parental consent for minors to obtain abortions, twenty-four-hour waiting periods, and spousal notification, among others. Some, but not all, of these laws were upheld in *Planned Parenthood v. Casey* (1992), which confirmed the basic holding of *Roe v. Wade* while also modifying it in significant ways. Meanwhile, pro-choice groups have increased their own lobbying activities to defend the *Roe v. Wade* decision from attack. Since the early 1980s, no Democratic presidential nominee has been able to escape the requirement of professed support for the decision.

President George W. Bush's appointment of Samuel Alito to replace the more moderate Sandra Day O'Connor on the U.S. Supreme Court fed the growing expectation that *Roe v. Wade* might be overturned by the increasingly conservative Supreme Court in the not-so-distant future. What effect would the overturning of *Roe v. Wade*

Pro-life protesters in Washington, DC, march in opposition to the Supreme Court's decision in *Roe v. Wade*.

have on the American political landscape? On www.cengage.com/dautrich/americangovernmentbrief/2e, find the Politics InterActive link for details on what life might look like if *Roe v. Wade* were overturned, including links that provide information about the issues surrounding Court decisions on abortion in historical, popular, and global perspectives.

★ SUMMARIZING WHAT YOU HAVE LEARNED ★

★ Types of Law

- Law encompasses the authoritative rules made by government. The term *civil law* refers to statutes enacted most often by legislative bodies; common law consists of the rulings handed down by judges that establish precedents. Other types of law include criminal, civil, constitutional, and administrative law.

★ The Structure of the U.S. Legal System

- Each of the fifty states has its own court system, which includes trial courts and appellate courts.
- Article III of the U.S. Constitution established the judicial branch of the federal government and created the U.S. Supreme Court.
- Federal district courts are the trial courts. Decisions may be appealed to the U.S. courts of appeals, whose decisions may be reviewed by the U.S. Supreme Court. The decision of a state supreme court that raises federal constitutional issues may also be brought directly to the U.S. Supreme Court.

★ The Adversarial System of Justice

- The American legal system is an adversarial system of justice, in which opposing parties contend against each other for a result favorable to themselves, and judges act merely as independent referees.
- In the United States, disputes between parties may be settled through civil litigation. Those accused of crimes are prosecuted through a criminal law system. The vast majority of criminal prosecutions are settled by plea bargaining.

★ Judicial Review and Its Implications

- Chief Justice John Marshall's opinion in *Marbury v. Madison* (1803) established the Supreme Court's authority to review the constitutionality of any act passed by Congress.

★ Limitations on Courts

- Courts in the United States cannot initiate lawsuits, they can only hear true controversies, their decisions affect only those parties that are part of the case, and they have no ability to enforce their decisions.

★ Electing and Appointing Judges

- State judges are selected in various ways depending upon the jurisdiction in question: Some are appointed by governors or legislatures; others must run in elections; still others are chosen by a merit plan system.
- All federal court judges are nominated by the president and must be confirmed by the U.S. Senate.

★ How a Case Proceeds within the U.S. Supreme Court

- In order to grant a writ of certiorari to review a case, four of the nine justices must agree.
- After briefs are filed and oral arguments are heard, the justices vote on the merits of the case and issue their majority opinion accordingly. Concurring and dissenting opinions may also be issued.

★ Why the Justices Vote the Way They Do

- Various factors influence a judge's decision making, including legal precedents, new circumstances, ideological attitudes, personal traits, intracourt politics, and external pressures.
- The unanimous opinion in *Brown v. Board of Education* was produced by Chief Justice Earl Warren; *Roe v. Wade* survived in part because several justices took note of external politics.

CourseMate

Key Terms

Amicus curiae briefs (p. 246)
Appellate jurisdiction (p. 240)
Briefs (p. 246)
Civil law (p. 231)
Class action lawsuit (p. 239)
Common law (p. 231)
Complaint (p. 234)
Concurring opinion (p. 247)

Defendant (p. 234)
Discovery (p. 235)
Dissenting opinion (p. 247)
Grand jury (p. 235)
Indictment (p. 236)
Judicial review (p. 237)
Litigation (p. 234)
Majority opinion (p. 247)

Original jurisdiction (p. 240)
Plaintiff (p. 234)
Plea bargain (p. 236)
Solicitor general (p. 246)
Standing (p. 239)
Writ of certiorari (p. 245)

Resources

Books and Articles

Abraham, Henry J. *Justices, Presidents, and Senators: A History of the U.S. Supreme Court Appointments from Washington to Clinton.* Lanham, MD: Rowman & Littlefield, 2007.

Baum, Lawrence. *American Courts: Process and Policy.* Boston: Houghton Mifflin, 2007.

Baum, Lawrence. *The Supreme Court.* Washington, DC: CQ Press, 2006.

Dahl, Robert. "Decision-making in a Democracy: The Supreme Court as a National Policy-Maker." *Journal of Public Law*, vol. 6 (1957): 279–295.

Epstein, Lee, and Jack Knight. *The Choices Justices Make.* Washington, DC: CQ Press, 1998.

Maltese, John A. *The Selling of Supreme Court Nominees.* Baltimore: Johns Hopkins University Press, 1995.

McCloskey, Robert G. *The American Supreme Court.* 4th ed. Chicago: University of Chicago Press, 2004.

Rosenberg, Gerald. *Hollow Hope: Can Courts Bring About Social Change?* Chicago: University of Chicago Press, 1993.

Segal, Jeffrey A., and Harold J. Spaeth. *The Supreme Court and the Attitudinal Model Revisited.* New York: Cambridge University Press, 2002.

Toobin, Jeffrey. *The Nine: The Secret World of the Supreme Court.* New York: Doubleday, 2007.

Yalof, David A. *Pursuit of Justices: Presidential Politics and the Selection of Supreme Court Nominees.* Chicago: University of Chicago Press, 1999.

Internet Sources

http://www.uscourts.gov (the home page of the U.S. federal judiciary, which includes information about the U.S. Supreme Court, the U.S. courts of appeals, U.S. district courts, and U.S. bankruptcy courts).

http://www.findlaw.com (the most comprehensive source of no-cost legal research available on the Internet; includes a legal search engine and links to organizations, law schools, and so on).

http://www.supremecourtus.gov (the U.S. Supreme Court's own Web site, which features recent decisions, briefs, and other important information about the nation's highest court).

http://www.oyez.org (this Web site features a searchable database of select Supreme Court opinions and audio excerpts of oral arguments from the Supreme Court; also includes a virtual tour of the U.S. Supreme Court building).

10 Public Opinion

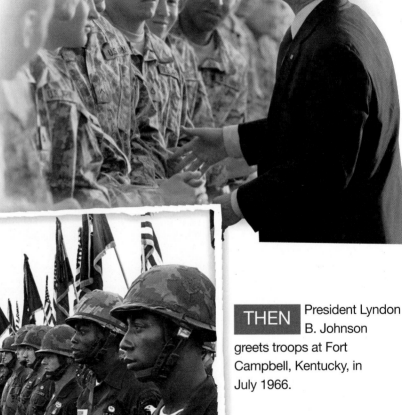

NOW President George W. Bush greets troops at Fort Benning, Georgia, in January 2007 as they prepare for deployment to Iraq.

AP PHOTO/GERALD HERBERT

THEN President Lyndon B. Johnson greets troops at Fort Campbell, Kentucky, in July 1966.

CORBIS

NOW &THEN

The Highs and Lows of Presidential Popularity

The nation was in crisis due to the tragic events of that day. In the wake of the tragedy, a stunned nation was willing to put its partisan differences aside. The record-breaking high approval ratings registered by the president in the days that followed the national tragedy confirmed that the nation was rallying behind its leader, giving him the benefit of the doubt and hoping that he would lead the nation through the crisis. As a result, the president and his administration would benefit from an influx of political capital during his initial year in office, allowing the president to embark on an unusually ambitious agenda for change. Over the course of time, however, the president's honeymoon period with the public was destined to come to an end; he would see his popularity slowly erode following the White House's decision to fight a war that played out over many years and eventually cost many American lives. Just as his young presidency had benefitted from record-high approval ratings in the wake of a national tragedy, his time in office would end with exceedingly low approval ratings as a result of a long and unpopular war.

NOW & THEN

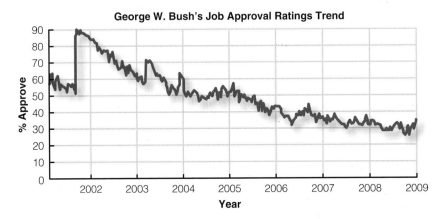

George W. Bush's Job Approval Ratings Trend

% Approve (y-axis: 0, 10, 20, 30, 40, 50, 60, 70, 80, 90)

Year (x-axis: 2002, 2003, 2004, 2005, 2006, 2007, 2008, 2009)

Source: The Gallup Organization. © 2009 The Gallup Organization.

NOW The young presidency of George W. Bush was stunned on September 11, 2001, by the terrorist attacks on the World Trade Center in New York City and on the Pentagon in Washington, DC. The nation's citizens were shocked as well. In this time of extreme national crisis, Americans of all ideological persuasions dropped their partisan leanings and threw their support behind Bush, hoping that the tough-talking Texan was the right man to lead the nation through the tragedy. A Gallup poll conducted after the attacks showed that Bush did, in fact, register the highest approval ratings—90 percent—ever recorded by the polling organization. Americans gave President Bush every benefit of the doubt as he responded to the events of that day. Benefiting from this rally-around-the-flag sentiment, Bush was dealt a hand of enormous political capital and presidential power, and in 2003 he used that capital to launch a war that deposed Iraqi dictator Saddam Hussein and removed his government from power, basing his decision to attack on intelligence that Saddam Hussein had been developing weapons of mass destruction. Bush quickly claimed victory, but the declaration turned out to be premature: the U.S. army and its allies found no weapons of mass destruction, and the invasion touched off a civil war between hostile Iraqi factions that would fester throughout the Bush presidency, costing thousands of American lives and hundreds of billions of dollars. By the time Bush was settling into his final year in office in 2008 a full five years after the invasion of Iraq, his approval ratings had reached a Gallup Poll record low of 25 percent.

THEN On the evening of November 22, 1963, just hours after President John Kennedy was assassinated in Dallas, Texas, Vice President Lyndon Baines Johnson took the presidential oath of office aboard Air Force One. The new president and his nation were still in shock at the events that had unfolded earlier that day. Glued to the television, the nation wondered who was responsible and whether the nation's security was at risk. They looked to the new president for hope and leadership, and Democrats as well as Republicans quickly rallied to support him. In a Gallup poll conducted shortly after Johnson took the oath, a near record 79 percent approved of his performance, affording him considerable presidential power. Johnson would use his lofty position in the following year and a half to push for civil rights legislation, secure a landslide election victory, and initiate comprehensive "Great Society" legislation aimed at improving education and defeating poverty. He also used his position to escalate a war against the communist threat in Vietnam, Laos, and Cambodia. President Johnson first deployed 3,500 U.S. combat units to the ground war in 1965. Initially, the public overwhelmingly supported the deployment. Over the next five years, however, the Johnson administration sent more and more combat troops to Vietnam to fight against the communist-backed North Vietnamese army and the guerrilla-type tactics they employed. The war continued to rage on with no end in sight as the number of American casualties grew and the costs of the war mounted. All of this took a serious toll on President Johnson's standing in the polls, as his popularity gradually declined to a low of 35 percent during his final year in office. Like George W. Bush, Lyndon Johnson saw the highest of highs and the lowest of lows in the court of public opinion.

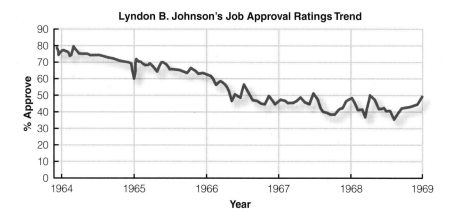

Lyndon B. Johnson's Job Approval Ratings Trend

Source: The Gallup Organization. © 1970 The Gallup Organization.

For political leaders and citizens alike, the appetite for information on what the public thinks has always been hearty. Today, this appetite is fed through the large number of opinion polls whose results are disseminated through newspapers, magazines, television, radio, and the Internet. The methods of gauging public opinion have advanced quite dramatically over the nation's history, and this advancement has been driven in no small part by the obsession to know "what Americans think." The nation's democratic roots, featuring a commitment to majoritarian rule and the notion of "consent of the governed," raise public opinion to a lofty status in American politics. Indeed, the willingness of officials to heed the people's voice has become firmly entrenched in American political culture. Presidents, like many others in the political system, have also shown an obsession with keeping tabs on public opinion. A president's authority to govern is, in part, influenced by his standing in the polls. When public support is high, a president enjoys a great deal of persuasive power, as Presidents Johnson and Bush did in 1963 and 2001, respectively. When public support dropped for both presidents, each man was reduced to a weak lame duck with little or no power to influence American politics. Knowing this, modern presidential candidates invest heavily in conducting significant numbers of public opinion polls throughout their election campaigns. Even when they are victorious, they continue to invest in conducting polls while in office.

Scientific measurement of public opinion is a relatively recent phenomenon in American politics. But the significant role that public opinion plays in the formulation of policy is as old as American democracy itself. Understanding what public opinion is, how it is expressed, how it forms, and how it is measured in contemporary politics is critical to understanding how American government works.

★ LO Understand both the theoretically important role that public opinion plays in American democracy and the tactical function public opinion plays in the policymaking process

Public Opinion in American Politics

The concept of public opinion is central to the American system of government. But the way public opinion is gauged and its relevance and uses in the American political system have changed over the nation's history. The U.S. Constitution begins with the words "We the People," highlighting the important role of the *public* in the creation of the government. Nonetheless, there is no mention of the term *public opinion* in the Constitution. The word *democracy* literally translated (from its Greek roots *demos kratos*) means "rule by the people," and thus, the opinions of the public take on a particularly important role in governing. The American system of government was founded on a set of democratic principles, first articulated by Plato and Aristotle and later popularized by political philosophers of the eighteenth-century Enlightenment, such as Montesquieu.[1] These principles herald the role of the public in governing and in consenting to what government does.

From the time of the founders up through the present day, the virtues of public opinion and its role in American democracy have been continually extolled. James Madison argued that the "public voice" and its formal role in voting provided primary justification for adopting the proposed Constitution. Borrowing from the political theories of John Locke, Madison acknowledged that government must serve the "will of the people." Andrew Jackson's presidency encouraged and empowered the "common man" to express his opinion for the purpose of influencing government.

Political leaders recognize that public opinion plays not only a theoretically important role in our democratic form of government but an important tactical role as well. Political scientist E. E. Schattschneider, in an influential book titled *Semisovereign People*, argued that "public opinion can emerge as a key factor in any political context" and that public opinion often is responsible for determining the outcome of important political battles. Long before Schattschneider, President Abraham Lincoln expressed this idea based on his own experiences, saying: "Public sentiment is everything. With public sentiment, nothing can fail; without it, nothing can succeed."[2]

Although most scholars, elected leaders, and everyday citizens would agree that **public opinion** is and should be very important in our system of government, the concept remains hard to define and measure. Many scholars regard public opinion as simply the summation of individual opinions on any particular issue or topic. Political scientist V. O. Key Jr., however, defined public opinion more specifically as "those opinions held by private persons which government finds it prudent to heed." As an input in the American political system, public opinion must not only exist, Key argued, but it must also be "heeded" or at least heard by those making policy decisions.[3]

Public opinion is a vague, though important, concept. It is regularly used by presidents to justify their policies, by political candidates to mount campaigns, by interest groups to promote their causes, by journalists to describe public preferences, and by scholars to understand the American government. Today, public opinion polls—for better or worse—have become the yardstick through which public opinion is understood and evaluated. The barrage of polls released daily by major media organizations provides a plethora of data defining the American psyche. There are, however, numerous methods through which public opinion in America is expressed.

Public opinion
The summation of individual opinions on any particular issue or topic.

How Is Public Opinion Expressed?

The formal constitutional mechanism by which public opinion influences the federal government is the free, open, and regular election of House members. Since ratification of the Seventeenth Amendment in 1913, the direct election of U.S. senators has served as yet another constitutional means for the expression of public opinion. Chapter 14 covers this form of expressing public opinion in detail. Voting is one important expression of public opinion and provides guarantees that officials are responsive to voters. In many state and local elections, voters are asked to respond to referendum questions, which empower the public to directly resolve policy issues. But there are a number of additional ways beyond voting in which public opinion has an influence on government. The First Amendment's guarantees that the people have the right to free speech, to peaceably assemble, and to petition their government pave the way for political rallies and protest rallies, which are important manifestations of public opinion.

★ **LO**

Learn the different ways in which public opinion may be expressed, including public opinion polls, rallies and protests, blogging, voting, and contributing time and money to campaigns

Supporting a candidate and engaging in attempts to elect an individual or political party to office through a monetary contribution or a contribution of time and effort are other ways that public opinion is expressed. Likewise, contributing time or money to an interest group or political action committee enables individuals to express their opinion indirectly and may have a significant impact on what government does.

Protesters at an April 2006 rally in Washington, DC, calling for American intervention to stop genocide in Darfur. Protests are an important expression of public opinion in the United States.

Public opinion is also expressed through the news media. Journalists often provide commentary on politics and public issues through radio talk shows, Web sites, editorial pages, and television news talk shows that provide perspectives on public opinion. Individual citizens may also use the media to express their opinion through letters to the editor. In addition, members of the public often choose to express their opinion directly to elected officials by contacting them, via either a letter or e-mail, a phone call, or the Internet, for their views on a particular issue.

Yet perhaps the most visible and widely used expression of public opinion in contemporary politics is the public opinion poll. Most major and many smaller media organizations today regularly conduct polls on politics and policy issues and publish the results of those polls in the form of news stories. The *USA Today/Gallup* poll, the CBS/*New York Times* poll, and the NBC/*Wall Street Journal* poll are only a few examples of media-based polls that, on a regular basis, provide data on American public opinion.

The Levels of Public Opinion

★ LO Distinguish between the different levels of public opinion, from broad values and beliefs, to partisan and ideological orientations, to attitudes and opinions on specific items

Public opinion exists at three basic levels: the broad level of values and beliefs, an intermediate level of political orientations, and the specific level of preferences about particular topics.

Values and Beliefs

At the highest, most abstract level are the values and beliefs of the American people. **Values** are the broad principles underlying American political culture that citizens support and adhere to; they represent that which people find most important in life. **Beliefs** are the facts that derive from values that people take for granted about the world. Although there are a number of values that Americans hold dear, political scientist Samuel Huntington has identified four politically relevant values that are widely accepted in the American political culture and serve as the basis for defining political beliefs on which there is great consensus in America: liberty, equality, and the rule of law.[4]

The vast majority of Americans support the idea of basic freedoms and liberties, such as freedom of religion and freedom of speech. These liberties are embedded in our political culture and serve as the basis for many government policies. Because Americans value liberty, for example, they believe that people should have the right to choose or not choose a religion, the right to publicly disagree with the president or the party in power, and the right to publish articles or news stories without government retribution.

Values
The broad principles underlying American political culture that citizens support and adhere to.

Beliefs
The facts that derive from values that people take for granted about the world.

Shaping Public Opinion, One Blog at a Time

Though many politically aware Americans still express their opinions on politics in traditional ways such as by writing letters to their local newspaper or by participating in live protests, millions of others have taken advantage of home computers with modems to post comments on the Internet through the use of political web logs, or "blogs." Blogs vary widely in form, but most feature some form of personal commentary, references to data, and links to other sources on the Internet related to the topic of discussion (often these links are to other political blogs).

Do blogs provide "objective journalism"? Most bloggers don't even aspire to that goal. Rather, they simply aim to provide up-to-date, personal perspectives on current political topics. Nor do readers hold most bloggers accountable for their lack of objectivity—liberals tend to flock to more liberal blogs such as *The Daily Kos* and *Talking Points Memo,* while conservatives frequent conservative sites such as *Powerline* or the blog of conservative author Michelle Makin. Indeed, many bloggers proudly state their political biases up front. Regardless, the danger remains that like-minded audiences will simply accept bloggers' opinions as the truth without any further research or reflection. Consider that Brigham Young University political

CAROL T. POWERS/THE NEW YORK TIMES/REDUX

Pictured here is Ana Marie Cox, founder of the popular "Wonkette," a blog about life in Washington.

scientist Richard Davis recently discovered that most people who closely follow both political blogs and traditional news media tend to believe the content on blogs is more accurate.

For Critical Thinking and Discussion

1. Do you go to blogs to shape your own political opinions? Why or why not?
2. Do you tend to visit blogs that reinforce your own biases and attitudes, or do you look for blogs that challenge your opinions?
3. What can bloggers add to coverage of an ongoing political event, such as a major party political convention, that traditional journalists may have difficulty capturing?

Likewise, a majority of Americans firmly value the concept stated in the Declaration of Independence that "all men are created equal." Regardless of economic status, race, or gender, the American public on the whole subscribes to the belief that all people should be treated equally under the law and that all people should have equal opportunities for economic success.

Finally, the value of the "rule of law" encourages a strong belief in the legitimacy of the U.S. Constitution, in the importance of elections as a way to configure government, and in the beliefs that the opinion of the majority should prevail, that those in the minority should have the right to challenge the majority, and that those accused of a crime should be entitled to fair procedures.

Unlike other levels of public opinion, values and beliefs are unique in that they generally receive a high level of support and consensus. Whether individuals are Democrats or Republicans, from the far right or the far left, elites or more representative of the masses, the vast majority generally subscribe to these broad values. Accordingly, values are the level of public opinion that defines our political culture; widespread agreement and support for them are thus critical to the maintenance of the American political system.

Political Orientations

Political orientations
The translation of values and beliefs into a systematic way of assessing the political environment.

Values and beliefs are very broad and abstract notions held by Americans that provide general guidance to people in thinking about politics. **Political orientations** are the translation of these values and beliefs into a systematic way of assessing the political environment. Although there may be broad consensus about values and beliefs among Americans, the translation of these values and beliefs into an organized way of thinking about politics and issues is considerably more varied.

The two primary ways Americans orient themselves toward political topics and issues are partisanship and political ideology. Partisanship, or party identification, which is discussed in Chapter 13, features a psychological attachment to one of the main political parties, generally either the Democrats or the Republicans.[5] A partisan identification provides an orienting mechanism for understanding how to apply one's values and beliefs to the political world. Consider, for example, the political debate over affirmative action policies. A Democratic orientation largely applies the value of equality and the belief that people of all races and creeds should enjoy equal opportunities, therefore suggesting support for affirmative action programs, which attempt to level the playing field and make corrections for policies that have historically benefited white males. A Republican orientation, on the other hand, generally places a higher priority on the value of individualism and the belief that government should not interfere with individual initiatives to succeed, thus suggesting opposition to affirmative action programs. Partisan orientation often helps people translate values into specific opinions.

Political ideology
A philosophical guide that people use to help translate their values and beliefs into political preferences.

Political ideology also provides an orientation for translating values into specific opinions. **Political ideology** is a philosophical guide that people use to help translate their values and beliefs into specific political preferences. The dominant ideologies in America are liberalism and conservatism. The contemporary **liberal ideology**, which is more closely associated with the modern Democratic Party, prefers that government take a more assertive role in the redistribution of economic resources but that government advocate positions that emphasize individual freedom on a range of social issues. Today's **conservative ideology**, which is more closely identified with the Republican Party, favors government activism in defense of more traditional values on social issues but prefers government restraint in economic redistribution.

Liberal ideology
A political orientation that favors a more assertive role in the redistribution of economic resources, but emphasizes individual freedom on a range of social issues.

The liberal and conservative camps largely agree on the basic values and beliefs of the American political culture—in the rule of law and majority rule and minority rights and in the idea that the free enterprise system will generally guarantee the most robust economy. But liberals and conservatives often differ when translating these values and beliefs into actual policies.

Conservative ideology
A political orientation that generally favors government activism in defense of more traditional values on social issues, but favors government restraint in economic redistribution.

Partisanship and political ideology are two very important topics in the study of American public opinion. They provide a framework for individuals to translate broad values and beliefs into preferences for issue positions and political candidates. These orientations help people to efficiently form opinions and express those opinions. Partisanship and political ideology also enable both political leaders and scholars to better understand why Americans think what they think about particular issues and vote the way they vote in elections.

The political orientations of Americans tend to be quite stable and lasting[6]—more so than the specific preferences that people have toward policies and political actors. The stability in American political orientations provides an order and consistency to American public opinion, which ultimately promotes stability in the political system as a whole.

Political Preferences

The most discussed level of public opinion is the particular **political preferences** that Americans have on policy issues, their attitudes regarding the performance of political leaders and institutions, and their candidate preferences in elections (see Figure 10.1). Support for the minimum wage, gun control proposals, the use of U.S. troops in fighting terrorism, abortion policy, campaign finance reform proposals, tax increases, or tax cuts are all specific policy issues on which the American public expresses opinions. In addition to policies, Americans also hold specific opinions about the

Political preferences
The attitudes people maintain regarding the performance of political leaders and institutions, their candidate preferences in elections, and specific policy issues.

FIGURE 10.1 American Political Preferences and Opinions on Selected Issues

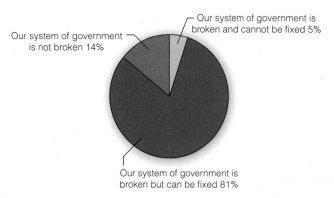

Which of the following comes closest to your view?

Our system of government is broken and cannot be fixed 5%

Our system of government is not broken 14%

Our system of government is broken but can be fixed 81%

Source: CNN/Opinion Research Corporation poll, February 2010.

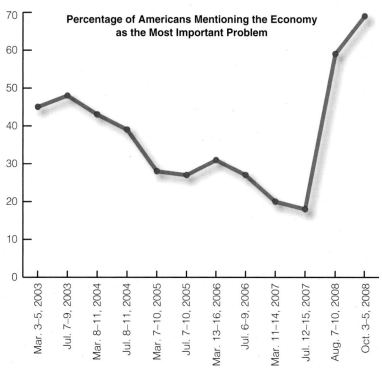

Percentage of Americans Mentioning the Economy as the Most Important Problem

The Gallup Organization regularly asks the American people what they think is the most important issue facing the country. A common answer is the economy, which jumped in late 2008 as the economy tumbled.

Source: The Gallup Organization. ©2003–2008 The Gallup Organization.

performance of their elected leaders such as the president, as well as their confidence in institutions such as Congress, the U.S. Supreme Court, and the military.

What Americans think about the minimum wage, the performance of the president, or the candidates in a political campaign is highly influenced by their political orientation. For example, an individual who identifies as a Republican and considers herself ideologically conservative is much less likely to say she approves of President Obama's performance than would a Democrat who considers himself liberal.

How Informed Is Public Opinion?

★ LO   Assess the mass public's level of knowledge about American politics and the capacity of the public to contribute to the political process

As discussed earlier in this chapter, American democracy relies on public opinion to choose leaders and inform public policy. This reliance is based on an important assumption about democracy—that citizens have the necessary information and skills to understand political issues and provide informed input. Since the time of Plato and Aristotle, political philosophers have dealt with questions about this important assumption: Is the public capable of democracy?

In the *Federalist Papers*, Alexander Hamilton and James Madison expressed concerns about the fickleness of public opinion and the potential "tyranny of the masses," which could lead to instability in governance.[7] Hamilton's solution to this problem was a republican form of government, in which the public chooses leaders who run the government, rather than a direct democracy in which the public rules directly.

Suspicions about the capacity of the public for meaningful contributions to governance were also articulated quite well by Walter Lippman in the early twentieth century.[8] Lippman, a well-known public opinion scholar, delivered withering attacks on ordinary citizens' lack of knowledge regarding politics. He argued that citizens invest very little energy and effort in acquiring information about politics, and as a consequence, the public lacks the necessary knowledge for their opinions to provide value. Subsequent research in the 1960s and 1970s, most notably by Philip Converse and his colleagues in *The American Voter*, used scientific surveys to support the argument that ordinary citizens tend to be ill-informed about political issues, ill-equipped to understand politics, and quite fickle in how they stand on issues.[9]

More contemporary studies indicate that the American public today is uninformed about politics. For example, a May 2008 national poll of 2,500 adult Americans found that

- 73 percent didn't know that the Bill of Rights specifically prohibits the establishment of an official religion in the United States.
- 79 percent couldn't identify the Gettysburg Address as the source of the phrase "Government of the people, for the people and by the people."
- 50 percent could not name the three branches of the federal government.
- 25 percent could not name one power of the federal government.
- 35 percent could not name at least one country that was an enemy of the United States during World War II.[10]

In addition, many surveys show that the public's level of expressed interest in politics is quite low. During the 2007 presidential primary campaign, for example, the Pew Research Center found that only one in five voters said that they were "very interested" in following the race (this represented an increase of seven percentage points over interest in the race in 2003). With such little knowledge of and lack of interest in politics, should public opinion even be considered an important factor in making public policy? How much confidence should we have in the outcome of elections when the voters know little about the candidates and the issues?

Some political scientists have come to the defense of the American public in this regard. V. O. Key Jr., in his work *The Responsible Electorate*, stated that although "many voters act in odd ways indeed," if one studies the electorate more carefully, one would find that "voters are not fools."[11] Key observed that "in the large, the electorate behaves about as rationally and responsibly as we should expect, given the clarity of the alternatives presented to it and the character of the information available to it." If political leaders don't rationally discuss issues and provide a framework for voters to use to understand politics, it is not the voters who should be blamed but rather the leaders. Considering this caveat, Key extolled the capacity of the public to form stable, responsible opinions and to contribute to the governing process.

Benjamin Page and Robert Shapiro extended Key's ideas in their book *The Rational Public*.[12] They used decades of public opinion poll data to show that over the long haul, public opinion on many issues remains fairly stable, and when it does change, it moves in logical directions. The aggregate responses of the public in polls, Page and Shapiro found, make sense and demonstrate rationality. They also found that the public makes distinctions between important policy areas and that public opinion tends to form meaningful patterns, consistent with a set of underlying beliefs and values.

The link between public opinion on an issue and public policy is a difficult one to establish. Page and Shapiro report that in the long run, there does seem to be a relationship between public attitudes on policy issues and the public policies that emerge from government. These researchers also argue that when public opinion shifts, a corresponding shift in public policy is likely to follow.

Political scientist Samuel Kernell has noted a more indirect link between public opinion and public policy: Political actors (most notably the president) who have high levels of public support are generally better able to get legislation passed.[13] For example, in 2003, President Bush was able to get Congress to pass a new tax cut package in part because of the high job performance ratings Americans gave him at that time. High levels of public support may be translated into an officeholder's greater political power to influence the legislative process.

How Does Public Opinion Form?

Through voting, opinion polls, protest rallies, communications with leaders, and newspaper editorials, public opinion is expressed and provides an important input for public policymaking. But how do individuals develop their particular political orientations, and how do they come to hold their specific political preferences? How do more deep-seated values and beliefs form? What influences the values that people hold, their partisan and ideological orientations, and their opinions on specific issues?

Political socialization is the process by which an individual acquires values, beliefs, and opinions about politics. Political socialization is a lifelong process, beginning in early childhood and continuing throughout an individual's life. The learning process that leads to the acquisition of values and opinions not only

★ LO
Recognize that political socialization is a lifelong process and know a number of important factors (such as the family, schools, friends, religion) that contribute to the development of political opinions

Political socialization
The process by which an individual acquires values, beliefs, and opinions about politics.

What the World Thinks about the United States

Polls often ask what Americans think about others. The Pew Global Attitudes project asks other nations what they think about Americans. One journalist, Andisheh Nouraee, had this take on a recent Pew survey about Americans:

The Pew Global Attitudes Project is an ongoing series of worldwide public opinion surveys designed to help Americans understand what the rest of the world is thinking about important issues. The [2006] survey asked 16,000 people in 15 countries what they think about several important political issues. Most important to us, the poll asked what people think about us . . . Sit back and enjoy the bad news: The world doesn't like us . . . only four [countries] had majorities who say they have a favorable opinion of the United States.

The United States' worst favorability ratings come from the Muslim countries in the survey. Only 30 percent of Indonesians and Egyptians view the U.S. favorably. In Pakistan, it's 27 percent; in Jordan, 15 percent; and in Turkey, only 12 percent of the people polled said they have a favorable opinion of the United States. Those numbers are especially disturbing when you consider that those countries are all considered friends of the U.S. And Turkey is not only a democracy, it's a member of NATO. If that's what our
Muslim friends think of us, imagine what our Muslim enemies must think.

The only country with a large Muslim population whose citizens view the U.S. favorably is Nigeria. Don't cheer up just yet, though. When Pew divided the Nigerian respondents into Muslims and Christians, they found that just 32 percent of Nigerian Muslims like us. Nigeria's overall pro-America numbers were so high, it turns out, because an astonishing 89 percent of Nigerian Christians like us. According to Pew, more Nigerian Christians view the U.S. favorably than the Americans do.

The other stunner from the "How they like us now?" survey is the sharp decline of the United States' favorability rating in Spain. Only 23 percent of Spaniards view the U.S. favorably this year, down from 41 percent last year. Remember, they're not only an ally, but they actually sent troops to Iraq when we asked. Of the 14 countries surveyed, only two of the countries have majorities who say they have some or a lot of confidence in Bush's international leadership. Those two countries: Nigeria and India.

In Great Britain, our greatest ally that isn't actually touching us, 30 percent of those surveyed say that they at least have some confidence in Bush's international leadership. In France, that number dips to 15 percent; in Spain, 7 percent; and in Turkey, just 3 percent of those surveyed said they have at least some confidence in Bush's international leadership. Three percent! That's one out of every 33 people. It makes me wonder if the people who said they have confidence in Bush even heard the question correctly. . . .

Source: Andisheh Nouraee, "What Do Foreigners Think of America These Days?: Don't Panic . . . Your War Questions Answered," Creative Loafing, July 5, 2006, accessed at http://atlanta.creativeloafing.com/gyrobase/Content?oid=oid%3A93423.

applies to politics, but it also applies to other orientations of people, including their beliefs about religion and culture.

Just as there are a number of factors and influences that lead individuals to consider themselves Democrats or Republicans or supporters of gun control or gun rights, there are also numerous factors and influences that lead people to choose a particular religion, such as Christianity or Buddhism, or to choose no religion at all. Socialization is important not only in the development of political learning for individuals but also in the transmission of fundamental beliefs and values of the American political culture from one generation to the next.

Although early political learning tends to be most profound, socialization to politics remains at work through a number of influences during a person's life. A number of factors and institutions, known as **agents of political socialization**, have been identified as having a particularly relevant impact on an individual's socialization to politics.[14]

Certainly, demographic factors such as race, ethnicity, gender, age, and economic status go a long way toward defining individuals' identities and can influence their political values. But a list of the most important agents of political socialization also includes such influences as family, friends and peer groups, schools, the media, and religion. Collectively, these agents promote the acquisition of the political values, beliefs, and opinions that an individual comes to hold.

Agents of political socialization
Factors that have a significant impact on an individual's socialization to politics.

Family

Because much time during the early years of a person's life is dominated by experiences with the family, many people develop values and beliefs consistent with those of their parents. Parents begin to teach their children about the political world early in the child's life. They transfer feelings about such concepts as authority, freedom, democracy, and racial prejudice to their children in formal and informal ways. By standing at attention during the playing of the national anthem or attending a Memorial Day service, parents are informally communicating important values about politics. Telling children that skin color should not affect how to think about a particular person or explaining why it is important to vote in an election is a formal way political information is communicated.

These early formal and informal cues from parents have a long-term and lasting impact on a child's political socialization. Over the years, researchers have found that children whose parents are more involved in politics tend to be more involved in politics themselves. The transference of party identification from parent to child is also significant. Children who grew up in homes where parents regard politics as important also tend to regard politics as important throughout their lives. Because children generally want to be like their parents, the many cues, both formal and informal, that they receive from their parents are a strong influence on the formation of political orientation.

ERIC FOWKE/PHOTOEDIT

Parents provide an important influence in socializing their children to appreciate American political values. Above, a father teaches his son to appreciate the values associated with Independence Day.

Friends and Peer Groups

As children grow older, they begin to interact with people outside their immediate family. They seek friendships with others and show a desire to get along with social groups. Children acquire a great deal of new political learning through their friends and associates, as well as from the social groups they seek to join. Often, the values, beliefs, and opinions of social peers are the same as or similar to those of the family, so friends and peers reinforce what was learned from parents. For example, wealthy people tend to live together in particular neighborhoods, and so as children from wealthy families find friends and peers, they are likely to find people who have been socialized by their parents in ways similar to themselves.

By the fifth or sixth grade, children become cognitively equipped to better understand the world of politics. Whereas previous learning tends to be based on

College Students Making Their Voices Heard

The economic recession of 2007–2010 slammed virtually all sectors of the American economy, including public higher education. Losses in state revenue and drops on college endowments forced many institutions to raise the cost of college tuition. As college boards of trustees began to approve sometimes large tuition hikes in 2009 and early 2010, a grassroots movement, spurred by the social networking site Facebook, various blogs, Twitter, and other types of social media, formed to speak out against these tuition increases. The Internet chatter culminated in a "March 4, 2010, Day of Action to Defend Public Education." Numerous rallies and marches to protest the cost hikes occurred on college campuses across the country that same day, including (1) more than 300 students blocking a major highway near the University of California at Davis; (2) fifteen students storming the chancellor's office at the University of Wisconsin–Milwaukee; and (3) more than 200 professors at the University of Illinois protesting pay cuts.

Protesters at the University of California express concern over college tuition increases on March 4, 2010 (picture from the March 5, 2010, *USA Today*).

AP PHOTO/BEN MARGOT

For Critical Thinking and Discussion

1. Have you participated in a protest rally or march on campus? If not, why not?

2. Marches and protests as an expression of public opinion are more common on college and university campuses than they are other in other venues. Why do you think colleges and universities tend to foster this form of expression in particular?

unquestioned acceptance of what is being communicated, young adults have the ability to critically analyze new information. This cognitive skill development comes at a time in life (young adolescence) when friends and peer groups are particularly influential. Thus, the desire to get along and to form social relationships has an important influence on political learning at this point in life.

The Schools

Part of the curriculum in many school systems across the United States focuses on the development of political values, such as respect for authority, legitimacy of our political institutions, patriotism, and capitalism. Classes in civic education and American government, the daily morning pledge of allegiance to the flag, and pictures of American presidents are just some of the mechanisms by which schools act as an agent of political socialization.

Schools serve as an important mechanism for the positive development of attitudes about basic American democratic values, thus promoting general positive attitudes about the legitimacy of the democratic system. Research conducted by David Easton and his colleagues in the 1950s and 1960s demonstrated that schools promoted a positive attachment to the concept of "democracy" by the third grade.[15] During the early grades, children acquire beliefs regarding a citizen's role in politics—obeying laws, voting, and paying attention to political events.

Political socialization from the school is not limited to elementary and high school. The college experience also has an important socializing effect on citizens' political development. College graduates tend to be more likely to vote and participate in politics, they are more likely to follow news and political campaigns, and they are better able to understand the political world in which they live. The effects of formal education, even beyond the specific civics education curriculum of the earlier grades, make an important positive contribution to an individual's political socialization.

The Media

Americans spend a great deal of time accessing news information and being entertained by the mass media. It is not surprising, then, that the media act as an important agent of political socialization as well. Information that citizens glean from media news coverage about political events and political campaigns has an impact on their values, beliefs, and opinions. Research has shown that heavy users of the news media are more politically informed than lighter users;[16] they are also more supportive of basic American values, such as individualism, equality, and free speech rights.

The media's impact as a socialization agent extends beyond the provision of news information. Entertainment television, the movies, talk radio, and other media forms also inspire various types of political learning. Studies have shown, for example, that entertainment television tends to promote negative stereotypes of women and minorities, which may reinforce negative attitudes about race or affirmative action. The use of Internet Web sites and blogs may also help shape a person's political outlook.

Religion

Throughout American history, religious organizations have played an important role in the political socialization process. The values of individualism and hard work were important influences in establishing a capitalist economy and continue to underpin economic policy in the United States. These values, based on the Protestant work ethic, continue to influence the socialization process. More recently, the Christian-based fundamentalist movement has utilized religious teaching to influence opinions about political issues. The Catholic Church's opposition to abortion affects many Catholics' position on that issue.

How Is Public Opinion Measured?

When Americans think about the term *public opinion* in contemporary politics, they often focus on the results of public opinion polls. A **public opinion poll** is a method of measuring the opinions of a large group of people by selecting a subset of the larger group, asking them a set of questions, and generalizing the findings to the larger group.

Public opinion poll
A method of measuring the opinions of a large group of people by asking questions of a subset of the larger group and then generalizing the findings to the larger group.

Polling Problems in Presidential Elections

"Dewey Defeats Truman"? "Gore defeats Bush"? Not so, as it turned out. Still, that didn't stop public opinion pollsters from convincing many in the media that Thomas Dewey would be elected president in 1948, and that Al Gore would be the winner in 2000. More than fifty years apart, the polls played an important role in two predictions that caused considerable confusion. Then, in 2008, the pollsters struck again. . . .

In 1948, polls leading up to Election Day predicted that New York Governor Thomas Dewey would defeat President Harry S. Truman. The Gallup poll, the Roper poll, and other opinion polling organizations consistently found Dewey ahead. The scientific sampling methods they employed had been used by these organizations in successfully calling the winner of every presidential race since

1936. The problem? All the major pollsters stopped their preelection polling at least two weeks before Election Day. In fact, Dewey did maintain a large lead throughout the campaign, a lead that had not changed up through mid-October. So the pollsters just stopped polling. Then, in the final weeks of the campaign, Truman's furious and aggressive campaign schedule began to make a difference, and voter opinions began to shift in favor of the incumbent president. Yet the pollsters didn't pick up these changes. Thus, their confident prediction that Dewey would win proved wrong, and the *Chicago Daily Tribune* became famous for its incorrect headline: "Dewey Defeats Truman."

In 2000, the presidential election between Republican George W. Bush and Democrat Al Gore proved once again the pollsters could be fallible. In the last few weeks of the campaign, many respected polling organizations showed a tight race between the two candidates. The Voter News Service (VNS), a company that conducted

Public opinion polls are not the only way public opinion in America is either expressed or understood, but polls have become the most obvious and important instrument for gauging public opinion. Polls provide information that elected leaders use in making public policy, thus providing an important way for public sentiment to influence public policy. Polls have also become a centerpiece of elections, used both by the candidates to shape a winning strategy and by journalists to provide coverage of campaigns.

Polling has become a huge industry in the United States. To the public, the most visible polls are those that are regularly conducted by media organizations, asking Americans what they think about a variety of topics, such as who they plan to vote for in an upcoming election, how they rate the job the president is doing, how they feel about the condition of the economy, and many other topics. Media polls are conducted with the purpose of broadcasting results as news stories. However, the polling industry extends far beyond media polls. Candidates at all levels conduct polls to identify strategies for waging a successful election campaign. Federal, state, and local government agencies conduct polls to evaluate the successes and failures of public programs. Interest groups conduct polls to promote their agendas.

Even though polls have come to play an important and visible role in American politics, the manner in which they are conducted is often misunderstood, and questions about their accuracy are often raised. What makes a poll "scientific"? How is it possible to interview 1,000 Americans and draw conclusions about how more than 200 million Americans think? How can two polls

polls of voters almost immediately after they exited the voting booth (aptly termed "exit polls"), was supported in 2000 by ABC, CBS, NBC, CNN, Fox, and the Associated Press. On Election Day that year, VNS conducted exit polls in each of the fifty states as a way of predicting the winner in each state, thus facilitating an accurate prediction of the Electoral College outcome. For each of the fifty states in the previous seven presidential elections, network exit polling correctly predicted the presidential winners. When the polls in Florida closed at 8 PM, VNS began tabulating its results, including its results in Florida, and sent the results to the media organizations that supported VNS. Based on the Florida exit poll data, the networks declared Gore the winner in Florida, which gave him enough Electoral College votes to win the election. Unfortunately, Florida was so close, and balloting was so complicated in that state, that the exit poll call was problematic. This flawed exit poll prediction thus complicated an already confusing election night for the television networks. It would take more than five weeks after Election Day, and a U.S. Supreme Court decision, to declare George W. Bush the winner in Florida and thus the winner of the presidential election.

In 2008, preelection pollsters struggled to accurately predict the outcome of several Democratic Party primaries. Most notable were the polls associated with the all-important New Hampshire primary. *USA Today*/Gallup, CBS, Fox, and a number of other organizations conducting polls in New Hampshire all concluded that Barack Obama would win the Democratic primary. Some of the polls indicated that Obama would defeat Hillary Clinton by more than 10 points. The nation and particularly the pollsters were surprised to find on election night that Clinton had defeated Obama. Clinton's surprise win in the nation's first primary came days after Obama's defeat of Clinton in the Iowa caucus and helped fuel a long and bitter battle for the Democratic nomination in 2008.

be conducted on the same topic and produce different findings? An understanding of polling techniques can help answer these questions.

Scientific Sampling

Polling procedures popularized by Dr. George Gallup in the 1930s relied on the principles of probability theory and focused on the sampling of the population under study.[17] Gallup's work helped usher in the modern era of public opinion research, characterized by scientific polling procedures. A *sample* is a subgroup of people from a population who are studied for the purpose of learning something about the whole population. Based on the laws of probability, it is possible to draw a sample from a population, administer a set of questions to those in the sample, and understand something about the entire population, within a known level of error.

A **scientific sample** is one that uses probability theory as a guide to selecting people from the population who will compose the sample. Random selection of respondents in the sample is key to achieving a scientific, or representative, sample. *Random sampling* is achieved by giving each possible respondent in the population a known chance of being selected in the sample. There are a number of ways of achieving a random sample.

Unscientific Polls and Pseudo-Polls

In a scientific poll, the results of the poll are generalizable to a population that is represented by the sample of people who are interviewed. **Unscientific polls**

Scientific sample
A randomly selected subgroup drawn from a population using probability theory.

Unscientific poll
A poll in which the sample of people interviewed is not representative of any group beyond those who register their opinion.

★ LO

Explain the differences between a scientific poll and an unscientific poll differ from scientific ones in that the sample of people who are interviewed is not representative of any group beyond those who register their opinion. There are many examples of unscientific polls in politics. What makes a poll unscientific is the way respondents are selected for the sample. If the vast majority of people in a population are given a chance of being sampled, then the poll is scientific. If not, then the sample represents nothing beyond itself. In an unscientific sample, some individuals in the population have no chance of being included. Many unscientific polls are conducted even today. A good example is the television call-in poll. Often, television news shows that deal with political topics will offer viewers an opportunity to call an 800 or 900 number to answer a poll question. These polls are unscientific because only those people who are viewing the show have an opportunity to respond. E-mail surveys conducted by CNN.com and ESPN.com are similarly unscientific surveys. The sample of people who call in is not representative of any group beyond the callers themselves.

Recently, some unscrupulous political campaigns and political action committees (PACs) have been disguising themselves as pollsters for the purpose of planting messages with voters rather than measuring public opinion. Some of these campaigns or PACs present themselves as pollsters for the purpose of fund-raising as well. These phone calls have come to be known as **pseudo-polls**. As the term implies, there is no polling going on with a pseudo-poll. Pretending to be pollsters, callers often contact tens of thousands of voters and ask hypothetical (that is, untrue) questions about their political opponents such as, "Did you happen to know that John Smith is reported to have beaten his wife in the past—does this make you any less likely to support him in his race for senator?" Respondents to the call believe they are being interviewed by a legitimate polling firm and take away from the conversation a contrived and false message about a political candidate. This type of pseudo-poll is called a "push poll" because the intention of the call is to "push," or influence, people to vote a particular way.

Sample Size

A fundamental characteristic of a scientific public opinion poll is the nature of the procedures used to draw a sample from the population. The size of the sample is also a factor in poll quality. **Sampling error** is the term used to indicate the amount of error in the poll that results from interviewing a sample of people rather than the whole population under study. Sampling error is largely a function of sample size: The larger the sample size, the less sampling error with the poll. However, there is a law of diminishing returns associated with increasing the size of the sample.

For example, a national scientifically drawn sample of 200 Americans has a sampling error of about + or −7 percent at the 95 percent level of confidence. This means that with a sample of 200, chances are 95 in 100 that the sample will produce results within seven points above or below the survey result. By increasing the sample size by 400 respondents, from 200 to 600, the sampling error is reduced to + or −4 percent. An additional 600 respondents in the sample, bringing the sample size to 1,200, reduces the sampling error to + or −3 percent.

Media organizations that report poll findings often attempt to convey information about the poll to help the reader/audience understand the sampling error associated with the results. Typically, a news report on a poll will include a statement like this: "The survey was conducted by telephone with a random sample

Pseudo-poll
Phone calls from members of political campaigns or PACs who present themselves as pollsters for the purpose of planting messages with voters rather than measuring public opinion.

Sampling error
The amount of error in a poll that results from interviewing a sample of people rather than the whole population under study; the larger the sample, the less the sampling error.

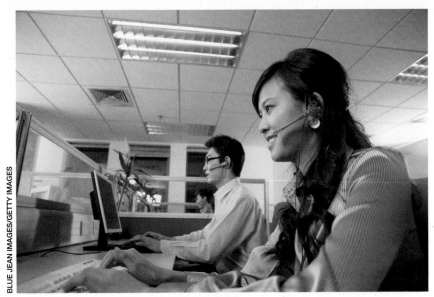

A telephone interviewer for a public opinion polling firm asks a randomly selected voter whom she will vote for in an upcoming election.

of 1,200 American adults. Sampling error for the survey is + or −3 percent at the 95 percent level of confidence."

What does this statement mean? Suppose the poll found that 60 percent of the respondents approved of the job that Barack Obama was doing as president. The statement indicates that there was a "random sample" of American adults. This means that the poll was a scientific poll, and the results can be generalized to the full American adult public.

With any scientific poll, there is sampling error, and probability theory allows us to calculate what the sampling error might be. This calculation is thus expressed as a "confidence interval," or range, which is reported to be + or −3 percent of the poll result (or a six-point range). The level of confidence typically reported is at the "95 percent level of confidence" (meaning that 95 of 100 similarly conducted polls would produce results in this range). Thus, what the statement says, then, is that we can be 95 percent confident that the approval rating for President Obama is somewhere between 57 and 63 percent.

In addition to random selection and sample size, the quality of the sample is affected by "nonresponse" error. Once a sample is selected, it is necessary to contact and conduct interviews with those in the sample. Rarely is it possible to obtain an interview with 100 percent of those sampled. Some people refuse to be interviewed, some are not home when contacts are made, and others screen their phone calls through an answering machine or caller ID system. Nonresponse is problematic when those who do not respond tend to answer the questions differently from those who do respond. The goal is to achieve as high a response to the poll as possible to limit possible nonresponse error.

Modern-day scientific polls of Americans and voters typically use a probability technique known as **random-digit dialing (RDD)** to obtain scientific telephone samples. RDD uses known information about telephone area codes and exchanges and randomly assigns the last four digits to these. Because about

Random-digit dialing (RDD)
A probability technique for scientific telephone polling that randomly assigns the last four digits to known information about telephone area codes and exchanges.

90 percent of the households in the United States have active telephone lines, almost everyone living in a house with a telephone has some chance of being selected in the sample.

Asking Questions on Polls

★ LO   Identify criteria for asking unbiased poll questions

Accurate and reliable polls require not only scientific sampling procedures but also significant attention to the way polling questions are asked. The way a question is worded can have a large impact on the type of answers given by survey respondents. Consider the following example of a question asked on a national survey conducted by the Roper Organization in 1993: "Does it seem possible or does it seem impossible to you that the Nazi extermination of the Jews never happened?" More than one in five respondents to the poll indicated that they thought it was possible that the Holocaust never happened. The results from this question led to a series of news stories expressing concern that nearly one quarter of the American public questioned the reality of the Holocaust. However, researchers noted an important problem with the wording of the question; namely, it included a double negative. It is difficult for respondents, particularly in a telephone interview (where they are not looking at the words of the question), to interpret what it means to "seem impossible" that something "never happened." The confusing question led to the exaggerated survey result. To test the notion that the question was confusing, the Gallup organization instead asked this question in a 1994 survey: "In your opinion, did the Holocaust definitely happen, probably happen, probably not happen, or definitely not happen?" In this form of the question, only 2 percent said that the Holocaust probably did not happen, and 0 percent said that it definitely did not happen.

Another example of how wording can influence the responses to a question involves two questions, on separate surveys, intended to measure attitudes about the legality of flag burning. A CBS/*New York Times* poll asked, "Should burning or destroying the American flag as a form of political protest be legal or should it be against the law?" Fourteen percent said it should be legal, and 83 percent said it should be against the law. A Gallup poll asked the question this way: "The Supreme Court ruled that burning the American flag, though highly offensive, is protected under the free speech guarantee of the First Amendment to the Constitution. Do you agree or disagree?" In answering this question, 38 percent agreed that flag burning should be legal—fully 24 percentage points higher than what was found with the CBS/*New York Times* question. In this case, the context in which Gallup framed the question—that the Supreme Court said flag burning was legal based on the First Amendment—produced the different result.

The polling community of practitioners and scholars has, over the years, conducted a number of experiments to test how question wording can influence the results of polls. Listed here are of some of the key recommendations for constructing good poll questions:

1. **Avoid double negatives in questions** (as in the Holocaust example cited earlier).

2. **Keep the question as simple as possible, using words that people with a limited vocabulary might understand.**

3. **Don't include more than one question within a question—such an error is called a double-barreled question.** An example of a double-barreled

question is, "Do you approve or disapprove of the job that President Obama is doing in handling the economic and domestic affairs of the nation?" Respondents might have different answers to the president's performance in economic versus other domestic affairs.

4. **The questions should not lead the respondent to a particular answer.** An example of a leading question is, "Do you approve of the job that Barack Obama is doing as president?" Because only the "approve" option is stated in the question, some respondents might answer "yes, they approve," when they might have answered that they "disapprove" had that option been provided as well.

5. **Don't expect honest answers to socially unacceptable response questions.** For example, using illegal drugs is not only illegal but regarded as socially unacceptable. So one should not necessarily expect all drug users to answer honestly a question about their own use of drugs.[18]

Interpreting Public Opinion Data

★ LO

Assess the findings from a poll along the dimensions of direction, intensity, and continuity of public opinion

Understanding public opinion requires attention not only to the scientific aspects of sampling and the wording of questions but also to the analysis and interpretation of the results of a poll. In assessing results, analysts are concerned with three important characteristics of public opinion data: direction, intensity, and continuity.[19]

To understand the **direction** of public opinion, the analyst seeks to find which position or preference a majority of people hold as their opinion. On most topics, there are two possible directions in which public opinion might lean—a positive direction or a negative direction. For example, with respect to presidential approval, respondents might either approve or disapprove of the job the president is doing. Similarly, the public might either trust or distrust their political leaders, or they might support or oppose a proposal for a policy that makes it more difficult to buy a handgun. On any given opinion question, direction is a basic characteristic that the analyst seeks to gauge.

Direction (of public opinion)
A tendency toward a particular preference, usually (though not always) characterized as either positive or negative.

Intensity is also an important characteristic of public opinion. Often, the analyst seeks not only to find the direction of opinion but also to determine how strongly or how committed the public feels about the opinion it holds. Consider the responses to the following question asked to a national sample of Americans in 2000: "Do you agree or disagree with this statement—companies should be allowed to advertise tobacco products on television?" Those polled were asked a follow-up question: "Do you strongly or mildly (agree/disagree) with this?" The results were as follows:

Intensity (of public opinion)
The degree of strength or commitment the public feels about the opinion it holds.

Strongly agree	24 percent
Mildly agree	27 percent
Mildly disagree	10 percent
Strongly disagree	37 percent

The direction of opinion in this case swings only marginally in agreement that companies should be able to advertise tobacco on TV. A bare majority, 51 percent, agreed with this statement, and 47 percent disagreed. The direction of opinion only modestly endorses the statement. However, the follow-up question sheds additional light on the intensity of opinion. Among those who agree, they are about evenly divided, 24 percent to 27 percent, between strongly and mildly agreeing. Those who disagree are much more intense in their feelings, with 37 percent strongly and only 10 percent mildly disagreeing.

Continuity is a third important characteristic of public opinion. Political preferences may remain very stable over time, they may gradually change, or they may fluctuate wildly over short periods of time. Continuity (or "changeability," its opposite) is often an important dimension of public opinion. The presidential approval rating is often analyzed from the context of the continuity/change dimension. When major political events occur, we often see change.

Making the Connection

Public opinion plays an important role in any system of government. Even authoritarian regimes such as the French government under King Louis XVI in the late eighteenth century, czarist Russia in the early twentieth century, and the Soviet Union in the late twentieth century were susceptible to being overthrown by the forces of the popular will. But in a democratic society, public opinion is freely expressed and willingly heeded by those running the government. In contemporary American politics, there are a variety of ways in which public opinion may be expressed. As Presidents Lyndon Johnson and George W. Bush quickly learned, public opinion can change drastically over a president's term, keeping chief executives and other public officials continuously accountable to the popular will.

Modern technology and the advancement of social science research have enabled political scientists, journalists, political candidates, and elected leaders to measure accurately and understand better not only what public opinion is but also how and why it changes. Modern presidents have the resources of scientific public opinion polls at their disposal and use them quite extensively. But although the scientific opinion poll is a modern phenomenon, the importance of public opinion has always been central to the life of American politics.

From March 22 to March 26, 2010, four separate organizations conducted national polls measuring approval of President Barack Obama's job performance. Gallup placed Obama's approval rating at 51 percent; the Rasmussen Poll found that 48 percent approved of Obama's performance; the Quinnipiac Poll said 45 percent approved; and the *Washington Post* found that it was 53 percent. What might account for the differences between these four polls' findings? Is it sampling error? The wording of the question used to measure presidential job approval? The way the different pollsters went about selecting a sample? The way the questions were administered to respondents?

Use the links below to find out how these organizations conduct their polls and how they measure presidential approval. What are the differences in the methodology of these various pollsters, and how might those differences contribute to different findings?

- http://www.gallup.com
- http://www.rasmussenreports.com
- http://www.quinnipiac.edu
- http://www.washingtonpost.com

On www.cengage.com/dautrich/ americangovernmentbrief/2e, find the Politics InterActive link for details about the presidential approval rating and how other major polling organizations measure it and what they have found.

The Gallup Poll, which has conducted preelection polls for CNN and *USA Today*, tracks voters' intentions throughout the fall campaigns. This graph shows Gallup's tracking from early September through the end of October in the 2008 presidential race.

Source: The Gallup Organization. © 2008 The Gallup Organization.

Chapter Summary

★ Public Opinion in American Politics

- Public opinion plays an important role in ensuring that citizens' beliefs are embraced in a democracy; public opinion also plays a tactical role for political officials, influencing the outcome of many important political battles.

★ How Is Public Opinion Expressed?

- Public opinion may be expressed through a variety of means, including public opinion polls, voting, free speech and assembly, the support of particular candidates for political office, and the contribution of time and efforts to interest groups.

- The news media also serve as an outlet for public opinion, and many members of the public express their opinions directly to elected officials through letters, phone calls, or e-mails. Blogs have become an increasingly popular way for individuals to express their views on issues.

★ The Levels of Public Opinion

- Public opinion exists at its most abstract level in the form of values and beliefs; it exists in a more specific form through political orientations, which translate values and beliefs into a systematic way of assessing political realities, and in an even more specific way in the form of particular political preferences.

★ How Informed Is Public Opinion?

- Many noted scholars in the early and mid-twentieth century argued that the public lacks the necessary knowledge for their opinions to provide value. Contemporary surveys continue to confirm that the public maintains a low interest in politics generally and that most Americans are uninformed about basic political facts.

- By contrast, a number of other scholars beginning with V. O. Key Jr. in the 1960s have argued that regardless of its specific knowledge of politics, the public as a whole behaves quite rationally over the long haul, expressing stable opinions that move (if at all) in logical and meaningful directions based on their values and beliefs.

★ How Does Public Opinion Form?

- Individuals' opinions are shaped in part by political socialization; impressions formed during youth often last well into adulthood. Opinions are also shaped by demographics (race, ethnicity, gender, age, and so on), family members, friends and peer groups, schools, the media, and religious organizations.

★ How Is Public Opinion Measured?

- Public opinion polls measure the opinions of a large group of people by selecting a subset of the larger group and then generalizing the findings from the small group back to the large group. To ensure that the poll is scientific, the sample must be chosen randomly using probability theory through techniques such as random-digit dialing.

- The way questions on a poll are worded is also an important factor in assessing polls.

★ Interpreting Public Opinion Data

- The proper interpretation of public opinion data requires attention to the direction, intensity, and continuity of the public's expressions. With regard to the third characteristic, political preferences may fluctuate wildly over short periods of time.

CourseMate

Key Terms

Resources

Books and Journals

Delli Carpini, Michael X., and Scott Keeter. *What Americans Know About Politics and Why It Matters.* New Haven, CT: Yale University Press, 1996.

Fowler, Floyd. *Survey Research Methods.* Newbury Park, CA: Sage Publications, 1995.

Hibbing, John R., and Elizabeth Theiss-Morse. *Congress as Public Enemy: Public Attitudes Toward American Political Institutions.* Cambridge: Cambridge University Press, 1995.

Igo, Sarah. *The Averaged American.* Cambridge, MA: Harvard University Press, 2007.

International Journal of Public Opinion (quarterly journal that serves as a source of public opinion analysis for academics and polling professionals).

Key, V. O., Jr. *The Responsible Electorate.* New York: Alfred A. Knopf, 1960.

Key, V. O., Jr. *Public Opinion and American Democracy.* New York: Alfred A. Knopf, 1967.

Page, Benjamin I., and Robert Y. Shapiro. *The Rational Public: Fifty Years of Trends in Americans' Policy Preferences.* Chicago: University of Chicago Press, 1992.

Public Opinion Quarterly (quarterly journal that features important theoretical contributions to opinion and communication research, analyses of current public opinion, and investigations of methodological issues involved in survey validity).

Schattschneider, E. E. *The Semisovereign People: A Realist's View of Democracy in America.* New York: Holt, Rinehart and Winston, 1960.

Stonecash, Jeffrey M. *Political Polling: Strategic Information in Campaigns.* New York: Rowman & Littlefield, 2003.

Traugott, Michael W., and Paul J. Lavraskas. *The Voter's Guide to Election Polls.* New York: Chatham House, 2000.

Zaller, John. *The Nature and Origin of Mass Opinion.* Cambridge: Cambridge University Press, 1992.

Internet Sources

http://www.gallup.com (the Web site for Gallup poll data).

http://www.aapor.org (the home page for the American Association for Public Opinion Research, the association for pollsters and people who study polls).

http://www.ropercenter.uconn.edu (Web site for the Roper Center for Public Opinion Research, which includes the largest collection of public opinion data in the world).

NOW Former lobbyist Jack Abramoff.

THEN Rep. Oakes Ames (R-MA) served in Congress from 1863 to 1873.

NOW & THEN

Lobbying Scandals with a Ring of Familiarity

The relationship between government and private interests has always been difficult to navigate. Lobbying legislators to favor or oppose certain legislation may be a time-honored practice, and yet so-called legislative favors granted in return for some financial interests can quickly cross the line and betray the public trust. Interest groups that advocate their position in the halls of Congress sometimes cross that line. In one instance, private financial interests hoped to capitalize on the greed of certain members of Congress, who were willing to accept rewards from these organizations in return for providing a piece of the expanding government largesse. The group's original cause may well have been noble, but once the public trust was violated, public faith in the entire operation was compromised. And because corruption knows no bounds, even the original cause of the interest groups was eventually undermined by those who tried to circumvent the rules of the political process.

NOW & THEN

AP PHOTO/GERALD HERBERT

NOW During the past two decades, many Native American tribes—buoyed by passage of the 1988 Indian Gaming Regulatory Act—have undergone a rags-to-riches story. Millions of Americans have visited tribe-run casinos located on reservations where gaming is now permitted. Many Native American tribes benefited from that federal legislation, and in the 1990s tribal leaders wanted to press their advantage further. Thus several tribes, including the Mississippi Choctaw, hired lobbyist Jack Abramoff to represent them before Congress. Abramoff proved especially effective in this role, helping defeat federal legislation that would have assessed the unrelated business income tax (UBIT) on Native American casinos. House Majority leader Tom DeLay (R-TX) was one of many House members who played a role in this and other victories. According to some media reports, Abramoff may have done more than just "argue forcefully" on the tribes' behalf: he allegedly spent millions of dollars to influence politicians. In addition to offering many members of Congress free meals at his restaurant, Abramoff maintained four skyboxes at major sports arenas for political entertaining at a cost of over $1 million a year. Joining Abramoff on one vacation in 2000 was DeLay, whose airfare to London and Scotland was allegedly charged to an American Express card issued to Abramoff.

Abramoff also defrauded the very Native American tribes he had been hired to serve. By overbilling Indian gambling interests and orchestrating lobbying activities against his own clients, Abramoff attempted to play both sides of the fence. Abramoff pleaded guilty to numerous charges in 2006. The Abramoff lobbying scandal led to the downfall of House Majority leader DeLay and to charges brought against many other members of Congress and their aides.

THEN Immediately after the Civil War, railroads were the dominant economic interest in Washington, DC. Seeking legislative support, the Union Pacific Railroad in particular exerted pressure on well-known Congressmen of the time such as Representative James Brooks (D-ME), and Senators James Harlan (R-IA) and James Willis Patterson (R-NH). Ironically, the key individual responsible for that pressure was a fellow Congressman, Oakes Ames (R-MA). As an influential member of the House, Ames obtained contracts for his family firm for the construction of the Union Pacific; he even installed his brother Oliver Ames as president of the railroad in 1866. In 1872 the railroad established a front company, known as Crédit Mobilier, as part of a financial scam to funnel money back to the railroads through their own construction contracts. Ames then allowed members of Congress to purchase railroad shares at face rather than market value; in return, the members agreed to ignore illegal corporate transactions and to help produce dividends for the railroads they now owned. Ames's scheme eventually ensnared the sitting vice president of the United States, Schuyler Colfax, as well as his successor as vice president, Henry Wilson. Ames was censured after a House investigation; Colfax was nearly impeached. In addition, Ames's actions nearly ruined the Union Pacific railroad, which went bankrupt in the 1870s. But at a time when corruption laws were still in their infancy, many politicians escaped with nothing more than "the embarrassment of public exposure."

LIBRARY OF CONGRESS PRINTS AND PHOTOGRAPHS DIVISION WASHINGTON, DC.

D uring these two critical periods in American history, private groups and economic interests exerted their will on the public institutions of government to such a great extent that all distinctions between public and private seemed to break down. No one could question the importance of the railways during the post–Civil War period; meanwhile Native Americans—downtrodden for so long in American society—had finally risen to a position of economic prominence in the 1990s, and their success was welcomed in many corners. Unfortunately, the aggressive lobbying on behalf of these two groups went too far.

Interest groups today play a central role in formulating public policy, directing the regulation of certain industries, and even influencing important court decisions. Indeed, there is little doubt about the size and magnitude of their influence throughout the American political system. Of course the vast majority of interest groups are law-abiding, positive forces in government. A key issue remains, however: How far do we allow such groups to press their interests in government before they become a negative force in democracy?

This chapter assesses the workings and performance of American politics from the perspective of interest group activity. What are interest groups? How do they work? Who belongs to them? Which ones are more and less powerful? How do they exert influence on what government does?

★ LO Appreciate the function of interest groups as a mechanism by which groups of people attempt to influence government to advance shared goals

Pluralism and the Interest Group System

The U.S. political system provides numerous opportunities for people to influence public policy. Voting in elections to choose leaders offers one such opportunity. The guarantees of freedom of speech to speak one's mind about political issues and freedom of the press to critically assess issues and leaders' performance are others. Public opinion polls are yet another mechanism that solicits input from the masses.

But perhaps the most natural—and arguably the most influential—form of public input into government arrives by way of the activities of interest groups. James Madison, in Federalist No. 10, admonished that "the latent causes of faction are thus sown in the nature of man."[1] By faction, Madison was referring to what we now term interest groups. Madison was concerned about the potential influence of factions on the government. But at the same time, he understood that people were by nature drawn toward the organization of collective interests and the use of that organization to influence government action. Madison expected that if enough interest groups vied to influence policy, they would cancel each other out.

What Is an Interest Group?

Interest group
An organization of people with shared goals that tries to influence public policy through a variety of activities.

An **interest group** (also referred to as a "pressure group" or "organized interest") is an organization of people with shared goals that tries to influence public policy through a variety of activities. Every individual has interests, and interest groups are a mechanism for people with shared goals to protect or advance their own interests. People can try to influence government on their own—such as by calling or writing their elected representatives to voice their opinion or by voting in an election. Another way people can influence government is by joining a group that is organized to accomplish an objective.

Senior citizens, for example, have a shared interest in securing cost-of-living adjustments (COLAs) in the Social Security system that disburses checks to them each month. Every year, the president and Congress determine the percentage rate increase in the COLA. The larger the increase, the higher will be an individual's monthly Social Security check. Each individual senior citizen might call his or her representatives in Congress to try to influence the vote for a larger COLA increase. Another way senior citizens may try to influence government is by joining and supporting AARP (formerly the American Association of Retired Persons), an interest group that, among other activities, tries to influence government to approve large increases in the annual COLA for Social Security. AARP is large, with many resources and lobbyists to influence legislators. Although an individual citizen's call to a representative may carry some weight, it is no match for the vast resources and activities of the AARP.

Interest groups link people with government policies. The linkage created by interest groups is constitutionally protected by the First Amendment, which guarantees the people's right "to peaceably assemble and petition the government for redress of grievances." People assembling in groups that carry out activities to foster group members' goals is a common activity in Washington, in the fifty state capitals, and in thousands of local governments.

Alexis de Tocqueville, a Frenchman who toured the United States in the early 1830s and observed the early workings of the U.S. political system, was struck by the extent to which group association and activity dominated the American system. In his now-classic 1835 book *Democracy in America*, de Tocqueville praised the extent to which group activity underpins American democracy.[2] More than French citizens and other Europeans that he observed, De Tocqueville found that Americans were particularly prone to organize in groups and use their associations to influence the political process.

Pluralism refers to the theory that public policy largely results from a variety of interest groups competing with one another to promote laws that benefit members of their respective groups. By contrast, **majoritarianism** refers to the theory that public policy is a product of what majorities of citizens prefer. Whereas the majoritarian perspective focuses on public opinion, voting results, and mass representation to describe how democracy in America actually works, the pluralist perspective suggests that in fact "the majority rarely rules."

Political scientist Robert Dahl, an architect of pluralist ideas, suggested in *A Preface to Democratic Theory* that the American people are represented in government primarily through interest group activity.[3] The products of public policy are largely a function of support for and membership in interest groups that compete for influence through activities such as lobbying. The U.S. political system, according to Dahl, offers a number of "access points" for any given group to provide input. These access points include Congress, executive branch offices, the courts, elections, and the news media. David B. Truman, another political scientist, has advanced the notion that group activity and mobilization are natural consequences of shared concerns.[4] The free and open competition among groups advances the democratic system, just as a free and open marketplace of ideas promotes the adoption of the best ideas in society.

The Pros and Cons of Interest Groups

The political power that emanates from groups of people organizing for the purpose of influencing government outputs can be quite strong. "Are interest

★ LO
Define pluralism as the theory that public policy is largely the product of a variety of different interest groups competing with one another to promote laws that benefit members of their respective groups

Pluralism
The theory that public policy largely results from a variety of interest groups competing with one another to promote laws that benefit members of their respective groups.

Majoritarianism
The theory that public policy is a product of what majorities of citizens prefer.

★ LO
Assess both the benefits and criticisms of the interest group system in the United States

In the Words of French Political Philosopher Alexis de Tocqueville

Alexis de Tocqueville, a French observer of the American political system, praised the role that interest groups played in American politics. After touring the United States in the early 1830s, de Tocqueville wrote *Democracy in America*, published in 1835, in which he made the following observations about interest groups, or "associations" as he referred to them, in the United States:

> The [citizen] of the United States learns from birth that he must rely on himself to combat the ills and trials of life. . . . If some obstacle blocks the public road halting . . . traffic, neighbors at once form a deliberative body; this improvised assembly produces an authority which remedies the trouble before anyone has thought of the possibility beyond that of those concerned . . . associations are formed to combat moral troubles; intemperance is fought in common. Public security, trade and industry, and morals and religion all provide the aims for associations in the United States. There

> is no end to which the human will despair of attaining by the free action of the collective power of individuals.

> When a political association is allowed to form centers of action at certain important places in the country, its activity becomes greater and its influence more widespread. There men meet, active measures are planned, and opinions are expressed with that strength and warmth which the written word can never attain.

> Freedom of association has become a necessary guarantee against the tyranny of the majority. In the United States once a party has become predominant all public power passes into its hands. . . . The most distinguished men of the opposite party . . . must be able to establish themselves outside of it. . . . The omnipotence of the majority seems to me such a danger to the American republics that the dangerous expedient used to curb it is actually something good. Here I would repeat something which I have put in other words when speaking of municipal freedom: no countries need associations more—to prevent either the despotism of parties or the arbitrary rule of a prince—than those with a democratic social state.

groups good or bad for American democracy?" is a question akin to the old cliché "Is the glass half full or half empty?" The answer, of course, depends on one's perspective. Madison himself recognized that interest groups were powerful and that they could be dangerous. But he also acknowledged that factions could not be eliminated. Channeling them into productive devices for promoting public input was a primary challenge his generation faced in framing the government.

The Pros. Many observers today sing the praises of an interest group system that advances the interests of the people. Their arguments in support of interest groups include the following:

- Interest groups provide all groups in society with an opportunity to win support for their ideas and positions. The vast number of interest groups represents a wide array of political opinions, economic perspectives, and social class differences.

- By their very nature, humans seek out others who have ideas similar to their own. Joining groups and working for the interests of the group are natural inclinations of citizens and should be encouraged as methods of representation in our democracy.

- The right of association is a basic right protected implicitly by the First Amendment to the U.S. Constitution, which affords individuals the right "peaceably to assemble."

- A wide array of diverse groups in society—rich and poor, urban and nonurban, male and female, Northern and Southern, liberal and conservative—potentially may organize and attempt to influence government. The system is fair in that it gives all groups an equitable opportunity to compete.

The Cons. Many other observers of the U.S. political system are quite critical of the power exerted by interest groups. In *The Power Elite*, C. Wright Mills characterizes interest groups as a tool of the political elite rather than a system that enables broad participation in influencing public policy.[5] Along this line, many criticize the ability of wealthy corporations and individuals to exert disproportionate influence on government through well-financed interest group activities. John Heinz and his colleagues argue further that the influence of interest groups is contingent on a number of factors and that their influence may be quite limited.[6] Other criticisms of interest groups include the following:

- Use of interest groups to make public policy is unfair because groups supported by the wealthy have far greater resources to promote their interests in the political system.

- Large corporations exist to maximize profits. They dominate the interest group system and tend to be ruthless in achieving their policy goals. The interest group system thus promotes the advancement of interests that do not always strive for the common good.

- The amount of interest group activity is so great that it has made it difficult to get things done in government. Too many groups are operating, slowing down the policymaking process to a state of gridlock in many areas.

- Interest group leaders are not elected, distinguishing them from many of the policymaking institutions that have been constitutionally ordained—such as Congress and the executive branch. Thus, interest group dominance of the political system is an affront to democracy.

- Interest groups work to concentrate benefits for the few while distributing costs to the many.

Interest Groups in Action

Interest groups have always played an important role in American politics. Even in the colonial period, groups such as the Sons of Liberty gathered members, collected donations, and organized protests to achieve the goal of American freedom from British taxation. The Sons of Liberty were successful in their aims because they tied their actions to the economic interests of their members. As Madison acknowledged, economic interests tend to be the type of concerns that are most salient to people and thus move them to collective action.

In 1886, the American Federation of Labor (AFL) was formed as the first broad-based national labor union. The AFL was originally established to advocate the rights of craft unions and ensure the terms of union contracts. Organized and led by Samuel Gompers for forty years, it attracted many members and raised funds to promote laws benefiting organized labor. The AFL was the principal advocate for establishing a cabinet department, the U.S. Department of Labor, to administer labor programs. This department continues to serve as one of the largest executive departments in the nation. In the 1950s, the AFL merged with the Congress of Industrial Organizations (CIO) to create the AFL-CIO, an interest group still very active in promoting the labor agenda.

The National Association of Manufacturers (NAM) was organized in 1885 for the purpose of advancing the interests of the manufacturing businesses. Although setting protective tariffs was its core objective, the NAM also became a primary opponent of the AFL and other labor interest groups. The goals of organized labor (such as higher wages for workers, better working conditions, increased benefits, and job security) and the goals of business owners (maximizing profits) often came into conflict.

Tensions between labor and business interests intensified with the tremendous growth of the American economy beginning in the late 1800s and continued to mount as the economy expanded. Large companies, focusing on maximizing profits (which in turn appealed to shareholders), opposed laborers' demands for increased wages, better working conditions, and worker benefits. Today, labor and business interest groups continue to be among the largest and most powerful interest groups in the nation.

The Growth of Interest Groups

★ LO Understand the reasons for the growth of interest groups in the United States during the twentieth century

Perhaps the most significant factor leading to an increase in the number of interest groups has been the overall growth in government. Interest groups attempt to advance their agenda by influencing various aspects of government. As the number of government programs and agencies has expanded, along with their reach, opportunities for influencing what government does through interest group activities have expanded as well.

The New Deal programs of the 1930s and the Great Society programs of the 1960s led to tremendous growth in the federal government and huge increases in the federal budget. Government began to assume a more active role not only in promoting its economic policies but in promoting social policies as well. In response, a vast number of interest groups formed. Both proponents and opponents of a more active government organized interest groups to advocate their views. As the number of interest groups advocating economic issues expanded, so too did the number of groups promoting ideological perspectives, positions on single issues, and political reforms.

Although interest groups have been part of the American system since its beginning, the number of groups has increased dramatically over the past half-century. Between 1960 and 2007, the number of official associations increased by 400 percent (from 5,843 to 23,298); the total amount of lobbying spending in Washington increased from $1.43 billion in 1998 to $3.47 billion in 2009; and from 1998 through 2009 the total number of registered lobbyists in Washington, DC, increased from 10,403 to 13,739.[7] Major political developments, such as the antiwar movement, the civil rights movement, and the Watergate scandal of the Nixon administration, mobilized a better-educated mass public to become increas-

AARP: The Behemoth of Interest Group Politics

AARP boasts over 40 million members, making it one of the largest interest groups in America. A principal reason for AARP's popularity is that its eligibility for membership is straightforward: One must be fifty years of age or older. Formerly known as the American Association of Retired Persons, AARP adopted its acronym as its official name in 1999, as its activities broadened beyond those directly related to advocating for the interests of retirees. In 2009, AARP reported spending about $30 million in lobbying government activities at the state and federal levels.

AARP now not only advocates for its membership, but it also provides a wide variety of services, including Medicare Supplemental insurance, discounts on rental cars, cruise and vacation packages, long-term care insurance, and legal services.

The size of AARP, along with the broad scope of its activities, have invited criticisms and led to some controversies. For example, 60,000 members quit the organization in 2009 over its endorsement of President Obama's health care reform proposals. The AARP also came under fire in 2003 for lobbying in favor of the Medicare Prescription, Drug, Improvement and Modernization Act. An Annenberg Public Policy Report concluded that AARP had a conflict of interest in advocating for this legislation because it earns income from the sale of health and life insurance policies, which benefit from the Act's provisions. Indeed, AARP concedes that it was paid over $650 million in royalties from insurance companies which sold products to AARP members through an AARP reference in 2008 alone. Meanwhile, those same member services and advocacy tactics—controversial as they may be—make AARP one of the largest and most successful interest groups in the American political system.

Members of the well-organized and very powerful AARP at a political rally.

WILLIAM THOMAS CAIN/GETTY IMAGES

---

ingly concerned about political issues. This heightened concern about social and political issues fostered a significant amount of new interest group activity. The sophisticated use of mass-media technologies such as television, the computer, and the Internet has facilitated the ability of groups to emerge and flourish.

Another factor contributing to the increase in interest group activity has been the escalating cost of financing political campaigns. As costs have increased, interest groups have come to play a greater role in supporting political parties and the election of candidates. The Federal Election Campaign Act of 1971 placed limits on individual and corporate contributions to political campaigns. As a means of financing campaigns through alternative methods, interest groups have formed **political action committees (PACs)**. Currently, PACs can contribute up to $5,000 directly to campaigns, as long as each PAC contributes to at least five different candidates in an election year. As we will see in Chapter 15, PACs are a source of much controversy because many political candidates have become dependent on PAC money to wage successful campaigns.

Political action committee (PAC)
The political arm of an interest group that promotes candidates in election campaigns primarily through financial contributions.

Iron Triangles, Issue Networks, and the Influence of Groups

The influence of interest groups is buoyed by the process in which public policy is created and modified. In any policy area, three key sets of actors interact to produce public policy: (1) congressional committees and subcommittees assigned to a specific policy area, (2) executive agencies of government that have the authority to administer policies in a particular area, and (3) private interest groups that have an interest in influencing that policy area. Members of congressional committees, managers of agencies, and leaders of interest groups all have vested interests in the specific policy area. As political scientist Theodore Lowi has noted, although these parties may not always agree on particular positions, they all seek to promote policies favorable to their interests, and they come to depend on one another for support and influence. Together, this network of actors dominates the development of public policies. This durable and seemingly impenetrable three-sided network has come to be known as the **iron triangle** of policymaking.[8]

The development of U.S. defense policy illustrates how iron triangles work. The armed services and defense committees and subcommittees in Congress are responsible for appropriating funds for defense contracts (such as for the building of new military aircraft). Members of Congress on these committees are committed to maintaining a strong national defense, and they control the purse strings for developing new defense systems. Leaders in the U.S. Department of Defense are responsible for implementing defense systems under the orders of the president and rely on congressional committees to fund strong systems. Private contractors such as Pratt & Whitney (an airplane engine manufacturer) employ the engineers and researchers to design superior systems and provide valuable information to the congressional committees and the Department of Defense.

The committees and the Department of Defense depend on Pratt & Whitney for advanced engine technologies, advice on aircraft design, and the capacity to produce cutting-edge aircraft engines. Pratt & Whitney benefits from winning federal contracts to produce defense systems. The congressional committees, Department of Defense managers, and corporate leaders and lobbyists from Pratt & Whitney are familiar with one another, depend on one another, and use one another in the development of defense systems. The iron triangle approach to public policymaking has institutionalized the role of interest groups in the exercise of American democracy.

Although an iron triangle refers to the interdependent relationship among legislators, bureaucrats, and lobbyists in a particular policy area, it is also possible to identify a broader set of actors who all have a vested interest in an area of public policy and try to collectively influence their policy area. Political scientists have used the term **issue networks** to describe the broader array of actors beyond legislators, bureaucrats, and lobbyists who try to influence

RÜSTEM GÜRLER/ISTOCKPHOTO.COM

ALEX WONG/GETTY IMAGES

Musician Moby (left) with Congressman Edward Markey (D-MA) talk to the press at a news conference on Internet freedom in 2006. Moby and Markey both support limiting the influence of giant companies on the Internet.

Iron triangle
A three-sided network of policymaking that includes congressional committees (and subcommittees) in a specific policy area, executive agencies with authority over that area, and private interest groups focused on influencing that area.

Issue network
The broad array of actors (beyond just the iron triangle) that try to collectively influence a policy area in which they maintain a vested interest.

a particular policy area. These include congressional staff people, journalists or other members of the media who often report on the policy area, and researchers who have done work on and are experts in the policy area.[9]

Membership in Groups

★ LO

Assess material, purposive, and solidary benefits as reasons why people join interest groups

Many Americans belong to interest groups, and many businesses, nonprofit organizations, and public entities belong to interest groups as well. It is estimated that about four in five citizens belong to at least one interest group. Many of the more common groups Americans belong to include labor unions (such as the AFL-CIO, which boasts a total of about 11 million members), professional associations (such as the 240,000 physicians and medical students who belong to the American Medical Association), and organizations such as the AARP to which many of the nation's senior citizens belong. As many as 3 million businesses across the United States belong to the U.S. Chamber of Commerce.[10]

Although the number of Americans who belong to interest groups is high, certain types of people are more likely than others to engage in interest group activity. Americans with higher incomes and greater resources, and those who are better educated and employed in professional occupations, are much more likely to belong to groups. Those with more financial resources tend to better appreciate the utility of group membership and interest groups' impact on the political process; wealthier individuals are also more likely to have the resources to support interest group activities. Thus, many critics of interest group politics charge that the pluralist model of democracy favors the upper middle class and upper class of society. Because those with more resources can and do support interest groups, they are more likely to influence public policy to their financial advantage.

Various reasons have been proposed to explain why people or organizations might join and support certain interest groups. One is that they receive specific, tangible benefits from membership. These are referred to as the **material benefits** of group membership.[11] For instance, local units of the National Education Association (NEA) work for its teacher members to win salary increases, and so the benefits of membership often produce a favorable material benefit to teachers in the form of higher wages. Many interest groups provide their members with other material benefits such as health and auto insurance discounts, magazine subscriptions, and free products.

Interest groups often appeal to many people for the **purposive benefits** (or expressive benefits) they provide.[12] Purposive rewards are those that do not directly benefit the individual member but benefit society more generally. Some interest groups, for example, are committed to the goal of improving the environment and promoting policies that better protect the natural environment. The Sierra Club is one such organization that endorses these goals, and members of the Sierra Club receive purposive benefits from membership and support of the group's activities.

The **solidary benefits** of membership, or the satisfaction that individuals receive from interacting with like-minded individuals for a cause, offer a third type of incentive for interest group membership.[13] Solidary benefits derive less from the interest group's goals and more from the process of interacting with others to achieve a goal. For example, a union worker who attends a labor rally to support increases in a new contract may receive satisfaction from simply being with colleagues in support of a cause.

Material benefits (of group membership) The specific, tangible benefits individuals receive from interest group membership, such as economic concessions, discounts on products, etc.

Purposive benefits (of group membership) Rewards that do not directly benefit the individual member, but benefit society as a whole.

Solidary benefits (of group membership) Satisfaction that individuals receive from interacting with like-minded individuals for a cause.

What Makes Some Groups More Powerful Than Others?

Although there are thousands of interest groups operating in the United States, some groups are more successful than others in promoting their cause and affecting public policy to their liking. There are three general characteristics of an interest group, which may have significant bearing on how powerful that group's influence will be in Washington:

1. **The size of the membership.** There is, undoubtedly, power in numbers. The larger the number of members of an interest group, the more powerful that group will be in affecting public policy. Large membership alone makes elected leaders responsive to a group's concerns. An interest group with a large number of members can increase its power and influence by convincing its members to vote for a candidate or candidates. A good example of a group that exhibits strength through numbers is the American Farm Bureau Federation (AFBF), which boasts 4.7 million members and has proven especially effective at promoting policies that provide large subsidies and other benefits to American farmers. A bilateral trade agreement between the United States and Russia in late 2006 was a testament to AFBF influence, as it substantially expanded the export market for U.S. farmers.

2. **The wealth of the members.** The number of members is an important indicator of the potential amount of money that interest groups might be able to raise. But just as important is the wealth of the membership. Certain interest groups enjoy a huge advantage when it comes to the average wealth of its members. For example, the American Trial Lawyers Association (ATLA) is made up of trial lawyers who, by virtue of their occupation, are quite wealthy when compared to average Americans. Thus, whereas the number of members of the ATLA is only about 60,000, the wealth of its membership and the consequent level of financial contributions from members provide sufficient resources to make it an especially powerful interest group in Washington.

3. **The dedication of members to the goals of the group.** In addition to the number of members and wealth of members, groups that have a loyal following based on members' commitment to the cause of the group can be a powerful resource.[14] The National Right to Life Committee (NRLC) is a good example. The NRLC organized and began to solicit members and contributions in 1973, after the *Roe v. Wade* decision legalized abortion. NRLC's members tend to be dedicated to right-to-life positions and willing to contribute much time, effort, and resources to advance its pro-life agenda.

Types of Interest Groups

Although interest groups represent a wide array of interests in American society, there are two basic types of interest groups: economic groups and noneconomic groups. Many groups engage in both economic and noneconomic pursuits, but most can be classified as either primarily economic or noneconomic in nature.

Economic Groups

Although the specific goals of different interest groups vary greatly, the vast majority of groups in America have goals that are economic in nature. Two of every three interest groups in America are **economic interest groups**, or groups that exist to promote favorable economic conditions and economic opportunities for their members. Economic groups also tend to be the largest and most powerful groups because members of such groups maintain a vested personal financial stake in having the group achieve its goals. Economic groups also tend to be the best organized and most influential interest groups.

There are thousands of interest groups that focus primarily on advancing the economic goals of their members. These groups include private businesses, labor unions, business and industry associations, and professional associations.

Business Groups. The largest companies in the nation and the world typically maintain internal units that function as an interest group for the company. General Motors (GM) and IBM, for example, have their own interest groups. Such companies typically have wide and varied interests. GM, for example, is affected by environmental laws (tougher air pollution laws often require GM to spend more on technologies to reduce emissions from their cars), labor laws (increases in the minimum wage require higher pay for some workers), and product safety laws (increased safety standards might increase the cost of assembling a car). GM needs a well-staffed interest group to try to influence these and many other types of legislation.

Most businesses belong to associations, and often, these associations engage in interest group activities to advocate for the interests of their members. Some associations are very broad in scope, such as the U.S. Chamber of Commerce with its 3 million members. These businesses range from small neighborhood auto mechanics to large billion-dollar financial institutions. The Chamber of Commerce seeks to broadly advance the interests of business owners.

Another type of business association is a **trade association**. A trade association typically focuses on one particular industry, and members of the association are drawn exclusively from that industry. Businesses in a particular trade often face similar types of concerns, and the trade association looks out for the specific interests of a classification of businesses. For example, the American Society of Travel Agents (ASTA) is a trade association whose 24,000 member institutions include travel agencies, hotels, airlines, car rental agencies, and the like. ASTA promotes legislation and regulations favoring the travel industry.

Businesses, business associations, and trade associations have an advantage over associations and other organizations whose members are individual citizens or consumers. Businesses quickly see the advantage of joining an association, which collectively advocates for the interests of like businesses. Individuals, however, are less likely to join and contribute to an association that advocates for such things as consumer protection. Because there are so many consumers, an individual consumer is less likely to see a benefit in his or her own contribution. But because there are fewer businesses that belong to any given trade association, businesses are more likely to perceive a benefit from participating in the organization. As Mancur Olson, a well-known scholar on interest groups, put it, smaller groups are more likely to organize and associate because members can more

Economic interest group
An organized group that exists to promote favorable economic conditions and economic opportunities for its members.

Trade association
A business association that focuses on one particular industry, with membership drawn exclusively from that industry.

LO Explain the "free rider" problem that many interest groups face

Free rider
An individual who does not join or contribute to an interest group that is representing his or her interests.

readily see the benefits and "logic of collective action."[15] That is, people with common interests working together in groups are more effective than the same number of people working independently.

Certainly, members of smaller groups are more likely to perceive direct benefits from their membership; smaller groups are also less likely to suffer from the free rider problem. **Free riders** are those individuals who do not join or contribute to an interest group that is representing their interests. Thus, they enjoy the benefits of membership without paying for the costs. The free rider problem is more common in larger groups, which may have trouble convincing individuals to contribute due to each individual's perception that others will work to achieve the group's goal.

TABLE 11.1 Who Spends the Most on Lobbying?

In 2009, interest groups spent more than $3 billion on lobbying activities in Washington, DC. This table shows the biggest spenders from 1998 through 2009.

Organization	Total
U.S. Chamber of Commerce	$606,758,180
American Medical Association	$220,832,500
General Electric	$196,410,000
AARP	$175,702,064
American Hospital Association	$174,890,431
Pharmaceutical Research and Manufacturers of America	$173,403,920
AT&T Inc.	$150,471,757
Northrup Grumman	$143,005,253
Exxon Mobil	$138,886,942
National Association of Realtors	$138,417,380
Blue Cross/Blue Shield	$136,317,077
Business Roundtable	$134,030,000
Edison Electric Institute	$133,955,999
Verizon Communications	$132,534,841
Lockheed Martin	$122,430,423
Boeing	$121,528,310
General Motors	$106,914,000
Southern Co.	$104,620,694
Freddie Mac	$96,194,048

Source: Center for Responsive Politics, http://www.opensecrets.org.

Labor Unions. Whereas business groups promote the interests of companies and corporations, labor unions promote the interests of American workers. In the early 1940s, as many as 35 percent of workers in America were union members. Over the years, however, the percentage of union workers has declined. Today, only about 13 percent of workers belong to a union. An important reason for this decline relates to changes in the type of jobs that Americans hold. Skilled and unskilled laborers are most likely to be unionized, but these types of jobs represent an increasingly smaller proportion of the workforce. Professional and service jobs, which are less likely to be unionized, now dominate the American workforce, and so union membership has declined. Rather than unionizing, professionals tend to organize and join professional associations. Some professionals, however, have unionized. The largest union in the United States today is a teachers' union, the National Education Association.

Unions differ from professional associations in that the laws provide certain bargaining rights to unions. Union membership may be required for all employees as well. State laws vary on this issue. Some states are **open shop**, which means that employees in that state maintain the option of whether or not to join a certified union. Of course, in open shop states, workers who do not join the union may benefit from union activities without "paying the price"—another form of the free rider problem. Since 1947, the federal Taft-Hartley Act has technically banned the **closed shop**, which requires union membership as a condition of employment in a unionized workplace. Still, unions have successfully convinced some state legislatures that because all workers enjoy the benefits of union advocacy (for example, promoting pay increases and so on), all workers should at least be required to pay dues to the union. Thus, many states allow so-called **union shops**, which require that employees in unionized workplaces either join the union or pay the equivalent of union dues to it after a set period of time.

Professional Associations. Higher levels of education and advances in technology have transformed the American workforce over the past half-century. One of the major changes has been an increase in professional, technical, and service jobs and a decrease in the number of skilled and unskilled labor jobs. Professionals have organized to promote and protect their economic interests through membership in professional organizations, which lobby on their behalf.

Two large and growing classes of professionals are lawyers and medical doctors, both of which have high-profile and powerful interest groups—the American Bar Association (ABA) for lawyers and the American Medical Association (AMA) for doctors. The medical and legal professions are regulated by state governments, and the ABA and AMA have been quite successful in influencing the regulatory process—for example, by establishing licensing requirements for lawyers and doctors.

Noneconomic Groups

Economic groups exist primarily to advance the commercial and financial interests of their members. Whereas economic interests dominate pluralist activities, many other interest groups advocate for primarily noneconomic concerns. Three general categories of **noneconomic interest groups** are public interest groups, issue or ideological groups, and government groups.

Open shop
The law that allows employees the option of joining or not joining the certified union at a unionized workplace.

Closed shop
The law that requires employees to become members of the union as a condition of employment in unionized workplaces.

Union shop
The law that requires that employees in unionized workplaces either join the union or pay the equivalent of union dues to it after a set period of time.

Noneconomic interest group
An organized group that advocates for reasons other than their membership's commercial and financial interests.

Public interest group
An organized group that promotes the broad, collective good of citizens and consumers.

Public Interest Groups. **Public interest groups** promote the broad, collective good of citizens and consumers. Many public interest groups seek to promote political reforms that enhance the role of the public in the political process. The League of Women Voters is one such group. Initially formed as an interest group that promoted women's suffrage, the league has become a leading advocate for improving turnout among all citizens in elections. The League of Women Voters has also taken the lead in promoting candidate engagement on issues of importance to the voters by sponsoring campaign debates.

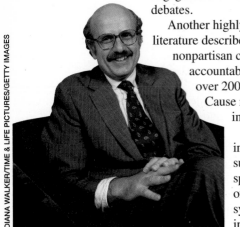

Another highly active public interest group is Common Cause. This group's literature describes itself in the following way: "Common Cause is a nonprofit, nonpartisan citizen's lobbying organization promoting open, honest and accountable government. Supported by the dues and contributions of over 200,000 members in every state across the nation, Common Cause represents the unified voice of the people against corruption in government and big money special interests."[16]

Common Cause promotes reforming the political system in ways that enhance the role of the average citizen. Thus, it supports laws limiting elected officials from taking gifts from special interests, banning large speaking honoraria for members of Congress, and reforming the presidential campaign finance system. Ironically, Common Cause also tries to limit the role interest groups play in the electoral process.

Fred Wertheimer, formerly the president of Common Cause.

Issue and ideological group
An organized group that focuses on specific issues and ideological perspectives.

Issue and Ideological Groups. Interest groups that focus on specific issues and ideological perspectives are known as **issue and ideological groups**. Abortion, women's rights, and the environment are just a few of the policy issues that have produced interest groups such as the National Right to Life Committee (pro-life), Americans for Free Choice (pro-choice), the National Organization for Women (NOW; women's rights), and the Sierra Club and the Nature Conservancy (both environmental groups). Each of these groups maintains effective lobbies on behalf of its positions.

Some groups have a broader focus than a particular issue or set of policy issues. These are known as ideological groups, and they promote a more general ideological approach on how government should deal with a host of issues. Both liberal and conservative ideological groups operate in the American pluralist system. The Americans for Democratic Action (ADA), for example, is an interest group that promotes government policies with a liberal orientation. Since 1947, the voting records of members of Congress on certain issues have served as the standard measure of political liberalism. The ADA supports candidates for office whose votes on key issues score a high "liberal quotient."

The Christian Coalition of America (CCA) is another ideological group that has become a lobbying powerhouse in recent decades; it offers a vehicle to become involved in influencing public policy. The CCA's agenda advocates pro-life positions, promotes the role of religion as a part of what government does, favors reducing tax burdens on families, and supports victims' rights.

Government Interest Groups. Most interest group activity organizes private concerns (of either individuals or businesses) for the purpose of influencing

YOUR PERSPECTIVE on American Government

"Before the Lecture Begins, Students from PIRG Have an Announcement. . . ."

If you have spent significant time on a college campus, you have probably heard about PIRG (Public Interest Research Group). PIRG is a federation of state-based public interest groups that, in the words of its website, "stand up to powerful special interests on behalf of the American public" (see http://www.uspirg.org/about-us). State PIRGs are particularly active in recruiting students on college campuses. At the start of the semester, student members of PIRG ask professors for a few minutes of class time to pitch PIRG-related activities to the class. For many students, this is their first exposure to an interest group. Those who join will quickly get involved in PIRG's public interest causes and sometimes even become interns and get course credit for the experience.

For Critical Thinking and Discussion

1. Does PIRG operate on your campus?
2. What other interest groups are active at your college?
3. Have you ever been asked to get involved in PIRG or another interest group's activities?
4. What kinds of interest groups are you most willing to support?

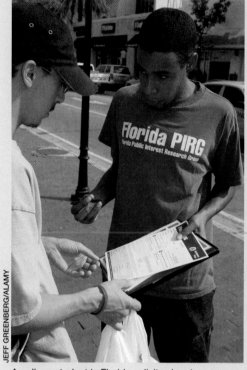

JEFF GREENBERG/ALAMY

A college student in Florida solicits signatures on a petition for Florida PIRG.

public policy. But private interests are not the only ones represented in the pluralist system. Groups representing the interests of governments also operate in this complex system.

Cities and states across the nation have organized to exert influence on the federal government. Most states and large cities employ their own lobbyists in Washington, DC. But states, cities, and other governments also organize collectively through a variety of interest groups, which are generally referred to as **intergovernmental lobbies**. The National League of Cities, for example, is an interest group that advocates for the broad interests of local governments. Not only do state and local governments lobby in Washington, DC, but foreign governments also organize and lobby. Many nations have embassies in the Washington, DC, area, and many of these embassies engage in interest group activities of their own.

Intergovernmental lobby
Any interest group that represents the collective interests of states, cities, and other governments.

★ LO   Identify the
activities interest groups
engage in to achieve their
goals and influence public
policy

How Interest Groups Achieve Their Goals

Interest groups engage in a number of activities to advance the goals of the group and influence public policy. These activities usually involve lobbying, supporting candidates and parties in election campaigns, mounting persuasion campaigns, and litigating.

Lobbying

Lobbying
The means by which interest groups attempt to influence government officials to make decisions favorable to their goals.

Interest groups attempt to influence elected and other public leaders to make decisions that are favorable toward the group's goals. **Lobbying** is the term that describes how interest groups go about influencing government officials. Lobbyists are the professionals who do the lobbying.

Lobbyists provide information to public officials with the hope that the information will convince the official to vote or act in a manner favorable to the group's interest. Lobbyists perform a valuable function to public officials by providing not only information and perspectives on issues but expertise as well. In the iron triangle system, lobbyists seek access to members of Congress and to managers in executive agencies in a particular policy area. Public officials come to depend on the lobbyists for information and knowledge. For example, managers in the Department of Defense and members of Congress on the armed services committees rely on lobbyists from Pratt & Whitney for information on emerging jet engine technologies, engine performance data, and other information, which allows the military to plan and improve the nation's defenses.

Similarly, the congressional committees responsible for workplace safety standards and the Occupational Safety and Health Administration (OSHA), the executive agency responsible for administering those standards, depend on the lobbyists representing labor unions and product safety groups for data and information on workplace hazards and recommendations for remediation. Of course, these same public officials are likely to be lobbied by business interests concerned about the increased costs associated with remediation of hazards.

Lobbyists communicate with public officials in many different ways, including formal presentations, written memos and policy papers, informal e-mails or notes, face-to-face meetings, or informal discussions over a meal or a drink. The most effective lobbyists are those who provide valuable, truthful information on policy issues and who make persuasive arguments. Having a good working relationship with public officials and a quality reputation provides the lobbyist with access to officials, which is crucial to the lobbyist's success.

A common perception of lobbying is that of a lobbyist offering money, gifts, trips, or other goods in return for a favorable action, such as a congressperson's vote on a particular bill. Though such activities do take place, in modern times, they have become the exception rather than the rule. The activities of lobbyists today are strictly regulated by federal and state governments. Lobbyist gift-giving and bribery of public officials is illegal in most states and can be prosecuted. States require lobbyists to provide financial statements, report expenses, and maintain official registration for interest groups and individuals who provide lobbying services.

Grassroots lobbying
Communications by interest groups with government officials through the mobilization of public opinion to exert influence on government action.

A form of lobbying that has been used more frequently in recent years is known as **grassroots lobbying**. The idea behind grassroots lobbying is that

High-Powered Lobbyists

Today, lobbyists are as important in policymaking as members of Congress themselves. But this is nothing new in American politics. Lobbying has been part of the American political system since the colonial era. Some of the nation's most successful lobbyists over time include the following:

Benjamin Franklin. Most students of American history recognize Benjamin Franklin as a founding father, political philosopher, and inventor/scientist. But Franklin was also a lobbyist and quite a successful one. The colonies of Pennsylvania, Georgia, and Massachusetts hired him to lobby on their behalf before the British Parliament from 1757 to 1770. Franklin's greatest lobbying success was securing the repeal of the Stamp Act in 1766.

Tommy Corcoran. "The Cork," as he was known in Washington circles, set the mold for today's most successful lobbyists. He was a trusted friend and adviser to President Franklin Delano Roosevelt during the New Deal era, when Corcoran successfully lobbied Congress on behalf of the White House for many new government programs, including the Securities and Exchange Commission, the Tennessee Valley Authority, and the Federal Housing Administration. He also placed hundreds of attorneys in jobs to run these New Deal agencies. A well-connected insider, The Cork established a private lobbying practice in 1942, where his many connections in government proved valuable for his private-sector clients. From the 1940s until the 1960s, he was the most powerful and influential lobbyist in Washington.

John Podesta. After serving as President Bill Clinton's fourth and final chief of staff from 1998 through 2001, John Podesta parlayed his top spot in the West Wing into a high-profile, influential, and lucrative lobbying career. He founded and is the current president of the Center for American Progress, a liberal think tank highly influential with Democrats in Congress. Podesta's understanding of White House operations earned him the position of director of the Obama–Biden transition team, where he played a key role in the selection of individuals to fill the highest level executive appointments. Today, he remains highly influential among Obama administration insiders, many of whom owe their appointment to him.

interest groups communicate with government officials by mobilizing public opinion to exert influence on government action. Because elected leaders are often quite sensitive to the opinions of voters, if a group can demonstrate that public opinion supports a particular position or that the public is willing to contact officials to express their view, officeholders will respond favorably because they want to enhance their chances of being reelected to office. Interest groups with a large number of members are particularly effective at grassroots lobbying, mainly because they can produce large numbers of potential votes in a given election. AARP, with more than 40 million members, has successfully used grassroots methods of lobbying to put pressure on Congress to protect the Social Security and Medicare systems—two primary goals of AARP.

Supporting Candidates and Parties in Elections

Interest groups are also quite active in electoral politics, providing resources for candidates and parties that support the interest groups' goals. PACs, described earlier in this chapter, are an important instrument through which interest groups provide financial support to candidates and political parties.

TABLE 11.2 Big Givers to Campaigns

These ten organizations were the biggest contributors to American political campaigns between 1989 and 2010. AT&T and the National Association of Realtors gave about equally to Democrats and Republicans, while the remaining top ten givers heavily tilted toward giving to Democratic Party candidates.

Organization	Contributions
AT&T, Inc.	$44,228,128
American Federation of State, County and Municipal Employees	$41,945,511
National Association of Realtors	$35,643,323
International Brotherhood of Electrical Workers	$31,544,407
Goldman Sachs	$31,544,275
American Association for Justice	$31,465,429
National Education Association	$30,162,867
Laborers Union	$28,993,900
Teamsters	$27,992,624
Service Employees International Union	$27,933,732

Source: Center for Responsive Politics, March 2010.

In addition to providing financial support to candidates, groups can play an important role in campaigns in other ways as well. For example, a labor union might endorse a candidate and communicate that endorsement to its members, urging members to vote for the candidate. A group might also use its resources to hire a phone bank to make "get out the vote" phone calls on behalf of a candidate or slate of candidates. Groups have also provided support by drafting speeches for candidates on policy matters or hosting rallies for office seekers.

Litigation

Interest groups have also become quite adept at using the court system as a means of achieving their goals. Groups regularly initiate lawsuits, request injunctions, defend members, and file briefs. Consumer product safety groups, for example, regularly file for injunctions in courts seeking to order companies to cease the sale of products that are unsafe.

Some interest groups focus primarily on the courts to achieve their goals. For example, the ACLU regularly initiates lawsuits in circumstances in which it believes the government is compromising individual civil liberties. The ACLU is very active in litigating gender discrimination cases. One of the advantages of interest group litigation is its capitalization of interest groups' financial resources; average citizens do not have sufficient resources to initiate so many lawsuits. Also, because interest groups often specialize in particular kinds of lawsuits, they are able to litigate more skillfully.

BETTMANN/CORBIS

ACLU attorney Ruth Bader Ginsburg in 1977. Sixteen years later Ginsburg became an associate justice on the U.S. Supreme Court.

Another way interest groups use the court system to exert influence is by the filing of amicus curiae ("friend of the court") briefs, which are companion briefs supporting an argument or set of arguments in an existing Supreme Court case.[17] Although the interest group is not a direct litigant in a matter, it can use an amicus brief to further or better articulate a position and thus aid litigants in their respective case.

Interest groups have also influenced the court system by engaging in lobbying activities to influence the appointment of judges. Pro-life and pro-choice groups are very active in supporting or opposing particular judicial nominees based on the nominees' position and past decisions on abortion cases. The American Bar Association uses a rating system to rank individuals nominated for federal judgeships that has become extremely influential in the appointment process.

Persuasion Campaigns

Many interest groups run media campaigns to persuade the public to support their position on issues. Some of this persuasion occurs during election campaigns when groups create and place ads intended to help a political candidate or political party achieve victory. But increasingly, groups have run such campaigns outside election campaigns to persuade or educate others to the group's way of thinking.

Groups have developed sophisticated public relations operations to communicate their positions. They use tactics such as "targeted mass mailings," in which they mail a pamphlet or other document to a large list of individuals that the group is attempting to influence. For example, the Americans for Democratic Action (ADA) maintains a list of voters who are not registered with any particular political party. The ADA often sends mailings to those on the list to try to persuade them to support the ADA's position on a particular issue. In addition to mass mailings, groups regularly use television, radio, newspapers, magazines, or even billboards to communicate positions and try to persuade. They also use the Internet to send messages to the wider public.

Making the Connection

Interest groups have become firmly entrenched within the American political landscape. Their influence is both certain and controversial. More than two centuries ago, James Madison expressed concerns about the influence of "factions." Today, many observers of American politics continue to express concerns about the influence of groups and the value of pluralism as a mode of governance. Nevertheless, interest groups offer an important and unique linkage between American citizens' varied interests and public policy. This does not diminish the importance of other linkages, such as free and open elections. But the linkage offered by interest groups is unique in that it allows citizens to exert influence by interacting with one another and collectively attempting to influence what government does.

Few would argue with the premise that interest groups have been responsible for leading the charge in promoting political and social policies that have significantly improved the lot of millions of Americans. At the same time, the relationship between interest groups and government actors can become uncomfortably close, if not downright corrupt. Nearly a century and a half apart, both the railways and the Native American tribes were interest groups that exerted a strong influence on government policymaking. Both sets of interests were well-respected for their contribution to the American landscape. Yet when Oakes Ames and Jack Abramoff, respectively, attempted to influence public policies and agreements using greed as an enticement, the democratic system suffered. Like everyone else in a democracy, interest groups must be free to press their own agenda, but not so free that they may trample the agendas of so many others.

POLITICS InterActive!

The Newest Way for Organized Interests to Influence Elections: 527s

Named after a section of the United States tax code, "527s" are a relatively new tool used by interest groups to try to influence the outcome of elections in America. A 527 group is a politically oriented organization that enjoys tax-exempt status under current law and thus is subject to no limits on the amount of soft money it can raise and spend. The group then uses the money it raised to develop and air "issue" advertisements. Although 527 groups cannot produce ads that directly tell voters which candidate or party to vote for in a particular election, they generally target positions on particular issues and craft advertisements that attempt to convince voters how they should think about those issues. Thus many 527 ads have amounted to negative attacks on the personality or character of particular candidates. In short, 527s have found a way to make an end run around the campaign finance system.

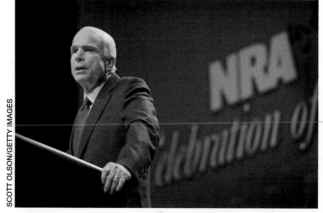

John McCain speaks at the annual meeting of the National Rifle Association, which endorsed him for president in 2008.

Spending by the 527s is significant. In 2008, 527 groups spent nearly $500 million on national, state, and local election contests. In the 2004 presidential election year, the 527s spent over $600 million. In the 2006 midterm election year, they spent $430 million.

Go to http://www.opensecrets.org/527s to find out which individuals and organizations provide the bulk of financial support to the 527s. Which industries have been most active in forming these groups? What kinds of ads have they produced? Who do you think benefits more—Democratic or Republican candidates—from the activities of 527 groups? Do these groups legitimately contribute to the "marketplace of ideas," or is this an example of "free speech run amuck"?

On www.cengage.com/dautrich/americangovernmentbrief/2e, find the Politics InterActive link for details on 527s. Consult as well the various links that relate to 527 advertisements. Historical, popular, and global perspectives on the 527s are also offered.

Chapter Summary

★ Pluralism and the Interest Group System

- Interest groups are a popular mechanism by which groups of people attempt to influence government to advance their shared goals.

- Pluralism is the theory that public policy largely results from a variety of interest groups competing with one another to promote laws that benefit members of their respective groups.

- Many praise the interest group system in the United States because it provides all groups in society with access and a fair opportunity to compete for influence over public policy.

- The interest group system is also criticized for allowing wealthy corporations and individuals a disproportionate influence on public policy, encouraging many groups to promote their own causes even if they run counter to the public interest, and significantly slowing down the policy-making process.

★ Interest Groups in Action

- The growth of interest groups in the United States during the twentieth century was a product of the tremendous growth of government in general over that same period and the increased concerns about political issues that are expressed by a better-educated mass public.

- Interest group influence over public policy is theoretically informal; in reality, interest group participation has become ingrained in the process through structures such as iron triangles and issue networks.

- Individuals tend to join or support interest groups to receive material benefits, purposive benefits (those that benefit society more generally), and solidary benefits based on individuals' satisfaction from interacting with like-minded people in pursuit of a goal.

- Large interest groups must always concern themselves with the problem of "free riders," those who benefit from interest group activities on their behalf without ever joining or contributing to that interest group.

- The most successful interest groups tend to maintain a large membership of individuals, at least some of whom are wealthy, as well as a loyal following based on members' commitment to the cause.

★ Types of Interest Groups

- Economic interest groups that pursue favorable monetary benefits for their members include business groups such as industry trade associations, labor unions, and professional associations. Non-economic interest groups that pursue goals other than the commercial interests of their members include public interest groups, issue or ideological groups, and government interest groups.

★ How Interest Groups Achieve Their Goals

- Interest groups achieve their goals through lobbying activities, supporting candidates in election contests, litigating, and mounting persuasion campaigns.

Key Terms

Closed shop (p. 295)

Economic interest group (p. 293)

Free rider (p. 294)

Grassroots lobbying (p. 298)

Interest group (p. 284)

Intergovernmental lobby (p. 297)

Iron triangle (p. 290)

Issue and ideological group (p. 296)

Issue network (p. 290)

Lobbying (p. 298)

Majoritarianism (p. 285)

Material benefits (of group membership) (p. 291)

Noneconomic interest group (p. 295)

Open shop (p. 295)

Pluralism (p. 285)

Political action committee (PAC) (p. 289)

Public interest group (p. 296)

Purposive benefits (of group membership) (p. 291)

Solidary benefits (of group membership) (p. 291)

Trade association (p. 293)

Union shop (p. 295)

Resources

Books

Berry, Jeffrey M. *The Interest Group Society*. New York: Longman, 1997.

Cigler, Alan, and Burdett Loomis, eds. *Interest Group Politics*, 7th ed. Washington, DC: CQ Press, 2006.

Goldstein, Kenneth M. *Interest Groups, Lobbying and Participation in America*. New York: Cambridge University Press, 1999.

Lowery, David, and Holly Brasher. *Organized Interests and American Government*. New York: McGraw-Hill, 2004.

Olson, Mancur. *The Logic of Collective Action: Public Goods and the Theory of Groups*. Cambridge, MA: Harvard University Press, 1965.

Rozell, Mark J., Clyde Wilcox, and David Madland. *Interest Groups in American Campaigns: The New Face of Electioneering*. Washington, DC: CQ Press, 2005.

Salisbury, Robert H. *Interests and Institutions: Substance and Structure in American Politics*. Pittsburgh, PA: University of Pittsburgh Press, 1992.

Tocqueville, Alexis de. *Democracy in America*. Edited by J. P. Mayer. Garden City, NY: Harper Perennial, 1988.

Internet Sources

http://www.opensecrets.org (Web site of the Center for Responsive Politics; includes facts and figures relating to lobbying activities, associations giving to political candidates, PACs, and sources of support for interest groups).

http://www.aflcio.org (AFL-CIO).

http://www.nlc.org (National League of Cities).

http://www.uschamber.org (U.S. Chamber of Commerce).

12 The Media and Politics

NOW The Obama White House web page promoting its health care reform bill in 2009.

On the webpage:

HEALTH CARE

Health Reform in Action

Health reform makes health care more affordable, holds insurers more accountable, expands coverage to all Americans and makes our health system sustainable.

HEAR MORE STORIES ▶

COURTESY OF WHITEHOUSE.GOV

THEN A still shot from a TV news broadcast in 1963 showing Birmingham, Alabama, firemen hosing down protesters.

CHARLES MOORE/BLACK STAR/ALAMY

NOW & THEN

A New Medium Assists in the Cause of Landmark Legislation

? *The battle being waged was the culmination of decades of debate that had thus far resulted in little legislation of any consequence. Now the president and his congressional allies were emboldened, and they sought to pass landmark legislation—but would they be able to overcome all the legislative hurdles that stood in their path? Their initiative this time would find an unexpected ally in the form of a powerful new medium. Those who tried to misrepresent the legislation would be held accountable; misleading arguments by the opposition could be verified thanks to a medium that offered unprecedented and convenient access to information. Public opinion was still bitterly divided on the reform, but this new medium would help the president win the highly contentious legislative battle. Indeed, without the help of this new medium, the president's persistent leadership might not have proved adequate to the challenge.*

LEARNING OBJECTIVES
★ WHAT YOU WILL LEARN ★

The Media in American Politics

★ Understand the purpose and evolution of the Federal Communications Commission

★ Describe the various functions that the media serve in the American political system

Historical Development of the Media

★ Appreciate the evolution from a partisan press to a media focused on objectivity

★ Explain how changes in technology have transformed the nature of the media

The Mass Media Today

★ Understand the large variety of media that cover news and provide opinion about government and politics, including both traditional media and "new" media

★ Assess changes in audience and readership patterns, and the impact of those changes on news coverage

★ Learn that the ownership of media organizations is concentrated in large corporations

The Effects of the Media

★ Describe the different theories that have been developed to explain the effect that exposure to news has on viewers/readers

Criticisms of the News Media

★ Identify common criticisms of media coverage of politics, including bias, sensationalism, and the concentration of corporate ownership

NOW & THEN

the WHITE HOUSE *PRESIDENT BARACK OBAMA* ★ ★ ★ ★ ★ Get Email Updates Contact Us

BLOG   PHOTOS & VIDEO   BRIEFING ROOM   ISSUES   *the* ADMINISTRATION   *the* WHITE HOUSE   *our* GOVERNMENT

HEALTH CARE

Health Reform in Action

Health reform makes health care more affordable, holds insurers more accountable, expands coverage to all Americans and makes our health system sustainable.

HEAR MORE STORIES ▶

00:00   00:00   Share | Embed

HEALTH CARE AT A GLANCE   ABOUT THE NEW LAW   RELIEF FOR YOU   MYTHS & FACTS   HEALTH CARE NEWS   50 STATES 50 STORIES

NOW   Early in his presidency, Barack Obama was determined to achieve legislative success on a subject that had proved elusive to so many of his predecessors: comprehensive health care reform. Franklin Roosevelt was forced to remove compulsory health care provisions from the social security legislation in 1935; Harry Truman had seen his proposal for national health care defeated as well. More recently, President Bill Clinton had made health care reform the centerpiece of his first term as president, only to see his plan soundly defeated in 1994 by a well-organized opposition. In these earlier battles, the American Medical Association and other opponents capitalized upon public fears that the legislation might separate individuals from their own doctors; many citizens had been overwhelmed by media campaigns that monopolized the airways with negative aspects of the legislation. The Obama administration's efforts to pass health care would not be so hindered, thanks in part to the Internet, which delivers virtually unlimited amounts of information to the vast majority of American homes. The Internet effectively brought the full debate over health care out into the open, exposing backroom deals and revealing the exaggerations inherent in arguments made both for and against the various bills under consideration. Ultimately the Obama administration took advantage of the Internet to sell its plan to the far left as well as the far right. The legislation eventually overcame all obstacles in its path, including a Republican party-line filibuster, which it cleared by just one vote. President Obama was thus able to seize the upper hand by a narrow margin. Had the public not been privy to the immense amounts of information pouring forth from the Internet, the arguments against the administration's plan might once again have proven too difficult to overcome.

THEN Health care reform was not the only proposed change to benefit from a new medium that reached millions. President John F. Kennedy's assassination in 1963 did not end his administration's hopes that it might see civil rights legislation pass before the 1964 presidential election. In fact, Kennedy's successor, Lyndon Johnson, pressed for civil rights legislation beginning in early 1964. Past presidents had tried and failed to pass civil rights laws: In 1947 President Truman was rebuffed in his hopes for legislation that addressed segregation. President Eisenhower pursued a centrist agenda on civil rights, but the best he could achieve was to establish a bipartisan civil rights commission and a civil rights division in the Justice Department; the 1957 Civil Rights Act had such a narrow impact that it proved a disappointment to civil rights leaders. Kennedy's ambitious civil rights agenda might have met a similar fate had the plight of African Americans in the South not been seen by the rest of the nation through extensive and unprecedented television coverage. Footage from television cameras allowed viewers at home to witness police officials directing full-pressure water hoses on African American school children, police dogs set loose on civil rights demonstrators, and numerous brutal beatings. Donations to the civil rights movement increased dramatically once the public outside the South became an eyewitness to these dramatic events, and legislative leaders from both parties soon felt public pressure to overcome the objections of opponents. After waiting out a fifty-four-day filibuster, the Senate eventually joined the House in approving major civil rights legislation. On July 2, 1964, President Lyndon Johnson signed the Civil Rights Act into law. Clearly the "small screen" had played a large role in the process.

A different still shot from a television report showing another Birmingham fireman hosing down protesters in 1963.

BETTMANN/CORBIS

C onsider the following facts about media consumption in the United States: The average American spends more time watching television than working or going to school. All forms of media considered, the average person is engaged in media consumption for 3,500 hours each year; that's almost 40 percent of the 8,760 hours that exist in a year. There are more TV sets per household than there are toilets. The media clearly have a pervasive presence in the everyday life of most Americans. From listening to radio "shock jocks" like Howard Stern, to watching popular television shows such as *American Idol*, to catching up on the latest news from around the world on CNN or a newspaper web page, Americans make ample use of the media sources available to them.

The news media serve a number of important political functions in the United States and operate through a large and growing number of outlets. Political leaders constantly monitor and attempt to influence news stories printed in newspapers and broadcast on television. Voters' primary source of information about political candidates and political issues is the news media. The technologies of television and the Internet allow citizens to observe events on the battlefield, look into the eyes of presidential candidates, and watch tragedies unfold such as the devastation unleashed on New Orleans and other parts of the Gulf Coast by Hurricane Katrina in 2005—many of these events unfold live from around the world in front of viewers in their own homes. Not only do the media serve as an important information source, but they also help set the political agenda, provide perspective and commentary on issues and political candidates, and help keep government accountable to the people.

★ LO Understand the purpose and evolution of the Federal Communications Commission

The Media in American Politics

Most news media organizations in the United States are owned by private companies, which, like most other private companies, seek to make a profit. Unlike other industries, however, the media enjoy a special constitutionally granted protection. The First Amendment to the U.S. Constitution specifically provides that "Congress shall make no law . . . abridging the freedom . . . of the press." When the First Amendment was adopted in 1791, the press was mostly a small collection of newspapers and magazines. Over the years, the press, now more commonly referred to as the media, has expanded to include radio, television, book publishers, music producers, the Internet, and motion pictures.

The argument for a free press in the United States today largely rests upon the concept of the "free marketplace of ideas," a phrase coined by Supreme Court Justice Oliver Wendell Holmes in his dissenting opinion in *Abrams v. United States* (1919), which suggests that allowing people to freely communicate their ideas will provide a larger variety of ideas to consider. Encouraging the publication and dissemination of a wide variety of political ideas offers citizens a diversity of opinions and perspectives and facilitates the free flow of information about local, national, and global events. Of course, for ideas to flow freely, government must be prevented from using its power to stifle perspectives with which it disagrees.

Government Regulation of the Media

Congress created the Federal Communications Commission (FCC) in 1934 to regulate the electronic media (primarily radio and eventually television) through the licensing of broadcasters and creating rules for broadcasters to follow. The FCC does not have authority to regulate the print media, such as newspapers. In fact, regulation of print media is rare, and courts have consistently treated the right of print media to publish free of government regulation. Some electronic media require broadcast frequencies that are scarce and thus need to be regulated to ensure the orderly transmission of programs.

Among the tools that the FCC may employ to regulate the activities of broadcasters is the threat of revoking a license or fining a station for violating its rules. The FCC has used these tools to limit the language and type of sexual material that broadcasters might use. For example, the FCC imposed fines on the owners of radio stations that broadcast shock jock Howard Stern. Stern's program often includes graphic descriptions of sexual acts and sex games, as well as language that the FCC deems unacceptable. Some of the stations that were fined then dropped Stern's show from their program schedule. To avoid further legal battles with the FCC, in 2005 Stern moved his show to a satellite radio station, which is not subject to FCC regulations because satellite radio is purchased by users and does not rely on the public airwaves.

One of the most celebrated instances of the FCC clamping down on material in broadcast transmission involved comedian George Carlin's "Seven Dirty Words" skit, which satirized attitudes toward vulgar language. In the skit, Carlin continually repeated the seven words that you can't say on TV or radio. The piece was played on a radio station licensed to the Pacifica Foundation. Prior to playing the piece, the announcer warned the audience about its content. Nevertheless, a listener complained to the FCC, and the FCC in turn warned the radio station not to replay the piece. The station challenged the FCC's authority to regulate programming content, and the case made its way to the U.S. Supreme Court in *FCC v. Pacifica Foundation* (1978).[1] In that case, the Supreme Court upheld the FCC's power to regulate the broadcast media on the criteria of indecent material.

The FCC's **equal time rule** mandates that radio and TV stations must offer equal amounts of airtime to all political candidates who want to broadcast advertisements. This rule also now includes a provision requiring that if a station broadcasts the president's State of the Union message, then that station must also provide free airtime for the opposing political party to broadcast a response.

From 1950 through the late 1980s, the FCC also enforced the so-called fairness doctrine, requiring broadcasters to set aside time for public affairs programming. The proliferation of news sources and technologies for transmitting electronic messages during the 1980s effectively ended the FCC's fairness doctrine requirements. These changes in technologies also resulted in the passage of the 1996 Telecommunications Act, which shifted the emphasis of government policy from regulating to facilitating competition. This law deregulated cable television providers, eliminated monopolies held by local phone companies, and allowed local phone companies to provide long-distance phone services. The Telecommunications Act transformed the FCC from a regulator of the telecommunications industry into an aggressive supporter of competition within that industry.

Functions of the Media in American Politics

Throughout the history of the United States, the media have come to serve a number of functions in the political system, all of which promote the free flow of information to the public. Principal functions of the media include (1) providing objective coverage of events, (2) facilitating public debate, and (3) serving as government watchdog.

Equal time rule
The FCC mandate that radio and TV stations offer equal amounts of airtime to all political candidates who want to broadcast advertisements.

★ LO
Describe the various functions that the media serve in the American political system

Providing Objective Coverage of Events. The media's most basic role involves monitoring events around the nation and the world and communicating those events to the public. Through modern communications technologies, the media have become proficient at reporting major events as they happen. Live coverage of presidential addresses, campaign debates, war operations, prominent trials, natural disasters, and other important world events have made their way almost instantaneously onto front-page headlines and into television's round-the-clock news coverage.

Providing information about news and events is perhaps the most basic and most important function of the media. Factual news information is an essential component of evaluating events and forming political opinions. Operating free of government control, the U.S. media can provide objective coverage of events to the American public. **Objectivity** refers to the media reporting events factually, accurately, fairly, and equitably—an important goal for many journalists. In addition to providing factual information about events, objective journalism requires signaling when important events occur and providing perspectives on all sides of an issue or policy debate. The goal of objectivity, however, is itself the subject of some debate. Objectivity is hard to define and measure, and journalists sometimes take a shortcut by trying to give equal weight to all sides without making any judgments of their own. This approach permitted Senator Joseph McCarthy to falsely but very publicly accuse people of being Communists in the 1950s; it let cigarette companies get away with denying that smoking causes cancer; and it prolonged the current national debate on global warming. Journalism professor Philip Meyer has advocated for a science-based definition of objectivity by getting journalists to seek more independent verification of facts.[2]

Numerous media formats strive to provide objective coverage of news information. Most of the content of newspapers (with the notable exception of the editorial pages) is aimed at objectively covering news events and politics at the global, national, and local levels. The twenty-four-hour cable news channels, such as CNN, Fox News, and MSNBC, provide news of events on a continuous basis. Many other formats are aimed at providing an objective look at news information to readers and viewers.

Moreover, the proliferation of cable television has broadened the role of the media as provider of information. Channels like the Biography Channel, the History Channel, local government access channels, and C-SPAN now offer programming that gives historical context to local, national, and international events.

Facilitating Public Debate. In addition to monitoring and reporting events, the media also facilitate public dialogue and debate on important political issues. By helping frame issues, offering perspectives on how a problem might be solved, and providing context and commentary on political campaigns, the media serve a vital role in a democratic system that depends heavily on voters to make informed choices in elections.

The media facilitate public debate through a variety of forms, both print and electronic. Newspaper editorials provide perspectives on policy debates and political candidates. Syndicated columnists such as David Broder, Anna Quindlen, and George Will publish columns in numerous newspapers around the nation on a regular basis, presenting their own perspectives on issues. Most newspapers dedicate space on their editorial pages for citizens to write opinion pieces ("op-eds") and letters to the editor offering their point of view. Many news

Objectivity
The journalistic standard that news reporting of events must be factual, accurate, fair, and equitable.

magazines adhere to a liberal or conservative approach in discussing issues or evaluating candidates for office. *The Nation*, for example, has a liberal perspective, whereas *The National Review* presents a conservative perspective. Even magazines devoted to one perspective or another, however, usually offer a forum for readers to assess issues. Radio talk shows that offer perspectives on politics, such as those of conservative radio talk show host Rush Limbaugh or liberal political commentator Ed Schultz, also facilitate public debate, as do television programs like MSNBC's *Countdown with Keith Olbermann* and Fox News' *Hannity's America*, which often feature debates between the anchors and their ideological opponents.

These media formats go beyond objectively reporting news to analyzing events and presenting arguments from varying ideological perspectives that readers and viewers can evaluate and use in forming their own opinions about public policies and political candidates.

Government Watchdog. Since the founding of the nation, American political culture has been characterized by a healthy skepticism about government. To govern is to have power, and in the minds of many, power corrupts. The federal system that divides power between the federal government and state and local governments; the system of shared power among the legislative, executive, and judicial branches of government; and the system of checks and balances among these three branches are mechanisms that help guard against the potential abuse of government power. The news media also help prevent the abuse of government power through their role as government watchdog. In this role, the media are sometimes referred to as the fourth branch of government, or the "fourth estate," checking the power of the other branches. Rooting out corruption and abuses of power through investigative journalism is a core function of the American media, no less important today than it was two centuries ago.

More than a century ago, a group of journalists, who came to be known as "muckrakers" (they were given this name by President Theodore Roosevelt), investigated and exposed corporate and political corruption in American life, including the corrupting effect of corporate contributions on presidential candidates who won office.[3] In the late 1800s, corporate wealth was concentrated in a handful of companies in the railroad and banking industries, and those companies bought favors and influence with various presidential administrations. The muckrakers exposed the rash of influence peddling and by doing so helped spawn new laws curbing corporate contributions to federal campaigns.

Perhaps the best-known case of the media uncovering and exposing government corruption was the investigative reporting of *Washington Post* reporters Bob Woodward and Carl Bernstein in the early 1970s concerning the Watergate corruption scandal of President Richard M. Nixon's administration. Their work led in part to Nixon's resignation in 1974 for his role in covering up the details of the Republican-led break-in of Democratic National Headquarters in the Watergate Hotel during the 1972 presidential campaign.[4] Woodward and Bernstein largely depended on an anonymous administration source, who came to be known as "Deep Throat," for information that ultimately exposed the White House cover-up of a number of criminal activities in Nixon's 1972 campaign for reelection. It was not until thirty years later, in 2005, that Mark Felt, who at the time of the Watergate break-in was deputy director of the FBI, publicly announced that he was in fact Deep Throat.

The media also exercise their watchdog function through television programs such as *60 Minutes*, *Dateline*, and *Meet the Press* and through Internet Web sites set up by groups like Common Cause, which provides data on the negative influence of corporate donations on political campaigns. The media also carry out their watchdog function through books. For example, the 2008 book *What Happened* by Scott McClellan, former press secretary to President George W. Bush, severely criticized the president and top Bush administration officials for waging a propaganda campaign to convince the American public that war with Iraq was necessary.[5]

Historical Development of the Media

Before the American Revolution, the news media consisted of a handful of newspapers that were published by printers.[6] A printer's main job was not to publish a newspaper but rather to prepare official documents (such as marriage licenses, deeds to land, and government documents), political pamphlets, and religious books. Newspapers of the time mostly featured notices of public events and advertisements for local merchants. These early newspapers carried little information about politics or news events.

The political events that led up to the American Revolution and the events of the Revolution itself changed the nature and functions of the colonial newspapers. Many colonists were intensely interested in the disputes with Great Britain and eager for news about the battles of the Revolution. Newspapers responded to these interests with news stories about the events. Stories about the economic turmoil of the post-Revolution period, particularly the bitter partisan fight between the Federalists and Anti-Federalists over ratification of the Constitution, also appeared in the nation's early newspapers.

The Era of the Partisan Press

★ LO   Appreciate the evolution from a partisan press to a media focused on objectivity

The Federalist/Anti-Federalist battle ushered in the **partisan press era**, a period characterized by newspapers supporting a particular political party. This period lasted from the late 1700s through the mid-1850s. Newspapers advocating the Federalist position that favored a stronger central government included John Fenno's *Gazette of the United States* and Noah Webster's *American Minerva*. The Anti-Federalists and later the Jeffersonian-Republicans, who supported states' rights, had their own partisan newspapers, such as the *National Gazette* and the *National Intelligencer*.

Partisan press era
The period from the late 1700s to the mid-1800s when newspapers typically supported a particular political party.

Partisan newspapers appealed mostly to readers who already agreed with the political positions advocated by those publications. Partisan-oriented news eventually became big business, and government printing contracts to partisan publications became a regular part of the spoils system.

During the early nineteenth century, a number of technological developments had a significant impact on the newspaper business. The invention of the rotary press in 1815 enabled the mass production of newspapers. The invention of the telegraph and the development of the telegraph system across the United States in the 1840s provided for the widespread electronic dissemination of news information. The expansion of the railroad system across the nation facilitated the mass distribution of newspapers across the continent. These developments allowed newspapers to print news events more quickly and distribute their publications to a larger number of people in a shorter period of

Can the Media Be Trusted to Tell the Truth?

A frequent question raised by critics of the news media is whether or not Americans can trust the truthfulness of news stories. Periodically during the course of American history, journalists have sensationalized stories as a way to "shock" audiences and increase sales of their own publications. Sometime these journalists play loose with the facts, and even fabricate stories outright. Those tactics may work to increase profits in the short run, but the cost to the reputation of American journalism has been significant indeed. Consider the following two cases:

In 1898, William Randolph Hearst was a wealthy newspaper magnate on a mission to incite a war against Spain. During the late 1800s, many American journalists had engaged in what has come to be known as "yellow journalism" to attract more readers and bolster the profits of newspaper owners. The yellow journalism of the late nineteenth century was marked by sensational photos, hoaxes, and even some fake interviews. Hearst, a leading practitioner of the art, became the owner and publisher of nearly thirty newspapers including the *San Francisco Examiner*, the *New York Journal*, and the *Chicago American*. In 1898, his newspapers' coverage of the explosion of the battleship *Maine* in Havana Harbor suggested that Spain was responsible for the blast, even though no hard evidence existed. Many historians believe that Hearst's accounts played a role in leading the United States to war with Spain in the Spanish-American War. He used the techniques of yellow journalism to build a media empire, but at the same time his methods eroded public confidence in news reporting in general, and in his own publications in particular.

In 1998, Matt Drudge was another culprit in the increasing public dismay with the media. Drudge and his *Drudge Report** certainly personify many of the problems that plague the reputation of the news media in the Internet age. Touted as a top

William Randolph Hearst.

CORBIS

Internet "news" source, the *Drudge Report* first became famous in 1998 for its coverage of the President Bill Clinton/White House intern Monica Lewinsky sex scandal. As the first to report over the Internet the lurid sexual details of White House encounters between Clinton and twenty-one-year-old Lewinsky, the *Drudge Report* "scooped" the story. Scandal surrounding the sexual encounters between Clinton and Lewinsky provided the material that attracted Drudge's readers to his website. Yet as fast as Drudge has been to report stories, he has sometimes proven to be quite unreliable. Rumors, rather than substantiated facts, serve as the basis for many of his stories. Early in 2004, Drudge "revealed" unsubstantiated stories about alleged marital affairs of Democratic presidential candidate John Kerry. None of the stories proved to have any basis in fact. Critics charge that when Drudge's stories fail to materialize, he doesn't hesitate to exaggerate the facts to increase his readership. Recent polls show that confidence in the news and newsmakers has dropped since the increase in sensationalized news that dates back at least to the 1980s.[†]

Matt Drudge.

AP PHOTO/MICHAEL CAULFIELD

*The *Drudge Report* can be found at http://www.drudgereport.com.

[†]See the 2006 General Social Survey, conducted by the National Opinion Research Center at the University of Chicago.

time. These technologies also helped reduce production costs, making newspapers affordable for most Americans. The term *penny press* aptly described the low cost of newspapers during the early to mid-nineteenth century.

By the 1850s, newspapers found that they could increase their circulation by distancing themselves from particular partisan positions. Eyeing ever-larger markets, newspapers began to appeal to all Americans. Journalists began to tout the goals of objective reporting of the facts rather than providing a biased or partisan perspective on events. By the end of the nineteenth century, the technological innovations and the desire of newspaper publishers to reach larger numbers of readers and maximize profits through the selling of advertisements had transformed the newspaper industry from a mostly partisan press to one focused on objective reporting of the news.

The Emergence of Electronic Media

★ LO Explain how changes in technology have transformed the nature of the media

The development of the radio in the early twentieth century provided a new means for Americans to get information about politics. Most notably, communication from the media source to the audience was instantaneous. In addition, the technology allowed political leaders to communicate directly with the American people. The first radio station was KDKA in Pittsburgh, established in 1923. The first network of radio stations, which was established in 1926 as the National Broadcasting Company (NBC), provided common programming and newscasts that were made available to the first truly mass audiences.

Franklin Delano Roosevelt, elected president in 1932, used the radio to deliver comforting and inspiring messages to the nation, then suffering in the midst of the Great Depression. FDR's weekly radio addresses, which the president called "fireside chats," represented the first significant use of this medium by a political leader to communicate to the nation's people. In addition to FDR's fireside chats, radio commentators such as Father Charles Coughlin (Detroit's anti-Semitic "fighting priest") and Louisiana Senator Huey Long popularized radio as a medium that could provide a great deal of political commentary and debate. During World War II, Americans eager for news about the progress of the war turned to the radio for information. Edward R. Murrow's live radio reports from London during the Nazi bombings of that city and from other battle sites captivated the nation.

A number of technological advancements have had a large impact on the scope and importance of the news media through American history, but none has had a more profound influence than the invention of television. In the post–World War II boom of the American economy, the nation quickly adopted TV as its primary medium for getting news about politics and the world. NBC and CBS developed the standard TV news show format in the early 1950s with a fifteen-minute daily news program. The program featured a news anchor reading the news, supported by film footage and reporters. This format—now modified into a half-hour program produced each evening—continues to be widely used today by all the major networks.

A defining moment in revealing the political power of electronic media was the live television broadcast of the debates between Republican Richard Nixon and Democrat John Kennedy, candidates in the presidential election of 1960. For the first time, all Americans were able to watch a live debate between the candidates. Many observers credit Kennedy's favorable TV performance as an important factor contributing to his razor-thin victory over

Nixon in the November election. During the first of three televised debates, Kennedy won over the audience with his relaxed and self-assured manner before the camera; by contrast, Nixon seemed nervous and uncomfortable. Nixon prepared for the debate by studying briefing documents but spent little time practicing debate style. Kennedy, on the other hand, spent a great deal of time practicing answers to questions out loud. For the two days prior to the first debate, Kennedy and his inner circle of advisers didn't leave the practice session in their hotel room. On the night of the debate, a tanned Kennedy looked strong and healthy. He wore a navy blue suit that contrasted sharply with the light walls of the TV studio. Nixon, on the other hand, looked ill and underweight. Just before the debate, he had been hospitalized with an infection and was exhausted from a hard week of campaigning. He wore makeup to cover up his five o'clock shadow and dressed in a light gray suit that blended into the background.

The candidates debated the important issues, and both did well in articulating their positions. But TV analysts reported that Kennedy won the debate. His stage presence, practice addressing the camera, tanned complexion, hand gestures, and commanding appearance compared favorably to the somber, pale Nixon. It was a lesson that no future presidential candidate would forget.

Interestingly, research on this debate[7] reveals that those who listened to the debate on the radio thought Nixon won, whereas those who watched the debate on TV tended to think that Kennedy won, proving that the medium through which events are communicated can indeed influence the way people evaluate those events. That the medium itself may have an important effect on the way people receive and perceive news was suggested by communications researcher Marshall McLuhan, who summarized this idea with his memorable phrase "the medium is the message."[8] Live broadcasts of presidential campaign debates have been a part of every presidential election contest since 1976.[9]

Television has transformed virtually every aspect of political campaigns and government policymaking. Prior to TV, the vast majority of voters never saw more than a still picture of the candidates, and most learned about them from reading newspaper accounts of their statements, speeches, and activities. Television, however, has allowed viewers to observe candidates live and in action and to see how they deliver a speech and respond to questions. Television has also given candidates the opportunity to develop an "image" through carefully planned media appearances and strategically designed political advertisements.

The Mass Media Today

Today's mass media include a variety of channels of communication through which news content is disseminated to audiences. Channels of communication may be either print or electronic. Print media include newspapers, magazines, and books. Electronic media include television, radio, the Internet, and movies. In addition, forms of content on any medium may be classified as either news or entertainment. In newspapers, for example, the first section of most publications is devoted entirely to news stories and editorials. Subsequent sections might include other information such as sports news or business news. Typically, there is an entertainment section that includes movie reviews, comics, crossword puzzles, recipes, and so forth. Television stations also provide news programming in the forms of news broadcasts, investigative reporting shows, and political talk shows. Entertainment programming takes the form of sit-coms, soap operas, reality TV programs, and drama shows.

Even media sources that are intended primarily to provide entertainment programming sometimes include content that may fall within the realm of politics. One very popular show that combines news with comedy is *The Daily Show*, hosted by political comedian Jon Stewart. During recent presidential elections, the cable television station MTV broadcast programming that attempted to increase voter turnout among young people.

The Print Media

The modern print media mostly include newspapers, magazines, and books. Use of these print media has declined in recent decades. *Time* and *Newsweek* are popular weekly magazines devoted to providing in-depth coverage of current events, although their readership has also declined as consumers of news increasingly turn to electronic sources of information. These and other news magazines often rely on photojournalism to support their longer stories to engage readers.

A century ago there were about 2,200 newspapers published daily; today there are only about 1,500 daily newspapers—a 30 percent decline—purchased by about 76 million readers. Once the prime source of news for Americans, newspapers now take a backseat to television as the nation's main news source (see Figure 12.1). Just as the number of newspaper readers declined following the widespread adoption of television within American households in the 1950s, today the Internet seems to be becoming a more popular source of news, and as a result, the number of newspaper readers is falling further.

FIGURE 12.1 The News Sources That Americans Use

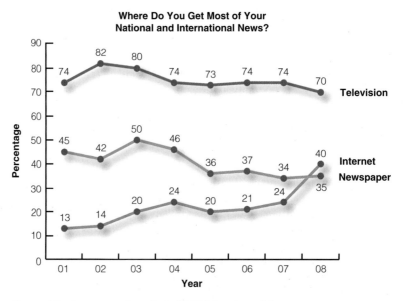

Source: http://pewresearch.org/pubs/1066/internet-overtakes-newspapers-as-news-source.

Wire services provide a clearinghouse for news as it is occurring. The largest wire service by far is the Associated Press (AP). The AP employs a large number of reporters throughout the nation and around the world to write stories on news events. Newspapers and television and radio stations that are members of the AP share the news services it produces. Using the AP as their news source allows smaller regional newspapers and local TV and radio stations to cover events from around the world in an efficient, informative, and cost-effective manner.

The Electronic Media

The major electronic media are television, radio, and the Internet. Television and radio have played an important role in American politics for many decades, and the Internet has been responsible for more recent changes in the news and the way Americans use the news. The Internet along with other relatively new media technologies such as DVDs, fax machines, cell phones, satellites, and cable TV have come to be known as the **new media** (or *digital media*), which have revolutionized the news business at every level.

Television. With its mass adoption by households in the early 1950s, television became and has remained the primary source of news for most Americans. More than 98 percent of households in the United States report having at least one television set. News programming on TV is provided mostly by broadcast television networks and their local affiliates. The broadcast networks include ABC, CBS, and NBC. Cable television stations, such as CNN, Fox News, and MSNBC, provide twenty-four-hour news programming as well. Other cable stations, such as C-SPAN and local public access stations, provide specialized coverage—for example, the live broadcast of congressional debates and committee meetings.

The defining characteristic of television is its visual nature.[10] The implied "reality" of seeing video of events, or live broadcasts of events, can be quite powerful. Compared to the written word, the spoken word, or even still pictures, video communicates events "as they are" and so is regarded by viewers as more

★ LO
Assess changes in audience and readership patterns, and the impact of those changes on news coverage

New media
Media outlets that rely on relatively newer technologies for communicating, such as the Internet, DVDs, fax machines, cell phones, satellites, cable TV, and broadband.

Left: Katie Couric of *CBS Evening News* became the first female solo anchor on a major network's evening news.
Right: Brian Williams, NBC's evening news anchor.

JOHN P. FILO/CBS/LANDOV

AP PHOTO/REED SAXON

trustworthy and "real." Many argue that film footage of reporters covering the Vietnam War contributed to the erosion of public support for America's involvement there. The daily barrage of video showing dead soldiers brought new meaning to Americans' understanding of war and influenced President Lyndon Johnson's decision not to seek reelection in 1968. In 2004, video of Americans captured and mutilated by Iraqi insurgents as a protest against the U.S. military occupation of Iraq captured a great deal of attention and reduced support for the Bush administration's policy. Likewise, vivid pictures of American mistreatment of Iraqi detainees at Abu Ghraib prison did not help the Bush administration's effort to defeat the Iraqi insurgents.

New satellite technologies further facilitate the live and instantaneous coverage of events not only around every corner of the globe but also from the moon, Mars, and Jupiter. The new high-tech satellites provide an opportunity for people to view events as they occur even from the outer reaches of the universe, such as the live pictures sent back from satellites on the 2004 U.S. spaceship mission to Mars.

Talk radio
A specialized form of radio programming on which one or more hosts provide commentary and often invite listeners to call in to the show and offer their own opinions.

Radio. Contemporary radio largely carries commercial music programming, with several minutes of each hour allotted to news, sports, traffic reports, and weather forecasts. A number of radio stations carry a specialized form of radio programming referred to as **talk radio**, in which one or more hosts provide commentary and often invite listeners to call in to the show and offer their own opinions. Talk radio steadily gained popularity in the late 1980s and early 1990s, marked by a growing interest in political talk shows, such as

AP IMAGES/PAUL DRINKWATER

BILL PUGLIANO/GETTY IMAGES

The Rush Limbaugh Show. Soon, increasing numbers of commuters with cell phones began to take time while sitting in traffic to listen to these shows and call in to offer their own views.

Some of the more popular call-in shows focus on politics. The hosts often provide an ideological perspective on policies, issues, and political candidates and campaigns. Listeners of a particular ideological persuasion enjoy hearing what the

Left: Keith Olbermann hosts the more liberal news commentary program, *Countdown with Keith Olbermann*, on the cable television station MSNBC. Right: Popular radio talk show host Rush Limbaugh, a favorite of conservatives across America.

host and others have to say, and a small number call in to offer their own views. Many local radio stations provide political talk radio programs, ranging from very modestly ideological debates to extremely partisan ones. Several nationally syndicated shows have also attracted an especially large listening audience, such as conservative commentator Rush Limbaugh's show.

A trend in ownership of radio is the purchase of smaller, local radio stations by large media organizations. Critics of this trend contend that the large corporate owners typically impose standardized programming through satellite feeds, thus depriving them of their local character.

The Internet. In 1993, a group of students at the University of Illinois developed MOSAIC, the first graphical Internet browser. It allowed users to view pictures and color images on the World Wide Web. MOSAIC soon went commercial and became Netscape, and by the mid-1990s, it was attracting tens of millions of users. Coupled with huge worldwide increases in sales of personal computers through the 1990s, the ease and user-friendliness of accessing the Internet made the medium an attractive source of news and information for people around the world.

The Internet's rise as a mass medium has many implications for news, information, and the American political system. One such effect is the way people use the Internet compared with other news sources. From the viewers' perspective, watching television is a passive activity. Once they've tuned into a particular channel, viewers have no other choice but to get whatever news is being presented. They cannot ask questions or seek specific answers to questions they might have. Likewise, listening to a radio broadcast is a fairly passive activity for listeners unless, of course, they choose to call in to the show. While reading a newspaper, people can pick and choose the articles they prefer to read. However, newspapers are also limited in the amount of content they can provide, and readers cannot query a newspaper to get answers on specific questions they might have.

The Internet, however, allows users to pursue exactly the kind of news and information they are interested in. Search engines such as Google and Yahoo allow Internet users to find whatever they are looking for. Furthermore, most news websites include a "search" feature that allows users to search the website and/or newspaper database for information relevant to a particular query.

Unlike other media, the Internet also enables individual users to be their own mass publisher. Most word processing packages include the option of "save as web page." A simple set of keystrokes enables users to place information, data, and graphics on their own web page. Web design software enables users to put a web page on a server and thus make that page available to millions of other Internet users to access. In this way, Internet users can publish material that is accessible to a mass audience.

The Internet has transformed the flow of news and information about politics in other ways as well. It has become a common source of information about political campaigns because candidates for office often create a web page and post it on a server for voters to access. A wide variety of "chat rooms" and online forums serve as venues for users to post their opinions, ask questions, and engage in dialogue on political issues. **Blogs** (derived from the term *weblogs*) have also become popular among many Internet users. In 2008, for example, the significant amount of fundraising and voter communication by Obama supporters substantially buoyed that campaign's success. Blogs provide a combination editorial page, personal web page, and online diary offering personal observations in real time about news events and issues. Some of the more popular blogs are published by journalists and political commentators.

About 60 percent of Americans report that they use personal computers on a regular basis, and most of these PCs are connected to the Internet. Those who use the Internet are more likely to be younger, middle- and upper-class, better educated, and nonminority—a disparity that has been referred to as the **digital divide**. Greater access to the Internet facilitates access to news and information, and those who have access clearly enjoy an advantage. However, as computers and Internet access costs decline, and as younger generations with computer skills replace older generations, the digital divide is likely to

Blogs
Internet sites that include a combination of editorial page, personal web page, and online diary of personal observations in real time about news events and issues.

Digital divide
The large differences in usage of the Internet between older and younger people, lower- and middle/upper-class people, lesser and better educated people, and minority groups and nonminority groups.

You and Your Blog Can Make a Difference

Political blogs have significantly changed the way that people across the country participate in American politics. They offer anyone with a computer and access to the Internet the opportunity to publish their political opinions in the mass media, to share ideas and perspectives with others, and to debate and challenge the positions of those with whom they disagree. Of the literally millions of political blogs to be found on the Internet, most are associated with a particular partisan or ideological perspective.

While political bloggers may be found all around the world, Americans between the ages of eighteen and thirty-five have been especially active in contributing their ideas in this particular marketplace, sometimes termed the "blogocracy." Some of their efforts have had a significant impact on political events. For example, during the 2006 Virginia Senate campaign, a supporter of Democratic candidate Jim Webb was following Webb's opponent, incumbent Senate George Allen, with a video camera. Annoyed at being followed, Allen referred to the Webb supporter as a "Macaca," which is a term that refers to a species of monkey and is considered an ethnic slur. The videotaper, S. R. Sidarth, was also a blogger, and immediately posted the video of Allen's slur on YouTube. Many other blogs and national news organizations began to cover the clip of Allen's slur. The posting is credited both with clinching Webb's narrow victory in the race, and in stifling Allen's presidential ambitions for 2008.

Another way some bloggers have influenced politics is through the "moneybomb," a blog-driven grassroots fundraising campaign that is usually generated over a short period of time: Supporters use the blogs to create a frenzied atmosphere to quickly raise money. Bloggers who supported Massachusetts GOP senate candidate Scott Brown initiated a moneybomb for him in his 2010 special election once Brown came within striking distance of winning Ted Kennedy's reliably Democratic seat. The effort raised $10 million.

ML HARRIS/GETTY IMAGES

College students, like the one pictured, can publish blogs from anywhere on campus.

For Critical Thinking and Discussion

1. Have you ever posted comments on a blog, whether your own, a friend's, or simply as a reply to another blogger's comments?

2. Find a blog that aligns with your own political interests or attitudes and read at least a week's worth of posting and comments. What do you notice? Do opinions tend to get debated or echoed within that blog?

3. What are the advantages and disadvantages of engaging in this form of political participation?

become less and less pronounced. Public libraries have provided another remedy to the digital divide. In 1996, 28 percent of all libraries had public access to the Internet. Today, 95 percent of libraries offer Internet access to patrons. Eager to gain access, the number of visitors to public libraries has increased by nearly 20 percent since 2002.

Ownership of the Media

Learn ★ LO that the ownership of media organizations is concentrated in large corporations

The framers of the Constitution were clearly committed to the freedom of the press. Government ownership of the press was then and is today regarded as a threat to the basic freedoms that Americans enjoy. If government controls the news and the flow of information to citizens, it holds too much power. Private ownership of the media allows for the free and open exchange of ideas. Ironically, some today argue that the concentration of ownership of the news media by large nonmedia corporations, such as General Electric and the Disney Corporation, has stifled diversity in news content and blurred the line between what is news and what is entertainment. One large corporation that owns multiple media outlets has become the norm, whereas in the past most media outlets were independently owned. It is also argued that ownership of media organizations by a conglomerate such as General Electric (GE) might compromise the objectivity of the news. When NBC, which is owned by GE, reports on a story about GE, might that story be biased?

The big three television networks—ABC, CBS, and NBC—have dominated television viewership since the early 1950s. By 1956, more than nine in ten stations were affiliated with one of these networks. Over the past several decades, the growing popularity of cable and satellite TV has challenged the predominant position of the three networks. With hundreds of channels now available, the three networks' share of the viewing market continues to shrink. This competition led the networks to focus on greater efficiencies in the day-to-day operation of their businesses. By the mid-1980s, all three networks had experienced a change in corporate ownership, and all three are now part of "vertically integrated" corporations that are involved in video production as well as national and local distribution. In the late 1980s, competition between the networks further increased with the addition of the Fox Network.

NBC is currently owned by the mega-corporation General Electric; the CBS network, formerly owned by Viacom, is now its own corporation; the Disney Corporation owns and operates the ABC network; and Fox, the newest of the major networks, is owned by the News Corporation.

Not all television and radio stations in the United States are privately owned. The Public Broadcasting Act of 1967 created the Corporation for Public Broadcasting (CPB), which is responsible for distributing federal funds to support public, noncommercial radio and television stations. These stations have had a difficult time surviving economically in a marketplace dominated by commercial interests. CPB funds the Public Broadcasting Service (PBS), which was formed in 1969 to distribute programming to the nation's public television stations. CPB-funded radio programs are distributed by National Public Radio (NPR), American Public Media, and Public Radio International to member stations.

The Effects of the Media

Describe the ★ LO different theories that have been developed to explain the effect that exposure to news has on viewers/readers

There is no doubt that Americans rely on the media for news and information about politics. What is less clear is the influence that media exposure has on citizens' opinions (Does watching a news story on the increase in crime rates make the viewer more fearful of crime?) and behavior (Does reading an article about Barack Obama's community organizing experiences lead a reader to vote for or against him on Election Day?).

Researchers can quite easily gauge the exposure and use of the media. It is much more difficult, however, to identify the impact of media exposure on opinions and behavior. Citizens are constantly bombarded by news stories from a variety of different media. Isolating how one news story, or even several stories in one medium, influences opinions or behaviors is very hard to determine.

Despite the difficulty of proving media effects, political leaders and candidates for election certainly act as though the effects are powerful. Leaders constantly try to influence campaign stories and news stories to favor their own positions. Presidents use press conferences to send messages and attempt to win public support. Candidates buy advertising time to try to influence voters. Political parties orchestrate events at party conventions to send favorable partisan messages to voters.

Early research studies of media effects examined how citizen exposure to media content during a campaign influenced how they voted. In classic books on the subject (such as *The Voter Decides* and *The American Voter*), the media were credited with having little or no effect on voters' decisions. These studies, which led to a theory known as **minimal effects theory**, found that deep-seated, long-term political attitudes had a much greater influence on the vote decision.[11] Such enduring and preexisting attitudes lead to selective perception and retention of news content. People evaluate news material from their own partisan perspective (selective perception) and tend to process and remember the material more consistent with their preexisting attitudes (selection retention).[12]

Moreover, preexisting attitudes often influence what kinds of news people choose to pay attention to in the first place (selective exposure). Psychologists suggest that people's desire to achieve cognitive consistency and avoid cognitive dissonance explains why they process new information in such a way as to assimilate it with existing attitudes. These early studies that found "minimal effects" were largely focused on partisan elections and attempted to evaluate the effects of media exposure on the vote decision.

Subsequent research, though not refuting the findings of the media's minimal effects on partisan behavior, examined other areas where media exposure might have an impact. **Social learning theory**, for example, argued that viewers imitate what they view on television through observational learning.[13] Television's focus on sex and violence has led to a large number of studies that try to assess whether exposure to such material leads viewers to become more violent with reduced moral standards. Some of this research suggests that viewers do learn negative, antisocial behavior from TV.

Some communications researchers have advanced the notion of *priming*,[14] which suggests that the activation of one thought also activates other thoughts, and exposure to media provides cues to people on this thought-activation process. For example, watching the Road Runner beat up on Wile E. Coyote in the old Warner Brothers cartoon may make one child act violently against another child after watching the cartoon. The rash of injuries related to the show *Jackass* is another example of the priming theory.

Critics of media often use social learning and priming theories to advocate for government controls of the media. The Telecommunications Act of 1996, for example, required television set manufacturers to include a V-chip in new units to allow parents to block programs they did not wish their children or families to view. Another law passed in 1997 required the television industry to develop a rating system for television shows based on the show's level of sex, violence,

Minimal effects theory
The theory that deep-seated, long-term political attitudes have much greater influence on an individual's vote decisions than does news media coverage.

Social learning theory
The theory that viewers imitate what they view on television through observational learning.

The Commercial Success of Fox News

The Fox News Channel, created by Australian media mogul Rupert Murdoch in 1996, is today the nation's most watched cable news network. Because its opinion shows are hosted by well-known conservative commentators such as Bill O'Reilly, Glenn Beck, and Sean Hannity, many believe that Fox's news format, too, is designed to promote conservative political programming. However, Fox News maintains that its news programming, which runs from 9 AM to 4 PM and 6 PM to 8 PM daily, remains fair and unbiased.

Along with O'Reilly, Beck, and Hannity, Fox News airs shows hosted by former Arkansas Governor (and Republican presidential candidate) Mike Huckabee, Shepard Smith, Greta Van Susteren, and Neil Cavuto. All of these shows typically rank in Neilson's top ten cable news shows. Fox's primary competition within the cable news industry comes from CNN and MSNBC. For the past few years, however, Fox News has decisively won the battle for viewers; in fact, the size of the Fox audience is larger than that of CNN and MSNBC combined. By the end of 2009, Fox News ranked second in the Neilson ratings for all cable networks (behind only the USA Network), while CNN and MSNBC ranked fifteenth and twenty-sixth, respectively.

Often a target of Fox News commentators, the Obama administration has been especially critical of this popular news outlet. In October 2009, the Obama administration's then director of communications, Anita Dunn, declared that her bosses were

Fox News conservative talk show host Bill O'Reilly draws a very high audience for his nightly cable TV show, *The O'Reilly Factor*.

going to take on Fox: "We are going to treat them the way we would treat an opponent. . . . We don't need to pretend that this is the way legitimate news organizations behave." Despite these and other criticisms, Fox News has continued to increase its domination of cable news programming.

For Critical Thinking and Discussion

1. What do you think accounts for the success of Fox News? Why has it been so much more successful than CNBC or CNN in attracting large audiences?

2. Do you think that Fox's coverage of the news is truly "objective," or does it reflect a conservative perspective? Likewise, does MSNBC's news programming reflect a liberal perspective?

and profanity. Studies that demonstrated a connection between TV exposure and negative behavior were important pieces of evidence used to promote support for the V-chip requirement and the TV ratings system.

The **cultivation theory** of media effects suggests that heavy television exposure helps develop an individual's overall view of the world.[15] According to this theory, the emphasis on violence and crime in both news and entertainment programming would lead the heavy viewer to overestimate and be disproportionately concerned about the extent of crime and violence.

A final theory of media effects is best known as **agenda setting**. This theory suggests that although the effects of exposure may be minimal or difficult to

Cultivation theory
The theory of media effects that suggests that heavy television exposure helps develop an individual's overall view of the world.

Agenda setting theory
The theory that holds that
although the effects of
television exposure may be
minimal or difficult to gauge,
the media are quite influential in telling the public what
to think about.

gauge, the media are quite influential in telling the public what to think about. For example, Monica Lewinsky's affair with President Bill Clinton was a lead story in the news throughout 1998, and the prominent placement of that story in numerous media outlets helped keep it a popular topic of conversation. Daily news coverage of the number of soldiers and civilians killed in Iraq focuses public attention on the U.S. military engagement there.

The media set the public agenda for the issues and activities that many Americans choose to think about and talk about. Prominently placed and frequently repeated headlines in newspapers, lead stories on television news shows and on talk radio, and highlighted stories on well-trafficked websites set the stage for public discourse. Citizens pick up a newspaper or flip on an all-news TV station to become informed about what is happening in their community, the nation, and the world. In this sense, the news media have a powerful impact on public debate.[16] As news media scholar Doris Graber has noted, "When media make events seem important, average people as well as politicians discuss them and form opinions. This enhances the perceived importance of these events and ensures even more public attention and, possibly, political action."[17]

Criticisms of the News Media

★ LO   Identify
common criticisms
of media coverage of
politics, including bias,
sensationalism, and the
concentration of corporate
ownership

Although Americans rely on the media for information about what is going on in the nation and around the world, the news media are also the subject of a number of criticisms. For example, despite the vast array of news sources available, most news programming follows a standard format that makes it appear the same to the public. Many newspapers are owned by a handful of publishers (such as the Tribune Company and Gannett) and follow a standard format for news. Similarly, just a few companies own many of the nation's radio stations and TV stations and employ a similar format in their programming. Critics charge that this concentration in ownership could result in a handful of companies promoting their own political objectives.

Another criticism of the private ownership of the media stems from the premise that the media, like most other privately owned companies, are in business primarily to make money. For the media, increasing profits requires attracting larger audiences and more readers, and as many media companies have found, providing higher-quality news programming on politically important topics does not always guarantee increased audience ratings or numbers of readers. Rather, news that provides more entertainment tends to attract larger audience shares.

Often, the result is news that is characterized by "sensationalized" content. Stories that highlight or exploit crime, violence, disasters, personal conflicts, competition, and scandals tend to increase the sale of newspapers and improve the ratings of TV news programs. Thus, the profit motive of private ownership drives companies in the news business to disproportionately cover events that include sensationalized content. Stories like the death of Michael Jackson, the foibles of *Jon and Kate Plus Eight*, and the extramarital affairs of John Edwards, Tiger Woods, New York Governor Eliot Spitzer, and South Carolina Governor Mark Sanford all received a tremendous amount of coverage at the expense of other, more important stories.

Sensationalism extends to coverage of elections as well. Studies of election coverage have found that most news dwells more on stories about the candidates' personal background than on their positions on the issues. Political scientists note

Foreign Press: All Obama, All the Time

President Obama's political opponents often like to complain that he is more popular abroad than he is at home. There may be good reason for this frustration, dating back to Obama's exceedingly positive treatment by the foreign press during his 2008 run for the presidency. *Politico*'s Michael Calderone took special note during that campaign of how the German press seemed to be rooting for Obama to win:

Christoph von Marschall, the Washington bureau chief of the Berlin-based newspaper Der Tagesspiegel, *wrote in Sunday's* Washington Post *about the "dirty little secret" of the Obama campaign: snubbing the foreign press. But lack of access hasn't stopped the ink from flowing. Barack Obama's face adorns newspaper and magazine covers worldwide, as reporters flock to foreign capitals for the presumptive Democratic presidential nominee's five-country tour following stops in Afghanistan and Iraq.*

Marschall, for one, said that he's written several Obama-related pieces already this past week, and will continue over the next few days, focusing on the trip's impact on the U.S. election. Back in Berlin, he estimated that 10 to 15 reporters will cover Obama's upcoming speech from various angles, filling up column inches in the newspaper's national, local and cultural pages. . . . Toby Harnden, U.S.

editor of the Daily Telegraph, *told* Politico *that it's almost as if the overwhelmingly popular Obama had been "designed by a committee of Europeans" with the goal of creating their ideal American presidential candidate.*

. . . . In an effort to satisfy voracious reader appetites for all things Obama, Der Spiegel *published a 6,300-word story, with the candidate adorning the cover. The font was nabbed from Germany's version of "American Idol." "Europeans have fallen in love with the Democrat, mostly because he's not Bush," Cordula Meyer and several* Der Spiegel *colleagues wrote. . . . "The German press, looking from Berlin, behaves as if the election of Obama is a foregone conclusion," said Josef Joffe, publisher-editor of* Die Zeit, *a weekly German newspaper. "He's being celebrated like a victorious Roman general who comes back from the conquest of Gaul or something."*

CARSTEN KOALL/GETTY IMAGES NEWS/GETTY IMAGES

Barack Obama addresses a crowd of enthusiastic Germans in June 2008.

Source: Michael Calderone, "Foreign Press: All Obama, All the Time," *Politico*, June 22, 2008 (www.politico.com/news/stories/0708/11972.html).

that this emphasis on covering "character" issues rather than policy positions characterizes modern presidential election campaign news. Another common criticism of the news media is that they are politically biased. Some critics, for example, charge that corporate owners of media organizations are more likely to hold a conservative ideology, which is reflected in their news products. Others cite studies indicating that journalists and reporters tend to hold a more liberal philosophy and that this orientation seeps into their stories. Certainly, there is evidence to support the assertions that owners and managers are more conservative than the citizenry as a whole and that journalists are more liberal. But the issue of whether personal ideology or partisanship is reflected in news stories is less clear. In some elections, research has demonstrated that newspaper and TV news programs have shown a pro-Republican bias, whereas in others it has found a pro-Democratic bias.[18]

Making the Connection

The media serve a number of important functions in the American political system. In addition to providing information, signaling events, and "watchdogging" what government does, the media also provide an infrastructure that leaders use to communicate with citizens. In the examples used at the outset of this chapter, we saw how Presidents Johnson and Obama took advantage of relatively new media (television and the Internet, respectively) to successfully win long-term political struggles to pass civil rights and health care reform legislation.

Technological innovations have served to change the forms and nature of the media throughout the course of American history. These changes have opened up new opportunities for presidents and other leaders to help shape a political agenda and successfully bring an important policy idea to fruition. These changes have also had the effect of bringing news and information to audiences with more and more speed and efficiency.

The America media remain as important a political institution as any in our system of government. Americans' demand for information, the appetite of journalists to keep tabs on government performance, and political leaders' reliance on the media to communicate with citizens all serve to make the media stronger today that they have ever been.

POLITICS InterActive!

Comedy Television: A New Rite of Passage for Presidents and Candidates

The night of March 3, 2008, presented a crucial moment in Senator Hillary Clinton's bid for the Democratic presidential nomination. She trailed Senator Barack Obama in the delegate count, and with a dwindling number of contests remaining on the calendar, the following day's primaries in Texas and Ohio could make or break her campaign. How did she choose to spend her time, her most precious commodity, on this critical evening? Hanging out via satellite with Jon Stewart on Comedy Central's *The Daily Show*, a daily half-hour political satire, usually targeted at politicians such as Clinton. "It is pretty pathetic," Clinton joked via satellite from Austin, Texas, with Stewart. "I only wish you were out on the campaign trail with us . . . you could make fun of us in person rather than by remote."

Two years later, on March 10, 2010, President Barack Obama found himself in the midst of a crucial national tour to sell his health care reform legislation to the American people. The president took precious time during this campaign to make a rare stop at *The David Letterman Show*, reaching an audience that might not watch the nightly news programs or cable news networks. Facing some criticism that his health care proposals had racist overtones, the President quipped to Letterman: "I think it's important to realize that I was actually black before the election." Letterman responded: "How long have you been a black man?"

Americans, and particularly younger Americans, increasingly rely on comedy shows for their political news. Comedic commentary on politicians and political events has become a prime source of news for many Americans, and presidents and candidates know that all too well. Stops on *The Daily Show*, Comedy Central's *The Colbert Report*, *The Tonight Show with Jay Leno*, and *The David Letterman Show* can do wonders for book sales, presidential aspirants, and presidents who are trying to advance a policy goal. So long as television comedians strike a chord with these prized audiences, future presidential candidates will continue to seek out appearances on these shows at every opportunity.

President Obama appears on the *Tonight Show with Jay Leno* in an effort to promote his administration's legislative agenda in March 2009.

On www.cengage.com/dautrich/americangovernmentbrief/2e, find the Politics InterActive link for a discussion of comedy news shows. Note how *The Daily Show*'s coverage of elections in particular can affect an election campaign. Consult as well the various links that explore how the structure of the American news media has changed, and where these comedy news shows fit in the new pecking order.

Chapter Summary

★ The Media in American Politics

- Congress created the Federal Communications Commission (FCC) in 1934 to regulate the electronic media through licensing of broadcasters and creating rules for broadcasters to follow. The FCC does not have authority to regulate the print media because the courts have consistently treated the right of print media to publish free from government regulation.

- The media serve a number of important functions in the political system, all of which promote the free flow of information to the public. These functions include providing objective coverage of events, facilitating public debate, and serving as government watchdog.

★ Historical Development of the Media

- From the nation's founding through the 1850s, news in America was largely provided by a partisan press, made up of newspapers supported by a particular political party.

- Over the past 150 years, the standards for news reporting have become less focused on serving political party interests and more focused on "objectivity."

- Technological change has greatly altered the news media. The invention of the rotary press in 1815 facilitated the mass printing of newspapers; the railroad system provided for speedy distribution of papers; the invention of the radio provided instantaneous coverage of events as they unfolded; and television brought taped and live footage of news events into people's homes.

★ The Mass Media Today

- Today's mass media comprise large and varied types of news outlets, including radio, television, books, newspapers, and magazines. They also include the so-called new media facilitated by the Internet, satellites, cell phones, broadband, and other new technologies.

- Corporate ownership of news media outlets today is characterized by large nonmedia corporations, such as General Electric and the Disney Corporation. Some argue that this concentration of large corporate ownership has stifled diversity in news content and blurred the line between what is news and what is entertainment.

- Although the big three television networks—ABC, CBS, and NBC—have dominated television viewership since the early 1950s, the growing popularity of the Fox network, as well as cable and satellite TV, have begun to offer stiff competition.

- The Public Broadcasting Act of 1967 created the Corporation for Public Broadcasting (CPB), which is responsible for distributing federal funds to support public, noncommercial radio (NPR) and television (PBS) stations.

★ The Effects of the Media

- The effects of exposure to news on readers/viewers are the subject of much debate. A number of theories—including social learning, minimal effects, cultivation, and agenda setting—seek to explain how the news media influence what people think about politics.

★ Criticisms of the News Media

- Media performance is often the subject of criticism. Some of the major sources of discontent with media performance include the concentration of corporate ownership of media outlets, sensationalized coverage of relatively unimportant events, and ideological bias in news reporting.

CourseMate

Key Terms

Agenda setting theory (p. 326)

Blogs (p. 321)

Cultivation theory (p. 325)

Digital divide (p. 321)

Equal time rule (p. 311)

Minimal effects theory (p. 324)

New media (p. 319)

Objectivity (p. 312)

Partisan press era (p. 314)

Social learning theory (p. 324)

Talk radio (p. 320)

Resources

Books

Anderson, David M., and Michael Cornfield, eds. *The Civic Web: Online Politics and Democratic Values.* Lanham, MD: Rowman & Littlefield, 2003.

Dautrich, Kenneth, and Thomas Hartley. *How the News Media Fail American Voters.* New York: Cambridge University Press, 1999.

Epstein, Edward. *News from Nowhere.* New York: Random House, 1973.

Graber, Doris A. *Mass Media and American Politics.* Washington, DC: CQ Press, 2004.

Iyengar, Shanto, and Jennifer A. McGrady. *Media Politics: A Citizen's Guide.* New York: W. W. Norton, 2006.

Jamieson, Kathleen Hall, and Paul Waldman. *The Press Effect: Politicians, Journalists and the Stories That Shape the Political World.* New York: Oxford University Press, 2003.

Meyer, Philip. *Precision Journalism: A Reporter's Introduction to Social Science Methods.* Lanham, MD: Rowman & Littlefield, 2002.

Murray, David, Joel Schwartz, and S. Robert Lichter. *It Ain't Necessarily So: How the Media Remake Our Picture of Reality.* New York: Penguin Books, 2002.

Patterson, Thomas E. *The Mass Media Election: How Americans Choose Their President.* New York: Praeger, 1980.

Schroeder, Alan. *Presidential Debates: Forty Years of High-Risk TV.* New York: Columbia University Press, 2000.

Thurber, James A., Candice J. Nelson, and David A. Dulio, eds. *Crowded Airwaves: Campaign Advertising in Elections.* Washington, DC: Brookings Institution Press, 2002.

Internet Sources

http://www.people-press.org (the site for the Pew Research Center for the People & the Press, which provides polling and other data on the news media).

http://www.mediaresearch.org (a media "watchdog" Web site containing a variety of reviews and research on media issues).

http://www.freedomforum.org (the site for the Freedom Forum Foundation, with information and analysis on news media issues and First Amendment debates).

http://www.knightfdn.org (the site for the Knight Foundation, an organization that provides programs and research on journalism topics).

13 Political Parties

 NOW Tea Party activists wearing themed costumes march in a tax-revolt rally in 2009.

THEN A rally of the Populists' movement in Willowdale Township, Kansas, during the early 1890s.

NOW & THEN

An Upstart Political Movement Takes on the Two-Party System

The two major political parties waged a ferocious battle in the midterm election campaign. The majority party, which controlled the White House and both houses of Congress, believed its recent electoral successes had given it a mandate to act. Accordingly, it used its strong majorities to muscle through landmark legislation. The opposition party was energized by "smaller government" enthusiasts who celebrated their status within the party of "No!" They denounced the majority as reckless "tax and spend," big government fanatics. In this era of deep skepticism about government, a new political movement was also taking shape. Frustrated with both major parties, this group of crusaders used an anti-elitist appeal to lash out at the establishment. The opposition party clearly benefitted from this new movement, as it was more closely aligned to the new group's ideology. This association led to strong gains for the opposition party on Election Day. And yet having benefitted from their links to this new anti-government movement, the party that now seized control of Congress soon faced a dilemma of its own: Should it embrace the upstarts' more radical, anti-government agenda—and in the process risk painting their entire party as out of touch with the political mainstream?

NOW & THEN

Marco Rubio, a successful Republican Tea Party candidate from Florida, tells supporters after his 2010 Senate election victory: "Our nation is heading in the wrong direction and we have both parties to blame."

AP PHOTO/ALAN DIAZ

marcorubio

NOW In 2009 and 2010, President Barack Obama and the Democrats muscled through an economic stimulus bill and landmark legislation addressing health care and financial reforms. The Republican minority held firm in its opposition to unprecedented spending, happily embracing their status as the party of "No." As deficits ballooned, the Republicans viewed the 2010 elections as an opportunity to reverse their electoral misfortunes in 2006 and 2008. At the same time, a political movement known as the "Tea Party" arrived on the political scene. Espousing principles of "fiscal responsibility," "adherence to the Constitution," and limited government, the Tea Party opposed what it regarded as excessive government spending by both major parties. The Tea Party movement had aided the cause of the more extreme conservative GOP contestants in primary contests, as its energetic band of followers occasionally frustrated Republican moderates. Still, the vast majority of Tea Party movement supporters were Republicans, and in the 2010 midterm elections the GOP recaptured the House and reduced the Democratic margin in the Senate. Tea Party candidates such as Rand Paul of Kentucky and Marco Rubio of Florida celebrated their Senate election victories with warnings that the Republican Party could not take their support for granted. For Republican congressional leaders in the new 112th Congress, a significant challenge lay ahead. Just how determined would Tea Party Republicans be in advancing their more extreme agenda? Would such an agenda threaten Republican gains in the years to come?

THEN After winning the White House and securing majorities in both houses of Congress in the 1888 elections, Republicans looked to the upcoming elections of 1890 and 1892 with considerable trepidation. Republican President Benjamin Harrison and his administration had significantly expanded the federal government's powers: the Republicans raised import duties to protect American businesses against global competition, expanded the money supply through the issuance of certificates backed by silver, increased pensions for military veterans, and passed the Sherman Anti-Trust Act to regulate the power and growth of monopolies. Democrats now became the party of "No!" With the 1890 elections approaching, they berated the "billion dollar" Congress for raiding the treasury, and voters quickly took to the Democrats' anti-silver, small government message to give them back control of Congress. The subsequent arrival of the "People's Party," known also as "Populists," soon complicated matters for Democrats eager to oust Harrison from office in the 1892 election. The Populists were radicals who crusaded against banks, railroads, and elites in general; their natural allies were the Democrats, and after running some candidates of their own, the Populists eventually supported William Jennings Bryan, the Democratic nominee for president in 1896. Democrats benefitted in the short term from the Populists' energetic following, but in 1894 and beyond, the Populists occasionally allied with like-thinking Republicans, forcing Democrats to rethink the benefits of allying themselves too closely with a radical political movement.

A cartoon from 1896 depicts William Jennings Bryan at the head of an army of fellow Populists, preparing to attack Washington, DC.

IN BATTLE ARRAY, — AND THERE 'S NOT MUCH DOUBT ABOUT THE RESULT.

P olitical movements organized around an anti-government, anti-establishment message are not uncommon in American politics. The "Know Nothing" movement was a nativist American political group that opposed major party positions on immigration and naturalization in the 1840s and 1850s; Father Charles Coughlin and Huey Long offered a form of anti-business populism in the 1930s. The Populist movement of the 1890s and the Tea Party movement of more recent times fall in line with that tradition, exciting an enthusiastic and passionate base of followers. Though such movements rarely break through with successful presidential candidates of their own, they do affect congressional and presidential elections significantly in the short run: the party in power may find itself on the short end of this sudden burst of enthusiasm, and the outparty can benefit greatly from the movement's skepticism over government. But then the political party that benefits electorally from the upstart movement must accommodate its new partner, and in the process it may be forced to stray far from more mainstream policy positions. So goes the challenge of major political parties, which may gain in the short term from such political movements, but then must learn to live with them without losing their mass appeal.

Political parties are the lifeblood of American politics. New laws are enacted through the debate and negotiation of party leaders in government; individuals are recruited and promoted as political candidates through the apparatus of the political party structure; voters evaluate campaigns and candidates largely through a partisan looking glass. At the national, state, and local levels, the two major political parties set the tone, control the agenda, and run the government. Parties have been the dominant organizational framework through which our government has worked for more than 200 years, even though the U.S. Constitution makes no mention of parties.

More than 60 years ago, the American Political Science Association (APSA) focused the scholarly community's attention on what it referred to as responsible party government.[1] The "responsible party government" model depicts the proper role of parties as organizations that offer clear programs and policy positions to voters. Voters make choices on the basis of those programs, and when victorious in elections, the party works toward achieving

Parties are also important in other democracies around the globe. Left: British Prime Minister David Cameron of the Conservative Party. Right: Israeli Prime Minister Benjamin Netanyahu of the Likud Party.

Senators Who Leave Their Party Loyalties Behind

Only twenty individuals in U.S. Senate history have been willing to leave their political party while serving as an incumbent senator (six of those switched from the Republican Party to the short-lived "Silver Republican party" during the 1890s). Senators may switch parties for any of several reasons, including (1) because their views are no longer aligned with their current party; (2) because they hope to increase power by moving from the minority party to the majority party; and (3) because the party base within their constituency is threatening to defeat renomination, while the opposing party offers greater prospects for nomination. This final rationale was offered by Senator Arlen Specter of Pennsylvania, who switched from the Republicans to the Democrats in April 2009 to avoid impending defeat in the 2010 Senate Republican primary. (The switch failed to save him, as Specter lost the Democratic primary instead.) Regardless of his motives, the move had key implications for the Obama administration's legislative agenda, as it laid the groundwork for a filibuster-proof Democratic majority.

While Specter's defection was clearly significant, it did not actually shift control over the Senate from one party to another. By contrast, consider the following two cases in which a party switch brought a change in partisan control of the Senate:

In 1953, Senator Wayne Morse of Oregon formally abandoned the Republican Party, to which he had been affiliated as a U.S. senator for eight years. Though reelected to office as a Republican in 1950, Morse formally became an independent at the beginning of the 1953 legislative session. Following the defection, what had been an even split between the ninety-six senators was suddenly transformed into a 48–47 advantage for the Democrats. Morse's control over the levers of power proved short-lived, however, as the death of nine senators and the resignation of another led to many reversals of party control during the course of the 83rd Congress, which convened between 1953 and 1955. In 1955 Morse formally switched allegiances to the Democratic Party and remained a Democrat until his death in 1974. As a senator, Morse was well known for his proclivity to defy his party's leadership . . . no matter which party that happened to be at a given time.

In 2001, only five months into the first session of the 107th Congress, Senator Jim Jeffords (R-VT) left the Republican Party to become an independent caucusing with the Democrats. Before his defection, the Senate had been exactly split (50–50) between the Republicans and the Democrats; Vice President Dick Cheney had thus cast the deciding vote in favor of his fellow Republicans' control. Jeffords' switch—spurred by the Senate Republicans' refusal to fully fund the Individuals with Disabilities Education Act—gave the Democrats a 50–49 advantage and thus a majority in the Senate.

those programs and policies. At the time of the next election cycle, voters hold the party accountable for what it has accomplished.

The extent to which parties actually resemble the responsible party model has been the subject of much debate over the past half century. Moreover, despite the large role parties play in the American political system, many observers argue that parties are organizationally weak, particularly when compared to parties in other democracies around the world. Whereas most European parties have clearly defined constituencies based on social class, regional, ethnic, or religious division, American political parties are often ideologically vague, aligning with broader constituencies and gravitating toward more centrist positions on issues. And despite their prevalence in politics, there are indications that the influence of parties is on the decline.

The founders who drafted the Constitution designed a federal system without political parties. They envisioned a system that would be run by independent-minded people who served out of a sense of civic virtue. James Madison's Federalist No. 10 deplores "factions," as he calls them. Madison and his colleagues largely looked upon parties (the equivalent of extremely large factions) as tools of the politically ambitious that would tend to promote corruption and bias in the political system.

Despite some of the founders' disdain for political parties, they have become central to the American political system. E. E. Schattschneider, a well-regarded student of American politics, observed in 1942 that "democracy is unthinkable, save in terms of the parties."[2] The Democratic and Republican parties not only have become important political institutions in their own right, but they play a central role in running government at all levels, and they organize and provide context to voters.

Political party
An organization that seeks to win elections for the purpose of influencing the outputs of government.

A **political party** is an organization that seeks to win elections for the purpose of influencing the outputs of government. Parties are typically guided by a political philosophy rooted in particular values and an ideological approach to governing. The philosophy, values, and ideological approach generally lead to specific issue positions espoused by leaders of a party and the candidates who run for office under a party's label. Some minor parties focus less on the unrealistic assumption that they might win elections and more on articulating an ideological approach to governing and supporting particular issue positions. As in any organization, parties include leaders as well as citizens. In American politics, parties provide an important link between citizens and their leaders, playing a key role in recruiting citizens and relying on them for support at election time.

★ LO Explain how a party system developed in the United States despite the founders' attempt to create a political system without parties

History of Political Parties in the United States

Even though the founders frowned on political parties and made no provision for them in the federal government they designed, not long after the first government under the new U.S. Constitution took office in 1791, a number of the architects of the Constitution became strong advocates of particular parties.[3] Perhaps more than anything else, this contradiction serves to highlight not only the importance of political parties to the practice of democracy but also the necessity of parties. In the United States, competition between the political parties has kept any one group or faction from becoming too powerful for too long. The Constitution provides various safeguards against the accumulation of power in the form of checks and balances. Paradoxically, although parties are not mentioned at all in the Constitution, competition between political parties has proven to be a significant check against tyranny.

The First Parties in America

The history of political parties in the United States traces back to colonial America, when supporters of the English Crown aligned with the British Tory Party, and advocates of a new independent American nation aligned themselves with the British Whig Party. Benjamin Franklin and other founders still considered themselves Tories up through the early 1770s, and during the American Revolution, colonists who supported Britain were called Tories or Loyalists. The period following the war ushered in new challenges as leaders of the new American nation debated the relationship that should exist between the national government and the state governments. Ultimately, this debate created two new parties (or "factions" as many still called them in the eighteenth century). The U.S. Constitution that replaced the Articles of Confederation significantly enhanced the structure, power, and importance of the national government. The debate over ratification of the new Constitution pitted the Federalists, who supported a stronger federal government, against the Anti-Federalists, who opposed a strong federal government and supported state sovereignty.[4]

More formal, identifiable political parties emerged and began to assume the critical function of supporting candidates for elective office during the first administration of George Washington. Once again, the issue that spurred the emergence of parties as vehicles for nominating candidates was the distribution of power between the federal and state governments under the Constitution. The Federalists continued to support a stronger federal government and the policies of the Washington administration, which promoted the power of the national government. Most Federalists also favored maintaining close ties with Great Britain. President Washington did not consider himself a member of the Federalist Party; he despised parties and refused to endorse their presence in the politics of the new country. Yet many of Washington's supporters, led by Alexander Hamilton, organized the Federalist Party and used the organization to recruit candidates for office.

The Federalist Party was soon challenged by the Democratic-Republican Party, which asserted that the Washington administration was assuming greater powers than those the Constitution granted to the federal government. It also criticized the federal government's favorable relations with Britain, preferring France as a closer European ally. As early as 1792, the Democratic-Republicans were organized and led by Thomas Jefferson and James Madison—the same Madison who ten years earlier had authored in Federalist No. 10 perhaps the most eloquent argument *against* factions that has ever been written. In the congressional elections of 1792, Democratic-Republican candidates won a majority of seats in the House of Representatives. George Washington was unopposed for president, but the Democratic-Republicans backed George Clinton against Federalist John Adams for the vice presidency. Adams, however, won reelection to the vice presidency by an electoral vote margin of 77 to 50.

By the time of the election of 1800, the parties were highly organized. Each of the two political parties endorsed a slate of candidates for president and vice president to avoid the problem of having two separate parties occupy those offices. The party organization selected presidential electors, who dutifully cast their constitutionally granted two votes to their party's candidates. The Federalists nominated both John Adams and Charles Pinckney, whereas the Democratic-Republicans endorsed Thomas Jefferson and Aaron Burr. Jefferson and Burr each received seventy-three electoral votes, thus producing an Electoral College tie for the presidency. By the provisions of the Constitution, the election was then to be decided by the House of Representatives. After a fair amount of debate and politicking, the House eventually selected Jefferson on the thirty-sixth ballot. Clearly the system of selecting the president needed to be modified from one that did not recognize the importance of political parties in the electoral process to one that did.

The Twelfth Amendment deferred to the reality of parties in presidential elections. Ratified prior to the election of 1804, this amendment formally separated the Electoral College vote for president and vice president. Rather than having electors cast two ballots for president, electors were now to cast separate votes for president and vice president.

The election of 1800 marked the beginning of the end for the Federalist Party. The Federalists would never again win a presidential election, and their strength in Congress diminished steadily over the next two decades. The Democratic-Republicans enjoyed party dominance to such an extent that the Federalists were virtually extinct after the election of 1820. Interestingly, this lack of competition from the Federalists during the first two decades of the nineteenth century had the effect of fragmenting the Democratic-Republicans. In 1824, the Democratic-Republican Party put forth several sectional candidates, but no candidate received a majority of electoral votes. (Andrew Jackson won ninety-nine votes, John Quincy Adams took eighty-four, and another seventy-four votes were scattered among other candidates.) Eventually, the House of Representatives decided in favor of Adams. The result was a Democratic-Republican Party in disarray.

A Second Party System Emerges

★ LO Trace the historical development of the modern Democrat and Republican Parties

Disillusioned by the outcome of the 1824 election, Andrew Jackson eventually formed a new political party, the Democratic Party, which remains one of the two major parties still competing in American politics today. Jackson's support in 1824 derived from many of the new states that had been added to the union as a result of westward expansion. Many such states, including Jackson's home state of Tennessee, allowed voters to choose presidential electors directly, rather than following the traditional practice of authorizing the state's congressional delegation (known as the *congressional caucus*) to choose electors. Because he received more popular votes than John Quincy Adams in 1824, Jackson felt the presidency was rightfully his that year. Those who remained loyal to John Quincy Adams began calling themselves the National Republicans. The next presidential election would be a contest essentially between two splinter groups (Democrats and National Republicans) of the now defunct Democratic-Republicans.[5]

Jackson took his case directly to the people and ran for president again in 1828, this time as a Democrat. He ran a populist campaign, arguing that the people should have a greater say in selecting the president. Jackson's theme caught fire with the voters, and the nation's continuing westward expansion, along with voting reforms and increased suffrage in eastern states, expanded the role of voters in selecting presidential electors. Thus, in a campaign that was essentially decided by the people, puritanical John Quincy Adams proved no match for the flamboyant Jackson, still revered as the general who led American forces to victory in the Battle of New Orleans, the final military engagement of the War of 1812. And Jackson's newly established Democratic Party emerged as a national force to be reckoned with.

The election of 1828 also permanently changed the nature of campaigns and, with them, the nature of parties. The precedent for a presidential election influenced by the masses was now set, and the era of congressional delegations selecting presidential electors was over. Parties quickly recognized the need to organize in states and localities to accommodate the new process of selecting presidential electors. Party organizations became larger and more powerful as they developed into critical instruments in campaigns. This era also established the tradition of holding **national party conventions**. These conventions drew together party delegates from across the states for several purposes. First, the

National party convention
A large meeting that draws together party delegates from across the nation to choose (or formally affirm the selection of) the party's presidential and vice presidential candidates.

AMERICAN GOVERNMENT In Global Perspective

The Importance of Having Honest Two-Party Elections

The 2009 Pew Global Attitudes Survey queried people from around the world about a variety of democratic ideals that characterize American political culture. One of those ideals is the value of "honest two-party elections." This graph shows the percentages of both middle-class and lower-income citizens from countries around the world who say that honest two-party elections are "very important."

A Chilean voter casts a ballot in Santiago during a recent national election. Since democracy was restored to Chile in 1990, voters in that nation tend to place high value on honest two-party elections, as shown on the right.

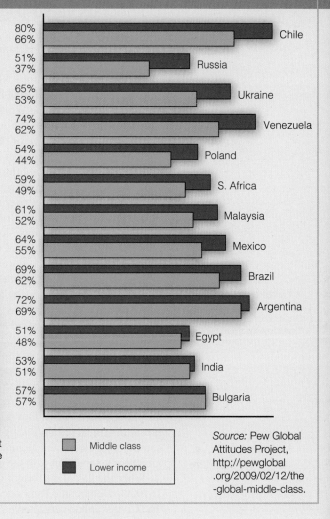

Country	Middle class	Lower income
Chile	80%	66%
Russia	51%	37%
Ukraine	65%	53%
Venezuela	74%	62%
Poland	54%	44%
S. Africa	59%	49%
Malaysia	61%	52%
Mexico	64%	55%
Brazil	69%	62%
Argentina	72%	69%
Egypt	51%	48%
India	53%	51%
Bulgaria	57%	57%

■ Middle class
■ Lower income

Source: Pew Global Attitudes Project, http://pewglobal.org/2009/02/12/the-global-middle-class.

delegates were responsible for choosing the party's presidential candidate and vice presidential candidate. Second, the delegates articulated their **party platform**, a document outlining the party's position on important policy issues. Third, the conventions coordinated the activities of parties across the states. National party conventions remain a central event both in the presidential selection process and in the organization of modern political parties in general.

The Democratic Party held its first national party convention in 1832, once again nominating Andrew Jackson for president, who then won re-election in the fall. Several years later, a new political party, the Whigs, emerged as a principal competitor to the Democrats. By the 1840s, the Democrats and Whigs dominated not only election contests but also leadership and committee assignments in Congress. Soon, those two parties became the primary vehicles through which legislation was sponsored and then shepherded through the Congress.

Party platform
A document outlining the party's position on important policy issues.

★ LO   Define "criti-
cal elections" and party
realignment and dealign-
ment in the United States
and cite examples of their
occurrence

The Modern Party System in America: Democrats versus Republicans

The year 1856 marked the first presidential election when the precursors to the modern Democratic and Republican parties faced off for office. Democratic nominee James Buchanan defeated Republican candidate John Fremont by 174 to 114 electoral votes. Since 1856, every presidential election but one has featured the Democrats and Republicans as the only two major political parties in serious contention for the White House. (The lone exception occurred in 1912, when former Republican President Theodore Roosevelt, the nominee of the newly formed Progressive or "Bull Moose" Party, ran second to Woodrow Wilson, the Democrat. Incumbent President William Howard Taft, the Republican nominee, finished a distant third.) In 1860, Democratic Party support for states' rights and Republican Party support for national power and preservation of the Union divided the parties over the issue of slavery. Republican Abraham Lincoln's successful campaign that year helped his party capture the presidency and a majority in both houses of Congress. It also precipitated the Civil War. With the eventual secession of eleven southern and Democrat-heavy states, the Republican Party came to dominate politics for the next decade.

Critical election
An election that produces sharp changes in patterns of party loyalty among voters.

Like the election of 1828, the election of 1860 is considered by many scholars to be a **critical election** in the modern era of American parties. The theory of critical elections, developed by political scientist V. O. Key Jr., posits that certain elections can be characterized as producing sharp changes in patterns of party loyalty among voters.[6] This occurred in 1860 when voter support for parties realigned along the issue of slavery, based primarily on a North versus South division. Until 1860, the Democratic Party had enjoyed support from urban and industrial areas in both the North and the South and the demographic and social groups associated with those regions. The Civil War shifted these alignments to a North–South division, thus rendering the 1860 contest a critical election. The theory of critical elections suggests that every such election is accompanied by some type of electoral realignment,[7] a lasting reconfiguration of how certain groups of voters align with the parties.

When the last of the former Confederate states was readmitted to the Union in 1870, the Democratic Party once again began to assert itself in national politics. The Civil War had cemented a "solid South" stronghold for the Democratic Party that would continue for a century. Republicans remained the favored party in the northern and midwestern states, although some major cities in the North (including New York City) tended toward the Democratic Party. Republicans dominated the presidency for the remainder of the century, winning six of the next eight presidential contests.

A third realigning election in the modern party era occurred in 1896. That election did not result in a clear shifting of voter preferences from one party to another; rather, it marked the rise of the Republican Party to a near total consolidation of power and voter support in the northern and western states, as well as the continued Democratic Party dominance in southern states. Republican candidate William McKinley won the 1896 election and, with it, a realignment of new allegiances to the Republican Party. Indeed, the only Democrat to capture the presidency between 1896 and 1932 was Woodrow Wilson.

In 1912, the Republican Party's progressive and conservative wings split, giving the Democrats the White House and a majority in both houses of Congress.

Within six years, however, Republicans regained control of Congress and were well positioned to retake the White House in 1920. During the sixty-two-year period from 1870 to 1932, the two major parties developed their party organizations and shored up their voting coalitions. They institutionalized their power in Congress by creating the party caucuses and electing party leaders. Also during this period, the Democrats and Republicans developed party organizations so strong that the two-party Democrat–Republican system would become permanently institutionalized in American politics.

A fourth realigning election in the modern party era resulted from shifting party allegiances in the midst of the Great Depression. Republican President Herbert Hoover was elected in 1928, less than a year before the stock market crash of 1929 sent the economy into a tailspin. Hoover and the Republicans adopted some limited measures to deal with the economic disaster, but they maintained their party's traditional conservative faith in the dynamics of the market to solve economic problems. Franklin Delano Roosevelt, the Democratic candidate opposing Hoover in 1932, advocated a substantially larger and more activist role for government in dealing with the Depression. Roosevelt's pledge of a "New Deal" and an activist government won the support of the urban working class, people of lower socioeconomic status, new immigrants, and many Catholics and Jews. The shift in allegiances from the Republican Party to the Democratic Party in 1932 (FDR carried forty-two states and 60 percent of the vote) had a lasting impact on voters. Adding the "New Deal coalition" to the "solid Democratic South" resulted in Democratic Party domination of American politics for at least the next thirty-six years. The policies of Democratic Presidents Roosevelt, Harry Truman, John F. Kennedy, and Lyndon Johnson during this era, supported by large Democratic majorities in Congress, were the product of the powerful New Deal coalition established in 1932.

Since 1968, however, both the New Deal coalition and the Democrats' solid grip on the South have declined.[8] At the same time, the century-long southern hostility toward the Republican Party of Abraham Lincoln has diminished, as many conservatives in the South have become attracted to the Republican Party and its socially conservative agenda. Between 1969 and 2010, the Democrats controlled the White House for just fourteen years, whereas the Republicans held the White House for twenty-eight years. During that same period, the Democrats controlled both chambers of Congress for twenty-four years and the Republicans for ten years, with eight years of split majorities in the House and Senate. No clear critical elections appear to have occurred over this time frame, and few patterns in voter realignment are obvious. Indeed, some political scientists have argued that the term *dealignment* best describes the behavior of voters since the 1960s.[9] **Dealignment** refers to the decline in both voter attachment to parties and clarity of party coalitions.

The 2010 election results provided new evidence of voters' lack of attachment to either of the two major political parties. After successive election cycles in which the Democratic party took significant strides toward reestablishing itself as a lasting majority, many of the same independents and disaffected Republicans who voted for Democrats in 2006 and 2008 returned to the Republican fold in 2010. As a consequence, the Republicans retook control of the House and reduced the Democrats' margin of control in the Senate to just 6 seats. More telling, many voters cast their lot with so-called Tea Party candidates who had criticized both major parties for their extravagant

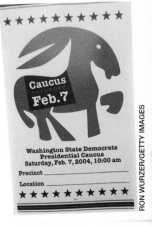

The elephant (above) is the symbol of the Republican Party. The donkey is the symbol for the Democratic Party.

Dealignment
A decline in voter attachment to parties and in clarity of party coalitions.

spending during the previous decade. As the Democrats and Republicans struggle with their long-term political identities, movements like the Tea Party will continue to hold their feet to the fire, threatening long-term party attachments that had been so prevalent in the past.

★ LO   Identify and explain the three broad functions of political parties

The Functions of Political Parties

Political parties serve a number of critical functions in the American political system at the national, state, and local levels of government. They give organizational coherence to both the operations of popular elections and the management of government. The functions that political parties serve have become inseparable from the principles that define how Americans choose leaders and how elected leaders formulate and administer public policies.

Contesting Elections

Free and open elections are the hallmark of the American republican form of government. With winning elections as their principal goal, political parties promote the prominence, competitiveness, and significance of elections in America. By winning elections and occupying seats in the government, members of the party can influence public policy. The larger the number of elective seats that a party controls, the greater the party's potential influence on policy outcomes. Thus, contesting elections lies at the core of a political party's functions.

To contest elections most effectively, the two major parties in the United States have developed a large set of party organizations. These organizations, which operate at the national, state, and local levels, are engaged in a number of activities directed toward winning elections. These activities include fundraising, organizing events and meetings, providing funding to candidates who are running for office, recruiting and organizing volunteers who want to work for the election of candidates, and purchasing services (for example, polling services, political advertisements, campaign materials such as bumper stickers, direct mail to homes, and so forth) to promote the election of candidates. Many election contests feature a candidate from the party currently in office (the incumbent candidate) defending his or her record against an alternative candidate from the party out of power.

The fact that political parties are organized to contest elections and offer alternative proposals for making public policy promotes the responsiveness of elected officials to the voters: By offering voters alternative candidates more in line with public opinion, parties provide an effective mechanism for voters to remove leaders from office through elections. Because the vast majority of elections feature a Democratic candidate running against a Republican candidate, the alternative candidates offered by the Democratic and Republican parties also serve to organize the process of competitive elections in the United States. Some elections include independent or third-party candidates, and in some elections, a Democratic candidate or a Republican candidate runs unchallenged. But most election contests feature some form of competition between candidates from the two major parties.

Recruiting and Nominating Candidates

Political parties are the main vehicles through which candidates for office are recruited and screened. The fact that parties exist to win elections gives them

The Republicans versus the Democrats . . . at a College Campus Near You

The College Republican National Committee and the College Democrats of America are two extremely active organizations, maintaining chapters on college campuses in all fifty states. These chapters serve as both an active recruiting tool for party membership and to support partisan activities in elections. Campus chapters for these groups provide a forum for students to discuss issues, participate in social events, hear speakers in their party, organize letter writing campaigns and phone banks, and conduct voter registration drives.

The College Republicans were founded in 1892. They have fifty state federations, more than 1,800 college chapters, and over 250,000 members. The College Republicans have served as a launching pad for many GOPers who have gone on to prominent political careers, including Grover Norquist, president of Americans for Tax Reform; U.S. Senators Rick Santorum and Roger Wicker; Rick Davis, campaign manager for John McCain's 2008 presidential bid; and Karl Rove, Fox News contributor and former political advisor to George W. Bush, to name just a few. The College Democrats, founded in 1932, can also boast of its history of launching great Democratic political careers, including that of Democratic National Committee chair and former Virginia Governor Tim Kaine, former Vermont Governor Howard Dean, and House Speaker Nancy Pelosi. Interestingly, former Democratic Senator and later Secretary of State Hilary Clinton was the president of the Wellesley College chapter of the College Republicans. If you

AP PHOTO/LINGBING HANG

A meeting of the College Republicans on the campus of West Virginia University.

are an aspiring Democrat or Republican looking for a place to launch a political career, your college's chapter of Democrats or Republicans may be the place to start. Or, if you feel strongly about one of the parties, your college chapter is a place where you can make a difference.

For Critical Thinking and Discussion

1. Does your college maintain chapters for the College Democrats and College Republicans? If so, which one is more popular on your campus? Does their relative popularity reflect the relative popularity of the two parties in the local region or the state?

2. If you are already a member, what kind of activities does your chapter engage in that help promote the national party's cause?

the incentive to recruit candidates to run for office under the party label. Parties want to find candidates who will represent the party well, and thus, they provide a "weeding out" process resulting in higher-quality candidates.

Most recruiting and promoting of candidates begin at the local party level. Individuals interested in politics often donate their time and efforts to working for political parties by, among other things, attending and participating in party meetings, distributing campaign literature, and driving candidates to campaign events. Local organizations tend to reward this service work with nominations for local offices, such as a seat on a local school board or a planning and zoning board. Successful candidates for these local offices often move up through the ranks of the local party organization to earn the endorsement and nomination of their party for higher office.

Providing a Framework for Voters to Make Vote Choices

Political parties also provide a useful framework for voters who must choose among candidates for elective office. Without even knowing the names of particular candidates for office, voters may be cued in to those candidates' political, ideological, and policy perspectives on the basis of a candidate's party. Most voters associate the political parties with at least broad approaches to governing, if not positions on specific policy issues. For example, on the role that government should play in fixing economic problems, most voters perceive the Democratic Party as more likely to support an active role for government, whereas Republicans are perceived as having a more "hands off" approach, preferring economic problems to correct themselves through the free market.

The organizational framework for voters to assess candidates is the political party. This framework helps voters more easily process and evaluate campaign information. Party labels thus offer voters an efficient shortcut mechanism for choosing among candidates. For instance, the Democratic Party and candidates running under that label are often regarded by voters as more liberal or left of center in their position on issues, whereas candidates under the Republican Party label are viewed as more conservative or right of center. **Party identification** is the psychological feeling of attachment that an individual has to a particular political party. This psychological connection influences other attitudes (such as one's position on gun control) as well as voting behavior. Party identification begins to form early in a person's life and generally remains quite stable throughout his or her lifetime. The authors of *The American Voter*, a classic book on American voting behavior, described party identification as "generally a psychological identification which can persist without legal recognition or evidence of formal membership."[10] Party identification serves an important role in forming attitudes on particular issues and making vote decisions.

Scientific surveys usually measure party identification by asking questions such as: "Generally speaking, do you think of yourself as a Republican, a Democrat, an independent, or what?" Scholars began measuring party identification in the 1950s, and research on the concept has revealed several important findings. First, although the number of independents has grown slightly over the years, there are many more party identifiers than there are independents. Indeed, the majority of Americans today identify with a political party. Second, whereas the Democratic Party had more identifiers than the Republican Party from the mid-1940s to the 1980s, the number of Democrats and Republicans is nearly equal today. As a consequence, the two major parties enjoy pretty much equal amounts of support from the American public. Third, despite these shifts, party identification in the electorate is quite resistant to change. Thus, from one election to another, voting patterns remain remarkably stable and rarely deviate from either a Democratic or Republican victory. Fourth, party identification plays a very important role in helping voters make voting decisions: The vast majority of

Party identification
The psychological attachment that an individual has to a particular party.

Partisan Differences on Social Issues

Americans who consider themselves Democrats tend to have different perspectives on social issues than those who consider themselves Republicans. The following data from a May 2010 Gallup Poll indicate how partisan groups differ on what is considered to be morally acceptable.

Percentage Viewing Matters as "Morally Acceptable," by Party ID
Ranked by party difference (Democrat vs. Republican)

	Democrat %	Independent %	Republican %	Difference pct. pts.
Gay or lesbian relations	61	61	35	26
Abortion	51	39	26	25
The death penalty	52	66	76	24
Embryonic stem cell research	68	62	47	21
Having a baby outside of marriage	61	59	41	20
Premarital sex	67	64	47	20
Buying/Wearing clothing made of animal fur	54	61	67	13
Divorce	73	74	61	12
Doctor-assisted suicide	52	46	40	12
Cloning animals	34	32	27	7
Suicide	18	16	11	7
Gambling	64	60	59	5
Extramarital affairs	7	7	3	4
Medical testing on animals	58	57	62	4
Cloning humans	11	7	8	3
Polygamy	6	12	5	1

Source: Gallup Poll, May 2010. © 2010 The Gallup Organization.

Republican identifiers vote for Republican candidates, and the vast majority of Democratic identifiers vote for Democratic candidates.[11]

Party identification is also an important concept for candidates and party leaders in plotting campaign strategies and contesting elections. As political scientist Philip Converse has noted, a **normal vote** can be expected for any given election contest.[12] That is, a certain percentage of voters can be expected to cast a ballot for the Democrats, whereas another predictable percentage can be expected to vote for the Republicans. The strategy designed to win an election and the

Normal vote
The percentage of voters that can be expected with reasonable certainty to cast a ballot for each of the two major political parties.

chances that the strategy will result in a victory largely depend on the normal vote distribution. The larger the margin of one party's normal vote, the less competitive the race. The competitiveness of the race can also be influenced by the number of the nonpartisan voters.

Although party identification is defined as a psychological attachment that an individual has to a particular political party and is regarded by political scientists as an attitude, formal membership in a political party is generally associated with the process of voter registration. In addition to making a citizen eligible to vote, the voter registration process in many states includes registering as a member of a political party. In some states, membership in a political party is a necessary precondition for voting in that political party's primary elections to select the candidates who will represent the party in a general election. States with open primaries do not limit the nomination process to voters of one party. State laws govern how a citizen becomes a member of a political party and thus eligible to vote in the party's primary election contests. In most states, it is possible to register to vote without being a member of any particular party. The rules for becoming a member of a party vary widely from state to state.

FIGURE 13.1 Partisan Voting in Congress

Every year, *Congressional Quarterly* measures the percentage of partisan votes taken in the House and Senate. A roll call vote is considered partisan if a majority of one party votes against a majority of the other. The percentage of partisan voting has hovered around a relatively high 50 percent in the House for the past two decades and stayed there during 2009, at 51 percent. But in the Senate, it was a whopping 72 percent—the highest percentage of partisan votes ever tallied in that chamber.

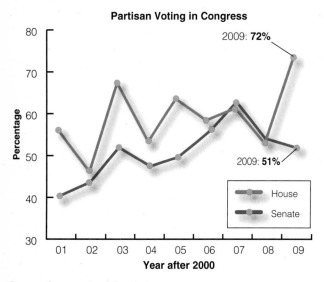

Partisan Voting in Congress

2009: **72%**

2009: **51%**

House
Senate

Percentage

Year after 2000

Source: Congressional Quarterly.

Providing Organization for the Operations of Government

The majority party organizes its respective institution to accomplish the task of governing.[13] The leadership organization in the House and Senate is based primarily on majority-party leadership. The top leadership position in the House of Representatives is the Speaker of the House, who is always chosen by the majority-party caucus of the House. The chief leadership position in the Senate is the majority leader, who is selected by the majority-party caucus in the Senate. Members of the majority party chair committees in both houses of Congress. Leaders in Congress then try to implement the campaign pledges and platforms advocated by their party during the previous election campaigns. The executive branch, headed by the president, includes various departments and agencies that conduct the work of the federal government. Partisanship and loyalty to the president's political party are important factors that influence whom the president appoints to lead these agencies and departments.

The policy agenda and important policy decisions are largely the result of the political party organization and partisan leadership of these key branches of government. The greater a party's control over the key governing institution, the more power that party has in influencing public policy. When the Democratic Party has a majority in both the House and the Senate and occupies the presidency, the Democratic Party has virtual control over what laws get passed. For example, the 1932 elections brought FDR, a Democrat, into the White House and resulted in increased Democratic majorities in both houses of Congress. The result of this dominance was passage of numerous laws promoting active government involvement in dealing with the Great Depression.

Divided government, on the other hand, refers to split party control of Congress and the presidency.[14] Because both houses of Congress are required for passing new laws, when the majority party in at least one house of Congress differs from the party occupying the presidency, a form of divided government exists. For example, beginning in January 2007, the Democrats controlled both houses of Congress while the Republican President George W. Bush was still in the White House. The presence of divided government often makes it difficult for either party to advance its policy goals and objectives.

Divided government
Split party control of Congress and the presidency.

Whereas the first 150 years of the republic were mostly characterized by one party controlling both branches of government, the last half-century has been dominated by divided government. For example, during the eight years that Republican Ronald Reagan was president, the Democrats held a majority of seats in the House of Representatives, and they continued to do so through Republican George H. W. Bush's administration that followed. During the administration of Democratic President Bill Clinton, the Republicans maintained a majority of seats in both houses for the last six of Clinton's eight years in office. The Democratic Party ended divided government—at least for a two-year period—with Barack Obama's 2008 presidential election victory over Republican nominee John McCain. In addition, the Democratic Party caucuses increased their margins in both the House of Representatives and the Senate for the 111th Congress. Those large margins of control proved short-lived, however, as the Republicans in 2010 gained over 60 House seats to retake the majority in that chamber and reduced Democratic margins in the Senate as well. Divided party government thus returned to Washington once again in 2011.

Many observers of American politics question the rationality of an American electorate that so often sends one party to the presidency yet keeps the opposite party in control of Congress. The stalemate or gridlock that may result from divided government is problematic to some. Still, many Americans believe that divided government has its benefits; certainly, divided control tends to intensify the checks and balances on power envisioned by the framers of the Constitution.

Why a Two-Party System?

Political parties are an integral part of many of the world's democracies. Contemporary party systems are largely a product of the unique characteristics, history, issues, and social class structure of any given nation.

Although party systems in a democracy vary in numerous ways, they may generally be classified into one of two general types: (1) two-party systems and (2) multiparty systems. The United States features a two-party system, dominated by the Democratic and Republican parties.[15] The vast size and organizational structure of the two major parties, coupled with the fact that these

Two-party system
A party system dominated by two major parties that win the vast majority of elections.

Multiparty system
A political system in which many different parties are organized on the basis of political ideologies, economic interests, religion, geography, or positions on a single issue or set of issues.

two parties win the great majority of elections, appropriately classify the United States as a **two-party system**. Other democracies feature as many as ten parties of relatively equal stature. The nations with **multiparty systems** typically include parties organized on the basis of political ideologies (such as the socialist party or conservative party), particular economic interests (such as the agricultural party or the industrial party), religion, geography, or positions on a single issue or set of issues.

In the United States, there is a wide range of ideological views, economic interests, religious orientations, ethnic groups, and geographic disparities. Other nations with such a wide diversity of interests typically rely on multiple parties to represent these different components of the population. However, in the United States, a two-party model has persisted now for more than two centuries.

Reasons for the Two-Party System in the United States

★ LO   Understand the historical and legal factors that contributed to the development of the two-party system in the United States

What factors contribute to the American two-party model? A key factor is the Electoral College system for selecting the president of the United States. To win the presidency, a candidate must obtain a majority, not simply a plurality, of votes in the Electoral College. Naturally, this requirement encourages groups of voters to align with one of the major political parties, lest their votes be wasted. Minority groups, such as blue-collar union members, which have no chance of achieving a majority of votes as a single unified party, have found it in their best interest to support one of the two major parties in a presidential election. Being part of a winning coalition yields more influence than being in a smaller unified group with no chance of winning.

A second important factor that promotes the two-party system is the winner-take-all process that prevails in selecting members of Congress. In U.S. congressional elections, only the candidate with the most votes in a single district wins the seat. For example, in a race for a Senate seat, if the Democratic candidate receives 40 percent of the vote, the Republican 35 percent, the Reform Party candidate 15 percent, and the Green Party 10 percent, the Democratic candidate with the 40 percent plurality is elected to Congress.

A third factor promoting the two-party system is the ideological nature of public opinion in America. Most Americans are ideologically centrist, or moderate, with few considering themselves strong ideologues. The lack of strong ideological differences helps explain why only two parties dominate American politics. Neither the Democratic nor the Republican Party can afford to be too strongly ideological because it would risk building a winning coalition in elections.

A fourth factor promoting the two-party system is the laws and regulations that govern campaigns in United States, which tend to benefit the major parties at the expense of third parties. For example, to qualify for matching federal funds for presidential campaigns and many state gubernatorial campaigns, candidates must demonstrate a minimum level of support in prior elections and/or primary elections. Most minor parties, however, are eligible to receive such funds only after the election is over. They receive public funding in federal elections, for example, if (1) they receive 5 percent of the popular vote and (2) they appear on the ballot in at least ten states. Because money to finance a campaign is necessary during, rather than after, the campaign, third parties are at a serious disadvantage. The lack of a history and lack of public interest in third-party primary elections preclude most from receiving federal or state funding in these elections. For a third party's candidate to appear on election ballots in the states, the party must meet a number of criteria, including petitions supporting the candidate and often significant fees.

Minor and Third Parties

★ LO
Explain the role that third parties have played in U.S. elections

Despite the dominance of the Republican and Democratic parties over the past century and a half, a number of third parties have contested elections in the United States. A recent third party of note was the Green Party, from which Ralph Nader launched his presidential campaign during the 2000 election.* Most third-party candidates fail to register even one percentage point of the popular vote in presidential elections, and few third-party candidates are found in the U.S. Congress, in state legislatures or governorships, or in local government. For the past 150 years, not one president has been elected who did not run as either a Democrat or Republican.

Even the few-and-far-between third-party candidacies that have attracted a sizable percentage of popular votes in presidential elections have experienced only short-lived success (see Table 13.1). The Progressive or "Bull Moose" Party

TABLE 13.1 Important Third-Party Candidacies in Presidential Races

Third parties are by no means a new phenomenon in American politics. Despite their tendency to be short-lived and their relative lack of success in capturing elective office, third-party movements endure, often affecting which major-party candidate wins office. The following is a select list of third parties, their respective candidates, and their vote totals in presidential elections.

Year	Party	Candidate	% of Popular Vote
1832	Anti-Masonic	William Wirt	8
1856	Know-Nothing	Millard Fillmore	22
1892	Populist	James Weaver	9
1912	Bull Moose	Theodore Roosevelt	27
1912	Socialist	Eugene V. Debs	6
1924	Progressive	Robert La Follette	17
1948	States' Rights	Strom Thurmond	2
1948	Progressive	Henry Wallace	2
1968	American Independent	George Wallace	14
1980	National Unity	John Anderson	7
1992	United We Stand America	Ross Perot	19
1996	Reform	Ross Perot	9
2000	Green	Ralph Nader	3
2004	Independent	Ralph Nader	1

* Nader was technically the Green Party candidate for president in 1996 as well, but he was only on 22 state ballots that year, and his candidacy labored under a self-imposed spending limit of $5,000. In the 2004 presidential election the Green Party candidate was Texas attorney David Cobb; Nader ran as an independent in 2004.

of Theodore Roosevelt, for example, garnered 27 percent of the vote in 1912 but failed to establish itself as a permanent threat to the two major parties. Its success was largely based on Roosevelt's stature and popularity, and by 1916, he had returned to the Republican fold. Likewise, Ross Perot, running as an independent in the 1992 presidential race, captured nearly 20 percent of the popular vote. But his attempt to match his 1992 success met with disappointment in his 1996 bid, when he took only 9 percent of the popular vote. By 2000, Perot's Reform Party showed up as barely a blip in the vote totals.[16]

While third parties face a number of obstacles, they continue to persist. Despite their limited success in winning important government positions, they often have substantial influence on the outcome of elections. Third-party candidates in hotly contested presidential races have on occasion siphoned off enough votes from one of the major-party candidates to provide an Electoral College victory to the other major party. Twice since 1832 a third party has won more than

TABLE 13.2 Third Parties Today

Despite the lack of electoral success by third parties, many continue to operate in the United States today. Listed here are a few of them, along with a description of their reason for being.

Party	Description
1. Natural Law Party	This party advocates "all-party" government, which it defines as "bringing together the best ideas, programs, and leaders from all political parties and the private sector to solve and prevent problems." The party argues that bringing the individual lives of people and national policies into harmony with the "natural law" will best solve the nation's problems.
2. Constitution Party	This party bases the foundation of its political activities on religious principles of Christianity. It argues that the U.S. Constitution established a "republic under God, rather than a democracy."
3. Reform Party	Ross Perot ran as a candidate in the 1992 presidential election under the organization "United We Stand America." He ran to protest the leadership of both the Republican and Democratic parties and won 19 percent of the popular vote. In 1996, Perot reorganized under the Reform Party name and won 9 percent of the popular vote. Former Republican Pat Buchanan was a Reform Party candidate for president in 2000, receiving 0.5 percent of the popular vote.
4. Libertarian Party	This party endorses the notion that government should be small and limited, interfering as little as possible with the lives of citizens. The Libertarian Party argues that "individuals have the right to exercise sole dominion over their own lives [and] they have the right to live in whatever manner they choose so long as they do not interfere with the rights of others." Libertarians place a premium on individual liberties and personal responsibility.
5. Socialist Party	Whereas the Libertarians support a very limited role for government, the Socialist Party supports active government involvement in providing equitable distributions of resources in society. Socialists endorse a strong government role in providing health care, jobs, housing, and education, among other public programs. Although Bernie Sanders won election in 2006 as a U.S. senator from Vermont running as a self-described "Democratic Socialist," he does not belong to the Socialist Party.
6. Green Party	The foundation of the Green Party rests on pro-environmentalist positions like "Green" parties in other democracies, such as Germany and France. In the United States, the Green Party is also identified with a number of social justice causes, including feminism, promotion of diversity, and global responsibility. Green Party candidate Ralph Nader took 2.7 percent of the popular vote in the 2000 election, finishing in third place.

20 percent of the popular vote in a presidential race, and five times during this period, a third party has won at least 10 percent of the popular vote.

Party Organizations

Political parties exist through party organizations at the national, state, and local levels. Although most elected government officials are members of the Democratic or Republican parties, political parties also exist as organizations outside the government. These party organizations, which often count millions of volunteers among their members, articulate positions on issues; enlist members from the public at large; recruit candidates who will run under the party label for elective office; raise money from individuals, corporations, and interest groups; and provide organizational and campaign services to candidates who are running for office.

Andrew Jackson is regarded as the father of the **national party organization**. Up until the election of 1828, a party's candidates for president and vice president were nominated by the party congressional caucus. Jackson changed this process by establishing a national party convention to be held several months before a presidential election. The convention brings together state and local party leaders to nominate the party's candidates for president and vice president. In addition to party leaders, the national conventions today include delegates from the states elected by members of the party in presidential primary elections.

Since the middle of the nineteenth century, both the Democratic and Republican national party organizations have been run by a **national committee**, which oversees the conduct of the presidential campaign and develops strategy for each party's congressional elections as well. The national committees, consisting of state and local party representatives, are run by a **national committee chair** chosen soon after the presidential election has concluded.

★ LO
Learn how party organizations operate at the national, state, and local levels, including how they define party platforms and help their candidates win elections

National party organization
The institution through which political parties exist at the national, state, and local levels, primarily focused on articulating policy positions, raising money, organizing volunteers, and providing services to candidates.

National committee
The committee that oversees the conduct of a party's presidential campaign and develops strategy for congressional elections.

National committee chair
The head of the national committee for one of the two major parties.

Barack Obama accepts the presidential nomination of the Democratic Party at that party's national convention in 2008.

PAUL J. RICHARDS/AFP/GETTY IMAGES

At the national level, the committees, chairs, and party organization largely provide a supportive role during the presidential campaign. Once providing a core advisory role to a presidential candidate, the national organizations today are more involved in helping their candidate raise money and campaign for office. Strategy, planning, and advising are now handled mostly by the candidate's own campaign staff, which typically includes a media consultant, a pollster, a campaign manager, and various other campaign consultants. The modern-day national party organization is also less influential in determining who the nominee will be and more responsive to the victorious candidate's personal campaign staff. They do maintain greater influence in assisting state and local party efforts to win elections by providing polling and media consulting services, campaign management services, and financial resources.

In the modern era, state and local party organizations tend to be more influential in the nomination of candidates, in developing and organizing campaigns, and in providing a cue to voters about their vote selections. Voters pay less attention to campaigns in state and local elections and therefore depend more on partisan cues in their choice of candidates. State legislative and local election campaigns generally have limited resources to mount significant image-building campaigns for candidates. Candidates are thus more dependent on the resources of the state and local party organizations for financing. Local party organizations provide "get out the vote" services by funding phone banks to contact voters directly. State and local organizations also fund and make available polling services and media consulting services to candidates in less visible races. Benefiting from these services, candidates for local and state offices may feel the need to be more responsive to the party organizations.

Local party organizations also provide the grassroots workforce for soliciting mass participation in political activities. These activities include implementing voter registration drives, organizing political fund-raisers and rallies, and staffing phone banks to make direct contact with voters urging them to vote for their party's candidates. Local organizations also provide the mechanism for identifying and recruiting talented citizens to become candidates for elective office. They provide the "farm team" for potential candidates for higher offices, such as governor, member of Congress, and senator.

Are Parties in Decline?

★ LO Learn the factors that have contributed to a decline in political parties over the past few decades and assess the future prospects for the parties

Many political scientists contend that the political party is in a state of decline in America. Bolstering this claim is the dealignment thesis described earlier in this chapter, which holds that voters today are less attached to parties and tend to be more independent minded than they were up through the 1960s. Political scientist Martin Wattenberg argues that increased negativity toward the parties has contributed to party decline.[17] Wattenberg suggests further that the mass media have contributed to this decline by neglecting to cover parties. Prior to the 1960s, voters depended mainly on parties to provide information about political issues and candidates; now voters turn to the media as the prime information source. Furthermore, the medium of television allows candidates today to bypass parties and appeal directly to the public for support. Many candidates now run campaigns that de-emphasize parties and focus primarily on the candidate's image.

Scholars have also noted a decline in the organizational linkages between officeholders and the political parties. Patronage, the practice by which victorious parties offer loyal party members jobs in government, declined substantially during the past century. Under the patronage system, parties were able to retain the strong support of many of their members by offering the prospect of a good government job if the party was victorious. The civil service and other reforms seriously limited a political party's ability to offer jobs or other favors in return for supporting the party. Although these reforms have eroded the power of parties, they have also improved the quality of government officials and reduced corruption in government affairs.

Changes in the way candidates are nominated by a party have also reduced the power of party organizations. Until recently, parties exerted powerful control over the process by which an individual becomes a candidate wearing the party label in a general election. Without endorsement of the party organization, candidates for president, Congress, and state and local office once were virtually precluded from running under the party label. However, reforms in the 1960s and 1970s reduced the party organization's role in the nomination process. The **direct primary election**, which provides for the nomination of a candidate based on an open election among all party members, has empowered rank-and-file party members rather than party leaders to choose the party's nominees. Direct primaries make it easier for candidates who are not necessarily approved by the party organization to wear the party label in a general election.

Direct primary election An open election, rather than an election by party leaders, to choose candidates for the general election.

Some scholars, however, are not so convinced that parties are on the decline. They argue that although certain aspects of parties are declining, in other ways, parties are showing a resurgence in relevance.[18] For example, parties have adapted quite well to candidate-centered campaigns by servicing candidate organizations. In 2008, the Democratic Party supported some candidates who actually de-emphasized their party identification and thus helped forge victories for Democrats in congressional districts that were considered moderate to conservative. Additionally, party-line voting in the House and the Senate has been highly disciplined in recent years. In the 110th Congress (2007–2008), for example, senators voted with their party's position on legislation an average of 83 percent of the time. Not much changed during the 111th Congress: When health care reform came up for a series of final votes in the Senate in late 2009 and early 2010, all 100 senators voted down the line with their party leadership's position on the issue.

Whether they are declining or not, at the moment, parties remain alive and quite active in American politics. Even though voter partisanship may have waned, party identification still remains a strong determinant of vote choice. Although the parties may be less visible to voters, they continue to exert considerable influence over voting decisions. The Democratic and Republican party organizations are well funded and include millions of party workers. Party organizations provide money and expertise to candidates to help them achieve electoral success. The president remains the recognized leader of the party label he wears, and the party with a majority of seats in each house of Congress maintains clear control of the legislative agenda. Although the power of the party may have declined, it is clear that "the party" is far from over in American politics.

Making the Connection

The founders never intended for a two-party system to take hold in the republic they so carefully designed; and yet two-party systems have dominated U.S. politics for over two centuries, beginning with the rivalry between Federalists and the Democratic-Republicans in the 1790s, and extending all the way up to the present, when the Democrats and modern-day Republicans take turns controlling our government. Sometimes both major parties—despite all their built-in political advantages—lose touch with passionate strains of popular opinion. This is most likely to occur when the public grows increasingly skeptical about government as a whole.

In such instances, an upstart political movement may suddenly arrive on the scene, connecting with the interests of a segment of the electorate that seeks a brand new means of influencing government. In the 1890s it was the "People's Party" (also known as the Populists) that made its voice heard; in 2010 the Tea Party movement lent its support to numerous anti-government candidates and helped to shift party control of Congress in the process. If history is a guide, those movements tend to be short-lived, exerting significant influence in a series of election cycles before one or both of the major parties bring the movement's energetic set of followers into their own party's fold. Will the major political party that is most successful in this regard be willing to incorporate the upstart movement's ideas into their policy agenda as well? That was the dilemma that faced the Democratic Party in the 1890s, and which faces the Republican Party in 2011 and beyond.

POLITICS InterActive!

A Democrat Even a Republican Nominee Could Love

Senator Joseph Lieberman of Connecticut has always been something of a political enigma. In 1998, he was the first prominent Democrat to publicly chastise Bill Clinton for the poor judgment the president exercised in his affair with Monica Lewinsky. However, the following year Lieberman voted against removing Clinton from office by impeachment. While voting as a classic liberal on social issues, Lieberman has cultivated his reputation as an extreme conservative on military and war issues. Indeed, he was one of the Senate's strongest advocates for continued prosecution of the controversial war in Iraq. And although Lieberman was tapped as the Democratic Party's nominee for vice president in 2000, his status as a Democrat became tenuous after the party's voters in Connecticut rejected him as their nominee for the Senate in 2006. Lieberman ran for re-election that fall as an independent, and coasted to victory.

Lieberman continued to caucus with the Democrats after his 2006 election victory, securing that party's narrow, 51–49 margin of control in the Senate. Still, the Democratic leadership in the 110th Congress could no longer take his support for granted. That became clear early in the 2008 presidential campaign when Lieberman declared his support for Republican Senator John McCain's candidacy over all the Democratic contenders for the White House, including his own home state colleague, Senator Christopher Dodd (D-CT). A serious contender to be McCain's choice for vice president (McCain chose Alaska Governor Sarah Palin instead), Lieberman even received a prominent speaking position at the 2008 Republican National Convention.

Senator Joseph Lieberman (I-CT), right, with 2008 Republican presidential candidate John McCain at the Republican National Convention.

JOE RAEDLE/GETTY IMAGES

On www.cengage.com/dautrich/americangovernmentbrief/2e, find the Politics InterActive link for a discussion of the narrow working margin in the Senate during the 110th Congress, and a list of the moderate Democrats and Republicans who were considered most influential when no one party enjoyed a large margin of control. Compare the party dynamics of the Senate during the 110th Congress with the Senate that followed in the 111th Congress that took office in January 2009. How were they different? How were they the same? For example, what can a majority do with a sixteen- or eighteen-seat margin that it cannot do when the Senate is more closely divided? What about with a twenty-seat margin? Consult as well the various links that relate to other famous mavericks that have confounded their own party leadership time and time again.

Chapter Summary

★ History of Political Parties in the United States

- Because many of the founders frowned on parties and other factions, the Constitution nowhere mentions or contemplates parties. Nevertheless, the debate over ratification of the Constitution gave rise to two parties: the Federalists and the Anti-Federalists. The United States has had a two-party system ever since.

- Every presidential and congressional election since 1796 has featured some form of party competition. National party conventions and national party organization originated during Andrew Jackson's presidency. The Democratic and Republican parties have dominated since 1856.

- Certain elections, such as those of 1860, 1896, and 1932, are considered "critical elections" because they produced sharp and lasting changes in patterns of party loyalty among voters.

- Some political scientists have termed the era since 1968 as a period of dealignment, characterized by a decline in voter attachment to parties and in clarity of party coalitions.

★ The Functions of Political Parties

- The two major parties have developed large organizations that exist at the national, state, and local levels. They assist in fund-raising for candidates, recruiting and organizing volunteers to work for candidates, and purchasing political services to promote the election of candidates.

- Party identification develops early in a person's political life, psychologically connecting the individual to a political party, which in turn influences other attitudes and voting behavior.

- Majority-party leadership in Congress organizes that branch to accomplish the task of governing. Partisanship also influences a president's policy positions and appointments.

- When divided party government exists, it becomes difficult for either party to advance its policy goals and objectives.

★ Why a Two-Party System?

- The U.S. party system has been dominated by Democrats and Republicans since the election of 1856. This two-party system is perpetuated by several factors, including the need for a majority of Electoral College votes (not just a plurality) to win the presidency outright and a winner-take-all system that makes it especially hard for third parties to succeed to any degree.

- Third-party candidates rarely attract a significant percentage of popular votes in presidential elections because voters perceive that votes for such a candidate would be wasted and because various legal barriers make it hard for third-party candidates to receive government funding.

★ Party Organizations

- The two major political parties have organizations at the national level, at the state level in all fifty states, and at the local level in most cities and towns across the nation. These organizations are active in developing party platforms, recruiting candidates to run for office, and providing financial support and other resources to aid the candidates electorally.

★ Are Parties in Decline?

- The decline of patronage and the prevalence of the direct primary election have contributed to the belief that parties are now in decline. Regardless, party identification remains an especially strong determinant of vote choice in America today.

CourseMate

Key Terms

Resources

Books

Aldrich, John H. *Why Parties? The Origin and Transformation of Party Politics in America.* Chicago: University of Chicago Press, 1995.

Beck, Paul Allen. *Party Politics in America*, 5th ed. New York: Longman, 1997.

Bibby, John F. *Politics, Parties and Elections in America.* Belmont, CA: Wadsworth, 2002.

Blevins, David. *American Political Parties in the 21st Century.* New York: McFarland, 2006.

Conley, Richard S. *The Presidency, Congress and Divided Government.* College Station: Texas A&M University Press, 2002.

Green, John C., and Daniel Shay, eds. *The State of the Parties: The Changing Role of Contemporary American Parties.* Lanham, MD: Rowman & Littlefield, 1996.

Keith, Bruce E., David E. Magleby, Candice J. Nelson, Elizabeth Orr, Mark C. Westlye, and Raymond E. Wolfinger. *The Myth of the Independent Voter.* Berkeley: University of California Press, 1992.

Milkis, Sydney M. *The President and the Parties: The Transformation of the American Party System Since the New Deal.* London: Oxford University Press, 1993.

Rosenstone, Steven J., Roy L. Behr, and Edward H. Lazarus. *Third Parties in America.* Princeton, NJ: Princeton University Press, 1984.

Wattenberg, Martin P. *The Decline of American Political Parties, 1952–1996.* Cambridge, MA: Harvard University Press, 1998.

Internet Sources

Web sites of various political parties:

http://www.natural-law.org (Natural Law Party).

http://www.constitutionparty.com (Constitution Party).

http://www.gp.org (Green Party).

http://www.rnc.org (Republican Party).

http://www.democrats.org/ (Democratic Party).

Other useful Web sites:

http://www.fec.gov (Federal Election Commission Web site).

http://www.electionstudies.org/ (information on partisanship and party identification from the National Election Study can be found at this Web site).

14 Voting and Participation

NOW Barack Obama, campaigning for the presidency in 2008.

THEN John F. Kennedy, campaigning for the presidency in 1960.

NOW &THEN

A Young, Charismatic Campaigner Energizes Voters and Overcomes the Weight of History

One of the youngest candidates ever to run for the presidency, this Democrat burst on the national political scene sporting a remarkable talent for energizing the base of a party that had been shut out of the White House for the past eight years. Young people newly drawn to electoral politics were attending his political rallies in droves. Yet a significant obstacle stood in his way: Americans had never before elected to the White House someone from his demographic group. He incurred other attacks as well, first from his formidable Democratic Party rival from the U.S. Senate, and later from his Republican opponent, each of whom attempted to convince voters that this new brand of politician was in fact an intellectual elitist out of touch with mainstream America. All these attacks proved unsuccessful. A majority of Americans responded to his message of change by electing him president of the United States. In connecting with voters and winning the presidential race, this new president overcame the weight of history by becoming the first person in his demographic group to occupy the Oval Office.

The Legal Structure for Voting

* ★ Assess the role of state governments in managing elections

* ★ Evaluate the effect of various constitutional amendments on the expansion of voting rights in the United States

* ★ Appreciate the wide diversity of voter registration systems implemented in the fifty states

Exercising the Franchise

* ★ Assess the influence of different factors in influencing voter turnout, including interest in politics, sense of civic duty, the perception that one's vote can make a difference, education, income, age, and social group pressures

* ★ Explore the influence of political campaigns on turnout and in affecting "high stimulus" elections

* ★ Compare and contrast voter turnout in the United States with voter turnout in other democracies

Making a Vote Choice

* ★ Understand the various factors that explain vote choices

Political Participation Beyond the Voting Booth

* ★ Appreciate the many forms of political participation beyond voting, including communicating concerns to officials, civil disobedience, and protest activities

CourseMate

NOW & THEN

CHRIS CARLSON/AP PHOTO

NOW A mere state senator from Illinois, Barack Obama burst on the political scene with a fiery, impassioned keynote speech at the 2004 Democratic National Convention. Not only was he young, charismatic, and a gifted orator, but he was also African American. Though the Democrats were defeated in the 2004 presidential contest, Obama was elected to the U.S. Senate. Soon thereafter he capitalized on the popularity and fame of his keynote speech to launch his own run for the presidency in 2008. His youth and vigor attracted record numbers of new voters to the Democratic Party, raised voting turnout in Democratic primaries to record numbers, and helped him defeat well-known U.S. Senator and former First Lady Hillary Clinton for the Democratic presidential nomination. Campaigning on an agenda for "change," Obama's youth and energy contrasted sharply with the more somber personality of his eventual Republican opponent, Senator John McCain. After eight years of Republican rule from George W. Bush in the Oval Office, voters were looking for something new and altogether different—and they found it in the charismatic and inspirational Obama. Ultimately voter turnout reached new highs in 2008, helped in no small part by Obama's electric candidacy. Voters from recent Republican strongholds including Colorado and Virginia—states that went for Republican George W. Bush in 2000 and 2004—helped the young Democrat make political history as the first African American to win the White House.

THEN Nearly a half century before Obama's historical run, Senator John F. Kennedy of Massachusetts exploded on the nation's political map with his own run at the vice presidency during the Democratic National Convention of 1956. He eventually lost the nod to fellow Senator Estes Kefauver of Tennessee, who became the choice of presidential nominee Adlai Stevenson. Still, the youthful and charismatic Kennedy had caught the eye of his party faithful (as well as the nation at large) with his convention appearance and narration of the keynote film. Four years later he capitalized on that stardom to mount his own successful campaign for the Democratic presidential nomination. Kennedy was young, charismatic, and a gifted and inspirational speaker, yet he had his own glass ceiling to overcome—Kennedy was Catholic, and no Catholic had ever made it all the way to the White House. Kennedy's youthful energy proved an asset throughout the campaign, first in helping him overcome a formidable primary challenge from Senate Majority Leader Lyndon Johnson and later in his hard-fought general election contest against his Republican opponent, Vice President Richard Nixon. Kennedy generated considerable voter interest by drawing large crowds at political rallies and high turnout in primary contests. His general election campaign called for a "New Frontier" of change for America, mobilizing many new voters in the process. Kennedy's charisma contrasted sharply with the rather dull personality of his Republican opponent, Richard Nixon. After eight years under Republican Dwight D. Eisenhower, voters from such Republican strongholds as Michigan and Pennsylvania—both states that twice went overwhelmingly for Eisenhower—helped Kennedy make history as the first (and so far, only) Catholic to occupy the White House.

PAUL SCHUTZER/TIME LIFE PICTURES/GETTY IMAGES

Democratic presidential hopeful Senator Barack Obama (D-IL) and his wife Michelle at a rally in St. Paul, Minnesota, in June 2008.

Representative democracy
System of government in which citizens elect the individuals who are responsible for making and enforcing public policy.

Majoritarianism
The principle that the choice that is supported by the most voters is the choice that prevails.

Voting
The political mechanism that ensures that the majority will rule.

olitical participation takes many forms in American politics.[1] At the core of participation is the act of voting. Open and free elections held on a regular basis are the hallmark characteristic of a democratic government. Voting provides the critical linkage between citizens' preferences and governmental authority. The United States is not a direct democracy in which every citizen is invited to deliberate the issues and vote on public policy. Rather, the U.S. system is a **representative democracy**, sometimes referred to as an indirect democracy or republican form of government, in which citizens choose the individuals who are then responsible for making and enforcing public policy. The people do not rule directly, but they have the opportunity to exercise power vicariously by choosing as their leaders individuals they prefer.

The core principle underlying representative democracy is **majoritarianism**, or majority rule, which means that among the choices presented to voters, the choice that is supported by the most voters (that is, receives the most votes) is the choice that prevails. When a majority makes its choice, the consent of the governed is satisfied. Given the diversity of opinions and interests among people in our society, it is unrealistic to assume that all, or even most, voters will agree on one choice. But the will of the people is accomplished when the majority decides.

Voting is the mechanism that ensures the majority will rule. Times change, and so do people's opinions and preferences. Therefore, representative democracy not only requires an election in the selection of leadership but also requires that elections occur on a regular basis so that the government's authority reflects changing majority views. Regular and periodic elections allow the majority of voters to continue to exercise ultimate control over the direction of public policy.

In this chapter, we explore historical and legal factors related to who has the right to vote, how Americans exercise their right to vote, and the factors that influence the making of a vote choice. Voting, of course, is not the only way citizens participate in the political process. They also contribute time and money to parties and candidates, write letters and contact public officials, express thoughts on policy issues and political candidates in blogs, attend town meetings and rallies, and engage in protests such as sit-ins, boycotts, and marches. We examine these forms of political participation as well.

The Legal Structure for Voting

The **franchise**, or suffrage, is the right to vote. When speaking about majority rule, it is important to ask, "majority of whom?" Article I, Section 4 of the U.S. Constitution assigns the system of voting, including the definition of who is granted suffrage, to the states. Voting registration, voter eligibility, methods of casting ballots, and the tallying of official results are all functions reserved for states. The original Constitution prescribes eligibility requirements for federal officeholders (representatives, senators, and the president) and lays out the system for selection of the president and vice president, but it says nothing about who can vote in elections for these officials. Constitutional amendments have been ratified and federal laws have been passed that prevent states from discriminating in granting suffrage rights; but technically, there exists no absolute constitutional right to vote in the first place.

Toward Universal Suffrage

The states have exercised significant authority in defining who is eligible to vote. For many years, states regularly denied minorities, women, young adults, Native Americans, and the poor the right to vote for officeholders at the local, state, and national levels of government. In addition, a number of states prescribed property ownership requirements that prevented many people from being eligible to vote. Some states at various points in the nation's early history sought to broaden the right of suffrage. New Jersey, for example, allowed women the right to vote in the early 1800s, and some northern states provided for black suffrage prior to the Civil War.[2] But the goal of **universal suffrage**—or the right of all citizens to vote—has been an elusive one throughout American history. Restrictions on voting rights have systematically denied the right of particular groups of people to participate in choosing their leaders.

Two centuries of government under the Constitution, however, have been marked by steady progress toward the goal of extending the franchise to all Americans. In the first federal elections in 1788, voting rights were limited to white men who owned property; in the most recent federal elections of 2008, all citizens of the United States age eighteen or older (who were not otherwise prohibited from voting due to a felony conviction or some similar offense) enjoyed the legal right to vote. Enfranchisement was not achieved quickly, nor did it happen as the result of one or two events. Rather, the process of extending the right to vote to all American adults occurred over centuries of time and with much opposition.

The Civil War presented the first major challenge to the disenfranchisement of a particular class of people, namely, African Americans. Prior to the Civil War, African American slaves not only did not have the right to vote; they had no rights at all. In the infamous U.S. Supreme Court decision *Dred Scott v. Sanford* (1857), the Court ruled that slaves were property, that they had

★ LO
Assess the role of state governments in managing elections

Franchise (or suffrage)
The right to vote.

★ LO
Evaluate the effect of various constitutional amendments on the expansion of voting rights in the United States

Universal suffrage
The idea that all citizens in a nation have the right to vote.

AMERICAN GOVERNMENT In Historical Perspective

When One Vote Made the Difference

Does your vote matter? Few elections are decided by one vote. However, there have been very important elections throughout American history that prove the exception rather than the rule. In some instances, a single vote made a huge difference. According to PBS's "The Democracy Project," these important elections were decided by a handful of votes:

1846 One vote decided on war with Mexico. In 1846, the Mexican army invaded Texas and President Polk asked for a Declaration of War. The Senate did not want to go to war, and the declaration passed by only one vote. The United States won the war against Mexico and with that victory added five states—Arizona, New Mexico, Nevada, Utah and California.

1867 One vote gave the United States the state of Alaska. The Alaska Purchase of 1867 was ratified by just one vote—paving the way for the territory to be America's largest state when it became part of the United States in 1958.

1876 One vote gave Rutherford B. Hayes the presidency of the United States. In the 1876 presidential election, Samuel Tilden received a half million more popular votes than Hayes. The Electoral College was not in agreement about who should be America's next leader. A special commission was formed to make the final decision. The commission decided, although Hayes had lost the actual vote by the citizens of the United States, he

had won the electoral vote by just one ballot: 185 to 184.

1916 One vote in each of the voting districts of California reelected President Wilson. If Wilson's op-ponent, Charles E. Hughes, had received an addi-tional vote in each one of California's voting precincts, he would have defeated Wilson.

1948 One vote per voting precinct gave Harry Truman the presidency. If Truman's opponent, Thomas E. Dewey, had received one vote more per precinct in Ohio and California, there would have been a tie and the House of Representatives would have decided the election. And because Dewey had more support in the House than Truman, Dewey would have won.

© 2012 CENGAGE LEARNING

Source: http://pbskids.org/democracy/vote/onevote2004.html.

Fifteenth Amendment
The amendment to the Constitution that guaranteed the franchise regardless of race, color, or any previous condition of servitude.

no rights under the law, and that they were not and could never become legal citizens of the United States. Immediately after the surrender of Confederate forces in 1865, President Abraham Lincoln gave an address suggesting that freed slaves be given the franchise. The idea met with some resistance, even among the northern states. However, the so-called Civil War amendments not only ended the institution of slavery (the Thirteenth Amendment) and granted citizenship to former slaves (the Fourteenth Amendment), but the **Fifteenth Amendment**, passed in 1870, guaranteed that "the right of citizens of the United States to vote shall not be abridged by the United States or any state on account of race, color, or any previous condition of servitude." The Fifteenth Amendment was the first formal action granting the federal government the power to enforce voting rights over the states.

The Fifteenth Amendment, however, did not deter some officials from the former Confederate states from finding ways to deny African Americans their newly won voting rights after Reconstruction ended in 1877. Threats, beatings, destruction of property, and other intimidation tactics, often ignored by local police, effectively kept blacks from coming to the polls on Election Day.[3] In addition, some states sought legal means to prevent blacks from voting. They passed laws instituting a **poll tax** that required individuals to pay a fee before being allowed to vote; they required potential voters to pass a **literacy test** to prove that they could read and write. Because most blacks were poor, they were often unable to pay the poll tax (usually about $30). Blacks also tended to have less education (in some states, it had been illegal to teach slaves to read and write), so they frequently could not pass the literacy tests, which were often deliberately difficult and unfairly applied to minorities to prevent them from voting. From the late 1800s through the first half of the twentieth century, these methods posed a substantial barrier to black turnout in federal elections, which typically was about 10 percent. These laws also depressed turnout of poor people in general.

The civil rights movement of the 1960s addressed the problems associated with the disenfranchisement of blacks. Two important products of this movement were the Twenty-fourth Amendment and the Voting Rights Act of 1965. The **Twenty-fourth Amendment**, passed in 1964, outlawed poll taxes by making unconstitutional any law that made payment of a tax a voting eligibility requirement in federal elections.[4] The Voting Rights Act of 1965 denied states the right to use literacy tests as a requirement for voting; it also provided African Americans with protection from intimidating tactics that had been used to keep them away from the polls.

The past century also witnessed the enfranchisement of women. Though passage of the Fifteenth Amendment in 1870 granted African American men the legal right to vote, women would not receive the same constitutional guarantee until 1920 with the passage of the **Nineteenth Amendment**. In 1848, some 200 delegates—women and men—met in Seneca Falls, New York, to issue a call for women's rights, including the right to vote. The Civil War years diverted the nation's attention from women's rights to other pressing problems.[5] Attempts to include a women's right to vote in the Fifteenth Amendment proved unsuccessful, although women began voting in some states well before passage of the Fifteenth Amendment. By the late nineteenth century, some of the new western states, such as Utah, Wyoming, Colorado, Idaho, Washington, and California, enacted women's suffrage laws. Despite continued opposition from leaders, including President Woodrow Wilson and many states in the Northeast, popular sentiment and a well-organized lobbying effort eventually led to the passage of the Nineteenth Amendment.

Three other groups have successfully won the right to vote through federal legislation and constitutional amendment. Until the early twentieth century, Native Americans had neither citizenship nor voting rights, but federal laws passed in 1924 made it illegal for states to deny Native Americans the franchise. In 1961, the **Twenty-third Amendment** to the Constitution gave residents of the District of Columbia the right to vote in presidential elections. Because the District is not a state, its residents had not been allowed to

Poll tax
The requirement that individuals pay a fee before being allowed to vote.

Literacy test
The requirement that individuals prove that they can read and write before being allowed to vote.

Twenty-fourth Amendment
The constitutional amendment that outlaws poll taxes.

Nineteenth Amendment
The constitutional amendment that guarantees women equal voting rights.

Twenty-third Amendment
The constitutional amendment providing electoral votes to the District of Columbia, thus giving District residents the right to vote in presidential elections.

participate in presidential elections. The Twenty-third Amendment allocates electoral votes to the District using the same formula by which electoral votes are allocated to a state: the total number of representatives it would have in the House, if it were a state, plus two. Today, the District of Columbia has a total of three electoral votes. In 1971, in the midst of the Vietnam War when many young Americans were dying in battle, Congress passed and the states ratified the **Twenty-sixth Amendment**, which lowered the voting age to eighteen in all local, state, and federal elections.

Twenty-sixth Amendment
The constitutional amendment that lowered the voting age to eighteen in all local, state, and federal elections.

Although the administration of election and voting rules is largely controlled by the states, a significant number of federal laws and constitutional amendments have extended voting rights in the United States. Collectively, these laws prevent states from discriminating against particular groups of citizens with respect to their right to vote. Unfortunately, racism and other forms of discrimination continue to exist and thus continue to affect voting rights in America. Subtle forms of discrimination, including intimidation tactics by groups such as the Ku Klux Klan, may scare individuals into not voting. But more overt discriminatory tactics, supported by some state and local laws, have largely been erased. As a society, the United States, over many years, has progressed toward the democratic ideal of universal suffrage. Today in the United States, the only adults legally disenfranchised are convicted felons in prison (forty-seven states), on probation (twenty-nine states), and on parole (thirty-two states).

★ LO Appreciate the wide diversity of voter registration systems implemented in the fifty states

Voter Registration Laws

Just as the extension of the franchise has evolved over the years, so has the system of voter registration. Most states today have voter registration systems in which individuals must qualify to become eligible to vote. The responsibility for qualifying lies with the individual. States do not compile and maintain a list of individuals who are eligible to vote. Rather, individuals must take it upon themselves to demonstrate their qualifications and file the appropriate paperwork to become eligible.

Massachusetts, in 1800, was the first state to require individuals to register to vote.[6] A handful of states followed Massachusetts's lead, but not until after the Civil War did most states adopt voter registration systems. Many of the voter registration systems that were adopted between the 1870s and the early 1900s made it harder for immigrants, the less educated, and those less familiar with the political system to vote. A leading force behind the institution of voter registration systems was the populist movement of the late nineteenth century, which largely included white, middle-class, native-born Americans. In the northern states, registration laws were intended to make it more difficult for new European immigrants to vote; in the West, the intention was to make voting by new Chinese and Japanese immigrants more difficult; in the South, registration was aimed at limiting the black vote; and the source of concern in the Southwest was Mexican immigrants. Most states today still rely on some form of self-initiated voter registration, which continues to present an obstacle to voting. A person must first find out how to register, remember to register in advance of Election Day, and then spend time registering. Many states require proof of age and citizenship, and many also impose a length-of-residence qualification, requiring potential voters to prove that they have resided in the state for a specified period of time.[7]

A number of organizations and public interest groups have lobbied state legislatures and Congress to simplify and ease voter registration requirements to allow more people to vote on Election Day, including those who fail to register in advance of the election. North Dakota is the only state that does not currently require registration, and three states—Maine, Minnesota, and Wisconsin—permit voters to register on Election Day. The National Voter Registration Act of 1993, often called the **Motor Voter law**, mandates that when an individual applies for or renews a state driver's license, the state must also provide that individual with voter registration materials. The idea behind the law is that combining the process of registering to vote with the more routine task of obtaining a driver's license makes voter registration easier. Research suggests that although this law has increased voter registration, it has not increased actual turnout.[8]

Motor Voter law
The federal law that mandates that when an individual applies for or renews a state driver's license, the state must also provide that individual with voter registration materials.

Exercising the Franchise

★ **LO**
Assess the influence of different factors in influencing voter turnout, including interest in politics, sense of civic duty, the perception that one's vote can make a difference, education, income, age, and social group pressures

A number of factors explain why people decide to cast a ballot on Election Day. An individual's interest in politics is one important factor. People who are more interested in politics tend to follow news about campaigns to a much greater degree than those who are less interested, and those who are more interested are more likely to vote.

Interest in politics, however, is only one factor that leads people to vote. Another is a person's sense of civic duty, or the belief that being a good citizen requires one to vote. Many people who are not very interested in politics show up to vote nonetheless because they have a sense of civic duty.[9] From a young age, most Americans are socialized to believe that participating in elections is characteristic of the good democratic citizen, and so they feel an obligation to cast a vote even though they may not be particularly interested in elections and campaigns.

Another factor that influences some people to vote is the perception that their vote can have an impact on the outcome of an election. Individuals who feel strongly about a particular issue, set of issues, or a candidate may want to vote on the theory that if the election is close, their vote might actually make a difference in the outcome. Indeed, the sense that one's vote can make a difference contributes to higher turnout in elections that are perceived to be close.

Finally, for some people, social group pressure can be a motivating factor in deciding to vote. Voting is often regarded as the "right" thing to do, and some people feel that casting a ballot is expected of them by others. This sense of social pressure to do what is acceptable by society's standards can increase the likelihood that a person will vote.

Who Turns Out to Vote?

An individual's interest in politics and attentiveness to news about politics and campaigns, sense of civic duty, and sense of political efficacy (that is, the belief that one's vote can make a difference) all lead to higher rates of **voter turnout**, which is the percentage of eligible voters who show up to vote on Election Day. In addition to these "political" factors that help distinguish between citizens who are more or less likely to vote, there are a number of demographic characteristics that also help explain turnout. A person's gender, age, and level of education are all related to the decision to vote (see Figure 14.1, p. 370).

Voter turnout
The number of people who turn out to vote as a percentage of all those eligible to vote.

FIGURE 14.1 Differences in Voter Turnout among Demographic Groups in 2008 Presidential Election

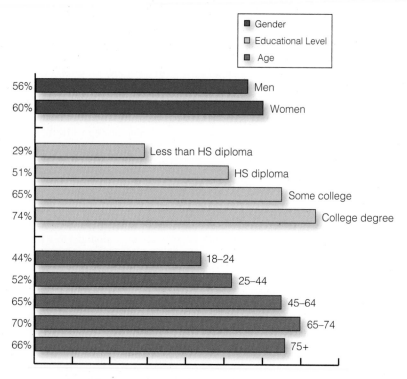

Source: Current Population Survey, U.S. Bureau of the Census 2008.

In many elections, younger people tend to pass up the opportunity to vote at greater rates than middle-aged and older people do. Youth nonvoting is often attributed to the more transient nature of younger people's lives.[10] At about age eighteen, many young people leave their parents' home to go to college, to take a job, or to start their careers. Younger Americans are less rooted in a community, have had less time to register to vote, and are experiencing major changes in their social and personal situation. Voting tends to be less of a priority under these changing circumstances. As people age, buy a home, have a family, and reside in a particular community for a period of time, they become more socially attached and are more likely to vote.

Two other demographic groups are substantially more likely to vote: better-educated Americans[11] and wealthier Americans.[12] These two factors are related because higher levels of education also lead to higher relative affluence and social status. The process of being educated sharpens a person's mind, improves the individual's ability to understand problems in society, and equips him or her to deal with complex information, such as the issues discussed in political campaigns. Education also enhances a person's appreciation for democracy and sense of civic duty. A better understanding of the issues and appreciation for the democratic process encourage higher levels of voter participation.

Courting the Youth Vote

Candidates and political parties often try to increase turnout as a means of enhancing their candidates' prospects in an election. However, nonpartisan organizations may engage in special efforts to encourage the so-called youth vote in particular. These organizations may target young voters primarily for two reasons: (1) young voters represent the future of American democracy, and (2) youth turnout has tended to be lower than turnout among older Americans. Even in 2008—when youth vote increased substantially as compared to past presidential elections—barely more than half of eligible voters aged eighteen to twenty-nine voted, leaving that group well behind turnout rates of the electorate as whole (more than 60 percent or more of eligible Americans voted in 2008).

Among the many organizations that run programs to encourage young voters to exercise their voting rights are the following:

- **Rock the Vote**, which claims to have registered more than 2 million new voters in 2008 alone;

- **18 in '08**, which provides programs on college campuses and produces documentaries that encourage youth voting and other political participation;

- **CIRCLE** (Center for Information and Research on Civic Learning and Engagement), which conducts research on the dynamics of young people's voting behavior (see http://www.civicyouth.org);

- **YouthVote.org**, a website that provides a plethora of information for young people to learn how to register to vote and why it is important to do so.

For Critical Thinking and Discussion

1. Have you ever been approached by a group or organization asking you either to register to vote or to turn out to vote in a particular election?

2. Did they make a special appeal to you on the basis of your age? How important was that appeal in your decision to vote (or not vote)?

3. Why do you think college-age students turn out in relatively lower numbers?

Why Don't People Vote?

Despite the numerous factors that motivate people to vote, many in fact do not vote. Voter turnout is a measure of how engaged Americans are in voting in any given election contest. High turnout is considered a healthy sign for a democratic system. It implies that people are engaged in political issues, spend the time to contribute to the system, and take responsibility for selecting leaders. Lower turnout is often viewed as a by-product of alienation, mistrust, and lack of confidence in the political system.

Economist Anthony Downs originally offered an explanation for nonvoting based on a theory known as *rational choice*.[13] He argued that voters might decide not to vote because they reason that the costs of obtaining and understanding information about candidates and campaigns outweigh the benefits of making a vote choice. It is a rational choice, therefore, to decide not to vote or to vote on the basis of certain "shortcuts" such as a candidate's political party.

★ **LO**

Explore the influence of political campaigns on turnout and in affecting "high stimulus" elections

Elections are plentiful in the United States and are held for many different offices at many different levels of government. Turnout varies from one type of election to another. Some elections draw much more media attention and thus engender more interest than others. Some feature much more political advertising and so provide more cues to voters. Some elections are inherently viewed as more important and so inspire a greater sense of civic duty among voters.

In 1966, political scientist Angus Campbell and his colleagues identified five factors that distinguish between "high-stimulus" elections (in which turnout tends to be higher) and "low-stimulus" elections (in which turnout is generally lower).[14] The factors that characterize a high-stimulus election are

- Greater levels of media coverage
- Higher significance of the office
- Campaigns in which voters assign high importance to an issue
- More attractive candidates
- Perceptions of a close race

Campbell and his colleagues argue that events external to voters may stimulate interest in elections and thus increase the likelihood that individuals will turn out to vote on Election Day. For example, when big issues such as war and peace are at stake, people are more likely to take an interest in the election and vote.

FIGURE 14.2 Voter Turnout in U.S. Congressional and Presidential Elections

The following shows trends in voter turnout from 1960 through 2008 for presidential year elections and midterm congressional elections.

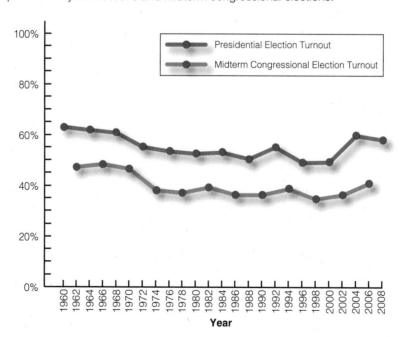

Presidential elections tend to produce the highest levels of turnout because

■ They are heavily covered by the media;

■ There is more spending on political advertisements, particularly on television, thus making the campaign more visible to voters; and

■ The presidency is the most significant office in the U.S. political system.

In presidential races where an issue important to many voters is at stake—such as problems with the economy in 1992, the Vietnam War in 1968, or the war with Iraq and terrorism in 2008—turnout tends to be especially high. Races for higher office typically deal with bigger issues and feature candidates who are more attractive to voters. For these reasons, turnout in presidential races, and to a lesser extent in contests for U.S. senators and state governors, tends to be higher than turnout in elections for lower state offices and local races.

Voting in the United States Compared with Other Democracies

★ LO

Compare and contrast voter turnout in the United States with voter turnout in other democracies

Many observers of elections note that voter turnout rates are lower in the United States than they are in other democracies. From 1992 through 2000, the average turnout rate in the United States for presidential elections was 52 percent. Over the same period, the average turnout rate in all federal elections (including midterm congressional races) was 45 percent. During roughly the same period of time, turnout in other nations, as shown in Figure 14.3, was much higher.

Several explanations have been offered to account for both the lower turnout rates in the United States compared with other democracies as well as the trend toward declining rates of turnout in the United States over the past half century.

1. **There are a large number of elections in America, making the opportunity to participate less of a novelty.** U.S. turnout rates may be lower than those in other democracies of the world simply because there are so many elections held in the United States.[15] The U.S. system of federalism produces several layers of government—national, state, and local. At the federal level, elections are held for president, the Senate, and the House of Representatives. At the state level, there are gubernatorial races as well as elections for other statewide offices, including attorney general, state treasurer, and other state agency heads. At the local level, there may be elections for mayor, city council, sheriff, local judges, and so on. Furthermore, for many of these offices, there are two elections: a primary election to elect the party candidate and a general election to determine the office winner. Also, in many states and localities, there are often special elections on referendum questions and bond issues. Opportunities for participation in elections in the United States are so plentiful that they have become commonplace events. The vast number of elections may help explain lower rates of voting in any one contest. Switzerland, which also has a large number of elections, has relatively low turnout compared with other democracies.

2. **Tuesdays are workdays.** Traditionally, most elections in the United States have been held on Tuesdays. Most working people work on Tuesday, and so it may be inconvenient or difficult for many voters to find the time to vote on this day. People report having less and less free time in our society, which can account in part for declining turnout. In many other countries,

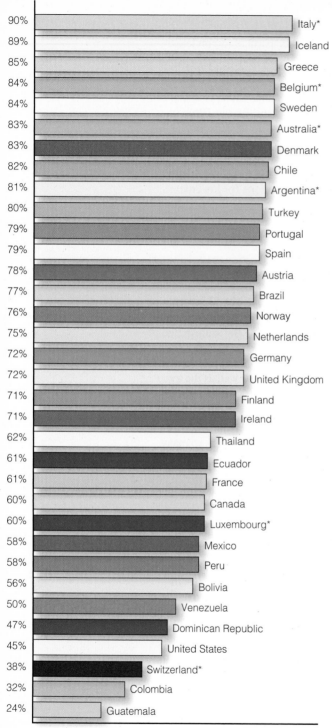

90%	Italy*
89%	Iceland
85%	Greece
84%	Belgium*
84%	Sweden
83%	Australia*
83%	Denmark
82%	Chile
81%	Argentina*
80%	Turkey
79%	Portugal
79%	Spain
78%	Austria
77%	Brazil
76%	Norway
75%	Netherlands
72%	Germany
72%	United Kingdom
71%	Finland
71%	Ireland
62%	Thailand
61%	Ecuador
61%	France
60%	Canada
60%	Luxembourg*
58%	Mexico
58%	Peru
56%	Bolivia
50%	Venezuela
47%	Dominican Republic
45%	United States
38%	Switzerland*
32%	Colombia
24%	Guatemala

*Denotes a country that has compulsory voting laws.

Source: International Institute for Democracy and Electoral Assistance.

elections are held on weekends or over a period of a number of days, making it easier for people to find the time to cast a vote.

3. **Voting in the United States usually requires advance registration.** As described earlier in this chapter, voters in most U.S. states are required to register to vote prior to Election Day. In other countries, voter registration is often automatic; that is, citizens of legal age are automatically registered to vote. Thus, voters simply need to show up at the voting place on Election Day. In countries where registration is automatic, 100 percent of eligible voters are thus registered; in the United States, where registration is usually a separate process, typically about 70 percent of eligible individuals have registered to vote.

4. **Over the past fifty years, perceptions both that participation can make a difference in what government does (that is, voters' sense of "internal efficacy") and that government is responsive to the people ("external efficacy") have declined.** Many researchers have concluded that the decline in political efficacy, which is accompanied by declines in political trust and in confidence in political institu-

FIGURE 14.3 Voter Turnout around the World

Voter turnout varies a great deal from one country to another. This figure depicts average voter turnout from 1991 through 2000 in a number of the world's democracies. The turnout rates are expressed as the percentage of the voting age population that actually voted in national elections. For the United States, the percentage includes both presidential and midterm congressional elections.

tions, has produced lower rates of voter turnout.[16] As people come to feel that they are less able to influence the system and that the system is less responsive to them, they may become less likely to vote.

5. **Extensions of the franchise lead to short-term declines in turnout.** Ironically, events that have expanded the franchise have been followed by lower rates of voter turnout. Following passage of the Fifteenth Amendment in 1870, which enfranchised former male slaves, the turnout rate dropped in 1872; passage of the Nineteenth Amendment in 1920, granting women the right to vote, led to an overall drop in turnout; and passage of the Twenty-sixth Amendment in 1971, which lowered the voting age to eighteen, led to lower turnout rates. One explanation for this phenomenon is that many newly eligible voters are not yet registered to vote and may require some time and socialization to get into the habit of voting.

6. **Voting in the United States is not compulsory.** Some democracies, including the United States, regard the franchise as a right. Accordingly, citizens have the opportunity to exercise their right to vote, or they may choose not to vote. By contrast, some democracies have compulsory voting laws requiring citizens to vote. These nations assert that voting is a citizen's responsibility. Belgium, in 1892, was the first country to adopt compulsory voting. According to the International Institute for Democracy and Electoral Assistance, thirty-two countries have compulsory voting laws on the books. Twenty-four countries enforce these laws to some degree, and of them, nine—Australia, Belgium, Cyprus, Fiji, Luxembourg, Nauru, Singapore, Switzerland, and Uruguay—have strict enforcement policies.

   Punishments for not voting in countries with compulsory voting laws include large fines, possible imprisonment (although imprisonment is generally the punishment for not paying a fine), and disenfranchisement. In Belgium, individuals who do not vote in four elections over a fifteen-year period are stripped of their voting rights. In Bolivia, voters are given vouchers after they vote, and these vouchers are needed to receive a salary from a bank during a three-month period after an election. In Greece, it is very difficult to get a passport or driver's license without showing proof of having voted.

   Many arguments can be made in favor of or against compulsory voting laws, but one thing is certain: Countries with compulsory voting laws have much higher turnout rates than countries without such laws. In Italy, for example, where lists of nonvoters are publicized, turnout has been around 90 percent. Though compulsory voting laws certainly increase turnout, many critics argue that the right to vote implicitly includes the right not to vote, just as the right to practice the religion of one's choice also includes the right not to practice a religion.

7. **There has been a decline in "social capital."** Political scientist Robert Putnam has noted a general decline in **social capital**, which is the extent to which individuals are socially integrated into their community.[17] Over the past half-century, Americans have become less socially connected because they are not as likely to be members of organizations such as political parties, labor unions, civic groups, or even bowling leagues. As

Social capital
The "social connectedness" of a community, or the extent to which individuals are socially integrated into their community.

reasons for this decline, Putnam cites the increase of women in the workforce and corresponding reduction in the amount of time that women have available to spend on social and community activities. Other factors for the decline include the increase in residential mobility, and technological innovations like radio, television, and the Internet. People today are more likely to stay home and watch TV or surf the Internet and less likely to engage in social activities with other people. Voting is, in part, a social activity. The decline in social capital may be responsible, at least in part, for the general decline in voting.

★ LO Understand the various factors that explain vote choices

Making a Vote Choice

After an individual registers to vote and makes a decision to vote, the final phase of the voting decision is to make a choice among the candidates who are running for office. In covering American politics, the news media spend a tremendous amount of time and resources analyzing how voters will vote in a contest, particularly in presidential elections. For this reason, preelection polling has become a centerpiece of American political campaign strategy as well as news coverage. Years before a presidential election takes place, media polls query American voters on the potential candidates and assess the level of support voters offer these candidates. Months before the election, daily tracking polls monitor how voters are thinking and changing from day to day.

Likewise, political scientists' primary focus of research on American political behavior is on how voters make up their minds about whom they will vote for. Research has identified a number of different factors that act as cues to individual voters in helping them make a vote decision. Collectively, these factors are referred to as "determinants of vote choice."

Candidate Familiarity

The most basic voting cue is simple name recognition and familiarity with a candidate. Many voters pay little attention to politics and political campaigns. Recognizing the name of a candidate on a ballot, then, offers an important voting cue. If voters recognize one candidate's name and no others, they are much more likely to vote for the name they recognize. Likewise, the more familiar voters are with a candidate, the more likely they are to vote for that candidate. In lower-visibility elections, such as primaries and local elections, name recognition plays a large role in the voting decision. However, even in statewide and presidential races (particularly presidential primaries), familiarity with a candidate can be an important cue to voters. High name recognition and voter familiarity propelled Hillary Clinton to the top of the pack at the outset of the Democratic presidential primaries during the 2008 campaign. In many congressional House races, incumbents tend to win reelection at rates in excess of 90 percent in large part because voters recognize their names and are less familiar with the challengers.

Party Identification

Political parties play many important roles in the American political system. Often, voters form a psychological attachment to a party that helps them organize their political information and offers an important cue to vote choice.

Television Presidents Paving the Way for Voter Open-Mindedness

When Barack Obama became the first African American to take the oath of office as U.S. president in 2009, he overcame racial barriers thought to be impenetrable just two decades earlier, when many voters dismissed Jesse Jackson's run for the presidency as a sideshow. Still, those among the tens of millions who watched Obama's inauguration as the forty-fourth president should be forgiven if the whole thing seemed just a bit familiar. Consider that on October 29, 2002, almost six years before Obama's election victory, viewers of the popular Fox series *24* were greeted by a television breakthrough of sorts, when African American character actor Dennis Haysbert was introduced in his new role as U.S. President David Palmer. More than four years later, on January 14, 2007, *24* fans were introduced to the sight of yet another African American president: This time it was David Palmer's brother Wayne (played by D. B. Woodside).

Other historical breakthroughs in television's depiction of the American presidency are notable as well. On May 14, 2007, the fictional Latin American Congressman Matthew Santos (played by Jimmy Smits) was sworn is as the new U.S. president in the final episode of the critically acclaimed drama series *The West Wing*. Women presidents have also appeared in prime time, both in the short-lived 2005 drama series *Commander in Chief* (Academy Award–winning actress Geena Davis played President Mackenzie Allen), as well as in the seventh season of *24*, when Allison Taylor (played by Cherry Jones) became the latest fictional chief executive in that series.

For his part, Dennis Haysbert has argued that his role as an African American president may have actually benefited Barack Obama: "If anything, my portrayal of David Palmer, I think, may have helped open the eyes of the American people." This may be a case of reality not so much mimicking popular culture as being influenced by its more open-minded mores.

For Critical Thinking and Discussion

1. What role does race or gender play in voters' assessments of candidates?
2. Can a fictional television series influence the way voters think about real-life candidates and their political viability? If so, how?
3. Do historical electoral breakthroughs (such as the election of the first African American or woman as president) require that voters first undergo a fundamental change in attitudes?

Pictured above are Dennis Haysbert as President David Palmer on *24*, Geena Davis as President MacKenzie Allen on *Commander-in-Chief*, and Jimmy Smits as President Matthew Santos on *The West Wing*.

Source: Simon Reynolds, "Haysbert: '24' President Helped Obama," Digitalspy.com, July 2, 2008.

FIGURE 14.4

Accuracy of the Gallup Poll in Predicting Voter Behavior

Preelection polls offer candidates, journalists, and voters detailed information on the dynamics of an election contest. How well the polls actually predict vote choices is a frequently voiced concern. One of the best-known opinion polls in the United States is the Gallup Poll, which has been conducting preelection polls since the 1936 presidential election. This figure shows Gallup's prediction for the percentage of the vote that the winner would receive in each presidential election from 1936 to the present, along with the actual percentage of the vote that the winner got on Election Day. Only once did Gallup make an incorrect prediction—in 1948, it predicted that Dewey would defeat Truman.

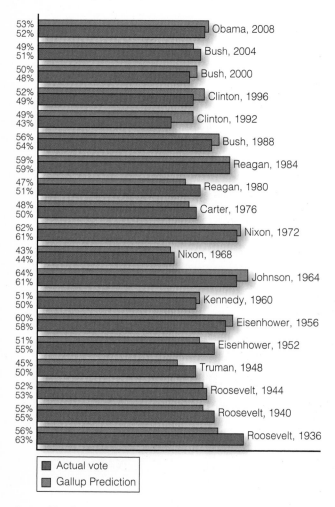

53% / 52%	Obama, 2008
49% / 51%	Bush, 2004
50% / 48%	Bush, 2000
52% / 49%	Clinton, 1996
49% / 43%	Clinton, 1992
56% / 54%	Bush, 1988
59% / 59%	Reagan, 1984
47% / 51%	Reagan, 1980
48% / 50%	Carter, 1976
62% / 61%	Nixon, 1972
43% / 44%	Nixon, 1968
64% / 61%	Johnson, 1964
51% / 50%	Kennedy, 1960
60% / 58%	Eisenhower, 1956
51% / 55%	Eisenhower, 1952
45% / 50%	Truman, 1948
52% / 53%	Roosevelt, 1944
52% / 55%	Roosevelt, 1940
56% / 63%	Roosevelt, 1936

■ Actual vote
■ Gallup Prediction

Source: The Gallup Organization.
©1936–2008 The Gallup Organization.

As discussed in Chapter 13, *party identification* is the term for this psychological attachment to a political party. Party identification tends to be a long-term predisposition; once it forms, it usually remains with an individual over the course of his or her life. Party identification, then, is an important determinant of vote choice.[18]

Party identification is particularly powerful in influencing a vote decision in lower-profile political races, where those who identify with a political party are most likely to turn out to vote, and those who turn out usually vote for the candidate associated with their political party.[19]

Although party identification and its impact on vote choice have been in a state of decline,[20] two thirds of voters continue to identify with one of the major parties, and thus, party identification remains the single best predictor of how an individual might vote in an election. Identifying with a partisan perspective provides a shortcut for voters in making candidate choices.

Issue Voting

For voters who identify as Democrats, the Democratic Party's candidate is likely to hold an issue position that they favor; the same is true for voters who identify as Republicans. For voters who identify as independents, however, a candidate's party does not serve as a determinant of vote choice. For these voters, a candidate's position on a particular issue or set of issues is a voting cue.

Voting on the basis of issues is more likely to occur in certain types of elections.[21] First, when a particular issue captures the attention of many people in the electorate, voters are more likely to use a candidate's position on that issue to form a vote decision. For example, in the 1968 presidential race, American involvement in the Vietnam War was a central concern for many voters, and many voted on the basis of the two candidates' positions on the war.[22] In the 2008 presidential race, Barack Obama and John McCain held substantially different positions on American policy in the Iraq war, an issue of primary importance to many voters. Those voters cast a vote largely on the basis of the candidates' position on the war.

Second, issue voting occurs more often when an issue is of particular personal concern to a voter. In 2008, for example, American voters were concerned about a poorly performing economy and the crisis on Wall Street, and thus many cast a vote on the basis of the candidates' proposals for addressing the economic crisis. Third, issue voting is much more likely to occur when the candidates hold clearly distinct positions on issues.

Anthony Downs's rational choice approach to understanding voting turnout also applies to making a vote choice. Downs suggested that in making a choice, voters examine the issue positions of the candidates and assess how close they are to the voters' own positions. The candidate whose positions on the issues are closer to the voter's earns the vote.

Issue voting is often regarded as the most sophisticated type of voting behavior. Notions of the "ideal democratic citizen" describe such a person as someone who is informed about issues, has developed a position on those issues, and then compares that position to the positions of the candidates. Voting on the basis of such a calculation requires political knowledge and attentiveness to campaigns. Although issues remain important to many voters and take on higher levels of importance under certain circumstances, most research indicates that other shortcut factors, such as party identification, are more commonly used to make choices.

© 2012 CENGAGE LEARNING

Retrospective Voting

In issue voting, a voter assesses the candidates' issue positions and casts a vote based on which candidate the voter thinks will do a better job in dealing with that issue in the future. However, a voter's past experience with a candidate or a political party also can be an important determinant of vote choice. **Retrospective voting**, a concept developed by political scientist Morris Fiorina, posits that evaluations of incumbents' past performance in office provide important cues for voters in deciding whether to vote for that incumbent.[23] Voters who believe that an incumbent has done a good job are likely to vote for the officeholder, whereas if they judge that an incumbent's job performance has been poor, they are likely to vote against the officeholder. Voter assessments of the economy and the performance of the president in handling economic conditions are especially important in a voter's retrospective evaluation of an incumbent. Bill Clinton's victory over incumbent George H. W. Bush in the 1992 presidential election was largely the result of voters' negative evaluations of Bush's handling of the nation's economy. Likewise, Ronald Reagan's defeat of incumbent President Jimmy Carter in 1980 was based on voters' perception that Carter performed poorly in dealing with economic problems and the Iranian hostage crisis.

In retrospective voting, the evaluation of the incumbent provides the determination of vote choice. In other words, a voter's assessment of the incumbent's job performance provides a shortcut decision rule on voting for or against the incumbent. Pollsters often measure this assessment through a "job approval rating" question. The percentage of voters who approve of the incumbent's job performance often reflects the percentage of the vote that the incumbent receives in a reelection bid.

Retrospective voting
An explanation of vote choice that asserts that voters' evaluations of a candidate's past performance in office provides an important cue for vote decisions.

Candidates for office often try to encourage voters to think retrospectively if it is in their strategic interest to do so. In the 1980 presidential campaign, while the nation was experiencing economic problems and an extended international crisis with hostages being held in Iran, challenger Ronald Reagan defeated incumbent Jimmy Carter in part by asking the voters, "Are you better off today than you were four years ago [before Carter took office]?" Similarly, in 1992, challenger Bill Clinton questioned the integrity of President George H. W. Bush by repeating a TV clip of the president saying "Read my lips, no new taxes"—a pledge Bush had made in 1988 but did not keep.

Candidate Image Voting

The image, personal traits, and other characteristics of the particular candidates in a campaign can also influence the way people vote. Especially in higher-stimulus elections, where candidates make ample use of television advertisements to build an image, voter perceptions of candidates' qualities are important. Perceptions of candidate image include such characteristics as honesty, trustworthiness, leadership ability, concern for voters, integrity, intelligence, and sense of humor.

In today's media age, candidates have found that image development is an efficient means of persuading swing voters how to vote. Thus, candidates often use television advertising to build their own favorable image or, conversely, to depict their opponents as having negative image characteristics. Visual images on television are useful in conveying symbolic, image-oriented messages. Bill Clinton in 1996 built a successful campaign around a theme that he would continue to improve the nation's economic future (his theme was captured in the slogan "building a bridge to the twenty-first century"). Ronald Reagan in 1984 cemented his strong leadership image in his campaign for reelection (with the TV ad slogan "It's morning again in America").

★ LO Appreciate the many forms of political participation beyond voting, including communicating concerns to officials, civil disobedience, and protest activities

Political Participation Beyond the Voting Booth

Although voting tends to be the most popular form of political participation in the United States, it is by no means the only way Americans participate. In a 2008 survey conducted by the Intercollegiate Studies Institute, 46 percent of Americans said they have actively tried to influence others how to vote, 48 percent said they have attended a political meeting or rally, 24 percent have worked on a political campaign, 40 percent have contributed money to a political campaign, 64 percent have signed a petition, and 25 percent have sent a letter to the editor.

Although all of these forms of political participation enrich American political culture, activities that are intended to protest something often gain the most visibility. One recent protest movement that gained a national following is the so-called Tea Party movement. Beginning in early 2009, a series of antitax protests emerged in response to the federal government's increase in spending to combat the economic recession. The Tea Party protests challenged the Barack Obama-Democratic Party policies of deficit spending and comprehensive reform of the nation's health care insurance system. The term *Tea Party* was chosen strategically to reference the Boston Tea Party, whose goal was to protest Britain's taxation policies toward the colonies during the American Revolutionary period. "TEA" is also used as an acronym for "taxed enough already." In addition to organizing protest rallies across the nation (annually on April 15, or "tax day," for example), Tea Party organizers were particularly active during the summer and fall of 2009 in voicing their concerns at congressional Democrats' constituent meetings promoting health care reform proposals.

The Tea Party also influenced a number of congressional races in the 2010 midterm elections. The movement helped conservative Republicans such as Rand Paul (R-KY) and Marco Rubio (R-FL) coast to general election victories in the Senate. At the same time, some Tea Party-supported candidates who won their GOP primary election against more moderate Republican candidates (such as Christine O'Donnell, who defeated the more moderate governor, Mike Castle, in the primary) were defeated in the general election.

Protests can take one of three forms: legal protests in which citizens play by the "rules of the game" to speak out against a government policy, acts of nonviolent civil disobedience, and illegal protest activities that often include violence.

Marches, sit-ins, and rallies are forms of legal protests; such activities are designed to call attention to an issue that the protesters feel is not receiving adequate attention in the standard political process. Protesters are exercising their First Amendment right "peaceably to assemble and to petition the government for a redress of grievances." Many legal peaceful protests have raised awareness of an issue to a level that forces the normal legislative process to address it. A number of protest movements paved the way for substantial changes in public policy. Protests against the Vietnam War during the late 1960s and early 1970s, for example, influenced American withdrawal from the Vietnam War. After World War I, protests among women's groups demanding the right of women to vote led to the adoption in 1920 of the Nineteenth Amendment granting women suffrage. Small groups of individuals who feel strongly about an issue and are willing to spend the time and effort to make their case often begin successful protests.

Protests make for good television because they generally feature conflict, a grievance, and individuals who are outspoken about the particular cause. Well-organized groups who engage in protests on hot-button issues, such as environmental groups, pro-life or pro-choice groups, and anti-death penalty groups, have become adept at informing the news media about the protests ahead of time and engaging articulate speakers to

AP PHOTO/ED REINKE

Republican U.S. Senate candidate Rand Paul addresses supporters at his primary election victory celebration in Bowling Green, KY, on May 18, 2010. Paul, who was backed by the Tea Party movement, went on to win in the general election and now represents Kentucky in the Senate.

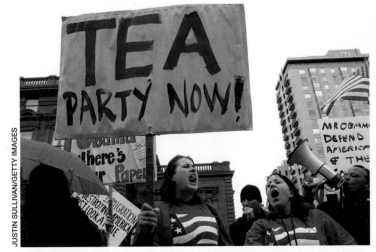

JUSTIN SULLIVAN/GETTY IMAGES

Members of the Tea Party movement protest outside a hotel in San Francisco before President Obama arrives for a fundraiser on May 25, 2010.

© 2012 CENGAGE LEARNING

make their case. The media attention often provides protesters with an opportunity to ensure that their causes reach the policy agenda of governing institutions.

The second type of protest behavior, civil disobedience, involves protesters engaged in illegal but nonviolent activity. The goal of the protesters is to break laws that they feel are unjust, and the protesters willingly accept the consequences for breaking the law. Blacks protesting segregation laws in the southern states during the 1950s and 1960s would intentionally break those laws as a way of drawing attention to the problem of segregation.

Finally, a third type of protest behavior involves violent protests. In 1992, a number of rioters in south central Los Angeles took to the streets after a jury acquitted several white police officers in a case where the officers had been caught on videotape brutally beating a black man they had stopped for a traffic violation. The rioters were protesting accusations of racial bias in the Los Angeles criminal justice system. The protesters looted businesses, stopped traffic, pulled a white truck driver out of his vehicle and severely beat him, and caused much damage to property.

Making the Connection

Barack Obama, like John F. Kennedy, inspired historic numbers of Americans to participate in the political process by casting their ballots. In both 2008 and 1960, these young, energetic candidates mobilized millions of new and first-time voters. Their emergence on the political scene altered the political landscape by tipping the balance of the turnout among certain demographic groups (Obama's candidacy increased turnout among African Americans, while Catholics rushed to the polls to vote for Kennedy) and thus shifted the White House from one party to another. While voter turnout does not often exceed the 60 percent mark as it did in 1960 and 2008, majorities of adult Americans do regularly participate in presidential elections every four years, and in doing so they help influence decisions about the future of the country.

Americans participate not only by voting in elections. As in the historic elections of 1960 and 2008, millions of Americans regularly participate in rallies for political candidates, contribute money to interest groups and political campaigns, and donate time to political causes that are of concern to them. Outside of elections, many Americans regularly write letters to the editor, post entries on political blogs, sign petitions, and speak to their elected officials. Participation is part and parcel of the American political culture.

POLITICS InterActive!

Genetics and Political Participation

For decades political scientists have used empirical methods in an attempt to unwrap the mysteries of why some people participate in politics and others do not. "Rational choice" theorists have used a cost-benefit analysis to explain such participation, based on the premise that if the perceived costs outweigh the perceived benefits, an individual will "sit out" an election. Others have used social-psychological explanations such as the perceived benefits of group membership, the strength of a person's attachment to a political party or candidate, and the level of interest in the campaign or the candidates. Still others have focused on additional factors such as a sense of civic duty, proximity to the polling place, and barriers to registration. Some of the research has identified patterns of participation, but no clear and convincing factors have been identified that consistently explain participation with any large degree of confidence.

PHOTODISC/GETTY IMAGES

Some recent research, however, may now hold the key to unlock the mystery of political participation. A study released by a group of political scientists in 2008 found a strong relationship between an individual's genetic makeup and his or her propensity to participate in politics. The research found that individual genetic differences account for a significant amount of variation in political participation, even after controlling for the effects of many of the more common factors researchers have associated with participation, such as education, age, income, socialization factors, and attitudes. The researchers—James H. Fowler, Laura A. Baker, and Christopher T. Dawes—discussed the findings of their study in an article entitled "Genetic Variation in Political Participation" published in the May 2008 issue of the *American Political Science Review*. In conducting their study, the researchers examined a national panel of over 800 twins, along with nearly 400 twins in southern California. They discovered that a wide variety of political activity, including running for office, attending political rallies, and contributing money to candidates and parties, could be partially explained by genetic factors.

On www.cengage.com/dautrich/americangovernmentbrief/2e, find the Politics InterActive link for details on the role of genetics and political participation. Consult as well the various links that relate to biological factors and politics. Historical, popular, and global perspectives on the issue are also presented.

Chapter Summary

★ The Legal Structure for Voting

- Traditionally, the states and not the federal government have had authority in running elections. However, state attempts to disenfranchise certain groups have been thwarted by constitutional amendments and federal laws. Although the goal of universal suffrage may not be fully realized today, over the centuries, the United States has moved closer to this goal.

- The constitutional amendments that have limited states' ability to disenfranchise voters include the Fifteenth Amendment (guaranteeing African American men the franchise), Nineteenth Amendment (women's suffrage), Twenty-fourth Amendment (outlawing poll taxes), and Twenty-sixth Amendment (guaranteeing the vote to those eighteen years of age).

- States are responsible for maintaining a system of voter registration, and the systems vary widely from state to state. Only one state (North Dakota) does not require voters to register to vote as a prequalification to voting. Through the Motor Voter law, the federal government has tried to encourage higher levels of voter registration.

★ Exercising the Franchise

- Among the factors that have been identified as relating to a citizen's propensity to vote are interest in politics, sense of civic duty, the perception that one's vote can make a difference, level of education, level of income, age, and social group pressure.

- The nature of the times and type of political campaign can also influence turnout. High stimulus elections, in which the issues are very important or the races are more visible, tend to produce higher voter turnout. Presidential elections generally promote the highest levels of turnout, and the less visible local races inspire the lowest levels of turnout.

- Although there has been a general declining trend in voter turnout in the United States over the past six or seven decades, recent presidential and midterm congressional elections have seen a modest increase in voting. This may be the result of voter concerns about U.S. military involvement in Iraq.

- Voter turnout in the United States tends to be lower than turnout in other democracies. Reasons that account for the lower U.S. turnout are the fact that there is no compulsory voting in the United States, the wide variation in states' voter registration requirements, the vast number of U.S. elections, and the tradition of holding elections on a weekday.

★ Making a Vote Choice

- A number of factors serve to explain the vote choices that voters make. These "determinants of the vote" include name recognition and candidate familiarity, party identification, the convergence between candidate issue positions and voter issue preferences, retrospective evaluations of the candidates' past performance, and voter assessment of the personal characteristics of the candidates.

★ Political Participation beyond the Voting Booth

- Although voting provides the critical link between people and government output in a representative democracy, there are many other ways that citizens participate beyond voting, ranging from writing or contacting an official about a concern to civil disobedience and protest activities.

CourseMate

Key Terms

Resources

Books

Alvarez, R. Michael, and Thad Hall. *Electronic Elections: The Perils and Promises of Digital Democracy.* Princeton, NJ: Princeton University Press, 2008.

Conway, M. Margaret. *Political Participation in the United States.* Washington, DC: CQ Press, 2000.

Flanigan, William H., and Nancy H. Zingale. *Political Behavior in the American Electorate*, 12th ed. Washington, DC: CQ Press, 2009.

Niemi, Richard, Herbert F. Weisberg, and David Kimball. *Controversies in Voting Behavior*, 5th ed. Washington DC: CQ Press, 2010.

Patterson, Thomas E. *The Vanishing Voter: Public Involvement in an Age of Uncertainty.* New York: Alfred A. Knopf, 2002.

Rosenstone, Steven J., and John Mark Hansen. *Mobilization, Participation and Democracy in America.* New York: Macmillan, 1993.

Teixeira, Ruy A. *The Disappearing American Voter.* Washington, DC: Brookings Institution Press, 1992.

Internet Sources

http://www.electionstudies.org (home to the American National Election Studies, which includes survey data on voter opinion and behavior for national elections since 1948).

http://www.fairvote.org (Web site of the Center for Voting and Democracy; includes a host of articles, data, and information on voting rights and voting turnout).

http://www.cawp.rutgers.edu/ (Web site for the Center for American Women and Politics at Rutgers University; contains data, program information, and fact sheets on the role of women in elections and voting).

http://www.civicyouth.org (Web site containing information on voting and participation geared toward younger voters).

NOW George W. Bush, campaigning for president in 2000.

THEN Rutherford B. Hayes, taking the presidential oath of office in 1877.

NOW &THEN

The Stolen Election?

? *All the experts were predicting a close election. The sitting president was not running for reelection, and so he would not play any visible role in the campaign. Politics, including the campaign itself, had been particularly divisive, due in part to heightened partisan tensions on Capitol Hill. Electorally, the partisan differences broke down by geography, as North and South lined up behind different candidates. But the hard-fought campaign finally ended, and Election Day drew to a close. All that remained was to count the votes and determine which candidate would be the next president. But Election Day came and went, and weeks passed following that first Tuesday in November without a declared winner. The Democratic Party's candidate had won the popular vote, but in presidential elections the Electoral College vote determines the winner. The vote margins in several states were very close, particularly in Florida. Voting irregularities in that state were the subject of considerable concern. The Electoral College outcome depended on the resolution of these voting disputes and the recount of the vote in certain districts, including some key districts in Florida. Ultimately, it was the U.S. Supreme Court, and that body's Republican appointees, that decided the election: by the Court's ruling, the new president would be the Republican Party candidate—and not the Democratic Party candidate who had received more popular votes. Millions of Americans were left frustrated with a process that seemed to only marginally reflect the public's will.*

NOW & THEN

RHONA WISE/AFP/GETTY IMAGES

A judge evaluates a questionable ballot due to a "hanging chad" after the 2000 presidential election in Florida.

NOW George W. Bush, the Republican Party candidate for president, was not declared the winner of the November 7, 2000, presidential election until more than a month had passed. Democrat Al Gore won the popular vote by about 500,000 votes. But on the evening of the election, with a number of states showing very close presidential races, the outcome of the electoral vote remained in question.

The campaign had been an especially hard-fought contest. The sitting president, Bill Clinton, played only a minimal role in the campaign, as the Gore campaign feared the scandals that rocked Clinton's second term might hurt Gore as well. Politically, the nation was largely divided along partisan lines, with Democrats providing the basis for Gore's coalition in the Northeastern states and Republicans contributing the strongest block for Bush in the South. The vote margins were close in a number of states—New Mexico, New Hampshire, Oregon, and Pennsylvania, to name a few. But the closest race, and the one that eventually became mired in controversy regarding voting irregularities, was in Florida with its twenty-five electoral votes.

In the weeks following Election Day, as votes in that state were recounted, lawyers for both the Bush and the Gore campaigns filed suits over how to count partially punched out paper ballots that still contained confetti-like bits of paper (the so-called hanging chads). Florida's Republican Secretary of State, Katherine Harris, reported directly to Governor Jeb Bush, the brother of George W. Bush; she also had been George W. Bush's Florida campaign co-chair the year before. Not surprisingly, Harris formally certified the results of the Florida vote in favor of George W. Bush before the recounts were concluded. Eventually, it was the court system, and in particular the U.S. Supreme Court, that decided the controversial election. By a 5–4 decision (the five justices in the majority were all conservatives appointed by Republican presidents), the Court ruled that the vote recounts must cease and that Harris's vote certification would stand.

THEN Some 124 years earlier, the election of 1876 was similarly mired in controversy, with many observers later referring to it as the "stolen election."[1] Like the 2000 campaign, the 1876 contest was expected to be close. The sitting president, Ulysses S. Grant, whose administration was plagued by political scandals, stayed clear of the campaign. Partisan differences that lingered after the Civil War remained a source of tensions in the reconstructed United States. Northern states provided the foundation of an electoral coalition for the Republicans whereas southern states amassed a voting bloc for the Democrats. The popular vote count across the nation gave Democratic candidate Samuel Tilden a 250,000-vote margin over Republican candidate Rutherford B. Hayes. Disputes over the vote counts in several states, including South Carolina, Louisiana, and especially Florida, left the winner of the contest in doubt for more than two months after Election Day.

Each candidate claimed that he had won the popular vote in Florida; the Democratic electors sent one set of Electoral College vote counts to the U.S. Senate, and the Republican electors sent their own vote count. The Republican-controlled Senate appointed a commission, with an equal number of Democrats and Republicans, plus one "neutral" Supreme Court Justice (who happened to be a Republican). The commission, by one vote, awarded all of the disputed electoral votes to Hayes, the Republican, who was declared the winner.

CORBIS

T he U.S. Constitution calls for a presidential election every four years and congressional elections every two years. Without skipping a beat, the United States has met this constitutional requirement for more than two centuries. Through a Civil War, two world wars, and several major economic depressions, elections—the hallmark of American democracy—have taken place like clockwork.

In designing this representative democracy, the founders intended a system that demanded accountability from elected officials. Elections for president and Congress provide this accountability. Regular and free elections are the linchpin underlying democracy in America. Every year, Americans are invited to cast ballots in elections for many local, county, and statewide races, but no election receives more attention than the race for the presidency.

American Presidential Elections in Historical Perspective

The U.S. constitution says nothing about political parties or the process by which individuals become candidates for the presidency. The founders assumed that electors, chosen by the states (and heavily influenced by the House of Representatives), would identify and evaluate potential candidates, and then the Electoral College would select the chief executive.[2] Parties, or "factions," were frowned on; the selection of president was intended to be the product of a select group of rational, wise men making choices at a lofty level above partisan politics.

Although their intentions for presidential selection were noble, the founders' expectations about how a president would actually be chosen proved to be quite naive. Political parties quickly became the framework for contesting presidential elections. Today, each of the two major parties holds nomination contests in the fifty states to select the party's candidate in the general election; the nominees compete in the general election.

The presidential selection process that has evolved over the past two centuries of U.S. nationhood is long and complex. The manner in which the 2012 selection process will occur is not based on some elaborate constitutional design. Rather, this complicated and quirky process is the result of more than 200 years of modification and evolution. Over the years, two distinct phases of the presidential selection process have developed: the nomination phase and the general election phase.

The Nomination Phase

In the nomination phase of the presidential election process, the political parties select specific people to run as the presidential and vice presidential candidates in the general election. This duo is referred to as the "party ticket." The Constitution did not account for a nomination phase because the founders did not anticipate that a two-party system would emerge. The first two presidential elections did not even include political parties. Rather, the electors from the states all agreed that George Washington should be president in 1789 and again in 1792. Nevertheless, divisions within the federal government erupted, and political alliances began to form during Washington's administration. These alliances resulted in the first two major political parties, the Federalists

AMERICAN GOVERNMENT In Global Perspective

A Presidential Candidate Captures the Imagination of Foreigners

Egyptian political scientist and former parliamentarian Mona Makram Ebeid attended the 2008 Democratic National Convention in Denver, Colorado. Upon his return to Egypt, he wrote a piece in the *Egypt Daily News* (on October 7, 2008) calling Barack Obama a charismatic leader in a nation that represents the world's "emotional centrality."

> . . . Obama has thrived in his career by turning campaign stops into emotional experiences. He has thrived also because of big crowds and small donors. At his convention speech, he looked like a star of a rock concert and the crowd responded accordingly. Attendees chanted, danced and shook miniature American flags in unison. His speech hit the kind of emotional high notes that have thrilled his followers. I believe that this success was due to his cleverly setting himself as a breakthrough candidate who was uniquely well placed to "turn the page of history" at a moment when so many voters are frustrated with the Bush administration's record of failures and alarmed at the prospect of American decline . . .

> The US presidential elections are watched with passion around the world not because of America's power but because of its emotional centrality. . . . The rest of the world would certainly embrace a less fearful and more open post-9/11 America. Choosing Barack Obama, a symbol of hope, would do more to restore the image of the United States in the world than anything else. A rejection of the promise he represents would be a symptom of that nation's historical decline. . . .

The rapt faces of attendees at the 2008 Democratic National Convention in Denver reflect the historical moment as Barack Obama becomes the first African American to win the nomination for president from one of the nation's two major political parties.

---

and their opponents, who eventually became known as the Democratic-Republicans. In 1796, when Washington decided not to seek a third term, each of these parties sought to win the presidency by recruiting and supporting candidates.[3]

The Federalists in Congress supported John Adams, and the Democratic-Republicans threw their support to Thomas Jefferson. Electors, who were largely chosen by state legislatures, followed the cues of their partisan leadership in casting their electoral votes, and Adams, the Federalist-supported candidate, won the general election with seventy-one electoral votes, whereas Jefferson received sixty-eight electoral votes. The nomination process in 1796 reflected a significant level of party discipline in the casting of ballots among electors. In the elections of 1800, 1804, and 1808, both the Federalists and the Democratic-Republicans used informal meetings and discussions to choose a party nominee. Democratic-Republicans dominated electoral politics from 1812 through 1828, as the Federalist Party eventually disappeared.

In 1824, however, a significant split occurred within the Democratic-Republican Party. Andrew Jackson, who had the support of many common people, challenged party favorite John Quincy Adams. Jackson won both the popular vote and a plurality of the electoral vote, but no candidate received a majority of electoral votes. By constitutional provision, the election was sent to the House of Representatives, which voted Adams the victor. Jackson then founded a new party, the Democratic Party,[4] which is, of course, one of the two major parties still in existence today. Jackson and his followers believed in the enfranchisement of all white men rather than just the propertied class; during what became known as the Jacksonian era, white male suffrage dramatically expanded throughout the country. Specifically, more and more state political parties adopted open caucuses, in which party members formally met to provide input as to whom their party should nominate for elective office.

Electoral reforms during the Progressive Era of the early 1900s opened participation in the nomination process to a greater number of Americans. The direct primary gave voters an opportunity to cast a ballot for delegates, who would in turn be sent to a national convention for the purpose of choosing a presidential nominee. The state of Florida was the first to hold a direct primary in a presidential election, in 1900. Although direct primaries did allow greater numbers of people the opportunity help select delegates, until the 1960s, it was still the political elite of a party (governors, mayors, party chairs, and other officials) that selected most of the delegates and thus had the most input in choosing the party's presidential nominee.

The political unrest of the 1960s, spurred by anti–Vietnam War activism, led to further changes that gave voters in primaries even more weight in selecting party nominees. Benefiting from the increased percentage of convention delegates chosen through open primaries, Jimmy Carter, the little-known governor of Georgia, won the Democratic Party's nomination in 1976. A political outsider, Carter was able to appeal directly to average voters. Carter not only won the nomination, but he also went on to win the presidency that year. His victory demonstrated to candidates in both the Democratic and Republican parties that securing sufficient numbers of delegates to win the nomination requires direct appeals to voters, whether through party caucuses or, more likely, through party primary contests.

The General Election Phase

The unanticipated emergence of political parties not only established a nomination process, but it also forced a change in the founders' design for selecting presidents. The founders intended the state legislatures to pick well-qualified "electors," who would meet on a specified day in their state to decide who was the best choice to become president. At the end of the day, these electors would then cast votes for president. The states then sent their vote totals to the president of the U.S. Senate (the sitting vice president), who counted the votes before Congress. The candidate with a majority of votes became president, and the second-place finisher became vice president. If no one candidate received a majority of the votes, the election was to be decided by the House of Representatives, with each state delegation having one vote to select the new president. The Senate was to select the vice president.

The Comeback Kids of Presidential Elections

Losing a presidential election can be an enormous letdown, but it hasn't stopped a number of high-profile losers from making a comeback. Six men who lost a general election contest have come back to be elected president.

In 1796, Thomas Jefferson lost a bitter campaign to John Adams by only three electoral votes. Jefferson came back to defeat Adams in 1800 and win reelection in 1804.

In 1808, James Monroe lost his bid for the White House in the nomination process but then went on to win the 1816 election and ran unopposed in 1820 (the only other presidential candidate to run unopposed was George Washington).

In 1824, Andrew Jackson lost his initial bid for the presidency to John Quincy Adams in a contest that was decided by the House of Representatives (because no candidate received a majority of electoral votes). In 1828, Jackson came back to defeat Quincy Adams and then won reelection in 1832.

In 1836, William Henry Harrison unsuccessfully ran for the presidency (he was defeated by Martin Van Buren). But like Jackson and Jefferson before him, Harrison avenged his loss with another run at the man who defeated him and won the election of 1840. Harrison never had the opportunity to run for reelection because he died a month after taking office.

In 1884, Grover Cleveland won the election but was defeated by Benjamin Harrison (William Henry Harrison's grandson) in 1888. Cleveland and Benjamin Harrison ran again in 1892, and this time Cleveland defeated Harrison, thus becoming the first and only chief executive to serve two nonconsecutive terms.

In 1968, the "comeback kid" was Richard Nixon, who had served eight years as vice president under President Dwight Eisenhower. In 1960, Nixon ran against John F. Kennedy and lost. Nixon then ran for governor of California but lost that race as well. Despite Nixon's quip to the press after his gubernatorial loss that "you won't have Nixon to kick around anymore," he won the Republican nomination in 1968 and defeated Hubert Humphrey in a very close contest. Nixon won reelection in 1972 by a landslide but midway through his term was forced to resign as a result of the Watergate scandal.

In the 1800 presidential race, nearly all of the Federalists voted for John Adams and Charles Pinckney (sixty-five and sixty-four votes, respectively), and all of the Democratic-Republicans voted for Jefferson and Aaron Burr, each of whom received seventy-three votes. Although it was generally agreed that Jefferson was the leader of the Democratic-Republican ticket, Burr challenged Jefferson in the House (because the election was a tie, the House state delegations had to choose the new president). Ultimately, the House decided in favor of Jefferson, who became president, with Burr then becoming vice president. It was clear that the presidential election system needed fixing.[5]

The Twelfth Amendment to the Constitution, passed in 1804, provided for separate balloting for president and vice president by requiring that electors designate one of their two votes for president and the second of their two votes for vice president. This amendment greatly reduced the possibility that future elections would end in a tie.

Several other amendments to the Constitution have altered the presidential selection process. The Twenty-second Amendment, ratified in 1951, limits presidents to two four-year terms in office (or ten years if a vice president serves out the term of a president). The Twenty-third Amendment, ratified in 1961, provides the District of Columbia with three electoral votes. Because the District is not a state, it has no senators or voting members in the House.

The modern presidential selection system is an amalgamation of the founders' design, modified by constitutional amendments and changes that occurred over time. This all makes for a complex system of picking a president. Although there are many caveats and exceptions to the rules, the contemporary presidential selection process generally consists of five stages.

1. **The prenomination campaign.** After a new president is selected, potential candidates for the next presidential election (four years hence) begin to explore the possibility of running. The ability to raise money, garner support from key leaders in the party, and attract the attention of the news media all contribute to each candidate's decision of whether to enter the race.

2. **The nomination campaign.** From January through June of the presidential election year, parties in each state hold either a primary or caucus in which the party delegates from the state commit to candidates. Each party has different criteria for allocating the number of delegates a state will get. The candidate who receives a majority of delegates wins the party nomination.

3. **The national conventions.** Each political party holds a national convention during the summer to showcase their candidate. Prior to the convention, the candidates select their vice presidential running mates. Although the conventions used to play an important role in defining the party platform and selecting the party's nominee, today the conventions are largely publicity events for the ticket and other stars in the party, as well as an opportunity to critique the opposing party.

4. **The general election campaign.** Because national party conventions today generally affirm rather than choose party nominees, presidential candidates usually begin waging their general election campaigns before the conventions, as soon as it becomes clear who will be the two major-party nominees. (These decisions generally occur some time in spring of the election year.) Most recent campaigns have included a series of televised debates between the presidential and the vice presidential candidates and a significant amount of advertising and campaigning in key states.

5. **The Electoral College decision.** The winner of the presidential election is decided on the basis of the vote count in the Electoral College. The number of electoral votes for each state is equivalent to the state's allotment of House members plus two (for the state's two U.S. senators). In all but two states, the candidate who wins the popular vote automatically receives all of the electoral votes from that state. (Currently, in Maine and Nebraska, the votes for president are counted for each congressional district; candidates get one elector for each district they win, and the candidate who wins the state overall gets an additional two electors.) Nationwide, the candidate who receives an outright majority of electoral votes wins the election.

The Prenomination Campaign

Although the presidential campaign officially begins with the first state contest for delegates in January of the election year, the real campaign for president

Left to right, former North Carolina Senator John Edwards, Illinois Senator Barack Obama, New Mexico Governor Bill Richardson, and New York Senator Hillary Rodham Clinton spar with each other during a debate among Democratic nominees early in 2008. While Edwards and Richardson struggled to win delegates, and thus bowed out of the nomination contest before it had formally concluded, Obama and Clinton continued to battle over the Democratic nomination all the way until June.

actually begins much earlier, soon after the previous presidential election has concluded. As part of the **prenomination campaign**, behind-the-scenes candidates who are thinking about making a run often begin to "test the waters" by talking to party insiders, shoring up early commitments of support, lining up a campaign staff, beginning a fund-raising operation, traveling around the country making speeches and appearances, setting up "exploratory committees" to assess the feasibility of making a formal declaration of official candidacy, and then making the official announcement. Shortly after the 2004 election, Senators John McCain and Barack Obama established exploratory committees and began raising money for their 2008 campaigns.

The prenomination campaign also marks the beginning of the "weeding out" process. Early on, many would-be candidates find insufficient support from party insiders. Others cannot raise sufficient funds to be competitive. Some tire too quickly of the arduous and time-consuming schedule necessary for launching a run for the presidency. These and other obstacles begin the process of narrowing the field of candidates.

For the 2008 election, with no incumbent president or vice president in contention, more than ten candidates from each of the two major parties seriously explored their presidential prospects during late 2006 and early 2007.

The **invisible primary** is the competition between candidates seeking the party nomination for front-runner status. A candidate gains front-runner status by winning broad support from important people within the party, raising more money than others, and achieving top position in the public polls conducted by leading news organizations. Front-runners tend to receive more coverage in the news, thus promoting their name recognition and popularity as candidates.

Within the Democratic Party, the invisible primary leading up to the early 2008 primaries and

Prenomination campaign
The political season in which candidates for president begin to explore the possibility of running by attempting to raise money and garner support.

Invisible primary
The competition among candidates seeking the party nomination for front-runner status prior to the primaries and caucuses.

Arizona Senator John McCain and former Massachusetts Governor Mitt Romney, here seen engaging in a testy dialogue during a debate among Republican presidential hopefuls in late 2007. McCain eventually defeated Romney and several other rivals to secure the 2008 Republican nomination. Once McCain's nomination was secure, Romney transformed from being McCain's foremost critic into one of his steadfast supporters and even garnered serious consideration from McCain for the vice presidential nomination later that summer.

caucuses began as a battle primarily among former First Lady and U.S. senator from New York Hillary Clinton, former North Carolina senator and 2004 vice presidential candidate John Edwards, Illinois Senator Barack Obama, Delaware Senator Joseph Biden, Connecticut Senator Christopher Dodd, Governor Bill Richardson of New Mexico, and Ohio Congressman Dennis Kucinich. On the Republican side, the contest for the 2008 nomination shaped up initially as a battle among Arizona Senator John McCain, actor and former Tennessee Senator Fred Thompson, former Massachusetts Governor Mitt Romney, and former New York City Mayor Rudolph Giuliani. The long list of initial contenders also included former Arkansas Governor Mike Huckabee, former South Carolina Congressman Duncan Hunter, Texas Congressman Ron Paul, and Colorado House member Tom Tancredo.

The fortunes of individual candidates can change in a hurry once the invisible primary has concluded. By the end of the invisible primary period in late 2007, it became clear that based on their fund-raising and showing in the national polls, the list of major contenders for the Democratic Party nomination would be limited to Senators Clinton, Edwards, and Obama. On the Republican side, the invisible primary concluded with Romney and Giuliani at the top of the pack.

★ LO   Identify the function of primaries and caucuses, and explain how the timing of those contests plays a role in the outcome of the nomination process

The Nomination Campaign

The invisible primary may go a long way toward winnowing the field down to a handful of realistic contenders for major-party nominations; still, as Mitt Romney and Rudy Giuliani learned in early 2008, money and attention can take you only so far; contenders for the presidency must ultimately deliver victories in state primaries and caucuses or risk seeing their financial and volunteer support dry up in a hurry. Given the reduced importance of party conventions in influencing nomination decisions in the modern era, success in the earliest primaries and caucuses may be crucial.

Primaries and Caucuses

Presidential primary
A statewide election to select delegates who will represent a state at the party's national convention.

Open primary
An election that allows voters to choose on the day of the primary election the party in which they want to vote.

Closed primary
An election that requires voters to declare their party affiliation ahead of time.

The nomination of a candidate by a political party is the product of state-to-state contests in which delegates are committed to those candidates seeking the party's nomination. There are two basic methods by which states allocate delegates: presidential primary elections and caucuses.[6] A **presidential primary** is a statewide election to select delegates who will represent a state at the party's national convention.[7] In this election, voters choose among delegates who are committed to a particular candidate. The delegates who win go to the national convention and cast their vote for a party nominee to run in the general election. In 2008, forty-three states used the presidential primary method of delegate selection. There are two types of primaries held by states. The less common approach is the **open primary**[8] in which voters can show up at the voting booth on the primary Election Day and declare whether they want to vote in the Democratic Party primary or the Republican Party primary; they then cast their vote in the primary they have chosen. A **closed primary**[9] election, by contrast, requires voters to declare a party affiliation ahead of time. When the voters show up to vote on the primary Election Day, they are eligible to vote only in the party in which they are registered. Many states that use the closed primary have modified their requirements by allowing voters who have previously declared no party affiliation to show up at the polls on the primary Election Day, declare a party, and thus, vote in that party's primary.

A handful of states, including Iowa, Nevada, and Maine, do not hold presidential primary elections at all; instead, they use the caucus method to select delegates for the national party convention. In the **caucus** method, party members are invited to attend local meetings at which they choose delegates who make a commitment to a candidate for the party nomination. These delegates in turn attend more regionalized meetings and select delegates from that group. Depending on the size of the state and the number of regions, this process continues until a slate of delegates attends a statewide convention, or caucus. At this statewide caucus, attendees again vote for a slate of delegates, who are committed to a candidate, to send to the party's national convention.

Democratic Senators Hillary Clinton and Barack Obama, early front-runners in the Democratic race, at a debate in June 2007.

The first state contest for delegates, normally the Iowa caucus, launches the process by which delegates from the states commit to candidates for the party nomination. About one week after the Iowa caucus comes the New Hampshire primary,[10] which has traditionally been the first state primary election in which delegates commit to candidates.[11] Each of the fifty states (along with the District of Columbia, the U.S. Virgin Islands, American Samoa, and Guam) holds either a caucus or primary election, and in each of these contests, delegates commit to candidates. The calendar of state caucuses and primaries, beginning in January and extending into June, is referred to as the **nomination campaign**. Through the nomination campaign, a candidate attempts to win a majority of delegates in the caucus and primary contests to lay claim to be the winner of the party's nomination.

Caucus
A method of choosing party nominees in which party members attend local meetings at which they choose delegates committed to a particular candidate.

Nomination campaign
The political season in which the two major parties hold primaries and caucuses in all the states to choose party delegates committed to specific candidates.

The Traditional Importance of the Iowa and New Hampshire Contests

Iowa and New Hampshire are small states with relatively few delegates. The Iowa Democratic caucus in 2012 will have fifty-two delegates at stake, while in the 2012 New Hampshire Democratic primary, a total of just thirty-one delegates will be at stake. To win the Democratic nomination, a candidate needs to amass support from more than 2,200 delegates. In pure delegate count, larger states, such as California with 448 delegates, Florida with 220, and New York with 276, are much more important. Why, then, do Iowa and New Hampshire enjoy such disproportionately great influence in the nomination process? The answer is timing. Iowa and New Hampshire have so much influence over the nomination campaign not because of the number of delegates they offer but because they have traditionally been the first two contests held. The news media focus a tremendous amount of attention on these initial competitions. Winners of the Iowa and New Hampshire contests receive a great amount of attention in the news, whereas losers tend to get written off as "unelectable."

The importance of these early contests has led to a phenomenon known as **frontloading**,[12] a trend that has occurred over the past five or six presidential elections in which states have moved their primary or caucus contests earlier in the year to attract greater attention from the candidates and the media. A state that holds its contest early makes itself more important in the nominee selection process. In 1988, the time between the Iowa caucus and the date by which most states had chosen their convention delegates was more than twenty weeks.

In 2008, the majority of delegates were selected within a four-week period, from January 3 to February 5. The rush to move the contests earlier actually caused considerable confusion in the Democratic nomination race in 2008. In an attempt to ensure that New Hampshire would remain the first contest, the Democratic National Committee passed a rule that any state that moved its primary earlier than February 5 (Super Tuesday) would forfeit its delegates. Nevertheless, the states of Michigan and Florida both moved their primaries to January, disqualifying both states' primary outcomes, which had favored Clinton. Ironically, the closeness of the race between Obama and Clinton throughout the spring of 2008 meant that considerable attention would be paid to later contests held in Pennsylvania, North Carolina, and Indiana.

For 2012, both major political parties have agreed to somewhat reverse the frontloading process. Specifically, no primary or caucus will occur prior to the Iowa caucus on January 16. Also, only Iowa, New Hampshire, South Carolina, Florida, and Nevada will be allowed to hold contests before February. States that allocate their delegates proportionate to the vote outcome will be permitted to hold contests as early as the first Tuesday in March, as a way to encourage greater voter representation. States that allocate all delegates to the contest winner (the "winner-take-all" states) may hold contests beginning on the first Tuesday in April. This plan is intended to spread out the primaries and caucuses, giving candidates more time to campaign in more states, and at the same time, preserve the unique role that Iowa and New Hampshire have played in the nomination process. The tentative slate of contests can be seen in Table 15.1 (all contests are primaries unless otherwise noted).

The Nominating Conventions

The national conventions for the Democratic and Republican parties were once used to discuss the party platform and, most important, to choose the candidate who would represent the party in the general election. The images of the smoke-filled back rooms where deals were cut and delegates were lobbied to throw their support behind a particular candidate were very real. For most of our nation's history, the major parties selected candidates for the presidency in this way. Much of the brokering and deal making took place by skilled political operators at the national conventions.

The 1968 Democratic National Convention, held in Chicago, was characterized by a great deal of divisiveness and discord, much of which was captured on national network television. Vietnam War protesters outside the convention hall were beaten by Chicago police under the direction of Chicago mayor and "political boss" Richard J. Daley. Tension reigned inside the convention center as well, with antiwar supporters of Eugene McCarthy and George McGovern

Frontloading
The recent trend of states moving their primaries and caucuses earlier in the year to attract greater attention from the candidates and the media.

★ LO Describe
the role of national party conventions

clashing with the party regulars supporting Hubert Humphrey. Television brought the negative images of the divided Democratic Party into American homes, seriously damaging the Democratic ticket. Four years later, television coverage again captured a disunited Democratic Party at the national convention in Miami, where delegates fought into the wee hours of the morning to select a party nominee (George McGovern finally won the nomination). The Democrats were not the only party to suffer discord and division. In 1976, grassroots support for Ronald Reagan spoiled any momentum incumbent President Gerald Ford hoped to generate at the Republican National Convention.

By the mid-1980s, both major political parties, recognizing the influential role that television was playing in election politics, had begun to adjust their agenda for the national conventions. With the frontloading process allowing candidates to capture a majority of delegates prior to the national convention, the parties began to choreograph their conventions and use them as advertisements for the party ticket. Today's conventions tend to avoid airing any intraparty differences. Instead, they are "anointing" ceremonies for the party ticket. They feature popular members of the party endorsing the nominees and include prerecorded videos highlighting the nominees' record of public service and family values.[13]

TABLE 15.1 Tentative Schedule of Primaries and Caucuses for the 2012 Presidential Election (determined at the time this book went to print)

Primaries and Caucuses 2012	State
Monday, January 16	*Iowa caucuses*
Tuesday, January 24	New Hampshire
Saturday, January 28	*Nevada caucuses,* South Carolina
Tuesday, January 31	Florida
Tuesday, February 7 (Super Tuesday)	Alabama, California, Connecticut, Delaware, Georgia, Missouri, New Jersey, New York, Oklahoma, Tennessee, Utah
Saturday, February 11	Louisiana
Tuesday, February 14	Maryland, Virginia
Tuesday, February 21	Wisconsin, *Hawaii GOP caucuses*
Tuesday, February 28	Arizona, Michigan
Tuesday, March 6	*Minnesota caucuses*, Massachusetts, Ohio, Rhode Island, Texas, Vermont
Tuesday, March 13	Mississippi
Tuesday, March 20	*Colorado caucuses,* Illinois
Tuesday, April 24	Pennsylvania
Tuesday, May 8	Indiana, North Carolina, West Virginia
Tuesday, May 15	Nebraska, Oregon
Tuesday, May 22	Arkansas, Idaho, Kentucky
Tuesday, June 5	Montana GOP, New Mexico, South Dakota

At the 2008 Democratic national convention, for example, a video of Barack Obama's life highlighted his experience as a community organizer in Chicago and his commitment to his family. His wife and brother-in-law spoke on his behalf. Former President Bill Clinton and Senator Hillary Clinton added words of praise for the ticket, and vice presidential candidate Joe Biden delivered his own "prime time" speech promoting Obama. Likewise, speakers at the Republican National Convention touted John McCain's military service. His wife, Cindy McCain, offered a brief testimonial on his behalf as well, and McCain's vice presidential running mate, Sarah Palin, gave a stirring speech that was widely regarded as the highlight of the convention.

The 2012 GOP and Democratic nominating conventions remain important political events. Rather than playing a crucial role in selecting the party nominee and debating the policy positions of the party, however, these conventions provide a week-long forum for the parties and their nominees to introduce themselves to voters and to formally kick off the general election campaign.

The General Election Campaign

A number of factors provide context for understanding general election campaigns in the American political system. These include whether or not an incumbent is running, the candidate's pick for the number-two spot on the ticket, the strategy for achieving a winning coalition of states, the presidential debates, political advertisements, and finally, the vote in the Electoral College.

Incumbent Race versus Open Election

General election campaigns for president are highly visible, very well funded, and among the most noteworthy of events in the American political system. Sometimes, the contest is an **incumbent race**, or one between a sitting president and a challenger, such as the 2004 contest between President George W. Bush and challenger John Kerry. In an incumbent race, the focus of the campaign tends to revolve around the performance of the incumbent over the past four years. In this sense, incumbent races are often viewed as a referendum on the performance of the current occupant of the White House.

In all, there have been eleven incumbents who lost their bids for another term. Five of these incumbent losses occurred over the past 100 years: In 1912, Woodrow Wilson defeated President William Howard Taft; in 1932, Franklin Delano Roosevelt defeated President Herbert Hoover; in 1976, Jimmy Carter defeated President Gerald R. Ford; in 1980, Ronald Reagan beat President Carter; and in 1992, Bill Clinton defeated President George H. W. Bush.

The 2012 presidential contest is likely to pit the Democratic incumbent President Barack Obama against a Republican challenger, with Obama's record as president serving as the main focus of the campaign. At the time this book went to press, the list of possible Republican presidential contenders in 2012 was a long one, headed by former Governor Mitt Romney of Massachusetts, Governor Haley Barbour of Mississippi, former Governor Mike Huckabee of Arkansas, former House Speaker Newt Gingrich, former Pennsylvania senator Rick Santorum, and 2008 vice presidential candidate Sarah Palin.

In **open elections**, neither candidate is an incumbent. That was the case in 2008, when neither a president nor a sitting vice president ran for president. In

Incumbent race
General election race pitting a person currently holding the office against a challenger.

Open election
General election race in which neither candidate is the incumbent. (Open elections for Congress are normally called "open seat elections.")

Getting Involved in Political Campaigns

Politics is very much on the minds of college-age Americans today. In 2008, a record 35.6 percent of college freshmen said that they had frequently discussed politics in the past year. (The previous high was 33.6 percent in 1968, at the height of the Vietnam War.) In the most recent presidential campaign, college students were more interested and more active than ever before. Students who work on election campaigns may find themselves performing such simple tasks as stuffing envelopes or walking door-to-door to distribute leaflets. Those who are technologically savvy may assist campaigns in other ways—for example, by helping to create Facebook profiles or fan pages on the Internet. In 2008 College Republicans nationwide socially networked through a website called Student Tools for Online Republican Mobilization, or STORM. Have you ever volunteered time to work on a political campaign? About 11 percent of college freshmen in 2008 said they did. (This figure was up by about three percentage points from 2004.) More college freshmen also report that they are likely to engage in a political protest (6.1 percent in 2008, as compared to 4.9 percent in 1966).

CHRIS HONDROS/GETTY IMAGES

Ohio State University students shown here are volunteering at the Obama campus headquarters on Election Day, November 4, 2008.

For Critical Thinking and Discussion

1. Why do you think your peers were so energized about the 2008 presidential election?

2. Do you think college students' participation made a difference in 2008?

3. Do you think the trend toward increased college student participation will continue in the 2012 presidential race?

Note: Data presented are from "Presidential Race Raised Student Political Involvement" by Mary Beth Marklein in *USA Today*, January 22, 2009.

---

fact, 2008 was the first election in eighty years to feature such an open-ended contest. (Although neither President Harry Truman nor Vice President Alben Barkley was a major-party nominee in 1952, both pursued the Democratic nomination for a short period of time before dropping out of the race.) The last truly open-ended election occurred in 1928, when neither President Calvin Coolidge nor Vice President Charles Dawes were ever serious candidates for their party's nomination.[14]

The Choice of a Vice Presidential Candidate

Another important aspect of campaign strategy is the selection of the vice presidential running mate. Significant amounts of thought and fanfare go into the selection. Vice presidential candidates are quite visible on the campaign

★ LO

Assess the various factors that contribute to the selection of vice presidential running mates trail and can provide a boost to the ticket. Democrat Barack Obama, who had been criticized by Republicans as being inexperienced, particularly in the area of foreign policy, selected Delaware Senator Joe Biden as his running mate in 2008. Biden's three-plus decades of experience in the Senate along with his chairmanship of the Senate Foreign Relations Committee figured largely in his selection as Obama's running mate. Republican John McCain's choice of Alaska Governor Sarah Palin appealed to social conservatives in his party (who were initially not very enthusiastic about McCain) and was intended to capture the attention of female voters who no longer had Hillary Clinton as an option. Unfortunately for Republicans, the selection of the forty-four-year-old Palin also led to excessive scrutiny of McCain's selection process for the vice presidential slot, especially after Palin stumbled in several of her initial interviews with the mainstream media.

The vice presidential candidates in 2008 were Democrat Delaware Senator Joe Biden (top) and Republican Alaska Governor Sarah Palin (above).

Gathering a Winning Coalition of States

A central feature of any general election campaign is each candidate's plan to put together a coalition of states sufficient to win a majority of electoral votes. At the outset of the campaign, states may be divided into three categories: strong Republican states, strong Democratic states, and the so-called **battleground** (or "swing") **states**, those which either candidate has a reasonable chance of winning.

In 2008 both the Republican nominee, John McCain, and the Democratic nominee, Barack Obama, set their sights on all twelve of the battleground states. John Kerry's narrow Electoral College loss to President George W. Bush in 2004 (Kerry fell short of the winning total by just eighteen Electoral College votes) pointed Obama's way to victory: If he could hold all of Kerry's winning states, while picking up just one or two of the battleground states won by Bush, he could secure victory. Accordingly, Obama invested considerable resources in the battleground states of Ohio and Florida, either of which would provide him with the necessary margin for success. Obama's campaign also focused its attention on three battleground states that Bush had won comfortably: North Carolina, Virginia, and Colorado. Meanwhile the McCain camp was on the defensive, fighting to hold onto all these states, while looking for a breakthrough in Pennsylvania, where Kerry had won in 2004. On Election Day 2008, Obama's strategy reaped rewards for the Democratic ticket: Obama won a clear majority of the twelve battleground states and thus coasted to victory in the Electoral College.

★ LO Analyze strategic campaign objectives that focus on securing a winning coalition of states

Battleground states
States identified as offering either major-party candidate a reasonable chance for victory in the Electoral College.

★ LO Evaluate the role of televised presidential debates and television advertising

The Presidential Debates

The media and the public have come to expect that a presidential campaign will feature debates between the presidential candidates and sometimes between the vice presidential candidates as well. Candidates may not believe it is in their strategic interest to debate their opponents (for example, a candidate who is ahead in the polls might prefer to play it safe and not run the risk of losing a debate and perhaps the lead in the campaign). Still, both major-party candidates usually agree to debate so that they aren't portrayed as being "afraid" to do so. (The history of presidential debates dating back to 1960 is discussed in further detail in Chapter 12.)

The schedule of debates and the rules governing their conduct are the product of intense negotiation between the campaigns. In 2008, the detailed set of rules for the four debates included instructions that the candidates could not cross over a line on the stage separating them, time limits on answering questions and offering rebuttals, and a restriction for the final two presidential debates that the candidates could not ask direct questions of each other.

Democratic presidential nominee Barack Obama and Republican presidential nominee John McCain shake hands before their second presidential debate.

Despite the large amount of attention both the campaigns and the media pay to the debates, the impact that debates have on the election outcome is unclear. Many researchers have documented that those who tend to watch the debates already have moderate to strong convictions regarding whom they want to win, and these convictions often shape how an individual voter evaluates the candidate's performance in the debates. Though polls sometimes show that the voters tend to identify a debate "winner," there is far less evidence to show that this has any impact on voter intentions. The first of the debates often gets the most attention, and yet many of the media-dubbed winners of first debates, whether Walter Mondale in 1984, Michael Dukakis in 1988, Ross Perot in 1992, or John Kerry in 2004, have ended up on the short side of the electoral vote count on Election Day. In 2008 Barack Obama performed well in all three of his debates against John McCain, and while those performances alone did not secure his final victory, polls indicated that they helped reassure many undecided voters that the junior senator from Illinois was indeed ready to be president. Some observers of elections indicate that although debates may not have a direct impact on vote intentions, they can change the dynamics of a campaign, which in turn may influence the outcome.[15]

The Advertising

Television advertisements have become a staple of presidential campaign strategies.[16] They are used to heighten name recognition, communicate core messages to voters, and offer reasons one should vote for (or against) a particular candidate. Television advertising uses a variety of different techniques to accomplish these goals. The most controversial of these techniques is the attack or "negative" ads that candidates often use to portray their opponents in a bad light.[17] Television ads can be very effective at convincing voters to support a candidate—particularly voters who are undecided on any particular candidate or who are politically independent rather than identifying themselves as a Democrat or a Republican. Other forms of campaign communication (such as televised debates, political news columns, political talk shows on radio and TV, and news broadcasts) are provided in formats that appeal to voters who are interested in the campaign and have already made up their mind about whom they will vote for. However, televised advertisements may be placed during certain shows or at certain times when independents and undecided voters are tuning in. The unsuspecting audience is captive to the short advertisement, which provides a unique opportunity for a campaign to attract votes.

★ LO Explain the Electoral College system

The Electoral College Vote

Unlike elections for most public offices in the United States, the outcome of the popular vote does not necessarily determine who wins the presidential election. The winner of the presidential election is the candidate who receives a majority of the 538 votes in the **Electoral College**. As the opening to this chapter demonstrated, in the highly controversial 1876 and 2000 presidential elections, the popular vote winner lost the presidential race. Similarly, John Quincy Adams won the 1824 election despite losing the popular vote, as did Benjamin Harrison in 1888.

Electoral College
The constitutional mechanism by which presidents are chosen. Each state is allocated Electoral College votes based on the sum of that state's U.S. senators and House members.

How does the Electoral College work? The Constitution allocates each state a certain number of electoral votes based on the sum of the number of senators (two) plus representatives (currently, anywhere from one to fifty-three) that a state has in the U.S. Congress. The Twenty-third Amendment to the Constitution allocated three electoral votes to the District of Columbia. The number of seats a state has in the House of Representatives may change as a result of the official census conducted every ten years. Thus, the number of electoral votes that a state has may change as well. The total number of electoral votes remains fixed at 538, and a candidate must receive a majority—270—to win the presidency (see Figure 15.1).

FIGURE 15.1 The Electoral College Map

This map of the states depicts the number of electoral votes each state had as a result of the 2000 U.S. census. The states shaded in red are those states whose electoral votes were cast for Republican John McCain in 2008. The blue states' electoral votes went to Democrat Barack Obama.

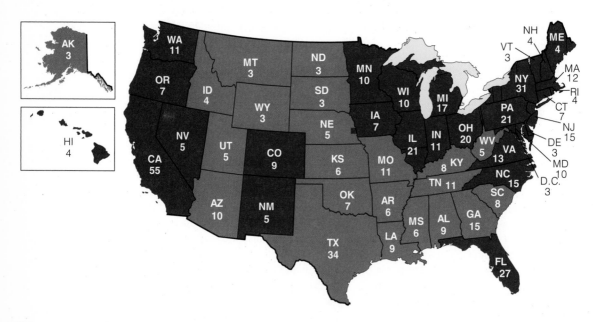

The minimum number of electoral votes possible for any one state is three because the Constitution guarantees to each state two senators and one House member. A number of states have three electoral votes: Vermont, Wyoming, North Dakota, South Dakota, Alaska, Montana, and Delaware. California currently has the largest number of electoral votes with fifty-five (fifty-three members of the House and two senators).

Even small states with as few as three electoral votes can influence the outcome of an election. In 2000, George Bush received 271 electoral votes, only one vote more than the 270 majority he needed to win. Had just one of the small states that gave Bush its three electoral votes voted for Gore, Bush would not have won the election.

Over the past sixty years, the U.S. population has shifted with the southern and western states gaining population and the northeastern and midwestern states losing. Consequently, the number of electoral votes in states such as Florida, California, Texas, and Arizona has grown, and the number of votes allocated to states like New York, Pennsylvania, Ohio, and Illinois has declined. Early projections from the 2010 census indicate that this trend will continue, which should add even more electoral strength to some regions, while subtracting from others. Based on figures from the Bureau of the Census, it is likely that the 2012 electoral vote count in Texas will swell from thirty-four to thirty-seven. The following states are likely to gain one additional electoral vote: Arizona, Florida, Georgia, Nevada, South Carolina, Utah, and Washington. By contrast, Ohio's total will decline from twenty to eighteen, and each of the following states are likely to lose one electoral vote: Illinois, Iowa, Louisiana, Massachusetts, Michigan, Minnesota, New Jersey, New York, and Pennsylvania.

Article II of the Constitution gives the state legislature of each state the authority to appoint **electors**, one for each electoral vote that a state has been allocated. During the first few presidential elections, most states used the state legislature to select the individuals who would be the state's electors.[18] By 1860, however, states gradually shifted to using the popular vote outcome in the state to allocate electors, or the so-called unit rule. The **unit rule** (or "winner take all" system) means that the candidate who receives the most votes among the popular votes cast for president in a state will receive all the electoral votes from that state. At present only two states, Maine and Nebraska, do not use the unit rule. Rather, in those states, the popular vote winner in each congressional district receives the electoral vote from that district, and the two votes that derive from the state's Senate seats are awarded to the statewide popular vote winner. In 2004, voters in Colorado defeated a referendum to allot electoral votes as Maine and Nebraska currently do.

The significance of the unit rule is illustrated by the outcome of the 2000 presidential election. In Florida, which had twenty-five electoral votes, the popular vote distribution between Bush and Gore was very close. For nearly one month after the election, controversies surrounding the vote count and the ballot in Florida left uncertain which candidate won the most popular votes in the state. What loomed in the balance was all of Florida's twenty-five electoral votes—and the election victory. Without Florida, Gore had 267 electoral votes, just three votes shy of victory, whereas Bush had 246. Because the unit rule applied to Florida's twenty-five votes, all twenty-five would be allocated on the basis of which candidate received the most popular votes.

Electors
Individuals appointed to represent a state's presidential vote in the Electoral College; in practice, voters in presidential elections vote for a slate of electors committed to a particular candidate, rather than voting directly for the candidate.

Unit rule
The system in forty-eight states by which the candidate who wins the most votes among popular votes cast for president in a state receives all the electoral votes from that state; also known as the "winner take all" system.

Appealing to Voters the Old Fashioned Way . . . by Writing a Book

Stump speeches, TV ads, press conferences, and visits to the county fair are staples in a modern presidential candidate's campaign playbook. More recently, a new item has been added to this list: authoring a book. Putting one's name on a book provides the candidate with an unfiltered opportunity to comprehensively make the case for his or her candidacy and gain credibility with voters. Back in 1999, the year before his first run for the presidency, John McCain wrote *Faith of My Fathers: A Family Memoir*, in which he described his grandfather's, father's, and his own commitment to the U.S. Navy. In 2008, just as he was embarking on his successful quest to become the Republican presidential nominee, he followed up with *Why Courage Matters: The Way to a Braver Life*. Barack Obama, the 2008 Democratic nominee, has written several books. In *Change We Can Believe In* (2008) and *The Audacity of Hope* (2008), he described his views of how to bring about change to American politics. In *Dreams from My Father*, written four years earlier, he described his earlier life as a son of a black father and white mother. Other candidates also put their pen to work on their own behalf: Republican candidate Ron Paul wrote *The Revolution: A Manifesto* (2008), in which he expounded his vision of a libertarian approach to governing. Democratic hopeful Hillary Clinton wrote *Living History* (2003) to promote the role she played as First

Lady during the Clinton administration and perhaps to pave her road to the presidency five years later.

Critics charge that these books are filled with vague platitudes that offer only a limited glimpse into the candidates' real positions. Moreover, in many cases ghostwriters (perhaps one of the candidate's own campaign speechwriters) are largely responsible for the language used. Still, no one expects these campaign "tomes" to go away soon, if only because they provide an excuse for candidates to embark on a book-signing tour that can serve to kick off a future presidential campaign. Possible candidates for the 2012 Republican nomination have wasted no time putting pen to paper in preparation for their own potential campaigns. Sarah Palin wrote *Going Rogue: An American Life* (2010), in which she chronicled growing up in Alaska and her life as a vice presidential candidate. That same year, Mitt Romney wrote *No Apology: The Case for American Greatness*, which touted the impressive contributions of America to the world. You should have little problem finding these and other campaign books at a bookstore near you.

For Critical Thinking and Discussion

1. Have you read any books written by a presidential candidate? If so, did the book change the way you viewed the candidate? Did you become more or less supportive of the candidate?

2. How much influence do you think candidate-authored books have? How would you compare the influence of a book to the influence of television ads or a candidate's web page?

The founders' original intent in creating the Electoral College was to keep the presidential selection process out of the direct hands of the people. They felt that the people were best represented by the House of Representatives, whose members were elected directly by voters. But the founders questioned the ability of the general public to select the chief executive. Rather, they believed that the more knowledgeable, wise, and politically thoughtful members of each state's legislature should be empowered with the authority to appoint electors who would choose from the best of the best.

Yet as the meaning of democracy changed and as American politics opened up to greater political participation, states began to use the popular vote as a means of allocating their electoral votes. Why, then, do we continue to use this rather complicated, indirect system for voters to choose their president? Why not simply use the sum total of the popular vote to choose a winner? The most basic answer is explained by politics, not necessarily logic. The Electoral College system benefits smaller states. For example, Wyoming's population of approximately 494,000 represents 0.17 percent of the potential popular vote. But its three electoral votes constitute 0.56 percent of the electoral vote total. Because every state starts off with two electoral votes (for its two U.S. senators), smaller states end up with disproportionately more voting power in the Electoral College than in the popular vote. In recent years, the states that benefit from the Electoral College system have tended to be dominated by Republican legislatures. Because changing the Electoral College system requires a constitutional amendment and because amendment procedures require approval by three fourths of the state legislatures, any attempt to change the system is unlikely to win the support of a sufficient number of state legislatures, enough of which are small enough to benefit from the Electoral College. Despite the many proposals that have been offered to reform or eliminate the Electoral College, it seems likely, at least for the foreseeable future, that the Electoral College is here to stay.

Campaign Funding

★ **LO**

Understand the impact money has on presidential campaigns, and recognize the laws governing campaign finance

Waging a political campaign, particularly a presidential campaign, is expensive.[19] In 2008, all the candidates together raised more than $1.7 billion, nearly double the amount raised in 2004, and more than four times the amount raised in 2000. Barack Obama's campaign alone raised $745 million. Campaign financing, then, is one of the most important functions of a political campaign. Hiring a professional staff to develop and implement a successful campaign, producing and airing TV commercials and radio spots, renting campaign headquarters office space, conducting polls to monitor the course of the campaign, and producing buttons, bumper stickers, and signs all cost money. Good candidates have demonstrated a high capacity for raising money to wage a campaign.

Sources of Funding

Where do campaigns find financial support? They find money from individual citizens, from interest groups and political action committees, and from political parties. Companies, groups, and individuals all have vested interests in the political system, and each may provide support (including monetary contributions) to promote candidates who advocate their own positions on issues. Our system of politics encourages people and groups to participate in the political process, and this participation includes financial contributions to campaigns. Indeed, giving money to candidates may be seen as a healthy sign that people are engaged in the political process and want to participate in making a difference.

Beginning in the 1970s, parties and candidates turned to political action committees (PACs) to address the new realities of political campaigns, particularly regarding fund-raising and limits on individual contributions. PACs are the arms of interest groups that raise and give money to political candidates. Any group that wishes to participate in financing campaigns must create a PAC and register it with the Federal Election Commission (FEC). There are more than 4,000 PACs currently registered with the federal government (see Figure 15.2). Of the $1 billion raised by House and Senate campaigns in 2008, about 32 percent came from the fund-raising efforts of PACs.

In addition to individual and PAC contributions, the political parties play an important role in financing political campaigns. Both major parties have national and statewide committees, which raise money and give money to candidates to fund campaigns. In 2000, the national party committees each collected and spent about $200 million to help fund their candidates. Typically, the parties support House and Senate candidates, particularly those who have a competitive chance of winning.

FIGURE 15.2
The Growth of Political Action Committees

The federal campaign finance legislation of the 1970s was the first vigorous attempt to monitor and regulate the money that was raised and spent on political campaigns. These laws applied to the regulation of hard money, which was money raised directly by and spent by the political candidates. They influenced the creation of political action committees (PACs), which raise and spend soft money—funds for political campaigning independent of the political candidates. In 1974, there were only 608 PACs registered with the federal government; by 2002, 4,027 PACs were registered. This figure shows the total amount of receipts and expenditures of all PACs registered with the federal government from the 1975–1976 election cycle to the 2007–2008 election cycle.

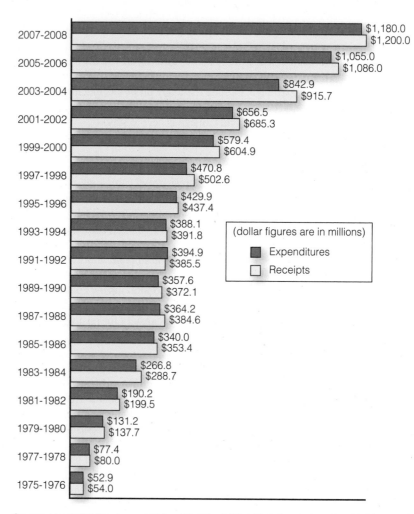

(dollar figures are in millions)
■ Expenditures
□ Receipts

	Expenditures	Receipts
2007-2008	$1,180.0	$1,200.0
2005-2006	$1,055.0	$1,086.0
2003-2004	$842.9	$915.7
2001-2002	$656.5	$685.3
1999-2000	$579.4	$604.9
1997-1998	$470.8	$502.6
1995-1996	$429.9	$437.4
1993-1994	$388.1	$391.8
1991-1992	$394.9	$385.5
1989-1990	$357.6	$372.1
1987-1988	$364.2	$384.6
1985-1986	$340.0	$353.4
1983-1984	$266.8	$288.7
1981-1982	$190.2	$199.5
1979-1980	$131.2	$137.7
1977-1978	$77.4	$80.0
1975-1976	$52.9	$54.0

Source: Harold W. Stanley and Richard G. Niemi, *Vital Statistics on American Politics 2004–2005*, 103 (Washington, DC: CQ Press, 2006). Copyright ©2006 CQ Press, a division of Sage Publications. Data for 2005-2008 are from www.fec.gov/press/press2009/2009041 5pac/20090424pac.shtml.

Another important source of campaign funding comes from the individual candidates' House and Senate campaigns. Members of Congress who hold safe seats are very effective at raising money for their own campaigns. These campaigns, because they are for safe seats, tend not to need a great deal of funding. So the incumbents use their campaign war chests to help fund the campaigns of their colleagues in more competitive races. Often, they do so through the formation of a PAC.

Though not the norm, some candidates for federal office use their own money to fund their campaigns. In 1992 and 1996, independent presidential candidate Ross Perot spent millions of dollars of his personal fortune (Perot's personal wealth is in the billions of dollars). Similarly, Democrat Jon Corzine of New Jersey spent more than $50 million of his own money to win a U.S. Senate seat in 2000 (his Republican competitor spent over $30 million of his own money).

The federal government and a handful of state governments (including Arizona, Connecticut, North Carolina, and Maine) also maintain some form of public campaign financing. Although candidates cannot be forced to participate in public financing schemes, which restrict their expenditures, the government may entice their participation by offering them significant public funds in return for their agreement to abide by personal campaign spending limits. The federal government's presidential election financing system allows major-party candidates to draw on funds received when taxpayers check a box on their tax returns agreeing to donate to the fund. In 2008, presidential candidates were eligible to receive approximately $85 million each if they agreed to limit their campaign expenditures. Democrat Barack Obama declined public financing and continued to privately raise funds through the general election—a decision based on his widespread success in raising campaign money during the primaries. By rejecting the use of such public financing, he was able to freely spend throughout the general election campaign without regard to any federally imposed limits. John McCain, however, a longtime champion of campaign finance reform and public financing, accepted the $85 million and its spending limits.

In recent presidential election cycles, candidates have been able to take advantage of the Internet as yet another means of fund-raising. In 2000, Bill Bradley raised more than $2 million via the Internet for his campaign for the Democratic presidential nomination. (He ended up losing his bid for the nomination to Al Gore.) Then, in the 2004 race for the Democratic presidential nomination, a little-known former governor from the small state of Vermont, Howard Dean, waged an impressive campaign by tapping into the vast potential of the Internet and online fund-raising. His followers, who came to be known as "Deaniacs," tended to be younger Americans, a group much more inclined to use the Internet, to IM (instant message), and to blog. The Dean campaign translated this orientation of his followers into the most successful Internet fund-raising campaign that American politics had ever seen. As Wired.com reported during the nomination campaign in early 2004:

> The biggest news of the political season has been the tale of this small-state governor who, with the help of Meetup.com and hundreds of bloggers, has elbowed his way into serious contention for his party's presidential nomination. . . . Dean has used the Net to raise more money than any other Democratic candidate. He's also used it to organize thousands of volunteers who go door-to-door, write personal letters to likely voters, host meetings, and distribute flyers.

Dean raised an unprecedented $40 million in his campaign for the nomination. This amount exceeded that of all his competitors for the nomination, and the vast bulk of his campaign war chest was derived from small, individual donations solicited through the Internet. Although Dean's campaign collapsed after the candidate suffered unexpected losses in Iowa and New Hampshire and although most of his $40 million war chest was depleted by the first primary contest, Dean's success at Internet fund-raising was nonetheless quite impressive. Then in 2008 Barack Obama's campaign substantially increased the stakes in fund-raising through the Internet by raising over $200 million through that medium. His appeal to voters through the Internet represents a significant achievement in the use of this new technology in campaign politics. As Americans increasingly come to rely on the Internet, it is likely that political candidates will follow Dean's and Obama's examples and harness this technology for fund-raising and other campaigning.

Regulating Campaign Financing

Congress and the states have passed many and varied laws to regulate the conduct of campaign contributions. These laws are not intended to prevent individuals or groups from giving money. Rather, they attempt to prevent a "quid pro quo," or a donation in return for an elected official voting or acting in a certain way in direct response to accepting the campaign gift.

The first significant piece of federal legislation aimed at regulating campaign financing was the **Federal Election Campaign Act (FECA)**, passed in 1971 and amended in 1974. The law required that all federal candidates accurately disclose campaign contributions and document all campaign expenditures. Subsequent amendments to FECA imposed legal limits on campaign contributions by individuals ($1,000 to each candidate per election cycle; $5,000 to PACs per year; and $20,000 to national party committees per year). Additionally, FECA imposed an outright ban on certain campaign contributions by corporations, unions, national banks, and foreign nationals, among others.

All these provisions targeted so-called **hard money** contributions that go directly to candidates and their campaign committees. FECA did little to stem the influx of **soft money** funds to political parties and political advocacy groups that are not contributed directly to candidate campaigns and that do not expressly advocate the election of a particular candidate. In the two decades following FECA, the two major political parties have strategically spent soft money on administrative and party-building activities, as well as on issue ads that do not specifically promote an individual candidate but that nevertheless attempt to affect the election outcome.

The **Federal Election Commission (FEC)** was established in 1974 to enforce all campaign financing rules and regulations, including limits on campaign contributions. Today, the FEC is the federal agency in charge of enforcing election laws. Provisions for public funding of presidential campaigns were subsequently passed in 1976 and 1979.

Critics have voiced a number of complaints about the system of campaign finance regulations. For one thing, the original limits on individual contributions—fixed by legislation in the 1970s—were never indexed to inflation. This oversight was addressed in legislation in 2002 which mandated that limits be indexed for inflation every two years. For example, in 2005–2006,

Federal Election Campaign Act (FECA)
The federal legislation passed in 1971 that established disclosure requirements and restricted individual campaign contributions.

Hard money
Donations made directly to political candidates and their campaigns that must be declared with the name of the donor (which then becomes public knowledge).

Soft money
Money not donated directly to a candidate's campaign, but rather to a political advocacy group or a political party for "party building" activities.

Federal Election Commission (FEC)
The agency created in 1974 to enforce federal election laws.

individuals were able to give up to $2,100 to candidates and up to $26,700 to national party committees.

Another complaint concerns the failure of the system to adapt to modern campaign dynamics. As a result of frontloading, presidential primary elections are now bunched up earlier and earlier in the general election campaign; yet the strict limits on expenditures imposed on those who accept public financing do not really account for these new campaign realities, which compel candidates to spend a considerable amount of their money during a relatively short period of time.

In recent years, advocates of campaign finance reform have focused their greatest criticism on soft money in the form of **independent campaign expenditures**. These are monies that PACs or individuals spend to support political campaigns but that do not directly contribute to them. FECA banned the unlimited use of independent expenditures to directly support the election of one candidate or the defeat of another candidate, but those funds could still be used to build the party as a whole. For example, a PAC can produce and support a political advertisement that endorses a particular party's position on an issue and pay for the airtime to broadcast that ad on television. The money for the ad is not donated to a campaign per se but instead is spent on services that support the campaign; thus, the money spent is considered an "independent" expenditure. The U.S. Supreme Court in **Buckley v. Valeo** (1976)[20] ruled that Congress could limit campaign contributions consistent with the First Amendment but that it could not limit independent campaign expenditures or personal money spent by candidates on behalf of their own campaigns. Twenty years later in *McConnell v. F.E.C.* (2003),[21] the Court extended that ruling to apply to spending by political parties as well. Thus, political parties themselves often sponsor television ads that talk more generally about issues facing the country without mentioning any individual candidate or race; of course, most political experts acknowledge that these ads may have a significant impact on individual campaigns.

The most recent reform attempts have focused on soft money and independent campaign expenditures. Senators John McCain (R-AZ) and Russell Feingold (D-WI) were particularly critical of the loopholes in campaign financing that have allowed soft money to go unregulated by the Federal Election Commission. They cosponsored legislation designed to better regulate the way campaigns are financed and how the money is spent. In 2002, Congress passed the **Bipartisan Campaign Reform Act (BCRA)**, popularly known as the McCain-Feingold Act, which prohibited national parties and candidates for federal office from accepting soft money (i.e., that which is not subject to regulation by the FEC). The BCRA also raised limits on contributions to a particular candidate for federal office from $1,000 to $2,000. Meanwhile, the U.S. Supreme Court in 2010 struck down as unconstitutional several other provisions of the BCRA, including certain limits on corporate and union funding of broadcast ads right before an election.

Congressional Campaigns and Elections

Although presidential elections typically receive the most attention from the media and the public, many other elections also occur regularly, including those that send members to the two houses of Congress. In each presidential election year, all 435 seats in the House of Representatives are contested, as are one third of the seats in the Senate. Midway between successive presidential

Independent campaign expenditure
Political donations that PACs or individuals spend to support campaigns, but do not directly contribute to the campaigns.

Buckley v. Valeo (1976)
The 1976 Supreme Court opinion that held that spending money to influence elections is protected First Amendment speech, and that prohibited limitations on independent expenditures or personal money spent by candidates on their own campaigns.

Bipartisan Campaign Reform Act (BCRA)
Also called the McCain-Feingold Act, the federal legislation that (1) restricted soft money spent by political parties, (2) regulated expenditures on ads that refer to specific candidates immediately before an election, and (3) increased limits on hard money donated directly to candidates and their campaigns.

elections are the **midterm congressional elections**, in which all 435 House seats are contested again and one third of the Senate seats are voted on (senators serve six-year terms, and the 100 Senate elections are staggered so that about one third of the seats are contested every two years).

Midterm elections for Congress differ from presidential-year elections in important ways.[22] First, voter turnout tends to be lower in the midterm contests. Without the large-scale attention the presidential race receives, voter interest and engagement in the midterm elections are lower, and thus, turnout tends to suffer. Even in the highly charged midterm elections of 2006, voter turnout was just 41 percent, almost fifteen percentage points below voter turnout figures for the preceding presidential election.

Second, midterm elections fail to offer congressional candidates what has come to be known as the **coattail effect**. In a presidential election year, the names of candidates for Congress typically are listed below the name of their party's candidate for president on the ballot. Thus, voters' selection of congressional candidates may be influenced by their choice for president. The congressional candidates, in effect, ride the coattails of the presidential candidate.[23] For the coattail effect to be apparent, the outcome of the presidential race typically needs to be a landslide victory for the winner, such as in 1984 when President Ronald Reagan soundly defeated Democrat Walter Mondale. For the first time in decades, the 1984 elections ushered in a Republican majority to the U.S. Senate. By contrast, George W. Bush's narrow victory in 2004 did not appear to produce a coattail effect.

Third, in midterm elections, there has been a discernible trend—though often not very strong—that favors congressional candidates in the party opposite the president's party. When a president wins, especially by a large margin, the coattail effect distorts what would normally occur in any given congressional race. Yet in midterm elections, without the president's name at the top of the ballot, the absence of the coattail gives the advantage to the opposing party. In the modern era, the party in opposition to the president has managed to regain control of Congress only in the midterm elections when the president's popularity is waning. Thus, in 1946 and then in 1994, the Republicans wrestled both houses of Congress back from the Democrats at midterm elections during the presidencies of Democrats Harry Truman and Bill Clinton, respectively. More recently in 2006, voters upset about the state of the war in Iraq dealt a devastating blow to the Republicans' control of Congress: Although many Republican incumbents in the House and Senate were ousted from office that year, not one Democratic House member or senator lost a seat in the 2006 midterm elections. The Democrats successfully rode the public's antiwar sentiment to regain control of both houses of Congress midway through the second term of Republican President George W. Bush. In the 2008 congressional races, the Democrats increased their majorities in both houses.

True to form, the 2010 midterm elections once again offered a rebuke to the political party holding the White House. Running on a platform that opposed Democratic spending initiatives and promised to rein in the size of government, Republican House candidates transformed a 178-seat minority into a 240-seat majority. By taking more than 60 seats away from the Democrats, Republicans enjoyed a level of midterm election success not seen by either party in decades. Republicans were also successful in the Senate, shrinking the Democrats' 18-seat margin of control down to just 6 seats.

More important than presidential coattails or any other factor in congressional elections, however, is the **power of incumbency**. Incumbent members of Congress, particularly those in the House, are returned to office by voters at amazingly high rates. In a normal year of House races, an incumbent who is running for reelection stands a better than 90 percent chance of returning to office.[24] What accounts for such a high return rate? First, name recognition of the candidate is a significant factor in lower-profile congressional races, and incumbents, because they have been in office, tend to have higher name recognition than do challengers. Second, the vast majority of congressional districts and thus the vast majority of seats in Congress are dominated by either the Republican Party or

Power of incumbency
The phenomenon by which incumbent members of Congress running for reelection are returned to office at an extremely high rate.

TABLE 15.2 Safe Seats in Congress

The vast majority of the 435 seats in the House of Representatives, each of which is contested every two years, and the 100 U.S. Senate seats, each of which is contested every six years, are safe seats for incumbents who are running for reelection. Even if there is not an incumbent running for reelection, most of these seats tend to be safe for one of the two major political parties. The 2010 midterm elections proved to be a bit of an anomaly, as 51 Democratic House incumbents in all lost their general reelection bids.

The table below shows the number of incumbents defeated and the number of seats that switched from one party to another in each congressional election since 1980.* Keep in mind that in each election year, 435 House races and thirty-three or thirty-four Senate races are usually contested.

Year	Incumbents Defeated	Open Seats Where Party Changed	Total Changes	Incumbents Defeated	Open Seats Where Party Changed	Total Changes*
	House of Representatives			**Senate**		
1980	30	11	41	9	3	12
1982	23	8	31	2	2	4
1984	16	6	22	3	1	4
1986	6	15	21	7	3	10
1988	6	3	9	4	3	7
1990	15	6	21	1	0	1
1992	24	19	43	4	0	4
1994	35	26	61	2	6	8
1996	21	14	35	1	3	4
1998	6	11	17	3	3	6
2000	6	12	18	6	2	8
2002	4	8	12	3	1	4
2004	5	5	10	1	7	8
2006	22	9	31	6	0	6
2008	17	13	30	5	3	8
2010**	53	10	63	2	4	6

* Figures include only shifts from one major party to the other party.

** Results from 2010 midterm elections include only those races decided as of November 5, 2010.

Source: Harold W. Stanley and Richard G. Niemi, *Vital Statistics on American Politics 2005–2006* (Washington, DC: CQ Press, 2006), 48–49. Copyright ©2006 CQ Press, a division of Sage Publications; updated by authors.

A dejected Senator Russ Feingold (D-WI) concedes defeat on November 2, 2010. Feingold served three terms in the U.S. Senate, but could not hold on for a fourth term against the electoral tide that swept many Republicans into office in 2010.

Safe seat
A congressional seat from a district that includes a high percentage of voters from one of the major parties.

Marginal seat
A seat in a congressional district that has relatively similar numbers of Democratic and Republican voters.

Franking privilege
The traditional right of members of Congress to mail materials to their constituents without paying postage.

the Democratic Party. Congressional seats from districts that include either a high percentage of Democratic voters or a high percentage of Republican voters are dominated by their respective majority party and are referred to as **safe seats**. A far smaller number of districts tend to have similar numbers of Democratic and Republican voters and are known as **marginal seats**. In the periodic redistricting of congressional districts, political parties try to configure districts to their own partisan advantage. This maneuvering tends to create a large number of safe seats and often very few marginal seats (see Table 15.2 on page 413).

Finally, incumbent members of Congress enjoy financial advantages, such as the **franking privilege**, which allows members to mail materials to their constituents without paying postage.

NOW & THEN

Making the Connection

Elections and campaigns are central features of the republican form of government in the United States. The number of elections is many, the cost of campaigns is high, and the process for selecting the nation's chief officeholder, the president of the United States, is long and complex. Several times in the nation's history, the complicated procedure for selecting a president has resulted in considerable controversy, as in the elections of 1876 and 2000. Yet through these controversies and many others, the U.S. political system has maintained free, open, and regular elections since George Washington was unanimously chosen as the nation's first president in 1789. U.S. presidential elections evoke a great deal of passion, engage the interest of millions of voters, persuade vast numbers of citizens and groups to contribute large amounts of money, and focus attention on the great issues of the day. Thus, campaigns and elections duly serve their purpose in providing an important connection between Americans and their government.

One significant development in the financing of the 2008 presidential primaries and caucuses was the success Democratic candidate Barack Obama enjoyed in raising so many small donations using the Internet. According to the nonpartisan Campaign Finance Institute, Obama raised $101 million in small individual contributions of $200 or less up through March 31, 2008. The vast majority of these small donations were made through the Internet. As compared to larger donations solicited directly from individuals, these Internet donations offered Obama numerous advantages: They provided his campaign with broad-based funding at very little cost, as compared to more expensive methods such as events, telemarketing, and direct mail; they required little time or effort on the part of the candidate himself; they filled the campaign's coffers without the risk of influence buying that accompanies larger contributions from a smaller number of individuals. Howard Dean, a candidate for the Democratic nomination in 2004, became the first presidential candidate to tap funds so successfully in this way—his campaign raised $50 million in the third quarter of 2003 with an average donation size of $80. In 2008, Obama refined and built on Dean's model, helping Obama secure his party's presidential nomination.

On www.cengage.com/dautrich/americangovernmentbrief/2e, find the Politics InterActive link for information about the Internet campaign financing phenomenon, including analysis of which candidates have benefited the most from Internet donations in recent election cycles. Historical, popular, and global perspectives on the issue are also presented.

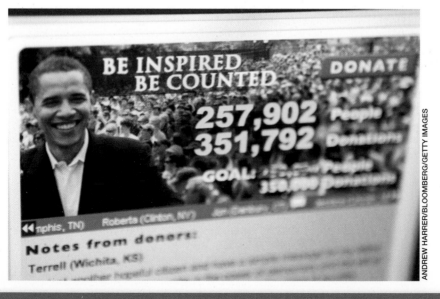

ANDREW HARRER/BLOOMBERG/GETTY IMAGES

Chapter Summary

★ SUMMARIZING WHAT YOU HAVE LEARNED ★

★ American Presidential Elections in Historical Perspective

- The system for choosing U.S. presidents includes two distinct phases: a nomination phase (during which major-party nominees are chosen) and a general election phase (in which a new president is selected).

- From 1796 up through the 1830s, the nomination process was dominated by officials of the two major parties who chose party nominees based on informal discussions. Andrew Jackson and the Democratic Party he founded gave the "common man" increased influence in choosing nominees; by the twentieth century, electoral reforms such as the direct primary gave voters in many states a formal opportunity to cast a ballot for delegates, who would in turn choose their party's nominees at a national convention.

★ The Prenomination Campaign

- Modern presidential elections begin with a prenomination campaign waged by potential candidates to raise money and gain the support of key party leaders. A candidate's failure to raise sufficient funds in this "invisible primary" may cause him or her to drop out of the race before any formal primaries or caucuses have been held.

★ The Nomination Campaign

- Nomination campaigns focus on attaining victories in presidential primaries and caucuses. The Iowa caucus and the New Hampshire primary have traditionally come at the beginning of the nomination calendar, and so they tend to disproportionately influence the final outcomes. In recent elections, many states have attempted to move their primaries and caucuses up on the calendar in a process known as frontloading.

- National party conventions used to play an important role in helping choose party nominees; today, they are mostly made-for-television affairs, anointing the party ticket with speeches offering testimonials to the nominees.

★ The General Election Campaign

- General election races may be either incumbent races (pitting a sitting president against a challenger) or open elections (with no incumbent in the race). In the former, the election often amounts to a referendum on the performance of the president over the previous four years.

- Presidential candidates choose their running mates (the vice presidential candidates) strategically to address specific weaknesses of the presidential candidate or to boost the ticket's prospects in certain geographic areas.

- To win the presidency, a candidate must put together a coalition of states sufficient to win a majority of the 538 Electoral College votes, which are allocated to each state based on the sum of the number of senators and the number of representatives. The candidate who does well in battleground states will normally win the 270 or more votes necessary to secure a majority.

- Televised debates between major presidential candidates occurred for the first time in 1960 and have been held in every presidential election since 1976. These debates tend to receive a large amount of attention from the press and the public, but their impact on the final election outcome remains unclear.

★ Campaign Funding

- Campaign funding is critical to the success of individual candidates. Election laws since 1974 have limited the amount individuals or organizations can give to candidates (hard money). The Bipartisan Campaign Reform Act (BCRA) went a step further, restricting expenditures to political parties or advocacy groups that are theoretically independent of specific candidates or campaigns (soft money). The Federal Election Commission enforces all such limitations that have been upheld as constitutional by the U.S. Supreme Court.

- In congressional elections, the power of incumbency is more important than any other factor. Unlike the case in midterm elections, congressional elections that coincide with presidential elections tend to garner greater voter turnout, and members of the successful presidential candidate's party sometimes benefit from the coattail effect.

CourseMate

Key Terms

Battleground states (p. 402)

Bipartisan Campaign Reform Act (BCRA) (p. 411)

Buckley v. Valeo (1976) (p. 411)

Caucus (p. 397)

Closed primary (p. 396)

Coattail effect (p. 412)

Electoral College (p. 404)

Electors (p. 405)

Federal Election Campaign Act (FECA) (p. 410)

Federal Election Commission (FEC) (p. 410)

Franking privilege (p. 414)

Frontloading (p. 398)

Hard money (p. 410)

Incumbent race (p. 400)

Independent campaign expenditure (p. 411)

Invisible primary (p. 395)

Marginal seat (p. 414)

Midterm congressional elections (p. 412)

Nomination campaign (p. 397)

Open election (p. 400)

Open primary (p. 396)

Power of incumbency (p. 413)

Prenomination campaign (p. 395)

Presidential primary (p. 396)

Safe seat (p. 414)

Soft money (p. 410)

Unit rule (p. 405)

Resources

Books

Abramson, Paul R., John H. Aldrich, and David W. Rohde. *Change and Continuity in the 2008 Elections.* Washington, DC: CQ Press, 2010.

Edwards, George. *Why the Electoral College Is Bad for America.* New Haven, CT: Yale University Press, 2004.

Magleby, David B., ed. *Financing the 2000 Election.* Washington, DC: Brookings Institution Press, 2002.

Mayer, William G., and Andrew Busch. *The Frontloading Problem in Presidential Nominations.* Washington, DC: Brookings Institution Press, 2003.

Wayne, Stephen J. *The Road to the White House 2008*, 8th ed. Boston: Wadsworth, 2008.

Internet Sources

http://www.electoral-vote.com (a Web site that uses polling data from each state to estimate and map the Electoral College vote outcome; provides historical data on Electoral College outcomes and statewide polls).

http://www.livingroomcandidate.org/ (the Museum of the Moving Image produces this valuable site, which contains televised campaign advertisements of candidates since the 1952 election).

http://www.opensecrets.org (this site, maintained by the Center for Responsive Politics, contains a wealth of information about PACs, campaign finance, and links to the Federal Election Commission's data).

16 American Economic Policy

NOW Traders and other businessmen linger outside the New York Stock Exchange on September 15, 2008, the day Lehman Brothers filed for bankruptcy.

THEN Crowds flock in front of the New York Stock Exchange on October 24, 1929 ("Black Thursday"), the first day of that year's Wall Street crash.

NOW & THEN

When the Greed and Arrogance of Financial Institutions Demand a National Solution . . .

 America's capitalist system was in a state of crisis. At least one major financial institution had already failed, and others were on the brink of collapse. While a select number of well-placed individuals exploited the lax regulatory environment, millions of others fell victim to financial institutions that took excessive risks with their money and capital. Many of these institutions were also less than candid with their investors. The President of the United States—bolstered by a legislative branch controlled by his own party—favored decisive action to regulate those institutions. With the public up in arms about the excesses of Wall Street, the administration's efforts were guaranteed to win some support from the opposition party as well. When wealthy financial institutions driven by greed and arrogance defraud so many citizens of their hard-earned savings and investments, a new agenda to regulate such bad behavior becomes that much more difficult to derail.

NOW & THEN

President Barack Obama, flanked by advisors, speaks on the state of financial reform legislation in January 2010.

JIM WATSON/AFP/GETTY IMAGES

NOW The "Great Recession" of 2007–2010 was marked by the collapse of Lehman Brothers, the government bailout of numerous other financial institutions at taxpayer expense, and significant downturns in stock markets around the world. This was not a routine down cycle by any measure—Wall Street insiders and titans of the financial world had contributed heavily to this financial collapse. The U.S. banking system was suffering a major liquidity crisis brought on by (1) predatory lending practices; (2) an upsurge in subprime lending to borrowers with weak credit histories, (3) the incorrect pricing of risk on complex assets such as derivatives; and (4) the rise of the shadow banking system, in which nonbank financial institutions were lending money free of regulations. Investment banks sold investments to unwitting clients even as they were secretly betting against those same investments. Critics complained that the regulatory system had failed to keep up with financial innovations; regulators had also made ill-advised policy decisions, such as to relax the net capital rule, which enabled investment banks to substantially increase their debts. Finally, even some institutions that received federal bailout money were paying executives outlandishly high salaries. On July 21, 2010, President Obama signed into law sweeping new legislation aimed at cracking down on banks and Wall Street—the Dodd-Frank Wall Street Reform and Consumer Protection Act increased oversight of risky financial institutions, ended taxpayer bailouts, and introduced brand new rules covering executive compensation and corporate responsibility. It also created the Consumer Financial Protection Bureau. A handful of Republicans, though disagreeing with some of the proposals, still voted for the final reform.

THEN In 1933, banks and other financial institutions were staring into an abyss of their own making. Since the beginning of the republic, Congress had never dared to comprehensively regulate either the offer and sale of securities or the trading of those securities through a secondary market. But the Wall Street Crash of 1929 had led to the failure of some major banks and the vast majority of Americans had seen their stock holdings disappear. Congressional investigators in 1932 and 1933 turned up considerable evidence of fraud and irresponsibility on Wall Street. Specifically, the banks and their affiliates had ignored plain conflicts of interest in their dealings, and had regularly engaged in underwriting unsound securities to pay off bad bank loans; competing banks had even "pooled operations" to artificially support the price of bank stocks. Wall Street insiders like Joseph Kennedy—father of the thirty-fifth president—used inside information about stocks to make millions. Even worse, the officers at many of these once revered institutions had also been playing by their own rules. The powerful banker, J. P. Morgan Jr., admitted under oath that his firm had employed "preferred lists," which enabled influential persons to buy securities at less than the market price. Congress passed the Securities Act of 1933 to set penalties for filing false information about stock offerings, and the Securities Exchange Act of 1934, which formed the Securities and Exchange Commission to regulate stock exchanges and end rampant insider speculation that had ruined so many. Democrats and Republicans alike who had railed against the excesses of Wall Street were now determined to end the era of unregulated securities and regulations. In truth, the public anger that raged against those men had given them little choice.

BETTMANN/CORBIS

The well-known financier J. Pierpoint Morgan Jr. listens intently during a Senate Banking and Currency Committee inquiry into his affairs in 1933.

T hough most Americans tend to subscribe to the value of "capitalism" in the abstract, the reality is a bit more complicated. When economic times are turbulent, the American public expects government to intervene on its behalf, and politicians who sit on their hands with a "wait and see" approach to an economic crisis may find themselves out of office long before the actual crisis has passed. When there is obvious wrongdoing, demands for government action may be even louder and more vehement. Certainly that is what happened in the early 1930s during the Great Depression, and then more recently during the Great Recession of 2007–2010. In both instances, banks and other financial institutions capitalized on a lax regulatory environment, and millions of innocent shareholders blamed the loss of their savings not just on the economic down cycle, but also on Wall Street insiders who, they felt, had stacked the system against them. When the public feels cheated, Washington must respond with major proposals for financial reform, and that is exactly what happened in both instances. The commitment to laissez-faire capitalism in the abstract proves little match against the lethal combination of a financial crisis and an outraged citizenry. Under those circumstances, members of both political parties can usually find some common ground; if they don't, they just might find an electoral pox befalling both of their partisan houses.

★ LO Define the various stages in which the public policymaking process unfolds

Public policy
The set of laws, regulations, and rules that affect the whole of society.

An Overview of the Policymaking Process

Public policy refers to the set of laws, regulations, and rules that affect the entire society. In the United States, the term *public policy* has come to be associated in particular with the response of public institutions—usually in the form of some principle, plan, or formal course of action—to events and conditions that occur both inside and outside the government.

Because the responsibilities and interests of private and public institutions often overlap, some battles that are waged primarily among private parties may still fall under the general subject of public policy; after all, government may seek to enact laws or regulations aimed at monitoring such disputes. Antitrust laws, for example, offer a public policy response to disputes that arise between competing private companies such as Microsoft and Netscape. Microsoft's dominance of the market for operating systems on personal computers afforded it the leverage and market power to demand that hardware manufacturers such as Dell and Gateway refuse to install other non-Microsoft products such as search engines; those demands in turn made it hard (some say impossible) for companies such as Netscape to compete. Government regulators feared that without some form of competition, Microsoft would eventually be in a position to gouge consumers with artificially high prices on all its products. Thus, the regulation of Microsoft and the agreements it made with manufacturers quickly became a matter of public policy in the 1990s, even though those agreements were technically between private entities.

Although the policymaking process tends to vary considerably from one subject area to another, most policies unfold in five separate stages.

- The *recognition/definition stage*, in which objectives to be fulfilled and goals to be pursued through policy are first identified and defined according to how the problem fits within existing policy categories and then prioritized;

- The *formulation stage*, in which various alternative courses for this policy are considered, and a preferred course is selected;

- The *adoption (or legitimation) stage*, in which the policy under consideration assumes the authority of law through ratification by Congress or through regulations issued by the relevant administrative agencies;

- The *implementation stage*, in which a bureaucratic agency translates law into action through the adoption of administrative regulations and the dedication of agency resources to carry out the policy; and

- The *evaluation stage*, in which the policy is assessed for its worth and effectiveness in meeting its original objectives and goals.

This chapter focuses on economic policymaking, which encompasses all the legislative and rule-making initiatives that affect the management of wealth and resources within this country. For much of its history, the United States maintained one of the world's most entrepreneurially free economies, with minimal government regulation. The government's mostly hands-off approach to economic matters survived until the early part of the twentieth century, when the federal government began to insert itself more regularly into the economy. At first, government involvement was directed at antitrust matters and corporate abuses such as the employment of child labor; by the 1930s, government involvement had begun to take a variety of new forms, as federal agencies actively oversaw the monetary system, supported struggling businesses, regulated the stock and bond markets, and otherwise reinforced the economic infrastructure as a whole. Indeed, immediately following the frightening events on Wall Street that occurred in September 2008, few from either political party questioned the wisdom of increasing government oversight of Wall Street. Today, the government's role in managing the economy is significant; elections are often decided by voter perceptions of success or failure in this area. Overseeing the economy includes two distinct forms of policymaking: fiscal policymaking and monetary policymaking.

Theories and Practice in Fiscal Policy

★ LO
Recognize the different theories that justify decisions to craft fiscal policy

Fiscal policy is concerned with how to raise revenue through taxation and how to spend the revenue generated. Many economists believe that the nation's fiscal policy has direct implications for unemployment, measured as the percentage of the workforce that wants to work and is not currently employed, and **inflation**, or consistent increases in the prices of goods and services. The primary instrument by which the federal government manages fiscal policy is the *federal budget*, a comprehensive plan laying out what the government will spend for its various programs during the coming fiscal years and how it expects to raise the money to pay for them.

Fiscal policy can be thought of as lying on a spectrum. At one end of the spectrum is the policy of minimal government interference in the economy, in which the government exercises little or no budget-making power by authorizing only minimal spending, taxation, and regulation of private business practices. At the opposite end of the spectrum is the policy of considerable government intervention in the economy, perhaps by taxing citizens or by offering subsidies to farmers in return for their agreement not to overproduce certain commodities.

A variety of economic theories explain the decision to craft fiscal policy at a given point along the fiscal policy spectrum. For example, the economic doctrine known as **laissez-faire** (a French phrase meaning, literally, "leave us alone") guided the fiscal policy that prevailed for much of the eighteenth and

Fiscal policy
Decisions by the federal government that relate to raising revenue through taxation and spending the revenue that is thereby generated.

Inflation
The overall general upward price movement of goods and services in an economy, normally measured by the consumer price index (CPI).

Laissez-faire economics
Fiscal policy theory that favors minimal intervention in the nation's economy.

nineteenth centuries in the United States.[1] Laissez-faire favors less intervention in the economy, allowing businesses to conduct their affairs more or less free from governmental regulation. The theory came under attack toward the end of the 1800s, when increasing industrialization led to more frequent financial panics, bouts of severe unemployment, corrupt business practices, and the abuse of workers, especially in big cities. Government's involvement in the economy gradually increased, and in the 1930s, widespread public support for President Franklin Roosevelt's New Deal programs, enacted to address the problems of the Great Depression, effectively spelled the end of laissez-faire theory as the guiding principle for the nation's fiscal policy.

Keynesian economic theory
Fiscal policy theory that favors government taxation and spending during difficult economic times.

Many of FDR's New Deal policies were based on **Keynesian economic theory**, named for the British economist John Maynard Keynes. Keynesian theory argues that the government should increase spending when economic times are bad as a way of raising total demand. Total demand for goods and services, according to this theory, is the key determinant of whether the economy is performing well.[2] The economic recovery that occurred during World War II, when federal military spending increased significantly, is often used to support the validity of Keynesian theory. Administrations that attempted to draw on the theory quickly learned that although government spending may forestall or even end a **recession**—defined as an economic slowdown characterized by high unemployment, reduced productivity, or some other negative economic indicators—it may also bring about other economic problems such as inflation and chronically high deficits. Barack Obama's administration also adopted a Keynesian approach to addressing the financial crisis of 2007–2010. President Obama adopted that approach while aware of the risks that higher deficits might pose to his chances for reelection in 2012.

Recession
An economic slowdown characterized by high unemployment, reduced productivity, or other negative economic indicators.

Supply-side economics is an alternative to Keynesian economics, arguing that rather than increasing government spending, cutting taxes (and cutting government spending that such taxes help to fund) is the preferred way to increase economic productivity and spur the economy. According to supply-side theory, high taxes take money out of the economy that would otherwise be invested in goods and services; thus, by decreasing taxes, money flows back into the economy, stimulating business, new jobs, and overall productivity. While campaigning for the presidency in 1980, Ronald Reagan seized on this theory to propose that a program of tax cuts, spending cuts, and balancing the budget was the best way to get the economy out of recession. (As president, Reagan did secure passage of a large tax cut, but federal spending and deficits also multiplied during his eight years in office.)[3]

Supply-side economics
Economic theory that favors cutting taxes as a way of increasing economic productivity.

★ LO Define the different measures used to assess the success or failure of fiscal policy

Assessing the Economy's Performance

Just as different economic theories guide the crafting of fiscal policy, different measures are used to assess whether the nation's fiscal policy has been a success. Listed here are several economic measures regarded as especially significant indicators of general economic performance.

Gross domestic product (GDP)
An estimate of the total money value of all the goods and services produced in the United States in a one-year period.

- **Gross domestic product (GDP)** is an estimate of the total money value of all the goods and services produced in the United States in a given one-year period. When GDP improves, workers are producing more in fewer hours, allowing employers in turn to increase wages without raising prices.

Consumer price index (CPI)
An index of prices for goods and services regularly traded in the U.S. economy

- The **consumer price index (CPI)** is an index of prices for goods and services regularly traded in the U.S. economy. A sustained rise over time in the CPI

indicates that inflation is on the rise and consumers' buying power is on the decline. Although critics argue that the CPI overstates inflation by at least 1 percent per year, the government still relies heavily on the CPI in defining tax brackets and spending for certain entitlement programs, such as cost-of-living adjustments for Social Security recipients.

The Great Recession of 2007–2010 claimed many workers' jobs. Here, individuals wait their turn to claim unemployment benefits in early 2010.

- The *unemployment rate* measures the percentage of people unemployed and actively looking for work in the U.S. labor market. Although a major goal of the economic programs of most Western governments (including the United States) is to keep unemployment relatively low, full employment remains an elusive goal due to seasonal factors, voluntary job changes, and routine shifts in economic conditions such as the rise in interest rates that assist some businesses (e.g. apartment rental firms) and hinder others (e.g. construction companies and home loan financing companies).

- The **budget deficit** is the amount of money spent by the U.S. government over and above what it collects in taxes and other revenue in a single year. A **budget surplus**, on the other hand, is the amount by which the U.S. government's revenue exceeds its spending in a given fiscal year. The federal government has posted annual budget surpluses just eleven times since 1931, including four straight years from 1998 through 2001.

- The **national debt** is the total sum of the outstanding debt obligations of the U.S. government, largely generated through the sale of interest-bearing U.S. savings bonds, U.S. treasury notes, and U.S. treasury bills to individuals or organizations. It represents the accumulated total of all government budget surpluses and deficits of past years as well.[4]

- The *Dow Jones Industrial Average* is perhaps the most widely used indicator of the overall condition of the stock market where publicly owned companies are actively traded each business day. "The Dow" is actually just a price-weighted average of thirty actively traded blue chip stocks (that is, from large companies), but its prominence on network newscasts each evening testifies to the important status it holds in the minds of consumers.

- *Housing starts* are a measure of the number of U.S. residential building construction projects begun during a specific period of time. Many experts believe that a decline in housing starts is one of the first signs of an approaching economic downturn, and thus, it is one of the first indicators consulted by those trying to assess the overall direction of the economy.

- The *consumer confidence index* measures the public's evaluation of the economy by asking a representative sample of Americans how they feel about the current condition of the economy, their personal financial situation, and their prediction about the future of the economy.

Budget deficit
The amount of money spent by the U.S. government beyond that which it collects in taxes and other revenue in a single year.

Budget surplus
The amount by which the U.S. government's revenue exceeds its spending in a given fiscal year.

National debt
Total sum of the federal government's outstanding debt obligations.

Assessing the All-Important Consumer Confidence Measure

Reported monthly, the consumer confidence index, or CCI, is an economic indicator that measures American consumer optimism/pessimism regarding the state of the economy. CCI is an important figure for policymakers in particular, who use it to identify and predict trends in the economy. It is also used by the Federal Reserve Board to help make decisions about changes in the prime rate. The CCI report sometimes has an effect on stock indexes as well.

The CCI is calculated by the Conference Board, an independent research organization that conducts a monthly scientific survey of 5,000 Americans. CCI was first measured in 1967 and was indexed at 100 in 1985 (that year's measurement was not much higher or lower than it had been in the eighteen years preceding it). An increase in the CCI may indicate increases in actual consumption, while a decline normally predicts a decrease in consumer spending. The monthly calculation of CCI is based on responses to five questions on the survey regarding

- Current business conditions in the United States
- Expectations about how business conditions might change in the next six months
- Current employment conditions in the United States
- Expectations about how employment conditions might change in the next six months
- Expectations about how one's own income situation might change in the next six months

The chart below shows how the CCI changed from June of 1997 through the beginning of the Great Recession of 2007–2010.

For Critical Thinking and Discussion

1. When faced with a down-trending CCI index, the government has a variety of options it can exercise, including issuing tax rebates or taking other fiscal or monetary actions to stimulate the economy. What do you think is the best way to instill a positive outlook in consumers?

2. Are consumers likely to react positively when the federal government takes bold actions, or do such moves only serve to confirm the consumers' sense that economic times are worsening?

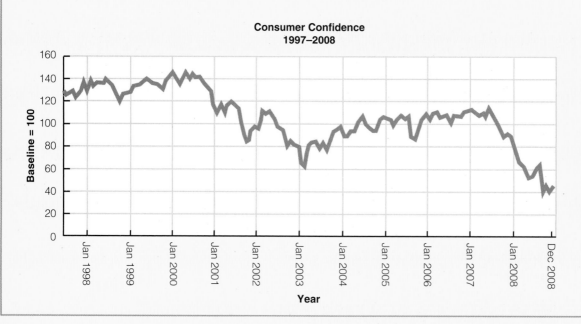

Consumer Confidence 1997–2008

- *Balance of trade figures* (also called net exports) measure the sum of the money gained by a given economy by selling exports minus the cost of buying imports. When a country exports more than it imports, the country has a trade surplus, whereas the reverse situation denotes a trade deficit. The United States has posted an annual trade deficit dating back to the 1970s; this is perhaps a testament to the rising purchasing power American consumers enjoy around the world. Economists often debate whether such chronic trade deficits are a bad thing.

In an effort to gauge the state of the economy as a whole, economists have attempted to combine these measures and others into some all-purpose economic indicator. For example, the *misery index*, measured by adding the inflation rate to the unemployment rate, is a rough indicator of how badly the economy is performing. Jimmy Carter capitalized on an exceedingly high misery index for 1975 to defeat incumbent President Gerald Ford, only to be victimized by an even higher misery index in 1979, which may well have cost Carter reelection in 1980.

The Federal Budget-Making Process

★ LO

Analyze the budget-making process, how it unfolds, and the roles played by Congress and the president in the process

The budget process begins when federal agencies formulate their budget requests and pass them on to the Office of Management and Budget (OMB). A part of the Executive Office of the President, the OMB determines whether the agency's budget proposals are in accord with the president's program and then uses those proposals to prepare an overall budget for the coming fiscal year, setting guidelines for estimating revenue and allocating spending.[5]

After receiving the president's proposals, Congress offers its own budget resolution for the fiscal year based on its own projections for revenue. The appropriations committees of the House and the Senate are primarily responsible for such budget formulation. Each of the two committees plans overview hearings during which the OMB director and representatives of federal agencies discuss the president's budget priorities. Each of the appropriations committees must eventually pass ten to twelve appropriations bills to keep the government running. House appropriations bills generally cover the topic areas listed here, with some variations from year to year.

1. Agriculture, rural development, and related agencies

2. Science, the Departments of State and Justice, and related agencies

3. Defense

4. Transportation, Treasury, Housing and Urban Development, the Judiciary, the District of Columbia

5. Energy and water development

6. Foreign operations, export financing, and related programs

7. Homeland Security

8. Interior, Environment, and related agencies

9. Labor, Health and Human Services, and Education

10. Military Quality of Life and Veterans Affairs

All appropriations bills originate in the House; after the House Appropriations Committee has reported the bills to the full House, and after the full House has passed each measure, the Senate Appropriations Committee takes its turn revising the House version. After Senate subcommittee work has been completed on the House bills, the Senate Appropriations Committee marks up its own versions of the bills and reports them to the Senate for floor action.

Congress created separate House and Senate budget committees during the 1970s to oversee the budget process. The Budget and Impoundment Act of 1974 required Congress to set a maximum spending figure for the total budget and for each of several broad funding categories based on projections of future revenue. These figures are prepared by the Congressional Budget Office (CBO), which reports to Congress, and the OMB, which reports to the president. When the CBO and the OMB differ widely on estimates, as has happened frequently in recent years, Congress tends to side with its own agency. The House and Senate budget committees may require cuts in spending to ensure that the overall budget targets can be reached. Eventually, the House and Senate must reconcile their competing versions of the budget and secure additional votes from their members for approval of the final budget bill, which is then presented to the president for signature.

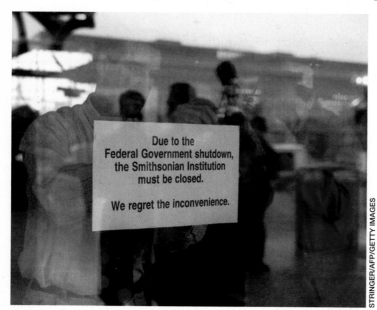

The Smithsonian Institution was among many government sites that were forced to close during the 1995 government shutdown.

All these legislative obstacles must be navigated over a period of eight months, extending from the first Monday in February (when the president's budget proposal is delivered to Congress) through October 1 (when the new fiscal year begins). If Congress and the president cannot agree on a final budget over this period of time, Congress may be forced to pass "continuing resolutions" to allow the government to keep running while final budget negotiations continue.[6] Occasionally, Congress and the president are at such loggerheads that a budget showdown occurs. In late 1995, the Republican Congress, led by House Speaker Newt Gingrich, insisted that President Bill Clinton sign a budget bill with spending cuts that Clinton's administration had strenuously opposed. When Congress refused to keep passing continuing resolutions, the resulting impasse led to two government shutdowns totaling twenty-seven days, during which all federal government institutions and buildings were forced to close.[7] Even after congressional leaders buckled under to the White House and reopened the government in January 1996, the fiscal year 1996 budget was not fully enacted until April 24, 1996, almost six months late.

Even though the Senate and House budget committees have brought more fiscal restraint to the budget process, some within and outside Congress attempted to introduce bolder budgetary reforms in response to the $200 billion deficits of the mid-1980s. The Gramm-Rudman-Hollings Act of 1985 set annual targets for reducing the deficit and required the General Accounting Office (GAO) to determine whether automatic spending cuts would take effect if Congress passed budgets that missed the established deficit target. In 1986, the Supreme Court struck down the act as unconstitutional because the GAO, accountable only to Congress, could not legally perform what were essentially "executive" acts.[8] The Budget Enforcement Act of 1990 set deficit targets that could be adjusted due to unforeseen economic changes; however, the act did not compensate for unexpected spending increases by requiring offsetting cuts elsewhere.

Of course, the central problem of the budget process—that it allows the federal government to spend more money than it takes in—remained in place even with such reforms. In recent years, Congress has debated passing a balanced budget amendment to the Constitution, which would require that annual federal spending be kept at or below revenue collected during the year. Proponents of the amendment argue that it would force free-spending lawmakers to become accountable: Just as many taxpayers must live off their income (or even considerably less), the government should be expected to do likewise. Opponents of the amendment counter that the government—in accordance with Keynesian principles—might want to engage in deficit spending during times of recession as a method of economic stimulation. They also note that the federal government must be able to spend freely to defend the national security of the United States, even if that means running up large deficits. (Although recent versions of the amendment would allow Congress to waive the requirement in case of war or military conflict, critics argue that even more flexibility is necessary.) The Balanced Budget Amendment has been passed in one house but defeated in the other on five separate occasions since 1982. In 1995 and again in 1997, the amendment failed by a single vote in the U.S. Senate.

Taxation Policy

Taxation policies tend to fall into one of two general categories. **Redistributive tax policies** aim to provide a social safety net to meet the minimum physical needs of citizens. Such policies accomplish this by following Robin Hood's principle of "taking from the rich and giving to the poor." For example, taxes that are channeled directly into public assistance programs are redistributive. **Distributive tax policies**, on the other hand, are intended to promote the interests of all economic classes equally. Taxes that are directed toward the maintenance of national parks or the national highway system theoretically benefit all citizens.

All governments need revenue to pay the salaries of government workers and to fund its various activities. In July 1789, just four months after the creation of a new government, Congress passed its first revenue-raising bill: Specifically, it levied **tariffs**, which are taxes on imported foreign goods. Up until the Civil War, tariffs provided approximately 90 percent of the federal government's revenue; yet as that war evolved into a long-lasting conflict, the Union needed far greater revenues than even high tariffs could provide. The exponential growth of the federal government after the Civil War exacerbated these demands further. Thus, in the late nineteenth and early twentieth centuries, the federal government was forced to look elsewhere for major sources of funding. Eventually, it started to draw more heavily on internal sources of revenue, including payroll taxes, corporate income taxes, and individual income taxes.

★ LO
Understand the different categories of tax policy and the evolution of tax policy in American history

Redistributive tax policies
Taxation policies that aim to provide a social safety net to meet the minimum physical needs of citizens.

Distributive tax policies
Taxation policies intended to promote the interests of all classes equally.

Tariff
A tax on imported goods, charged at the time the goods are received in port.

The Sixteenth Amendment to the U.S. Constitution authorizes Congress to tax an individual's increase in wealth, whether that wealth comes from wages, benefits, bonuses, or any other form of income. The fairness of individual income taxes, which now provide nearly half of all revenue that flows into the U.S. treasury, remains a subject of contentious debate. The federal government has traditionally imposed a **progressive tax** on incomes. With a progressive tax, the tax rate on an individual's income increases as the amount of income gets larger. Although President Reagan signed tax reform legislation in 1986 to cut top rates and close various loopholes, the personal income tax system still remained mostly progressive. In 2010 the tax system featured rates that go up in several stages to a high of 35 percent for all wages earned over $373,650. Conversely, a tax that charges all individuals the same amount, regardless of income, is called a **regressive tax** because it exacts a larger percentage of income from the lower-wage earner than it does from the high-income earner. Most state sales taxes are regressive because they apply equally to every purchaser: For example, both a poor person and a wealthy person pay the same amount of sales tax for a gallon of gasoline, but that amount constitutes a higher percentage of the poor person's income.

Some people confuse regressive taxes with **flat taxes**. Unlike regressive taxes, flat taxes tax all entities at the same rate *as a proportion of income*. Thus, with a flat tax, a rich person may pay far more in total taxes than a poor person, although the two are still being taxed at the same percentage rate. In 1996 and 2000, presidential candidate Steve Forbes proposed that the federal government impose a flat tax of 15 percent on all income earned in the United States. Forbes argued that such a system would spread the tax burden more evenly, stop penalizing Americans for working harder to earn more, and dramatically simplify the current system.[9] Forbes's proposals have not fared well in the political arena; currently, neither of the two major parties is putting its weight behind a truly flat income tax for Americans.

During the past century, Congress has also imposed corporate income taxes, which today make up just less than 10 percent of the government's revenues. Other important revenue sources include federal taxes on gasoline, communications services, estates, large financial gifts, and customs duties. And if these revenue sources fall short of projected expenditures in the form of a deficit, the federal government must make up the difference by borrowing money in the form of issuing U.S. savings bonds, treasury bills, and the like.

Americans commonly complain about the high taxes they pay, and politicians frown on tax increases and support tax cuts for that very reason. Despite all the complaints about high taxes, Americans' tax burden is quite low when compared with the tax burdens of people in other developed countries. Although U.S. citizens pay an income tax rate somewhere between 10 percent and 35 percent, citizens of Sweden pay twice that amount—between 33 percent and 60 percent of their income—to the Swedish government. Taxes paid by citizens in France, Germany, and Great Britain also tend to be higher (as a percentage of their income) than those paid by citizens of the United States.

Progressive tax
A tax whose effective rate on an individual's income increases as the person's income rises.

Regressive tax
A tax that charges individuals the same amount, regardless of income.

GLEN DAVIS/FORBES

In his 2005 book, two-time presidential candidate Steve Forbes argued for a simplified flat tax form that would be the size of an index card.

Flat tax
A tax policy that draws money from all entities at the same proportion of their income.

"What about Us?" The Chinese Reaction to the U.S. Fiscal Stimulus Plan

When Congress approved a $787 billion fiscal stimulus plan in early 2009, the impact of that policy was felt worldwide. On the positive side, if the Obama administration's Keynesian approach to the economic crisis helped solve the ills of the global economy as well, so much the better from the perspective of America's many trading partners. On the other hand, some countries quickly learned that the devil was in the details: The stimulus plan specifically required that all spending on public works and building projects use only U.S.-made goods such as iron and steel. Exceptions to that rule kicked in only when the United States was already obligated to accept foreign-made goods, under multilateral and bilateral trade pacts—thus Canada, the European Union, and Japan could still import goods for use under the stimulus plan. Yet what about other countries like India, Brazil, Russia, and China? According to China's official news agency, Xinhua ("China View"), the "Buy American" requirement of the U.S. economic stimulus package amounts to trade protectionism that could actually harm the world economy instead of helping it:

Increased borrowing by the United States to fund its massive stimulus package could cause the depreciation of U.S. dollar-denominated assets, Chinese economists have told [news agency] Xinhua. Being the largest holder of U.S. Treasury securities, China has reason to be concerned about that possible depreciation, the economists said. The $787 billion stimulus bill, the American Recovery and Reinvestment Act, is designed to jolt the ailing U.S. economy by providing government spending and tax cuts for both individuals and businesses . . . but trade protectionism will also cause catastrophic effects to some poor countries, making the current financial crisis one of a humanitarian crisis as well. . . .

Source: China View, February 18, 2009 (http://www.chinaview.cn).

Of course, such comparisons are not altogether fair; for example, Sweden, as part of its welfare system, provides all its citizens with an extensive tax-funded public child care system, dental care, and a ceiling on health care costs. England's tax-funded national health care service offers its citizens "free" services as well.

Spending Policies: Dividing the Pie

Budget surpluses are a rarity in modern American politics because the federal government has demonstrated time and again its capacity to spend taxpayer money. Government spending topped $3.7 trillion in fiscal year 2010 alone. Although the president is legally responsible for proposing budgets and has the power to veto spending decisions, Article I of the Constitution grants Congress exclusive power to lay and collect duties "to pay the debts and provide for the common defense and general welfare of the United States." In reality, Congress allots funds from the U.S. treasury to federal departments and agencies and then gives them **budget authority**, which allows them to incur obligations to spend or lend that money. Budget authority for a fiscal year is essentially like permission for an agency to enter a contract. It is not the same thing as how much the agency will spend in that fiscal year; that amount is called **outlays**.

★ LO

Assess the differences between mandatory and discretionary spending by government

Budget authority
The power of federal departments and agencies to incur obligations to spend or lend money.

Outlays
The money federal departments or agencies actually spend in a given fiscal year.

Mandatory spending
Federal government spending that is not controlled by annual budget decisions; includes entitlements such as Medicare and Social Security.

Discretionary spending
Forms of federal government spending that Congress can modify or eliminate in any given year, including spending on education, the environment, and national defense.

Where does taxpayer money go? The truth about government spending might surprise you. Spending tends to fall into two general categories. **Mandatory spending** refers to spending not controlled by annual budget decisions; these funds are automatically obligated by virtue of previously enacted laws and may not be modified by annual budget decisions (although they can be modified by repeal or modification of the original legislation). Most mandatory spending occurs in the form of entitlements: government spending such as Social Security, Medicare (national health insurance for seniors), and veterans benefits that must be paid to anyone meeting specific eligibility requirements. President Franklin Roosevelt's New Deal programs and President Lyndon Johnson's Great Society programs substantially expanded the number of entitlements, forcing future lawmakers to grapple with those entitlements when they considered reforms of their own. Since 1995, nearly two thirds of all government spending has been mandatory, almost double the percentage of mandatory spending outlays of the early 1960s (see Figure 16.1).

Discretionary spending encompasses all those spending categories that Congress does have the power to modify or eliminate in a given year. Budgeting

FIGURE 16.1 Where Do Federal Tax Dollars Come From and Where Do They Go?

Mandatory spending (required by law) represents such a large percentage of the budget (approximately two thirds of all government spending) that lawmakers often complain that their hands are tied as they wrestle with ways to cut costs. Unlike most spending on our national defense, which Congress authorizes each year at its discretion, entitlements such as Social Security, Medicare, and the food stamp program are examples of mandatory spending categories. The two pie charts shown here illustrate sources of federal revenues and the allocation of federal spending in fiscal year 2010.

Federal Revenues—FY 2010

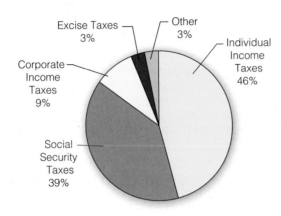

Excise Taxes 3%
Other 3%
Individual Income Taxes 46%
Corporate Income Taxes 9%
Social Security Taxes 39%

Federal Spending—FY 2010

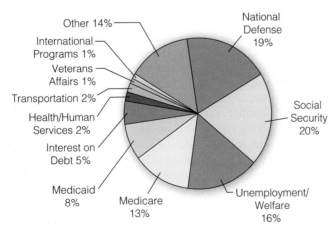

Other 14%
International Programs 1%
Veterans Affairs 1%
Transportation 2%
Health/Human Services 2%
Interest on Debt 5%
Medicaid 8%
Medicare 13%
National Defense 19%
Social Security 20%
Unemployment/ Welfare 16%

Source: Budget of the U.S. Government Fiscal Year 2011, Historical Tables, published by the Executive Office of the President.

is normally a give-and-take process between Congress and the president concerning the most appropriate levels of discretionary spending. Most federal spending on education, the environment, and national defense is based on discretionary spending outlays. When an administration's critics accuse the president of not being fiscally conservative enough with government spending, their criticisms usually focus on government spending as a whole; in fairness, however, only discretionary spending really lies within the president's immediate influence. In the eight years the Clinton administration was responsible for the federal budget (1994 through 2001), discretionary spending increased by an annual average of 3.4 percent; during the George W. Bush administration, discretionary spending increased by an average of 10.5 percent annually.

Year in and year out, one particular mandatory spending category—Social Security spending—tops all the other categories. In fiscal year 2008, the federal government spent $608 billion on the program, and Social Security expenditures in excess of $700 billion are anticipated in future years. Among the discretionary program outlays, national defense has traditionally constituted the largest part of the budget. In 1962, the federal government allotted $52.3 billion to defense, almost ten times the amount earmarked to any other discretionary program category. Nearly a half century later, in 2009, over $660 billion was allotted to national defense. The growth in discretionary spending during the past decade can be attributed in part to the George W. Bush administration's desire to increase spending on defense and homeland security in the wake of the terrorist attacks of September 11, 2001, and the Obama administration's willingness to continue most of those same defense policies. Increases in discretionary spending during the first year of the Obama administration were also influenced by the $787 billion stimulus plan Congress passed to jumpstart the economy.

Theories and Practice in Monetary Policy

Monetary policy is the means by which the government controls the supply and price of money in the economy. Although this may seem like a nonpolitical, technical function, the exercise of monetary policy can have profound implications on unemployment rates and inflation and thus is the focus of considerable political interest.

With few exceptions, the **Federal Reserve System**, which is headed by the **Federal Reserve Board** ("the Fed"), determines monetary policy in the United States. Since 1913, this independent agency has acted as the nation's central bank, supervising and regulating all of the nation's banks and providing financial information to the public. In addition to the Federal Reserve Board, Congress established twelve nonprofit Federal Reserve Banks to serve as the operating arms of the central banking system. By law, all "member banks" in the United States (which includes all national banks and many state banks) must maintain fractional reserves—a portion of their deposits that must be kept on hand or at the Fed to satisfy any demands for withdrawal. (Most fractional reserves are kept in accounts at the Federal Reserve Banks.) The Federal Reserve Banks in turn issue stock and pay dividends to member banks as partial compensation for the lack of interest they pay on member banks' required reserves. The Federal Reserve Board sets all rules and regulations for the Federal Reserve Banks.[10]

Perhaps the single most important responsibility of the Federal Reserve is to set the **discount rate** that all member banks and other depository institutions

★ LO Understand the origins and development of the Federal Reserve System in the United States

Monetary policy
Regulation of the money supply and interest rates by a central bank, such as the U.S. Federal Reserve Board, in order to control inflation and stabilize the currency.

Federal Reserve System
The central banking system of the United States, which controls the nation's money supply.

Federal Reserve Board
The Federal Reserve System's Board of Governors, which votes on monetary policy in the United States, supervises the nation's banks by setting rules for the twelve Federal Reserve Banks, and engages in open market operations.

Discount rate
The rate (expressed as a percentage) that all Federal Reserve member banks and other depository institutions will be charged by the Federal Reserve Banks to borrow short-term funds.

will be charged to borrow short-term funds. A high discount rate makes it more expensive for member banks to borrow money from the Federal Reserve Banks but more profitable for banks to lend money (because they'll secure greater interest on their investment). The opposite is true when the Federal Reserve lowers the discount rate: Banks are more apt to borrow money because it is cheaper, whereas lending money to others becomes less profitable. A second important function of the Federal Reserve is engaging in **open market operations**, in which it buys and sells government securities as a means of controlling the national money supply; buying bonds increases the amount of money in circulation, whereas selling has the opposite effect. Finally, the Federal Reserve sets the **reserve requirements** of member banks, determining the minimum liquid assets each bank must keep on hand to back customer loans. Any of these actions has the effect of either tightening or loosening the overall money supply.

In recent years, it has become common for investors to eagerly anticipate the Federal Reserve's next announcement that it plans to adjust the interest rate up or down.[11] Although hardly an exact science, the Federal Reserve's setting of a new discount rate can affect the economy in profoundly important ways. Why would the Federal Reserve choose to raise the discount rate? The primary goal of the Federal Reserve is to stabilize the economy and prevent dangerously wide fluctuations that can upset the economy. Although politicians may benefit in the short run from a quickly growing economy, the Federal Reserve may fear the eventual onset of high inflation. Under such circumstances, it may seek to tighten the money supply (the total amount of money available in the economy at a particular point in time) by increasing the discount rate. Such a move may be politically unpopular because interest rates throughout the economy tend to rise along with the discount rate, making it harder for individuals to borrow money for houses and consumer goods. Investments by businesses may similarly be curtailed.

On the flip side, the Federal Reserve may choose to lower the discount rate as a way to stimulate investment and spur the economy forward. Lower interest rates allow individuals to borrow and invest more for consumer goods and real estate, and businesses can borrow more money for capital investment. Some economists believe lower interest rates also keep unemployment at a minimum because businesses are better able to maximize their production capacity.

When Congress enacted the Federal Reserve Act in 1913, it sought to ensure that the Federal Reserve could act independently of partisan political considerations, which often demand short-term fixes to the economy. Each of the Fed's seven members serves a term of fourteen years. Once appointed and confirmed, a board member may not be removed from office except through a cumbersome impeachment process for serious criminal violations. The president also determines (with the consent of the Senate) who will serve as Federal Reserve chair for a period of four years, although in practice the chair is often reappointed several times.

Few officials in history have faced a more daunting challenge than Ben Bernanke, the current Federal Reserve Chair who was first appointed by President George W. Bush in January 2006. Bernanke replaced Alan Greenspan, the legendary chairman who presided over an unprecedented period of high economic growth and low inflation during his nineteen years at the helm of the Fed.

Bernanke's challenge grew significantly in late 2008 when, during his first term as Federal Reserve Chairman, he presided over the biggest economic

Open market operations
The buying and selling of government securities by the Federal Reserve Board as a means of controlling the national money supply.

Reserve requirement
The minimum liquid assets each bank must keep on hand to back customer loans.

Hurricane Relief That Calls for a "Hands-on" President

As an overall matter, the president provides the broad direction of economic policy but leaves it to agency heads and bureaucracies to see that the policy is carried out effectively. Of course, disaster relief is one exception to that rule. When nature strikes with harsh consequences, the nation wants to know that its president is on the scene, not leaving FEMA workers and other subordinates to offer sympathy to the victims. Two presidents, both of whom hailed from Texas, learned that lesson the hard way.

On September 5, 1965, Hurricane Betsy, a category 4 storm with winds in excess of 150 miles per hour, slammed into Louisiana. New Orleans was hit especially hard, as three quarters of the city was left underwater. President Lyndon B. Johnson followed coverage of the storm from his office in Washington, DC. Preparing for two busy days ahead in the nation's capital, he was not inclined to visit the Gulf Coast. That all changed after Senator Russell Long (D-LA) and other lawmakers from the region urged the president to come immediately to New Orleans to survey the damage. Senator Long in particular felt that Johnson must reach out to citizens and give a human face to the federal government. Heeding the advice, Johnson hurried to New

Orleans; his motorcade stopped repeatedly along the water-swept streets, allowing the president to personally reach out to the storm's victims. "I want them to know they're loved," LBJ said at the time. This was one instance in which the president's personal touch wasn't just nice. It was necessary.

On August 30, 2005, Hurricane Katrina, also a category 4 storm with winds of up to 175 miles per hour, barreled into Louisiana and southern Mississippi. The levees protecting New Orleans were once again breached, but this storm proved among the deadliest ever, as more than 1,300 fatalities and over $100 billion in damage were attributed to Katrina. At the time the storm hit, President Bush was vacationing at his ranch in Crawford, Texas. Returning to Washington, DC, in the days immediately following the hurricane, President Bush was captured by one photographer surveying the damage from Air Force One as it passed overhead on its way to the nation's capital. Many found the photograph troubling, as it seemed to present an image of a president out of touch with what was happening below. Eventually, Bush did visit New Orleans, and he too reached out to the victims. Like LBJ, Bush had failed to see right away that entrusting subordinates to on-site activities is never enough in the context of natural disasters. At least in this context, policy administration requires a human face—that of the president of the United States.

---

collapse since the Great Depression. Bernanke approached the crisis by proposing initiatives designed to save the world economy rather than simply to shape U.S. monetary policy. Under his leadership the Federal Reserve Bank ratcheted down interest rates to zero; lent money to mutual funds, hedge funds, foreign banks, investment banks, manufacturers, insurers, and other borrowers; jump-started stalled credit markets and revolutionized housing finance in the United States by purchasing mortgage bonds in bulk. *Time* magazine named Bernanke its "Person of the Year" in 2009 for these efforts, and President Obama reappointed Bernanke to a second term in 2010, though not without overcoming resistance from some senators who feared the Federal Reserve Bank had grown too powerful under Bernanke's leadership.

As is the case with the government's financial policy, its choice of monetary policy can significantly affect the overall direction of the nation's economy. Still, not all sectors will be affected evenly by these policies. A general rise in interest rates, for example, may deflate the housing market but

A New Orleans neighborhood destroyed by Hurricane Katrina.

leave other sectors relatively unaffected. Thus, in discussing overall economic policy, it is sometimes useful to focus on more specific policy areas that shed light on how government intervention in public policy matters sometimes makes a difference. Though numerous sectors of the economy offer opportunities for analysis, the remainder of this chapter focuses on a topic that continues to challenge federal and state officials to consider innovative policy solutions: emergency and disaster relief policy.

Emergency and Disaster Relief Policy

Define and ★ LO assess the role that FEMA plays in assisting the victims of natural disasters

The U.S. Federal Emergency Management Agency (FEMA) has existed in one form or another for more than two centuries, providing relief after disasters that leave citizens homeless, penniless, or in need of significant medical care. Whenever the president of the United States declares a state of emergency in some affected geographic region, FEMA is able to exercise its power to coordinate federal relief efforts and offer assistance to individuals and governments to help them rebuild homes, businesses, and public facilities.

Until quite recently, many Americans may have taken FEMA's role for granted; that changed as a result of the events following Hurricane Katrina's ravaging of the Gulf Coast in August 2005. The failure of President George W. Bush to pay an immediate visit to the areas in southern Louisiana and Mississippi most affected by the hurricane led to a precipitous drop in his approval ratings. FEMA Director Michael Brown also came under intense scrutiny; Brown was criticized both for FEMA's slow response to the disaster and for his own apparent disconnect with FEMA's on-site activities. (Brown resigned within weeks of the disaster.) Three years later, in September 2008, Hurricane Ike bore down on the Texas coast near Galveston, where it was destined to become the third costliest hurricane in U.S. history. This time federal officials were conscious of the role that citizens have come to expect the federal government to play in attending to damaged areas and in providing emergency relief to the victims of disasters.

Perhaps the most controversial issue facing administrations responsible for disaster relief concerns whether they should attempt to rebuild homes and infrastructure in stricken areas that are just as likely to experience similar disasters in the future. Critics of FEMA claim that bureaucratic involvement at taxpayer expense increases the likelihood that sentimental value will affect the agency's decision making; they argue that if private companies were required to carry out the duties of FEMA, reconstruction would occur only in safer areas. This issue is likely to reemerge in the years to come as officials determine the extent to which government subsidies should help to rebuild New Orleans, much of which remains susceptible to hurricane damage in the future. By the end of 2005, FEMA had already distributed the first $20 million installment of a $120 million community disaster loan to the city of New Orleans.

Making the Connection

Major economic crises serve to provide an unexpected jolt to the American political system. When such crises occur, political officials must revisit old understandings and assumptions about economic policymaking, or risk being perceived as defending the very same economic interests that contributed to and exacerbated the current economic disaster. In 1933 and 2009, new presidents and their newly established administrations targeted the economic elites of Wall Street that had benefitted financially at the expense of millions of average citizens and their modest savings. The "old rules" no longer worked.

The Roosevelt administration helped push through two major pieces of legislation (the Securities Act of 1933 and the Securities Exchange Act of 1934) that, for the first time in history, held corporate financiers liable whenever they provided false information or traded on inside information not available to the public. More than three quarters of a century later, the Obama administration and the Democrat-controlled Congress passed major legislation to reduce taxpayer-funded bailouts of financial institutions, restrict executive compensation, regulate corporate responsibility, and offer new protection for consumers. The preference so many Americans normally express for capitalism in the abstract gave way in both these cases to new public demands that the government hold Wall Street and its financial institutions accountable. Economic policymaking accounts for these new political realities when such crises arise; the public expects nothing less.

Former Fed Chairman Greenspan: A Legacy of Forcefulness

When he was first approached in 1987 about the possibility of becoming the chairman of the Federal Reserve Board, Alan Greenspan wasn't interested. As an economist working in New York, Greenspan preferred more mechanical types of economic analysis that drew on hard accounting principles, and he viewed the central task of the Federal Reserve—to make economic predictions—as a near impossibility. But he eventually accepted the position when President Reagan offered it to him, and Greenspan's emphasis on low interest rates during his nearly nineteen years in the position helped make him the most renowned Fed chairman in history. It even earned him a share of credit for an economic recovery that stretched throughout the 1990s with inflation rates and interest rates near record lows.

In fact, Greenspan became such a respected figure that even a simple appearance by him before Congress became a market-shifting event. For example, immediately after President Clinton in 1993 unveiled his economic plan aimed at deficit reduction, Greenspan told the Senate Banking Committee that Clinton's plan was both "serious" and "credible." Within a week of that endorsement, long-term interest rates began to fall, much to the delight of Clinton administration officials. Aware of his impact, Greenspan took great care to avoid offering sound bites that might be misinterpreted in the media. Indeed, he was often accused of using "constructive ambiguity" to promote incomprehensibility (and no doubt a degree of mystery) about his own opinions.

Greenspan was a cult figure in Washington, DC, in the 1980s and 1990s; yet as with all such figures, the passage of time provides new perspectives that are not all positive. In congressional testimony he provided in 2008, Greenspan acknowledged that he had been "partially wrong" in opposing the regulation of derivatives and lending institutions. Democratic members of Congress complained that by supporting President George W. Bush's proposal to privatize social security, Greenspan showed he was less than independent. Nobel Prize–winning economist (and *New York Times* columnist) Paul Krugman agreed, arguing that Greenspan's support for Bush betrayed the trust normally placed in a Federal Reserve chairman. Regardless, Greenspan's legacy as a dominant figure in economic policymaking is not likely to be forgotten anytime soon.

On www.cengage.com/dautrich/americangovernmentbrief/2e, find the Politics Interactive link for a detailed discussion of the challenges that faced the current Federal Reserve chairman, Ben Bernanke, and how they differ from the challenges faced by Greenspan. Did the economic crisis that began in 2007 fundamentally alter the role played by the modern Federal Reserve chairman? Must the Fed chair be a more active figure in the American political system today? You will also find information to help you understand the modern Federal Reserve Board that Alan Greenspan shaped over two decades as well as historical, popular, and global perspectives on the Fed.

Chapter Summary

★ SUMMARIZING WHAT YOU HAVE LEARNED ★

★ An Overview of the Policymaking Process

- The policymaking process generally unfolds in five stages: a recognition/definition stage, a formulation stage, an adoption stage, an implementation stage, and an evaluation stage.

★ Theories and Practice in Fiscal Policy

- Fiscal policy is concerned with the raising of revenue through taxation and the spending of whatever revenue has been generated. The federal budget, which lays out a comprehensive plan of government spending, is the primary means by which government carries out fiscal policy.

- Laissez-faire capitalism, which favors minimal government interference in the economy, dominated the U.S. economy for much of the eighteenth and nineteenth centuries; however, beginning in the 1930s, the government began to apply the principles of Keynesian economic theory, which favors government spending during difficult economic times. During the past quarter century, some presidents have turned to supply-side economics, which favors cutting taxes as a way of increasing economic productivity.

- The most significant indicators of U.S. economic success or failure include the nation's gross domestic product, the consumer price index, the unemployment rate, the budget deficit, and the Dow Jones Industrial Stock Average.

- Today's budget-making process is dominated by the president, who proposes an initial budget that will serve as the framework for all budget negotiations. Congress responds initially through its appropriations and budget committees, which in turn formulate budget proposals based on its own projections for future revenue. Occasionally, Congress and the president struggle to find a compromise, and in some extreme cases, the federal government has been forced to shut down until some compromise can be reached.

- Taxation policies may be redistributive (benefiting the poor at the expense of the rich) or distributive (promoting the interests of all economic classes equally).

- A large percentage of taxpayer funds goes to mandatory spending (usually in the form of entitlements such as Medicare and Social Security) that is unaffected by annual budget decisions. Discretionary spending categories include defense, education, and the environment.

★ Theories and Practice in Monetary Policy

- The Federal Reserve supervises the nation's monetary policy by setting the discount rate that its Federal Reserve Banks may charge member banks to receive loans and by determining the minimum assets banks must keep in hand, called the reserve requirements. When the Federal Reserve lowers the discount rate, it may stimulate economic investment, but it risks setting off higher inflation rates.

★ Emergency and Disaster Relief Policy

- The thorny politics of natural disaster relief has also provided a challenge to federal officials.

CourseMate

Key Terms

Budget authority (p. 431)

Budget deficit (p. 425)

Budget surplus (p. 425)

Consumer price index (CPI) (p. 424)

Discount rate (p. 434)

Discretionary spending (p. 432)

Distributive tax policies (p. 429)

Federal Reserve Board (p. 434)

Federal Reserve System (p. 434)

Fiscal policy (p. 423)

Flat tax (p. 430)

Gross domestic product (GDP) (p. 424)

Inflation (p. 423)

Keynesian economic theory (p. 424)

Laissez-faire economics (p. 423)

Mandatory spending (p. 432)

Monetary policy (p. 434)

National debt (p. 425)

Open market operations (p. 435)

Outlays (p. 431)

Progressive tax (p. 430)

Public policy (p. 422)

Recession (p. 424)

Redistributive tax policies (p. 429)

Regressive tax (p. 430)

Reserve requirement (p. 435)

Supply-side economics (p. 424)

Tariff (p. 429)

Resources

Books

Dye, Thomas. *Understanding Public Policy.* New York: Prentice Hall, 2001.

Forbes, Steve. *Flat Tax Revolution: Using a Postcard to Abolish the IRS.* New York: Regnery, 2005.

Greider, William. *Secrets of the Temple: How the Federal Reserve Runs the Country.* New York: Simon & Schuster, 1989.

Kingdon, John. *Agendas, Alternatives and Public Policies*, 2nd ed. New York: Addison-Wesley, 1997.

Phillips, Kevin. *Bad Money: Reckless Finance, Failed Politics, and the Global Crisis in American Capitalism.* New York: Viking Adult, 2008.

Stone, Deborah. *Policy Paradox: The Art of Political Decision Making*, rev. ed. New York: W. W. Norton, 2001.

Weisman, Steven R. *The Great Tax Wars: Lincoln to Wilson—The Fierce Battles over Money and Power That Transformed a Nation.* New York: Simon & Schuster, 2002.

Internet Sources

http://www.federalreserve.org (the official site of the Federal Reserve Board).

http://www.fema.gov (the official site of the Federal Emergency Management Agency; includes a history of the agency, its strategic plan, and information about active disasters and emergencies).

http://www.atr.org/ (the official site for Americans for Tax Reform, one of the most influential organizations in the country pushing for lower taxes).

NOW President Barack Obama, celebrating passage of comprehensive health care reform on March 23, 2010.

JEWEL SAMAD/AFP/GETTY IMAGES

THEN President Theodore Roosevelt, at Yosemite Park.

CORBIS

NOW &THEN

When a President Scales Back His Goals to Achieve Major Social Policy Reforms

The problem had been festering for decades. To address it, the energetic young president demanded sweeping, vigorous policy reforms. Although leaders of both parties conceded the need for some degree of change, the president's proposals soon met with considerable skepticism in Congress. Even some members of the president's own party feared he was trying to do too much too soon. As a result, the policy-making process was suspended in legislative gridlock. With the window for comprehensive reform starting to close, the president considered various compromises. In the end, a more modest version of the president's proposals would become law. The president may not have gotten all that he wanted, but what he did achieve represented a policy breakthrough, and he would get much of the credit for making it happen. By his willingness to compromise, he made this breakthrough possible.

LEARNING OBJECTIVES
★ WHAT YOU WILL LEARN ★

The Nature and Practice of Crime Policy

★ Compare and contrast the two principal models of criminal justice policymaking

The Welfare State

★ Contrast the U.S. welfare state model to that found in other Western democracies

Policies and Programs for the Poor

★ Understand the role of welfare policies in addressing the needs of the poor

The Social Security System

★ Assess the state of the Social Security system, its prospects, and reforms

Health Care Policy

★ Compare America's health care system to European systems with universal care

★ Assess efforts to overhaul the nation's health care system, including the 2010 legislation

Other Policy Areas

★ Understand the role the EPA has played in advancing national environmental policy

★ Assess education policy, including the expanded role of the federal government in requiring local schools to meet standards

★ Consider how energy policy is determined in the United States, including the mandates and programs that encourage efficiency

★ Understand the history of immigration policy in the United States and current proposals to restrict illegal immigrants

CourseMate

NOW & THEN

JEWEL SAMAD/AFP/GETTY IMAGES

NOW America's health care system had been an issue of growing national concern for decades. Spiraling costs and widespread complaints about limited access to care forced the issue to the forefront of the political agenda once again in 2009. Approaching the issue from a position of considerable political strength, President Barack Obama argued for an expansion of health insurance to cover all of the uninsured, caps on premium increases, and provisions that allowed people to retain their coverage when they left or changed jobs. In addition to universal coverage, a centerpiece of his proposed reform was the promise of a government insurance plan, known as the "public option," to compete with the corporate insurance sector to reduce costs. He soon met opposition not just from Republicans across the board, but from moderate Democrats such as Senators Max Baucus (D-MT) and Mary Landreau (D-LA). They believed the costs of universal coverage and the public option proposal made health care reform less attractive. To achieve the votes needed to overcome a Republican filibuster in the Senate, disappointed House leaders and a frustrated White House soon deferred to political reality: on March 23, 2010, President Obama signed into law health care reform legislation that followed the more moderate Senate model almost exactly: it lacked universal coverage and featured no public option. Still, the legislation amounted to a sweeping overhaul of the U.S. health care system aimed at mandating coverage and lowering costs. From the perspective of the White House, it was better to pass significant legislation that met many of the President's goals than to do nothing at all.

THEN President Theodore Roosevelt's romanticism about nature and the wilderness dated back to his days as an amateur rancher in the badlands of North Dakota during the late 1880s. As his political career progressed, he watched with frustration as conglomerate trusts abused the environment in the name of industrial progress. He believed that natural resources were like a family trust—they existed to be used, but they had to be used wisely. At the outset of his administration, Roosevelt announced that the conservation of forest and water resources would be considered a national issue of vital importance.[1] By executive order he designated many federal tracts as game reserves, and he reserved more than 150 million acres in all as national forest reserves protected from unregulated strip mining. Yet to effectively conserve resources, there was only so much the president could do without Congress; business interests had successfully lobbied the legislative branch to go slow in protecting many aspects of the environment. Roosevelt prevailed to a degree when Congress passed the Transfer Act of 1905, moving the management of forest reserves over to the Bureau of Forestry, where it became known as the U.S. Forest Service. But he was frustrated in other ways, as Congress refused his entreaties to pass laws protecting the nation's water resources. Roosevelt moved his environmental agenda forward, but he was denied more comprehensive forms of reform. So goes the plight of the nation's chief executive, who must accept significant compromises when he pushes for landmark legislation.

CORBIS

Grand policy-planning strategies are often unrealistic in a system where passing laws of any kind is so difficult. The separation of governmental powers, the involvement of interest groups at every stage of the process, and the intense media scrutiny all conspire to slow down policymaking mechanisms if not grind them to a halt. Officials must often resort to breakthroughs that fall short of their campaign promises and overall objectives.

In the 1950s, Professor Charles E. Lindblom described the domestic policymaking process as the "science of muddling through."[2] Lindblom's view challenged the prevailing rational-comprehensive model of policymaking, in which rational decision makers utilized scientific analysis and sound logic to develop public policy. Lindblom felt that this model was unrealistic because of the political and human factors involved in the process. Even landmark legislation that stands the test of time is often a product of compromises between the president, Congress, and other political factors. Political scientists Bryan Jones and Frank Baumgartner have argued that public policy can be explained by "punctuated equilibrium," in which long periods of stability are broken up by sudden and abrupt change.[3] In the case of environmental laws at the turn of the twentieth century and health care reform at the outset of the twenty-first century, big solutions to policy problems were imperfect from the president's perspective—but that didn't make them any less significant.

The term **social policy** refers to the rules, regulations, and policymaking pertaining to the quality of life, welfare, and relations of human beings in the United States. There are many different types of social policy, and in this chapter, we review some of the major ones: crime policy, welfare policy, social security policy, health care policy, environmental policy, education policy, energy policy, and immigration policy. In each instance, we will consider the evolution of social policy within the overall framework of policymaking discussed in the previous chapter.

Social policy
Rules, regulations, and policymaking pertaining to the quality of life, welfare, and relations of human beings in the United States.

Crime control model
Criminal justice policymaking model that views the controlling of criminal behavior as the system's most important function.

★ **LO**   Compare and contrast the two principal models of criminal justice policymaking

Former New York City mayor Rudolph Giuliani, seen here in 2007, campaigning for the presidency on his record of reducing the city's crime rates during the mid-1990s.

MARIO ANZUONI/REUTERS/LANDOV

The Nature and Practice of Crime Policy

Perhaps the most fundamental way modern societies manage relations among human beings residing within their jurisdictions is through the use of a comprehensive criminal justice system. Democratic systems must strike a careful balance between maintaining public order and protecting individual freedom; the rules and practices of the criminal justice system determine where and how that balance will be struck. For example, especially severe and strict forms of law enforcement could prove effective at making citizens safe but only at a very high cost in taxpayers' money and possibly some loss of individual freedom as well.

In 1968, social scientist Herbert Packer defined two different models of criminal justice policymaking: the "crime control model" and the "due process model."[4] The **crime control model** views the control of criminal behavior as the most important function of criminal justice. Packer depicts the crime control model as a type of "assembly line justice" because it tries to move cases quickly and efficiently through the system. The process requires that police and prosecutors make crucial judgments about defendants' guilt early in the process; the crime control model thus relies extensively on negotiations between defense attorneys and state prosecutors early on to avoid the uncertainty and high costs associated with a full-blown trial. In theory, the guilty will be routinely pressed to enter plea bargains, whereas the innocent should hope to see their indictments dismissed early in the process. Of course, the quick nature of this process increases the likelihood that public officials and defense attorneys will not always make the best judgments.

By contrast, in the **due process model**, the principal goal is justice, which focuses just as much on acting to protect the innocent as it does on convicting the guilty. Stressing the adversarial process and the need for hearings, the model endeavors to guarantee that all criminal justice decisions will be based on reliable information at every stage of the process, with the government forced to meet far higher standards than the accused along the way. By placing a premium on protecting the rights of individuals, some guilty defendants may go free simply because the state has not met its high burden of proving guilt "beyond a reasonable doubt."[5]

The American system of criminal justice can be characterized as a tug of war between both these models, with no-name, relatively run-of-the-mill, usually poor defendants generally falling into the crime control "assembly line," whereas bigger-name, higher-profile, and wealthy defendants are far more likely to experience the due process model.

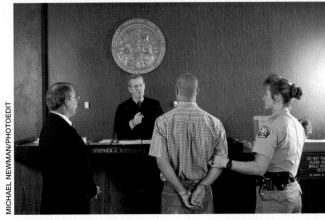

MICHAEL NEWMAN/PHOTOEDIT

A defendant being arraigned in one of the nation's criminal courtrooms.

Due process model
Criminal justice policymaking model that views the attainment of justice—which includes protection of the innocent—as the principal goal of the system.

The Welfare State

The term **welfare state** refers to a social system in which the state assumes a considerable degree of responsibility for citizens in matters of health care, employment, education, and retirement income. In its ideal form, a welfare state is expected to do more than merely guarantee a minimum level of subsistence in these matters; thus, welfare states do not simply ensure a "safety net" for their citizens. (Naturally, these welfare states require higher levels of taxation than do more strictly capitalist systems.) The actual amount of welfare provided varies widely from nation to nation. Nearly all modern welfare states fall somewhere on a spectrum between pure **capitalism** (an economic system in which all or most of the means of production are privately owned under competitive conditions) and **socialism** (an economic system in which all or most of the means of production are owned by the community as a whole). Most welfare states have this much in common: They ensure that whatever welfare is provided is done so in universal fashion. In short, they tend to cover every person who meets welfare standards as a matter of right rather than discretion.

Fiercely protective of its capitalist origins, the U.S. government vigorously resisted assuming broad welfare state functions up until the 1930s, when the

Welfare state
Social system in which the state assumes a considerable degree of responsibility for citizens in matters of health care, employment, education, and retirement income.

Capitalism
Economic system in which all or most of the means of production are privately owned under competitive conditions.

Socialism
Economic system in which all or most of the means of production are owned by the community as a whole.

Innovative Crime Policies through the Years

For as long as crimes have been committed, politicians have sought to implement public policies that address the "crime problem"—so much the better for the reelection prospects of public officials who can more rightfully claim to be "law and order" politicians who "clean up the streets" for honest citizens. In recent years, even Congress has sought its share of credit for reducing crime, passing with overwhelming bipartisan support an act prohibiting possession of guns in school zones and a federal carjacking act, among other crime-fighting initiatives. Of course, politicians disagree vehemently on the best method for fighting crime; sometimes, the innovative new methods of the moment can be relegated to the dustbin of law enforcement within a few decades.

During the mid to late nineteenth century, law enforcement agencies increasingly believed that even evil wrongdoers had the power within themselves to resist the temptation to commit crimes, as long as they embraced discipline and hard work. Thus, law enforcers

A vagrant is hauled off by city policemen as part of law enforcement's emphasis on public order maintenance.

devoted large portions of their budgets to discouraging "rowdy and undisciplined behavior," even though such minor offenses were not always committed by bad or evil people. City police officers in particular drastically increased the number of arrests they made for drunkenness and vagrancy on the theory that those smaller, less "harmful" crimes contributed to a general state of moral decline. No less notable a law enforcement official than Theodore Roosevelt, New York City police commissioner in the mid-1890s, saw police work as "a fight to clean up vice to promote the advance of civilization and decency." This emphasis on public order maintenance receded somewhat after the turn of the century, especially in the 1920s, as police officers increasingly viewed themselves as "professional crime fighters" who needed to focus on more serious offenses such as murder, rape, and burglary. "Order maintenance," by contrast, was de-emphasized.

From the 1940s through the 1970s, the theory of rehabilitation, which argued that convicted offenders could be restored to a constructive place in society by means of training, therapy, or other methods, played a dominant role in the treatment of criminal

---

★ **LO** Contrast the U.S. welfare state model to that found in other Western democracies

Great Depression exposed the harsh realities that unfettered capitalism can occasionally impose on the masses. It wasn't until the Great Society legislation of the mid-1960s that the federal government actively expanded the reach of the welfare state to include the provision of education, health care, and assistance to the poor.

Compared with other Western democracies in Europe and elsewhere that have embraced the welfare state on behalf of their citizens, the U.S. welfare state model is far less comprehensive and ambitious. Why the reluctance to go further? Welfare continues to be seen as "taking something" without contributing offenders across the nation. Most state criminal justice systems relied on indeterminate sentencing, featuring no fixed release date set by a judge, on the grounds that prisoners who knew in advance when they would be released would have little motivation to participate in treatment or therapy programs while they were incarcerated. By the 1980s, this model was increasingly questioned by scholars who challenged whether there was any clear and provable link between poverty and low self-esteem on the one hand and criminal activities on the other hand. Indeterminate sentences soon gave way to fixed and determined sentences that allowed wardens and other public officials to more effectively manage the criminal populations under their charge.

In the 1980s, a new version of an older theory gained momentum once again. In 1982, social scientists James Q. Wilson and George Kelling wrote an article titled "Broken Windows: The Police and Neighborhood Safety." In a modern spin on the public order theories advanced more than a century earlier, they argued that disorderly behavior left unregulated and unchecked signals to residents that they are and will continue to be unsafe. By contrast, quickly cleaning up vandalism, such as fixing broken windows right away, deters further petty crimes and antisocial behavior in the short run and deters major crimes in the long run. It also encourages law-abiding residents to stay put rather than flee the neighborhood. Wilson and Kelling's "broken windows" theory attracted widespread national attention in the 1980s and again in the early 1990s when New York City Mayor Rudolph Giuliani spoke of "quality of life" and "zero tolerance" in his approach to cleaning up crime in New York City. Subway fare dodgers were soon prosecuted to the full extent of the law, and New York City police also rid the streets of "squeegee men," who demanded payment for cleaning the windshields of drivers entering the city, even when the drivers did not ask for and often did not want the service provided. Sociologists today disagree over how much, if anything at all, zero tolerance contributed to the overall drop in crime in New York City and other urban centers that focused on addressing such petty offenses, as many other crime-fighting initiatives were taking place simultaneously.

CLEVE BRYANT/PHOTOEDIT

Wilson and Kelling's "broken windows" theory argued that even minor disorderly conduct, if left unregulated, signals to law-abiding residents that they will never be safe.

in return, so the notion of a state built around this premise remains objectionable to many Americans. Indeed, many Americans (and the political parties that curry favor with them) view welfare recipients as going against the grain of the work ethic and thus getting a "free ride" based on the efforts of others. Although the miserable conditions associated with the Great Depression went a long way toward debunking the belief that the poor are always responsible for their own plight, Americans are still reluctant to see the federal government install a system of social welfare similar to what has been established in many European democracies.

Realistic Options for National Service

In the early 1960s, young people in the United States who wanted to help change the world considered joining the Peace Corps, a government agency charged with "increasing international mutual understanding." More than 200,000 have taken up that call, working for the Peace Corps in 139 different countries. But for all the opportunities the Peace Corps provided for international service, it lacked an outlet to serve the United States at home. That changed in 1993 when the National Community and Service Trust Act created AmeriCorps. Since its creation, AmeriCorps has sent over a quarter of a million young people to communities in the United States to support the start-up of innovative new national programs, including City Year, Public Allies, and Teach for America. It also brought vital resources to established programs, including Boys and Girls Club, Big Brothers Big Sisters, Justicecorps, and the American Red Cross.

COURTESY OF AMERICORPS

Like any government program, AmeriCorps has its share of critics. Some have alleged that the program diverts young people participating in the program from attaining higher levels of education on their own behalf or that it delays the start of their careers. Critics also charge that AmeriCorps sends the wrong message by implying that volunteers should be paid for community service work (full-time members who complete their service earn a Segal AmeriCorps Education Award of $4,725).

For Critical Thinking and Discussion

1. Would you consider joining AmeriCorps or some other form of national service before embarking on your own career? Why or why not?

2. Should AmeriCorps "volunteers" be paid even a minimal scholarship amount?

★ LO Understand the role of welfare policies in addressing the needs of the poor

Policies and Programs for the Poor

The Great Depression created a significant change in attitudes about welfare programs and led directly to broader government involvement. New Deal programs such as the Works Progress Administration and the Federal Emergency Relief Administration provided public jobs and emergency aid. Aid to Dependent Children (later called Aid to Families with Dependent Children, or AFDC) supplemented existing state programs by providing money to poor single mothers unable to work and partake in federal jobs programs.[6] More a public charity than an entitlement, AFDC money went to the extremely poor, and its benefits were often below prevailing minimum wages.

President Lyndon Johnson's Great Society program of the mid-1960s substantially expanded federal welfare programs. As part of his administration's "war on poverty," a federal food stamps program was initiated in 1964; the federal government also gave money to community service programs such as Legal Aid, medical clinics in poor neighborhoods, and the Head Start preschool education program for disadvantaged children. The **Medicare** program was created to provide health insurance for the elderly in general, whereas **Medicaid** became the first federal program to provide limited health care services to the poor.[7]

Medicare
Federal program that provides health insurance for the elderly.

Medicaid
Federal program that provides limited health care services to the poor.

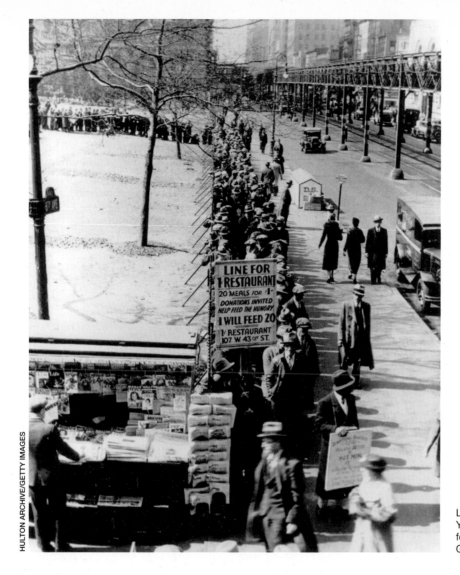

Long lines of people in New York City waited patiently for handouts during the Great Depression.

Mismanagement slowed the progress of the war on poverty; the outbreak of riots and crimes in the inner cities—where much of the antipoverty legislation was targeted—further doomed legislative support for the expansion of such programs.

Once established into law, the welfare reforms of the mid-twentieth century were not free of controversy. Activists complained that AFDC benefits were not high enough to bring poor families out of poverty, trapping them in their economic plights for the foreseeable future. Additionally, approximately 25 percent of those defined as poor by federal law were still not receiving any form of federal benefits under the current program. Conservatives were also frustrated, charging that the incentives of the welfare system encouraged poor mothers to stay home without actively seeking employment or even to have more children as a means of increasing government payments.

As a presidential candidate in 1992, Bill Clinton promised to "end welfare as we know it"; four years later, with the Republicans firmly in control of Congress, President Clinton was presented with legislation that held him to those very words. In 1996, Congress passed and Clinton signed into law the Personal Responsibility and Work Opportunity Reconciliation Act, which replaced AFDC with the TANF (Temporary Assistance to Needy Families) program. TANF devolved much of the former AFDC program back to the states, scaled back the food stamps program, and required welfare recipients to work or at least actively look for work. The law also imposed a five-year limit on receiving benefits, overthrowing the previous system of providing indefinite benefits to those who met federal eligibility requirements.[8] In its first few years, the program succeeded in decreasing state caseloads by as much as 50 percent. Still, critics charged that it penalizes the truly needy; additionally, because "last hired" individuals tend to be the first ones fired during more difficult times, many have returned to welfare since 2001, increasing caseloads during the past decade.

The Social Security System

★ LO Assess the state of the Social Security system, its prospects, and reforms

Social Security has frequently been called the "third rail" of American politics: Any politician who touches it is sure to get shocked into submission.[9] The specter of millions of older Americans living in poverty as a result of the Great Depression led to the establishment of Social Security in 1935 as a sort of national pension system. The system was originally intended to be a self-sufficient "pay-as-you-go" system: Workers and their employers would pay dedicated Social Security taxes, and these funds would then be disbursed in the form of pension payments to current retirees. During its early years, the Social Security system often ran surpluses because the ratio of workers to beneficiaries remained high. In the 1950s, Congress even broadened the system's coverage and raised minimum benefits to lower-income contributors.

Unfortunately, the severe economic strains of the 1970s, including high inflation, substantially eroded the Social Security trust fund, which contains securities redeemable to make payments to retirees whenever contributions are not sufficient to pay benefits. Minor reforms have been implemented to increase Social Security taxes and raise the retirement age, shoring up the trust fund for the time being. Still, some economists fear that the Social Security system will become weaker in the years ahead, as a greater percentage of the disproportionately large baby boom generation (those born between 1946 and 1964) reaches retirement age during the first decade of the twenty-first century.[10] By the year 2025, when all baby boomers will be eligible for Social Security, the system may face solvency issues. Through the use of tax incentives, the federal government has recently played a role in encouraging people to put aside extra savings for retirement. As a result, millions today directly invest a substantial portion of their savings in the stock market through the use of tax-favored retirement vehicles such as Individual Retirment Accounts (IRAs). Not only do such vehicles help provide an extra retirement cushion, they also have helped to ensure that a stream of investment capital continues to flow into publicly traded companies on the stock market, which in turn contribute to the well-being of the economy.

Health Care Policy

The U.S. health care system today differs in important ways from the public-run systems found in other modern industrial nations. France, Great Britain, and other European democracies have all adopted systems of **universal health care**, in which full access to health care is provided to citizens at government expense. In the United States, health care has remained a privately operated activity, in which patients secure health care insurance and enter into relationships with physicians largely outside government control. The **Patient Protection and Affordable Care Act of 2010 (PPACA)** and subsequent legislation passed by Congress (most notably the Health Care and Education Reconciliation Act of 2010) penalize some citizens who do not obtain health care insurance. Still, the recent legislation does not provide any form of public–sponsored health care plans (other than "health insurance exchanges" that organize the marketplace for the purchase of private health insurance in more cost-efficient ways), and federal laws do not assign doctors to patients. Consequently, Americans still have more choice in doctors and facilities than do citizens in most other parts of the world.

Ensuring that society's oldest and poorest citizens receive adequate health care was a primary concern of U.S. health care laws even before the 2010 legislative reforms. Since 1965, the Medicare program has provided health insurance as a Social Security benefit to retirees; amendments to the program in 2003 limited the costs of prescription drugs for seniors. More recently, the federal government extended the reach of Medicare to small, rural hospitals and facilities. The poor sometimes receive health insurance through grants to the states as part of the Medicaid program; the PPACA expanded Medicaid eligibility as well. Beginning in 2014, persons with income levels up to 133 percent of the poverty line will qualify for coverage. Additionally, federal legislation dictates the rules to be followed by **health maintenance organizations (HMOs)**, which are prepaid group practice arrangements that attempt to limit costs through flat monthly rates.[11] Yet the defining characteristic of health care in the United States—patients' reliance on private, voluntary health plans—continues with government incentives and penalties playing a significant role in the process.

Significant criticisms of the health care system in the United States remain. Most of those who do have health insurance receive it through group plans offered by their employers, and the 2010 legislation did little to reverse that reality. Thus when employees change jobs, their health insurance coverage is normally disrupted. Additionally, in 2009 one in seven Americans under sixty-five still did not have health insurance. While the PPACA is expected to significantly lower this figure, it will not guarantee universal coverage by any means.

Finally, health insurance is not the same as actual health care. Many continue to be hindered by a lack of access to primary care: More than 20 million people in the United States live in rural areas or inner-city neighborhoods that have a shortage of physicians to meet their basic health care needs.[12] Rural residents are particularly disadvantaged: According to the U.S. Department of Health and Human Services, residents of rural areas maintain the highest death rates for unintentional injuries generally and for motor-vehicle injuries specifically, due in large part to the shortage of physicians in such areas. Thus health care delivery practices will continue to be a problem, no matter how far government extends the scope of health care insurance coverage.

★ LO Compare America's health care system to European systems with universal care

★ LO Assess efforts to overhaul the nation's health care system, including the 2010 legislation

Universal health care
National health care system in which full access to health care is provided to citizens at government expense.

Patient Protection and Affordable Care Act (PPACA)
The main federal legislation passed in 2010 that overhauled the health care system by expanding Medicaid and guaranteeing health care coverage for select groups of citizens. The law was amended a week later by the Health Care and Education Reconciliation Act of 2010.

Health maintenance organization (HMO)
Prepaid group medical practice arrangement that attempts to limit health care costs through the establishment of flat monthly rates.

Other Policy Areas

Environmental Policy

★ LO Understand the role the EPA has played in advancing national environmental policy

Contemporary environmental policy was crafted piecemeal during the 1960s and early 1970s.[13] The National Environmental Policy Act of 1969 imposed restrictions on all federally funded projects that might cause damage to the environment; the 1960 Clean Water Act and the 1963 Clean Air Act spelled out specific requirements to be met by all businesses whose activities might cause pollution. The 1964 Federal Wilderness Act protects more than 650 million acres of federal land in forty-four states from logging, mining, oil and gas drilling, off-road vehicles, and further road building. Perhaps the single biggest governmental commitment to the environmental movement came with the creation of the **Environmental Protection Agency (EPA)** in 1970. The EPA coordinates all the above programs into a single regime of law enforcement; it also issues regulations spelling out the requirements of vague legislative initiatives to control the quality of the environment.[14]

Environmental Protection Agency (EPA)
Federal agency that administers and enforces all of the nation's environmental programs and spells out the requirements of legislative initiatives to control the quality of the environment.

In recent decades, the EPA has been much more active in tightening pollution standards and regulating environmental risks more closely, including those that affect wildlife as well as humans. However, the EPA was allotted a mere $10.5 billion in fiscal year 2010, considerably less than that earmarked for competing programs such as transportation ($73 billion). As long as future administrations must concern themselves with economic productivity and the cultivation of new energy sources, future EPA administrators are likely to find themselves torn between two masters: the environment and their own bosses.

Education Policy

★ LO Assess education policy, including the expanded role of the federal government in requiring local schools to meet standards

Education has traditionally been a state and local responsibility. The movement to create taxpayer-funded public schools, which began in the 1840s and gained momentum in the 1860s, was seen as a local, community responsibility. This approach to education policy helps explain the widespread variations in quality and administration of school programs across the nation: The public school systems created by many state legislatures in the mid-twentieth century were marked by harshly unequal per-pupil expenditures between white schools and segregated black schools. The federal government's involvement in education during this period occurred mainly as an outgrowth of its functions as supervisor of veterans' affairs. For example, the Servicemen's Readjustment Act of 1944, popularly known as the G.I. Bill of Rights, provided for college or vocational education for returning World War II veterans, as well as one year of unemployment compensation.

By the early 1960s, a wave of educational reform had swept Washington, DC. Following the Supreme Court's unanimous ruling in *Brown v. Board of Education* (1954) that declared racially segregated schools unconstitutional, federal legislators decided national educational problems demanded national solutions. President Lyndon Johnson's Great Society program included not only the Head Start program to assist disadvantaged preschool children but also the Elementary and Secondary Education Act of 1965, which offered the first comprehensive federal aid program for public education in the United States. Since then, the federal government has funded nearly 7 percent of public education, amounting to approximately $30 billion annually. Higher education students have been

And the Oscar Goes to . . . the Former Vice President?

Political officials will use any medium at their disposal to move issues of social policy onto the national political agenda. FDR took to the radio airwaves to build support for his social security proposal; John F. Kennedy used the live press conference to hint at a potential overhaul of the nation's immigration policy; and a slew of presidential candidates in recent years have become best-selling authors, reaching millions with their proposals to overhaul health care or education policy. However, the cinema has never been a politician's best friend, perhaps because moviegoers demand strict entertainment for the high prices they pay at the local cineplex. Yet in 2006, former Vice President Al Gore defied this conventional wisdom. Gore's documentary film, *An Inconvenient Truth*, was the centerpiece of his campaign to educate citizens about the dangers of global warning.

The idea for the documentary came from environmental activist Laurie David, who witnessed Gore's presentation at a town hall meeting. David was impressed enough to convince film director and producer Davis Guggenheim (whose credits include *24* and *NYPD Blue*) to adapt the presentation into a film. In addition to winning the 2007 Academy Award for Best Documentary film, *An Inconvenient Truth* has raised international public awareness of climate change and reenergized the environmental movement. The documentary has even been included in schools' science curricula in some foreign countries. Still, while Gore's film placed climate change squarely on the national agenda for discussion, no formal legislation was anywhere close to passage at the time this book went to press.

For Critical Thinking and Discussion

1. Why do you think the medium of film proved so effective at depicting the climate change crisis?

2. How important was it to have a former vice president as the movie's central figure? Do you think the film would have been produced without Gore's participation? Why or why not?

3. When the former vice president provided testimony to Congress, the reviews of his performance were mixed, with some Republican members of Congress expressly critical of his position. Once global warning was placed on the congressional agenda, would another spokesman have been more effective at helping to steer potential bills through Congress? Why or why not?

LAWRENCE BENDER PRODS./THE KOBAL COLLECTION/ERIC LEE

Former Vice President Al Gore, now a prominent environmental activist, lecturing about global warming.

helped indirectly by federal spending, and more directly by a federal student loan program that provides $10 billion in loans each year. If you received a student loan from a commercial bank, it may well be guaranteed by the federal government, which pays nearly $3 billion in defaulted student loans to banks each year.

The federal government's greater economic role in education has led to some sacrifice in local and state autonomy in education matters. Federal spending on local education is often accompanied by conditions that state administrators must

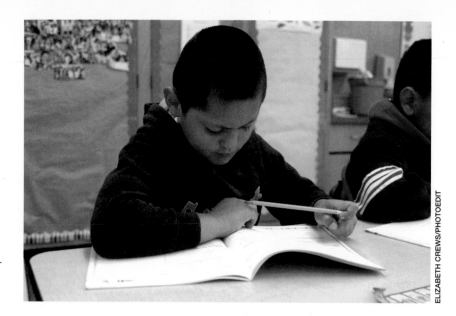

An elementary school student taking a standardized test as mandated by federal "No Child Left Behind" legislation.

ELIZABETH CREWS/PHOTOEDIT

follow. For example, amendments to the Elementary and Secondary Education Act in recent years have required public and private schools alike to offer an "individualized education program" for students with disabilities. Concerns have also been raised about the content of curricula and the quality of teaching. The states have implemented various reforms to improve standards for the training of teachers and the testing of students. In 2002, President George W. Bush signed the **No Child Left Behind Act**, which required mandatory testing of students to meet basic competencies.[15] This policy has proven controversial because it means schools with a high percentage of low-income or underprivileged children can be labeled as "failures" under the policy. Penalties for failing to meet standards include the forced hiring of tutors and other academic assistants, substantially straining the economic burdens on these schools.

No Child Left Behind Act
Federal legislation passed in 2002 that requires mandatory testing of students to meet basic competencies.

★ LO Consider how energy policy is determined in the United States, including the use of mandates and programs that encourage energy efficiency

Energy Policy

The 1973 energy crisis—which arose when Middle East oil-producing companies collectively proclaimed a six-month oil embargo on the United States—made energy a popular topic of discussion in the United States. Though Americans constitute only 5 percent of the world's population, in most years they consume more than a quarter of the world's energy. According to the Department of Energy, the United States currently receives 87 percent of its energy from fossil fuels: The largest such source is oil (40 percent), followed by natural gas (24 percent) and coal (23 percent). (Oil is primarily consumed as fuel for cars, buses, trucks, and airplanes.) The remaining 13 percent is supplied by nuclear power, hydroelectric dams, and miscellaneous renewable sources such as rain, sunlight, and wind.

Though Congress has passed numerous energy policy acts aimed at conservation and the further development of renewable energy sources, the

United States continues to lack a comprehensive long-term energy policy. The fashioning of legislation designed to reduce supply disruptions and price volatility over the long term has run into continuous political obstacles, as lawmakers balance those objectives with competing goals such as the need to protect the environment. While gasoline supply problems during the past decade have spurred calls for expanding U.S. refining capacity and transport systems for oil, national and local environmental regulations, along with local community sentiment, have created significant obstacles for policymakers hoping to implement such policies.

The 2010 Deepwater Horizon Oil Spill in the Gulf of Mexico was estimated to have covered nearly 4,000 square miles at its peak.

Critics of American energy policy often cite America's dependence on foreign oil as perhaps the most troubling problem of all—over half of the oil Americans use is imported, and the United States holds less than 2 percent of the world's oil reserves. Perhaps that explains why so many politicians continue to press for America to fund the development of domestic petroleum sources in Alaska and elsewhere. All momentum for such development was at least temporary halted, however, by the 2010 Deepwater Horizon oil spill in the

President Obama talking to fishermen affected by the 2010 oil spill in the Gulf.

Gulf of Mexico, which was caused by an explosion on an offshore oil drilling platform owned by BP, a British oil company. The explosion created a traveling oil slick in the Gulf covering an area of nearly 4,000 square miles. In the wake of the worst oil spill disaster in U.S. history, a debate over U.S. energy policy in general has been renewed once again, with America's offshore oil drilling policies coming under increasing scrutiny. During the 2008 presidential election campaign, Republican vice presidential candidate Sarah Palin, then the governor of Alaska, repeated the slogan "Drill, baby, drill" in numerous stump speeches to trumpet her support of offshore drilling. That position may not prove so popular, however, in the wake of the 2010 Deepwater Horizon oil spill in the Gulf.

Immigration Policy

The United States has long prided itself as a "nation of immigrants," and with good reason: Immigration has served as a major source of population growth and cultural change throughout much of American history. Even after the federal government began to place significant restrictions on immigration beginning in the 1920s, natives of foreign lands continued to enter the United States in significant numbers. According to the most recent figures, the United States continues to accept more immigrants as permanent residents each year than all other countries in

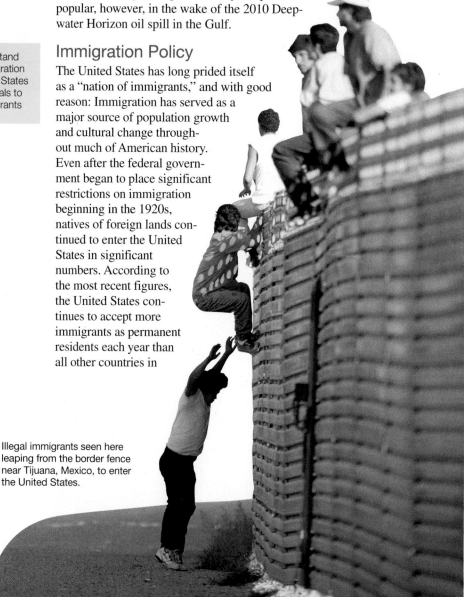

Illegal immigrants seen here leaping from the border fence near Tijuana, Mexico, to enter the United States.

AP PHOTO/LENNY IGNELZI

the world combined. Currently the foreign-born share of the U.S. population is approximately 10 percent, with the vast majority of recent immigrants (8 in 10) hailing from countries in Latin America and Asia.

While the diversity of the American people has contributed to America's strength, the assimilation of so many foreign natives into the citizenry has not been free of controversy. When specific ethnic populations emigrate in large waves, they are often subject to discrimination; language barriers contribute further to the difficulties many immigrants face in trying to gain employment or otherwise be socialized in the United States. Meanwhile, many legal immigrants have to wait years for applications to be processed.

Additionally, the ranks of illegal immigrants began to swell in the 1970s. Since the 1990s the number of illegal immigrants has outpaced the number of legal immigrants, causing public officials to wonder whether federal immigration policies are broken. Each year more than a half million people either enter the United States illegally or overstay their visas. Immigration raids have proved ineffective, netting relatively few arrests and placing the burdens of the system onto immigrant families. Undocumented aliens create numerous problems for authorities: Many receive health care from hospital emergency rooms without payment; they also tend to take jobs away from both legal immigrants and native-born Americans, increasing the resentment they suffer from the rest of the population.

Given the heated public debate on the subject, few were surprised when the state of Arizona passed its own stringent immigration law in 2010, authorizing police officers to detain anyone suspected of being in the country illegally. The law also made the failure to carry immigration documents a crime. Though the Obama administration immediately challenged the law's constitutionality in court, other states appeared ready to pass similar laws in response to the public's growing frustration over the illegal immigration problem.

In 2009 the Obama administration signaled its willingness to consider proposals to strengthen border controls and crack down on employers hiring illegal aliens, while at the same time allowing undocumented aliens to pay fines, learn English, and then possibly go to the back of the line for the opportunity to become U.S. citizens.

"GIVE ME YOUR TIRED, YOUR POOR, YOUR HUDDLED MASSES YEARNING TO BREATHE FREE, THE WRETCHED REFUSE OF YOUR TEEMING SHORE. SEND THESE, THE HOMELESS, TEMPEST-TOST TO ME, I LIFT MY LAMP BESIDE THE GOLDEN DOOR!"

© 2012 CENGAGE LEARNING

NOW & THEN

Making the Connection

Social welfare policy in the United States has been a source of continued frustration for many. This nation's status as one of the richest nations in the world over the past century might imply a responsibility on the part of the government to spread around those riches so that each person is assured at least a minimum level of subsistence and welfare, as well as the right to enjoy such public goods as clean water and clean air. At the same time, the U.S. capitalist system tends to foster a "pull yourself up by your bootstraps" culture, which is at odds with any public policy efforts leading to the systematic provision of goods and services to needy people. U.S. culture has instead traditionally emphasized a reliance on churches and other nonprofit organizations to provide that level of security. In the modern era, the U.S. government has attempted to strike a balance between these two positions to the satisfaction of few.

Prior to the New Deal, the government's role in providing social welfare was quite limited. Since the 1930s, and especially since the 1960s, the government's social welfare functions have increased substantially. Of course, innovative social welfare policies do not emerge overnight. The controversy that sur-rounds governmental welfare policies often invites as much resistance as it does cheerleading, and presidents must learn to scale back their dreams to ensure some form of victory in the short term. Theodore Roosevelt's attempt to establish landmark environmental conservation policy met with resistance in Congress; his administration managed to create 150 million acres of national forest reserves and a national forest service to look out for them, but little else. President Barack Obama entered office in 2009 with hopes of passing comprehensive health care reform featuring universal coverage and a government-run public option; by the time the smoke cleared in March 2010, his administration had managed to trans-form the system in significant ways, yet universal coverage and a "public option" were nowhere to be found in the final bills. Roosevelt and Obama—even with a generally supportive Congress on their respective sides—had to scale back their goals . . . or risk achieving nothing at all. Clearly Charles Lindblom's "science of muddling through" is a policymaking process for the patient only, even in the case of policy reforms that are considered groundbreaking in many respects.

POLITICS InterActive!

Social Security: The Third Rail of American Politics

The Social Security Act of 1935 essentially introduced U.S. citizens to the welfare state. The primary purpose of the law was to provide adequate income to American retirees at a time when an economic depression was making it difficult for many seniors to make ends meet. Social Security today has become a central feature of American work life and retirement. Without this public retirement system, more than half of America's senior citizens would have incomes below the poverty level.

The retirement portion of today's Social Security system requires American workers and their employers to provide the revenue to keep the system afloat, while payments are made to retirees. Payment benefits are based on a formula that takes into account the amount of money a retiree contributed to the system and the age at which that individual retired. Because revenues currently outpace outlays, the system today is financially healthy. Most economists agree, however, that the financial security of the Social Security system will soon be threatened because payments to Social Security recipients will start to outpace contributions to the system within the next decade. The source of this imbalance is the large population of baby boomers who are now beginning to retire, drawing money from the system rather than contributing to it. Although a number of proposals have been offered to fix this impending problem, none so far have been adopted. The administration of President George W. Bush proposed a number of measures to privatize the system, but the nation's focus on international events, a poorly performing stock market (which would be used to accomplish privatized retirement savings accounts under the Bush plan), and strong opposition from the Democrats doomed these proposals.

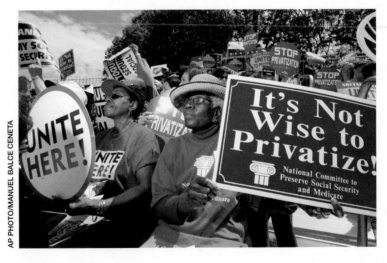

AP PHOTO/MANUEL BALCE CENETA

On www.cengage.com/dautrich/americangovernmentbrief/2e, find the Politics InterActive link for details on the politics of Social Security. Consult as well the various links that provide historical, popular, and global perspectives on the Social Security system.

Chapter Summary

★ SUMMARIZING WHAT YOU HAVE LEARNED ★

- Social policy refers to the rules, regulations, and policymaking pertaining to the quality of life, welfare, and relations of human beings in the United States. There are many different types of social policy, including crime policy, welfare policy, social security policy, health care policy, environmental policy, education policy, energy policy, and immigration policy.

★ The Nature and Practice of Crime Policy

- Democratic governments must strike a delicate balance between maintaining public order and protecting individual freedom. Especially severe and strict forms of law enforcement would make citizens safe but with a very high cost to taxpayers and possibly some loss of individual freedom as well.

★ The Welfare State

- The welfare state is a social system in which the state assumes a considerable degree of responsibility for citizens in matters of health care, employment, education, and retirement income. The actual amount of welfare provided varies widely from nation to nation. Most modern welfare states fall somewhere on a spectrum between pure capitalism and pure socialism.

- The United States generally resisted any meaningful attempt to provide welfare benefits to all citizens until the 1930s.

★ Policies and Programs for the Poor

- President Lyndon Johnson's Great Society programs of the mid-1960s further advanced welfare programs in the United States, introducing such programs as Medicare and Medicaid.

★ The Social Security System

- Social Security is a retirement benefit program for members of the U.S. workforce. Although it has provided retirement income for millions of retirees since 1935, many economists predict that the system will eventually be forced to pay out significantly more than it brings in.

- A number of proposals to privatize Social Security have been suggested; however, to date, the U.S. Congress has enacted no major policy changes, and the crisis on Wall Street in September 2008 put off all discussion of privatization for the time being.

★ Health Care Policy

- The U.S. health care system contrasts sharply with systems found in other western democracies that feature universal health care.

- Criticisms of the U.S. system focus on limitations on access and excessively high costs. The 2010 federal legislation addressed various inequities in the insurance industry, but it did not address these access-to-care issues.

★ Other Policy Areas

- Environmental policy was crafted piecemeal beginning in the 1960s; the Environmental Protection Agency (EPA) is the principal agency responsible for administering the Clean Air Act and other federal programs.

- Education has traditionally been a state and local responsibility. LBJ's Great Society of the 1960s included programs to assist disadvantaged preschool children and programs offering federal aid for public education and low-cost student loans for college.

- The United States has no comprehensive energy policy; public officials worry that with America's continued dependence on foreign oil, the nation will continue to experience supply disruptions and price volatility.

- Despite the pride Americans take in their country's position as a "nation of immigrants," the political system has struggled in its efforts to address the illegal immigrant problem, as well as issues of assimilation and discrimination.

CourseMate

Key Terms

Capitalism (p. 447)

Crime control model (p. 446)

Due process model (p. 447)

Environmental Protection Agency (EPA) (p. 454)

Health maintenance organization (HMO) (p. 453)

Medicaid (p. 450)

Medicare (p. 450)

No Child Left Behind Act (p. 456)

Patient Protection and Affordable Care Act (PPACA) (p. 453)

Socialism (p. 447)

Social policy (p. 446)

Universal health care (p. 453)

Welfare state (p. 447)

Resources

Books

Beland, Daniel. *Social Security: History and Politics from the New Deal to the Privatization Debate.* Lawrence: University Press of Kansas, 2005.

Blank, Rebecca. *It Takes a Nation: A New Agenda for Fighting Poverty.* Princeton, NJ: Princeton University Press, 1998.

Friedman, Thomas L. *Hot, Flat, and Crowded: Why We Need a Green Revolution—and How It Can Renew America.* New York: Farrar, Straus, and Giroux, 2008.

Gore, Albert, Jr. *An Inconvenient Truth: The Planetary Emergency of Global Warming and What We Can Do About It.* New York: Bloomsbury Books, 2006.

Patterson, James T. *America's Struggle Against Poverty.* Cambridge, MA: Harvard University Press, 1994.

Skocpol, Theda. *Social Policy in the United States.* Princeton, NJ: Princeton University Press, 1995.

Internet Sources

http://www.epa.gov (the official Web site of the Environmental Protection Agency, which features information on environmental projects and programs, news and events, as well as rules and regulations).

http://www.ssa.gov (the official Web site of the Social Security Administration, which includes information on services, benefits, research and data, Social Security laws, and other frequently asked questions about Social Security in the United States).

http://www.welfaretowork.org (the official Web site of the Welfare to Work Partnership, a nonpartisan group organized to help businesses hire people on public assistance).

http://www.medicare.gov (the official U.S. Web site on the Medicare program, which features information about Medicare enrollment and the Medicare Prescription Drug Improvement and Modernization Act of 2003).

18 American Foreign Policy

NOW President George W. Bush, speaking to U.S. Marines at Camp Pendleton in California.

DAVID MCNEW/GETTY IMAGES

THEN President Woodrow Wilson (in top hat) marching in a Liberty Loan Parade during World War I.

HULTON ARCHIVE/GETTY IMAGES

NOW & THEN

A Domestic Focus Yields to International Realities

During his campaign for the presidency, he repeatedly criticized previous administrations for engaging in foreign policy initiatives that overextended America's military abroad. In fact, he openly questioned the need to send troops to countries where the nation's interests were not immediately threatened. His position squared well with public attitudes of the time: foreign policy barely registered on the public's radar throughout the presidential campaign. Eventually he was elected president on the strength of his ambitious domestic agenda. Yet once elected, dramatic events tipped the political scales in favor of increased U.S. involvement abroad. This same chief executive who had campaigned against international forays by American forces went before a joint session of Congress to demand immediate military action in another part of the world. More active participation in international conflicts, the president believed, would increase the U.S. government's leverage to dictate the future international order. This president's primary legacy would not be any lasting successes achieved in the domestic sphere; rather, he would be best remembered for his actions as commander in chief of the U.S. armed forces and for his attempts to spread democracy as part of a new international order he helped to create.

LEARNING OBJECTIVES
★ WHAT YOU WILL LEARN ★

The Constitutional Framework of American Foreign Policy

* ★ Discuss the formal powers of Congress and the president to conduct foreign policy under the Constitution

The Roots of American Foreign Policy

* ★ Trace the history of U.S. foreign policy from American independence to the present

* ★ Compare different approaches to foreign policy including isolationism, pacifism, and expansionism

* ★ Understand the role of manifest destiny and America's shift to internationalism in the twentieth century

* ★ Consider America's approach to the Cold War, including theories of containment

* ★ Describe current foreign policy in the Middle East, including the ongoing war on terrorism

The Structure of American Foreign Policymaking

* ★ Explain how foreign and military policy is conducted by the executive branch

* ★ Describe the bureaucratic structures that implement foreign policy, including the State Department, the National Security Council, and various intelligence agencies

* ★ Understand how public opinion shapes foreign policy, especially since the 9/11 attacks

Foreign Policy Dilemmas for the Twenty-first Century

* ★ Appreciate how the preemption doctrine is used to justify aggressive military actions in the Middle East

* ★ Learn about the nature of U.S. foreign aid and the role of the United Nations

CourseMate

NOW & THEN

DAVID MCNEW/GETTY IMAGES

NOW Although the son of a president who had led the nation into war in the early 1990s, President George W. Bush never imagined that his tenure in office would be dominated by military operations in Afghanistan, Iraq, and other countries as part of his own administration's war on terrorism. Indeed, he viewed his father's failed bid for reelection in 1992 as a warning that Americans wanted their chief executives to emphasize issues at home—in particular, the state of the economy, health care, and domestic law enforcement issues. But the events of September 11, 2001, shifted the new president's priorities: reacting swiftly to the terrorist attacks on the World Trade Center and the Pentagon, Bush directed his primary focus to foreign policy matters. Over the next year and a half, the Bush administration would (1) shepherd through Congress the USA Patriot Act, giving federal law enforcement officials countless new tools to fight the war on terrorism; (2) establish a new cabinet-level bureaucratic structure called the Department of Homeland Security, charged with coordinating the nation's defense against military threats; and (3) send U.S. troops into both Afghanistan and Iraq, toppling the governments of each of those nations in succession. Less than two years after criticizing those who had advocated an increased U.S. role as an international policeman, George W. Bush had proven his readiness to flex U.S. military power overseas.

THEN President Bush was not the first American chief executive to see his own carefully conceived domestic agenda swept away in the face of unanticipated foreign policy demands. Woodrow Wilson ran for president twice as the Democratic candidate most closely associated with progressive domestic reforms. Who would have imagined that he would one day become the president responsible for unprecedented military interventions overseas? To be sure, Wilson's first term in office focused on addressing the ill effects of the Industrial Revolution at home, even as World War I was being fought in Europe. Not even the German sinking in 1915 of the British liner *Lusitania*, with 128 Americans aboard, could shift Wilson from his isolationist position. The following year Wilson even campaigned successfully for reelection on the slogan "He kept us out of the war." After Wilson's second inauguration, however, the war began to hit home as Germany resumed its policy of unrestricted submarine warfare in the Atlantic: German subs sank three American merchant ships in early 1917. These acts led Wilson to condemn the German campaign before Congress, as he urged Americans to fight to make the world "safe for democracy." U.S. involvement in World War I eventually tipped the military balance in favor of the Allies; it also cemented Wilson's status as a key player in shaping the treaty for peace following the war.[1]

Both George W. Bush and his predecessor of nearly a century ago, Woodrow Wilson, faced similar dilemmas. Foreign policy always seems to sit on the back burner of American politics—at least until the nation is unexpectedly attacked. Then, even those leaders who were elected on a platform of noninterventionism lead the charge for military solutions. Franklin Delano Roosevelt's aggressive domestic agenda lost considerable steam by the end of his second term, as the United States turned its attention increasingly to the looming threat of World War II. Just as dramatically, the expansion of the Vietnam War brought an abrupt halt to Lyndon Johnson's domestic agenda beginning in the summer and early fall of 1965.[2]

Wilson and Bush alternated first as beneficiaries and then later as victims of this inexorable pull toward foreign policy priorities. Each man, by his words and actions, contributed heavily to the shape of U.S. foreign policy during his presidency, and the American people would eventually issue blame or credit to each of them according to the success of his policies in the world arena. Yet presidents do not act alone in making foreign policy. As we shall see, other actors within and outside government also play a role in influencing America's foreign policy. The political activities of these other actors provide an enlightening window into the American political system as a whole.

★ LO   Discuss the formal powers of Congress and the president to conduct foreign policy under the Constitution

The Constitutional Framework of American Foreign Policy

A nation's foreign policy comprises all of its activities directed at conducting relations with other countries, including military operations and diplomatic activities (such as the building up of trade practices and the making of treaties). In the 200-plus-year history of the United States, few have disputed the federal government's exclusive authority to manage the nation's foreign policy. Indeed, two of the three original cabinet departments created by Congress were the Department of State and the Department of War, a sign of just how important these two functions would be to the nation.

Article I of the Constitution gives Congress the exclusive power to declare war, raise armies, punish maritime crimes, and regulate foreign commerce. Under Article II, the president is empowered as commander in chief to conduct the course of war. The founders' intent in separating the power to command from the power to fund the military was to check the war power from being abused. The Constitution also gives the president the authority to negotiate treaties and to appoint and receive ambassadors.

Perhaps the most basic elements of foreign policy during the eighteenth and nineteenth centuries were the treaties the United States entered into with foreign nations. Because the Senate alone was vested with the authority to ratify such treaties (by a two-thirds vote), many expected that this small legislative body (there were just twenty-six senators at the outset) would exert a strong influence over the nation's foreign policy.

Within the next two centuries, control over foreign affairs, including the power to make war, would shift from Congress to the White House. Fundamental changes in America's role in world affairs during the twentieth century spurred this transfer of power. America's ascendancy to superpower status in the early part of the twentieth century led to U.S. involvement in world affairs. The presidency was well suited to respond to these new demands on America's

Presidential Dominance of the War-Making Power

The Constitution vests Congress alone with the authority to declare war; the president's role as commander in chief is theoretically limited to making strategic decisions about how to wage war and, arguably, to repelling unexpected attacks from foreign powers. In reality, however, the president has come to dominate the declaration and exercise of war-making power in everything but name.

In 1861, President Abraham Lincoln waged "war" for almost three months against the Confederate states without even calling Congress into session. From April 12 (the day the Southern rebels first fired on a federal military installation at Fort Sumter in South Carolina) through July 6, Lincoln proclaimed a blockade of the Southern states, increased the size of the army, expended funds for military purposes without congressional approval, and suspended the writ of habeas corpus (which limited the holding of prisoners without a trial). Although Lincoln defended each of these measures as defensive in nature, critics of his administration complained that he exceeded his constitutional authority. In at least one respect, the Supreme Court agreed: In 1866, it declared the suspension of habeas corpus unconstitutional.

In 1964, President Lyndon Johnson secured near unanimous consent from Congress for passage of the Gulf of Tonkin resolution, which authorized the White House to use armed military force to protect U.S. soldiers in South Vietnam and to deter further aggression from North Vietnam. Congressional leaders believed at the time that they were merely helping Johnson assume a stronger defensive posture in the wake of numerous North Vietnamese gunboat attacks on U.S. destroyers. But in subsequent years, Johnson interpreted the resolution to provide him with a virtual blank check for further military action in Vietnam. He eventually sent close to half a million troops to fight in what remained an undeclared war and ordered the offensive bombing of North Vietnamese strongholds, all on the basis of the Gulf of Tonkin resolution's slim grant of war-making authority.

In 2003, President George W. Bush ordered U.S. military forces (joined by troops from Great Britain and smaller contingents from Australia and Poland) to invade Iraq in order to "disarm Iraq of weapons of mass destruction, to end Saddam Hussein's support for terrorism, and to free the Iraqi people." The previous year Congress had passed a joint resolution to authorize the use of United States Armed Forces against Iraq. Though the resolution further authorized the administration to use "any means necessary to do so," it specifically supported and encouraged diplomatic efforts by President Bush to "strictly enforce through the UN Security Council all relevant Security Council resolutions regarding Iraq." Ultimately the UN refused to authorize the invasion. Accordingly, critics of the Bush administration's legal rationale for the invasion contended that Congress authorized military action only in conjunction with the UN—the legal right to determine how to enforce UN resolutions rested theoretically with the Security Council alone, not with individual nations like the United States. Still, President Bush's military policy lay almost entirely within his own administration's discretion: The U.S. invasion forces remained in Iraq for nearly a decade.

attention; within the three branches of government, the single chief executive is best positioned to respond to sudden changes in circumstances around the globe in a quick and forceful manner. Unlike Congress, the president can use the "bully pulpit" of the office to communicate policies and generate support for the administration's goals. Highly activist presidents, including Theodore Roosevelt, Woodrow Wilson, and Franklin Delano Roosevelt, capitalized on these assets by communicating frequently with world leaders and their own publics on pressing affairs around the world.

A napalm strike erupts in a fireball near U.S. soldiers in Vietnam in 1966.

Two presidencies theory
Theory articulated by political scientist Aaron Wildavsky that posits the existence of a more powerful presidency in foreign affairs and a more limited presidency in the domestic sphere.

War Powers Resolution
Largely ignored congressional policy that restricts the president's power to engage in war except (1) when Congress has declared war, (2) when Congress has specifically granted the president permission to use armed forces, or (3) when the nation is under attack. The resolution further requires the president to report to Congress whenever American forces are entered into hostilities.

Although the Constitution appears to give Congress primary authority over foreign and military affairs, the large and often unwieldy Congress has proven no match for modern presidents on the world stage. Political scientist Aaron Wildavsky's **two presidencies theory** posits the existence of a more powerful presidency in foreign affairs and a more limited presidency in the domestic sphere. Of course, the president's dominance over foreign affairs hasn't stopped Congress from at least trying to reassert its authority in this realm.

In 1973, with public opinion shifting against military involvement around the globe, Congress passed the **War Powers Resolution**, overriding President Richard Nixon's veto in the process. The resolution theoretically restricted the president's power to engage in war to instances in which Congress had declared war or specifically granted the president permission to use armed forces or to cases when the nation was under attack. The resolution required the president to report to Congress whenever American forces were entered into hostilities and attain congressional permission to engage those forces for more than sixty days. Every president since Nixon has either evaded or ignored the War Powers Resolution, arguing that it unconstitutionally infringes on the president's war powers. In fact, no court to date has ever ruled definitively on whether the president must comply with the law's provisions.

With some exceptions, the rise of the president to become the key actor in foreign affairs was a twentieth-century development. Initially, the founders' hopes for an American foreign policy built on consensus among the political branches of government were for the most part realized. But this new decision-making apparatus faced severe tests in the decades following the American Revolution.

★ LO
Trace the history of U.S. foreign policy from American independence to the present

The Roots of American Foreign Policy

As a new nation with a limited military, the United States was at first heavily dependent on maintaining good foreign relations to avoid disadvantageous military engagements. Fortunately, the great distance that separated America from western European superpowers provided a measure of protection from frequent threats and incursions. More than two centuries later, the nation's status as a military superpower affords it far more leverage in its relations with foreign powers. Still, with advances in communications and transportation effectively shrinking the size of the global community, the United States must expend considerable resources and energy to successfully navigate through an increasingly complex foreign policy landscape. American foreign policy has always stood front and center in the list of U.S. government priorities.

The Isolationist Tradition and the Monroe Doctrine

The successful transition of the former British colonies in America into an independent nation was the product of astute foreign policy initiatives by some high-profile figures. George Washington's Continental Army struggled for victories throughout the war for American independence; American fortunes in the war were raised only after Benjamin Franklin helped convince France in 1778 to join the war on the side of the colonies. Indeed, many historians and analysts attribute the Americans' victory over Britain to this crucial Franco-American alliance, which provided the colonies with resources to threaten British ships off the waters near the Atlantic Coast. However, under the leadership of President George Washington, the newly formed United States of America set aside the alliance with France and declared formal neutrality when England and revolutionary France went to war in 1793. In his farewell address to the nation in 1796, Washington urged his fellow Americans to steer clear of permanent alliances of any kind.

During the nation's early years, the United States maintained a foreign policy marked by **isolationism**, defined as opposition to both (1) interventions in distant wars (that is, outside the Western Hemisphere) and (2) involvement in permanent military alliances. The policy of isolationism dominated America's foreign affairs for nearly a century and a half, preserving America's freedom to refuse to act until the very last minute and, in most cases, allowing it to forgo intervention altogether. Isolationism is distinguished from **pacifism**, a policy that refuses to sanction any military conflict and opposes all war making. Consistent with its general policy of isolationism, during the nineteenth century, the United States fought wars in lands that bordered the nation or lay within U.S. boundaries in 1812 (against Britain), in 1846 (against Mexico), and in 1898 (against Spain in the Caribbean). Finally, the policy of military isolationism did

★ LO

Compare different approaches to foreign policy including isolationism, pacifism, and expansionism

Isolationism
Foreign policy doctrine that opposes intervention in distant wars and involvement in permanent military alliances.

Pacifism
Doctrine of foreign relations that refuses to sanction any military conflict and that opposes all war making.

Challenged for his lack of foreign policy experience, Democratic presidential candidate Barack Obama traveled to the Middle East and Europe in the summer of 2008 to meet with a number of foreign leaders. The candidate is seen here meeting with Israeli president Shimon Peres in Jerusalem.

Monroe Doctrine
U.S. foreign policy that proclaimed North and South America unavailable for future colonization by any European power and that declared that any such colonization would be viewed as an act of war on the United States.

not mean complete isolation from the world's culture or commerce, as Americans enthusiastically learned from other nations and welcomed visitors and products from abroad throughout this period.

America's brand of military isolationism never applied to the Western Hemisphere. On December 2, 1823, President James Monroe declared the nation's commitment to a foreign policy that would eventually become known as the **Monroe Doctrine**. Specifically, Monroe proclaimed that both North and South America should not be considered "as subjects for future colonization by any European power" and that the United States would consider any efforts by Europeans to colonize these areas "as dangerous to our peace and safety."

Expansionism and the Birth of a Superpower

★ LO Understand the role of manifest destiny and America's shift to internationalism in the twentieth century

Expansionism
Doctrine that favors a country expanding its own territory and influence.

Manifest destiny
U.S. policy of the mid-nineteenth century that advocated acquiring lands and occupying the entire American continent from one ocean to the other.

Meanwhile, the United States practiced a policy of expansionism on the North American continent. **Expansionism** is the doctrine of increasing the territory or economic influence of one's own country. The policy began as a systematic effort to pursue what many American officials viewed as the nation's defining ideology: its **manifest destiny** to acquire lands and occupy the entire continent from the Atlantic to the Pacific Ocean. America's purchase of the massive Louisiana Territory from the French in 1803 more than doubled the land size of the United States at the time. The federal government went on to annex Florida after conquering Spanish holdings there between 1817 and 1819. Resolution of border conflicts with Great Britain in the 1840s established the northeastern boundary of Maine and of the Oregon territory. The United States annexed the independent Republic of Texas in 1845 and, following a successful war against Mexico in 1846–1848, gained all of present-day California, Nevada, and Utah and parts of present-day Arizona, New Mexico, Colorado, and Wyoming.

Up until World War I, the United States remained primarily separate from the rest of the world militarily. Even the outbreak of World War I in 1914 produced no immediate change in U.S. foreign policy; President Woodrow Wilson openly proclaimed U.S. neutrality in the dispute and, between 1915 and 1917, continually attempted mediation among the warring parties. Only when those efforts to settle the war failed, and Germany began to relentlessly attack U.S. vessels in 1917, did America enter the war on the side of the Allies—Great Britain, France, Italy, and Russia.

By the end of World War I, the European Allies owed more than $11 billion to the United States, making America a creditor nation for the first time in its history. Other world powers looked to the United States for guidance and resources to help construct a new international order, and together with President Wilson, in 1919, they drafted the Versailles Treaty, which established a system of reparations and called for the creation of a League of Nations, which was intended to arbitrate international disputes and thereby avoid future wars. Yet preferences for a policy of isolationism still ran strong throughout America. After an overconfident Wilson engaged in a series of political missteps in selling the Versailles Treaty to the public, the Republican-controlled U.S. Senate balked at the risk that the League of Nations might force the U.S. president to engage in military action; the Senate wanted Wilson to modify those aspects of the League covenant, but he refused. Facing an unyielding president on the issue, the Senate voted against U.S. membership in the League, which thereafter proved ineffective in maintaining peace and preventing aggression and was eventually dissolved in 1946. Thus, American isolationism continued to prevail in the years between the two world wars.

As a second world war approached in the late 1930s and early 1940s, President Franklin Roosevelt made clear where the sympathies of the U.S. government lay, first by utilizing a lend-lease program with Britain to supply that country with arms at little or no cost and later by

AP PHOTO

President Woodrow Wilson (far right) meeting with European leaders in Paris to discuss war reparations in January 1919.

increasing economic pressures on the Japanese in the Pacific.[3] The Japanese attack on Pearl Harbor on December 7, 1941, propelled the United States into the war against Germany, Japan, and Italy.

U.S. involvement in World War II proved critical to the final outcome: American soldiers and resources were an important component in the success of the D-Day invasion of France and much of western Europe in 1944. The United States detonated two atomic bombs over Japan in August 1945, forcing the Japanese to surrender. After the war, the European victors looked to the United States again to help keep international peace. This time, they were not disappointed, as they had been when the U.S. Senate refused to support the League of Nations three decades earlier. In 1945, the United States joined the newly created **United Nations (UN)**, an international organization formed to promote and maintain international security and peace.

After World War II, America's prevailing foreign policy changed from one marked by isolationism to one featuring **internationalism**; the United States now actively participated in a process that collectively secured the political independence and territorial boundaries of other countries by a system of economic and military sanctions against aggressor nations. In fact, America went even further than other nations in this regard. The **Marshall Plan** (formally the European Recovery Program) introduced by Secretary of State George Marshall in 1947 provided $13 billion in loans to Western European countries whose economies had been ravaged by World War II.

Foreign Policy during the Cold War

Out of the wreckage of World War II emerged two global military and political superpowers, the United States and the Soviet Union, locked in what would become a half-century-long struggle called the **Cold War**.[4] This conflict over ideological differences (the promotion of democracy by the United States versus the promotion of communism by the Soviet Union) lasted from 1945 until the dissolution of the Soviet Union in 1991 and was carried on by a variety of methods, including economic warfare, arms buildups, and tense diplomacy. Postwar leaders in the United States believed that the nation had fought in World War II to protect self-determination and open trade, and together with

United Nations (UN)
International organization formed after World War II to promote and maintain international security and peace.

Internationalism
Doctrine that favors active participation of the nation in collective arrangements that secure the political independence and territorial boundaries of other countries.

Marshall Plan
The 1947 U.S. policy that provided loans and aid to Western European countries whose economies had been ravaged by World War II.

Consider America's approach to the Cold War, including theories of containment

Cold War
The nearly half-century struggle over ideological differences between the United States and the Soviet Union. Waged through economic warfare, arms buildups, and tense diplomatic talks, the Cold War never broke out into a sustained military engagement between the two nations and ended with the dissolution of the Soviet Union in 1991.

**North Atlantic Treaty
Organization (NATO)**
A military, political, and
economic alliance of nations
formally bound to protect
self-determination and open
trade in Western Europe.

Warsaw Pact
Formal alliance of nations
within the Soviet sphere during the Cold War.

Truman Doctrine
Doctrine articulated by
President Harry Truman in
the late 1940s by which
money and resources were
provided to support and
sustain non-Communist
governments in areas strategically vital to the United
States.

Containment
U.S. foreign policy that
sought to restrict Soviet
power (and Communist
influence) to its existing
geographical sphere.

Domino theory
Theory that held that
Communist takeovers of
countries in Southeast Asia
and elsewhere would be
followed by subsequent
Communist takeovers of
nearby countries.

other Western European nations, including Great Britain and France, it formed military, political, and, at times, economic alliances. Formally created in 1949, the **North Atlantic Treaty Organization (NATO)** bound the United States to the military defense of Western Europe. Meanwhile, the Soviet Union in the late 1940s dominated its Eastern European neighbors, including Poland and Romania. In 1955, those nations and others within the Soviet sphere formed the **Warsaw Pact**.

In 1947, President Harry Truman articulated the **Truman Doctrine**, which provided money and resources to sustaining non-Communist governments in areas strategically vital to the United States, such as the Mediterranean and the Middle East. American foreign policy during the Cold War generally adhered to a policy of **containment**—restricting Soviet power to its current geographic sphere and resisting any efforts to expand Communist influence. When the Soviets in 1949 blockaded the city of Berlin (a West German city located entirely within Soviet-controlled East German territory), the United States air-lifted supplies to the city for nearly a year. Aerial reconnaissance allowed the Cold War adversaries to keep a more careful eye on each other beginning in the 1950s. It also led to the Cuban missile crisis in October 1962, when President John F. Kennedy's demands that the Soviet Union remove missiles from nearby Cuba led to a tense standoff with the Soviets and nearly ignited a nuclear war. U.S. military involvement in both the Korean and Vietnam Wars was spurred by U.S. government fears of a total Communist takeover of those two coun-tries. Most U.S. presidents during the Cold War subscribed to some version of the **domino theory**, which posited that Communist takeovers of these South-east Asian countries would be followed by takeovers of Taiwan, India, Iran, and possibly other nations as well.

The American military failure in the Vietnam War in particular led offi-cials at every level of the American government to revisit some of the most fundamental premises of U.S. foreign policy, including the theory of contain-ment.[5] The American phase of that war, extending from the early 1960s until 1973, proved longer lasting and more divisive than any other war involving the United States.[6] The conflict eventually left 58,000 Americans dead or missing and cost the U.S. government more than $167 billion. Despite all the bloodshed, the United States accomplished none of its aims in the war:

to repel North Vietnam aggression, help negoti-ate a lasting peace, and encourage South Viet-nam as a self-sufficient republic.

During the 1970s, the United States and the Soviet Union engaged in a period of some-what eased tensions, or limited détente. During this time, they agreed on several strategic arms limitation treaties (SALT I and SALT II) that set

A distraught President
Ronald Reagan and Soviet
leader Mikhail Gorbachev
leaving their unsuccess-
ful arms limitations talks
in Reykjavik, Iceland, in
October 1986.

BETTMANN/CORBIS

restrictions on nuclear missiles.[7] But such détente proved short-lived, as confrontations in underdeveloped Third World nations continued to inject tensions into the Cold War landscape. President Ronald Reagan, denouncing the Soviet Union as an evil empire, outlined a new defense plan, the controversial **Strategic Defense Initiative (SDI)**, an antimissile system based on the use of lasers and particle beams to shoot down Soviet nuclear missiles in outer space.[8]

The Cold War formally came to a close in 1991, when Soviet Premier Mikhail Gorbachev resigned his position with the Soviet government amid extremely difficult economic times. In addition to the former Soviet-bloc countries, ten former Soviet republics, including Russia, declared their independence.[9] Following the end of the Cold War, U.S. leaders redirected their foreign policy thinking toward a new world order characterized by conflicts in the Third World, a war on terrorism, and threats of nuclear attack from both terrorists and rogue nations.

New World Order and New World Disorder

U.S. responsibilities around the world have not decreased much at all in the aftermath of the Cold War. In his January 1991 State of the Union speech, President George H. W. Bush spoke of the onset of a **new world order**, in which numerous nations would work together for the purpose of securing

Strategic Defense Initiative (SDI)
A theoretical antimissile system based on the use of lasers and particle beams to shoot down Soviet nuclear missiles in outer space.

New world order
President George H. W. Bush's description of the post–Cold War world, in which nations would work together for the purpose of securing collective peace, security, freedom, and the rule of law.

collective peace, security, freedom, and the rule of law.[10] Maintaining this new world order has been a challenge for American political leaders ever since.

Further complicating the foreign affairs landscape was the looming presence of China. Still a Communist nation, China is a crucial market for U.S. goods and products, given that it contains one fifth of the world's population. In the 1990s, both Presidents George H. W. Bush and Bill Clinton emphasized the need for liberalization of global trade, and in 1993, Congress approved the North American Free Trade Agreement (NAFTA), which lifted trade barriers such as protective tariffs and investment restrictions between the United States and Canada and Mexico. Of course, economic concerns do not eliminate other interests; tragic human rights abuses in Somalia and Bosnia put pressure on the George H. W. Bush and Clinton administrations to intervene on humanitarian grounds in those countries. The balance both presidents struck in those instances, providing limited aid but no military assistance, prompted criticisms that they had failed to wield America's superpower status in the most appropriate fashion.[11]

The U.S. Government Confronts the Middle East

★ LO Describe current foreign policy in the Middle East, including the ongoing war on terrorism

Although the Cold War has ended, among the current generation of policymakers, the specter of the Vietnam War continues to cast a large shadow on foreign policy deliberations. Discussions of American military intervention since the early 1970s have occurred with the lessons of the Vietnam War looming ominously in the background. Some hawkish conservatives even complain of what they call a "Vietnam syndrome," in which the problems of Vietnam produce an undesirable pacifism on the part of American leaders. Politicians live in fear of supporting yet another war in which public support is flimsy, the military objectives are unclear, and an exit strategy remains ill defined. American interventions in the Balkans and Somalia in the 1990s were limited by fears that increased U.S. involvement in those countries would escalate into another Vietnam. During the first Persian Gulf War of 1991, Joint Chiefs of Staff Chairman Colin Powell urged the nation to avoid Vietnam-like entanglements in which fear of escalation placed the military in an essentially unwinnable conflict.

President George W. Bush's administration faced inevitable comparisons between the Vietnam War and U.S. intervention of Iraq in 2003. When the military failed to unearth "weapons of mass destruction" cited as partial justification of the war, critics of the Iraqi intervention argued that U.S. interests in the region were just as unclear as they had been in Southeast Asia during the 1960s. Furthermore, the U.S. military's failure to contain rebel insurgents even after taking control of Baghdad invited comparisons to guerrilla war in North Vietnam. In response, President Bush proclaimed that the Iraqi invasion had both removed a brutal dictator, Saddam Hussein, from power and restored a democratic government, in the form of duly held elections, to the previously oppressed nation. Up through the end of his presidency, Bush continued to claim that his administration was committed to having

During his campaign for the presidency in 2008, Barack Obama visited Germany, where he was warmly received by thousands of Europeans.

AP PHOTO/JENS MEYER

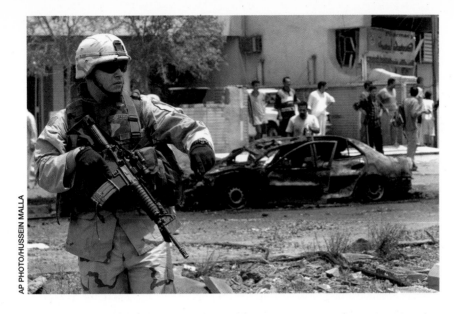

A U.S. soldier guarding the scene of a car bomb explosion in Baghdad.

the American military stay in Iraq until democracy and stability were established, a clear attempt to distinguish this event from the nation's tenuous hold of the South Vietnamese city of Saigon, which the United States abandoned in 1975.

Militarily, the greatest threats to U.S. security during the first decade of the twenty-first century appear to lie in two areas of the world: the Middle East and North Korea. More of the U.S. government's attention in recent decades has been focused on the former locus of conflict. Since it first recognized the newly created independent nation of Israel in 1948, the United States has been committed in its support for that country as a political haven for Jews. Meanwhile, Israel has emerged as a modernized democratic presence in a region of the world dominated by Arab countries largely hostile to Western economic power and its cultural domination. U.S. support for Israel has assured the United States of a friendly ally in the Middle East, yet it has also at times run counter to fundamental principles of self-determination, as U.S. officials have been forced to confront another dilemma—what to do with the tens of thousands of Palestinian refugees uprooted from their homes in the years following Israel's occupation of former Palestinian territory.

Navigating the New World Order After the September 11 Attacks

The events of September 11, 2001, refocused the U.S. government's foreign policy energies toward a global war on terrorism. After a short-lived war in Afghanistan that purportedly expelled the Al-Qaeda terrorist network from that country, the George W. Bush administration turned its attention back to Saddam Hussein's government in Iraq, which it accused of supporting terrorism abroad and concealing weapons of mass destruction. After less than six weeks of fighting, American military forces liberated the country of Hussein's dictatorial government during the spring of 2003.

Yet the aftermath of the Iraq War has proved highly problematic, with insurgent forces in and around the nation's cities posing an ever-present threat to the more than 150,000 American forces who remained there as part of the occupation.[12] By early 2007, over 3,000 Americans had died in Iraq, and Congress began putting pressure on the Bush administration to lay out a timetable and plan for eventual American withdrawal. Rejecting those entreaties, in early 2007 President Bush increased by over 20,000 the number of troops deployed to Iraq in what came to be known as the "Iraq War Troop Surge of 2007." (Administration officials attributed a general drop in violence in Iraq during 2007–2008 to this increased military presence.) As one of the first moves in his presidency, Barack Obama announced an 18-month withdrawal window for combat forces in Iraq, with approximately 50,000 troops remaining in the country after 2011 "to advise and train Iraqi security forces and to provide intelligence and surveillance."

President Obama's announcement did not spell a pullback from the Middle East as a whole, however: In December 2009 he confirmed plans to escalate U.S. military involvement in Afghanistan by deploying an additional 30,000 troops. The Obama administration cited the recent strengthening of the Taliban, a Sunni Islamist political movement that has supported terrorist training camps in the region, as the reason for increasing its military presence in that country. Threats of nuclear and biological terrorism remain ever present in the Middle East, where terrorists continue to operate underground. In the past decade, North Korea has also emerged as a potential nuclear threat. Critics charge that the end of the Cold War has ushered in a "new world disorder," featuring ever-shifting alliances and grave terrorist threats from entities not formally associated with any specific nation.

Within this constantly shifting international terrain, America continues to search for its role and identity in the twenty-first-century. In *Colossus: The Rise and Fall of the American Empire*, British-born Harvard Professor Niall Ferguson argues that like the great British Empire of old, the United States needs to embrace its imperial character and commit to more securely establishing the types of democratic institutions around the world that foster long-term prosperity.[13] In another influential book, *Soft Power: The Means to Success in World Politics*, Joseph Nye argues that rather than relying on unilateralism and military power, the United States should endeavor to win the voluntary cooperation of foreign governments.[14] Is the United States an empire? Does it want to be? In light of the difficulties U.S. military forces have faced in postwar Iraq, many of these questions will continue to be debated in the years ahead.

The Structure of American Foreign Policymaking

The Constitution designates specific roles for the president and the Senate in making U.S. foreign policy. Yet over the course of two centuries, the president of the United States and the executive branch that reports to the president have assumed an increasingly significant role in the process, rendering Congress, interest groups, and citizens themselves less significant in foreign policymaking.

The Role of the Executive Branch

Many actors and institutions attempt either formally or informally to influence American foreign policy. The president of the United States sits squarely

★ LO Explain how foreign and military policy is conducted by the executive branch

at the center of foreign policymaking—within the federal government, the president often dictates its terms with little interference from the other branches.[15] On the positive side, presidential dominance of foreign policy allows the U.S. government to act immediately and decisively in response to developments abroad. The quick responses to the bombing of Pearl Harbor, the threat of nuclear missiles in Cuba, and the 9/11 terrorist attacks might not have been possible had the principal decision makers been a legislative body or council. Although the president is at the center of foreign policymaking, other executive branch departments and agencies help formulate and implement foreign policy.

The **Department of State**, headed by the secretary of state, maintains primary responsibility for many foreign policy programs. State Department programs include diplomatic missions to other countries, foreign aid to developing nations, and contributions to **international organizations** (official entities of international scope or character, usually established by treaty, such as the World Bank and the International Monetary Fund). During the latter half of the twentieth century, the secretary of state emerged as a principal spokesperson for the U.S. government on all foreign policy matters.

Military power is an important factor in U.S. foreign relations. The **Department of Defense** plays a critical role in helping formulate and implement U.S. foreign policy by managing the nation's military. The secretary of defense is the principal civilian adviser to the president on military matters. On the military side, the president is advised by the **Joint Chiefs of Staff (JCS)**, which consists of the chief officers of the four branches of the armed forces (army, navy, air force, and marines) as well as the JCS chair and vice chair. The JCS delivers the president's orders to the military commands involved in a particular operation.

In 1947, the National Security Act established the **National Security Council (NSC)** as an advisory body to the president, coordinating information about foreign, military, and economic policies that affect national security. By law, the NSC must include the president, vice president, and the secretaries of state and defense. But recent presidents have also appointed a national security adviser to supervise the council and monitor the implementation of national security decisions made by the president. Dating back to the 1960s, the national security adviser has served as both a key adviser and policymaker for most modern presidents.[16]

Although not directly responsible for formulating the administration's overall foreign policy direction, other agencies and executive branch officials also influence aspects of foreign policy. In the aftermath of the 9/11 terrorist attacks, the Bush

Department of State
Executive branch agency that is primarily responsible for most foreign policy programs within the executive branch, including diplomatic missions, foreign aid, and contributions to international organizations.

Describe the ★ LO
bureaucratic structures that implement foreign policy, including the State Department, the National Security Council, and various intelligence agencies

International organization
Entity of international scope or character, usually established by treaty, such as the World Bank or the International Monetary Fund.

Department of Defense
Executive branch agency that is responsible for managing the nation's military and advising the president on all military matters.

Secretary of State Hillary Clinton, left, is sworn in to office by Vice President Joseph Biden, right, as her husband (former President Bill Clinton), daughter Chelsea, and mother Dorothy Rodham look on.

ALEX WONG/GETTY IMAGES

Joint Chiefs of Staff (JCS)
Group of chief officers of the four branches of the armed forces as well as a JCS chair and vice chair, which advises the president on military matters and delivers the president's orders to the military.

National Security Council (NSC)
Advisory body to the president charged with coordinating information about foreign, military, and economic policies that affect national security.

Department of Homeland Security (DHS)
Executive branch agency established in 2002 to coordinate government entities in protecting U.S. citizens against terrorism within the nation's borders.

Central Intelligence Agency (CIA)
Federal agency charged with evaluating and disseminating intelligence information, performing public relations functions that affect international perceptions of the United States, and engaging in overt and covert operations at the direction of the president.

Military-industrial complex
The vast network of defense industries in America (including manufacturers of weapons, missiles, aircraft, and so forth) and their allies in the federal bureaucracy.

★ **LO** Understand how public opinion shapes foreign policy, especially since the 9/11 attacks

administration sought to create a unified security structure to coordinate the protection of U.S. citizens against terrorist threats within the nation's own borders. Accordingly, Congress in 2002 established the **Department of Homeland Security (DHS)**. Various governmental divisions responsible for U.S. security have been brought under DHS control, including border and transportation security, infrastructure protection, the U.S. Coast Guard, the U.S. Secret Service, the Federal Emergency Management Agency (FEMA), and the bureau of citizenship and immigration services. The DHS secretary is responsible for overseeing the efforts of more than 180,000 government employees in the department's efforts to strengthen U.S. borders, provide for intelligence analysis and infrastructure protection, and improve the use of science and technology to combat terrorist threats. The DHS is also responsible for formulating a comprehensive response and recovery capability in the event of an unexpected threat.

The National Security Act of 1947 created the **Central Intelligence Agency (CIA)** to correlate, evaluate, and disseminate intelligence information from throughout the world that affects national security. Unlike the NSC, the CIA is also responsible for disseminating propaganda or performing public relations functions on behalf of the U.S. government and for engaging in overt or covert activities at the direction of the president.

The term **military-industrial complex** refers to the vast network of defense industries in America, such as manufacturers of weapons, missiles, aircraft, submarines, and so forth, and their bureaucratic allies. The complex as a whole maintains a keen interest in foreign policymaking that is concerned with defense and national security. These industries expanded during the Cold War as U.S. defense budgets rose to as much as 40 percent of annual federal spending. In the late 1990s, defense spending amounted to just 15 percent of the budget, generating ever more feverish efforts by members of the military-industrial complex to either increase that allotment or shift the focus of defense spending to weapons and resources that meet their own areas of expertise.

SEAN ADAIR/REUTERS/CORBIS

Top officials at the Central Intelligence Agency faced some public criticism for failing to anticipate the terrorist attacks of September 11, 2001. In 2004, President Bush appointed a director of national intelligence to coordinate all intelligence information in the future.

American Foreign Policy and Public Opinion

Public opinion on foreign policy issues is a central concern for key actors in the U.S. foreign policymaking arena, including the president, in part because those actors won't keep their jobs for long if they ignore popular sentiments. When the public punishes officials at the polls for their

"Jaywalking" and Americans' Lack of Knowledge of World Affairs

Though American political leaders emphasize the interconnectedness of global institutions and leaders, Americans tend to be far more inward looking. Comedians like Jay Leno have turned the common person's relative lack of knowledge into a form of late night entertainment. As the host of NBC's *The Tonight Show*, Leno enjoys taking cameras out on the street to tape one of his most popular segments, "Jaywalking." Since 2000 he has been asking random people questions about current news and other topics. Most of the responses shown in the segments are outrageously incorrect; for example, one person believed that Abraham Lincoln was the first president,

Jay Leno interviews a pedestrian on Melrose Avenue in Los Angeles for a "Jaywalking" segment on *The Tonight Show*.

and another could not identify a picture of Hillary Clinton. Sometimes the questions are of the "What color is the White House?" variety. And when Leno asks people on the street about foreign affairs, the answers tend to be especially entertaining—and distressing:

- Leno: "What country is the Panama Canal located in?" Answer: "I have no idea."
- Leno: "Who lives at the Vatican?" Answer: "Um . . . the Vaticans?" (After Leno provided the clue that "he wears a tall hat," one person guessed: "Abraham Lincoln?")
- Leno: "Where would you find Guantanamo Bay?" Answer: "Somewhere in Vietnam."

Recent "Jaywalking" videos can be found at *The Tonight Show* website, at http://www.nbc.com/the-tonight-show/.

For Critical Thinking and Discussion

1. How important is it for citizens to have general knowledge about other countries in general, and U.S. foreign relations in particular?

2. Should standardized tests focus on social studies and civics, in addition to math and reading skills?

3. In your opinion, are sources of news on the Internet, such as Google news and Yahoo news, as effective at conveying information as more traditional media sources such as newspapers and magazines? How are they better and how are they worse?

ill-advised foreign policy decisions, observers are quick to criticize those officials for ignoring the will of the people.[17] Certainly, when President George W. Bush ordered a "surge" of 20,000 more U.S. forces in Iraq in early 2007, he was not responding to public opinion as much as he was hoping to shift it in a prowar direction. However, many political defeats occur because officials have misinterpreted public attitudes rather than ignoring them outright. Even Lyndon Johnson, whose Vietnam policy proved so unpopular that he was forced to drop out of the presidential election race in 1968, was known to have carried in his pajama pockets the results of public opinion polls about foreign policy.

Part of the challenge facing U.S. officials is that public attitudes toward foreign affairs often defy easy analysis and interpretation. Modern presidents have managed to generate considerable public support for foreign policy objectives that protect American jobs, control illegal immigration, or counter the illegal drug trade. By contrast, foreign policy initiatives that promote human rights or advance democracy abroad have been far less likely to garner support. Political scientist John Mueller offered the following four propositions to describe American public opinion concerning foreign policy:

1. Americans will tolerate a substantial loss of American lives only if the enemy is seen to be truly powerful and set on jeopardizing vital American interests;

2. The advantage to a president of a success in minor foreign policy ventures is marginal; the disadvantage to a president of a failure in such a venture is more than marginal;

3. If they are not being killed, American troops can remain in peacekeeping or other ventures virtually indefinitely with little public criticism; and

4. Although few concerns can turn the public's attention to foreign affairs, nuclear weapons retain the capacity to arrest the public's attention, and the same may hold for biological and chemical weapons.[18]

The thorny politics of foreign occupation that occurs following most military battles—when the victors must (at least temporarily) control the area that has been seized by military force—can weigh especially heavily in the court of public opinion. Public support for the war tends to tail off once the opposing armies have been defeated. If the occupation fails, the defeated or other hostile entities may seize the opportunity to reverse the war's outcome. America's military history features numerous successful military occupations, such as that over West Germany and Japan in the aftermath of World War II. By contrast, the George W. Bush administration invested more than $1 billion per day in the occupation of Iraq; yet far more American troops were killed during the occupation than during the brief six-week military conflict.

TODD HEISLER/THE NEW YORK TIMES/REDUX PICTURES

President Obama delivers an address to the UN General Assembly on September 23, 2009.

A Perspective on Obama's Afghan Strategy from the Other Side of the World

President Barack Obama's decision to significantly increase the U.S. military presence in Afghanistan was accompanied by a specific timetable: After boosting the Afghan army to over 130,000 soldiers, the United States planned to withdraw its own forces from that country starting in late 2011. Though such timetables have a tendency to change quickly, recent experiences in Vietnam and Iraq have led the American public to demand clear exit strategies from their military leaders—for better or worse. Although definite timetables may appeal to American sensibilities, strategists from the other side of the world may feel quite differently. Consider the reaction to timetables articulated by Dr. Shanthie Mariet D'Souza of the Institute for Defence Studies and Analyses, New Delhi, India, in December 2009:

The most widely and intensely debated aspect of the present strategy is setting the date of draw down of [American] forces. By fixing an arbitrary time frame of summer of 2011, especially when the strategy is just being unveiled, it runs the danger of working to the advantage [in propaganda] of the insurgents and their sponsors. The Taliban have posted a message on the Voice of Jihad web page in response to the new strategy—"You send more troops, we'll have more to kill." Also, the limited time frame will help carry their narratives further in the Pushtun heartland: "Americans have the watches; but we have the time." . . . [A]lthough the setting of a date for draw down of forces after 18 months ends a lot of speculation regarding American intentions in that country, and has provided some clarity to the domestic constituency and allies, it has sent a wrong message to the "friends and foes" in the region. . . .

Source: Atlantic Review, posted December 10, 2009 (http://www.atlanticreview.org).

Foreign Policy Dilemmas for the Twenty-first Century

★ **LO**

Appreciate how the preemption doctrine is used to justify aggressive military actions in the Middle East

Some foreign policy dilemmas of the twenty-first century, such as the problematic occupation of Iraq by U.S. forces after the 2003 Iraq War, represent new versions of age-old challenges that the U.S. government has faced on an intermittent basis since the nation's founding. Others represent unforeseen obstacles produced by circumstances unique to the modern, post–Cold War world. Regardless, American officials must always be on the lookout for foreign policy challenges that arise with little or no warning and that can overshadow all other aspects of the federal government's agenda if they are not kept under control. Officials must also be prepared to justify their actions according to some theory or well-articulated rationale, lest they be accused of conducting foreign policy "on the fly" with little real reason for endangering American resources and, in some instances, for putting American troops in harm's way.

Is the "Preemption Doctrine" Justifiable?

Only a year after the collapse of the Soviet Union in 1991, the first hint of a dramatic transformation in America's foreign policy could be seen. In 1992, several

Canadian Prime Minister Stephen Harper, right, chats with President Obama during a session at the G-20 Summit in Toronto, Canada, in June 2010.

Preemption doctrine
Doctrine of war making that reserves the right of the U.S. military to use advance strikes to stop rogue states from developing weapons of mass destruction.

Pentagon planners working in the George H. W. Bush administration drafted a policy statement asserting that the American government should assume a far more activist role in foreign affairs, especially in the Middle East. Their statement specifically reserved the right of the U.S. military to use advance strikes to stop rogue states from developing weapons of mass destruction. Later termed the **preemption doctrine**, this statement sparked considerable controversy after it was leaked to the *New York Times*. In 1997, one of its original authors, Paul Wolfowitz, joined Donald Rumsfeld and other conservative foreign policy advocates to warn President Bill Clinton that America's containment of Iraq had failed. They urged the government to shift its focus to the outright removal of Iraqi leader Saddam Hussein, who had remained in power even through the American military's conquering of his country during the Persian Gulf War of 1991. With George W. Bush's election as president in 2000 and the more intense focus on international terrorism that followed the September 11, 2001, attacks, the emphasis on preemption became ingrained in U.S. policy.

Even advocates of this doctrine do not dispute that preemption carries with it some significant risks. The fundamental paradox of preemption is that it can be effectively applied only to a country that lacks the capacity to retaliate. Although Iraq suffered from preemptive American attacks in the spring of 2003, North Korea and Iran—two nations similarly charged with posing international threats—are less likely to be targets of a U.S. preemptive attack because neither is viewed as so weak or vulnerable as was Saddam Hussein's regime. Critics of the preemption doctrine also charge that although this policy may be justified in the rare instance when a rival power's attacks are imminent, it cannot be justified to prevent attacks in the distant and more ambiguous future.

What Role Does Foreign Aid Play in the New International Order?

The American government's legacy of providing monetary aid to struggling nations and allies was first established on a monumental scale with the Marshall Plan to help Western European nations recover after World War II. Although humanitarian concerns continue to influence such aid, U.S. economic and national security interests also affect foreign aid decisions. Expanded foreign markets would purchase domestic products and agricultural goods, boosting the U.S. economy. New states would also be more likely to join the expanding capitalist world economy if U.S. aid contributed to their recovery and encouraged them to reject anticapitalist economic systems.

Because the dissolution of the Soviet Union has weakened some of the strategic rationale for foreign aid, there have been substantial reductions in such aid during the past decade. Critics of foreign aid also charge that much of the money provided by America goes to elites in the recipient nations rather than to those who need help. Defenders of aid respond that even when elites control a sizable portion of the aid, the recipient nation is able to expand its national output, which leads to higher living standards for all. But this "trickle-down" theory of foreign aid has been cast aside in recent years by experts such as economist Peter Boone of the London School of Economics. After assessing the experience of nearly 100 nations, Boone concluded that because foreign transfers only tend to increase government consumption (which has no positive effect on growth), foreign aid has had little or no impact on the recipient country's overall investment levels.[19]

The United States continues to be a leading contributor to such international aid institutions as the World Bank, which since 1945 has extended credit to nations for building and economic development. America also contributes substantially to the International Monetary Fund, which helps maintain the value of foreign currencies during times of crisis. But the heyday of foreign aid—when it served as a critical instrument of U.S. foreign relations—appears to be a thing of the past.

Does the United Nations Still Serve an Important Function?

The United Nations, founded at the conclusion of World War II, is structured around five separate governing bodies: (1) the General Assembly, which is made up of all member states (at present there are 192 member states); (2) the Economic and Social Council, which is made up of fifty-four members chosen by the General Assembly and serves primarily an advisory body to the General Assembly on matters of international economic and social cooperation; (3) the Secretariat, which supports the other UN bodies and carries out tasks as directed by the other bodies; (4) the International Court of Justice, the UN's judicial organ that has jurisdiction to try certain international war criminals and settles disputes submitted to it by duly authorized international entities; and (5) the Security Council, which maintains peace and security among nations by issuing resolutions that (at least in theory) are binding on UN members. The separation of the Security Council from the larger General Assembly is significant. As currently constituted, the Security Council consists of five permanent members (China, France, the Russian

Federation, the United States, and Great Britain) and ten nonpermanent rotating members. Each of the five permanent members maintains the absolute right to veto decisions of the all-important council, the only UN body with the power to authorize economic sanctions or military force. However, the General Assembly retains the exclusive power to enforce Security Council decisions.

The United States dominated the UN on all security issues during its first forty years, but as U.S. influence over the body has declined, calls have increased within Congress to reduce American aid to the organization and to ignore its dictates whenever American security interests were at issue. In 2003, America went to war in Iraq even though the UN Security Council was unwilling to offer advance authorization for any such military action. Yet immediately after the war with Iraq had concluded, the UN began relief and reconstruction activities in the war-torn nation, and began pushing for a resolution that would broaden international control over the region. Thus in the twenty-first century, the UN seems destined to play at least a limited role in international affairs, asserting its authority most strongly during peacekeeping and relief missions that follow military action.

Making the Connection

As much as individual presidents like to think they control the agendas of their presidencies, unforeseen crises have a way of scuttling such carefully laid plans and bringing new priorities to the table. Both Woodrow Wilson and George W. Bush may have anticipated that, given the American public's recent hesitancy to overextend its military commitments abroad, their terms in the White House would be spent mainly attending to domestic concerns. Woodrow Wilson managed to do just that during his first term, but nearly his entire second term was occupied with the management of World War I and its aftermath. George W. Bush had not even served a full year as president when the tragic events of September 11, 2001, launched his administration into a war on terrorism; domestic issues temporarily fell off the public's radar screen during these periods.

The president in particular enjoys considerable discretion in pursuing a foreign policy agenda; Congress and other governmental actors play only a subordinate role in such affairs. Actors outside government also have only limited influence to affect foreign policy decisions. Not surprisingly, many presidents, including most recently Presidents Nixon and Clinton, found foreign policy to be a welcome diversion from the scandals that were rocking their respective presidencies. At the same time, many foreign policy issues—relations with Russia, the Arab–Israeli conflict, the military occupation in Iraq, to name just a few—are among the most complicated and difficult issues a president faces. As a result, though some presidents enjoy short-term successes in foreign affairs, few are able to offer long-term solutions, and many only tend to exacerbate the problems faced by their predecessors.

A Growing Threat from Iran?

Since the overthrow of the Iraqi government by U.S. military forces in the spring of 2003, the American military has added the occupation of that country to its already sizeable list of responsibilities in Europe, the Pacific, and elsewhere. To meet these growing military demands, in February 2007 Secretary of Defense Robert Gates proposed that the United States increase the overall size of its military by nearly 100,000 troops. That would bring the total active-duty force of the United States to approximately 1.5 million soldiers and personnel.

Gates has publicly expressed concerns that the already stretched capacity of the U.S. military leaves it in little position to even rattle its sabers to gain leverage against upstarts such as Iran, which fired unarmed missiles on November 2, 2006, as part of a series of military war games. Since 1992, Iran has produced its own tanks, armored personnel carriers, guided missiles, submarines, and even one fighter plane. Meanwhile, Iran's current president, Mahmoud Ahmadinejad, has so far refused the demands of the UN Security Council to stop Iran's nuclear program, claiming that Iran's nuclear enrichment program is for peaceful purposes only. The Iranian presidential elections of 2009 produced a surprising landslide win for Ahmadinejad, followed by allegations of fraud and widespread protests.

EMMANUEL DUNAND/AFP/GETTY IMAGES

Mahmoud Ahmadinejad, president of Iran.

As one of the three members of President George W. Bush's original "axis of evil" (along with Iraq and North Korea), Iran's warlike gestures may ultimately force the U.S. government to once again exercise its military power in the Middle East. Indeed, despite offering prospects for improved U.S. foreign relations elsewhere, the Obama administration has backed increased sanctions on Iran for its nuclear program, and President Obama himself has condemned the Iranian government's mistreatment of international journalists covering the elections. Still, even if Secretary Gates's requests are met, is the United States really in a position to offer a military challenge to Iran at the same time that it is maintaining an occupying force in Afghanistan and Iraq? Furthermore, should it be prepared to do so?

On www.cengage.com/dautrich/americangovernmentbrief/2e, find the Politics InterActive link for the latest details on the military threat from Iran and a discussion of how the current administration is reacting to these threats. Consult as well the various links that provide historical, popular, and global perspectives on the Iran–U.S. relationship.

Chapter Summary

★ The Constitutional Framework of American Foreign Policy

- The federal government maintains exclusive authority over foreign policy in the United States. The president is the commander in chief and has the power to negotiate treaties and appoint and receive ambassadors; Congress has the power to declare war, raise armies, and regulate foreign commerce, among its other functions.

★ The Roots of American Foreign Policy

- Over two centuries, the practical power to make war has shifted from Congress to the president, who as commander in chief is far better suited to respond to sudden changes in circumstances around the world. Thus, the president has become even more powerful in foreign affairs than in domestic affairs.

- The United States adhered to a policy of isolationism from the time of its founding until the late nineteenth century, generally forgoing intervention in foreign wars during that period. However, in the mid-nineteenth century, the U.S. government practiced aggressive expansionism in North America; near the end of the century, it also annexed Hawaii and gained possession of the Philippine Islands.

- With its entry into World War I and World War II, the United States rose to the status of world superpower, with many smaller nations looking to the U.S. government to preserve international peace. America's foreign policy eventually shifted to an emphasis on internationalism, by which it participated in a system of collective security.

- The Cold War, pitting the United States against the Soviet Union from 1945 until 1991, was waged through economic warfare, arms buildups, and moments of tense diplomacy that fell short of direct military engagements between the two superpowers. The demise of Soviet-run regimes in Russia and elsewhere beginning in the late 1980s failed to decrease U.S. involvement around the world.

- The Middle East remains a source of great concern for U.S. foreign policy in the twenty-first century. After the 9/11 attacks, the federal government launched an aggressive war on terrorism. The U.S. military overthrew the governments of Afghanistan and Iraq in 2001 and 2003, respectively, as part of the war on terrorism.

- Although the continued occupation of Iraq by U.S. forces after the Iraqi war was a source of debate among political officials between 2003 and 2008, President Obama offered the prospect for a draw down of forces in Iraq; the Obama administration sought instead to redirect U.S. military strength to Afghanistan and elsewhere.

★ The Structure of American Foreign Policymaking

- In formulating foreign policy, the president is assisted by the secretary of state, the secretary of defense, the Joint Chiefs of Staff, the national security adviser, and the director of national intelligence.

- The Department of Homeland Security, created by an act of Congress in 2002, is responsible for border and transportation security, intelligence analysis, infrastructure protection, and all other government divisions that play a role in protecting the United States against terrorist threats.

- Public opinion concerning American foreign policy often defies easy interpretation. Many presidents have been punished at the polls for ill-advised foreign policy decisions, whereas others have essentially rescued their presidencies by engaging in successful foreign policy initiatives.

★ Foreign Policy Dilemmas for the Twenty-first Century

- Foreign policy dilemmas facing American officials in the twenty-first century include questions about when (if at all) a preemptive military attack is justified, whether the United States should increase or decrease foreign aid in general, and the role of the United Nations.

CourseMate

Key Terms

Central Intelligence Agency (CIA) (p. 480)

Cold War (p. 473)

Containment (p. 474)

Department of Defense (p. 479)

Department of Homeland Security (DHS) (p. 480)

Department of State (p. 479)

Domino theory (p. 474)

Expansionism (p. 472)

Internationalism (p. 473)

International organization (p. 479)

Isolationism (p. 471)

Joint Chiefs of Staff (JCS) (p. 480)

Manifest destiny (p. 472)

Marshall Plan (p. 473)

Military-industrial complex (p. 480)

Monroe Doctrine (p. 472)

National Security Council (NSC) (p. 480)

New world order (p. 475)

North Atlantic Treaty Organization (NATO) (p. 474)

Pacifism (p. 471)

Preemption doctrine (p. 484)

Strategic Defense Initiative (SDI) (p. 475)

Truman Doctrine (p. 474)

Two presidencies theory (p. 470)

United Nations (UN) (p. 473)

War Powers Resolution (p. 470)

Warsaw Pact (p. 474)

Resources

Books

Ferguson, Niall. *Colossus: The Price of America's Empire.* New York: Penguin Books, 2004.

Kissinger, Henry. *Crisis: The Anatomy of Two Major Foreign Policy Crises.* New York: Simon & Schuster, 2003.

Mead, Walter Russell. *Special Providence: American Foreign Policy and How It Changed the World.* New York: Routledge, 2002.

Nye, Joseph, Jr. *The Paradox of American Power: Why the World's Only Superpower Can't Go It Alone.* New York: Oxford University Press, 2002.

Wittkopf, Eugene R., and James M. McCormick. *The Domestic Sources of Foreign Policy*, 3rd ed. Lanham, MD: Rowman & Littlefield, 1999.

Woodward, Bob. *The War Within: A Secret White House History, 2006–2008.* New York: Simon & Schuster, 2008.

Internet Sources

http://www.defense.gov (the official Web site of the Department of Defense; contains information on all branches of the military, speeches and press resources, reports from the secretary of defense, and so on).

http://www.state.gov (the official Web site of the U.S. Department of State, featuring reports on world affairs, information about traveling and living abroad, and so forth).

http://www.un.org/english (the English-language Web site of the United Nations; includes daily briefings and information about breaking developments in world affairs, documents and maps, conferences and publications, and a link to a live UN webcast).

NOW A hospital waiting room crowded with patients in 2004.

SUSAN WATTS/NY DAILY NEWS ARCHIVE/GETTY IMAGES

THEN A line of poor people awaiting handouts of soup and coffee in New York City during the late 1920s.

HULTON ARCHIVE/GETTY IMAGES

NOW & THEN

State "Laboratories of Democracy" That Point the Way

? *The national government arrived late to the scene when it enacted a broad and comprehensive social program designed to benefit millions of needy Americans. Several state governments had already established their own programs, extending unprecedented new benefits to their own citizens. State legislators who sponsored the new programs celebrated their progressive policy innovations, arguing that they had succeeded where so many other states had failed. In the final analysis, these policies did not simply start a movement of similar initiatives in other states; they also offered a model of sorts for the federal government to enact its own national program years later. Innovative state policies had thus served an even greater purpose: they showed how state governments can effectively serve as "laboratories of democracy" for the nation as a whole.*

NOW & THEN

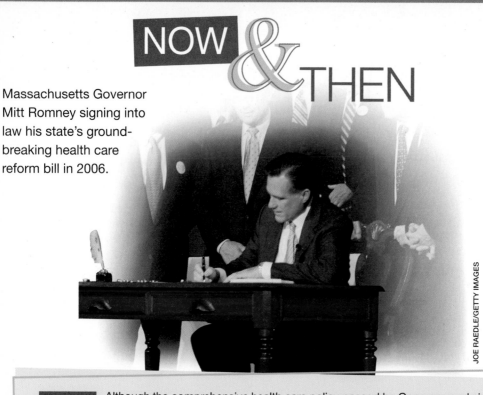

Massachusetts Governor Mitt Romney signing into law his state's ground-breaking health care reform bill in 2006.

JOE RAEDLE/GETTY IMAGES

NOW Although the comprehensive health care policy passed by Congress and signed into law on March 23, 2010, significantly expanded health care coverage to uninsured individuals across the country, it stopped short of the "universal coverage" President Obama and Democratic leaders had long been advocating. Supporters of universal health care coverage should have been forewarned: progressive state legislatures had debated the merits of their own health care initiatives in recent decades, and a handful had even made significant strides, but none had succeeded in guaranteeing complete universal coverage. Hawaii was the true pioneer in this regard: in the 1970s its legislature enacted a law that mandated employer-based health insurance for all employees not covered by collective bargaining. Later, in 1989, the Aloha state went a step further, subsidizing insurance coverage for Hawaiians unable to pay. Even so, 5 percent of Hawaii's population remained uninsured. Five thousand miles away in Boston, Massachusetts, the state legislature in 2006 passed legislation requiring all residents to purchase health insurance or face stiff legal penalties. Once again, however, ambiguous definitions of the term *affordable* meant that at least some Massachusetts residents would continue to be uninsured. Several state governments had expanded health care coverage, but they had failed to enact universal coverage for their populations. In 2010 the national government's health care reform plan similarly expanded coverage for millions, but it, too, failed to provide universal coverage.

THEN Even before passage of the Social Security Act in 1935, many states provided assistance to the elderly. Although state-sponsored "old-age pensions" were practically nonexistent before the onset of the Great Depression, thirty states passed some form of elderly assistance legislation between 1930 and 1935. Thus when President Franklin Roosevelt proposed the national system of Social Security legislation in 1935, he was able to learn and borrow from the three most successful state old-age pensions of that time: those in California, Massachusetts, and his own home state of New York, where as governor he had urged passage of such legislation. Unlike failed programs in other states, those three states did not require counties to "opt in" to the program to participate; all counties were enrolled automatically. Moreover, many of the failed state programs had trouble enrolling older citizens who were reluctant to "go on welfare"; the more successful state policies billed themselves instead as variations on employee savings programs. Accordingly, the national Social Security program passed by Congress was mandatory, and it too would be financed by payroll taxes, distinguishing it further from more traditional welfare programs. The state governments had once again performed a valuable service with their experimental policies, pointing the way to a national program that survives seventy-five years later. Franklin Roosevelt must have been especially proud, as the Old Age Pension Act of New York that he had signed into law as governor of that state helped pave the road to the Social Security Act he signed into law as president just a few years later.

New York State Governor Franklin Roosevelt, who signed into law the Old Age Pension Act of New York in 1930.

BETTMANN/CORBIS

As Supreme Court Justice Louis Brandeis argued in 1932, the states provide the nation as a whole with true laboratories for democracy:

Denial of the right to experiment may be fraught with serious consequences to the nation. It is one of the happy incidents of the federal system that a single courageous state may, if its citizens choose, serve as a laboratory; and try novel social and economic experiments without risk to the rest of the country.[1]

States provide the venue for experiments in policy and legal decisions, with some states having more liberal orientations and others tilting more conservative. In addition to taking on the issues of health care coverage and old-age pensions, state governments grapple with other concerns such as the right to die (as in Oregon's "Death with Dignity" Act) and the legal use of marijuana for pain relief (as in California). Throughout U.S. history, states have often taken the lead in experimenting with new ideas. Citizens and policymakers throughout the nation watch what the states do and monitor the impact and effectiveness of those experiments.

Historical Development of State and Local Governments

Colonial governments existed in America for more than a century before the war for American independence and the adoption of the U.S. Constitution. The thirteen colonies at the time of the American Revolution became the first thirteen states, each of which had an existing system of government when it became a state. These thirteen political systems were accustomed to operating quite independently. It was not until the American fight for independence from Great Britain that the colonies, out of necessity, began to work together in any coordinated way.

By the time of the Revolution, the colonies had well-established governments, with governors, legislatures, and court systems as well as numerous towns and cities, which had their own charters. Some of the colonies had already adopted a "bill of rights," identifying and trumpeting the individual liberties that their citizens enjoyed. Following the successful war for independence, the political establishments and governing structures of all thirteen states labored to maintain their own authority and governing power as the new federal government took shape. As discussed in Chapter 2, a critical problem with the first government of the United States, under the Articles of Confederation, was that the states retained too much authority. The framers at the Constitutional Convention in 1787, though granting greater authority to the federal government, were careful to retain authority for the states.

Article IV, Section 3 of the U.S. Constitution provides Congress with the power to admit new states. The initial step in the process for a territory or independent entity to become a state is for its governing legislature to submit a petition to Congress requesting that it be considered for statehood. Following congressional approval of the petition, the would-be state must then draft a state constitution, which has to include a provision for a republican form of government. Once Congress accepts the constitution, a bill can then be entered for accepting the territory into statehood. As with any other bill, the president must sign it to take effect.

Since the original thirteen colonies became states, thirty-seven states have been added to the union. Each of the fifty states has a constitution, a democratically elected governor and state legislature, and a judicial system. Within each state are thousands of cities, towns, and municipalities, chartered by the state. Each of the states enjoys governing authority within its borders and, under the rules of the federalist system, conducts relations with other states, provides citizenship status to its inhabitants, and plays a dominant role in certain policy areas. Although the fifty states are characterized by these qualities and are bound together politically and culturally, they widely vary in other ways. In some states, the state government is dominated by a strong governor (as in Maryland and New York); in other states, power is concentrated in the legislature (New Hampshire, Maine, Vermont, and South Carolina, for example). Some states have very populous state legislative districts (one legislator per about 300,000 citizens such as in California) and others have districts with far fewer constituents (such as Vermont with about one legislator for every 3,000 citizens). Some elect their state judges whereas others do not. In short, the governments that operate across the fifty states vary greatly.

Structure of State and Local Governments
State Constitutions

A **state constitution** is the fundamental law governing the structure and activities of state and local government. The only restriction on a state constitution is that it cannot conflict with the U.S. Constitution or federal laws and treaties. Just as the blueprint for how the federal government works is found in the U.S. Constitution, each of the fifty states has a state constitution that spells out who has power, how that power is shared, how policy is made, what rights citizens have, and how elections are to be conducted. Typically, however, state constitutions differ from the U.S. Constitution in that they tend to be more specific on policy issues and in describing the political party system.

The constitutions of the fifty states reflect each state's political, historical, and cultural diversity. Some of the state constitutions are very old. For example, the constitution for the Commonwealth of Massachusetts, which dates back to 1780, is older than the U.S. Constitution. In fact, the Massachusetts constitution is the oldest written constitution still in use in the world. By contrast, Georgia adopted a new constitution in 1983. The details and specificity of state constitutions varies widely as well, with Vermont's constitution containing only about 8,000 words, as compared to Alabama's, which contains over 340,000 words.

The early state constitutions emphasized many of the same themes that the U.S. Constitution stresses: that governmental power emanates from the people and that people possess the power to change the constitution. Early state constitutions also tended to place greater power in the state legislature and extend less to the governor. This policy reflected Americans' suspicion of kings and royal governors, given their experience in the revolutionary era. Between the American Revolution and the Civil War, most states rewrote their constitutions, often multiple times. These revisions reflected the need to strengthen the powers of the state's governor. Constitutional revisions also tended to provide for

Explain the function and forms of state constitutions and local government charters ★ LO

State constitution
The fundamental law governing the structure and activities of state and local government.

Failures in the Laboratories of Democracy

The statement of U.S. Supreme Court Justice Louis Brandeis that states should serve as "laboratories for democracy" has been trumpeted as a unique positive feature of American government. Examples are plentiful of the successes of state-driven initiatives; in the case of old-age pensions and health care, they eventually gave rise to sweeping national reforms. But the experiments have not always been successful. Indeed, sometimes they have been downright failures.

In 1865, the Thirteenth Amendment to the U.S. Constitution ended the practice of slavery in the United States. Prior to this amendment, many territories that applied for statehood found themselves caught in the national debate over the polarizing issue of slavery. In 1819, Missouri, a slave-owning territory, applied for statehood, but was rejected by the nonslavery states in Congress because it would tip the balance of states to slave-owning ones. Missouri was admitted in 1821, only after Maine was offered admission as a nonslave state. The legislatures in Missouri and Maine included clauses in their state constitutions regarding the legality of slave ownership, and this experiment worked, because both were successfully admitted. After Missouri's admission until the time of the Civil War, nine other states were admitted to the Union, each with an explicit provision in its constitution regarding slavery. The Thirteenth Amendment, of course, ended the experiment of gaining state admission on the basis of its policy on slavery.

In 1933, prohibition—the banning of the manufacture, sale, and transportation of intoxicating liquors—was repealed by the Twenty-first Amendment to the Constitution. The state of Maine in 1851 had been the first state to pass a law that made it illegal to make or consume alcohol within its borders. Eleven more states followed Maine's lead and had adopted prohibition laws by 1860. The movement continued to gain appeal and by 1919 Maine's initial experiment some seventy years earlier had become national policy with ratification of the Eighteenth Amendment to the U.S. Constitution. Support for prohibition, however, was short-lived. With northern Democrats such as Al Smith and Franklin Delano Roosevelt of New York leading the opposition to prohibition, the "noble experiment," as it was called, ended when ratification of the Twenty-first Amendment in 1933 repealed the Eighteenth Amendment.

In 2003, the state of California experimented with a new regulatory policy to deal with energy providers in the state. Over the previous few years, California had experienced severe shortages of energy. In order to deal with the shortages, the state negotiated long-term contracts with energy suppliers outside the state. What was described as a new and innovative policy of importing energy ended in disaster. When energy shortages occurred, the out-of-state suppliers delivered energy at hugely inflated costs, which was allowable under the deal negotiated by the state. The California experiment's failure served as a warning to other states that long-term contracts with out-of-state energy suppliers were not a good way to deal with energy shortages.

greater democratization of state institutions, including new provisions for popular elections of state officials, extensions of suffrage (by removing property ownership as a qualification for voting), and the promotion of local self-government rule. For example, the earliest New York State Constitution gave the governor the authority to appoint the mayors of cities; but an 1833 amendment provided for the popular election of city mayors.[2]

In the late 1800s and early 1900s, new state constitutions and amendments to existing constitutions focused on the growing demands placed on states from industrialization and urbanization. States began to include in their constitutions provisions for public health services to deal with urban health problems, public education for poor and working-class children, and regulation of the business environment to control or moderate monopolistic activities of the railroads and other industries. Also in the 1900s, a number of states passed provisions for initiative and referendum, measures that give a state's voters the right to pass laws directly (without having to go through the state legislature) and to veto laws passed by the state government).

Local Government Charters

There are more than 87,500 local governments in the United States.[3] These include units that govern cities, towns, counties, school systems, and special districts such as transit systems. Whereas the fifty state governments are sovereign units that coexist with the federal government, local governments are chartered by the state in which they exist. A local **charter** is a state law that grants a local government the authority to provide public services, enact and enforce regulations, and raise revenue to support its operations.

State governments exercise authority over local governments. Unlike the relationship between the federal government and state governments where states have the constitutional right to exist, local governments do not enjoy the same protections against state encroachment. In 1868, Judge John Forrest Dillon of the Iowa Supreme Court issued a ruling, which has come to be known as **Dillon's Rule**, that gives state governments clear authority over local governments. Dillon ruled that "municipal corporations owe their origins to and derive their power and rights wholly from the legislature . . . As it [the state] creates, so it may destroy."[4] Thus, a state government may issue directives ordering localities to do as it wishes. State governments can decide what local services must be provided, how school districts must be arranged, and so forth.

The most common type of local government is that which has been chartered by a state to manage and regulate local public services, such as fire and police protection, local roads, parks and recreation, libraries, sewer and water facilities, and the like. These are multipurpose local governments, and they are commonly referred to as a city, a town, a township, or a county or parish. There are about 40,000 of these types of local governments in the United States, and they range from large cities with millions of residents such as New York City, Los Angeles, Atlanta, Chicago, and Houston, to small towns with only a few hundred residents, or even fewer.

Most of these multipurpose local governments fall into one of three categories, although distinctions between them are by no means well defined:

1. **Counties.** All states have **counties** (called parishes in Louisiana and boroughs in Alaska), although the size, importance, and scope of activity of county governments vary quite a bit. Most states use counties to keep basic administrative data on the population such as birth and death records, voter registration records, and land ownership and usage records, as well as to administer elections and the local court system.[5] Across most of the United States, counties coexist with city or town governments, each of which retains authority for providing certain services.

2. **Cities.** The type of local government that has been chartered by a state to serve the needs of a more urbanized or densely populated area is typically referred to as a **city**. The more formal term for a city is municipality. Cities can be large, such as New York City; medium-size, like Little Rock,

Charter
A state law that grants a local government the authority to provide public services, enact and enforce regulations, and raise revenue to support its operations.

Dillon's Rule
The Iowa Supreme Court ruling establishing that state government maintains clear authority over local governments to issue directives ordering localities to do what the state wishes.

County
A form of local government that varies in importance and scope of activity across the states and usually coexists with city or town governments.

City
The type of local government that has been chartered by a state to serve the needs of an urbanized or densely populated area.

Arkansas; or small, like Burlington, Vermont. Large and often medium-size cities are characterized by an urban core, which places special demands on local government. In many cities, this urban core includes a central business district, often defined visually by the city's skyline of tall buildings. Maintaining the business district, making it attractive to businesses and visitors, and dealing with housing issues for the city's residents are just some of the special policy issues facing American cities. Many cities around the United States, however, are much smaller and are typically referred to as villages.

3. **Townships.** In rural areas of the states, towns or **townships** are the unit for which a local government is chartered. In addition, geographic outgrowths of cities are often referred to as towns or townships. In many states the county government provides various services for townships.

Other local governments that provide specialized services rather than a full array of local services are called special districts. The most common type of special district is a school district, which provides educational instruction and services. Another common type of special district is a water or sewerage authority. There are approximately 50,000 special districts across the fifty states, about one third of which are school districts.

Who Governs the States?

Like the federal government, all the states divide political power among three branches of government: an executive branch headed by a governor that is responsible for administering the law; a legislative branch, composed of legislators elected by the people to represent districts within a state, that has the authority to pass laws; and a judicial branch that interprets laws and settles disputes. The logic of this separation of powers is the same as that of the organization of the federal government: a distribution of power across numerous institutions so that no one person or institution accumulates excessive power that might undermine democracy.

The Governor. Every state has a governor, who is the head of the state's executive branch of government. In the early days of the new nation, governors were politically weak. Most held a term of one or two years. However, as most of the states found out, legislatures are best at debating public policy and passing laws, not administering state programs and policy. As state governments grew with the nation and states began to provide more services, it became clear that a strong governor was needed to ensure the effective administration of these programs. Over time, the office of governor became increasingly important.

Today, most governors are elected to terms of office of four years. In all the states, the candidate who receives the highest number of popular votes wins the governor's office. Many states set a minimum age and a minimum number of years of residency in the state for a person to be eligible to become governor.

Governors, like U.S. presidents, are the chief executive officers in their respective state and thus serve a variety of important roles in state government. First, as ceremonial leader of state government, the governor presides over major state events and represents the state around the nation and in Washington, DC. The governor is also the head of the state political party of which she or he is a member. More often than not, members of the governor's party in a state legislature take their cues from and follow the leadership of the governor when it comes to voting on legislation. As head of the party in the state, the governor typically has a great deal of influence in fund raising for the party and setting the tone and strategy for statewide elections.

Like the president, governors are the chief executives and managers of the state government. They choose the individuals who are the leaders of important state departments and agencies. In times of crisis or natural disaster in a particular state, governors typically take charge and direct response and relief efforts. In most states, the governor is the first and primary author of the state budget, which allocates money for the operations of the state departments and agencies. Whereas the state legislature is responsible for approving the budget, the governor's office is primarily responsible for setting spending priorities and negotiating wage and benefits packages for state employees.

The State Legislatures. All the states vest lawmaking authority in the state's legislature. In forty-nine of the fifty states, the state legislature is similar in structure to the U.S. Congress: a bicameral, or two-house, legislature that consists of a state senate and a state house (commonly referred to as a state general assembly). Only Nebraska has a unicameral, or one-house, state legislature.

© 2012 CENGAGE LEARNING

Though a majority in each house of the state legislature must pass a bill before it may become law, the governor also has a role in the legislative process. Governors may veto bills; to become law a vetoed bill must be approved by a supermajority (usually two thirds) of the state legislature. Legislatures also share with the governor some administrative functions, including the development of budgets for state agencies and the oversight of bureaucratic agencies.

There are 7,382 elected members of the fifty state legislatures across the nation, and the size of the legislature varies from state to state. The state legislature of California, the largest state in terms of population (about 35 million), has only 120 members (eighty in the state house and forty in the state senate). New Hampshire, a state that ranks forty-first in total population (about 1.3 million), has a state legislature of 424 members (400 in the house and twenty-four in the senate). Even the state of Vermont, ranked forty-ninth in population, has more state legislators than California, which has nearly fifty times its population.

Since the 1950s, most state legislatures have experienced a great deal of change. One aspect of the change relates to the types of people who are elected to serve. From 1970 to 1999, for example, the percentage of women legislators increased from 4 percent to 22 percent.[6] The percentage of African American legislators increased from 2 percent to 8 percent over the same thirty-year period.[7] Although their numbers in state legislatures are still disproportionately lower than their population size, women and certain racial groups now have greater representation and impact than they did decades ago.

Several U.S. Supreme Court decisions in the 1960s spurred a revolution of sorts in the development of state legislatures. These court decisions required the democratization of legislative apportionment to achieve the goal of "one person, one vote."[8] In many states today, the position of state legislator is a full-time job, and legislators receive a commensurate full-time salary. With the increase in talent in the legislature also came improved procedural changes and enhanced institutional capacity,[9] including the hiring of qualified professional staffs for legislative leadership and committees and significant improvement of the space and other resources in legislative office buildings and facilities.

Alan Rosenthal, the nation's foremost authority on state legislatures, has noted that the reapportionment decisions, changes in the composition of the legislatures, and resource enhancements led legislators to spend more time on the job. Legislatures began meeting more frequently and tackling larger issues. In many states, legislatures began to take a much more active role in overseeing the performance of state agencies and in developing budgets for agencies. Prior to the 1960s, governors clearly exerted more power than the legislature. The professionalization of most state legislatures, however, transformed state politics by empowering the legislative branch and thus balancing the power among the branches.

State Courts. Most criminal and civil law matters in the United States find their way into the legal system of one of the fifty states. All together, the state governments process nearly 35 million cases per year, which amounts to more than 95 percent of the nation's litigation. About a third of the cases in state legal systems relate to criminal matters. Although each state's system features its own set of unique characteristics and nuances, some common elements exist.

Every state maintains trial courts that do the bulk of work, processing cases at the lower levels of the state legal system. These trial courts (often called "district courts" or "circuit courts" depending on the state or locality) may themselves hear appeals from subordinate courts such as traffic courts; they also serve as sites for trials of more significant crimes. Thirty-nine of the fifty states have intermediate appellate courts, to which all appeals from trial courts must first be directed. All fifty states maintain at least one high supreme court. (Texas and Oklahoma have separate supreme courts for criminal and civil cases.) State supreme courts generally provide the final source of appeal for each state legal system. To appeal beyond the state supreme court directly to the U.S. Supreme Court, a losing party must first exhaust all the remedies available at the state level.

In theory, state courts must comply with pronouncements from the U.S. Supreme Court over the meaning of the Constitution and the Bill of Rights. The reality is much more complicated. During various periods of American history, rebellious state courts tried to evade certain Supreme Court pronouncements by distinguishing or limiting the Supreme Court ruling and on occasion even by denying the Supreme Court's jurisdiction over the matter. Although the U.S. Supreme Court can usually exert its will over defiant state courts, it must expend key institutional resources and prestige to do so.

Who Governs the Localities?

Local governments vary widely in how they are structured and usually take one of four forms:

★ LO Describe the various forms of local government that exist across the numerous municipalities in the United States

Mayor-council form
The form of local government, modeled on the executive and legislative branches of the federal government and the fifty state governments, in which the mayor is the executive and council is the legislative

1. **The mayor-council form. The mayor-council form** of government, the most common structure for local governments, is modeled on the executive and legislative branches of the federal government and the fifty state governments. The council is the legislative body and the mayor is the executive. The primary job of the council is to enact new laws and the main role of the mayor is to administer the local laws. However, legislative and executive authority is often shared through a system of checks and balances. For example, though ultimately the council is responsible for passing new laws, the mayor often sets the agenda or has the authority to veto a new law.

The power of the mayor in the mayor-council form varies. In localities with a *weak mayor system*, the mayor has no veto authority, has little or no control over appointments to head local agencies, and is not selected in a general election by voters, but rather by the council from within its own ranks. In cities with a *strong mayor system*, the mayor is directly elected by the voters of the locality. In such a system, the mayor has the true executive authority of selecting people to run local agencies and has the power to veto council legislation.

2. **The council-manager form.** The second most common local government structure is the **council-manager form**. The council-manager form attempts to remove politics from the management of the city and place it in the hands of a professional, nonelected manager. Typically, the manager is hired by the council for a period of time to run the government on a day-to-day basis. Under this system, the council holds all political and legislative authority. Together, the mayor-council format and the council-manager structure account for about 90 percent of all local governments in the United States.[10]

3. **The commission form.** A small number of localities use the **commission form** to run local government. Typically, each member of the commission is elected by the voters and has administrative authority over a specific area. For example, in Portland, Oregon, a six-member city commission serves as the city's government. One member serves as mayor and the other five each manage an area of the city, such as public works, public utilities, or public safety.

4. **The town meeting.** The **town meeting** is a form of local government found exclusively in some small towns in the New England states. In the town meeting, citizens vote on policy issues, people to manage certain town projects, and other matters that a town council or commission would normally vote on. The town meeting is the only remaining form of pure direct democracy left in the United States.

Council-manager form
The form of local government that places management of the city or town in the hands of a nonelected professional appointed by the council.

Commission form
The form of local government that features an elected group of commissioners with each commissioner having administrative authority over a specific aspect of government.

Town meeting
The form of local government found exclusively in some small towns in New England (and two Midwest states) in which all citizens are invited to vote on policy issues and management matters.

State Elections

★ LO

Assess how different states administer elections

States are responsible for administering elections. U.S. constitutional amendments and other federal legislation place some restrictions on what states can and cannot do in running elections. States cannot deny those at least eighteen years of age, women, or racial and ethnic minorities the right to vote; nor can they charge a fee as a voting requirement or require a literacy test. But beyond these federal protections granted to all U.S. citizens, states are responsible for carrying out and managing elections. As a result there are in reality fifty different systems of electing public officials. As of January 1, 2010, nine states allow voters to register to vote when they show up at the polls on Election Day (Connecticut allows the practice only in the case of presidential elections). Most other states mandate that voters register at least two weeks (and in some cases at least thirty days) before Election Day; North Dakota is the only state that maintains no requirement at all for voters to register before they cast a ballot.[11] Some states require that voters register with a particular political party; others do not. Some states require primary elections to select the party candidates; other states allow parties to hold conventions or caucuses to make these choices.

AMERICAN GOVERNMENT In Popular Perspective

The New England Town Meeting: Still Going Strong after 380 Years

New England is often viewed as somewhat quirky or peculiar. Nothing better illustrates that quirkiness than the region's continued reliance on the town meeting system of government. In a tradition dating back to the 1630s, citizens of small communities (normally 6,000 residents or fewer) throughout the New England states come together once a year to discuss the business of their town. The "town meeting" form of government offers perhaps the purest form of direct democracy, as all the citizens present (limited to legal voters within the community) approve the following year's budget, set the salaries for elected officials, and then vote on local statutes and laws. Although Michigan and Minnesota have also retained town meeting systems in some form, New England remains its principal locus, with every state in that region continuing to adhere to the centuries-old tradition.

Citizens who participate in open town meetings often take their role quite seriously, and they tend to jealously protect each meeting's participatory prerogatives. Former Vermont Governor Madeleine Kunin learned this lesson the hard way. In March 1988 she visited an open town meeting in the small town of Duxbury to explain her decision to support a controversial regional planning law. But when Governor Kunin stepped forward to address the meeting, a motion was raised from the floor to prevent her from doing so. After a vote, a second motion, and much discussion, Kunin was eventually allowed to address the meeting. So much for gubernatorial prerogative.

For Critical Thinking and Discussion

1. What are the advantages and disadvantages of governing small communities by the town meeting system?

2. If only a small percentage of the community's voters actually participate, is the system less legitimate?

3. Would you favor town meetings as a form of government in slightly larger communities (between 6,000 and 10,000 people)? Why or why not?

States also differ in the technologies they employ for voters to cast ballots. Some use paper ballots, others use levered voting machines, and still others use touch-screen computers. Some states allow counties or other political subdivisions to choose their own preferred voting mechanism. In addition, there are also variations in state requirements about the presentation of candidates on the ballot. Third-party candidates often must achieve a minimum number of signatures from voters to get on the ballot at all (and the number of signatures varies quite a bit from state to state). Some states use the **Indiana ballot** format, in which the name of the political party appears at the top of the column and candidates for the various offices appear below the party label, thus cuing the voters to partisan-based voting. Some states using this type of ballot include a lever or check box above the column to allow a voter to select all of a particular party's candidates in one stroke. Other states use a **Massachusetts ballot**, which organizes the slate of candidates according to the office they are seeking, indicating the candidate's party affiliation with a label.

Though all fifty states maintain a two-party electoral system, some states are so dominated by one of the two parties that the only meaningful competition occurs in the primary election or caucus that determines the dominant party's nominee. In some states, such as Wyoming, Idaho, and Utah, the Republicans

Indiana ballot
The voting ballot format in which the name of the political party appears at the top of the column and candidates for the various offices appear below the party label, thus cuing the voters to partisan-based voting.

Massachusetts ballot
The voting ballot format that organizes the slate of candidates according to the office they are seeking, indicating the candidate's party affiliation with a label.

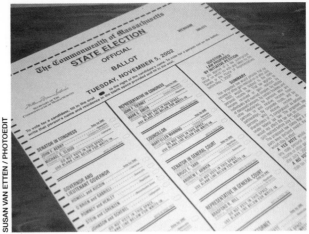

Left: An "Indiana ballot," with the name of the political parties heading the columns across the ballot. Right: A "Massachusetts ballot," which organizes the candidates on the basis of the office they are running for, with a party label associated with each candidate.

dominate the state legislature. In other states like Hawaii, the Democrats are largely in control. In still other states, such as Illinois, Michigan, and Pennsylvania, the parties are evenly balanced and competition for control of the state legislature is intense.[12]

Though many states authorize a primary runoff election to determine party nominees for office, only the state of Louisiana features a system of nonpartisan primary runoff elections.[13] Nebraska is the only state to hold nonpartisan elections for statewide office: Candidates are listed on ballots without party labels, and parties are forbidden from recruiting candidates. By virtue of a voter initiative in 2004 that restored a qualifying primary for partisan races, Washington is once again the only state in the country to hold so-called blanket primaries in which voters can cross party lines and choose candidates of either party on an office-by-office basis. Because the states control and manage all elections, there are fifty unique systems for voting. Although these fifty different systems provide for a great deal of color, nuance, and diversity in American campaigns and elections, it is difficult to summarize how all fifty state elections systems work. Despite all the variations, a useful framework for understanding campaigns and elections within the states begins with the state political party organizations.

State Party Organizations

All fifty states have a Democratic Party and a Republican Party organization. Though many other party organizations, like the Green Party, the Socialist Party, or the Libertarian Party, may be found in the states, the two major political parties tend to dominate campaigns and elections. Sometimes independent or third-party candidates are successful, but such victories are rare. Today, for example, only about twenty of the nearly 7,400 state legislative seats across the country are held by independents or members of a third party.[14] Party competition in the states is largely between the two major parties, the Democrats and Republicans.

Over the past several decades, candidates for high-profile races, such as the presidency and the U.S. Senate, generally have become less reliant on the parties to wage successful campaigns for office.[15] These federal races often attract the contributions of many donors. Once in office, federal elected officials also have access to a variety of campaign resources, including the franking privilege and easy access to and attention from the news media.

Most candidates for state elective offices do not enjoy these same resources. Thus, the state and local party organizations play a much more important role in the election politics of most state races. One exception, of course, are gubernatorial elections, which often do attract the attention of many donors as well as the news media. State parties once exercised greater control, leadership, and discipline over the nomination process and the conduct of general election campaigns, but today state parties typically do not control the nomination of candidates and the conduct of campaigns. They do, however, continue to play a large supportive role.[16] State political party organizations continue to serve a number of important roles in the elections of state officeholders. These include the following:[17]

- **Fundraising to help pay for election campaigns.** Campaigns for the state legislature, governor's office, or other statewide office often require the work of professional campaign staffers (such as a campaign manager, pollster, and media director) and support staff. These campaigns also need money to produce and place advertising in newspapers and on radio and television. The parties are highly organized for fund raising to help support their own candidates. Although individual candidates conduct some campaign fund raising, the state party organizations are an important source of money for waging political campaigns.

- **Providing campaign support services to candidates.** The state party organizations often purchase the services of campaign strategists, advertising agencies, organizers, and fund raisers. The party organizations also fund phone bank activities, as well as other activities to help their candidate's chances of winning at the polls. The parties also organize get-out-the-vote efforts on Election Day, which include calling party members to remind them to vote and providing rides and assistance to those who need help getting to the polling place.

- **Recruiting candidates and influencing the party nominating process.** In the past, the state and local party organizations, often through party bosses and political machines, had a great deal of control over the selection of the party's candidates. Laws controlling patronage, however, diminished the power of the political machines. In addition, the professionalization of campaigns and the ability of candidates to raise funds outside of the party system have also loosened the grip that the parties have on the nominations. The decades-long trend toward primary elections, rather than caucuses, as the dominant method for nominating candidates has reduced party influence even more. Still, the state parties remain very active in recruiting individuals who are good partisans, contribute to the party organization, and show the promise of winning in the general election.

- **Providing a framework for voters to help make a vote choice.** The states' two-party systems offer voters a simple general framework in most campaigns involving a choice between the Democratic and the Republican candidate. State parties develop a platform, ideological and issue-position perspectives, and advertising themes, and communicate these themes and perspectives to voters through campaign events and advertising. The regularized competition between the two major parties in political campaigns provides a familiar framework for voters within which to make their vote decisions.

The Democratic and Republican state party organizations each have a state committee consisting of those elected to represent localities plus other elected officials in the party, which oversees the parties' activities. This committee organizes state party conventions, where party members meet to create a party platform, recruit and sometimes nominate candidates for office, and develop fund-raising strategies. The committee also coordinates the activities of local party groups.[18]

Gubernatorial Elections

The highest state office is that of governor, so it's not too surprising that gubernatorial elections tend to attract relatively higher levels of voter interest. Gubernatorial elections generally feature significant party competition, higher campaign budgets, and a considerable amount of news media attention.

Whereas many state legislative seats are often uncontested, rarely is a gubernatorial race without competition between the two major parties. In fact, gubernatorial races often include one or more third-party candidates. Though prior to the 1960s the Democrats tended to occupy a larger number of governorships, more recently the parties have been about equally successful.[19] Though Democrats have been more successful on the West Coast and in the southern states (winning 65 percent of those contests over the past forty years), more recently Republican gubernatorial candidates have been more successful in the South. In the Midwest, Republicans have won nearly two thirds of gubernatorial races since 1966.[20] As of January 1, 2010, twenty-six governors were Democrats and twenty-four were Republicans.

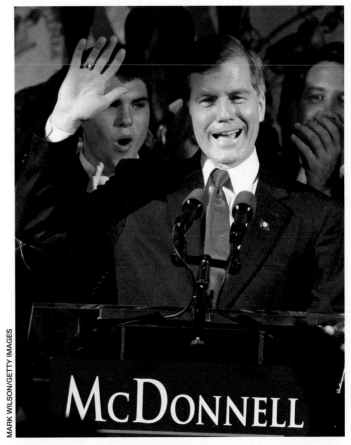

MARK WILSON/GETTY IMAGES

Pictured above is Republican Bob McDonnell at his victory speech on election night in November 2009. McDonnell defeated Democrat Creigh Deeds in a hotly contested gubernatorial race in Virgina.

Similar to the presidency, many states impose term limits on the governorship. Term limits have the effect of reducing the number of incumbents running for reelection. Therefore, though incumbency is still a powerful indicator of success, it is less influential overall in gubernatorial races than in lower-profile state legislative elections. However, incumbents who do run for reelection generally do quite well—in 2008, eight of the nine gubernatorial incumbents running for reelection were successful, similar to the pattern for incumbents in earlier years.[21] Of course incumbency is no guarantee to victory, especially in difficult economic times. Just ask Democrat Jon Corzine, the former governor of New Jersey, who lost his reelection bid in 2009 to Republican Chris Christie.

Though many states have gubernatorial term limits, Virginia is unique in that it prohibits governors from serving two terms consecutively. This restriction means that no gubernatorial races in that state feature an incumbent candidate.

State Legislative Elections

Corresponding to the wide variation in how legislatures represent citizens are the great differences in state legislative campaigns. In states with less populous districts, campaigns are likely to be characterized primarily by door-to-door canvassing for votes, lawn signs, bumper stickers, campaign buttons, and perhaps a town meeting–style debate. In larger constituencies, such as in California, campaigns tend to be highly professionalized, well funded, and characterized by television advertising. The nature of party competition also influences the competitiveness and conduct of a particular legislative seat. Nationally in 2009, 55 percent all state legislative seats were occupied by Democrats and 44 percent were held by Republicans,[22] offering the impression that the parties actively compete. But the national figures obscure the fact that one particular party tends to dominate many of these legislative seats.[23] In the 2004 state legislative races, for example, 35 percent of all legislative seats ran a candidate from only one political party. Further, in most instances, the one candidate in these districts was an incumbent up for reelection, indicating the power of incumbency in legislative races. Without any meaningful competition, the election campaigns in as many as one third of state legislative districts are merely formalities. Often, these noncompetitive elections do not even feature a campaign.

Other state legislative races, however, include some level of competition. In fact, the trend toward greater professionalization of legislative campaigns is apparent, including greater fund raising and financing, more advertising, and the use of hired professionals to manage and support the campaign. With the devolution of federal authority to the states in many policy areas, state governments have become more important in policymaking. Thus, interest groups, PACs, and individual contributors have come to realize that in many policy areas, winning state legislative races is critical to influencing public policy outcomes.

In the 1990s, many states adopted legislation creating limits on the duration of time an individual may serve as a state legislator. The 1995 Supreme Court decision that invalidated state laws that set term limits for members of the U.S. Congress[24] does not apply to state offices, so term limits for state office continue to be valid. In states where there are term limits, the power of incumbency has been reduced. In states with term limits, however, legislative efforts to coordinate

Yes, Virginia, You Too Can Run for Political Office

Student government offers college students the chance to get a taste of governing. Yet sometimes college students want something more: the chance to run for and serve in state or local government. Normally a college degree is considered a minimum qualification for a position in government—but not always. So before you put off into the future your own plans to seek higher office, consider the following five college-age politicians who sought positions in state and local government with some degree of success:

- In November 2000, eighteen-year-old Derrick Seaver of Minster, Ohio, won an open seat in Ohio's State House of Representatives.

- In November 2001, Jeffrey Dunkel was three months shy of nineteen when he was elected as mayor of Mount Carbon, Pennsylvania.

- In November 2005, voters in Hillsdale, Michigan, elected eighteen-year-old Michael Sessions to be their next mayor even though under local law he was not legally old enough to place his name on the ballot. Sessions still won as a write-in candidate.

- In November 2005, the city of Torrington, Connecticut, elected twenty-two-year-old Ryan Bingham to be its mayor.

- On May 16, 2006, Mark Harris, a twenty-one-year-old political science major at George Washington University, scored a stunning upset when he defeated five-term incumbent Thomas Stevenson in the Republican primary for the forty-second district in the Pennsylvania House of Representatives. Harris eventually lost to the Democratic candidate, Matt Smith, in the general election.

JEFFREY SAUGER/BLOOMBERG VIA GETTY IMAGES

MICHAEL SESSIONS
MAYOR

legislative agendas have been problematic due to the turnover in leadership positions such as those of legislative speakers, majority and minority leaders, and committee chairs. As a result, the executive branch of government in these states has become relatively more powerful.

Even with the term limits movement, incumbent state legislators still wield considerable electoral power. The return rate of incumbent legislators who run for reelection exceeds 90 percent. This is about the same return rate for incumbent U.S. House members who seek reelection. These data confirm that while there may be dissatisfaction with the performance of state legislatures (and the U.S. Congress) in general, the level of support for one's own state legislator (and member of Congress) remains high.

The term limits movement has subsided somewhat over the past decade. In fact, six of the twenty-one states that adopted term limits legislation eventually rescinded the term limits rules. Even in California, the six-year limit for members of the general assembly and eight-year limit for state senators are being debated.

State Judicial Elections

Unlike federal judges, who are appointed by the president with the advice and consent of the Senate, many state judges are selected by some form of judicial election. Thirty-eight of the fifty states currently elect members of their highest court, and more than 86 percent of state judges across the country must stand for election. Where one stands in the age-old debate over whether judges should be elected in the first place depends on one's view of the role judges should play in the state governmental system. Most local and state bar officials think that judges must possess a high level of expertise and thus they should be selected only by other well-qualified professionals such as attorneys; others see the judicial function as more akin to a form of policymaking and thus place a premium on holding judges accountable to the public at large through popular elections to the bench.

Certainly no other type of government official is selected by so many different methods. Judicial elections may be partisan or nonpartisan in nature. Partisan judicial elections (held in seventeen states) are usually more subdued affairs than partisan elections of other political officials. Still, judicial candidates must be prepared to campaign for their party's nomination and, if necessary, to make appearances and raise money for a general election campaign against a named opponent. A candidate for the bench must be cautious of how he or she campaigns for office: Discussion of court procedures and the proper qualifications of individuals is fair game, but any reference to how a candidate might rule on a specific case runs afoul of the Code of Judicial Conduct, which forbids judicial candidates' responses to substantive legal questions.

More than a century ago, progressives troubled by the prospect of judges engaging in partisan politics pressed for nonpartisan judicial elections in which all party labels were eliminated. Yet in practice, it is nearly impossible to eliminate the influence of political parties in judicial elections of any kind. Michigan, for example, requires that nonincumbent candidates for the state's supreme court secure the backing of a major party in order to get on the ballot; thus Michigan's judicial elections tend to have a partisan flavor, even though the candidates technically run on a nonpartisan ticket. Recently the Michigan Republican Party even ran a television commercial criticizing a Democratic judicial candidate by name for being soft on crime. Similarly, the Minnesota Republican Party voted to endorse candidates for the state appeals court and supreme courts in so-called nonpartisan judicial elections.[25]

In recent years, judicial elections have become expensive affairs. Of the twenty-two states that use head-to-head elections to choose members of the state's supreme court, nine states broke combined candidate fund-raising records in 2004. Two candidates in one record-setting 2004 race in Illinois combined to raise more than $9.3 million—a figure higher than that raised by candidates in eighteen U.S. Senate races that same year. Between 1993 and 2006, candidates for Alabama's top state court posts spent more than $48 million. State supreme court election races tend to attract record sums from business interests in particular, but groups interested in social issues or crime policies may also succeed in politicizing certain judicial elections, including even some retention elections. In the most famous instance, Crime Victims for Court Reform was at least partly responsible for causing the ouster of California Supreme Court Chief

Justice Rose Bird and two of her colleagues in 1986 after they voted against the death penalty. Television advertising has become an especially potent weapon in many recent judicial elections, further increasing the costs of running in judicial elections.

★ LO

Compare and contrast the referendum, initiative, and recall mechanisms and assess how they contribute to democratic governance in the states

Referendum, Initiative, and Recall

The American tradition of direct democracy dates back to the town meetings held in the New England colonies as early as the 1630s. Today the remnants of direct democracy can still be found at the state and local levels in the form of referenda and initiatives, and—in some extremely rare cases—in the form of recall elections.

Currently twenty-four state constitutions (mostly in the West) and countless numbers of local governments offer voters the opportunity to vote on **referenda**, which refer to popular votes to overturn legislation already passed at the state or local level. By contrast, an **initiative** consists of newly drafted legislation submitted directly to a popular vote as an alternative to adoption by a legislature. Although the process varies from state to state, there are usually three steps in the initiative and referendum process: (1) citizens petition to put a measure on the ballot for voter approval; (2) once a defined number of signatures of legally registered voters has been gathered, the proposition is then put on the ballot during an election; (3) if a majority votes in favor of the proposition, the initiative or referendum has passed.

Referendum
A question that appears on the ballot asking voters to approve or reject a policy action either recommended by the state legislature or already approved by the state legislature.

Initiative
A question that goes directly to the voters for approval or rejection without first having been proposed by the state legislature.

One of the most famous initiatives in modern times was California's Proposition 13, which severely limited property tax increases in the state. It passed in 1978 by a vote of 65 percent to 35 percent. More significantly, its passage presaged a "taxpayer revolt" throughout the country, which contributed in part to the election of Ronald Reagan to the presidency in 1980. Voter referenda on standing laws are no less significant. For example, in 1990 the Nevada legislature initiated a referendum on the state's abortion law, which conformed to the Supreme Court's pro-abortion rights decisions in *Roe v. Wade*. Eventually, an approving majority of more than 60 percent gave the law a degree of legitimacy and quieted organizations opposed to abortion in the process. Other frequent topics for such propositions include term limits, environmental laws, and affirmative action.

There are many passionate supporters and critics alike of the initiative and referendum process. Those who favor this form of direct democracy believe the process reengages voters with politics and democracy. It can also help resolve certain political problems that elected

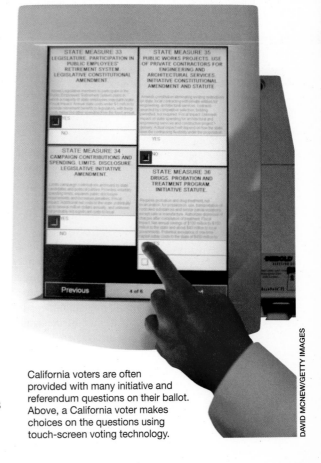

California voters are often provided with many initiative and referendum questions on their ballot. Above, a California voter makes choices on the questions using touch-screen voting technology.

DAVID MCNEW/GETTY IMAGES

Former California governor Gray Davis concedes defeat after the historic recall election in 2003. His wife and mother are by his side.

officials are unwilling to handle. Critics, however, complain that referenda undermine the concept of representative democracy. They also contend that the process has a substantive bias against civil rights and liberties, concepts that often fare poorly in polls of the citizenry. Finally, too many propositions on the ballot can make the entire voting procedure unwieldy and confusing for many citizens.

One significant downside to initiatives in particular is that they are often written by citizens who may not be able to see the unintended consequences of the proposals. Unfortunately, because most passed initiatives at the state level automatically become amendments to state constitutions, tinkering with or eliminating such measures can be especially challenging. Consider California's "Three Strikes and You're Out" proposition, which was passed in 1994 by an overwhelming vote of 72 percent. Once enacted, the initiative sent many individuals to jail for life on their third felony conviction, even when the third offense was considered relatively minor (in one case the provision was applied to a felon convicted of stealing a pizza). Naturally, the law produced controversial results, and many reformers proposed changes in it. One amendment—which scaled the law back by providing for drug treatment instead of life in prison for most of those convicted of possessing drugs—was passed by referendum six years later. Meanwhile, another proposed amendment, which would have required the third felony to be either "violent" and/or "serious" in order to result in a twenty-five-years-to-life sentence, was narrowly defeated in the amendment process. If the issue had been the subject of more flexible statutory law, it could have been more easily revised by the legislature to meet unexpected problems along the way.

Direct democracy can become especially controversial in those rare instances when voters attempt to remove an elected official from office in a **recall** election. Originally advocated by leaders of the Progressive movement during the late nineteenth century, the majority of states today allow recall elections in localities, but only nineteen states currently permit recall elections to oust statewide officers.

Recall
A ballot measure allowing voters to remove duly elected officials from office prior to the end of their term.

The first successful recall of a governor occurred in 1921, when North Dakota Governor Lynn Frazier was recalled.[26] Rather than starting a trend, however, the North Dakota case proved to be an aberration. For more than eight decades afterward, dozens of attempts to recall governors around the country failed. That streak ended in 2003 with the ouster of California Governor Gray Davis.

The recall mechanism places formidable obstacles in the way of removing a governor, no matter how unpopular he or she might be. Specifically, California law stipulates that recall of any statewide officer initially requires a petition by a number of voters equal to 12 percent of the previous vote for that office. In the case of Gray Davis, his opponents needed to gather 897,156 signatures to initiate a recall.

Opposition to Davis in 2003 was far greater than expected: Many citizens blamed him for the record state deficits that hit after the "dot-com" bubble exploded in the late 1990s. An electricity crisis in 2000–2001, in which the state had to resort to "rolling blackouts" and penalties for excessive energy use, was also laid at Davis's doorstep. Following his reelection in 2002 with just 47 percent of the vote, Davis's announcement in December 2002 that the state faced record budget deficits incited his opponents to attempt a recall in early 2003.

On July 23, 2003, California's secretary of state announced that there were more than 1.3 million valid signatures on the petition for Davis's recall. Once the petition was certified, Davis's recall was set to go before the voters on Election Day in 2003: If a majority favored his ouster at that time, the candidate with the plurality of votes in the same election would become the next governor. The challenge to succeed Davis as governor became something of a free-for-all, with a list of 135 candidates eventually appearing on the ballot. Once the popular Hollywood actor Arnold Schwarzenegger announced his candidacy on *The Tonight Show*, he became the immediate front-runner.

On Election Day, October 7, 2003, 55 percent of those voting favored the recall, making Davis only the second governor to be recalled in American history. Schwarzenegger was the clear victor in the vote to succeed Davis, garnering an impressive 48 percent of the votes in the crowded field. On November 13, 2003, Schwarzenegger was sworn in as California's thirty-eighth chief executive, putting an end to a political year in California marked at times by chaos. The 2003 recall election drew to the polls many voters who had never voted before. In that sense, democracy was certainly expanded.

Making the Connection

The fifty states in the United States of America differ, often dramatically and in many ways. The common thread is their commitment to a democratically elected government. But their political cultures are different, the dominance of their political orientations to the left or to the right varies, and their rules for electing and retaining elected officials differ. The power of their governors, as compared with that of the state legislature, varies, as do the ways in which the states charter localities and the forms of local governments they impose on them.

The variety found across the fifty state political systems, though confusing to some, produces some tremendous benefits, including the adaptability of governance to regional concerns and local cultures. But perhaps most beneficial to democracy in the United States as a whole is the capacity of states and localities to experiment with new policies, new laws, and new ways of thinking about democracy. New York, California, and Massachusetts experimented with government-run old-age pensions in the early 1930s; the federal government borrowed from these programs when it created the Social Security System in 1935. The Hawaii and Massachusetts legislatures struggled mightily to grant "near-universal" health care coverage for their citizens; the federal government's health care overhaul in 2010 accomplished many of the same objectives, although it similarly fell short of universal coverage. One thing remains certain: The wide variety of political cultures and governing institutions across the fifty states provides fertile ground for America's larger experiment with democracy to flourish.

J ust as the president delivers an annual State of the Union address to Congress, governors present an annual "state of the state" address to their respective state legislatures. This address provides each governor with the opportunity to outline a policy agenda and focus the attention of legislators and the media on proposals to achieve the governors' goals.

The National Governors Association (NGA) recently reviewed all of the state-of-the-state addresses made by governors in 2009 in a report titled *The Governors Speak 2009: A Summary of the State of the State Addresses of the Nations' Governors*. Not surprisingly, in 2009 most governors focused on the sharp downturn in economic conditions across the nation and the severe pains this was causing to state budgeting. In 2009, thirty-two governors described their state as in difficult budgetary distress, while only eleven said that their state was fiscally in good shape.

LINDA DAVIDSON/THE WASHINGTON POST/GETTY IMAGES

Maryland Governor Martin O'Malley delivers the "State of the State" address to Maryland's General Assembly in Annapolis on February 2, 2010.

Visit the NGA's Web site (http://www.nga.org) and click through its "state of the states" pages.

- How does your state stack up against others in terms of its fiscal situation?
- What are the common problems that governors identify as placing fiscal stress on the states?
- What does the governor of your state say about issues other than budget deficits that confront your state?

On www.cengage.com/dautrich/americangovernmentbrief/2e, find the Politics InterActive link for details on the "Governors' State of the State Addresses."

Chapter Summary

★ SUMMARIZING WHAT YOU HAVE LEARNED ★

★ Historical Development of State and Local Governments

- The thirteen colonies became the first thirteen states after the American Revolution. Thirty-seven more states entered the union since then through the process of congressional approval and presidential signature. Once a state enters the union, it enjoys sovereignty and cannot be altered or eliminated by the federal government.

- States have often taken the lead in experimenting with new ideas and potential reforms. Citizens and policy-makers throughout the nation watch what other states do and monitor the impact and effectiveness of their experiments. Other states and the federal government have often learned from successes and failures.

★ Structure of State and Local Governments

- Every state has a constitution defining the political structure of its government. The U.S. Constitution requires that all of the states maintain a republican form of government. All fifty states have executive, legislative, and judicial branches of government. State constitutions generally feature a bill of rights, rules for the conduct of state elections, and other provisions for the operation of state government.

- Local governments are created by a state government issuing a charter. Charters are issued for the establishment of a variety of types of local governments, including counties, cities, towns and townships, and special districts, such as school districts. States can alter, transform, enhance, and eliminate local governments, under the precedent known as "Dillon's Rule."

- Every state has a governor, who is the head of the executive branch of state government. The powers, duties, and terms of office for governors vary from state to state, although most governors have become more powerful state actors over the years, and most are elected to four-year terms.

- State legislatures vary across the fifty states. Forty-nine states have bicameral state legislatures, with a senate and a house; the exception is Nebraska, which has a unicameral legislature. In some states the legislative districts are very small, while in others the districts are quite large, with hundreds of thousands of constituents represented by each legislator. Some states have very professionalized legislatures, with full-time legislators and large staffs; other states have part-time legislators who earn no salary for their work.

- Most criminal and civil matters in the United States are adjudicated by state court systems. Every state has a trial court system, where a case is first heard, and a high court, which is the highest state appeals court. Many states also have intermediary appeals courts. With the exception of a possible review by the U.S. Supreme Court, the state high courts provide the final ruling on a state matter.

- Four forms of governance in localities are the mayor-council form, the council-manager form, the commission form, and the town meeting. In the mayor-council form, the mayor is the executive and the council is the legislative body. In the council-manager form, the council selects a professional city/town manager to run the government on a day-to-day basis. In the commission form, each member of the commission is elected and exercises administrative authority over a specific area. In the town meeting, decisions on policy issues and other matters are made by the voters participating.

★ State Elections

- States are responsible for administering elections, but U.S. constitutional amendments and federal legislation place some restrictions on what states can and cannot do in running elections. States cannot deny those at least eighteen years of age, women, or racial and ethnic minorities the right to vote; nor can they charge a fee as a voting requirement or require a literacy test. Beyond these federal protections granted to all U.S. citizens, states enjoy discretion in how they carry out and manage elections.

- Each state has both a Democratic Party organization and a Republican Party organization. Most candidates for the state legislature and local offices depend greatly on the support of their respective party organization for money and other resources to wage campaigns and compete for elective office. State party organizations raise funds, provide campaign services, recruit candidates to run for office, and offer a framework for voters to make voting decisions.

- Modern gubernatorial elections tend to be high-profile events, especially when compared to state legislative races. As many as one third of the nearly 7,400 state legislative seats are uncontested races, with only one candidate running in the general election. The trend, however, is toward more competition for state legislative seats, particularly in states where there is fierce competition between the parties.

- Thirty-eight of the fifty states hold popular elections for the selection of judges. Some states use partisan elections to select judges, in other states, judges run on nonpartisan ballots. Elective systems for judicial selection promote greater accountability to the public in judicial decision making.

- Referendum, initiative, and recall are election mechanisms that many states use to promote greater public participation in decision making beyond voting for candidates. The referendum seeks voter approval or rejection of a policy passed by the state legislature; the initiative allows voters to consider policies in the absence of legislative action. Recall allows voters to remove elected officials from office before the end of their term.

CourseMate

Key Terms

Charter (p. 497)

City (p. 497)

Commission form (p. 501)

Council-manager form (p. 501)

County (p. 497)

Dillon's Rule (p. 497)

Indiana ballot (p. 502)

Initiative (p. 509)

Massachusetts ballot (p. 502)

Mayor-council form (p. 500)

Recall (p. 511)

Referendum (p. 509)

State constitution (p. 495)

Town meeting (p. 501)

Township (p. 498)

Resources

Books

Dresang, Dennis L., and James J. Gosling. *Politics and Policy in American States and Communities.* New York: Longman, 2002.

Jewell, Malcolm E., and David M. Olson. *Political Parties and Elections in American States.* Homewood, IL: Dorsey Press, 1988.

Rosenthal, Alan. *Legislative Life: People, Process and Performance in the States.* New York: Harper & Row, 1981.

Van Horn, Carl E., ed. *The State of the States*, 4th ed. Washington, DC: CQ Press, 2006.

Internet Sources

http://www.ncsl.org (Web site for the National Conference of State Legislatures; provides a wealth of information for state lawmakers and for students of state government and politics, including data on who serves in state legislatures, historical and current election data, and reviews of policy issues and innovations in the states).

http://nga.org (Web site for the National Governors Association; provides detailed information about the nation's fifty governors and includes data on gubernatorial elections, current issues, op-eds from the nation's governors, and much more; the NGA is a valuable resource for the states' chief executives).

http://www.nlc.org (Web site for the National League of Cities; a comprehensive resource for information about the nation's cities; also provides data on trends in localities and links to a variety of municipalities and programs for cities).

Appendix

Declaration of Independence

In Congress, July 4, 1776.
A DECLARATION
By the Representatives of the United States of America,
In General Congress Assembled.

When in the Course of human Events, it becomes necessary for one People to dissolve the Political Bands which have connected them with another, and to assume among the Powers of the Earth, the separate and equal Station to which the Laws of Nature and of Nature's God entitle them, a decent Respect to the Opinions of Mankind requires that they should declare the causes which impel them to the Separation.

We hold these Truths to be self-evident, that all Men are created equal, that they are endowed by their Creator with certain unalienable Rights, that among these are Life, Liberty, and the Pursuit of Happiness—That to secure these Rights, Governments are instituted among Men, deriving their just Powers from the Consent of the Governed, that whenever any Form of Government becomes destructive of these Ends, it is the Right of the People to alter or abolish it, and to institute new Government, laying its Foundation on such Principles, and organizing its Powers in such Form, as to them shall seem most likely to effect their Safety and Happiness. Prudence, indeed, will dictate that Governments long established should not be changed for light and transient Causes; and accordingly all Experience hath shewn, that Mankind are more disposed to suffer, while Evils are sufferable, than to right themselves by abolishing the Forms to which they are accustomed. But when a long Train of Abuses and Usurpations, pursuing invariably the same Object, evinces a Design to reduce them under absolute Despotism, it is their Right, it is their Duty, to throw off such Government, and to provide new Guards for their future Security. Such has been the patient Sufferance of these Colonies; and such is now the Necessity which constrains them to alter their former Systems of Government. The History of the present kind of Great Britain is a History of repeated Injuries and Usurpations, all having in direct Object the Establishment of an absolute Tyranny over these States. To prove this, let Facts be submitted to a candid World.

He has refused his Assent to Laws, the most wholesome and necessary for public good.

He has forbidden his Governors to pass Laws of immediate and pressing importance, unless suspended in their Operation till his Assent should be obtained; and when so suspended, he has utterly neglected to attend to them.

He has refused to pass other Laws for the Accommodation of large Districts of People, unless those People would relinquish the Right of Representation in the Legislature, a Right inestimable to them, and formidable to Tyrants only.

He has called together Legislative Bodies at Places unusual, uncomfortable, and distant from the Depository of their public records, for the sole Purpose of fatiguing them into Compliance with his Measures.

He has dissolved Representative Houses repeatedly, for opposing with many Firmness his Invasions on the Rights of the People.

He has refused for a long Time, after such Dissolutions, to cause others to be elected; whereby the Legislative Powers, incapable of Annihilation, have returned to the People at large for their exercise; the State remaining in the mean time exposed to all the Dangers of Invasion from without, and Convulsions within.

He has endeavoured to prevent the Population of these States; for that Purpose obstructing the Laws for Naturalization of Foreigners; refusing to pass others to encourage their Migrations hither, and raising the Conditions of new Appropriations of Lands.

He has obstructed the Administration of Justice, by refusing his Assent to Laws for establishing Judiciary Powers.

He has made Judges dependent on his Will alone, for the Tenure of their Offices, and the Amount and Payment of their Salaries.

He has erected a Multitude of new Offices, and sent hither Swarms of Officers to harass our People, and eat out their Substance.

He has kept among us, in Times of Peace, Standing Armies, without the consent of our Legislatures.

He has affected to render the Military independent of and superior to the Civil Power.

He has combined with others to subject us to a Jurisdiction foreign to our Constitution, and unacknowledged by our Laws; giving his Assent to their Acts of pretended Legislation:

For quartering large Bodies of Armed Troops among us:

For protecting them, by a mock Trial, from Punishment for any Murders which they should commit on the Inhabitants of these States:

For cutting off our Trade with all Parts of the World:

For imposing Taxes on us without our Consent: For depriving us, in many Cases, of the Benefits of Trial by Jury:

For transporting us beyond Seas to be tried for pretended Offences:

For abolishing the free System of English Laws in a neighbouring Province, establishing therein an arbitrary Government, and enlarging its Boundaries, so as to render it at once an Example and fit Instrument for introducing the same absolute Rule into these Colonies:

For taking away our Charters, abolishing our most valuable Laws, and altering fundamentally the Forms of our Governments:

For suspending our own Legislatures, and declaring themselves invested with Power to legislate for us in all Cases whatsoever.

He has abdicated Government here, by declaring us out of his Protection and waging War against us.

He has plundered our Seas, ravaged our Coasts, burnt our Towns, and destroyed the Lives of our People.

He is, at this Time, transporting large Armies of foreign Mercenaries to compleat the Works of Death, Desolation, and Tyranny, already begun with circumstances of Cruelty and Perfidy, scarcely paralleled in the most barbarous Ages, and totally unworthy the Head of a civilized Nation.

He has constrained our fellow Citizens taken Captive on the high Seas to bear Arms against their Country, to become the Executioners of their Friends and Brethren, or to fall themselves by their Hands.

He has excited domestic Insurrections amongst us, and has endeavoured to bring on the Inhabitants of our Frontiers, the merciless Indian Savages, whose known Rule of Warfare, is an undistinguished Destruction, of all Ages, Sexes and Conditions.

In every stage of these Oppressions we have Petitioned for Redress in the must humble Terms: Our repeated Petitions have been answered only by repeated Injury. A Prince, whose Character is thus marked by every act which may define a Tyrant, is unfit to be the Ruler of a free People.

Nor have we been wanting in Attentions to our British Brethren. We have warned them from Time to Time of Attempts by their Legislature to extend an unwarrantable Jurisdiction over us. We have reminded them of the Circumstances of our Emigration and Settlement here. We have appealed to their native Justice and Magnanimity, and we have conjured them by the Ties of our common Kindred to disavow these Usurpations, which, would inevitably interrupt our Connections and Correspondence. They too have been deaf to the Voice of Justice and of Consanguinity. We must, therefore, acquiesce in the Necessity, which denounces our Separation, and hold them, as we hold the rest of Mankind, Enemies in War, in Peace, Friends.

We, therefore, the Representatives of the UNITED STATES OF AMERICA, in GENERAL CONGRESS, Assembled, appealing to the Supreme Judge of the World for the Rectitude of our Intentions, do, in the Name, and by Authority of the good People of these Colonies, solemnly Publish and Declare, That these United Colonies are, and of Right ought to be, FREE AND INDEPENDENT STATES; that they are absolved from all Allegiance to the British Crown, and that all political Connection between them and the State of Great-Britain, is and ought to be totally dissolved; and that as FREE AND INDEPENDENT STATES, they have full Power to levy War, conclude Peace, contract Alliances, establish Commerce, and to do all other Acts and Things which INDEPENDENT STATES may of right do. And for the support of this Declaration, with a firm Reliance on the Protection of divine Providence, we mutually pledge to each other our Lives, our Fortunes, and our sacred Honor.

John Hancock

Georgia:
Button Gwinnett
Lyman Hall
George Walton

North Carolina:
William Hooper
Joseph Hewes
John Penn

South Carolina:
Edward Rutledge
Thomas Heyward, Jr.
Thomas Lynch, Jr.
Arthur Middleton

Maryland:
Samuel Chase
William Paca
Thomas Stone
Charles Carroll of Carrollton

Virginia:
George Wythe
Richard Henry Lee
Thomas Jefferson
Benjamin Harrison
Thomas Nelson, Jr.
Francis Lightfoot Lee
Carter Braxton

Pennsylvania:
Robert Morris
Benjamin Rush
Benjamin Franklin
John Morton
George Clymer
James Smith
George Taylor
James Wilson
George Ross

Delaware:
Caesar Rodney
George Read
Thomas McKean

New York:
William Floyd
Philip Livingston
Francis Lewis
Lewis Morris

New Jersey:
Richard Stockton
John Witherspoon
Francis Hopkinson
John Hart
Abraham Clark

New Hampshire:
Josiah Bartlett
William Whipple

Massachusetts:
Samuel Adams
John Adams
Robert Treat Paine
Elbridge Gerry

Rhode Island:
Stephen Hopkins
William Ellery

Connecticut:
Roger Sherman
Samuel Huntington
Oliver Wolcott

New Hampshire:
Matthew Thornton

November 23, 1787

TO THE PEOPLE OF THE STATE OF NEW YORK

Among the numerous advantages promised by a well-constructed Union, none deserves to be more accurately developed than its tendency to break and control the violence of faction. The friend of popular governments never finds himself so much alarmed for their character and fate, as when he contemplates their propensity to this dangerous vice. He will not fail, therefore, to set a due value on any plan which, without violating the principles to which he is attached, provides a proper cure for it. The instability, injustice, and confusion introduced into the public councils, have, in truth, been the mortal diseases under which popular governments have everywhere perished; as they continue to be the favorite and fruitful topics from which the adversaries to liberty derive their most specious declamations. The valuable improvements made by the American constitutions on the popular models, both ancient and modern, cannot certainly be too much admired; but it would be an unwarrantable partiality, to contend that they have as effectually obviated the danger on this side, as was wished and expected. Complaints are everywhere heard from our most considerate and virtuous citizens, equally the friends of public and private faith, and of public and personal liberty, that our governments are too unstable, that the public good is disregarded in the conflicts of rival parties, and that measures are too often decided, not according to the rules of justice and the rights of the minor party, but by the superior force on an interested and overbearing majority. However anxiously we may wish that these complaints had no foundation, the evidence of known facts will not permit us to deny that they are in some degree true. It will be found, indeed, on a candid review of our situation, that some of the distresses under which we labor have been erroneously charged on the operation of our governments; but it will be found, at the same time, that other causes will not alone account for many of our heaviest misfortunes; and, particularly, for that prevailing and increasing distrust of public engagements, and alarm for private rights, which are echoed from one end of the continent to the other. These must be chiefly, if not wholly, effects of the unsteadiness and injustice with which a factious spirit has tainted our public administrations.

By a faction, I understand a number of citizens, whether amounting to a majority or a minority of the whole, who are united and actuated by some common impulse of passion, or of interest, adversed to the rights of other citizens, or to the permanent and aggregate interests of the community.

There are two methods of curing the mischeifs of faction: the one, by removing its causes; the other, by controlling its effects.

There are again two methods of removing the causes of faction: the one, by destroying the liberty which is essential to its existence; the other, by giving to every citizen the same opinions, the same passions, and the same interests.

It could never be more truly said than of the first remedy, that it was worse than the disease. Liberty is to faction what air is to fire, an aliment without which it instantly expires. But it could not be less folly to abolish liberty, which is essential to political life, because it nourishes faction, than it would be to wish the annihilation of air, which is essential to animal life, because it imparts to fire its destructive tendency.

The second expedient is as impracticable as the first would be unwise. As long as the reason of man continues fallible, and he is at liberty to exercise it, different opinions will be formed. As long as the connection subsists between his reason and his self-love, his opinions and his passions will have a reciprocal influence on each other; and the former will be objects to which the latter will attach themselves. The diversity in the faculties of men, from which the rights of property originate, is not less an insuperable obstacle to a uniformity of interests. The protection of these faculties is the first object of government. From the protection of different and unequal faculties of acquiring property, the possession of different degrees and kinds of property immediately results; and from the influence of these on the sentiments and views of the respective proprietors, ensues a division of the society into different interests and parties.

The latent causes of faction are thus sown in the nature of man; and we see them everywhere brought into different degrees of activity, according to the different circumstances of civil society. A zeal for different opinions concerning religion, concerning government, and many other points, as well of speculation as of practice; an attachment to different leaders ambitiously contending for pre-eminence and power; or to persons of other descriptions whose fortunes have been interesting to the human passions, have, in turn, divided mankind into parties, inflamed them with mutual animosity, and rendered them much more disposed to vex and oppress each other than to co-operate for their common good. So strong is this propensity of mankind to fall into mutual animosities, that where no substantial occasion presents itself, the most frivolous and fanciful distinctions have been sufficient to kindle their unfriendly passions and excite their most violent conflicts. But the most common and durable source of factions has been the various and unequal distribution of property. Those who hold and those who are without property have ever formed distinct interests in society. Those who are creditors, and those who are debtors, fall under a like discrimination. A landed interest, a manufacturing interest, a mercantile interest, a moneyed interest, with many lesser interests, grow up of necessity in civilized nations, and divide them into different classes, actuated by different sentiments and views. The regulation of these various and interfering interests forms the principal task of modern legislation, and involves the spirit of party and faction in the necessary and ordinary operations of the government.

No man is allowed to be a judge in his own case, because his interest would certainly bias his judgment, and, not improbably, corrupt his integrity. With equal, nay with greater reason, a body of men are unfit to be both judges and parties at the same time; yet what are many of the most important acts of legislation, but so many judicial determinations, not indeed concerning the rights of single persons, but concerning the rights of large bodies of citizens? And what are the different classes of legislators but advocates and parties to the causes which they determine? Is a law proposed concerning private debts? It is a question to which the creditors are parties on one side and the debtors on the other. Justice ought to hold the balance between them. Yet the parties are, and must be, themselves the judges; and the most numerous party, or, in other words, the most powerful action must be expected to prevail. Shall domestic manufactures be encouraged, and in what degree, by restrictions on foreign manufactures? are questions which would be differently decided by the landed and the manufacturing classes, and probably by neither with a sole regard to justice and the public good. The apportionment of taxes on the various descriptions of property is an act which seems to require the most exact impartiality; yet there is, perhaps, no legislative act in which greater opportunity and temptation are given to a predominant party to trample on the rules of justice. Every shilling with which they overburden the inferior number, is a shilling saved to their own pockets.

It is in vain to say that enlightened statesmen will be able to adjust these clashing interests, and render them all subservient to the public good. Enlightened statesmen will not always be at the helm. Nor, in many cases, can such an adjustment be made at all without taking into view indirect and remote considerations, which will rarely prevail over the immediate interest which one party may find in disregarding the rights of another or the good of the whole.

The inference to which we are brought is, that the *causes* of faction cannot be removed, and that relief is only to be sought in the means of controlling its *effects*.

If a faction consists of less than a majority, relief is supplied by the republican principle, which enables the majority to defeat its sinister views by regular vote. It may clog the administration, it may convulse the society; but it will be unable to execute and mask its violence under the forms of the Constitution. When a majority is included in a faction, the form of popular government, on the other hand, enables it to sacrifice to its ruling passion or interest both the public good and the rights of other citizens. To secure the public good and private rights against the danger of such a faction, and at the same time to preserve the spirit and form of popular government, is then the great object to which our inquiries are directed. Let me add that it is the great desideratum by which this form of government can be rescued from the opprobrium under which it has so long labored, and be recommended to the esteem and adoption of mankind.

By what means is this object attainable? Evidently by one of two only. Either the existence of the same passion or interest in a majority at the same time must be prevented, or the majority, having such coexistent passion or interest, must be rendered, by their number and local situation, unable to concert and carry into effect schemes of oppression. If the impulse and the opportunity be suffered to coincide, we well know that neither moral nor religious motives can be relied on as an adequate control. They are not found to be such on the injustice and violence of individuals, and lose their efficacy in proportion to the number combined together, that is, in proportion as their efficacy becomes needful.

From this view of the subject it may be concluded that a pure democracy, by which I mean a society consisting of a small number of citizens, who assemble and administer the government in person, can admit of no cure for the mischiefs of faction. A common passion or interest will, in almost every case, be felt by a majority of the whole; a communication and concert result from the form of government itself; and there is nothing to check the inducements to sacrifice the weaker party or an obnoxious individual. Hence it is that such democracies have ever been spectacles of turbulence and contention; have ever been found incompatible with personal security or the rights of property; and have in general been as short in their lives as they have been violent in their deaths. Theoretic politicians, who have patronized this species of government, have erroneously supposed that by reducing mankind to a perfect equality in their political rights, they would, at the same time, be perfectly equalized and assimilated in their possessions, their opinions, and their passions.

A republic, by which I mean a government in which the scheme of representation takes place, opens a different prospect, and promises the cure for which we are seeking. Let us examine the points in which it varies from pure democracy, and we shall comprehend both the nature of the cure and the efficacy which it must derive from the Union.

The two great points of difference between a democracy and a republic are: first, the delegation of the government, in the latter, to a small number of citizens elected by the rest; secondly, the greater number of citizens, and greater sphere of country, over which the latter may be extended.

The effect of the first difference is, on the one hand, to refine and enlarge the public views, by passing them through the medium of a chosen body of citizens, whose wisdom may best discern the true interest of their country, and whose patriotism and love of justice will be least likely to sacrifice it to temporary or partial considerations. Under such a regulation, it may well happen that the public voice, pronounced by the representatives of the people, will be more consonant to the public good than if pronounced by the people themselves, convened for the purpose. On the other hand, the effect may be inverted. Men of factious tempers, of local prejudices, or of sinister designs, may, by intrigue, by corruption, or by other means, first obtain the suffrages, and then betray the interests, of the people. The question resulting is, whether small or extensive republics are more favorable to the election of proper guardians of the public weal; and it is clearly decided in favor of the latter by two obvious considerations:

In the first place, it is to be remarked that, however small the republic may be, the representatives must be raised to a certain number, in order to guard against the cabals of a few; and that, however large it may be, they must be limited to a certain number, in order to guard against the confusion of a multitude. Hence, the number of representatives in the two cases not being in proportion to that of the two constituents, and being proportionally greater in the small republic, it follows that, if the proportion of fit characters be not less in the large than in the small republic, the former will present a greater option, and consequently a greater probability of a fit choice.

In the next place, as each representative will be chosen by a greater number of citizens in the large than in the small republic, it will be more difficult for unworthy candidates to practice with success the vicious arts by which elections are too often carried; and the suffrages of the people being more free, will be more likely to centre in men who possess the most attractive merit and the most diffusive and established characters.

It must be confessed that in this, as in most other cases, there is a mean, on both sides of which inconveniences will be found to lie. By enlarging too much the number of electors, you render the representatives too little acquainted with all their local circumstances and lesser interests; as by reducing it too much, you render him unduly attached to these, and too little fit to comprehend and pursue great and national objects. The federal Constitution forms a happy combination in this respect; the great and aggregate interests being referred to the national, the local and particular to the State legislatures.

The other point of difference is, the greater number of citizens and extent of territory which may be brought within the compass of republican than of democratic government; and it is this circumstance principally which renders factious combinations less to be dreaded in the former than in the latter. The smaller the society, the fewer probably will be the distinct parties and interests composing it; the fewer the distinct parties and interests, the more frequently will a majority be found of the same party; and the smaller the number of individuals composing a majority, and the smaller the compass within which they are placed, the more easily will they concert and execute their plans of oppression. Extend the sphere, and you take in a greater variety of parties and interests; you make it less probable that a majority of the whole will have a common motive to invade the rights of other citizens; or if such a common motive exists, it will be more difficult for all who feel it to discover their own strength, and to act in unison with each other. Besides other impediments, it may be remarked that, where there is a consciousness of unjust or dishonorable purposes, communication is always checked by distrust in proportion to the number whose concurrence is necessary.

Hence, it clearly appears, that the same advantage which a republic has over a democracy, in controlling the effects of faction, is enjoyed by a large over a small republic,—and is enjoyed by the Union over the States composing it. Does the advantage consist in the substitution of representatives whose enlightened views and virtuous sentiments render them superior to local prejudices and schemes of injustice? It will not be denied that the representation of the Union will be most likely to possess these requisite endowments. Does it consist in the greater security afforded by a greater variety of parties, against the event of any one party being able to outnumber and oppress the rest? In an equal degree does the increased variety of parties comprised within the Union, increase this security. Does it, in fine, consist in the greater obstacles opposed to the concert and accomplishment of the secret wishes of an unjust and interested majority? Here, again, the extent of the Union gives it the most palpable advantage.

The influence of factious leaders may kindle a flame within their particular States, but will be unable to spread a general conflagration through the other States. A religious sect may degenerate into a political faction in a part of the Confederacy; but the variety of sects dispersed over the entire face of it must secure the national councils against any danger from that source. A rage for paper money, for an abolition of debts, for an equal division of property, or for any other improper or wicked project, will be less apt to pervade the whole body of the Union than a particular member of it; in the same proportion as such a malady is more likely to taint a particular county or district, than an entire State.

In the extent and proper structure of the Union, therefore, we behold a republican remedy for the diseases most incident to republican government. And according to the degree of pleasure and pride we feel in being republicans, ought to be our zeal in cherishing the spirit and supporting the character of Federalists.

PUBLIUS

Federalist No. 51

February 8, 1788

TO THE PEOPLE OF THE STATE OF NEW YORK

To what expedient, then, shall we finally resort, for maintaining in practice the necessary partition of power among the several departments, as laid down in the Constitution? The only answer that can be given is, that as all these exterior provisions are found to be inadequate, the defect must be supplied, by so contriving the interior structure of the government as that its several constituent parts may, by their mutual relations, be the means of keeping each other in their proper places. Without presuming to undertake a full development of the important idea, I will hazard a few general observations, which may perhaps place it in a clearer light, and enable us to form a more correct judgment of the principles and structure of the government planned by the convention.

In order to lay a due foundation for that separate and distinct exercise of the different powers of government, which to a certain extent is admitted on all hands to be essential to the preservation of liberty, it is evident that each department should have a will of its own; and consequently should be so constituted that the members of each should have as little agency as possible in the appointment of the members of the others. Were this principle rigorously adhered to, it would require that all the appointments for the supreme executive, legislative, and judiciary magistracies should be drawn from the same fountain of authority, the people, through channels having no communication whatever with one another. Perhaps such a plan of constructing the several departments would be less difficult in practice than it may in contemplation appear. Some difficulties, however, and some additional expense would attend the execution of it. Some deviations, therefore, from the principle must be admitted. In the constitution of the judiciary department in particular, it might be inexpedient to insist rigorously on the principle: first, because peculiar qualifications being essential in the members, the primary consideration ought to be to select that mode of choice which best secures these qualifications; secondly, because the permanent tenure by which the appointments are held in that department, must soon destroy all sense of dependence on the authority conferring them.

It is equally evident, that the members of each department should be as little dependent as possible on those of the others, for the emoluments annexed to their offices. Were the executive magistrate, or the judges, not independent of the legislature in this particular, their independence in every other would be merely nominal.

But the great security against a gradual concentration of the several powers in the same department, consists in giving to those who administer each department the necessary constitutional means and personal motives to resist encroachments of the others. The provision for defense must in this, as in all other cases, be made commensurate to the danger of attack. Ambition must be made to counteract ambition. The interest of the man must be connected with the constitutional rights of the place. It may be a reflection on human nature, that such devices should be necessary to control the abuses of government. But what is government itself, but the greatest of all reflections on human nature? If men were angels, no government would be necessary. If angels were to govern men, neither external nor internal controls on government would be necessary. In framing a government which is to be administered by men over men, the great difficulty lies in this: you must first enable the government to control the governed; and in the next place oblige it to control itself. A dependence on the people is, no doubt, the primary control on the government; but experience has taught mankind the necessity of auxiliary precautions.

This policy of supplying, by opposite and rival interests, the defect of better motives, might be traced through the whole system of human affairs, private as well as public. We see it particularly displayed in all the subordinate distributions of power, where the constant aim is to divide and arrange the several offices in such a manner as that each may be a check on the other—that the private interest of every individual may be a sentinel over the public rights. These inventions of prudence cannot be less requisite in the distribution of the supreme powers of the State.

But it is not possible to give to each department an equal power of self-defense. In republican government, the legislative authority necessarily predominates. The remedy for this inconveniency is to divide the legislature into different branches; and to render them, by different modes of election and different principles of action, as little connected with each other as the nature of their common functions and their common dependence on the society will admit. It may even be necessary to guard against dangerous encroachments by still further precautions. As the weight of the legislative authority requires that it should be thus divided, the weakness of the executive may require, on the other hand, that it should be fortified. An absolute negative on the legislature appears, at first view, to be the natural defense with which the executive magistrate should be armed. But perhaps it would be neither altogether safe nor alone sufficient. On ordinary occasions it might not be exerted with the requisite firmness, and on extraordinary occasions it might be perfidiously abused. May not this defect of an absolute negative be supplied by some qualified connection between this weaker department and the weaker branch of the stronger department, by which the latter may be led to support the constitutional rights of the former, without being too much detached from the rights of its own department?

If the principles on which these observations are founded be just, as I persuade myself they are, and they be applied as a criterion to the several State constitutions, and to the federal Constitution it will be found that if the latter does not perfectly correspond with them, the former are infinitely less able to bear such a test.

There are, moreover, two considerations particularly applicable to the federal system of America, which place that system in a very interesting point of view.

First. In a single republic, all the power surrendered by the people is submitted to the administration of a single government; and the usurpations are guarded against by a division of the government into distinct and separate departments. In the compound republic of America, the power surrendered by the people is first divided between two distinct governments, and then the portion allotted to each subdivided among distinct and separate departments. Hence a double security arises to the rights of the people. The different governments will control each other, at the same time that each will be controlled by itself.

Second. It is of great importance in a republic not only to guard the society against the oppression of its rulers, but to guard one part of the society against the injustice of the other part. Different interests necessarily exist in different classes of citizens. If a majority be united by a common interest, the rights of the minority will be insecure. There are but two methods of providing against this evil: the one by creating a will in the community independent of the majority that is, of the society itself; the other, by comprehending in the society so many separate descriptions of citizens as will render an unjust combination of a majority of the whole very improbable, if not impracticable. The first method prevails in all governments possessing an hereditary or self-appointed authority. This, at best, is but a precarious security; because a power independent of society may as well espouse the unjust views of the major as the rightful interests of the minor party, and may possibly be turned against both parties. The second method will be exemplified in the federal republic of the United States. Whilst all authority in it will be derived from and dependent on the society, the society itself will be broken into so many parts, interests, and classes of citizens, that the rights of individuals, or of the minority, will be in little danger from interested combinations of the majority. In a free government the security for civil rights must be the same as that for religious rights. It consists in the one case in the multiplicity of interests, and in the other in the multiplicity of sects. The degree of security in both cases will depend on the number of interests and sects; and this may be presumed to depend on the extent of country and number of people comprehended under the same government. This view of the subject must particularly recommend a proper federal system to all the sincere and considerate friends of republican government, since it shows that in exact proportion as the territory of the Union may be formed into more circumscribed Confederacies, or States oppressive combinations of a majority will be facilitated: the best security, under republican forms, for the rights of every class of citizens, will be diminished; and consequently the stability and independence of some member of the government, the only other security, must be proportionately increased. Justice is the end of government. It is the end of civil society. It ever has been and ever will be pursued until it be obtained, or until liberty be lost in the pursuit. In a society under the forms of which the stronger faction can readily unite and oppress the weaker, anarchy may as truly be said to reign as in a state of nature, where the weaker individual is not secured against the violence of the stronger; and as, in the latter state, even the stronger individuals are prompted, by the uncertainty of their condition, to submit to a government which may protect the weak as well as the more powerful. It can be little doubted that if the State of Rhode Island was separated from the Confederacy and left to itself, the insecurity of rights under the popular form of government within such narrow limits would be displayed by such reiterated oppressions of factious majorities that some power altogether independent of the people would soon be called for by the voice of the very factions whose misrule had proved the necessity of it. In the extended republic of the United States, and among the great variety of interests, parties, and sects which it embraces, a coalition of a majority of the whole society could seldom take place on any other principles than those of justice and the general good; whilst there being thus less danger to a minor from the will of a major party, there must be less pretext, also, to provide for the security of the former, by introducing into the government a will not dependent on the latter, or, in other words, a will independent of the society itself. It is no less certain than it is important, notwithstanding the contrary opinions which have been entertained, that the larger the society, provided it lie within a practical sphere, the more duly capable it will be of self-government. And happily for the *republican cause*, the practicable sphere may be carried to a very great extent, by a judicious modification of mixture of the *federal principle*.

PUBLIUS

Presidents of the United States

Name of President	Dates of Service	Political Party Affiliation	Vice President(s)	Major Party Candidate(s) Defeated in General Election
George Washington	1789–97		Adams	
John Adams	1797–1801	Federalist	Jefferson	Jefferson
Thomas Jefferson	1801–09	Democratic-Republican	Burr/Clinton	Adams, Pinckney
James Madison	1809–17	Democratic-Republican	Clinton/Gerry	Pinckney, D. Clinton
James Monroe	1817–25	Democratic-Republican	Tompkins	King
John Quincy Adams	1825–29	Democratic-Republican/Democratic	Calhoun	Jackson
Andrew Jackson	1829–37	Democratic	Van Buren	J. Q. Adams, Clay
Martin Van Buren	1837–41	Democratic	Johnson	Harrison
William Harrison	1841	Whig	Tyler	Van Buren
John Tyler	1841–45	Whig	vacant	
James Polk	1845–49	Democratic	Dallas	Clay
Zachary Taylor	1849–50	Whig	Fillmore	Cass
Millard Fillmore	1850–53	Whig	vacant	
Franklin Pierce	1853–57	Democratic	King/vacant	Scott
James Buchanan	1857–61	Democratic	Breckinridge	Fremont
Abraham Lincoln	1861–65	Republican	Hamlin/Johnson	Breckinridge, Douglas, McClellan
Andrew Johnson	1865–69	Democratic	vacant	
Ulysses S. Grant	1869–77	Republican	Colfax/Wilson/vacant	Seymour, Greeley
Rutherford B. Hayes	1877–81	Republican	Wheeler	Tilden
James Garfield	1881	Republican	Arthur	Hancock
Chester Arthur	1881–85	Republican	vacant	
Grover Cleveland	1885–89	Democratic	Hendricks/vacant	Blaine

Name of President	Dates of Service	Political Party Affiliation	Vice President(s)	Major Party Candidate(s) Defeated in General Election
Benjamin Harrison	1889–93	Republican	Morton	Cleveland
Grover Cleveland	1893–97	Democratic	Stevenson	Harrison
William McKinley	1897–1901	Republican	Hobart	Bryan
Theodore Roosevelt	1901–09	Republican	vacant/Fairbanks	Parker
William Taft	1909–13	Republican	Sherman/vacant	Bryan
Woodrow Wilson	1913–21	Democratic	Marshall	T. Roosevelt, Taft, Hughes
Warren G. Harding	1921–23	Republican	Coolidge	Cox
Calvin Coolidge	1923–29	Republican	vacant/Dawes	Davis
Herbert Hoover	1929–33	Republican	Curtis	Smith
Franklin D. Roosevelt	1933–45	Democratic	Garner/Wallace/ Truman	Hoover, Landon, Wilkie, Dewey
Harry Truman	1945–53	Democratic	vacant/Barkley	Dewey
Dwight Eisenhower	1953–61	Republican	Nixon	Stevenson
John F. Kennedy	1961–63	Democratic	Johnson	Nixon
Lyndon Johnson	1963–69	Democratic	vacant/Humphrey	Goldwater
Richard Nixon	1969–74	Republican	Agnew/vacant/Ford	Humphrey, McGovern
Gerald Ford	1974–77	Republican	vacant/Rockefeller	
Jimmy Carter	1977–81	Democratic	Mondale	Ford
Ronald Reagan	1981–89	Republican	G. H. W. Bush	Carter, Mondale
George H. W. Bush	1989–93	Republican	Quayle	Dukakis
William Clinton	1993–2001	Democratic	Gore	G. H. W. Bush, Dole
George W. Bush	2001–2009	Republican	Cheney	Gore, Kerry
Barack Obama	2009–present	Democratic	Biden	McCain

Glossary

A

Administrative discretion The freedom of agencies to decide how to implement a vague or ambiguous law passed by Congress.

Administrative law A law that relates to the authority of administrative agencies and the rules promulgated by those agencies.

Affirmative action Programs, laws, or practices designed to remedy past discriminatory hiring practices, government contracting, and school admissions.

Agenda setting theory The theory that holds that although the effects of television exposure may be minimal or difficult to gauge, the media are quite influential in telling the public what to think about.

Agents of political socialization Factors that have a significant impact on an individual's socialization to politics.

Amendments Modifications or additions to the U.S. Constitution passed in accordance with the amendment procedures laid out in Article V.

Amicus curiae briefs Written documents filed by outside parties in the case with an interest in the outcome of the litigation expressing their own views on how the Court should decide a particular case.

Anarchy A state of lawlessness and discord in the political system caused by lack of government.

Anti-Federalists Those who opposed ratification of the proposed Constitution of the United States.

Appellate jurisdiction The authority of a court to review decisions handed down by another court.

Articles of Confederation The document creating a "league of friendship" governing the thirteen states during and immediately after the war for independence; hampered by the limited power they vested in the legislature to collect revenue or regulate commerce, the Articles eventually proved unworkable for the new nation.

Authoritarianism A form of government in which one political party, group, or person maintains such complete control over the nation that it may refuse to recognize and may even suppress all other political parties and interests.

Authority The ability of public institutions and the officials within them to make laws, independent of the power to execute them.

B

Bail An amount of money determined by a judge that the accused must pay to a court as security against his or her freedom before trial.

Battleground states States identified as offering either major-party candidate a reasonable chance for victory in the Electoral College.

Beliefs The facts that derive from values that people take for granted about the world.

Bicameral legislature A legislature composed of two separate chambers.

Bill A proposed law presented for consideration to a legislative body.

Bill of attainder An act of a legislature declaring a person (or group) guilty of some crime, and then carrying out punishment without a trial. The Constitution denies Congress the ability to issue a bill of attainder.

Bill of Rights The first ten amendments to the U.S. Constitution, which protect various rights of the people against the new federal government.

Bipartisan Campaign Reform Act (BCRA) Also called the McCain-Feingold Act, the federal legislation that (1) restricted soft money spent by political parties, (2) regulated expenditures on ads that refer to specific candidates immediately before an election, and (3) increased limits on hard money donated directly to candidates and their campaigns.

Block grants Grants from the federal government to the states that may be used at the discretion of states to pursue more generalized aims.

Blogs Internet sites that include a combination of editorial page, personal web page, and online diary of personal observations in real time about news events and issues.

Briefs Written documents filed by parties in an appealed case arguing why constitutional or statutory law weighs in favor of their respective positions.

***Brown v. Board of Education* (1954)** The 1954 U.S. Supreme Court decision that declared school segregation to be unconstitutional.

***Buckley v. Valeo* (1976)** The 1976 Supreme Court opinion that held that spending money to influence elections is protected First Amendment speech, and that prohibited limitations on independent expenditures or personal money spent by candidates on their own campaigns.

Budget authority The power of federal departments and agencies to incur obligations to spend or lend money.

Budget deficit The amount of money spent by the U.S. government beyond that which it collects in taxes and other revenue in a single year.

Budget surplus The amount by which the U.S. government's revenue exceeds its spending in a given fiscal year.

Bureaucracy An organization set up in a logical and rational manner for the purpose of accomplishing specific functions.

Bureaucratic adjudicating Determining the rights and duties of particular parties within the scope of an agency's rules or regulations.

C

Cabinet The collection of the principal officers in each of the executive departments of the federal government who serve as key advisers to the president.

Cabinet departments Those federal agencies that qualify as the major administrative organizations of the executive branch.

Capitalism Economic system in which all or most of the means of production are privately owned under competitive conditions.

Casework The direct assistance that a member of Congress provides to a constituent, community group, or a local or state official.

Caucus A method of choosing party nominees in which party members attend local meetings at which they choose delegates committed to a particular candidate.

Central Intelligence Agency (CIA) Federal agency charged with evaluating and disseminating intelligence information, performing public relations functions that affect international perceptions of the United States, and engaging in overt and covert operations at the direction of the president.

Charter A state law that grants a local government the authority to provide public services, enact and enforce regulations, and raise revenue to support its operations.

Checks and balances A system of limits imposed by the Constitution that gives each branch of government the limited right to change or cancel the acts of other branches.

City The type of local government that has been chartered by a state to serve the needs of an urbanized or densely populated area.

Civil law This term has two meanings: (1) legislative codes, laws, or sets of rules enacted by duly authorized lawmaking bodies such as Congress, state and local legislatures, or any executive authority entrusted with the power to make laws; (2) the body of noncriminal laws of a nation or state that deal with the rights of private citizens.

Civil liberties Those specific individual rights that are guaranteed by the Constitution and cannot be denied to citizens by government. Most of these rights are in the first ten amendments to the Constitution, known as the Bill of Rights.

Civil rights Those positive rights, whether political, social, or economic, conferred by the government on individuals or groups.

Civil Rights Act of 1964 The federal law that banned racial discrimination in all public accommodations, including those that were privately owned; prohibited discrimination by employers and created the Equal Employment Opportunity Commission to investigate complaints of discrimination; and denied public funds to schools that continued to discriminate on the basis of race.

Civil service The system whereby workers in the federal bureaucracy are supposed to be immune from partisan political maneuvering.

Civil Service Reform Act of 1978 The federal act that replaced the Civil Service Commission (the agency that oversaw federal hiring and firing practices) with the Office of Personnel Management (OPM) and the Merit Systems Protection Board (MSPB).

Civil War Amendments The Thirteenth Amendment (ratified in 1865) banished slavery from all states and U.S. territories. The Fourteenth Amendment (ratified in 1868) granted full U.S. and state citizenship to all people born or naturalized in the United States and guaranteed to each person "the equal protection of the laws." The Fifteenth Amendment (1870) forbade the denial or abridgement of the right to vote by any government on account of race.

Class action lawsuit A lawsuit filed by a large group of people with clearly defined common interests.

Closed primary An election that requires voters to declare their party affiliation ahead of time.

Closed rule A rule of procedure adopted by the House Rules Committee that severely limits the ability of members of Congress to amend a bill.

Closed shop The law that requires employees to become members of the union as a condition of employment in unionized workplaces.

Cloture A Senate debate procedure that permits that body to end debate and force a vote on a bill by a vote of sixty senators.

Coattail effect The potential benefit that successful presidential candidates offer to congressional candidates of the same political party during presidential election years.

Cold War The nearly half-century struggle over ideological differences between the United States and the Soviet Union. Waged through economic warfare, arms buildups, and tense diplomatic talks, the Cold War never broke out into a sustained military engagement between the two nations and ended with the dissolution of the Soviet Union in 1991.

Commission form The form of local government that features an elected group of commissioners with each commissioner having administrative authority over a specific aspect of government.

Common law Judge-made law handed down through judicial opinions, which over time establish precedents.

Complaint A document written by the plaintiff arguing why the court is empowered to hear the case and explaining why the plaintiff is entitled to some form of relief under the current law.

Concurrent powers Those powers shared by the federal and state governments under the Constitution.

Concurring opinion The opinion of one or more justices that agrees with the end result reached by the majority but disagrees with the reasons offered for the decision.

Confederation A system of government (or "league") in which two or more independent states unite to achieve certain specified common aims.

Conference committee A joint committee of Congress appointed by the House of Representatives and the Senate to resolve differences on a particular bill.

Congressional agencies Government bodies formed by and relied on by Congress to support members of Congress in performing their functions.

Congressional district A geographic region (either a state itself or a region located entirely within one state) whose residents select one member to represent it in the House of Representatives.

Congressional oversight Congress's exercise of its authority to monitor the activities of agencies and administrators.

Congressional personal staff A group of workers who assist an individual member of Congress in performing his or her responsibilities.

Conservative ideology A political orientation that generally favors government activism in defense of more traditional values on social issues, but favors government restraint in economic redistribution.

Constitutional Convention Meeting of delegates from twelve states in Philadelphia during the summer of 1787, at which was drafted an entirely new system of government to govern the United States.

Consumer price index (CPI) An index of prices for goods and services regularly traded in the U.S. economy

Containment U.S. foreign policy that sought to restrict Soviet power (and Communist influence) to its existing geographical sphere.

Continuity (in public opinion) A tendency for political preferences to remain generally stable over time.

Cooperative federalism The doctrine of federalism that affords Congress nearly unlimited authority to exercise its powers through means that often coerce states into administering and/or enforcing federal policies.

Council-manager form The form of local government that places management of the city or town in the hands of a nonelected professional appointed by the council.

County A form of local government that varies in importance and scope of activity across the states and usually coexists with city or town governments.

Crime control model Criminal justice policymaking model that views the controlling of criminal behavior as the system's most important function.

Critical election An election that produces sharp changes in patterns of party loyalty among voters.

Cultivation theory The theory of media effects that suggests that heavy television exposure helps develop an individual's overall view of the world.

D

Dealignment A decline in voter attachment to parties and in clarity of party coalitions.

Declaration of Independence Formal document listing colonists' grievances and articulating the colonists' intention to seek independence; formally adopted by the Second Continental Congress on July 4, 1776.

Defendant The target of a plaintiff's complaint.

Delegation of congressional power Congress's transferring of its lawmaking authority to the executive branch of government.

Democracy Form of government in which the people, either directly or through elected representatives, hold power and authority. The word *democracy* is derived from the Greek *demos*

kratos, meaning "rule by the people."

Department of Defense Executive branch agency that is responsible for managing the nation's military and advising the president on all military matters.

Department of Homeland Security (DHS) Executive branch agency established in 2002 to coordinate government entities in protecting U.S. citizens against terrorism within the nation's borders.

Department of State Executive branch agency that is primarily responsible for most foreign policy programs within the executive branch, including diplomatic missions, foreign aid, and contributions to international organizations.

Deregulation The elimination of government oversight and government regulation of certain activities.

Devolution The transfer of power and responsibilities for certain regulatory programs from the federal government back to the states.

Digital divide The large differences in usage of the Internet between older and younger people, lower- and middle/upper-class people, lesser and better educated people, and minority groups and nonminority groups.

Dillon's Rule The Iowa Supreme Court ruling establishing that state government maintains clear authority over local governments to issue directives ordering localities to do what the state wishes.

Direct democracy A system of government in which all citizens participate in making policy, rules, and governing decisions.

Direction (of public opinion) A tendency toward a particular preference, usually (though not always) characterized as either positive or negative.

Direct primary election An open election, rather than an election by party leaders, to choose candidates for the general election.

Discount rate The rate (expressed as a percentage) that all Federal Reserve member banks and other depository institutions will be charged by the Federal Reserve Banks to borrow short-term funds.

Discovery A stage of pretrial litigation in which the plaintiff and defendant have the right to learn what information the other side has about the case by requesting documents or materials, access to property, and/or examinations, or by offering answers to questions about the litigation either in written form or verbally at a deposition.

Discretionary spending Forms of federal government spending that Congress can modify or eliminate in any given year, including spending on education, the environment, and national defense.

Dissenting opinion The opinion of one or more justices who disagree with the result reached by the majority.

Distributive tax policies Taxation policies intended to promote the interests of all classes equally.

Divided government Split party control of Congress and the presidency.

Domino theory Theory that held that Communist takeovers of countries in Southeast Asia and elsewhere would be followed by subsequent Communist takeovers of nearby countries.

Double jeopardy clause The constitutional protection that those accused of a crime cannot be tried twice for the same crime.

Dual federalism The doctrine of federalism that holds that state authority acts as a limit on congressional power under the Constitution.

Due process model Criminal justice policymaking model that views the attainment of justice—which includes protection of the innocent—as the principal goal of the system.

E

Economic equality May be defined as providing all groups the equality of opportunity for economic success, or as the equality of results. In the United States, the latter has been the more common understanding of economic opportunity.

Economic interest group An organized group that exists to promote favorable economic conditions and economic opportunities for its members.

Electoral College The constitutional mechanism by which presidents are chosen. Each state is allocated Electoral College votes based on the sum of that state's U.S. senators and House members.

Electors Individuals appointed to represent a state's presidential vote in the Electoral College; in practice, voters in presidential elections vote for a slate of electors committed to a particular candidate, rather than voting directly for the candidate.

Enumerated powers Express powers explicitly granted by the Constitution such as the taxing power specifically granted to Congress.

Environmental Protection Agency (EPA) Federal agency that administers and enforces all of the nation's environmental programs and spells out the requirements of legislative initiatives to control the quality of the environment.

Equal time rule The FCC mandate that radio and TV stations offer equal amounts of airtime to all political candidates who want to broadcast advertisements.

Establishment clause The clause in the First Amendment that prohibits government from enacting any law "respecting an establishment of religion." Separationist interpretations of this clause affirm that government should not support any religious activity. Accommodationists say that support for a religion is legal provided that all religions are equally supported.

Exclusionary rule The legal rule requiring that all evidence illegally obtained by police in violation of the Bill of Rights must be "excluded" from admission in a court of law, where it might have assisted in convicting those accused of committing crimes.

Executive agreement A pact reached between the president and a foreign government that does not require the consent of Congress.

Executive Office of the President The staffers who help the president of the United States manage the rest of the federal bureaucracy.

Executive orders Rules or regulations issued by the chief executive that have the force of law and do not require the consent of Congress.

Expansionism Doctrine that favors a country expanding its own territory and influence.

Ex post facto laws A law that punishes someone for doing something in the past, at a time when the act was not illegal. The Constitution denies government the ability to write laws ex post facto.

F

Federal Election Campaign Act (FECA) The federal legislation passed in 1971 that established disclosure requirements and restricted individual campaign contributions.

Federal Election Commission (FEC) The agency created in 1974 to enforce federal election laws.

Federal Register The journal that publishes draft regulations that implement a federal program.

Federal Reserve Board The Federal Reserve System's Board of Governors, which votes on monetary policy in the United States, supervises the nation's banks by setting rules for the twelve Federal Reserve Banks, and engages in open market operations.

Federal Reserve System The central banking system of the United States, which controls the nation's money supply.

Federalism The doctrine underlying a system of government in which power is divided between a central government and constituent political subunits.

Federalist Papers A series of articles authored by Alexander Hamilton, James Madison, and John Jay, which argued in favor of ratifying the proposed Constitution of the United States; *The Federalist* Papers outlined the philosophy and motivation of the document.

Federalists Those who supported ratification of the proposed Constitution of the United States between 1787 and 1789.

Fifteenth Amendment The amendment to the Constitution that guaranteed the franchise regardless of race, color, or any previous condition of servitude.

Filibuster The action by a single senator or a minority of senators to block a bill from passage by refusing to end discussion.

Fiscal policy Decisions by the federal government that relate to raising revenue through taxation and spending the revenue that is thereby generated.

Flat tax A tax policy that draws money from all entities at the same proportion of their income.

Franchise (or suffrage) The right to vote.

Franking privilege The traditional right of members of Congress to mail materials to their constituents without paying postage.

Free exercise clause The religious freedom clause in the First Amendment that denies government the ability to prohibit the free exercise of religion. Debate over the clause has largely focused on whether government laws can force adherents of a certain religion to engage in activities that are prohibited by their religious beliefs or prevent them from performing acts that are compelled by their religious beliefs.

Free rider An individual who does not join or contribute to an interest group that is representing his or her interests.

Frontloading The recent trend of states moving their primaries and caucuses earlier in the year to attract greater attention from the candidates and the media.

Full faith and credit clause The provision in Article IV, Section 1 of the Constitution that forces states to abide by the official acts and proceedings of all other states.

G

Gerrymandering The drawing of House district boundaries to the benefit of one political party over another. The term is named for Elbridge Gerry, a Massachusetts delegate to the Constitutional Convention, who (as governor) redrew districts in this fashion to favor the Democratic-Republicans.

***Gibbons v. Ogden* (1824)** The Supreme Court case that held that under the Constitution a federal license to operate steamboats overrides a state-granted monopoly of New York waters.

Good faith exception An exception to the exclusionary rule that states if a search warrant is invalid through no fault of the police, evidence obtained under that warrant may still be admitted into court.

Government The collection of public institutions in a nation that establish and enforce the rules by which the members of that nation must live.

Government corporations Units in the federal bureaucracy set up to run like private companies that depend on revenue from citizens to provide their services.

Grand jury A jury whose duty it is to hear the evidence offered by a prosecutor and determine whether a trial is justified.

Grants-in-aid Grants from the federal government to states that allow state governments to pursue specific federal policies such as highway construction.

Grassroots lobbying Communications by interest groups with government officials through the mobilization of public opinion to exert influence on government action.

Great Compromise A proposal also known as the "Connecticut Compromise" that provided for a bicameral legislature featuring an upper house based on equal representation among the states and a lower house whose membership was based on each state's population; approved by a 5–4 vote of the state delegations.

Great Society A set of aggressive federal domestic policies proposed by President Lyndon Johnson and passed by Congress in the 1960s that further enhanced the role of the presidency.

Gross domestic product (GDP) An estimate of the total money value of all the goods and services produced in the United States in a one-year period.

H

Hard money Donations made directly to political candidates and their campaigns that must be declared with the name of the donor (which then becomes public knowledge).

Hatch Act of 1939 The 1939 law that insulated the civil service from partisan politics by prohibiting employee dismissals for partisan reasons and by prohibiting federal workers from participating in political campaigns.

Health maintenance organization (HMO) Prepaid group medical practice arrangement that attempts to limit health care costs through the establishment of flat monthly rates.

I

Impeachment The first step in a two-step process outlined in Article II, Section 4 of the U.S. Constitution to remove a president or other high official from office. The House of Representatives, by majority vote, may impeach if the official has committed "treason, bribery, or other high crimes or misdemeanors." The second step requires a conviction in the Senate by a two-thirds vote.

Incorporation The process by which the U.S. Supreme Court used the due process clause of the Fourteenth Amendment to make most of the individual rights guaranteed by the Bill of Rights also applicable to the states. Incorporation provided that state and local governments, as well as the federal government, could not deny these rights to citizens.

Incumbent race General election race pitting a person currently holding the office against a challenger.

Independent agency A department that focuses on a narrower set of issues than do higher-status cabinet departments.

Independent campaign expenditure Political donations that PACs or individuals spend to support campaigns, but do not directly contribute to the campaigns.

Indiana ballot The voting ballot format in which the name of the political party appears at the top of the column and candidates for the various offices appear below the party label, thus cuing the voters to partisan-based voting.

Indictment A decision by a grand jury authorizing the government to proceed to trial against the defendant.

Individualism The value that individuals are primarily responsible for their own lot in life and that promotes and rewards individual initiative and responsibility. This value underlies America's reliance on a capitalist economy and free-market system.

Inflation The overall general upward price movement of goods and services in an economy, normally measured by the consumer price index (CPI).

Initiative A question that goes directly to the voters for approval or rejection without first having been proposed by the state legislature.

Intensity (of public opinion) The degree of strength or commitment the public feels about the opinion it holds.

Interest group An organization of people with shared goals that tries to influence public policy through a variety of activities.

Intergovernmental lobby Any interest group that represents the collective interests of states, cities, and other governments.

Internationalism Doctrine that favors active participation of the nation in collective arrangements that secure the political independence and territorial boundaries of other countries.

International organization Entity of international scope or character, usually established by treaty, such as the World Bank or the International Monetary Fund.

Invisible primary The competition among candidates seeking the party nomination for front-runner status prior to the primaries and caucuses.

Iron triangle A three-sided network of policymaking that includes congressional committees (and subcommittees) in a specific policy area, executive agencies with authority over that area, and private interest groups focused on influencing that area.

Isolationism Foreign policy doctrine that opposes intervention in distant wars and involvement in permanent military alliances.

Issue and ideological group An organized group that focuses on specific issues and ideological perspectives.

Issue network The broad array of actors (beyond just the iron triangle) that try to collectively influence a policy area in which they maintain a vested interest.

J

Jim Crow laws Laws used by some southern states that required segregation of blacks and whites in public schools, railroads, buses, restaurants, hotels, theaters, and other public facilities. The laws excluded blacks from militias and denied them certain education and welfare services.

Joint Chiefs of Staff (JCS) Group of chief officers of the four branches of the armed forces as well as a JCS chair and vice chair, which advises the president on military matters and delivers the president's orders to the military.

Joint committee A committee comprising members of both the House and the Senate that is investigative in nature.

Judicial review The power of a court to declare acts of the other branches of government or of a subordinate government to be unconstitutional and thus invalid.

K

Katz test The legal standard that requires the government to attain a warrant demonstrating "probable cause" for any "search" that violates a person's actual and reasonable expectation of privacy.

Keynesian economic theory Fiscal policy theory that favors government taxation and spending during difficult economic times.

L

Laissez-faire economics Fiscal policy theory that favors minimal intervention in the nation's economy.

Layer cake federalism Description of federalism as maintaining that the authority of state and federal governments exists in distinct and separate spheres.

Legitimacy The extent to which the people afford the government the authority and right to exercise power.

Lemon test The legal test that determines if a government statute aiding public or private schools is an unconstitutional violation of the establishment clause. The statute is unconstitutional if the statute has no secular purpose, if its principal or primary effect advances or inhibits religion, or if it fosters "an excessive government entanglement with religion."

Libel Printing or disseminating false statements that harm someone.

Liberal ideology A political orientation that favors a more assertive role in the redistribution of economic resources, but emphasizes individual freedom on a range of social issues.

Limited government The value that promotes the idea that government power should be as restricted as possible.

Literacy test The requirement that individuals prove that they can read and write before being allowed to vote.

Litigation Any judicial contest, including all the events that lead up to a possible court event.

Lobbying The means by which interest groups attempt to influence government officials to make decisions favorable to their goals.

Logrolling The trading of influence or votes among legislators to achieve passage of projects that are of interest to one another.

Loose construction Constitutional interpretation that gives constitutional provisions broad and open-ended meanings.

M

Majoritarianism (1) The principle that the choice that is supported by the most voters is the choice that prevails; (2) the theory that public policy is a product of what majorities of citizens prefer.

Majority caucus The members of the party that has the majority of seats in a particular chamber.

Majority leader In the Senate, the controlling party's main spokesperson who leads his or her party in proposing new laws and crafting the party's platform. The Senate majority leader also enjoys the power to make committee assignments. In the House, the majority leader is the controlling party's second in command, who helps the Speaker to oversee the development of the party platform.

Majority opinion The opinion of a majority of members of the U.S. Supreme Court, which carries the force of law.

Majority rule The notion that the will of the majority should guide decisions made by American government.

Mandatory spending Federal government spending that is not controlled by annual budget decisions; includes entitlements such as Medicare and Social Security.

Manifest destiny U.S. policy of the mid-nineteenth century that advocated acquiring lands and occupying the entire American continent from one ocean to the other.

Marble cake federalism Description of federalism as intertwining state and federal authority in an inseparable mixture.

Marginal seat A seat in a congressional district that has relatively similar numbers of Democratic and Republican voters.

Marshall Plan The 1947 U.S. policy that provided loans and aid to Western European countries whose economies had been ravaged by World War II.

Massachusetts ballot The voting ballot format that organizes the slate of candidates according to the office they are seeking, indicating the candidate's party affiliation with a label.

Material benefits (of group membership) The specific, tangible benefits individuals receive from interest group membership, such as economic concessions, discounts on products, etc.

Mayor-council form The form of local government, modeled on the executive and legislative branches of the federal government and the fifty state governments, in which the mayor is the executive and the council is the legislative body.

McCulloch v. Maryland (1819) The Supreme Court case that established that Congress enjoys broad and extensive authority to make all laws that are "necessary and proper" to carry out its constitutionally delegated powers.

Medicaid Federal program that provides limited health care services to the poor.

Medicare Federal program that provides health insurance for the elderly.

Merit system A system of appointing and promoting civil service personnel based on merit rather than political affiliation or loyalty.

Midterm congressional elections Congressional elections held midway between successive presidential elections.

Military-industrial complex The vast network of defense industries in America (including manufacturers of weapons, missiles, aircraft, and so forth) and their allies in the federal bureaucracy.

Minimal effects theory The theory that deep-seated, long-term political attitudes have much greater influence on an individual's vote decisions than does news media coverage.

Minority caucus The members of the party that has a minority of seats in a particular chamber.

Minority leader The leader of the minority party in each chamber.

Miranda warning The U.S. Supreme Court's requirement that an individual who is arrested must be read a statement that explains the person's right to remain silent and the right to an attorney.

Monarchy A form of government in which one person, usually a member of a royal family or a royal designate, exercises supreme authority.

Monetary policy Regulation of the money supply and interest rates by a central bank, such as the U.S. Federal Reserve Board, in order to control inflation and stabilize the currency.

Monroe Doctrine U.S. foreign policy that proclaimed North and South America unavailable for future colonization by any European power and that declared that any such colonization would be viewed as an act of war on the United States.

Motor Voter law The federal law that mandates that when an individual applies for or renews a state driver's license, the state must also provide that individual with voter registration materials.

Multiparty system A political system in which many different parties are organized on the basis of political ideologies, economic interests, religion, geography, or positions on a single issue or set of issues.

N

National committee The committee that oversees the conduct of a party's presidential campaign and develops strategy for congressional elections.

National committee chair The head of the national committee for one of the two major parties.

National debt Total sum of the federal government's outstanding debt obligations.

National party convention A large meeting that draws together party delegates from across the nation to choose (or formally affirm the selection of) the party's presidential and vice presidential candidates.

National party organization The institution through which political parties exist at the national, state, and local levels, primarily focused on articulating policy positions, raising money, organizing volunteers, and providing services to candidates.

National Security Council (NSC) Advisory body to the president charged with coordinating information about foreign, military, and economic policies that affect national security.

National supremacy doctrine Chief Justice John Marshall's interpretation of federalism as holding that states have extremely limited sovereign authority, whereas Congress is supreme within its own sphere of constitutional authority.

Natural law According to John Locke, the most fundamental type of law, which supersedes any law that is made by government. Citizens are born with certain natural rights (including life, liberty, and property) that derive from this law and that government cannot take away.

Necessary and proper clause The clause in Article I, Section 8 of the Constitution that affords Congress the power to make laws that serve as a means to achieving its expressly delegated powers.

New Deal A set of aggressive federal domestic policies proposed by President Franklin Roosevelt in the 1930s and passed by Congress as a response to the Great Depression; it ultimately transformed the presidency into an institution marked by permanent bureaucracies and well-established repositories of power.

New Jersey Plan A proposal known also as the "small states plan" that would have retained the Articles of Confederation principle of a legislature where states enjoyed equal representation.

New media Media outlets that rely on relatively newer technologies for communicating, such as the Internet, DVDs, fax machines, cell phones, satellites, cable TV, and broadband.

New world order President George H. W. Bush's description of the post–Cold War world, in which nations would work together for the purpose of securing collective peace, security, freedom, and the rule of law.

Nineteenth Amendment The constitutional amendment that guarantees women equal voting rights.

No Child Left Behind Act Federal legislation passed in 2002 that requires mandatory testing of students to meet basic competencies.

Nomination campaign The political season in which the two major parties hold primaries and caucuses in all the states to choose party delegates committed to specific candidates.

Noneconomic interest group An organized group that advocates for reasons other than their membership's commercial and financial interests.

Normal vote The percentage of voters that can be expected with reasonable certainty to cast a ballot for each of the two major political parties.

North Atlantic Treaty Organization (NATO) A military, political, and economic alliance of nations formally bound to protect self-determination and open trade in Western Europe.

O

Objectivity The journalistic standard that news reporting of events must be factual, accurate, fair, and equitable.

Oligarchy A form of government in which a small exclusive class, which may or may not attempt to rule on behalf of the people as a whole, holds supreme power.

Open election General election race in which neither candidate is the incumbent. (Open elections for Congress are normally called "open seat elections.")

Open market operations The buying and selling of government securities by the Federal Reserve Board as a means of controlling the national money supply.

Open primary An election that allows voters to choose on the day of the primary election the party in which they want to vote.

Open rule A rule of procedure adopted by the House Rules Committee that permits amendments to a bill.

Open shop The law that allows employees the option of joining or not joining the certified union at a unionized workplace.

Original jurisdiction The authority of a court to be the initial court in which a legal decision is rendered.

Outlays The money federal departments or agencies actually spend in a given fiscal year.

Overriding a veto The power of the Congress to enact legislation despite a president's veto of that legislation; requires a two-thirds vote of both houses of Congress.

P

Pacifism Doctrine of foreign relations that refuses to sanction any military conflict and that opposes all war making.

Pardon The president's constitutional authority to relieve an individual of both the punishment and the guilt of violating the law.

Partisan press era The period from the late 1700s to the mid-1800s when newspapers typically supported a particular political party.

Party identification The psychological attachment that an individual has to a particular party.

Party platform A document outlining the party's position on important policy issues.

Patient Protection and Affordable Care Act (PPACA) The main federal legislation passed in 2010 that overhauled the health care system by expanding Medicaid and guaranteeing health care coverage for select groups of citizens. The law was amended a week later as the Health Care and Education Reconciliation Act of 2010.

Patronage The act of appointing people to government positions.

Pendleton Civil Service Reform Act The 1883 law that created a merit system for hiring many federal workers, protected them from being fired for partisan reasons, and set up a Civil Service Commission to oversee the hiring and firing process.

Plaintiff The party that chooses to initiate formal legal proceedings in a civil case.

Plea bargain A pretrial negotiated resolution in a criminal case in which the defendants seek to reduce their jail sentences by pleading guilty and in return prosecutors are willing to trade down the severity of the punishment.

Plessy v. Ferguson (1896) The Supreme Court case that upheld a Louisiana segregation law on the theory that as long as the accommodations between the racially segregated facilities were equal, the equal protection clause was not violated. The Court's ruling effectively established the constitutionality of racial segregation and the notion of "separate but equal."

Pluralism The theory that public policy largely results from a variety of interest groups competing with one another to promote laws that benefit members of their respective groups.

Pocket veto The indirect veto of a bill received by the president within ten days of the adjournment of Congress, effected by the president's retaining the bill unsigned until Congress adjourns.

Policy implementation The process of carrying out laws, and the specific programs or services outlined in those laws.

Political action committee (PAC) The political arm of an interest group that promotes candidates in election campaigns primarily through financial contributions.

Political culture The values and beliefs about government, its purpose, and its operations and institutions that are widely held among citizens in a society; it defines the essence of how a society thinks politically and is transmitted from one generation to the next.

Political equality A condition in which members of different groups possess substantially the same rights to participate actively in the political system. In the United States, these rights include voting, running for office, petitioning the government for redress of grievances, free speech, free press, and the access to an education.

Political ideology A philosophical guide that people use to help translate their values and beliefs into political preferences.

Political orientations The translation of values and beliefs into a systematic way of assessing the political environment.

Political party An organization that seeks to win elections for the purpose of influencing the outputs of government.

Political preferences The attitudes people maintain regarding the performance of political leaders and institutions, their candidate preferences in elections, and specific policy issues.

Political socialization The process by which an individual acquires values, beliefs, and opinions about politics.

Politics The way in which the institutions of government are organized to make laws, rules, and policies, and how those institutions are influenced.

Poll tax The requirement that individuals pay a fee before being allowed to vote.

Popular sovereignty The idea that the ultimate source of power in the nation is held by the people.

Pork-barrel legislation A government project or appropriation that yields jobs or other benefits to a specific locale and patronage opportunities to its political representative.

Power The ability to get individuals to do something that they may not otherwise do, such as pay taxes, stop for red lights, or submit to a search before boarding an airplane.

Power of appointment The president's constitutional power to hire and fire those charged with administrative authority to help execute federal laws, such as ambassadors, federal judges including those on the Supreme Court, and all other federal officers under the president's charge. Most of these appointments require the consent of the Senate.

Power of incumbency The phenomenon by which incumbent members of Congress running for reelection are returned to office at an extremely high rate.

Preemption The constitutional doctrine that holds that when Congress acts affirmatively in the exercise of its own granted power, federal laws supersede all state laws on the matter.

Preemption doctrine Doctrine of war making that reserves the right of the U.S. military to use advance strikes to stop rogue states from developing weapons of mass destruction.

Prenomination campaign The political season in which candidates for president begin to explore the possibility of running by attempting to raise money and garner support.

Presidential primary A statewide election to select delegates who will represent a state at the party's national convention.

President pro tempore In the absence of the vice president, the senator who presides over the Senate session. By tradition, this is usually the senator from the majority caucus who has served the longest number of consecutive years in the Senate.

Prior restraint The government's requirement that material be approved by government before it can be published.

Privatization The process of replacing government-provided services with services provided by the private sector.

Progressive tax A tax whose effective rate on an individual's income increases as the person's income rises.

Pseudo-poll Phone calls from members of political campaigns or PACs who present themselves as pollsters for the purpose of planting messages with voters rather than measuring public opinion.

Public interest group An organized group that promotes the broad, collective good of citizens and consumers.

Public opinion The summation of individual opinions on any particular issue or topic.

Public opinion poll A method of measuring the opinions of a large group of people by asking questions of a subset of the larger group and then generalizing the findings to the larger group.

Public policy The set of laws, regulations, and rules that affect the whole of society.

Purposive benefits (of group membership) Rewards that do not directly benefit the individual member, but benefit society as a whole.

R

Racial profiling The law enforcement practice of taking race into account when identifying possible suspects of crimes.

Random-digit dialing (RDD) A probability technique for scientific telephone polling that randomly assigns the last four digits to known information about telephone area codes and exchanges.

Reapportionment The allocation of a fixed number of House seats to the states.

Recall A ballot measure allowing voters to remove duly elected officials from office prior to the end of their term.

Recession An economic slowdown characterized by high unemployment, reduced productivity, or other negative economic indicators.

Redistributive tax policies Taxation policies that aim to provide a social safety net to meet the minimum physical needs of citizens.

Redistricting The act of redrawing congressional boundaries to achieve equal representation in each of the congressional districts.

Referendum A question that appears on the ballot asking voters to approve or reject a policy action either recommended by the state legislature or already approved by the state legislature.

Regressive tax A tax that charges individuals the same amount, regardless of income.

Regulations Rules or other directives issued by government agencies.

Regulatory agency A government body responsible for the control and supervision of a specified activity or area of public interest.

Reporting legislation The exclusive power of standing committees to forward legislation to the full House or Senate. Neither chamber can vote on a bill unless the committee votes to approve it first.

Representative democracy A form of government designed by the U.S. Constitution whereby free, open, and regular elections are held to allow voters to choose those who govern on their behalf and who are responsible for making and enforcing public policy; it is also referred to as indirect democracy or a republican form of government.

Reprieve The president's constitutional authority to reduce the severity of a punishment without removing the guilt for those who have violated the law.

Reserved powers Those powers expressly retained by the state governments under the Constitution.

Reserve requirement The minimum liquid assets each bank must keep on hand to back customer loans.

Retrospective voting An explanation of vote choice that asserts that voters' evaluations of a candidate's past performance in office provides an important cue for vote decisions.

Rules Committee A committee in the House of Representatives that determines the rules by which bills will come to the floor, be debated, and so on.

S

Safe seat A congressional seat from a district that includes a high percentage of voters from one of the major parties.

Sampling error The amount of error in a poll that results from interviewing a sample of people rather than the whole population under study; the larger the sample, the less the sampling error.

Scientific sample A randomly selected subgroup drawn from a population using probability theory.

Select committee A committee established by a resolution in either the House or the Senate for a specific purpose and, usually, for a limited time.

Senior Executive Service (SES) Since the late 1970s, a defined group of approximately 7,500 career professionals in the federal bureaucracy who provide continuity in the operations of the bureaucracy from one presidential administration to the next.

Separation of powers The principle that each branch of government enjoys separate and independent powers and areas of responsibility.

Shays's Rebellion Armed uprising by debt-ridden Massachusetts farmers frustrated with the state government.

SLAPS test A standard that courts established to determine if material is obscene based in part on whether the material has serious literary, artistic, political, or scientific value. If it does, then the material is not obscene.

Social capital The "social connectedness" of a community, or the extent to which individuals are socially integrated into their community.

Social contract From the philosophy of Jean-Jacques Rousseau, an agreement people make with one another to form a government and abide by its rules and laws, and in return, the government promises to protect the people's rights and welfare and promote their best interests.

Social equality Equality and fair treatment of all groups within the various institutions in society, both public and private, that serve the public at large,

including in stores, theaters, restaurants, hotels, and public transportation facilities among many other operations open to the public.

Socialism Economic system in which all or most of the means of production are owned by the community as a whole.

Social learning theory The theory that viewers imitate what they view on television through observational learning.

Social policy Rules, regulations, and policymaking pertaining to the quality of life, welfare, and relations of human beings in the United States.

Soft money Money not donated directly to a candidate's campaign, but rather to a political advocacy group or a political party for "party building" activities.

Solicitor general The lawyer representing the U.S. government before the U.S. Supreme Court.

Solidary benefits (of group membership) Satisfaction that individuals receive from interacting with like-minded individuals for a cause.

Sovereignty The supreme political power of a government to regulate its affairs without outside interference.

Speaker of the House The leader of the House of Representatives, responsible for assigning new bills to committees, recognizing members to speak in the House chamber, and assigning chairs of committees.

Spoils system The postelection practice of rewarding loyal supporters of the winning candidates and party with appointive public offices.

Standing The requirement that a party must be uniquely or

singularly affected by a controversy in order to be eligible to file a lawsuit.

Standing committee A permanent committee that exists in both the House and Senate; most standing committees focus on a particular substantive area of public policy, such as transportation, labor, foreign affairs, and the federal budget.

State constitution The fundamental law governing the structure and activities of state and local government.

State of the Union address An annual speech that the president delivers to Congress laying out the status of the nation and offering suggestions for new legislation.

Strategic Defense Initiative (SDI) A theoretical antimissile system based on the use of lasers and particle beams to shoot down Soviet nuclear missiles in outer space.

Strict construction Constitutional interpretation that limits the government to only those powers explicitly stated in the Constitution.

Strict scrutiny A legal standard set in *Brown v. Board of Education* for cases related to racial discrimination that tends to invalidate almost all state laws that segregate racial groups.

Supply-side economics Economic theory that favors cutting taxes as the way of increasing economic productivity.

Supremacy clause The provision in Article VI, Clause 2 of the Constitution that provides that the Constitution and federal laws override any conflicting provisions in state constitutions or state laws.

Symbolic speech Nonspoken forms of speech that might be protected by the First Amendment, such as flag burning, wearing armbands at school to protest a war, or camping out in public parks to protest the plight of the homeless.

T

Talk radio A specialized form of radio programming on which one or more hosts provide commentary and often invite listeners to call in to the show and offer their own opinions.

Tariff A tax on imported goods, charged at the time the goods are received in port.

Theocracy A form of government in which a particular religion or faith plays a dominant role in the government.

Three-Fifths Compromise A compromise proposal in which five slaves would be counted as the equivalent of three free people for purposes of taxes and representation.

Title IX The section of the Federal Educational Amendments Law of 1972 that prohibits the exclusion of women from an educational program or activity receiving financial assistance from the federal government. Courts have interpreted those provisions to force colleges and universities to provide as many athletic teams for women as they do for men.

Town meeting The form of local government found exclusively in some small towns in New England (and two Midwest states) in which all citizens are invited to vote on policy issues and management matters.

Township The name for the type of local government that typically serves rural areas or geographic outgrowths of cities.

Trade association A business association that focuses on one particular industry, with membership drawn exclusively from that industry.

Truman Doctrine Doctrine articulated by President Harry Truman in the late 1940s by which money and resources were provided to support and sustain non-Communist governments in areas strategically vital to the United States.

Twenty-fourth Amendment The constitutional amendment that outlaws poll taxes.

Twenty-second Amendment Passed in 1951, this constitutional amendment restricts any one person from being elected to the presidency "more than twice," or from acting as president for longer than two and a half terms.

Twenty-sixth Amendment The constitutional amendment that lowered the voting age to eighteen in all local, state, and federal elections.

Twenty-third Amendment The constitutional amendment providing electoral votes to the District of Columbia, thus giving District residents the right to vote in presidential elections.

Two-party system A party system dominated by two major parties that win the vast majority of elections.

Two presidencies theory Theory articulated by political scientist Aaron Wildavsky that posits the existence of a more powerful presidency in foreign affairs and a more limited presidency in the domestic sphere.

U

Union shop The law that requires that employees in unionized workplaces either join the union or pay the equivalent of union dues to it after a set period of time.

Unitary system of government A system of government in which the constituent states are strictly subordinated to the goals of the central government as a whole.

United Nations (UN) International organization formed after World War II to promote and maintain international security and peace.

Unit rule The system in forty-eight states by which the candidate who wins the most votes among popular votes cast for president in a state receives all the electoral votes from that state; also known as the "winner take all" system.

Universal health care National health care system in which full access to health care is provided to citizens at government expense.

Universal suffrage The idea that all citizens in a nation have the right to vote.

Unscientific poll A poll in which the sample of people interviewed is not representative of any group beyond those who register their opinion.

V

Values The broad principles underlying American political culture that citizens support and adhere to.

Veto The constitutional procedure by which the president refuses to approve a bill or joint resolution and thus prevents its enactment into law.

Virginia Plan A proposal known also as the "large states plan" that empowered three separate branches of government, including a legislature with membership proportional to population.

Voter turnout The number of people who turn out to vote as a percentage of all those eligible to vote.

Voting The political mechanism that ensures that the majority will rule.

Voting Rights Act of 1965 The federal law that invalidated literacy tests and property requirements and required select states and cities to apply for permission to the Justice Department to change their voting laws. As a consequence, millions of African Americans were effectively reenfranchised in the South.

W

War Powers Resolution Largely ignored congressional policy that restricts the president's power to engage in war except (1) when Congress has declared war, (2) when Congress has specifically granted the president permission to use armed forces, or (3) when the nation is under attack. The resolution further requires the president to report to Congress whenever American forces are entered into hostilities.

Warrant A document issued by a judge or magistrate that allows law enforcement to search or seize items at a home, business, or anywhere else that might be specified.

Warsaw Pact Formal alliance of nations within the Soviet sphere during the Cold War.

Welfare state Social system in which the state assumes a considerable degree of responsibility for citizens in matters of health care, employment, education, and retirement income.

Whip (majority and minority) Member of Congress elected by his or her party to count potential votes and promote party unity in voting.

White House chief of staff The manager of the White House staff, which serves the president's organizational needs, including speechwriting, advance work for presidential appearances, scheduling, congressional relations, public relations, and communications.

White House Office of Legislative Affairs A presidential office that serves as a liaison between the president and Congress. This office helps the president develop the strategy used to promote passage of the president's legislative agenda.

White House press secretary The person on the White House staff who plays an especially important role in briefing the press, organizing news conferences, and even briefing the president on questions that may be asked.

Writ of certiorari The formal term for an order by which the Supreme Court acts in its discretion to review a case from a lower court.

Notes

Chapter 1

1. http://curiouscapitalist.blogs
   .time.com/2010/11/03/why
   -the-u-s-midterm-elections
   -are-bad-for-the-global
   -economy/#ixzz14FGZu61g.
2. See Thomas Hobbes, *Leviathan*
   (London: A. Crooke, 1651).
3. For a collection of Rousseau's
   work, see Jean-Jacques
   Rousseau, *The Social Contract
   and Discourses*, translation
   and commentary by G. D. H.
   Cole (London: Guernsey Press,
   1983).
4. Harold Lasswell, *Politics: Who
   Gets What, When and How*
   (New York: McGraw-Hill, 1936).
5. John Locke, *Two Treatises of
   Government*, ed. Peter Laslett
   (Cambridge: Cambridge
   University Press, 1960).
6. Alexis de Tocqueville,
   Democracy in America, 1835,
   ed. Richard Hefner (New York:
   Penguin Books, 1956).
7. Robert Goidel, Donald A. Gross,
   and Todd G. Shields, *Money
   Matters* (Lanham, MD: Rowman
   & Littlefield, 1999), 17.
8. Morris Fiorina, *Culture War? The
   Myth of a Polarizing America*
   (New York: Pearson Longman,
   2005).

Chapter 2

1. Fred Anderson, *The War That
   Made America: A Short History
   of the French-Indian War* (New
   York: Viking, 2005).
2. Robert Middlekauff, *The
   Glorious Cause* (New York:
   Oxford University Press, 1982).
3. Events of these years are nicely
   recounted in Pauline Maier,
   *From Resistance to Revolution:
   Colonial Radicals and the
   Development of American
   Opposition to Britain, 1765–
   1776* (New York: W. W. Norton,
   1992).
4. *The Political Writings of Thomas
   Paine, Vol. 1* (Boston: J. P.
   Mendum Investigator Office,
   1870).
5. David McCullough, *John
   Adams* (New York: Simon &
   Schuster, 2001), 119; Joseph
   Ellis, *Founding Brothers* (New
   York: Knopf, 2000), 212–213.
6. Pauline Maier, *American
   Scripture: Making the
   Declaration of Independence*
   (New York: Vintage, 1998).
7. Merrill Jensen, *The Articles
   of Confederation: An
   Interpretation of the Social-
   Constitutional History of the
   American Revolution, 1774–
   1781* (Madison: University of
   Wisconsin Press, 1959).
8. For an account of
   Massachusetts public policy
   during this period, see Van
   Beck Hall, *Politics without
   Parties: Massachusetts 1780–
   1791* (Pittsburgh: University of
   Pittsburgh Press, 1972).
9. Robert Gross, ed., *In Debt
   to Shays* (Charlottesville:
   University of Virginia Press,
   1993).
10. Christopher Collier, *Decision in
   Philadelphia: The Constitutional
   Convention of 1787* (New York:
   Ballantine Books, 2007).
11. For a discussion of the
   founders' silence on slavery,
   see Joseph Ellis, *Founding
   Brothers* (New York: Knopf,
   2000), 81–119.
12. Jacob E. Cooke, ed., *The
   Federalist* (Middletown, CT:
   Wesleyan University Press,
   1961).
13. Saul Cornell, *The Other
   Founders: Anti-Federalism and
   the Dissenting Tradition in
   America 1788–1828* (Chapel
   Hill: University of North
   Carolina Press, 1999).
14. Henry Mayer, *A Son of Thunder:
   Patrick Henry and the American
   Republic* (Charlottesville:
   University of Virginia Press,
   1992).
15. Paul Murphy, *The Historic
   Background of the Bill of Rights*
   (New York: Taylor & Francis,
   1990).
16. See Jefferson–Madison
   correspondence republished in
   Philip Kurland, ed., *The Founders'
   Constitution* (Indianapolis:
   Liberty Fund, 2000).
17. One of the better recent works
   on Marshall's tenure at the
   Court is R. Kent Newmyer,
   *John Marshall and the Heroic
   Age of the Supreme Court*
   (Baton Rouge: Louisiana State
   University Press, 2002).
18. 17 U.S. 316 (1819).
19. See Robert Bork, *The Tempting
   of America* (New York: Simon &
   Schuster, 1990).
20. Lawrence Tribe, *Constitutional
   Choices* (Cambridge, MA:
   Harvard University Press, 2004).

21. John Hart Ely, *Democracy and Distrust* (Cambridge, MA: Harvard University Press, 1980).

Chapter 3

1. Stanley R. Sloan, *NATO, The European Union and the Atlantic Community: The Transatlantic Bargain Reconsidered* (New York: Rowman & Littlefield, 2002).
2. See *McCulloch v. Maryland*, 17 U.S. 316 (1819).
3. *Goodrich v. Department of Public Health*, 798 N.E. 2d 941 (Mass 2003).
4. In California, same-sex marriages were performed under the authority of a state supreme court ruling between June 16, 2008, and November 4, 2008, before a voter initiative reinstated that state's previous ban on the practice.
5. For example, in *Supreme Court of New Hampshire v. Piper*, 470 U.S. 274 (1985), the U.S. Supreme Court interpreted the privileges and immunities clause of Article IV to forbid states from excluding nonresidents from admission to the practice of law.
6. Stanley Elkins and Eric McKitrick, *The Age of Federalism: The Early American Republic 1788–1800* (New York: Oxford University Press, 1995).
7. 17 U.S. 316 (1819).
8. 22 U.S. 1 (1824).
9. H. W. Brands, *Andrew Jackson: His Life and Times* (New York: Doubleday, 2005).
10. *Railroad Retirement Board v. Alton Railroad Co.*, 295 U.S. 330 (1935); *Carter v. Carter Coal Co.*, 298 U.S. 238 (1936).
11. William E. Leuchtenburg, *The Supreme Court Reborn: The Constitutional Revolution in the Age of Roosevelt* (New York: Oxford University Press, 1995).
12. *Heart of Atlanta Motel v. United States*, 379 U.S. 241 (1964); *Katzenbach v. McClung*, 379 U.S. 294 (1964).
13. For an application of the term to welfare policy, see Pamela Wilson, *Welfare Policymaking in the States: The Devil in Devolution* (Washington, DC: Georgetown University Press, 2002).
14. David Savage, *Turning Right: The Making of the Rehnquist Supreme Court* (New York: Wiley, 1993).
15. 505 U.S. 144 (1992).
16. 521 U.S. 898 (1997).
17. 514 U.S. 549 (1995).
18. 529 U.S. 598 (2000).
19. 527 U.S. 706 (1999).
20. *New State Ice Co. v. Liebmann*, 285 U.S. 262, 311 (1932).
21. See BEA News Release No. 08-11, "State Personal Income Tax 2007" (Released March 26, 2008).

Chapter 4

1. David McCullough, *John Adams* (New York: Simon & Schuster, 2001), 504.
2. Antonin Scalia, "Law and the Winds of Change." Remarks made at the 24th Australian Legal Convention, Perth, West Australia, September 21, 1987.
3. Alexander Hamilton, James Madison, and John Jay, *The Federalist Papers,* Clinton Rossiter, ed. (New York: New American Library, 1971).
4. Jefferson–Madison correspondence in Philip Kurland, ed., *The Founders' Constitution* (Indianapolis, IN: Liberty Fund, 2000).
5. 32 U.S. 243 (1833).
6. Thomas Jefferson first coined that phrase in a letter he wrote as president to the Baptists of Danbury, Connecticut, in 1802. George Seldes, ed., *The Great Quotations* (Secaucus, NJ: Citadel Press, 1983), 369.
7. 319 U.S. 624 (1943).
8. 374 U.S. 398 (1963).
9. *Reynolds v. United States*, 98 U.S. 145 (1878).
10. 494 U.S. 872 (1990).
11. Carolyn N. Long, *Religious Freedom and Indian Rights: The Case of* Oregon v. Smith (Lawrence: University Press of Kansas, 2000).
12. Noah Feldman, *Divided by God* (New York: Farrar, Straus and Giroux, 2005).
13. 370 U.S. 421 (1962).
14. 374 U.S. 203 (1963).
15. 472 U.S. 38 (1985).
16. 403 U.S. 602 (1971).
17. 505 U.S. 577 (1992).
18. 530 U.S. 290 (2000).
19. 249 U.S. 247 (1919).
20. 341 U.S. 494 (1951).
21. 304 U.S. 144 (1938).
22. 395 U.S. 444 (1969).
23. Harry Kalven, *A Worthy Tradition: Freedom of Speech in America* (New York: Harper & Row, 1988).
24. 376 U.S. 254 (1964).
25. Anthony Lewis, *Make No Law: The Sullivan Case and the First Amendment* (New York: Vintage Books, 1992).
26. 403 U.S. 713 (1971).
27. 413 U.S. 15 (1973).
28. 521 U.S. 844 (1997).
29. John W. Johnson, *The Struggle for Students' Rights:* Tinker v. Des Moines *and the 1960s* (Lawrence: University Press of Kansas, 1997).

30. *Tinker v. Des Moines*, 393 U.S. 503 (1969).
31. 491 U.S. 397 (1989).
32. Robert Justin Goldstein, *Flag Burning and Free Speech: The Case of* Texas v. Johnson (Lawrence: University Press of Kansas, 2000).
33. Philippa Strum, *When the Nazis Came to Skokie: Freedom for Speech We Hate* (Lawrence: University Press of Kansas, 1999).
34. 528 U.S. 343 (2003).
35. Milton Heumann and Thomas W. Church, eds., *Hate Speech on Campus* (Boston: Northeastern University Press, 1997).
36. 554 U.S. _____ (2008).
37. 561 U.S. _____ (2010)
38. Lucas A. Powe Jr., *The Warren Court and American Politics* (Cambridge, MA: Belknap Press of Harvard University, 2002).
39. 389 U.S. 347 (1967).
40. 367 U.S. 643 (1961).
41. It should be noted, however, that a majority of states have chosen to use grand juries, even without being compelled to do so by the U.S. Constitution.
42. 384 U.S. 436 (1966).
43. Gary Stuart, *Miranda: The Story of America's Right to Remain Silent* (Tucson: University of Arizona Press, 2004).
44. 372 U.S. 335 (1963).
45. 536 U.S. 304 (2002).
46. 381 U.S. 479 (1965).
47. 410 U.S. 113 (1973).
48. N. E. H. Hull and Peter Charles Hoffer, Roe v. Wade: *The Abortion Rights Controversy in American History* (Lawrence: University Press of Kansas, 2001).
49. 505 U.S. 833 (1992).
50. 550 U.S. 124 (2007).
51. 539 U.S. 558 (2003).

Chapter 5

1. Juan Williams, *Eyes on the Prize: America's Civil Rights Years, 1954–1965* (New York: Penguin, 1988).
2. Louis R. Harlan, *Booker T. Washington: The Making of a Black Leader* (New York: Oxford University Press, 1975).
3. David Levering Lewis, *W. E. B. DuBois, 1868–1919: Biography of a Race* (New York: Owl Books, 1994).
4. 347 U.S. 483 (1954).
5. Eric Foner, *Reconstruction: America's Unfinished Revolution* (New York: Harper, 2000).
6. 109 U.S. 3 (1883).
7. 163 U.S. 537 (1896).
8. For a comprehensive account of the NAACP's strategy, see Richard Kluger, *Simple Justice* (New York: Vintage Books, 1975).
9. 358 U.S. 1 (1957).
10. Jennifer Hochschild, *The New American Dilemma: Liberal Democracy and School Desegregation* (New Haven, CT: Yale University Press, 1984).
11. See Taylor Branch, *Pillar of Fire: America in the King Years, 1963–65* (New York: Simon & Schuster, 1999).
12. Charles Whalen and Barbara Whalen, *Longest Debate: A Legislative History of the Civil Rights Act* (Santa Ana, CA: Seven Locks Press, 1984).
13. 438 U.S. 265 (1978).
14. 515 U.S. 200 (1995).
15. 539 U.S. 306 (2003).
16. 539 U.S. 244 (2003).
17. Michael Jones and Eileen Poe-Yamagata, *And Justice for Some* (Washington, DC: Building Blocks for Youth Press, 2000).
18. 208 U.S. 412 (1908).
19. 368 U.S. 57, 61 (1961).
20. 411 U.S. 677 (1973).
21. 429 U.S. 190 (1976).
22. U.S. Merit Systems Protection Board, "Sexual Harassment in the Federal Workplace: Trends, Progress, Continuing Challenges" (Office of Policy Evaluation, U.S. Merit Systems Protection Board Document).
23. 517 U.S. 620 (1996).

Chapter 6

1. Woodrow Wilson, *Congressional Government* (Baltimore: Johns Hopkins University Press, 1981; originally published in 1885).
2. For a good discussion of the Constitutional Convention and issues related to Congress, see Charles Stewart III, "Congress and the Constitutional System," in *Institutions of American Democracy: The Legislative Branch*, ed. Paul J. Quirk and Sarah A. Binder (New York: Oxford University Press, 2005).
3. Alexander Hamilton, James Madison, and John Jay, *The Federalist Papers* (Chicago: The New American Library of World Literature; reprinted in 1961).
4. Thomas Mann, *Unsafe at Any Margin: Interpreting Congressional Elections* (Washington, DC: Brookings Institution Press, 1978).
5. See, for example, *Baker v. Carr*, 369 U.S. 186 (1962); *Reynolds v. Sims*, 377 U.S. 533 (1964); *Wesberry v. Sanders*, 376 U.S. 1 (1964).
6. See James Madison, Federalist No. 63.
7. For a discussion of leadership in Congress, see Burdett A. Loomis, *The Contemporary Congress*, 3rd ed. (Boston: Bedford St. Martin's, 2000), chapter 6.

8. A classic work on congressional committees is Richard F. Fenno Jr., *Congressmen in Committees* (Boston: Little, Brown, 1973).

9. See Stephen S. Smith and Christopher Deering, *Committees in Congress,* 2nd ed. (Washington, DC: CQ Press, 1990).

10. See Roger Davidson and Walter Oleszek, *Congress and Its Members*, 4th ed. (Washington DC: CQ Press, 1994).

11. A classic piece on the topic is John Manley, "Wilbur Mills: A Study of Congressional Influence," *American Political Science Review* 63 (1969): 442–464.

12. Eric Redman, *The Dance of Legislation* (Seattle: University of Washington Press, 1974).

13. For a discussion of the motivations for senators to filibuster, see Sarah A. Binder and Stephen S. Smith, *Politics or Principles? Filibustering in the United States Senate* (Washington, DC: Brookings Institution Press, 1997).

14. Morris P. Fiorina, *Congress: Keystone of the Washington Establishment,* 2nd ed. (New Haven, CT: Yale University Press, 1989).

15. For a discussion of the presidential nominating process, see David A. Yalof, *Pursuit of Justices* (Chicago: University of Chicago Press, 2001).

16. Richard F. Fenno Jr., *Home Style: House Members in Their Districts* (Boston: Little, Brown, 1978).

Chapter 7

1. H. W. Brands, *Andrew Jackson: His Life and Times* (New York: Random House, 2005).

2. See *Ex Parte Merryman,* 17 Fed. Cas. 144 (1961).

3. See Clinton Rossiter, *The American Presidency* (Baltimore: Johns Hopkins University Press, 1987).

4. For an excellent history of the appointment process, see Michael J. Gerhardt, *The Federal Appointments Process: A Constitutional and Historical Analysis* (Durham, NC: Duke University Press, 2003).

5. Robert F. Kennedy Jr., *Thirteen Days: A Memoir of the Cuban Missile Crisis* (New York: W. W. Norton, 1999).

6. Mark Peterson, *Legislating Together: The White House and Capitol Hill from Eisenhower to Reagan* (Cambridge, MA: Harvard University Press, 1990).

7. Lee Hamilton and Jordan Tama, *A Creative Tension: The Foreign Policy Roles of the President and Congress* (Washington, DC: Woodrow Wilson Press, 2003).

8. Kenneth Mayer, *With the Stroke of a Pen: Executive Orders and Presidential Power* (Princeton, NJ: Princeton University Press, 2001).

9. The updated version of this work is Richard Neustadt, *Presidential Power and Modern Presidents: The Politics of Leadership from Roosevelt Through Reagan* (New York: Free Press, 1991).

10. Jules Witcover, *Crapshoot: Rolling the Dice on the Vice Presidency* (New York: Crown, 1991).

11. Bob Woodward, *Plan of Attack* (New York: Simon & Schuster, 2004).

12. For a comprehensive discussion of the various ways that modern presidents have organized the White House, see Stephen Hess, *Organizing the Presidency* (Washington, DC: Brookings Institution Press, 1988).

13. Bill Adler, *America's First Ladies* (New York: Taylor, 2002).

14. Samuel Kernell, *Going Public: New Strategies of Presidential Leadership* (Washington, DC: CQ Press, 1992).

15. See Kathleen Hall Jamieson and Paul Waldman, *The Press Effect: Politicians, Journalists, and the Stories That Shape the Political World* (New York: Oxford University Press, 2002).

16. John A. Maltese, *Spin Control: The White House Office of Communications and the Management of Presidential News* (Chapel Hill: University of North Carolina Press, 1992).

Chapter 8

1. For a good discussion of the themes of the 1980 campaign, see Theodore H. White, *America in Search of Itself: The Making of the Presidency, 1956–1980* (New York: Harper and Row), 1982.

2. See James Horn, Jan Ellen Lewis, and Peter S. Onuf, eds., *The Revolution of 1800: Democracy, Race, and the New Republic* (Charlottesville VA: University of Virginia Press, 2002).

3. See William Earl Weeks, "Louisiana Purchase" in *The Oxford Companion to United States History* (New York: Oxford University Press, 2001), 463.

4. See *Washington Monthly,* a periodical that regularly reports on the excesses and waste in the federal bureaucracy.

5. For a comprehensive discussion of the virtues of contemporary bureaucracy, see Charles T. Goodsell, *The Case for Bureaucracy* (Chatham, NJ: Chatham House Publishers, 1994).

6. Max Weber, chapters 11 and 12 in *Economy and Society,* ed. Guenther Roth and Claus Wittich (New York: Bedminster Press, 1968).

7. For a good discussion of organizational issues in the federal bureaucracy, see James Q. Wilson, *Bureaucracy: What Government Agencies Do and Why They Do It* (New York: Basic Books, 1989).

8. See Joel Aberbach, *Keeping a Watchful Eye: The Politics of Congressional Oversight* (Washington, DC: Brookings Institution Press, 1990).

9. Beverly Cigler, "The Paradox of Professionalization" in *Democracy, Bureaucracy and the Study of Administration,* ed. Camilla Stivers (Boulder, CO: Westview Press, 2001).

10. For a good discussion of the growth of the federal bureaucracy during the FDR years, see Brian J. Cook, *Bureaucracy and Self-Government: Reconsidering the Role of Public Administration in American Politics,* chapter 5: "Serving the Liberal State" (Baltimore: Johns Hopkins University Press, 1996).

11. David Osborne and Ted Gaebler, *Reinventing Government: How the Entrepreneurial Spirit Is Transforming the Public Sector* (New York: Penguin Books, 1993).

12. Harold S. Stanley and Richard G. Niemi, *Vital Statistics on American Politics, 2005–2006* (Washington, DC: CQ Press, 2006), 266.

13. Robert H. Wiebe, *The Search for Order: 1877–1920* (New York: Hill & Wang, 1967).

14. Data from the U.S. Bureau of Labor Statistics Web site: http://www.bls.gov/oco/cg/cgs041.htm.

15. See Ari Hoogenboom, *Outlawing the Spoils: A History of the Civil Service Reform Movement, 1865–1883* (Champaign: University of Illinois Press, 1961).

16. Bruce Maxwell, *Insider's Guide to Finding a Job in Washington* (Washington, DC: CQ Press, 2000), 74–75.

Chapter 9

1. For an account of the ways in which the Supreme Court's methods contribute to its image and status as an institution, see John Brigham, *The Cult of the Court* (Philadelphia: Temple University Press, 1987).

2. John Merryman, *The Civil Law Tradition* (Palo Alto, CA: Stanford University Press, 1985).

3. G. Alan Tarr and Mary Cornelius Porter, *State Supreme Courts in State and Nation* (New Haven, CT: Yale University Press, 1988).

4. 1 Cranch (5 U.S.) 137 (1803).

5. An important exception to the strict use of the adversarial approach in the American legal system comes in the form of structural reform litigation, a term that describes certain types of lawsuits brought against bureaucracies such as prisons, school systems, welfare systems, and so on. Judges in these types of cases often assume a more active "managerial approach" in the process, overseeing the implementation of remedies and occasionally taking a proactive role to ensure that the lawyers are properly representing their client's interests. For comprehensive analysis of one example of structural reform litigation in action, see Malcolm Feeley and Edward Rubin, *Judicial Policymaking and the Modern State: How the Court Reformed America's Prisons* (Cambridge: Cambridge University Press, 2000). Of course, the more traditional adversarial system still tends to predominate in most other forms of civil litigation.

6. See George Fisher, *Plea Bargaining's Triumph: A History of Plea Bargaining in America* (Palo Alto, CA: Stanford University Press, 2003); Milton Heumann, *Plea Bargaining: The Experiences of Prosecutors, Judges, and Defense Attorneys* (Chicago: University of Chicago Press, 1981).

7. James Eisenstein, Roy Flemming, and Peter Nardulli, *The Contours of Justice* (New York: Addison-Wesley, 1988).

8. The *Marbury* case is extensively discussed, along with Marshall's other contributions as a jurist, in R. Kent Newmyer, *The Supreme Court Under Marshall and Taney* (Arlington Heights, IL: Harlan Davidson, 1968).

9. 17 U.S. 316 (1819).

10. 1 Wheat (14 U.S.) 304 (1816).

11. 358 U.S. 1 (1958).

12. 347 U.S. 483 (1954).

13. 418 U.S. 683 (1974).

14. Bradley Canton and Charles Johnson, *Judicial Policies: Implementation and Input,* 2nd ed. (Washington, DC: CQ Press, 1999).
15. 370 U.S. 421 (1962).
16. Philip DuBois, *From Ballot to Bench: Judicial Elections and the Quest for Accountability* (Austin: University of Texas Press, 1980).
17. Sheldon Goldman, *Picking Federal Judges* (New Haven, CT: Yale University Press, 1997).
18. Barbara Perry, *A Representative Supreme Court* (Westport, CT: Greenwood Press, 1991).
19. John Maltese, *The Selling of Supreme Court Nominees* (Baltimore: Johns Hopkins University Press, 1995).
20. Ethan Bronner, *Battle for Justice: How the Bork Nomination Shook America* (New York: W. W. Norton, 1989).
21. Richard Pacelle, *Between Law and Politics: The Solicitor General and the Structuring of Race, Gender, and Reproductive Rights Litigation* (College Station: Texas A & M University Press, 2003).
22. 384 U.S. 436 (1966).
23. Jeffrey Segal and Harold Spaeth, *The Supreme Court and the Attitudinal Model* (Cambridge: Cambridge University Press, 1993), 246.
24. See, for example, Sheldon M. Novick, *Honorable Justice: The Life of Oliver Wendell Holmes, Jr.* (Boston: Little, Brown, 1989).

Chapter 10

1. Vincent Price, *Public Opinion* (Newbury Park, CA: Sage Publications, 1992), 5–22.
2. E. E. Schattschneider, *The Semisovereign People: A Realist's View of Democracy in America* (New York: Holt, Rinehart and Winston, 1960).
3. V. O. Key Jr., *Public Opinion in American Democracy* (New York: Alfred A. Knopf, 1961).
4. Samuel P. Huntington, *American Politics: The Promise of Disharmony* (Cambridge, MA: Harvard University Press, 1981).
5. The concept of partisanship and controversies surrounding it over the years are presented in Warren E. Miller and Merrill Shanks, *The New American Voter* (Cambridge, MA: Harvard University Press, 1996).
6. See M. Kent Jennings and Richard G. Niemi, *Generations and Politics: A Panel Study of Young Adults and Their Parents* (Princeton, NJ: Princeton University Press, 1981).
7. James Madison, Alexander Hamilton, and John Jay, *The Federalist Papers*, Federalist No. 51 (New York: Doubleday, 1966, originally published in 1788).
8. Walter Lippman, *Public Opinion* (New York: Harcourt Brace Jovanovich, 1922).
9. Angus Campbell, Philip E. Converse, Warren E. Miller, and Donald E. Stokes, *The American Voter* (New York: John Wiley, 1960).
10. Survey conducted by the Interscholastic Studies Institute.
11. V. O. Key Jr., *The Responsible Electorate* (Cambridge, MA: Belknap Harvard, 1966).
12. Benjamin I. Page and Robert Y. Shapiro, *The Rational Public: Fifty Years of Trends in Americans' Policy Preferences* (Chicago: University of Chicago Press, 1992).
13. Samuel Kernell, *Going Public: New Strategies of Presidential Leadership* (Washington, DC: CQ Press, 1997).
14. Jack Dennis, ed., *Socialization to Politics* (New York: John Wiley, 1973).
15. See, generally, David Easton, *A Systems Analysis of Political Life* (New York: John Wiley, 1965).
16. Michael S. Delli Carpini and Scott Keeter, *What Americans Know About Politics and Why It Matters* (New Haven, CT: Yale University Press, 1996).
17. Charles W. Roll and Albert H. Cantril, *Polls: The Use and Misuse in Politics* (New York: Basic Books, 1972).
18. An important book spelling out the variety of problems and issues with the wording of survey questions is Howard Schuman and Stanley Press, *Questions and Answers in Attitude Surveys* (New York: John Wiley, 1981).
19. For a more detailed discussion of these concepts, see W. Lance Bennett, *Public Opinion in American Politics* (New York: Harcourt Brace Jovanovich, 1980).

Chapter 11

1. James Madison, Federalist No. 10, in *The Federalist Papers* (New York: Mentor Books, reprint edition, 1961), 77.
2. Alexis de Tocqueville, *Democracy in America* (New York: Mentor Books, reprint edition, 1956).
3. Robert Dahl, *A Preface to Democratic Theory* (Cambridge: Cambridge University Press, 1956).
4. David B. Truman, *The Governmental Process* (New York: Alfred A. Knopf, 1951).

5. C. Wright Mills, *The Power Elite* (New York: Oxford University Press, 1956).

6. John P. Heinz, Edward O. Laumann, Robert L. Nelson, and Robert H. Salisbury, *The Hollow Core* (Cambridge, MA: Harvard University Press, 1993).

7. See http://www.opensecrets .org/lobbyists/index.asp.

8. See Theodore J. Lowi, *The End of Liberalism* (New York: W. W. Norton, 1979).

9. See William Gormley, "Regulatory Issue Networks in a Federal System," *Polity*, 18 (1986): 595–620.

10. See http://uschamber.com.

11. Mancur Olson, *The Logic of Collective Action: Public Goods and the Theory of Groups* (Cambridge, MA: Harvard University Press, 1971), 22–35.

12. Robert Salisbury, "An Exchange Theory of Interest Groups," *Midwest Journal of Political Science* 13 (1969): 1–32.

13. Peter B. Clark and James Q. Wilson, "Incentives Systems: A Theory of Organization," *Administrative Science Quarterly* 6 (1961): 129–166.

14. For a good discussion of the influence of group membership on group effectiveness, see Mancur Olson, *The Logic of Collective Action: Public Goods and the Theory of Groups* (Cambridge, MA: Harvard University Press, 1971).

15. Ibid.

16. See http://www.commoncause .org.

17. David Lowery and Holly Brasher, *Organized Interests and American Government* (New York: McGraw-Hill, 2004), 247.

Chapter 12

1. 438 U.S. 726 (1978).

2. See Philip Meyer, *Precision Journalism: A Reporter's Introduction to Social Science Methods* (Lanham, MD: Rowman & Littlefield, 2002).

3. The word *muckrakers* is derived from the idea that this group was "raking up the muck" from scandals and corruption of government and industry.

4. For a chronicle of the Watergate story, see Bob Woodward and Carl Bernstein, *All the President's Men* (New York: Simon & Schuster, 1974).

5. Scott McClellan, *What Happened: Inside the Bush White House and Washington's Culture of Deception* (New York: PublicAffairs, 2008).

6. For a thorough review of the history of news, see Mitchell Stephens, *A History of News: From the Drum to the Satellite* (New York: Viking Press, 1989).

7. Kurt Lang and Gladys Lang, *Television and Politics* (Edison, NJ: Transaction Publishers, 2001).

8. Marshall McLuhan, *Understanding Media: The Extensions of Man* (New York: McGraw-Hill, 1964).

9. For a good review of the process and impact of presidential debates, see Alan Schroeder, *Presidential Debates* (New York: Columbia University Press, 2000).

10. See Doris Graber, *Processing Politics: Learning from Television in the Internet Age* (Chicago: University of Chicago Press, 2001).

11. Mass communication researcher Joseph Klapper was a pioneer of the minimal effects (or limited effects) theory. He introduced the theory in a book titled *The Effects of Mass Communication* (New York: Free Press, 1960).

12. For a good discussion of selection retention, see D. Sears and J. Freeman, "Selective Exposure to Information: A Critical Review," in *The Process and Effects of Mass Communication*, ed. Wilbur Lang Schramm (Chicago: University of Illinois Press, 1972).

13. For a good discussion of social learning theory, see Albert Bandura, *Social Foundations of Thought and Action* (Englewood Cliffs, NJ: Prentice Hall, 1986).

14. See L. Berkowitz, "Some Effects of Thought on Anti- and Pro-Social Influences of Media Effects," *Psychological Bulletin* 95 (1984): 410–427.

15. A pioneer in developing cultivation theory was George Gerbner. See George Gerbner et al., "Growing Up with Television: The Cultivation Perspective," in *Media Effects: Advances in Theory and Research*, ed. Jennings Bryant and Dolf Zillman (Hillsdale, NJ: Lawrence Erlbaum, 1994), 17–41.

16. A number of studies have demonstrated the agenda-setting power of the media, including Maxwell E. McCombs, "The Agenda-Setting Approach," in *Handbook of Political Communications*, ed. Dan D. Nimmo and Keith Sanders (Thousand Oaks, CA: Sage, 1981), 121–140; and Shanto Iyengar and Donald R. Kinder, *News That Matters* (Chicago: University of Chicago Press, 1987).

17. Doris Graber, *Mass Media and American Politics* (Washington, DC: CQ Press, 2002), 207.
18. Kenneth Dautrich and Thomas H. Hartley, *How the News Media Fail American Voters* (New York: Columbia University Press, 1999), 92–95.

Chapter 13

1. "Toward a More Responsible Party System: A Report of the Committee on Political Parties, American Political Science Association," *American Political Science Review* 44, no. 3 (September 1950).
2. E. E. Schattschneider, *Party Government* (New York: Farrar and Rinehart, 1942).
3. See chapter 2 in John F. Bibby, *Politics, Parties and Elections in America*, 5th ed. (Belmont, CA: Wadsworth, 2002).
4. See Paul Finkelman and John Moore, "Political Parties," in *The Encyclopedia of American Political History*, ed. Peter Wallenstein and Paul Finkelman (Washington, DC: CQ Press, 2001).
5. See chapter 2 in John F. Bibby, *Politics, Parties and Elections in America*, 5th ed. (Belmont, CA: Wadsworth, 2002).
6. V. O. Key Jr., "A Theory of Critical Elections," *Journal of Politics* 16, no. 1 (1955): 13–18.
7. See Walter Dean Burnham, *Critical Elections and the Mainsprings of American Politics* (New York: W. W. Norton, 1970).
8. For a thorough analysis of how the American party system has changed since the New Deal, see Sidney M. Milkis, *The President and the Parties: The Transformation of the American Party System Since the New Deal* (New York: Oxford University Press, 1993).
9. Paul Allen Beck, "The Dealignment Era in America," in *Electoral Change in Advanced Industrial Democracies: Realignment or Dealignment*, ed. M. N. Dalton, T. T. Flanagan, and H. Beck (Princeton, NJ: Princeton University Press, 1984).
10. Angus Campbell, Philip E. Converse, Warren E. Miller, and Donald E. Stokes, *The American Voter* (New York: Wiley, 1960).
11. For a thorough discussion of the concept of party identification, see Warren E. Miller and J. Merrill Shanks, *The New American Voter* (Cambridge, MA: Harvard University Press, 1996).
12. Philip E. Converse, "The Concept of the Normal Vote" in *Elections and the Political Order*, ed. Angus Campbell, Philip E. Converse, Warren E. Miller, and Donald E. Stokes (New York: Wiley, 1966).
13. For a discussion of governance and the parties, see John W. Aldrich, *Why Parties? The Origin and Transformation of Political Parties in America* (Chicago: University of Chicago Press, 1995), chapter 7.
14. See Richard S. Conley, *The Presidency, Congress and Divided Government* (College Station: Texas A&M University Press, 2002).
15. For a good discussion of the rationale for America's two-party system, see Frank J. Sorauf, *Party Politics in America*, 5th ed. (Boston: Little, Brown, 1984).
16. For a good discussion of nineteenth- and twentieth-century third-party candidacies, see Steven J. Rosenstone, Roy L. Behr, and Edward H. Lazarus, *Third Parties in America*, 2nd ed. (Princeton, NJ: Princeton University Press, 1996).
17. Martin Wattenberg, *The Decline of American Political Parties* (Cambridge, MA: Harvard University Press, 1998).
18. See, for example, Jeff Cohen, Richard Fleisher, and Paul Kantor, eds., *American Political Parties: Decline or Resurgence?* (Washington, DC: CQ Press, 2001).

Chapter 14

1. For a comprehensive discussion of political participation, see M. Margaret Conway, *Political Participation in the United States*, 3rd ed. (Washington, DC: CQ Press, 2000).
2. For a discussion of the struggle for suffrage, see William H. Flanigan and Nancy H. Zingale, *Political Behavior of the American Electorate*, 9th ed. (Washington, DC: CQ Press, 1998), chapter 2.
3. See M. Margaret Conway, *Political Participation in the United States*, 3rd ed. (Washington, DC: CQ Press, 2000), chapter 5.
4. Some southern states continued to use the poll tax in state elections after passage of the Twenty-fourth Amendment. In 1996, the U.S. Supreme Court in *Harper v. Virginia State Board of Elections* outlawed the use of the poll tax in state elections as well as federal elections.

5. See Nancy McGlen and Karen O'Connor, *Women, Politics and American Society*, 2nd ed. (Upper Saddle River, NJ: Prentice Hall, 1998).

6. A thorough discussion of the development of states' voter registration systems can be found in Joseph P. Harris, *Registration of Voters in the United States* (Washington, DC: Brookings Institution Press, 1929).

7. A federal statute requires that the waiting period from becoming a state resident to being eligible to vote may not exceed thirty days.

8. Michael D. Martinez and David B. Hill, "Did Motor Voter Work?" *American Politics Quarterly* 27 (1999): 296–315.

9. See Lee Sigelman et al., "Voting and Non-voting: A Multi-Election Perspective," *American Journal of Political Science* 29 (November 1985): 749–765.

10. See Raymond E. Wolfinger and Steven J. Rosenstone, *Who Votes?* (New Haven, CT: Yale University Press, 1980), 44–46.

11. Norman H. Nie, Jane Junn, and Kenneth Stehlik-Barry, *Education and Democratic Citizenship in America* (Chicago: University of Chicago Press, 1996).

12. Todd G. Shields and Robert K. Goidel, "Participation Rates, Socioeconomic Class Biases and Congressional Elections: A Cross Validation," *American Journal of Political Science* 41 (1997): 683–691.

13. Anthony Downs, *An Economic Theory of Democracy* (New York: Harper and Brothers, 1957).

14. Angus Campbell, Philip E. Converse, Warren E. Miller, and Donald E. Stokes, *Elections and the Political Order* (New York: Wiley, 1966).

15. See Ivor Crewe, "As the World Turns Out," *Public Opinion* 4 (February–March 1981).

16. For a discussion of trends in political efficacy, see also M. Margaret Conway, *Political Participation in the United States*, 3rd ed. (Washington, DC: CQ Press, 2000), 51–53.

17. Robert Putnam, *Bowling Alone* (New York: Simon & Schuster, 2000).

18. The psychological concept of party identification is developed in Angus Campbell, Philip E. Converse, Warren E. Miller, and Donald E. Stokes, *The American Voter* (New York: Wiley, 1960).

19. For discussion of the role of party identification in forming vote choices, see Warren E. Miller and J. Merrill Shanks, *The New American Voter* (Cambridge, MA: Harvard University Press, 1996), and William H. Flanigan and Nancy H. Zingale, *Political Behavior of the American Electorate*, 9th ed. (Washington, DC: CQ Press, 1998).

20. See Martin P. Wattenberg, *The Decline of Political Parties, 1952–1996* (Cambridge, MA: Harvard University Press, 1998).

21. Warren E. Miller and J. Merrill Shanks, *The New American Voter* (Cambridge, MA: Harvard University Press, 1996), chapter 12.

22. See Norman Nie, Sidney Verba, and John Petrocik, *The Changing American Voter* (Cambridge, MA: Harvard University Press, 1979).

23. Morris P. Fiorina, *Retrospective Voting in American National Elections* (New Haven, CT: Yale University Press, 1981).

Chapter 15

1. See Ari Hoogenboom, *The Presidency of Rutherford B. Hayes* (Lawrence: University Press of Kansas, 1988).

2. See Lawrence D. Longley and Neal R. Peirce, *The Electoral College Primer* (New Haven, CT: Yale University Press, 1996).

3. For a good discussion of the development of parties in the early Republic, see Stanley Elkins and Eric McKitrick, *The Age of Federalism: The Early American Republic 1788–1800* (New York: Oxford University Press, 1993).

4. See Paul Finkelman and John Moore, "The Democratic Party," in *The Encyclopedia of American Political History*, ed. Peter Wallenstein and Paul Finkelman (Washington, DC: CQ Press, 2001).

5. See Tadahisa Kuroda, *The Origins of the Twelfth Amendment: The Electoral College in the Early Republic 1787–1804* (Westport, CT: Greenwood Press, 1994).

6. A thorough discussion of the nomination process as well as other aspects of the presidential campaign can be found in Stephen Wayne, *The Road to the White House 2008*, 8th ed. (Boston: Wadsworth Press, 2008).

7. Larry M. Bartels, *Presidential Primaries and the Dynamics of Public Choice* (Princeton, NJ: Princeton University Press, 1988).

8. See John F. Bibby, *Politics, Parties and Elections in America* (Chicago: Nelson-Hall, 1992), chapter 6.

9. Ibid.

10. For a good discussion of the relevance of the New Hampshire primary, see Dante J. Scala, *Stormy Weather: The New Hampshire Primary and Presidential Politics* (New York: Palgrave Macmillan, 2003).

11. Nevada disrupted this traditional ordering in 2008 when it scheduled its Republican and Democratic caucuses for January 19, three days before the New Hampshire primary. New Hampshire then moved its primary primary to January 8.

12. See William G. Mayer and Andrew Busch, *The Frontloading Problem in Presidential Nominations* (Washington, DC: Brookings Institution Press, 2003).

13. For a history of party conventions, see CQ Press's *National Party Conventions 1831–2004* (2005).

14. The supporters of Herbert Hoover, the Republican candidate in 1928, briefly considered putting Dawes on the ticket as the vice president once again, but backed down when the move was opposed by President Coolidge.

15. See Alan Schroeder, *Presidential Debates: 40 Years of High Risk TV* (New York: Columbia University Press, 1997).

16. See Darrell M. West, *Television Advertising in Election Campaigns 1952–1996* (Washington, DC: CQ Press, 1997).

17. For an analysis of the effects of negative ads on voters, see Richard R. Lau and Gerald M. Pomper, *Negative Campaigning: An Analysis of U.S. Senate Elections* (Lanham, MD: Rowman and Littlefield, 2004).

18. For a discussion of why the Electoral College was created and how it has changed, see Lawrence D. Longley and Neal R. Peirce, *The Electoral College Primer 2000* (New Haven, CT: Yale University Press, 1999), chapter 2.

19. See David B. Magleby and Candice J. Nelson, *The Money Chase* (Washington, DC: Brookings Institution Press, 1990).

20. *Buckley v. Valeo*, 424 U.S. 1 (1976).

21. *McConnell v. F.E.C.*, 540 U.S. 93 (2003).

22. For a thorough discussion of congressional elections, see Paul S. Herrnson, *Congressional Elections: Campaigning at Home and in Washington*, 2nd ed. (Washington, DC: CQ Press, 1998).

23. For a complete discussion of the coattail effect, see Gary C. Jacobson, *Electoral Origins of Divided Government 1946–1988* (Boulder, CO: Westview Press, 1990).

24. See Gary C. Jacobson, *The Politics of Congressional Elections*, 5th ed. (New York: Longman, 2001), chapter 3.

Chapter 16

1. Adam Smith's masterpiece, *The Wealth of Nations* (reprinted by New York: Modern Library, 1994), provides the foundation of modern economic theory and its defense of free market economies.

2. John Maynard Keynes's most famous work is *The General Theory of Employment, Interest, and Money* (New York: Harcourt Brace Jovanovich, 1936).

3. See David Stockman, *The Triumph of Politics: How the Reagan Revolution Failed* (New York: Harper & Row, 1986).

4. John Steele Gordon, *Hamilton's Blessing: The Extraordinary Life and Times of Our National Debt* (New York: Penguin, 1998).

5. Shelley Lynne Tomkin, *Inside OMB: Politics and Process in the President's Budget Office* (Armonk, NY: M. E. Sharpe, 1998).

6. See Allen Schick and Felix Lostracco, *The Federal Budget: Politics, Policy, Process* (Washington, DC: Brookings Institution Press, 2000).

7. Elizabeth Drew, *Showdown: The Struggle Between the Gingrich Congress and the Clinton White House* (New York: Touchstone, 1997).

8. *Bowsher v. Synar*, 478 U.S. 714 (1986).

9. Forbes's most recent proposal for a flat tax is discussed in Steve Forbes, *Flat Tax Revolution: Using a Postcard to Abolish the IRS* (Washington, DC: Regnery, 2005).

10. William Greider, *Secrets of the Temple: How the Federal Reserve Runs the Country* (New York: Simon & Schuster, 1989).

Chapter 17

1. Douglas Brinkley, *The Wilderness Warrior: Theodore Roosevelt and the Crusade for America* (New York: Harper, 2010).

2. Charles Lindblom, "The Science of Muddling Through," *Public Administration Review* 19 (Spring 1959): 79–88.

3. Bryan Jones and Frank Baumgartner, "A Model of Choice for Public Policy," *Journal of Public Administration Research and Theory Online* 15 (2006): 325–351.

4. Herbert Packer, *The Limits of the Criminal Sanction* (Stanford, CA: Stanford University Press, 1968).

5. For a discussion of criminal justice in America more generally, see George Cole and Christopher Smith, *The American System of Criminal Justice* (Belmont, CA: Wadsworth, 2001).

6. Kristen Lindenmeyer, *A Right to Childhood: The U.S. Children's Bureau and Child Welfare* (Urbana: University of Illinois Press, 1997).

7. Jonathan Oberlander, *The Political Life of Medicare* (Chicago: University of Chicago Press, 2003).

8. Jeffrey Lehman and Sheldon Danziger, "Turning Our Back on the New Deal: The End of Welfare in 1996," in *Race, Poverty and Domestic Policy*, ed. C. Michael Henry (New Haven, CT: Yale University Press, 2004).

9. Robert Hudson, ed., *The New Politics of Old Age Policy* (Baltimore: Johns Hopkins University Press, 2005).

10. See Paul Light, *Still Artful Work: The Continuing Politics of Social Security Reform* (New York: McGraw Hill, 1994).

11. Jan Gregoire Coombs, *The Rise and Fall of HMOs: An American Health Care Revolution* (Madison: University of Wisconsin Press, 2005).

12. William Gesler and Thomas Ricketts, eds., *Health Care in Rural North America: The Geography of Health Care Services in North America*

(Newark, NJ: Rutgers University Press, 1992).

13. For an especially readable introduction to environmental policy, see Daniel J. Fiorino, *Making Environmental Policy* (Berkeley: University of California Press, 1995).

14. For a more critical look at the EPA during much of its existence, see Mark K. Landy, Marc J. Roberts, and Stephen R. Thomas, *The Environmental Protection Agency: Asking the Wrong Questions: From Nixon to Clinton* (New York: Oxford University Press, 1994).

15. See Patrick J. McGuinn, *No Child Left Behind and the Transformation of Federal Education Policy, 1965–2005* (Lawrence: University Press of Kansas, 2006).

Chapter 18

1. H. W. Brands, *Woodrow Wilson, 1913–1921* (New York: Times Books, 2003).

2. Two of the best overviews of American foreign policy during the latter half of the twentieth century are Stephen Ambrose and Douglas Brinkley, *Rise to Globalism: American Foreign Policy Since 1938* (New York: Penguin, 1997); and Thomas Patterson, J. Garry Clifford, and Kenneth Hagan, *American Foreign Policy: A History* (New York: D. C. Heath, 1997).

3. Robert Dallek, *Franklin Delano Roosevelt and American Foreign Policy, 1932–1945* (New York: Oxford University Press, 1995).

4. D. F. Flemming, *The Cold War and Its Origins: 1917–1960* (New York: Doubleday, 1961).

5. David DiLeo, *George Ball, Vietnam and the Rethinking of Containment* (Chapel Hill: University of North Carolina Press, 1991).

6. Stanley Karnow, *Vietnam: A History* (New York: Penguin, 1997).

7. Robert Litwak, *Détente and the Nixon Doctrine* (Cambridge: Cambridge University Press, 1986).

8. John Newhouse, "The Missile Defense Debate," *Foreign Affairs* 80, no. 4 (July/August 2001).

9. John Lewis Gaddis, *The Cold War: A New History* (New York: Penguin, 2005).

10. One of the key architects of this new understanding was Bush's secretary of state, James A. Baker III. See James A. Baker III, *The Politics of Diplomacy* (New York: Putnam, 1995).

11. Many of these criticisms are discussed in Samantha Power's award-winning book, *A Problem from Hell: America and the Age of Genocide* (New York: Harper Perennial, 2003).

12. Perhaps the best book written to date about the problems in the military's 2003 intervention in Iraq is Michael Gordon and Bernard Trainor's *Cobra II: The Inside Story of the Invasion and Occupation of Iraq* (New York: Pantheon, 2006).

13. Niall Ferguson, *Colossus: The Rise and Fall of the American Empire* (New York: Penguin Books, 2005).

14. Joseph Nye, *Soft Power: The Means to Success in World Politics* (New York: PublicAffairs, 2005).

15. Louis Fisher, "Without Restraint: Presidential Military Initiatives from Korea to Bosnia," in *Domestic Sources of American Foreign Policy*, 3rd ed., ed. Eugene Wittkopf and James McCormick (Lanham, MD: Rowman and Littlefield, 1999), 141–155.

16. Geoffrey Kemp, "Presidential Management of the Executive Bureaucracy," in *United States Foreign Policy: The Search for a New Role*, ed. Robert J. Art and Seyom Brown (Upper Saddle River, NJ: Prentice Hall, 1993).

17. See William B. Quandt, "The Electoral Cycle and the Conduct of American Foreign Policy," *Political Science Quarterly* 101 (1986): 825–837.

18. John Mueller, "Public Opinion and Foreign Policy: The People's Common Sense," in *Domestic Sources of American Foreign Policy*, 3rd ed., ed. Eugene Wittkopf and James McCormick (Lanham, MD: Rowman and Littlefield, 1999), 51–60.

19. Peter Boone, "The Impact of Foreign Aid on Savings and Growth," *Center for Economic Performance Working Paper No 1265*, London, October 1994, 25–26.

Chapter 19

1. From the dissenting opinion of U.S. Supreme Court Justice Brandeis in *New State Ice Co. v. Liebman*, 1932.

2. For a very good review of the adoption and ratification of state constitutions in all 50 states, see http://www.thegreenpapers.com/slg/constitution/phtml.

3. 2002 Census of Governments, Vol. 1, No. 1, Government Organization. U.S. Census Bureau.

4. Judge John Dillon, *City of Clinton v. Cedar Rapids and Missouri River Railroad Co.* (Iowa, 1868).

5. Dennis L. Dresang and James J. Gosling, *Politics and Policy in American States and Communities* (New York: Longman, 2002), 99–100.

6. Conference of State Legislatures, "Women in State Legislatures" (1999).

7. Joint Center for Political and Economic Studies, "Black Elected Officials" (1999).

8. See *Baker v. Carr* (1962) and *Reynolds v. Sims* (1964).

9. For a good discussion of the professionalization of state legislatures, see Alan Rosenthal, *Legislative Life* (New York: Harper and Row, 1981).

10. Dresang and Gosling, *Politics and Policy in American States and Communities*, op. cit., 262.

11. Janelle Carter, "Bill Won't Force N.D. to Register," *Bismarck Tribune*, April 12, 2002, 6A.

12. For data on how all 50 states fare with respect to party competition over the last 50 years, see Harrold W. Stanley and Richard G. Niemi, *Vital Statistics on American Politics 2003–2004* (Washington DC: CQ Press, 2003), 21.

13. Michael Barone and Richard Cohen, *2004 Almanac of American Politics* (New York: National Journal Group, 2003), 693.

14. Data obtained from the Web site of the National Council of State Legislatures, http://www.ncsl.org.

15. For a complete discussion of the reduced influence of parties in campaigns and elections, see Martin P. Wattenberg, *The Decline of American Political Parties* (Cambridge, MA: Harvard University Press, 1998).

16. Barbara G. Salmore and Stephen A. Salmore, *Candidates, Parties, and Campaigns* (Washington, DC: CQ Press, 1989).

17. Kenneth Dautrich and David A. Yalof, "The State of State Elections" in *The State of the States*, 4th ed., ed. Carl Van Horn (Washington, DC: CQ Press, 2006), 17–19.

18. Malcolm E. Jewell and David M. Olson, *Political Parties and Elections in American States* (Homewood, IL: Dorsey Press, 2001).

19. Jerrold G. Rusk, *A Statistical History of the American Electorate* (Washington, DC: CQ Press, 2001), 438.

20. Harold W. Stanley and Richard G. Niemi, *Vital Statistics on American Politics 2003–2004* (Washington, DC: CQ Press, 2003), 20.

21. Ibid., 45.

22. See the national Conference of State Legislatures Web page, http://www.ncsl.org.

23. Drawn from an article by Tom Story on the National Council of State Legislatures Web page, http://www.ncsl.org.

24. *U.S. Term Limits, Inc., v. Thornton*, 514 U.S. 779 (1995).

25. See Anthony Champagne, "Political Parties and Judicial Elections," *Loyola of Los Angeles Law Review* 34, 1411–1427.

26. Dale Wetzel, "California Recall: North Dakota Blazed the Trail over 80 Years Ago," *Bismarck Tribune*, August 2, 2003, 1B.

Index

Note: Terms in **boldface** type are key terms defined in the glossary. Page numbers in *italics* refer to tables, figures, and boxed features. Page numbers preceded by the letter C are found in the annotated Constitution.